Discrimination at Work

The Psychological and Organizational Bases

Discrimination at Work

The Psychological and Organizational Bases

Edited by

Robert L. Dipboye
University of Central Florida

Adrienne Colella
Texas A&M University

Psychology Press
Taylor & Francis Group

New York   London

Senior Acquisitions Editor:	Anne Duffy
Editorial Assistant:	Kristin Duch
Cover Design:	Kathryn Houghtaling Lacey
Textbook Production Manager:	Paul Smolenski
Full-Service Compositor:	TechBooks

This book was typeset in 10/12 pt. Palatino Roman, Bold, and Italic.
The heads were typeset in Poppl Laudatio, Poppl Laudatio Bold, and Poppl Laudatio Bold Italic.

First published 2005 by

Lawrence Erlbaum Associates, Inc., Publishers

This edition published 2012 by Psychology Press

Psychology Press	Psychology Press
Taylor & Francis Group	Taylor & Francis Group
711 Third Avenue	27 Church Road, Hove
New York, NY 10017	East Sussex BN3 2FA

First issued in paperback 2014

Psychology Press is an imprint of the Taylor and Francis Group, an informa business

Library of Congress Cataloging-in-Publication Data

Discrimination at work : the psychological and organizational bases / edited by
   Robert L. Dipboye, Adrienne Colella.
      p.   cm.—(The Organizational Frontiers Series)
   Includes bibliographical references and indexes.
   ISBN 0-8058-5207-7 (cloth : alk. paper)
      1. Discrimination in employment—Research.   2. Industrial organization—Social
aspects—Research.   3. Prejudices—Research.   4. Stereotype (Psychology)—Research.
5. Diversity in the workplace—Management—Research.   6. Discrimination in
employment—Prevention—Research.   I. Dipboye, Robert L.   II. Colella, Adrienne,
1961–III. Series.

   HD4903.D573   2005
   331.13'3—dc22

                                                                    2004016293

ISBN 13: 978-0-8058-5207-3 (hbk)
ISBN 13: 978-1-138-00407-8 (pbk)

The Organizational Frontiers Series

The Organizational Frontiers Series is sponsored by The Society for Industrial and Organizational Psychology (SIOP). Launched in 1983 to make scientific contributions to the field, the series has attempted to publish books on cutting edge theory, research, and theory-driven practice in industrial/organizational psychology and related organizational science disciplines.

Our overall objective is to inform and to stimulate research for SIOP members (students, practitioners, and researchers) and people in related disciplines including the other subdisciplines of psychology, organizational behavior, human resource management, and labor and industrial relations. The volumes in the Organizational Frontiers Series have the following goals:

1) Focus on research and theory in organizational science, and the implications for practice.
2) Inform readers of significant advances in theory and research in psychology and related disciplines that are relevant to our research and practice.
3) Challenge the research and practice community to develop and adapt new ideas and to conduct research on these developments.
4) Promote the use of scientific knowledge in the solution of public policy issues and increased organizational effectiveness.

The volumes originated in the hope that they would facilitate continuous learning and a continuing research curiosity about organizational phenomena on the part of both scientists and practitioners.

SIOP Organizational Frontiers Series

SIOP Organizational Frontiers Series

Series Editor
Robert Pritchard
University of Central Florida

Dipboye/Colella: (2005) *Discrimination at Work: The Psychological and Organizational Bases.*

Griffin/O'Leary-Kelly: (2004) *The Dark Side of Organizational Behavior.*

Hofmann/Tetrick: (2003) *Health and Safety in Organizations.*

Jackson/Hitt/DeNisi: (2003) *Managing Knowledge for Sustained Competitive Knowledge.*

Barrick/Ryan: (2003) *Personality and Work.*

Lord/Klimoski/Kanfer: (2002) *Emotions in the Workplace.*

Drasgow/Schmitt: (2002) *Measuring and Analyzing Behavior in Organizations.*

Feldman: (2002) *Work Careers.*

Zaccaro/Klimoski: (2001) *The Nature of Organizational Leadership.*

Rynes/Gerhart: (2000) *Compensation in Organizations.*

Klein/Kozlowski: (2000) *Multilevel Theory, Research and Methods in Organizations.*

Ilgen/Pulakos: (1999) *The Changing Nature of Performance.*

Earley/Erez: (1997) *New Perspectives on International I-O Psychology.*

Murphy: (1996) *Individual Differences and Behavior in Organizations.*

Guzzo/Salas: (1995) *Team Effectiveness and Decision Making.*

Howard: (1995) *The Changing Nature of Work.*

Schmitt/Borman: (1993) *Personnel Selection in Organizations.*

Zedeck: (1991) *Work, Families and Organizations.*

Schneider: (1990) *Organizational Culture and Climate.*

Goldstein: (1989) *Training and Development in Organizations.*

Campbell/Campbell: (1988) *Productivity in Organizations.*

Hall: (1987) *Career Development in Organizations.*

Contents

I Psychological, Group, and Organizational Bases of Discrimination

II Understanding Discrimination Against Specific Groups

III Implications for Practice, Policy, and the Law

Series Foreword

This is the twenty-second book in the Organizational Frontiers Series of books initiated by the Society for Industrial and Organizational Psychology. The overall purpose of the Series volumes is to promote the scientific status of the field. Ray Katzell first edited the Series. He was followed by Irwin Goldstein, Sheldon Zedeck, and Neal Schmitt. The topics of the volumes and the volume editors are chosen by the editorial board or individuals propose volumes to the editorial board. The series editor and the editorial board then work with the volume editor(s) in planning the volume. During the writing of the volume, the series editor often works with the editor and the publisher to bring the manuscript to completion.

The success of the series is evident in the high number of sales (now over 45,000). Volumes have also received excellent reviews, and individual chapters as well as volumes have been cited very frequently. A symposium at the SIOP annual meeting examined the impact of the Series on research and theory in industrial and organizational psychology. While such influence is difficult to track and volumes varied in intent and perceived centrality to the discipline, the conclusion of most participants was that the volumes have exerted a significant impact on research and theory in the field and are regarded as being representative of the best the field has to offer.

This volume, edited by Robert Dipboye and Adrienne Colella, reflects new thinking and research in the area of discrimination. This volume identifies a large body of research and theory on the biases that can occur in the work place based on race, religion, national origin, sex, sexual orientation, age, physical disability, and other employee characteristics. However, the volume is not a simple repetition of what we know about each type of discrimination. Rather, the focus is on broadening our perspective on the entire issue and attempting to integrate disparate bodies of work.

There are several other strengths of this volume. It deals with discrimination at multiple levels of analysis from the individual to the organization as well as with social policy and legal issues. The section in the concluding chapter on implication for practice, policy and law is especially important in that it brings the academic issues to a practical level for organizations and policy makers. In the concluding chapter, the editors also present a model of discrimination that attempts to integrate the ideas on the preceding chapters.

Another major strength of the volume is how it identifies research needs. These are noted in many of the chapters, and the concluding chapter discusses specific improvements that future research could make in participants, settings, obtrusiveness, and degree of participant involvement. This concluding chapter also describes needed conceptual and empirical scholarship. This is particularly important because we want the volume to stimulate research. The more the questions and methodologies are developed by these experts, the better other researchers can use the information to do new research. For scholars who are interested in discrimination, this concluding chapter presents an excellent summary of the important issues and a roadmap for guiding future research. We all hope this volume will energize researchers and stimulate new ideas about how to understand and deal with discrimination in organizations.

The editors and chapter authors deserve our gratitude for clearly communicating the nature, application, and implications of the theory and research described in this book. Production of a volume such as this involves the hard work and cooperative effort of many individuals. The editors, the chapter authors, and the editorial board all played important roles in this endeavor. As all royalties from the Series volumes are used to help support SIOP, none of them received any remuneration. The editors and authors deserve our appreciation for engaging in a difficult task for the sole purpose of furthering our understanding of organizational science. This is also the first volume by our new Frontiers publisher, Lawrence Erlbaum Associates. We want to express our gratitude to Anne Duffy, our new Erlbaum editor, who has worked hard to move the series to Erlbaum. She has also been a great help in the planning and production of the volume.

—Robert D. Pritchard
University of Central Florida
Series Editor, 2003–2008

Preface

Many of the contributors to this book participated in a conference on workplace discrimination held at Rice University in May 2000. The idea behind the conference was to bring together major scholars in industrial and organizational psychology (I/O), who were doing research on the topic, with a few of the more active researchers in social psychology. For two stimulating days of presentations, posters, and roundtable discussions, we explored the research and theory relating to the various areas of workplace discrimination. The idea for the book came from the realization, reinforced in this conference, that there had been no attempt in the workplace discrimination literature to bring together the research and theory on the topic. We sought to bring together in one volume a review of the scholarly work on discrimination based on race, age, sexual orientation, gender, physical appearance, disability, and personality. In addition, we attempted to explore the multilevel antecedents and potential bases for a general model of discrimination in the workplace. Although social psychological research and theory have provided invaluable insights, an understanding of discrimination in the workplace and solutions requires incorporating factors at the organizational, individual, and group levels. We do not claim to have arrived at a definitive model, but we hope that the several initial attempts here will facilitate future attempts at integration of the diverse work on this topic.

In the review of the research related to specific areas of discrimination, we have intentionally focused on the groups that have received the most attention and have given relatively little attention to other ethnic and racial groups, such as Jews, Hispanics, and Native Americans. Our inattention was a reflection of the amount of research in the workplace and was not meant to suggest that discrimination against these other groups is infrequent or unimportant.

The reader should also be aware, as might be expected with a topic as controversial as this, that the authors in this volume probably differ to some extent in their views on the nature of discrimination and the preferred solutions. Consequently, the reader should not attribute the views expressed in any one chapter to the authors of another chapter. Although we did not poll the contributors, we suspect that there are points of agreement. For one, we probably agree that the inequality among various groups in our society is a problem that deserves the attention of industrial and organizational psychologists. We also probably agree that discrimination can be rigorously researched just as other topics in I/O psychology are researched and that the research should be held to the same standards as any other area. We probably agree that there are weaknesses in the previous work, as can be expected of any relatively new area of research. Finally, we also probably agree that we have learned much from the research that can contribute to our understanding and application and that workplace discrimination is a promising area for future research.

We owe thanks to many people who have assisted in various ways during the planning and writing of the book. First, we thank Neil Schmitt and Bob Pritchard, who were the chairs of the Frontiers Committee of the Society for Industrial and Organizational Psychology during its preparation. We thank Dean Robert Stein of the School of Social Sciences at Rice University, whose generous support of the discrimination conference at Rice in 2000 brought together what turned out to be the core contributors to this volume. We appreciate the assistance of our graduate student and clerical assistants and the social support of our spouses. To the extent that this book is well received, they deserve more than a small share of the credit.

—Robert L. Dipboye
University of Central Florida

—Adrienne Colella
Texas A&M University

Contributors

Winfred Arthur, Jr., is full professor and director of the graduate program in industrial/organizational psychology at Texas A&M University. His primary interests include: personnel psychology; testing, selection, and validation; human performance; team selection and training; training development, design, delivery, and evaluation; complex skill acquisition and retention; models of job performance; and meta-analysis. He has published numerous articles in *Journal of Applied Psychology, Personnel Psychology,* and other journals in human resource management and I/O.

Janet L. Barnes-Farrell is associate professor and director of the graduate program in industrial/organizational psychology at the University of Connecticut. Her primary fields of expertise include performance appraisal, workplace concerns of older workers, and issues of bias and fair treatment in a diverse workforce. Her research has appeared in a number of professional journals, including *Journal of Applied Psychology, Personnel Psychology, Human Resource Management Review, Journal of Business and Psychology, Organizational Behavior and Human Decision Processes, Psychology and Aging, Experimental Aging Research, Sex Roles,* and *Psychology of Women Quarterly.* She is a member of the editorial board for the *Journal of Applied Psychology* and frequently serves as an ad hoc reviewer of research in the field of work behavior.

Arthur P. Brief is the Lawrence Martin chair of business at Tulane University's A.B. Freeman School of Business and holds a courtesy appointment in the department of psychology. He is a recipient of the Freeman School's most prized award for teaching, the Wissner Award, and the Academic Leadership Award from the Aspen Institute. His scholarship, which focuses on two arenas, job related distress and ethical decision making in organizations, also has been award winning. He is currently co-editor of Lawrence Erlbaum Associate's Organization and Management Series. In 2003, Professor Brief became the editor of the *Academy of Management Review.* He is a fellow of the Academy of Management, the American Psychological Association, and the American Psychological Society.

Rebecca M. Butz is a PhD candidate in organizational behavior at the A.B. Freeman School of Business, Tulane University. Her research interests include discrimination in the workplace, group composition, and employee well-being.

Georgia T. Chao is an associate professor of management at Michigan State University. Her primary research interests lie in the areas of career development, organizational socialization, and international human resources development. She is a fellow of the Society for Industrial and Organizational Psychology and the American Psychological Association and currently serves on four editorial boards. She is the current secretary of the Society for Industrial and Organizational Psychology.

Donna Chrobot-Mason is an assistant professor of psychology at the University of Colorado at Denver. She earned her PhD from the University of Georgia in 1997 and worked in Human Resources at Xerox Corporation for four years. Donna conducts research in identity development, diversity management, and leadership across differences. Some of her specific research interests are organizational diversity climate as a competitive business advantage, diversity training theory and multicultural competency development, leader effectiveness in the face of demographic changes, and ethnic/racial and sexual identity development.

Jeanette N. Cleveland is a professor of psychology at Pennsylvania State University. She is the author of books, chapters, and papers dealing with performance appraisal, gender and diversity, and work and family issues. She was consulting editor for *Journal of Organizational Behavior* and has served or is currently serving on the editorial boards of *Academy of Management Journal, Journal of Vocational Behavior, Human Resource Management Review, Journal of Organizational Behavior, Journal of Applied Psychology,* and *International Journal of Management Reviews*. She is the author of over 30 articles and book chapters and is author or editor of a number of books including *Women and Men in Organizations: Sex and Gender Issues at Work* (with M. Stockdale & K. Murphy, 2000). She was elected member-at-large in 1997 of the Society for Industrial and Organizational Psychology and is a fellow of SIOP (Division 14) and APA. She is co-editor with Edwin Fleishman of LEA's Applied Psychology series.

Adrienne Colella has published research on several topics, including goal setting and feedback, utility analysis, and the recruitment and socialization of organizational newcomers. Currently much of her research focuses on disability issues in HRM. Her articles appear in major journals including the *Academy of Management Review, Journal of Applied Psychology, Personnel Psychology,* and *Human Performance*. She has been an investigator on grants or contracts from the Army Research Institute, the NPRDC, New Jersey Developmental Disability Council, and Rutgers University. She is a fellow of the American Psychological Association and the Society of Industrial/ Organizational Psychologists and a member of the Academy of Management. She serves on the editorial boards of the *Journal of Applied Psychology*, *Academy of Management Journal*, and *Human Resource Management Review*.

Elizabeth A. Deitch is a PhD candidate in industrial and organizational psychology from Tulane University. She conducts research addressing workplace discrimination based on race, gender, or sexual orientation, with an emphasis on the well-being of those who are the targets of discrimination on the job.

Robert L. Dipboye is the chair of psychology and a professor of psychology at the University of Central Florida. Previously he was Herbert S. Autrey professor of psychology and management at Rice University where he also served as department chair. He has published three books and over 50 articles and chapters. He is a fellow of the American Psychological Association, the Society of Industrial and Organizational Psychology, and the American Psychological Society and a member of the Society of Organizational Behavior. He has been on the editorial boards of the *Academy of Management Review*, the *Journal of Organizational Behavior*, and the SIOP Frontier Series and served as associate editor of the *Journal of Applied Psychology*. His research interests include personality (as it relates to work motivation and stress), employment discrimination, training, group behavior in organizations, leadership, and employee selection.

Dennis Doverspike, PhD, ABPP, is a full professor of psychology at the University of Akron, fellow of the Institute for Life-Span Development and Gerontology, and director of the Center for Organizational Research. In addition, he has over 30 years of experience working with consulting firms and with public and private organizations. His areas of specialization include job analysis, testing, and compensation.

John F. Dovidio is Charles A. Dana professor of psychology at Colgate University, where he is currently serving as provost and dean of the faculty. He (MA, PhD in social psychology from the University of Delaware) has been editor of *Personality and Social Psychology Bulletin* and associate editor of *Group Processes and Intergroup Relations* of the *Journal of Personality and Social Psychology*. He is a fellow of the American Psychological Association and of the American Psychological Society and served as president of the Society for the Psychological Study of Social Issues (SPSSI), Division 9 of APA. His research interests are in stereotyping, prejudice, and discrimination; social power and nonverbal communication; and altruism and helping. He has published over 100 books, articles, and chapters on these topics. He shared the 1985 and 1998 Gordon Allport Intergroup Relations Prize with Samuel L. Gaertner for their work on aversive racism and ways to reduce bias.

Michele J. Gelfand is an associate professor of psychology at University of Maryland—College Park. Her program of research focuses on three major areas. First, her research examines cultural influences on negotiation, with the goal of expanding the dominant paradigm that exists in the field. Second, her work centers on basic theoretical and methodological issues in cross-cultural psychology, namely conceptualizing and measuring dimensions of cultural variation, including individualism and collectivism and cultural tightness–looseness. Finally, her research focuses on workplace diversity, within which she examines issues of gender in organizations: cross-cultural organizational behavior; cultural influences on negotiation, mediation, justice, and revenge; workplace diversity; sexual harassment and discrimination; theory and method in assessing aspects of culture (individualism–collectivism; cultural tightness–looseness). She is the 2002 recipient of both the L. L. Cummings Award for Early Career Contributions of the Organizational Behavior Division of Academy of Management and the Ernest J. McCormick Award for Distinguished Early Career Contributions of the Society for Industrial and Organizational Psychology. She is an elected member of the Society for Experimental Social Psychology (SESP) and associate editor of *Applied Psychology: International Review*. She also serves on the editorial boards of several major journals.

Caren B. Goldberg is an associate professor at The George Washington University, where she teaches undergraduate, masters, and doctoral courses in human resource management. She has been honored with two departmental awards for her teaching. She has published research in the *Journal of Applied Psychology, Assessment, Journal of Business Research, Sex Roles, Journal of Organizational Behavior, Group and Organization Management*, and *Journal of Career Planning and Employment*. Professor Goldberg is on the editorial board of three of the top journals in HR, and she periodically reviews articles for numerous other journals. She served as Secretary of the HR division of the Academy of Management and was the division chair of the Southern Management Association's Human Resources/Dispute Resolution/Careers division.

Martin M. Greller (PhD, Yale University) is on the faculty of the Robert J. Milano Graduate School of Management and Urban Policy, New School University, in New York as the head of its human resource management program. He previously served as professor of management at the University of Wyoming and was on the faculty of Baruch College—City University of New York and New York University. He has been a consulting psychologist with RHR International and Director of Human Resource Planning and Development for The New York Times Company. He has published work on careers and feedback in *Journal of Applied Psychology*, *Academy of Management Journal*, *Human Relations*, *Human Resource Planning*, and *Journal of Vocational Behavior* and serves on the editorial boards of *Journal of Vocational Behavior* and *Human Resource Planning*. He served on the advisory board of University of Missouri's Multicultural Management Program and on the Community Council of Great New York's Task Force on Employment of Older Workers. He is a licensed psychologist in New York and New Jersey.

Michelle C. Haynes is currently a doctoral student in the Social/ Organizational Program at New York University. Her research interests include affirmative action, sex bias in the workplace, and judgment and decision making.

Michelle R. Hebl is the Radoslav Tsanoff associate professor of psychology and management at Rice University. She received her BA at Smith College in 1991, her MS at Texas A&M University in 1993, and her PhD at Dartmouth College in 1997. Her research focuses on the workplace discrimination and the barriers stigmatized individuals face in the hiring process, business settings, and medical community. She is the co-editor of the recently released *Social Psychology of Stigma*.

Madeline E. Heilman is professor of psychology at New York University. She received her PhD in social psychology from Columbia University. She is on the editorial boards of the *Journal of Applied Psychology* and *The Academy of Management Review*. Her current research focuses on sex bias in work settings, the dynamics of stereotyping, and the unintended consequences of preferential selection processes.

John H. Jackson (PhD, University of Colorado) is professor of management at the University of Wyoming. He is co-author of the best selling university HR text *Human Resource Management*. He worked in the telecommunications industry in human resources management for several years. Dr. Jackson has authored six other college texts and over 50 articles and papers, including those appearing in *Academy of Management Review, Journal of Management, Human Resources Management,* and *Human Resources Planning*. He has consulted widely with a variety of organizations on HR and management development matters. During the past several years, he has served as an expert witness in a number of HR-related cases. At the University of Wyoming, he is serving as chairman in the department of management and marketing. Professor Jackson has received the University of Wyoming's top teaching award. In addition, he designed one of the first classes in the nation on business environment and natural resources. He is on the board of directors of the Wyoming Business Council and the Wyoming Workforce Development Council.

Hannah-Hanh D. Nguyen, MA, is a doctoral candidate in the Industrial–Organizational Psychology program at Michigan State University. Nguyen's research interests include gender and diversity issues, stereotype threat effect, test-taking strategies, and cross-cultural research on women as managers.

Lisa Hisae Nishii joined the School of Industrial and Labor Relations as an assistant professor in July 2003. She received her PhD and MA in industrial and organizational psychology from the University of Maryland and her BA in economics from Wellesley College. She won the Milton Dean Havron Social Sciences Award for Outstanding Achievements as a doctoral student. Professor Nishii's research focuses on three main areas: cross-cultural HR and organizational behavior, diversity in the workplace, and strategic human resource management (SHRM). Her research has been published in the *Journal of Applied Psychology and Organizational Dynamics*, and she has co-authored several chapters. Several of her research papers have been nominated for awards, and a 2001 paper on cultural differences in cognitive representations of conflict in the U.S. and Japan won the Best Empirical Paper Award from the International Association of Conflict Management. Professor Nishii has also worked as an organizational consultant for several organizations on a variety of topics, including diversity management, service climate, selection systems, performance management, and leadership development.

Ramona L. Paetzold holds a JD from University of Nebraska and a DBA from Indiana University. She is an associate professor in the Human Resource Management area of the Department of Management at Texas A&M University. Her primary research interests are in the intersection of human resource management and employment law. Her work encompasses psycho-legal aspects of sexual harassment, disabilities and accommodations, and workplace violence. She has recently published in such outlets as the *Academy of Management Review, American Business Law Journal, North Carolina Law Review, Employee Rights and Employment Policy Journal*, and *Houston Law Review*. In addition to the above interests, she also teaches in the field of research methods, and has published works relating research methods to discrimination law. She is co-author of the book *The Statistics of Discrimination* (with Steven L. Willborn). Dr. Paetzold has served as senior articles editor for the *American Business Law Journal* and editor-in-chief of the *Journal of Legal Studies Education*. Her primary teaching responsibilities include employment law, employment discrimination law, research methods, and multivariate methods for management office.

Belle Rose Ragins is a professor of management at the University of Wisconsin—Milwaukee and the research director of the UWM Institute for Diversity Education and Leadership (IDEAL). Her current research examines the development of mentoring relationships and explores how gender and diversity affect mentoring. She has also researched the glass ceiling, sexual harassment, diversity, and sexual orientation in organizations. She has written more than 70 papers for presentation at national and international conferences and for publication in leading academic journals. She is co-author of the book *Mentoring and Diversity: An International Perspective*. She has received eight national awards for her research, including the Sage Life-Time Achievement Award for scholarly contributions to management, the American Society for Training and Development Research Award, the American Psychological Association Placek Award, and five best paper awards from the National Academy of Management. She has or is currently serving on the editorial review boards of the *Academy of Management Journal*, the *Journal of Applied Psychology, Personnel Psychology, Group & Organization Management*, and the *Journal of Vocational Behavior*. She was awarded the first Visiting Research Fellowship position at Catalyst, a national non-for-profit research and advisory organization working to advance women in business and the professions. She was a research advisor for 9-to-5, the National Association of Working Women. In 2004, she won the Mentoring Legacy award at the Academy of Management meeting.

Jana L. Raver is an assistant professor in organizational behavior at Queen's School of Business, Queen's University. Her research involves workplace diversity, interpersonal treatment and counterproductive work behaviors, and examining the cross-cultural generalizability of organizational theories. Her research in this area has also examined sexual harassment as a counterproductive behavior with negative implications for team-level interpersonal processes and financial outcomes. Within the domain of workplace diversity, her work has included an examination of employees' attributions regarding discrimination and how these relate to justice perceptions, organizational climate for diversity, organizational-level antecedents to discrimination, and the role of gender and relational self-construals in negotiations. Her paper (with Michele Gelfand) "Linking Sexual Harassment, Team Processes and Team Performance" was winner of the Dorothy Harlow Best Paper Award in the Gender and Diversity division of the Academy of Management 2003.

Christine M. Riordan, associate professor of management, received her undergraduate degree in engineering from Georgia Institute of Technology and her MBA and her PhD in management from Georgia State University. Prior to obtaining her PhD, she was employed as a human resource management specialist at Southern Company Services and as an account manager at OnLine Financial. Additionally, she has been a consultant for many organizations, such as AT&T and LOMA, Inc. Her current research concerns the effect of human resource management practices on group and organizational performance, the management of diversity, and corporate image. She frequently presents the results of her research at national and regional meetings and serves as an editorial reviewer for several major scholarly journals. Her research findings have appeared in journals such as *Journal of Management, Journal of Applied Psychology,* and *Journal of Business and Psychology*. She is active in several professional associations including the Academy of Management Association, American Psychological Association, Society for Industrial and Organizational Psychology, and the Southern Management Association. She is on the editorial board of the *Journal of Management*.

Bryan S. Schaffer is an assistant professor in the Department of Management & Accountancy at the University of North Carolina—Asheville. He earned a BS from the University of Florida, an MBA from Georgia State University, and a PhD in Organizational Behavior & Human Resource Management from the University of Georgia. At UNC—Asheville, he teaches courses in Foundations of Management, Organizational Behavior, and Human Resource Management. His research interests include relational demography, workplace discrimination, and group & team dynamics. Schaffer has published his work in peer reviewed journals and proceedings, including *Organizational Research Methods*, and has presented his work at various national academic conferences. He is a member of the Academy of Management, the American Psychological Association, and the Southern Management Association.

Benjamin Schneider is senior research fellow at Personnel Research Associates, Inc. and professor of psychology at the University of Maryland. He taught for many years at Maryland and also at Yale, MSU, Dartmouth, Peking University (China), IAE (France), and Bar-Ilan University (Israel). Dr. Schneider has two major streams of research, each of which has several subcategories. One research stream concerns the role of manager personality in understanding the structure, strategy, and climate/culture of organizations. His second stream of research concerns research directed at understanding organizational designs for service quality. He has consulted with numerous companies on issues of service quality and personnel selection. He won the SIOP year 2000 Distinguished Scientific Contributions Award. His academic accomplishments include more than 90 journal articles and book chapters, eight books, and appointment to the editorial review boards at various times of the *Journal of Applied Psychology* and other major journals. Professional recognition for his accomplishments include: election to fellowship in the American Psychological Association, the American Psychological Society, and the Academy of Management; president of the Organizational Behavior Division of the Academy of Management; and President of the Society for Industrial and Organizational Psychology. He has also been awarded the Society for Industrial and Organizational Psychology's 2000 Distinguished Scientific Contributions Award.

Lynn M. Shore is a visiting professor at the University of California, Irvine, and she joined the faculty at San Diego State University in the fall of 2004. Her research on the employee-organization relationship focuses on the influence of social and organizational processes. Her work on diversity has examined the impact that composition of the work group and employee/supervisor dyads has on the attitudes and performance of work groups and individual employees. She has published numerous articles in such journals as *Academy of Management Journals, Academy of Management Review, Journal of Applied Psychology, Personnel Psychology, Journal of Organizational Behavior, Human Relations,* and *Journal of Management.* Dr. Shore is a fellow of the American Psychological Association and the Society for Industrial and Organizational Psychology. She served as the chair of the Human Resources Division of the Academy of Management in 2001. Dr. Shore is an associate editor for the *Journal of Applied Psychology.*

Marcus M. Stewart, assistant professor of management at the University of Georgia, earned his BS and MBA at Bentley College in Waltham, Massachusetts and his PhD in organizational behavior at the University of North Carolina at Chapel Hill. His current research focuses on the effects of diversity on feedback processes, career management, and social justice. He teaches courses in organizational behavior and human resource management and has published his research in the *Journal of Applied Psychology.*

Dianna L. Stone is professor of management and psychology at the University of Central Florida. Her interests are in the areas of diversity and culture (especially race, disabilities, and Hispanics at work), reactions to personnel selection techniques, privacy in organizations, social justice, and human resource technology. She has published in the *Journal of Applied Psychology, Personnel Psychology, Academy of Management Review, Journal of Management and Organizational Behavior,* and *Human Decision Processes.* She currently serves as the associate editor for the *Journal of Quality Management and Research in Human Performance.* She is also the director of a research center at UCF named PRIMO (Partnership for Research on the Influence of Multiculturalism in Organizations). In addition, she is a fellow of the American Psychological Association and the Society for Industrial and Organizational Psychology.

Eugene F. Stone-Romero (PhD, University of California at Irvine) is professor of psychology at the University of Central Florida. He is a fellow of the Society for Industrial and Organizational Psychology, the American Psychological Society, and the American Psychological Association. He formerly served as an associate editor of the *Journal of Applied Psychology* and now serves on the editorial boards of several journals, including the *Journal of Applied Psychology*, *Personnel Psychology*, *Journal of Management*, and *Organizational Research Methods*. Professor Stone-Romero's current research interests include the influence of work-related values on work behavior, unfair discrimination in organizations, privacy in organizations, and determinants of work quality.

Kecia M. Thomas is associate professor and graduate coordinator for the Department of Psychology at the University of Georgia (UGA). She also holds an appointment in UGA's Institute for African-American Studies. Kecia is an industrial/organizational psychologist whose primary research interests are in the area of the psychology of workplace diversity. She has published research on the topics of recruitment, leadership, and careers in a number of psychology journals and has completed a text on diversity dynamics in the workplace.

Theresa K. Vescio is an assistant professor of psychology at Pennsylvania State University. She studies social attitudes and social cognition. Her primary research endeavors fall under the rubric of stereotyping and prejudice. Within this context, her work focuses on the following four areas: (1) how global societal stereotypes influence judgments of and behavior toward individual members of stereotyped groups; (2) how contact with individual outgroup members affects stereotypic representations of outgroups and intergroup prejudice; (3) intergroup categorization, perception and bias; and (4) how members of stereotyped groups define themselves and cope in the face of negative stereotyped perceptions of the groups to which they belong.

Carolyn Wiethoff is a clinical assistant professor in the management department of the Kelley School of Business at Indiana University—Bloomington. She holds a BA in philosophy and religion from Kean University in New Jersey, an MA in speech communication from Indiana University—Bloomington, and a PhD in management and human resources from the Fisher College of Business at The Ohio State University. Her research interests include the effect of nonvisible diversity (e.g., sexual orientation or religious differences) on individual and group behavior in organizations. She supplements this interest with research in the areas of trust and work teams.

Discrimination at Work

The Psychological and
Organizational Bases

1

An Introduction

Robert L. Dipboye
University of Central Florida

Adrienne Colella
Texas A&M University

When we first considered editing this volume on workplace discrimination, we had reservations because employment discrimination has been written about extensively in the social sciences. We wondered about what new thinking could be added—how could this volume move the frontier of employment discrimination research forward? How could this book distinguish itself from the myriad of other books on the topic? After some initial research, we concluded that such a volume was indeed needed to bring together a substantial, but disparate body of literature and to offer authors who have written extensively on the topic a forum for suggesting the next steps in workplace discrimination research. It is to these ends, integrating a great body of literature based on different theory and methodology and moving research in this area forward, that we hope this volume expands the frontier of workplace discrimination research.

This book is concerned with prejudice, stereotyping, and discrimination in the workplace. We refer to *prejudice* as the attitudinal and especially the affective biases that exist with regard to members of groups other than those to which one belongs. *Stereotyping* is used to refer to the cognitive biases against outgroup members and includes not only attributions of traits to members of these groups but also beliefs about these individuals.

Discrimination refers to the unfair behavioral biases demonstrated against these persons.

Although the title of this book suggests a focus solely on discrimination, the behavioral, affective, and cognitive components are intertwined; consideration of one requires consideration of the other two. Most of the authors in this volume were informed by the theory and research in social psychology on the cognitive and attitudinal bases of discrimination. However, as noted by Susan Fiske (1998), "Documenting discriminatory behavior has not been social psychology's strong suit. Like the attitude–behavior debacle that almost destroyed the foundations of persuasion research, a debacle threatens stereotyping research if it does not soon address behavior" (p. 374). Discrimination appears to have received much more attention in the organizational sciences; it is this literature that we will critically review and attempt to integrate.

Discrimination in its most general form is the differentiation among persons for the purpose of making decisions about those individuals and can occur on the basis of legitimate factors (e.g., merit or potential to perform a job). Our primary concern is with the discrimination that can occur against persons on the basis of characteristics that are inappropriate and irrelevant bases for employment decisions (e.g., group membership). We deal with the discrimination that can occur as persons prepare themselves for employment and that can occur in their treatment once they are employed and enter the organization. Discriminatory treatment includes the formal procedures used not only in selection, appraisal, compensation, placement, promotion, training, and working conditions but also in the more informal and subtle forms of discrimination, such as social exclusion. In this book, we explore discrimination that is well-intentioned and malicious, conscious and unconscious, legal and illegal, and related and unrelated to meaningful criteria of success. Regardless of the form it assumes, however, the effect is the same. One group of persons is placed at a disadvantage on the basis of group identity (Cox, 1993, p. 64), social category (Jones, 1986), stigma (Goffman, 1963), or ascribed characteristics (Messner, 1989, p. 71) relative to other groups with comparable potential, performance, or proven success (Cascio, 1998).

Diversity in the workplace has become a major topic of research in the organizational sciences over the past decade with numerous books and articles bringing attention to the benefits of a workforce that is heterogeneous in terms of race, gender, disability status, age, and sexual orientation. Despite this positive framing of the issue, unfair discrimination on the basis of these characteristics continues as a major barrier to achieving diversity and its benefits. There are profound inequalities in opportunity in the United States and other democratic societies despite the fundamental democratic premise that all people should have an equal chance at occupational success and the pursuit of happiness. Older workers are more likely to be unemployed and less likely to receive training and career counseling than younger workers (U.S. Department of Labor, 2002a). Relative to White workers, Black employees are paid much less, are more than twice as likely to be unemployed, are underrepresented in higher paid occupations, and are overrepresented in lower paid occupations (U.S. Dept. of Labor, 2002b). People with disabilities are more likely to be unemployed and are paid less than people who do not have disabilities (McNeil, 2000). Women are not only underpaid relative to men but also hold less prestigious positions, advance more slowly in organizations, and tend to be found in occupations that are predominately female (U.S. Dept. of Labor, 2002b). There are little data on gays and lesbians, but here again there is evidence of inequalities such as greater rates of termination (Croteau, 1996). A variety of factors is likely to determine labor market outcomes, and a question addressed to varying degrees in these chapters is how unfair discrimination in the workplace is involved in these inequalities.

During the past century, social scientists from a variety of disciplines have investigated discrimination, and over the last three to four decades scholars have directed substantial attention to discrimination in the work place. In this book, we summarize this previous scholarly work, examine the possible bases for integrating and interpreting this work, and set an agenda for future work. The passage of the Civil Rights Act of 1964, the Age Discrimination in Employment Act, and other laws prohibiting employment discrimination was a major impetus for the work on this topic in personnel psychology and human research management. It is our impression that much of the literature on I/O psychology stays within the framework of the law to educate and assist employers in how to best comply with these laws. The authors in this book were encouraged to go beyond existing legal thinking and incorporate a multidisciplinary perspective.

This book is organized into three parts: (I) The fundamental causes of discrimination; (II) research on discrimination against specific groups (e.g., race, sex, disability); and (III) the implications of research and theory for policy and practice aimed at reducing discrimination. We chose to divide the book into these three parts because they reflect the general lines of psychologically based research conducted in the area of employment discrimination. However, the chapters in each part also speak to issues addressed in other sections. For example, the Brief, Butz, and Deitch chapter on race in part II addresses the impact of the environment on discrimination, an issue that is also relevant to part I regarding the causes of discrimination.

The question addressed by the authors of the chapters in part I is as follows: How can we explain discrimination in organizations? A variety of models representing different perspectives have been proposed to understand discrimination at the level of the individual, the group, the organization, and the environment of the organization. This part examines the origins of discrimination from each of these perspectives.

In chapter 2, "Discrimination at the Level of the Individual: Cognitive and Affective Factors," John Dovidio and Michelle Hebl consider the cognitive and affective antecedents of discrimination. It is well established that people are "cognitive misers" and often take short cuts in their gathering and processing of information on others. Discrimination from this perspective is a consequence of the short cuts taken in processing of information on racial minorities, women, older employees, persons with disabilities, gays and lesbians, and other minority and historically disadvantaged groups. These affective factors reflect a very different process. In recent years, increasing attention has been given to how the stereotyping, prejudice, and discrimination of White persons are driven by unconscious, negative affect toward Black persons.

At another level of explanation are the relationships in which people are involved and the groups to which they belong in organizations. These group and relational level factors are the topic of the next two chapters: "Relational Demography Within Groups: Through the Lens of Discrimination" by Christine Riordan, Bryan Schaffer, and Marcus Stewart and "Group-Level Explanations of Workplace Discrimination" by Kecia Thomas and Donna Chrobot-Mason. Both chapters review evidence that discrimination is associated with friendships, social networks, and other informal relationships that emerge in an organization (Ibarra, 1993; Riordan & Shore, 1997). Although not officially sanctioned by the organization, these relationships often impact performance by defining who has access to information, physical resources, social support, status, and influence. Still another social factor is the normative pressure associated with group membership. Discrimination against a member of an outgroup may reflect conformity to what is expected of the person by peers and supervisors and may be independent of the private beliefs or attitudes.

Finally, discrimination can reflect a variety of factors at the level of the organization. Several of these factors are discussed by Michele Gelfand, Lisa Nishii, Jana Raver, and Benjamin Schneider in chapter 5, "Discrimination in Organizations: An Organizational-Level Systems Perspective." The authors consider structural factors such as firm size and gender and racial occupational segregation, and the existence of a specialized human resource management function. Other organizational factors discussed in this chapter include the policies of the organization, the core values that define the culture of the organization, the composition of the corporate board, and the philosophy and attitudes of the top leadership of the organization.

Whereas the authors of the chapters in part I address general underlying components of discrimination in organizations, the authors of the chapters in part II explore specific manifestations of discrimination including discrimination on the basis of race and ethnicity, gender, disability, age, sexual orientation, personality, and attractiveness. The first five forms of discrimination have been the focus of policy and law and have received the most attention in discussions of discrimination in the workplace. In each chapter, the authors examine how the particular type of discrimination is manifested in the entry of employees into an organization and their treatment in the workplace. Each chapter reviews research on biases against the target group in recruitment, selection, placement, performance appraisal, compensation, training and development, promotion, and work conditions.

In chapter 6, "Organizations as Reflections of Their Environments: The Case of Race Composition," Arthur Brief, Rebecca Butz, and Elizabeth Deitch address the topic of race discrimination. The discussion in this chapter is relevant to discrimination against a variety of historically disadvantaged groups, but the focus in their chapter is on African Americans. Special attention is paid to how an organization's environment can shape prejudice, stereotypes, and discrimination inside the organization. In chapter 7, "Gender Discrimination in Organizations," Jeanette Cleveland, Theresa Vescio, and Janet Barnes-Farrell examine discrimination based on the gender of employees. The authors consider factors at the individual, group, and organizational levels that influence both covert and blatant gender discrimination and that render the workplace unfriendly and uncomfortable for women. Particularly provocative is the authors' suggestion that sex discrimination is rooted in how men have constructed the idea of career success. The authors suggest that organizational scientists rethink what should define success in organizations.

In chapter 8, "Understanding Heterosexism at Work: The Straight Problem," Belle Rose Ragins and Carolyn Wiethoff address discrimination on the basis of sexual orientation. This chapter examines the extent that negative attitudes toward gays and lesbians spill over into their recruiting, hiring, and treatment in the workplace and the individual, group, and organizational factors that influence discrimination against persons who are gay, lesbian, bisexual, and transgendered. The authors also consider the factors associated with coming out in the workplace and the consequences of coming out on occupational success and physical and psychological well-being. In the next chapter, "Age Discrimination in the Workplace," Lynn

Shore and Caren Goldberg examine biases in the workplace against older employees, a topic that will receive increasing attention as the baby boom generation ages. The authors propose a model in which social comparison processes are at the core of age discrimination. In "Workplace Discrimination Toward Persons With Disabilities: A Call for Some New Research Directions," Adrienne Colella and Dianna Stone review the research on discrimination against persons with both physical and mental impairments. The authors review the published research on disability and suggest new directions for future research, such as greater attention to the roles of emotions and paternalism and a broader range of outcomes.

The chapters in part II are concerned mostly with groups for which there are policies and laws providing some level of protection. However, unfair discrimination occurs on the basis of other factors in addition to those that have been afforded legal protection. The chapters by Eugene Stone-Romero, "A Stigma That Can Lead to Workplace Discrimination: Personality," and Robert Dipboye, "Looking the Part: Bias Against the Physically unattractive as a Discrimination Issue" expand the discussion by exploring discrimination on the basis of personality and physical appearance. Stone-Romero uses Erving Goffman's (1963) theory of stigma to discuss character stigma resulting from attributions to individuals of traits that mark them as undesirable. Stone-Romero considers the potential of personality measures used to assess fit to the job and organization to stigmatize individuals as deficient in competence or character. The physical appearance of employees (or what Goffman called the "abominations of the flesh") can also serve as a major source of bias in decisions regarding hiring, promotion, and treatment. There is considerable evidence of bias against the physically unattractive in both the laboratory and field (Stone, Stone, & Dipboye, 1992). Dipboye considers whether this is an important bias that deserves separate attention and its potential role as a mediator of other forms of bias.

The third part of the book addresses the implications of research and theory in dealing with discrimination. This part will consider some of the issues and unanswered questions associated with attempts to solve the problem of discrimination. In chapter 13, "Achieving Diversity and Reducing Discrimination in the Work Place Through Human Resource Management Practices," Winfred Arthur and Dennis Doverspike examine the potential of selection, recruitment, training and development, and compensation to reduce discrimination. In "Using Law and Psychology to Inform Our Knowledge of Discrimination," Ramona Paetzold examines the implications of psychological research and theory for discrimination law and argues for changes in the law to reflect the findings of research. In chapter 15, "Combating Organizational Discrimination: Some Unintended

Consequences," Madeline Heilman and Michelle Haynes review a program of research showing that preferential treatment can stigmatize those it is intended to benefit. In "International Employment Discrimination: A Review of Legal Issues, Human Impacts and Organizational Implications," Georgia Chao and Hannah-Hanh Nguyen review how other countries deal with the issue of discrimination. This chapter highlights various international perspectives on discrimination and considers how we can incorporate global perspectives into our study of employment discrimination. The chapter by Martin Greller and John Jackson differs from the other chapters in this book in that the authors do not review research or theory and instead provide a case study. They report on how they were part of a team of social scientists that assisted legislative attempts to reduce the gender gap in wages in Wyoming ("Doing Research on Pay Equity in Support of the Political Process: The Wyoming Experience").

In "The Dilemmas of Workplace Discrimination," we conclude the volume with an assessment of the current state of the research and a summary of the major themes of the book. We call for a general framework that provides a general understanding of workplace discrimination as a complex, subtle, and dynamic phenomenon. In laying the foundation for a model, we suggest several new directions in research. We also consider some new directions for practical interventions in dealing with discrimination.

In conclusion, this Frontiers series volume should provide readers with a clear understanding of the psychologically based workplace discrimination research. The theory, methodology, and suggested implications of this research are put forth to allow scholars and scientist–practitioners to gain a comprehensive view of the field. Furthermore, much of the work in this volume discusses future directions for research on workplace discrimination. Our hope is that these ideas will ignite and guide future research and practice.

REFERENCES

Cascio, W. F. (1998). *Applied psychology in human resource management*. Upper Saddle River, NJ: Prentice-Hall.

Croteau, J. M. (1996). Research on work experiences of lesbian, gay, and bisexual people: An integrative review of methodology and findings. *Journal of Vocational Behavior, 48*, 195–209.

Cox, T. (1993). *Cultural diversity in organizations. Theory, research, and practice*. San Francisco: Berrett-Koehler.

Fiske, S. (1998). Stereotyping, prejudice, and discrimination. In D. Gilbert, S. Fiske, & G. Lindzey (Eds.). *The handbook of social psychology: Vol. 2*. (4th ed., pp. 357–411). New York: McGraw-Hill.

Goffman, E. (1963). *Stigma: Notes on the management of spoiled identity*. Englewood Cliffs, NJ: Prentice-Hall.

Ibarra, H. (1993). Personal networks of women and minorities in management: A conceptual framework. *Academy of Management Review, 18,* 56–87.

Jones, J. M. (1986). Racism: a cultural analysis of the problem. In J. F. Dovidio & S. L. Gaertner (Eds.), *Prejudice, discrimination and racism* (pp. 279–314). New York: Academic Press.

McNeil, J. M. (2000). *Employment, earnings, and disability.* Paper presented at the 75th Annual Conference of the Western Economic Association International, Vancouver, British Columbia.

Messner, S. F. (1989). Economic discrimination and societal homicide rates: Further evidence on the coast of inequality. *American Sociological Review, 54,* 597–611.

Riordan, C. M., & Shore, L. M. (1997). Demographic diversity and employee attitudes: An empirical examination of relational demography within work units. *Journal of Applied Psychology, 82,* 342–358.

Stone, E. F., Stone, D. L., & Dipboye, R. L. (1992). Stigmas in organizations: Race, handicaps, and physical attractiveness. In K. Kelley (Ed.), Issues, theory, and research in industrial/ organizational psychology (pp. 385–457). Amsterdam, Netherlands: Elsevier.

U.S. Department of Labor, Bureau of Labor Statistics (2002a). U.S. Department of Labor, *Employment and Earnings.* Washington, D.C.: U.S. Government Printing Office.

U.S. Department of Labor, Bureau of Labor Statistics (2002b). *Report on the American workforce.* Washington, D.C.: U.S. Government Printing Office.

I

Psychological, Group, and Organizational Bases of Discrimination

2

Discrimination at the Level of the Individual: Cognitive and Affective Factors

John F. Dovidio
Colgate University

Michelle R. Hebl
Rice University

Discrimination traditionally has been defined as unjustified negative actions that deny "individuals or groups of people equality of treatment" (Allport, 1954, p. 51). Discrimination occurs at many levels: cultural, social, institutional, and individual. Perhaps because of its multiple sources and manifestations, discrimination and perceptions of discrimination continue to be dominant forces within the lives of most minority group members in the United States (Gallup, 2002). Members of these groups traditionally have been underrepresented and disadvantaged socially, politically, and economically. This chapter examines the causes and consequences of discrimination in the workplace focusing on the individual level. We highlight the role that the cognitive and affective components of intergroup attitudes play in this process.

This chapter consists of five sections. The first section identifies basic intrapersonal and interpersonal processes that critically shape intergroup discrimination. In this section, we define the key terms of attitudes,

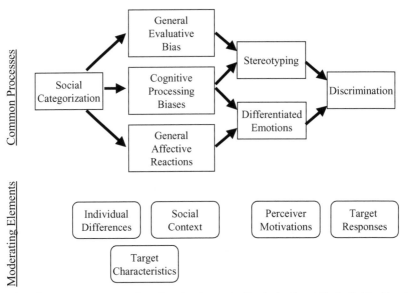

FIG. 2.1. Common processes and moderating factors in discrimination at the individual level.

prejudice, and stereotypes. The second section considers how basic cognitive and affective processes, which apply to intergroup relations in general, contribute to discrimination. We discuss how cognitive and affective factors operate independently and in concert to influence discrimination. These factors are summarized in the top half of Fig. 2.1. The third section explores factors, such as individual differences and qualities of target groups and their members, that moderate the influence of these basic processes. Although there are significant commonalities in process, there are also strikingly divergent ways in which different individuals react to members of specific stigmatized groups in various situations. These moderating elements are presented in the bottom half of Fig. 2.1. The fourth section illustrates possible manifestations of discrimination in the workplace. We examine how discrimination may be manifested both directly and indirectly. The fifth section summarizes conclusions and implications.

BASIC CONCEPTS

Three key concepts for understanding individual processes that produce discrimination are attitudes, prejudice, and stereotypes. *Attitudes* traditionally have been conceptualized as having both cognitive and affective elements. The cognitive component involves specific thoughts or beliefs about the attitude object. With respect to intergroup attitudes, cognitive processes include both the basic consequences of categorizing people into ingroups and outgroups (e.g., the tendency to see members of another group as similar to one another) and the types of generalizations that people make about particular groups. The affective component of attitudes relates to feelings and emotions associated with the attitude object. Although cognitive and affective intergroup orientations are often consonant, they may also be inconsistent. For instance, modern forms of prejudice have been described as involving a disassociation between affect and cognition, with feelings often being more negative than beliefs about members of other groups (Dovidio & Gaertner, 1998). Moreover, the relative contribution of the affective and cognitive factors to discrimination may vary across groups as a function of individual differences and group relations.

Prejudice is commonly defined as an unfair negative attitude toward a social group or a person perceived to be a member of that group. Prejudice serves fundamental functions. Like other attitudes, it provides a schema for interpreting the environment by signaling whether others in the environment are good or bad, thereby preparing people to take appropriate action. Prejudice may be reflected in general evaluative responses and may also involve emotional reactions, such as anxiety or contempt. In this chapter, we consider evaluative and affective aspects of prejudice separately.

A *stereotype* is a generalization of beliefs about a group or its members that is unjustified because it reflects faulty thought processes or overgeneralizations, factual incorrectness, inordinate rigidity, misattributions, or rationalizations for prejudiced attitudes or discriminatory behaviors (Dovidio, Brigham, Johnson, & Gaertner, 1996). Rather than representing an overall orientation toward a group, a stereotype represents a particular constellation of traits and roles associated with a group. Because stereotypes operate as coherent cognitive schemas, they fundamentally influence how information about a group or group member is acquired, processed, stored, and recalled (von Hippel, Sekaquaptewa, & Vargas, 1995). The activation of stereotypes typically produces an information processing advantage for stereotypical traits or other associations (Mackie, Hamilton, Susskind, & Rosselli, 1996). In addition, people do not typically attend to perceptual information that could disconfirm stereotypes (von Hippel et al., 1995), and they tend to view group members who are nonstereotypic as exceptions or representative of a subtype of the group. As a result of these processes, stereotypes are highly resistant to change.

Despite the traditional distinction between prejudice and stereotyping, researchers have also emphasized their commonalities and close relationship. For instance, prejudices and stereotypes encompass affective and cognitive responses. In addition, both prejudices and stereotypes do not have to be consciously endorsed to be influential; they may be activated both implicitly (automatically and without awareness) and explicitly (consciously, deliberately, and controllably). Whereas explicit prejudices and stereotypes typically are assessed using self-report measures, implicit prejudices and stereotypes typically are measured using response latency techniques or other (e.g., memory) cognitive tasks. Furthermore, prejudice and stereotyping share functional characteristics. Fiske (1998) observed that both are enduring human characteristics, have automatic aspects, have a degree of social utility, are mutable, and are influenced by other social structures. Finally, both are also rooted in categorical thinking about others. In the next section, we examine how social categorization and category-based responding influence intergroup relations and discrimination generally.

COMMON PROCESSES IN DISCRIMINATION

Discrimination, or unfair treatment, at the level of the individual has at its foundation the recognition that people belong to different social groups. Thus, we describe some of the causes and consequences of social categorization. As illustrated in the top of Fig. 2.1, we discuss key processes involved in social categorization, and then we consider how cognitive processes relate to stereotyping and affective reactions separately and how they can jointly influence discrimination.

Social Categorization and Social Identity

From a social categorization perspective, one universal facet of human perception essential for efficient functioning is the ability to sort people, spontaneously and with minimum effort or awareness, into a smaller number of meaningful categories. A critical aspect of social categorization is whether a person is perceived to be a unique individual, a member of the perceiver's group (the ingroup), or a member of another group (an outgroup). Although the basis of people's impressions ranges on a continuum from person-based, individuating qualities to group-based characteristics, because of ease and efficiency, people tend to rely more on group-based impressions (Fiske, Lin, & Neuberg, 1999). The tendency to categorize others as a member of a group rather than as an individual is stronger with greater salience placed upon the basis of categorization, greater "fit" of an individual to the prototype of the category, and more direct relevance of group membership to the situation. Situational factors (such as interdependence) or perceivers' motivations (such as a desire for accuracy) can produce more individuated impressions. Stereotypic impressions tend to strengthen, however, when perceivers rely on group-based information. Social identity theory (Tajfel & Turner, 1979) and self-categorization theory (Turner, 1985) further emphasize that when personal identity is salient, a person's individual needs, standards, beliefs, and motives primarily determine behavior; in contrast, when social identity is salient, collective needs, goals, and standards are primary.

As illustrated in Fig. 2.1, social categorization of others systematically influences how people react in terms of evaluations (general evaluative bias), how they think about others (cognitive processing biases and stereotyping), and how they feel (general affective biases and differentiated emotions). Although affective and cognitive reactions have been hypothesized to be separate systems, with affect being the more basic and immediate system (Zajonc, 1980), both processes are initiated with social categorization. Moreover, these processes jointly influence outcomes, which we consider next.

General Consequences of Social Categorization

One of the most basic forms of social categorization is the classification of people into ingroup and outgroup members. Even when the basis of the assignment is arbitrary, this mere categorization is sufficient to create an overall evaluative bias: People categorized as members of one's own group are evaluated more favorably than are those categorized as members of another group. This bias occurs spontaneously and is most pronounced for prototypical group members (see Gaertner & Dovidio, 2000, for a review).

Social categorization also influences how people process information about others in fundamental ways. Perceptually, when people or objects are categorized into groups, actual differences between members of the same category tend to be minimized and often to be ignored in making decisions or forming impressions, whereas between-group differences tend to become exaggerated (Turner, 1985). People retain more detailed and more positive information about ingroup than outgroup members, strategically recall why ingroup members are similar and outgroup members are dissimilar to the self, and work harder for ingroups (see Gaertner & Dovidio, 2000).

The process of social categorization also influences affective reactions. As Insko et al. (2001) demonstrated, categorization in terms of group membership rather than individual identity evokes greater feelings of fear and lower levels of trust in interactions with others. General anxiety may be aroused in intergroup settings for a number of additional reasons, such as unfamiliarity with group members, hostility, self-presentational concerns, and distrust (Stephan & Stephan, 1985).

The general evaluative, cognitive, and affective processes form the foundation for the development of more differentiated responses toward specific groups. These general tendencies translate into more specifically defined stereotypes and differentiated emotional reactions.

Stereotypes and Emotional Reactions

Closely related to the initial categorization of people as ingroup or outgroup members is the development of social stereotypes, which arise from individuals' needs to understand, predict, and control the environment. Once categorization occurs, members of other groups are viewed as similar to one another (the outgroup homogeneity effect) and as having common characteristics. Traits often are overemphasized in stereotypes of outgroups because dispositional attributions of this type offer stable explanations for the group's behavior, which enhance feelings of predictability. In addition, the content of specific group stereotypes (e.g., lazy, incompetent, emotional) frequently evolves from existing differences in group roles or statuses within a society and serves to justify and perpetuate these status differences (Jost, Burgess, & Mosso, 2001).

Intergroup affect can be aroused either broadly (e.g., intergroup anxiety) or uniquely (e.g., specific, differentiated emotions) in response to the nature of the group or the group stereotype. Jones et al. (1984) proposed that specific emotional reactions to groups and group members may be shaped by cultural factors. In particular, they hypothesized that any given society has implicit emotion rules that define how its societal members should feel and react toward members who are deviant. These feelings may involve anxiety and revulsion, anger, or sympathetic and nurturant feelings. For example, if people appraise an individual as violating ingroup norms, they may experience disgust, which in turn prompts avoidance. Such a reaction may be typical for stigmas, such as being gay or lesbian, which seem to be tied to the perceived violation of dominant (ingroup) norms and values.

Specific affective reactions to groups may also be a function of the way groups are stereotyped. Fiske, Cuddy, Glick, and Xu (2002) found that stereotypes are represented by separate dimensions associated with competence and warmth. Groups that are perceived as high in competence but low in warmth (e.g., rich people) tend to evoke envy, whereas those high in competence and high in warmth (e.g., Black professionals) produce admiration. Among groups viewed as low in competence, those who are high in warmth (e.g., elderly people) are associated with pity, whereas those also low in warmth (e.g., poor Black people) generate contempt.

As illustrated in Fig. 2.1, social categorization and social identity create a foundation for developing general biases; stereotypes and differentiated intergroup emotions provide specific mechanisms that influence the degree and form of discrimination toward particular groups.

Discrimination

Stereotypes are both prescriptive and descriptive (Eagly & Karau, 2002). Consequently, behaviors by members that violate stereotypic expectations, even though they may be positive and instrumental actions when considered objectively, can elicit negative emotions (such as fear, disgust, or anger). These negative emotional reactions can then trigger discrimination to maintain the status quo, which favors one's own group over others. For example, stronger perceptions that "Blacks are getting too demanding in their push for equal rights," an item from McConahay's (1986) Modern Racism Scale, are associated with more negative affect toward Blacks targets and with higher levels of discrimination by White individuals. Analogously, in terms of discrimination against women, Rudman (1998) found that women who were self-promoting were perceived as higher in competence than were those who were not self-promoting. However, self-promoting women were viewed to be less socially attractive and less likely to be hired than were self-promoting men and nonself-promoting women. Thus, to the extent that the specific content of stereotypes guides appraisals of group members and defines appropriate roles and behaviors, stereotypes can determine how people respond affectively and, ultimately, behaviorally to group members.

Besides their expression in overt discrimination, racial stereotypes and prejudice can shape interpersonal interactions in subtle but significant ways, such as through self-fulfilling prophecies. Regardless of their self-reported (and presumably conscious) racial attitudes, individual differences in automatically and unconsciously activated attitudes predict how friendly White individuals behave overall (Fazio, Jackson, Dunton, & Williams, 1995) and nonverbally (Dovidio, Kawakami, Johnson, Johnson, & Howard, 1997; Word, Zanna, & Cooper, 1974) toward a Black person. Furthermore, consistent with the operation of self-fulfilling prophecies, and as shown by Word et al. (1974), Black applicants who interact with interviewers displaying a less friendly nonverbal style perform significantly more poorly in the situation.

The elements identified in the top half of Fig. 2.1 offer a view of the types of factors that contribute to individual-level discrimination in general and in the workplace. These elements can best be conceptualized as factors that influence an individual's *propensity* to discriminate. The actual manifestation of discrimination, however, can be determined ultimately by other moderating elements. We consider these influences in the next section.

MODERATING FACTORS

As illustrated in the bottom half of Fig. 2.1, at least five types of moderators can influence cognitive and affective reactions to members of stigmatized groups and the basic expression of discrimination. The first three moderators (individual differences, social context, and target characteristics) largely influence the early stages depicted in Fig. 2.1, shaping social categorization processes; the nature of evaluative, cognitive, and affective biases that are elicited; and the manifestation of stereotypes and differentiated emotional reactions. The last two moderating factors (perceiver motivations and target responses) tend to influence the later stages depicted in Fig. 2.1.

Individual Differences

People differ systematically in their tendencies to perceive others in terms of group membership, in their propensity to see groups hierarchically, and in their willingness to endorse stereotypic characterizations and prejudicial attitudes openly. We consider three individual differences, the first of which is authoritarianism. Developed as a construct in the late 1940s, the authoritarian personality inventory was constructed to measure anti-Semitism and its correlates (Adorno, Frenkel-Brunswik, Levinson, & Sanford, 1950). The resulting personality structure largely reflected ethnocentrism, a tendency to think in rigid categories, a need to submit to authority, adherence to middle class values, and rationalized aggression.

Altemeyer (1996) continued Adorno et al.'s (1950) line of research by focusing on what he referred to as right-wing authoritarians, or people who specifically (a) submit to authorities, (b) exhibit aggression toward social deviants, and (c) maintain conventional beliefs. Those scoring high in right-wing authoritarianism are also more likely to endorse and defend the status quo and hold negative attitudes toward and limit the opportunities of stigmatized or oppressed individuals. Those high in right-wing authoritarianism are also likely to see the world as threatening and may feel more justified in discriminating against others as a way to maintain control (see also Crandall & Eshleman, 2003).

A second individual difference involves social dominance orientation (Pratto, Sidanius, Stallworth, & Malle, 1994). People high in social dominance orientation believe that group hierarchies are inevitable, see the world as involving competition between groups for resources, and view unequal social outcomes as a consequence of social hierarchies as appropriate. They tend to be high in prejudice toward a range of other groups. Individuals low in social dominance orientation, in contrast, are generally concerned about others' welfare, empathic, and tolerant of other individuals and groups (Pratto et al., 1994).

A third individual difference is the level of prejudice that people hold. Whereas authoritarianism and social dominance orientation may be related directly to overt biases, such as old-fashioned racism, other forms of bias have emerged as current norms and laws sanction open discrimination. Examples of contemporary racial biases include aversive racism (Gaertner & Dovidio, 1986), modern racism (McConahay, 1986), and symbolic racism (Sears, Henry, & Kosterman, 2000). A common, critical aspect these three different forms of contemporary bias is the conflict between the denial of personal prejudice and underlying unconscious negative feelings and beliefs.

Dovidio and Gaertner (2000), for example, proposed that aversive racism may be one factor that contributes to disparities in the workplace. At the time of hiring, aversive racism can affect how qualifications are perceived and weighed, in ways that systematically disadvantage Black relative to White applicants. Dovidio and Gaertner found that racial bias among Black applicants was not expressed when Black and White job candidates were clearly qualified or clearly unqualified for a position. However, when qualifications were not clear, bias against Black candidates emerged.

Measures of implicit attitudes and stereotypes, assessed using response latency techniques, have helped to identify who is likely to exhibit these types of subtle biases. In general, response time measures relate to a wide range of personal characteristics and orientations, such as self-esteem and political ideology (Jost, Glaser, Kruglanski, & Sulloway, 2003), and these measures have been used to increase the accuracy of predicting voting behavior, other political positions, and consumer behavior (Bassili, 1995; Fazio, Powell, & Williams, 1989). Using response time measures to assess implicit feelings about Blacks and self-report techniques to measure explicit attitudes, Dovidio, Kawakami, and Gaertner (2002) evaluated the effects of White individuals' unconscious (implicit) and conscious (explicit) attitudes on discrimination. Explicit attitudes shape deliberative, well-considered responses (e.g., overt judgments) for which people have the motivation and opportunity to weigh the costs and benefits of various courses of action, whereas implicit attitudes shape responses that are more difficult to monitor and control (e.g., some nonverbal behaviors). Thus, the relative impact of implicit and explicit attitudes is a function of the context in which the attitudinal object appears, the motivation and opportunity to engage in deliberative processes, and the nature of the behavioral response. We consider the role of the social context in the next section.

Social Context

As shown in Fig. 2.1, the social context, or composition and nature of the relationships between members of different groups, can systematically influence the salience of intergroup boundaries and the likelihood that people will be seen and categorized in terms of their group memberships. A critical aspect of the social composition of the workplace is the potential for "tokenism."

Kanter (1977) described a "token" in her seminal work as being a member of recognizable subgroup representing less than 15% of the total group. Tokens often report experiencing negative feelings of distinctiveness, vulnerability, and a loss of self-confidence (see Niemann & Dovidio, 1998). These feelings may have a number of organizational repercussions such as decreased performance, less favorable performance appraisals, and fewer opportunities to advance. Feelings of distinctiveness, based on race or gender, can also arouse "stereotype threat" in which people behave in ways that conform to the cultural stereotype of their group, even when such behaviors have an adverse effect on performance (Sekaquaptewa & Thompson, 2003; Steele, 1997).

Another aspect of the social context that influences whether social categorization will occur is the perceived functional relationship between the ingroup and outgroup. Theories based on functional relations often point to competition and consequent perceived threat as a fundamental cause of discrimination. Realistic group conflict theory (Campbell, 1965), for example, posits that in the context of perceived group competition, discrimination becomes an instrument for protecting the resources and opportunities for one's group. Contexts that arouse perceptions of group competition produce or increase the salience of ideologies that justify discrimination (Jost et al., 2001).

Alternatively, the social context may be structured in a way that reduces discrimination. The importance of the nature of the social context is also emphasized in the long tradition of work on the contact hypothesis (Allport, 1954). This hypothesis proposes that simple contact between groups is not sufficient to improve intergroup relations. Rather, prerequisite features must be present (e.g., equal status between groups, cooperative interaction, opportunities for personal acquaintance between the members, and norms that support interaction both within and outside of the contact situation). Both laboratory and field research generally support the improvement of intergroup relations and reductions of bias toward stigmatized individuals when these prerequisite criteria have been established (see Pettigrew & Tropp, 2000).

Intergroup contact, appropriately structured, can reduce bias and discrimination by influencing processes at the earliest stages of the model presented in Fig. 2.1. For instance, through cooperative interaction and the pursuit of common goals, people may *recategorize* others, who were originally viewed as outgroup members, as members of one larger, inclusive superordinate group (Gaertner & Dovidio, 2000), thereby redirecting the forces of ingroup favoritism related to social categorization. Intergroup contact can also decrease bias and discrimination by leading individuals to develop decategorized representations, that is, by perceiving others in terms of their unique qualities rather than their group membership, which can lead to personalized relationships (Miller, 2002). However, if the social context is competitive rather than cooperative, if the nature of the interaction reinforces stereotypes, or if members are stereotypic in their actions, contact can actually exacerbate rather than reduce bias.

Target Characteristics

Characteristics of the targets can influence whether they are initially perceived in categorical or personalized ways. When individuating information is unavailable, people are perceived primarily in stereotypic ways; when individuating information is present, perceivers base their judgments primarily on this information (Locksley, Borgida, Brekke, & Hepburn, 1980). In addition, when information about a person is available, the degree to which it is consistent with overall group stereotypes can determine whether perceptions of the person will be shaped by general group stereotypes (e.g., stereotypes of women), stereotypes of subtypes (e.g., stereotypes of business women), or the person's unique qualities.

Once a person is categorized as a member of a group, the nature of the stigmatizing elements that characterize the social category strongly influence whether and how discrimination will occur. As suggested earlier, the extent to which a person's membership in a negatively viewed outgroup (i.e., a stigmatized group) is perceived to be controllable is one of the strongest determinants of whether individuals will openly express negative feelings and beliefs and discrimination (Weiner, 1995). Those who possess stigmas that are perceived to be more controllable (e.g., homosexuality, obesity, alcoholism)—particularly when the person's failure to exercise control is seen as violating cultural values, such as the Protestant Ethic (Crandall & Martinez, 1996)—are regarded much more negatively and are generally the targets of open discrimination. In contrast, when group membership is perceived to be uncontrollable (e.g., as with stigmatizing conditions such as physical disabilities) individuals may often show ambivalent or even somewhat favorable reactions (Hebl & Kleck, 2002).

Another critical dimension is the perceived threat posed by the outgroup. Perceived threat can involve competition over scarce resources, symbolic challenge to one's cherished values, or personal peril (Stephan & Stephan, 2000). For example, overweight people disrupt normative values for thinness: They are seen as aesthetically displeasing, deviant from accepted standards, and viewed to possess a condition that is controllable (Weiner, 1995). Not surprisingly, then, overweight people face discrimination throughout all stages of the employment cycle (for a review, see Roehling, 1999). An example involving personal peril involves avoiding gay men or lesbians for fear that one will get AIDS or be recruited "over to the other side."

Stigma has negative consequences not only for stigmatized targets but also for nonstigmatized targets who are associated with stigmatized people (Neuberg, Smith, Hoffman, & Russell, 1994). This stigma-by-association effect applies to stigmatizing conditions, such as being gay and lesbian and overweight, and this generalization extends to others who may simply be physically close but not personally associated with a stigmatized person (Hebl & Mannix, 2003).

Motivations of the Individual

Another moderator (see Fig. 2.1) involves individuals' motivations toward members of socially stigmatized groups. In addition to individual- and group-level motivations that promote bias (e.g., through competition), people may also possess internal motivations to respond without prejudice (Devine, Plant, & Buswell, 2000). People who are high on this dimension consciously attempt to override the use of implicit, automatically activated stereotypes, engaging in a number of compensating strategies such as stereotype suppression (Monteith, Sherman, & Devine, 1998). Although this strategy is sometimes effective, it is also shown to have paradoxical "rebound" effects in which, after efforts to suppress stereotypes have been relaxed, increases in stereotyping and prejudicial responding occur (Macrae, Bodenhausen, Milne, & Jetten, 1994). Furthermore, Crandall and Eshleman (2003) suggest that rather than being motivated to suppress prejudice, individuals may frequently be motivated to justify their expressions of prejudice against certain groups (e.g., gay and lesbian or obese individuals).

Target Responses and Strategies

A fifth moderator is the way in which the target responds during interactions (see Fig. 2.1), such as differentially perceiving or strategically reacting to discrimination. Targets may adopt perceptual strategies of either denying or overestimating discrimination. Potential victims of discrimination frequently recognize that their group is discriminated against but tend to deny the same level of personal experience with discrimination (Crosby, 1984). This denial of personal discrimination may be functional; viewing oneself as a victim can lower one's self-esteem, lead to self-blame, and threaten one's sense of control (Crocker & Major, 1994). Denying discrimination, therefore, may help targets maintain a positive self-concept. In addition, targets who complain about being victims of discrimination are disliked and highly reprimanded (Kaiser & Miller, 2001), thereby reinforcing underestimation strategies.

Alternatively, when targets feel particularly vulnerable to discrimination but still feel able to exert some control, they become hypervigilant and may overestimate the amount of discrimination directed toward them (e.g., Hebl, Foster, Mannix, & Dovidio, 2002). To the extent that minority group members are sensitive to signs of rejection, dislike, or discrimination, they may weigh the negative, subtle signals more heavily than the positive overt signals (Vorauer & Kumhyr, 2001).

Given that individuals are able in some cases to identify themselves as victims of discrimination, the strategies that they use to deal with their potential victimization also determine interpersonal and interactional outcomes. Through concealment, Goffman (1963) observed, stigmatized individuals can avoid many negative outcomes by attempting to "pass," or appear nonstigmatized. However, a preoccupation with concealment leads to impaired judgments and behaviors and to long-term health risks (Cole, Kemeny, Taylor, & Visscher, 1996).

Another strategy involves acknowledgment, the overt mentioning or disclosing of one's stigma to others (e.g., Hebl & Kleck, 2002). There may be cases in which the stigma is not able to be concealed and is the primary focus of the interaction. In this case, a direct acknowledgment may actually reduce prejudice-related thought suppression and potentially accompanying negative affect, which can oftentimes activate stereotypes and biases more strongly (e.g., Macrae et al., 1994). Acknowledgment may also lead others to believe targets are well-adjusted and to seek out interactions they would normally avoid. For targets, acknowledgment leads to increased job satisfaction and decreased job anxiety, particularly if coworkers react well to acknowledgment (Griffith & Hebl, 2002).

Still another strategy is compensation. People who perceive or anticipate discrimination may engage in a range of compensatory behaviors. In the short run, they may be especially motivated to make a good impression. Miller, Rothblum, Felicio, and Brand (1995) found that that overweight individuals who feel immediately threatened by the possibility of discrimination act in more socially skilled ways than those who do not experience such threats. In the longer run, however, people may compensate by limiting their personal investment in an organization. King, Hebl, George, and Matusik (2003) showed that women working in the construction industry who reported discrimination appeared to compensate by engaging in less organizational citizenship behaviors or prosocial behaviors while maintaining the same level of performance and job-contingent behaviors as those not experiencing discrimination.

Up to this point, we have reviewed general processes that underlie individual-level discrimination. In the next section, we build upon these general principles and illustrate how they can produce discrimination and disparities in the workplace.

INDIVIDUAL-LEVEL DISCRIMINATION IN THE WORKPLACE

Individual-level cognitive and affective processes can produce workplace discrimination in various ways. For instance, prejudice can be manifested blatantly and openly in ways that provide visible barriers to employment and advancement. Biases may also operate indirectly, influencing perceptions and attributions, which, in turn, can produce disparate outcomes. Furthermore, biases can influence social interactions in ways that consistently disadvantage certain groups.

Direct Consequences for Employment-Related Decisions

Open expressions of bias, such as those assessed by self-report measures, continue to predict discrimination, including discrimination in hiring decisions, at the individual level. Nevertheless, the magnitude of this effect, in terms of both prejudice ($r = .32$) and stereotypes ($r = .16$) is modest (Dovidio et al., 1996). Open expressions of prejudice and negative stereotypes toward a variety of targets, however, have declined, and acceptance in social and work settings has increased (Schuman, Steeh, Bobo, & Krysan, 1997).

One factor that may account for limited overt discrimination is the current legal or normative constraints. The Civil Rights Act and other legislative initiatives prohibit discrimination against individuals based on gender, race, religion, national origin, age, physical disability, and pregnancy. Organizational-level polices and norms also influence the extent to which discrimination is manifested by employees. Institutional policies can act as interventions to the expression of discrimination. For instance, Griffith and Hebl (2002) compared companies that did and did not have organizational policies supporting gay and lesbian lifestyles (e.g., formal antidiscriminatory sexual-orientation policies, active support for gay/lesbian activities, and diversity training that specifically included gay and lesbian issues). Gay and lesbian employees who worked in these organizations, compared to those employed by organizations that did not have such policies, were much more likely to be "out," reported less job discrimination, experienced more favorable coworker reactions, and indicated more positive treatment from their supervisors. Similarly, Ragins and Cornwell (2001) found that gay and lesbian employees were less likely to report discrimination on the job when they worked in organizations with supportive policies or in locations with legislation against discrimination toward gay and lesbian individuals. Analogously, the degree to which an organizational authority condones discrimination relates to the extent to which people will discriminate in personnel selection decisions (Brief, Buttram, Elliott, Reizenstein, & McCline, 1995).

Indirect Consequences for Employment-Related Decisions

Although changes in laws and norms may be effective at limiting overt forms of personal discrimination, negative stereotypes and attitudes can still operate indirectly, for example, by biasing perceptions of attributes or credentials, by influencing decisions in situations in which discrimination would not be obvious, or by producing "backlash" to members of protected groups. For instance, Polinko and Popovich (2001) found that obese job applicants were rated as having more negative work-related attributes, and Hebl and Mannix (2003) showed that men who were in proximity to obese women were rated as less "professional" when they were in close physical proximity to an obese woman (regardless of their relationship) than when they were alone.

The consequences of biased perceptions and attributions can be significantly moderated by the "fit" between a candidate and a position (Heilman, 1983). For instance, women are discriminated against more for positions requiring male sex-typed behaviors (e.g., leadership, authority) than those requiring female sex-typed behaviors (e.g., nurturant, sensitive; Rudman & Glick, 2001). Heilman (2001) proposed that the scarcity of women in the upper level of organizations is a consequence of stereotypes of women that "result in devaluation of their performance, denial of credit to them for their successes, or their penalization for being competent" (p. 657).

Prejudice, as well as stereotypes, can operate indirectly to produce disparities. Even for people who appear nonprejudiced in their public responses, bias against members of stigmatized groups may be manifested when situations are complex, when the appropriateness of an applicant's qualifications are not entirely clear, or when decisions involve the assessment of multiple dimensions (Dovidio & Gaertner, 1998; Gaertner

& Dovidio, 1986). Consistent with this reasoning, outside of the laboratory in generally complex employment contexts, gender and racial biases in performance appraisals and hiring and promotion decisions are generally still observed (Bowen, Swim, & Jacobs, 2000; Powell & Butterfield, 2002). Moreover, supportive of the moderating factors identified in the laboratory, employment interview evaluations of Black and Hispanic applicants tend to be less favorable than those of White applicants, primarily when the interview session is less structured (Huffcutt & Roth, 1998), and when appropriate justifications arise, such as economic conditions that require layoffs (Elvira & Zatzick, 2002). In addition, White interviewers who are higher in measures of subtle racism, such as "modern racism" (McConahay, 1986), are more likely to discriminate against Black than White applicants in hiring when a business-related justification for not hiring the candidate is available (Brief, Dietz, Cohen, Pugh, & Vaslow, 2000).

Individual-level discrimination of this type may be further moderated by the degree of threat that an employment decision has for oneself or for one's group. For example, White individuals show more racial bias in their employment-related responses, particularly for attributions of personal qualities, when their decisions are perceived to threaten the traditionally advantaged status that they have had over Black individuals. Similarly, policies such as affirmative action that are designed to benefit members of other groups are resisted more strongly by people who view the consequences as more threatening to their group (Dovidio & Gaertner, 1996). In contrast, consistent with the principles of social identity discussed earlier, when a superordinate American identity is more salient, White individuals are more likely to support affirmative action policies that benefit members of American minority groups (Smith & Tyler, 1996).

Members of target groups themselves are also susceptible to self-stereotyping and self-attributional biases. Heilman and Alcott (2001) found that women who believed that others thought their selection to a higher status position was based on gender rather than merit anticipated that others held negative impressions of them and behaved in more timid, uncertain, and limited ways in their role as leaders.

Interaction Biases

Discrimination in the workplace can also occur indirectly through biases in how people interact with each other. Hebl et al. (2002), for instance, found that store managers did not discriminate against gay and lesbian job applicants, relative to heterosexual applicants, in terms of pursuing their candidacy. However, store managers were less friendly, interested, and helpful in their interactions with gay and lesbian candidates than with heterosexual candidates. Similarly, Hebl and Mannix (2003) demonstrated that salespeople displayed interpersonal discrimination with obese customers compared to thinner customers. Whether it is based on negative attitudes, which may not even be conscious (Dovidio, Gaertner, Kawakami, & Hodson, 2002), or intergroup anxiety and avoidant tendencies (Hyers & Swim, 1998), discrimination in interpersonal behaviors in the workplace can adversely affect members of minority groups indirectly, by creating impressions of discrimination in the workplace, and directly, by interfering with efficiency and productivity. In addition, the avoidant behavior associated with interpersonal discrimination can reduce the support and diminish the quality of mentorship for minority group members relative to majority group members (Ragins, 1999).

With regard to the experience of discrimination, Hebl et al. (2002) found that people's perceptions of being discriminated against were strongly related to interpersonal discrimination. Perceptions of discrimination, in turn, are associated with a range of negative work-related reactions: negative work attitudes among gay and lesbian employees (Ragins & Cornwell, 2001), greater job stress among Black women (Mays, Coleman, & Jackson, 1996), a mistrust and lack of responsiveness to critical feedback among Blacks (Cohen, Steele, & Ross, 1999), lower feelings of power and greater feelings of work conflict among women (Gutek, Cohen, & Tsui, 1996), and less organizational commitment among Hispanics (Foley, Kidder, & Powell, 2002).

The results of these studies suggest that although organizations may seem to be free of blatant discrimination, a closer, more interpersonal examination suggests that discrimination may be alive and well. According to Valian (2001), it is these small differences or "molehills" that accumulate to create "mountains" of differences. In a modeling study, Martell, Lane, and Emrich (1996) demonstrated that a 1% bias based on sex at the individual level can subsequently translate into a 15% bias against women in hiring at a societal level. In the case of targets who face discrimination, the negativity is still widespread and, although it has changed its appearance, the impact is still substantial.

CONCLUSIONS AND IMPLICATIONS

In summary, because discrimination at the individual level is rooted in many normal processes, such as social categorization, the potential for bias within organizations is significant. Although laws, organizational policies, and social norms appear to be effective in controlling overt forms of discrimination toward many groups, these interventions do not apply to all groups that may be victimized by discrimination (e.g., gay and lesbian individuals in many parts of the country), and particularly to members of groups whose stigmas are perceived to be controllable (e.g., overweight people). Moreover, because the psychological bases that underlie individual-level discrimination (e.g., stereotypes, negative affect) have not been addressed directly, discrimation will be readily manifested when changes in the social context signal discrimination is permissible (Crandall & Eshleman, 2003). The implications for an organization can be quite direct and immediate. Brief et al. (1995) demonstrated that MBAs show a propensity to discriminate in an obvious and blatant manner against minorities when they are told in an explicit manner that the CEO supports such discrimination.

The motivation for and causes of discrimination at the individual level also commonly do not reflect a malicious desire to harm those from other groups. As we have discussed, the conscious motivations of most White individuals is to treat Black individuals fairly: Polls and surveys about prejudice and intent to discriminate have shown consistent declines to low levels (Schuman et al., 1997). Instead, discrimination may arise out of unconscious psychological processes, making much of the discrimination that occurs unintentional. Because individuals also internalize egalitarian norms and principles but continue to harbor negative feelings and beliefs, often unconsciously (Gaertner & Dovidio, 1986), discrimination is frequently manifested in subtle and indirect ways, for example in how people interpret the actions of others and how they interact with them, which is not readily recognizable as discrimination.

These findings suggest at least three additional avenues of inquiry in organizations that go beyond a traditional focus on the effects of blatant expressions of prejudice and discrimination against minorities. One direction involves the effects of ingroup favoritism on disparities in outcomes between majority and minority group members. Research on social categorization demonstrates that people, particularly those with limited intergroup experience, typically feel more comfortable with members of their own group than with members of other groups (Pettigrew & Tropp, 2000), and that they are more open, self-disclosing, and helpful to members of their own group (Dovidio, Gaertner et al., 1997). When legally protected groups (such as women or racial and ethnic minorities) are involved, majority group members may also avoid minority group members out of a fear of behaving inappropriately, in way that might suggest prejudice or discrimination and place them in organizational or legal jeopardy (Gaertner & Dovidio, 1986).

This avoidant behavior likely results in less support and less senior sponsorship for minority group members than for majority group members in organizations. To the extent that mentoring, sponsorship, and informal organizational support foster the advancement of people within an organization, pro-ingroup biases can thus produce systematic disparities based on race, sex, and ethnicity within an organization. Receiving mentoring is associated with increased career satisfaction, salary compensation, job satisfaction, and the mitigation of discrimination (Chao, 1997; Dreher & Ash, 1990; Ragins, 1999). Although this process of ingroup favoritism may not represent discrimination in the classic form or within a strict legal definition (see Krieger, 1998), it is nevertheless a systematic bias that can place minority group members at a significant disadvantage within an organization relative to majority group members.

A second avenue for future research, within the field in general and in organizations in particular, is a focus on the interactions between majority and minority group members. As Devine and Vasquez (1998) observed about the area generally, "the literature has had very little to offer to help us understand the nature of the interpersonal dynamics of intergroup contact.... we do not know what happens when interaction begins" (p. 241). In organizations that depend on efficient and effective interactions, prejudice and perceptions of prejudice can have critical adverse effects. Implicit prejudice places particular cognitive demands on White individuals in interracial interactions that can deplete their resources to perform job-related cognitive tasks (Richeson & Shelton, 2003). Moreover, explicit, conscious prejudice and implicit, unconscious prejudice can have different effects. Dovidio, Kawakami, et al. (1997) found that self-reported prejudice predicted bias in overt decisions (i.e., how White interviewers evaluated Black relative to White applicants), whereas implicit prejudice (which was largely uncorrelated with explicit prejudice) predicted biases in nonverbal measures of friendliness (e.g., eye contact). Thus, because prejudice, stereotyping, and discrimination at the individual level involve attitudinal responses, both explicit and implicit, and behavioral reactions, both initiated and reciprocal, we propose that studying intergroup relations in dynamic interactions offers unique insights into understanding the underlying processes and outcomes.

A third direction for future research involves greater focus on the psychology of minorities. Although the traditional emphasis of research on prejudice and stereotyping at the individual level has been on majority group members, recent research has begun to emphasize the role of minorities. Minorities are not simply passive targets; they are actively involved, and their thoughts, feelings, and actions can moderate the nature of intergroup interactions and organizational outcomes. Minorities often approach intergroup interactions with guardedness and mistrust (Hyers & Swim, 1998). In addition, when conditions make their group membership salient, minorities are particularly susceptible to experiencing stereotype threat (Steele, 1997) or feelings of tokenism (Niemann & Dovidio, 1998; Sekaquaptewa & Thompson, 2003), which can interfere with their cognitive performance, even on tasks of considerable importance and relevance. However, minorities can also respond in ways that reduce the impact of stereotyping and prejudice, for example, by displaying individuating characteristics or emphasizing common group membership (Gaertner & Dovidio, 2000), and by facilitating intergroup communication and interaction (Hebl & Kleck, 2002; Miller & Myers, 1998). Future research, therefore, might productively consider how the attitudes and behaviors of minorities influence perceptions of and responses to discrimination and ultimately help to shape their advancement within organizations.

In conclusion, understanding the dynamics of individual-level discrimination, with a focus on both majority and minority group members, offers a more comprehensive view of how bias affects the lives of minority and stigmatized group members. Knowledge of the causes of discrimination (e.g., unconscious negative feelings, ingroup favoritism) and of the factors that promote its manifestation (e.g., ambiguous criteria) can also help guide policies and interventions that can effectively combat individual-level discrimination. To address discrimination at the individual level, it is important "to structure programs and policies that make people and organizations accountable for their actions, provide accurate assessment of patterns of bias, and initiate action to eliminate biases without necessarily demonstrating intentionality or eliminating all other possible explanations" (Dovidio, 1997, p. 4). Alternatively, employment situations can be structured to emphasize the importance of other identities (e.g., company or workgroup allegiance) that reduce the salience of social categorization based on race, sex, or other stigmatizing characteristics and redirect the forces of ingroup bias to improve intergroup attitudes and productivity within an organization (Gaertner & Dovidio, 2000). Clearly, despite substantial progress in addressing open forms of discrimination, discrimination is not yet "a thing of the past."

ACKNOWLEDGMENTS

Preparation of this chapter was supported by NIMH Grant MH 48721 to the first author. Correspondence should be sent to John F. Dovidio, Department of Psychology, University of Connecticut, 406 Babbidge Rd., Storrs, CT 06269–1020, e-mail: john.dovidio@uconn.edu, or to Michelle R. Hebl, 1600 S. Main Street–MS 25, Rice University, Houston, TX 77005, e-mail: hebl@rice.edu.

REFERENCES

Adorno, T. W., Frenkel-Brunswick, E., Levinson, D. J., & Sanford, R. N. (1950). *The authoritarian personality*. New York: Harper & Row.

Allport, G. W. (1954). *The nature of prejudice*. New York: Addison-Wesley.

Altemeyer, B. (1996). *The authoritarian specter*. Cambridge, MA: Harvard University Press.

Bassili, J. (1995). Response latency and the accessibility of voting intentions: What contributes to accessibility and how it affects vote choice. *Personality and Social Psychology Bulletin, 21*, 686–695.

Bowen, C., Swim, J. K., & Jacobs, R. R. (2000). Evaluating gender biases on actual job performance of real people: A meta-analysis. *Journal of Applied Psychology, 30*, 2194–2215.

Brief, A. P., Buttram, R. T., Elliott, J. D., Reizenstein, R. M., & McCline, R. L. (1995). Releasing the beast: A study of compliance with orders to use race as a selection criterion. *Journal of Social Issues, 51*, 177–193.

Brief, A. P., Dietz, J., Cohen, R. R., Pugh, S. D., & Vaslow, J. B. (2000). Just doing business: Modern racism and obedience to authority as explanations for employment discrimination. *Organizational Behavior and Human Decision Processes, 81*, 72–97.

Campbell, D.T. (1965). Ethnocentric and other altruistic motives. In D. Levine (Ed.), *Nebraska symposium on motivation* (Vol. 13, pp. 283–311). Lincoln, NE: University of Nebraska Press.

Chao, G. T. (1997). Mentoring phases and outcomes. *Journal of Vocational Behavior, 51*, 15–28.

Cohen, G. L., Steele, C. M., & Ross, L. D. (1999). The mentor's dilemma: Providing critical feedback across the racial divide. *Personality and Social Psychology Bulletin, 25*, 1302–1318.

Cole, S. W., Kemeny, M. E., Taylor, S. E., & Visscher, B. R. (1996). Elevated physical health risk among gay men who conceal their homosexual identity. *Health Psychology, 15*, 243–251.

Crandall, C. S., & Eshleman, A. (2003). A justification-suppression model of the expression and experience of prejudice. *Psychological Bulletin, 129*, 414–446.

Crandall, C. S., & Martinez, R. (1996). Culture, ideology, and antifat attitudes. *Personality and Social Psychology Bulletin, 22*, 1165–1176.

Crocker, J., & Major, B. (1994). Reactions to stigma: The moderating role of justifications. In M. P. Zanna & J. M. Olson (Eds.), *The psychology of prejudice: The Ontario symposium, Vol. 7. Ontario symposium on personality and social psychology* (pp. 289–314). Hillsdale, NJ: Lawrence Erlbaum Associates.

Crosby, F. (1984). The denial of personal discrimination. *American Behavioral Scientist, 27*, 371–386.

Devine, P. G., Plant, E. A., & Buswell, B. N. (2000). Breaking the prejudice habit: Progress and obstacles. In S. Oskamp (Ed.), *Reducing prejudice and discrimination* (pp. 185–210). Mahwah, NJ: Lawrence Erlbaum Associates.

Devine, P. G., & Vasquez, K. A. (1998). The rocky road to positive intergroup relations. In J. Eberhardt & S. T. Fiske (Eds.), *Confronting racism: The problem and the response* (pp. 234–262). Newbury Park, CA: Sage.

Dovidio, J. F. (1997, September). *Understanding contemporary racism: Causes, consequences, challenges*. Paper presented at the meeting of The President's Advisory Board on Race, Washington, DC [on-line]. Available: (http://clinton3.nara.gov/Initiatives/OneAmerica/pres.html).

Dovidio, J. F., Brigham, J. C., Johnson, B. T., & Gaertner, S. L. (1996). Stereotyping, prejudice and discrimination: Another look. In C. N. Macrae, C. Stangor, & M. Hewstone (Eds.), *Stereotypes and stereotyping* (pp. 276–319). New York: Guilford.

Dovidio, J. F., & Gaertner, S. L. (1996). Affirmative action, unintentional racial biases, and intergroup relations. *Journal of Social Issues, 52*(4), 51–75.

Dovidio, J. F., & Gaertner, S. L. (1998). On the nature of contemporary prejudice: The causes, consequences, and challenges of aversive racism. In J. Eberhardt & S. T. Fiske (Eds.), *Confronting racism: The problem and the response* (pp. 3–32). Newbury Park, CA: Sage.

Dovidio, J. F., & Gaertner, S. L. (2000). Aversive racism and selection decisions: 1989 and 1999. *Psychological Science, 11*, 319–323.

Dovidio, J. F., Gaertner, S. L., Kawakami, K., & Hodson, G. (2002). Why can't we just get along? Interpersonal biases and interracial distrust. *Cultural Diversity & Ethnic Minority Psychology, 8*, 88–102.

Dovidio, J. F., Gaertner, S. L., Validzic, A., Matoka, A., Johnson, B., & Frazier, S. (1997). Extending the benefits of recategorization: Evaluations, self-disclosure, and helping. *Journal of Experimental Social Psychology, 33*, 401–420.

Dovidio, J. F., Kawakami, K., & Gaertner, S. L. (2002). Implicit and explicit prejudice and interracial interaction. *Journal of Personality and Social Psychology, 82*, 62–68.

Dovidio, J., Kawakami, K., Johnson, C., Johnson, B., & Howard, A. (1997). The nature of prejudice: Automatic and controlled processes. *Journal of Experimental Social Psychology, 33*, 510—540.

Dreher, G. F., & Ash, R. A. (1990). A comparative study of mentoring among men and women in managerial, professional, and technical positions. *Journal of Applied Psychology, 75*, 539–546.

Eagly, A. H., & Karau, S. J. (2002). Role congruity theory of prejudice toward female leaders. *Psychological Review, 109*, 573–598.

Elvira, M. M., & Zatzick, C. D. (2002). Who's displaced first? The role of race in layoff decisions. *Industrial Relations, 41*, 329–361.

Fazio, R. H., Jackson, J. R., Dunton, B. C., & Williams, C. J. (1995). Variability in automatic activation as an unobtrusive measure of racial attitudes: A *bona fide* pipeline? *Journal of Personality and Social Psychology, 69*, 1013–1027.

Fazio, R. H., Powell, M. C., & Williams, C. J. (1989). The role of accessibility in the attitude-to-behavior process. *Journal of Consumer Research, 16*, 280–288.

Fiske, S. T. (1998). *Stereotyping, prejudice, and discrimination.* In D. T. Gilbert, S. T. Fiske, & G. Lindzey (Eds.), The handbook of social psychology (Vol. 2, 4th ed., pp. 357–411). New York: McGraw-Hill.

Fiske, S. T., Cuddy, A. J. C., Glick, P., & Xu, J. (2002). A model of (often mixed) stereotype content: Competence and warmth respectively follow from perceived status and competition. *Journal of Personality and Social Psychology, 82*, 878–902.

Fiske, S. T., Lin, M., & Neuberg, S. L. (1999). The continuum model: Ten years later. In S. Chaiken & Y. Trope (Eds.), *Dual process theories in social psychology* (pp. 231–254). New York: Guilford.

Foley, S., Kidder, D. L., & Powell, G. N. (2002). The perceived glass ceiling and justice perceptions: An investigation of Hispanic law associates. *Journal of Management, 28*, 471–496.

Gaertner, S. L., & Dovidio, J. F. (1986). The aversive form of racism. In J. F. Dovidio & S. L. Gaertner (Eds.), *Prejudice, discrimination, and racism* (pp. 61–89). Orlando, FL: Academic Press.

Gaertner, S. L., & Dovidio, J. F. (2000). *Reducing intergroup bias: The common ingroup identity model.* Philadelphia: The Psychology Press.

Gallup (2002). *Poll topics & trends: Race relations.* Washington, DC: The Gallup Organization [on-line]. Available: http://www.gallup.com/poll/topics/race.asp.

Goffman, E. (1963). *Stigma: Notes on the management of spoiled identity.* Englewood Cliffs, NJ: Prentice–Hall.

Griffith, K. H., & Hebl, M. R. (2002). The disclosure dilemma for gay men and lesbians: "Coming out" at work. *Journal of Applied Psychology, 87*, 1191–1199.

Gutek, B. A., Cohen, A. G., & Tsui, A. (1996). Reactions to perceived sex discrimination. *Human Relations, 49,* 791–813.

Hebl, M. R., Foster, J. B., Mannix, L. M., & Dovidio, J. F. (2002). Formal and interpersonal discrimination. A field study of bias toward homosexual applicants. *Personality and Social Psychology Bulletin, 28,* 815–825.

Hebl, M. R., & Kleck, R. E. (2002). Acknowledging one's stigma in the interview setting: Strategy or liability? *Journal of Applied Social Psychology, 32,* 223–249.

Hebl, M. R., & Mannix, L. M. (2003). The weight of obesity in evaluating others: A mere proximity effect. *Personality and Social Psychology Bulletin, 29,* 28–38.

Heilman, M. E. (1983). Sex bias in work settings: The Lack of Fit Model. *Research in Organizational Behavior, 5,* 269–298.

Heilman, M. E. (2001). Description and prescription: How gender stereotypes prevent women's ascent up the organizational ladder. *Journal of Social Issues, 57,* 657–674.

Heilman, M. E., & Alcott, V. B. (2001). What I think you think of me: Women's reactions to being viewed as beneficiaries of preferential selection. *Journal of Applied Psychology, 86,* 574–582.

Huffcutt, A. I., & Roth, P. L. (1998). Racial group differences in employment interview evaluations. *Journal of Applied Psychology, 83,* 179–189.

Hyers, L. L., & Swim, J. K. (1998). A comparison of the experiences of dominant and minority group members during an intergroup encounter. *Group Processes and Intergroup Relations, 1,* 143–163.

Insko, C. A., Schopler, J., Gaertner, L., Wildschut, T., Kozar, R., Pinter, B., Finkel, E. J., Brazil, D. M., Cecil, C. L., & Montoya, M. R. (2001). Individual–intergroup discontinuity reduction through the anticipation of future interaction. *Journal of Personality and Social Psychology, 80,* 95–111.

Jones, E. E., Farina, A., Hastorf, A. H., Markus, H., Miller, D. T., & Scott, R. A. (1984). *Social stigma: The psychology of marked relationships.* New York: Freeman.

Jost, J. T., Burgess, D., & Mosso, C. O. (2001). Conflicts of legitimation among self, group, and system: The integrative potential of system justification theory. In J. T. Jost & B. Major (Eds.), *The psychology of legitimacy: Emerging perspectives on ideology, justice, and intergroup relations* (pp. 363–388). New York: Cambridge University Press.

Jost, J. T., Glaser, J., Kruglanski, A. W., & Sulloway, F. J. (2003). Political conservatism as motivated social cognition. *Psychological Bulletin, 129,* 339–376.

Kaiser, C. R., & Miller, C. T. (2001). Stop complaining!: The social costs of making attributions to discrimination. *Personality and Social Psycholology Bulletin, 27,* 254–263.

Kanter, R. M. (1977). *Men and women of the corporation.* New York: Basic Books.

King, E., Hebl, M. R., George, J., & Matusik, S. (2003). *Negative consequences of perceived gender discrimination in male-dominated organizations: A field study.* Unpublished manuscript, Department of Psychology, Rice University, Houston, TX.

Krieger, L. H. (1998). Civil rights perestroika: Intergroup relations after affirmative action. *California Law Review, 86,* 1251–1333.

Locksley, A., Borgida, E., Brekke, N., & Hepburn, C. (1980). Sex stereotypes and social judgment. *Journal of Personality and Social Psychology, 39,* 821–831.

Mackie, D. M., Hamilton, D. L., Susskind, J., & Rosselli, F. (1996). Social psychological foundations of stereotype formation. In C. N. Macrae, C. Stangor, & M. Hewstone (Eds.), *Foundations of stereotypes and stereotyping* (pp. 41–78). New York: Guilford.

Macrae, C. N., Bodenhausen, G. V., Milne, A. B., & Jetten, J. (1994). Out of mind but back in sight: Stereotypes on the rebound. *Journal of Personality and Social Psychology, 67,* 808–817.

Martell, R. F., Lane, D. M. & Emrich, C. (1996). Male-female differences: A computer simulation. *American Psychologist, 51,* 157–158.

Mays, V. M., Coleman, L. M., Jackson, J. S. (1996). Perceived race-based discrimination, employment status, and job stress in a national sample of Black women: Implications for health outcomes. *Journal of Occupational Health Psychology, 1,* 319–329.

McConahay, J. B. (1986). Modern racism, ambivalence, and the modern racism scale. In J. F. Dovidio & S. L. Gaertner (Eds.), *Prejudice, discrimination, and racism* (pp. 91–125). Orlando, FL: Academic Press.

Miller, C. T., & Myers, A. M. (1998). Compensating for prejudice: How heavyweight people (and others) control outcomes despite prejudice (pp. 191–219). In J. K. Swim & C. Stangor (Eds.), *Prejudice: The target's perspective.* San Diego: Academic Press.

Miller, C. T., Rothblum, E. D., Felicio, D. M., & Brand, P. A. (1995). Compensating for stigma: Obese and nonobese women's reactions to being visible. *Personality and Social Psychology Bulletin, 21,* 1093–1106.

Miller, N. (2002). Personalization and the promise of contact theory. *Journal of Social Issues, 58,* 387–410.

Monteith, M. J., Sherman, J. W., & Devine, P. G. (1998). Suppression as a stereotype control strategy. *Personality and Social Psychology Review, 2,* 63–82.

Niemann, Y. F., & Dovidio, J. F. (1998). Relationship of solo status, academic rank, and perceived distinctiveness to job satisfaction of racial/ethnic minorities. *Journal of Applied Psychology, 83,* 55–71.

Neuberg, S. L., Smith, D. M., Hoffman, J. C., & Russell, F. J. (1994). When we observe stigmatized and "normal" individuals interacting: Stigma by association. *Personality and Social Psychology Bulletin, 20,* 196–209.

Pettigrew, T. F., & Tropp, L. R. (2000). Does intergroup contact reduce prejudice? Recent meta-analytic findings. In S. Oskamp (Ed.), *Reducing prejudice and discrimination* (pp. 93–114). Hillsdale, NJ: Lawrence Erlbaum Associates.

Polinko, N. K., & Popovich, P. M. (2001). Evil thoughts but angelic actions: Responses to overweight job applicants. *Journal of Applied Social Psychology, 31,* 905–924.

Powell, G. N., & Butterfield, D. A. (2002). Exploring the influence of decision makers' race and gender on actual promotions to top management. *Personnel Psychology, 55,* 397–428.

Pratto, F., Sidanius, J., Stallworth, L. M., & Malle, B. F. (1994). Social dominance orientation: A personality variable predicting social and political attitudes. *Journal of Personality and Social Psychology, 67,* 741–763.

Ragins, B. R. (1999). Gender and mentoring relationships: A review and research agenda for the next decade. In G. N. Powell (Ed.), *Handbook of gender & work* (pp. 347–370). Thousand Oaks, CA: Sage.

Ragins, B. R., & Cornwell, J. M. (2001). Pink triangles: Antecendents and consequences of perceived workplace discrimination against gay and lesbian employees. *Journal of Applied Psychology, 86,* 1244–1261.

Richeson, J., & Shelton, J. N. (2003). When prejudice does not pay: Effects of interracial contact on executive function. *Psychological Science, 14,* 287–290.

Roehling, M. V. (1999). Weight-based discrimination in employment: Psychological and legal aspects. *Personnel Psychology, 52,* 969–1016.

Rudman, L. A. (1998). Self-promotion as a risk factor for women: The costs and benefits of counterstereotypical impression management. *Journal of Personality and Social Psychology, 74,* 629–645.

Rudman, L. A., & Glick, P. (2001). Prescriptive gender stereotypes and backlash toward agentic women. *Journal of Social Issues, 57,* 743–762.

Schuman, H., Steeh, C., Bobo, L., & Krysan, M. (1997). *Racial attitudes in America: Trends and interpretations.* Cambridge, MA: Harvard University Press.

Sears, D. O., Henry, P. J., & Kosterman, R. (2000). Egalitarian values and contemporary racial politics. In D. O. Sears, J. Sidanius, & L. Bobo (Eds.), *Racialized politics: The debate about racism in America* (pp. 75–117). Chicago: University of Chicago Press.

Sekaquaptewa, D., & Thompson, M. (2003). Solo status, stereotype threat, and performance expectancies: Their effects on women's performance. *Journal of Experimental Social Psychology, 39*, 68–74.

Smith, H. J., & Tyler, T. R. (1996). Justice and power: When will justice concerns encourage the advantaged to support policies which redistribute economic resources and the disadvantaged to willingly obey the law? *European Journal of Social Psychology, 26*, 171–200.

Steele, C. M. (1997). A threat in the air: How stereotypes shape intellectual identity and performance. *American Psychologist, 52*, 613–629.

Stephan, W. G., & Stephan, C. W. (1985). Intergroup anxiety. *Journal of Social Issues, 41*, 157–175.

Stephan, W. G., & Stephan C. W. (2000). An integrated threat theory of prejudice. In S. Oskamp (Ed.), *Reducing prejudice and discrimination* (pp. 23–45). Hillsdale, NJ: Lawrence Erlbaum Associates.

Tajfel, H., & Turner, J. C. (1979). An integrative theory of intergroup conflict. In W. G. Austin & S. Worchel (Eds.), *The social psychology of intergroup relations* (pp. 33–48). Monterey, CA: Brooks/Cole.

Turner, J. C. (1985). Social categorization and the self-concept: A social cognitive theory of group behavior. In E. J. Lawler (Ed.), *Advances in group processes* (Vol. 2, pp. 77–122). Greenwich, CT: JAI.

Valian, V. (1998). *Why so slow? The advancement of women.* Cambridge, MA: MIT Press.

von Hippel, W., Sekaquaptewa, D., & Vargas, P. (1995). On the role of encoding processes in stereotype maintenance. In M. P. Zanna (Ed.), *Advances in experimental social psychology* (Vol. 27, pp. 177–254). San Diego: Academic Press.

Vorauer, J. D., & Kumhyr, S. M. (2001). Is this about you or me? Self- versus other-directed judgments and feelings in response to intergroup interaction. *Personality and Social Psychology Bulletin, 27*, 706–719.

Weiner, B. (1995). *Judgments of responsibility: A foundation for a theory of social conduct.* New York: Guilford.

Word, C. O., Zanna, M. P., & Cooper, J. (1974). The nonverbal mediation of self-fulfilling prophecies in interracial interaction. *Journal of Experimental Social Psychology, 10*, 109–120.

Zajonc, R. B. (1980). Feeling and thinking: Preferences need no inferences. *American Psychologist, 35*, 151–175.

3

Relational Demography Within Groups: Through the Lens of Discrimination

Christine M. Riordan
University of Georgia

Bryan S. Schaffer
University of North Carolina, Asheville

Marcus M. Stewart
University of Georgia

Employees today work in diverse environments, consisting of individuals who are heterogeneous in a variety of personal characteristics, including age, race, sex, sexual orientation, religion, and nationality. This increasingly diverse labor force has motivated both practitioners and scholars to continue developing an understanding of the nature, dynamics, and outcomes associated with diversity (e.g., Ely & Thomas, 2001). One major theoretical base that has emerged to predict and explain diversity and its associated phenomena is relational demography theory (Riordan, 2000; Williams & O'Reilly, 1998). Relational demography theory proposes that individuals compare their own demographic characteristics with the demographic composition of their social unit to determine if they are similar or dissimilar (Tsui, Egan, & O'Reilly, 1992; Tsui & O'Reilly, 1989). In turn, the level of demographic (dis)similarity to the social unit is proposed to affect individuals' work-related attitudes and behaviors.

Because relational demography theory focuses on the individual's re-actions to being similar or different from his/her workgroup on personal characteristics, it is commonly thought to be a direct test of the impact of diversity on individuals. To date, much of the research on relational de-mography within groups has focused on outcomes such as organizational commitment, turnover, job satisfaction, group cohesiveness, group com-munication, and perceptions of rewards, such as advancement opportuni-ties (e.g., Jackson et al., 1991; Riordan & Shore, 1997; Tsui et al., 1992; Zenger & Lawrence, 1989). The theoretical foundation of relational demography suggests that being different than others can negatively affect an individ-ual's attitudes and behaviors. For example, Wagner, Pfeffer, and O'Reilly (1984) found that within top management teams, managers who differed in age from the others were more likely to leave the organization. Similarly, Chatman and Flynn (2001) found that newcomers to workgroups (tenure dissimilarity to others) perceived work group norms as less cooperative than veteran group members.

Because relational demography theory suggests that demographic dis-similarity has negative effects on individuals, it is logical that perceptions of discrimination and exclusionary behaviors would be promixal outcomes of relational demography within groups. Yet, little research has actually examined the impact of relational demography within groups on discrimi-nation type outcomes such as racism and sexism. The purpose of this chap-ter, therefore, is to review the relational demography literature through the lens of discrimination.

We first briefly review the basic theoretical premises of relational de-mography theory. We then propose a model by which to examine relational demography through the lens of discrimination. Through this model, we give consideration to the factors and outcomes that accompany relational and group sources of discrimination and suggest directions for future re-search on relational demography and discrimination.

RELATIONAL DEMOGRAPHY THEORY

Five interrelated theoretical perspectives have been used to explain re-lational demography in the workplace context. The first two are Byrne's (1971) similarity-attraction paradigm, and Schneider's (1987) attraction-selection-attrition model. The third is the collective set of perspectives encompassing both social identity and self-categorization theories (Hogg & Terry, 2000). The final two perspectives are the value-in-diversity and tokenism hypotheses. The following sections briefly review these five pers-pectives and, where appropriate, note their relationship to discriminatory type outcomes, such as the formation of ingroups/outgroups, unequal reward allocations, and lack of attraction, trust, fit, and shared identity.

The Similarity-Attraction Paradigm

In 1954, the term *homophily* was introduced in social psychology to refer to the tendency for individuals to be attracted to others who share similar personal characteristics (cf. Lazarsfeld & Merton, 1954; Hinds, Carley, Krackhardt, & Wholey, 2000). These characteristics include attitudes, beliefs, and physical attributes. Similarity in this sense is thought to be an uncertainty reduction mechanism that facilitates individuals' decisions regarding group membership and their formations of personal identities. The phenomenon suggests that people who are similar will want to interact with one another and will share a base of reciprocal trust and affect that is lacking among dissimilar individuals (Hinds et al., 2000).

Drawing upon these principles, Byrne (1961, 1971) offered a model of interpersonal attraction and presented a set of variables that were thought to affect the inclination for individuals to be drawn to one another. The most important of these variables was perceived similarity. Perceived similarity to others is said to be important for interpersonal attraction because it helps individuals to make sense of their environments more effectively by way of validation (Festinger, 1954; Newcomb, 1961; Rand & Wexley, 1975). "To the extent that a person offers consensual validation by demonstrating similarity to us in some way, such an interaction will be perceived as being rewarding and lead to positive feelings toward this individual" (Rand & Wexley, 1975, p. 536). Early studies have supported this contention (Baskett, 1973; Golightly, Huffman, & Byrne, 1971; Pulakos & Wexley, 1983; Rand & Wexley, 1975) and support Byrne's (1961, 1971) paradigm.

Researchers adapted the similarity-attraction paradigm as one theoretical explanation for the effects of relational demography on individual attitudes and behaviors (e.g., Tsui & O'Reilly, 1989). Demographic characteristics are, for the most part, immediate and highly salient and thus can strongly affect members' attitudes and perceptions about the group. Similarity on salient characteristics can draw the group together, favorably shape members' feelings about the group, and facilitate the interactive processes among group members. This is because members who share similar backgrounds, or are similar in physical and visible characteristics, may find it easier to interact and cooperate within group settings. Demographic commonality among members can eliminate much of the need for prerequisite social screening processes that often takes place prior to constructive behaviors directed toward real progress. For example, a new group consisting of members who are very different from one another, with respect to age, gender, race, and education, will likely have more interpersonal variability in perspectives, values, and biases (because of demographic differences), and will thus have more obstacles to overcome as it works toward achieving task-related objectives. Groups with similar members will be able to focus on such objectives with fewer distractions impeding their progress.

Several studies in relational demography have used the similarity-attraction paradigm to generate and test hypotheses. Hinds and colleagues (2000) examined individuals' preferences to work with others who were similar to them in race and gender. People had a strong preference for working with others of the same race, but no support was found for the expectation that people would prefer working with others of the same gender. Elvira and Cohen (2001) predicted that turnover would be lower for women from a large financial firm when there were higher proportions of women employed at their job level. Results supported the similarity-attraction paradigm among women within the same organizational level. However, turnover was not influenced by the proportion of women above and/or below the target's rank, indicating relative rank within the organization was an important contextual factor negating similarity-attraction processes. Kirchmeyer (1995), in her study of Canadian managers, showed that employees who were most dissimilar in terms of age, education, and lifestyle perceived the lowest levels of job challenge and workgroup fit, consistent with similarity-attraction. However, gender dissimilarity was associated with higher job challenge, and cultural dissimilarity was not related to any of the job experiences. Wagner et al. (1984) discussed similarity-attraction in terms of its importance in a relational sense. Using the premise that similarity is a key factor in interpersonal attraction, and that interpersonal attraction is related to integration and ultimately turnover, Wagner et al. (1984) predicted that top management team members who are more similar to the group (in terms of age and date of organizational entry) would be less likely to leave the organization. They found partial support for this prediction. Age dissimilarity was related to higher turnover.

Although many studies have drawn on the similarity-attraction paradigm to explain the effects of relational demography, most have failed to examine the mechanisms behind these relationships (Riordan, 2000). Based on the theory, the obvious intervening variable that would be expected to play a role is liking, or attraction. We were able to identify only one study to date that has examined the intervening role of this variable. Riordan and Weatherly (1999) found that liking mediated the relationship between education similarity and perceptions of group organizational citizenship behaviors, specifically, group altruism and civic virtue.

Attraction-Selection-Attrition

Schneider's (1987) attraction-selection-attrition (ASA) model was a direct extension of the similarity-attraction paradigm. He argued that the attributes of people in the workplace (primarily attitudes, personality, and values), and the interpersonal context created by the mix of these attributes, are the fundamental determinants of organizational behavior. The ASA framework suggests that similar kinds of people will be attracted to the organization, which will begin to determine the makeup of the place. Organizations are said to further promote this homogeneity by recruiting and selecting individuals who are similar, only differing on specific competencies. The theory also suggests that people who do not fit the organization will likely leave. In this sense, the people who remain will be similar. As a result of these attraction, selection, and attrition processes, it is predicted that the resulting similarity will influence employees' attitudes, perceptions, and behaviors.

Whereas the ASA framework focuses primarily on characteristics that are related to personality or dispositions (Schneider, 1987), there are reasons to believe that the premises behind the model would also apply to demographic characteristics. The theory states that individuals are not randomly assigned to settings, but instead actively select situations where they feel most comfortable (or where they fit). Consistent with this reasoning, demographic characteristics, being highly visible to others, might very well serve as cues for people to assess such fit and thus influence the processes of attraction, selection, and attrition. Jackson et al. (1991) used the ASA model as a theoretical explanation in their study that examined demographic dissimilarity as it related to recruitment (selection) and turnover (attrition).

Despite efforts to increase and promote diversity in the workplace, the processes described by the ASA model may contribute to the formation of homogeneous ingroups and outgroups within the organization. Within social ingroups, there may be processes occurring related to attraction-selection-attrition, similar to those Schneider (1987) originally described. Considering the role of demographic similarity, this would suggest that people would be motivated to join social groups composed of individuals who share the same demographic characteristics (attraction). In addition, social groups should also have some type of gatekeeping function that would allow or deny access to similar or dissimilar individuals (selection). Finally, when individuals in the social group do differ on one or more salient characteristics, they will likely be motivated to become a member of other groups who share their demographic characteristics (attrition and selection into a new group). Thus, the examination of ingroup/outgroup processes via ASA is useful, with the focus being on the maintenance of homogeneity within an ingroup, not necessarily across several groups within the organization.

Discrimination, based on demographic characteristics, therefore can result in a more informal manner from the friendships and social networks that emerge in an organization (Riordan & Shore, 1997; Ibarra, 1995). Even when not officially sanctioned by organizations, the formation of ingroups/outgroups can define who has access to information and other resources needed to effectively perform in a job. Moreover, individuals who are commonly different from the majority in the organization, such as racial minorities, women, disabled persons, older individuals, and gays and lesbians, can be excluded from these informal relationships. Additionally, early in one's career, dissimilar individuals who are not a part of the ingroup may lack the mentoring that is often important to achieving success within organizations (Ragins, 1999; Thomas, 2001).

A recent study of doctoral students and advisors found that mentoring relationships tended to form among individuals who were similar in sex, race, and age (Turban, Dougherty, & Love-Stewart, 1997). Additionally, Ragins (1997) highlighted the challenges of stereotypes, attributions, lack of shared identity, and personal comfort in diversified mentoring relationships. These challenges may constrain the development activities provided and perceived in demographically dissimilar mentoring relationships. Overall, lack of networks, mentors, and role models for outgroup members reflect exclusion from informal relationships, with ingroup members acting as gatekeepers in the organization.

Social Identity and Self-Categorization Theories

Social identity and self-categorization theories also relate to the formation of ingroups and outgroups within organizations (Hogg & Terry, 2000). These theories are largely based on the assumption that to make social comparisons in their environments, individuals must first define themselves along some social criterion (or criteria). From a social-psychological perspective, this involves defining oneself and being defined by others as a member of some type of group (Tajfel & Turner, 1979). This can be accomplished by using salient characteristics in the immediate environment for differentiation purposes. Such social categorizations can facilitate the classification and ordering of the social environment in which one exists.

The characteristics by which social categorization is accomplished can include many factors, such as demographics, values, personality, attitudes, organizational and other group memberships. Perceptions of social groups based on these categorizations provide individuals with the means for forming their own social identities. For example, a Caucasian female may define or identify herself based on the characteristics she uses for social categorization: I am a female in my thirties, I am Caucasian, and I have a masters degree (Ashforth & Mael, 1989; Riordan, 2000). "These identifications are to a very large extent (inherently) relational and comparative: they define the individual as similar to or different from, as 'better' or 'worse' than, members of other groups" (Tajfel & Turner, 1979, p. 40).

Relational demography research, which is based on such comparative differences, often uses the concepts related to social identity as a theoretical foundation. In Ely's (1994) study of women's proportional representation as partners in law firms, it was concluded "social identity (theory) may link an organization's demographic composition with an individuals' workplace experiences" (p. 203). She found that women partners in firms with fewer senior women were less likely to experience positive outcomes, such as support from women peers and perceptions about advancement opportunities.

According to social identity and self-categorization theory, individuals categorize themselves and similar others as comprising the ingroup and categorize dissimilar others into the outgroup(s). Individuals' reactions to others are driven by needs to reduce uncertainty and to maintain or enhance their self-esteem (social identity needs). In an effort to favorably differentiate the ingroup from a relevant outgroup, dissimilarity or "otherness" is seen as a deficiency and is often the basis for derogation, stereotypes, and polarization directed toward outgroup members (Hogg & Terry, 2000; Tajfel & Turner, 1979; Williams & O'Reilly, 1998).

In an experiment designed to test the basic propositions behind social identity theory, Turner, Brown, and Tajfel (1979) expected that subjects would be willing to sacrifice monetary rewards to achieve positive group distinctiveness. In addition, they hypothesized that ingroup favoritism would be greater when rewards were higher and when the outgroup was more relevant, or had a more salient comparative meaning. Results of their study supported these hypotheses. Subjects sacrificed both group and personal incentives in favor of intergroup differences that put ingroups at an advantage relative to outgroups (Turner et al., 1979). In addition, ingroup treatment toward outgroup members (in terms of fairness and discrimination) was more derogatory when the outgroup was particularly relevant to ingroup members, in a social comparison sense.

In the work environment, demographic characteristics, such as age, gender, race, and education, may be particularly salient and will therefore likely be used for making ingroup/outgroup differentiations. Demographic characteristics are highly visible, and, thus, offer employees simple cues for making distinctions among other coworkers (Flynn, Chatman, & Spataro, 2001). In fact, social categorizations and ingroup/outgroup distinctions, based on demographics, are likely to take place even when formal work-groups or other divisions within the organization have already been established (Chatman, Polzer, Barsade, & Neale, 1998; Flynn et al., 2001). As a result, relational demography theories assert that within workgroups, social comparison processes based on demographics are likely to take place. Workgroup members who are demographically dissimilar to the rest of the group are expected to experience the unfavorable outcomes associated with being categorized in the outgroup.

Much of the relational demography research has drawn on social identity and self-categorization theories in an attempt to explain the effects of dissimilarity on various work-related outcomes (e.g., Chatman et al., 1998; Chatman & Flynn, 2001; Harrison, Price, & Bell, 1998; Harrison, Price, Gavin, & Florey, 2002; Jehn, Northcraft, & Neale, 1999; Tsui et al., 1992). For example, Pelled (1996) examined how dissimilarity with respect to race, gender, and tenure would affect one's perceptions of group conflict and performance. Consistent with social identity theory, she found that gender and tenure dissimilarity were related to higher levels of perceived conflict, ostensibly as a function of differences and difficulties in communicating and establishing effective norms across these subgroups (gender and tenure subgroups), and that these perceptions, in turn, were related to lower ratings of group performance. She did not find support for the effects of race dissimilarity.

Some researchers used a combined perspective from both the similarity-attraction paradigm and social identity and self-categorization theories to examine relational demography processes (e.g., Zenger & Lawrence, 1989). For example, Tsui et al. (1992) noted that such theories should be treated as complimentary. In their study of organizational attachment, they suggested that for an employee who is demographically different from others, "lower organizational attachment may be a consequence of two possible processes: (1) social isolation and lower interpersonal attraction due to attitudinal differences associated with demographic dissimilarity, and (2) incongruence stemming from one's self-categorization of the group and its actual demographic composition" (p. 554). Their results showed that race and age dissimilarity were both negatively related to organizational attachment (lower intentions to stay in the organization). They also found that race dissimilarity was negatively related to organizational commitment.

Harrison and colleagues (1998, 2002) and Chatman and Flynn (2001) extended and integrated research on the similarity-attraction hypothesis and social identity theory by considering the effects of time. These studies found that early in workgroup formation (or newcomer entry) dissimilar members experienced lower levels of affect toward the groups, and heterogeneous groups displayed less effective norms, attributable to similarity-attraction processes. Over time, however, and as per social identity theory, contact among workgroup members facilitated recategorization among group members, yielding greater group cohesiveness and more cooperative norms. In other words, as a function of shared and firsthand experience, group members had increasingly individuated information upon which to base their perceptions of each other rather than general and often negative stereotypes. Dissimilar group members reported improved perceptions of and identification with their workgroups over time, and workgroups exhibited more effective norms.

The Tokenism Hypothesis

The theory of tokenism considers the role of those who are such a small minority in groups (15% or less of the total group) that they are seen as symbols of a certain category, rather than as individuals (Kanter, 1977; Young & James, 2001). Because these individuals are highly visible, given the characteristics that differentiate them from other members, negative outcomes are typically predicted. Kanter (1977) suggested that three factors associated with tokenism could have an impact on an individual's performance at work.

First, increased visibility can create unfair or unequal performance pressure for the "token" individual, causing this person to either overachieve to meet expectations or to underachieve to alleviate other members' concerns about competition (Spangler, Gordon, & Pipkin, 1978; Young & James, 2001). Second, workgroup members will likely create boundaries based on an exaggeration of the differences between themselves and the token individual. This idea is consistent with the ingroup/outgroup distinctions that are described in social identity theory. These boundaries can lead to feelings of detachment and segregation for minority individuals, along with perceptions of exclusionary treatment. Finally, the workgroup may have certain beliefs and/or stereotypes that fit the characteristics of majority members, and therefore token individuals may often find themselves having to conform to the rest of the group, rather than challenging group norms or expectations (Spangler et al., 1978; Young & James, 2001).

Most studies using the tokenism hypothesis have examined the role of gender dissimilarity and its effects on minority members. For example, Young and James (2001) investigated the work experiences of male flight attendants, who represent token individuals in a female-dominated occupation. They found that token status led to increased role ambiguity, lower self-esteem, and perceptions of poor job fit. In turn, these negative outcomes were related to lower job satisfaction and organizational attachment. However, tokenism can apply to other demographic variables as well. Jackson, Thoits, and Taylor (1995) found that Black leaders in the United States, who were in work situations where they were outnumbered by Whites, exhibited higher levels of depression and anxiety, as compared to those in more balanced situations. Similarly, Li (1994) found that Asian minorities (tokens) in Caucasian majority groups displayed lower levels of performance and self-efficacy, relative to Asian participants in more balanced groups. The tokenism hypothesis is consistent with the basic principles of relational demography. An individual who is demographically dissimilar to the rest of his or her group members will likely experience unfavorable attitudes and behaviors, relative to individuals who are demographically similar to their respective group members (Riordan, 2000).

The Value-in-Diversity Hypothesis

Whereas each of the aforementioned theoretical perspectives have highlighted the negative or unfavorable consequences of demographic dissimilarity, some researchers have offered reasons why, or conditions under which, dissimilarity might be beneficial. Generally, this perspective, sometimes referred to as the "value-in-diversity hypothesis" (e.g., Ely & Thomas, 2001), attempts to explain how information and decision making can be positively affected by demographic heterogeneity in workgroups (Williams & O'Reilly, 1998). For example, Ancona and Caldwell (1992) found that functional background and tenure diversity in new product teams contributed to more positive managerial ratings of team innovation and to more positive ratings of overall effectiveness, respectively.

Two factors related to workgroup heterogeneity are suggested to contribute to overall improved group performance. First, employees in a diverse workgroup should have better access to informational networks outside of the group (Williams & O'Reilly, 1998). For example, Zenger and Lawrence (1989) stated that "If Mary, a new employee, works on a project with Bob, a 20-year veteran, Mary will probably find it easier to contact Bob's friends outside the project group as a result of her association with Bob" (p. 372). This type of external communication flow can improve group processes and performance (Katz, 1982; Zenger & Lawrence, 1989). Similarly, according to Granovetter's (1973; 1982) "strength in weak ties" hypothesis, demographically dissimilar group members contribute to workgroup creativity and performance by providing access to unique, nonredundant resources (e.g., networks, information) unavailable in majority group members' overlapping networks.

Second, demographically dissimilar employees should have a broader range of knowledge and experience than similar employees and can therefore add value to workgroups by providing new information that is much needed, especially for tasks related to product design, innovation, or complex problem solving (Ely & Thomas, 2001; Williams & O'Reilly, 1998). Overall, the benefits predicted by the value-in-diversity hypothesis have been associated with personal characteristics such as tenure, experience, education, and knowledge. Research has generally supported the hypothesis with regard to these characteristics with some exceptions (e.g., O'Reilly, Snyder, and Boothe, 1993).

Although some studies have found that diversity on these visible characteristics can be beneficial (Ely & Thomas, 2001), much less research has supported the hypothesis for more visible demographic characteristics such as race, age, and gender. For example, Watson, Kumar, and Michaelsen (1993) found that culturally diverse groups of undergraduate students (with respect to race and nationality), after several weeks of working together on a project, were more effective on task elements related to identifying problems and generating solution alternatives than homogeneous groups. Kirchmeyer and Cohen (1992) found that for culturally diverse groups, the use of frank and open discussions, the encouragement of a variety of opinions, and the careful critiquing of other members, helped the group make more valid and more important assumptions.

Finally, Cox, Lobel, and McLeod (1991), also using students as participants, found that diverse groups (e.g., a mix of Anglo American, Asian, Hispanic, and Black American members) displayed more cooperative behavior than groups that were more homogeneous (e.g., all Anglo American members). Each of these examples was a laboratory study using groups comprising either undergraduate or graduate college students. There have been virtually no organizational field studies that have supported the information and decision-making hypothesis when the measure of workgroup diversity has been based on visible demographic characteristics (Williams & O'Reilly, 1998; see Ely & Thomas, 2001, for an exception). Although the advantages of certain types of functional and background diversity may, in some cases, be related to improved group processes such as communication and even group performance, most of this research has focused only on group-level outcomes. That is, research has not really examined or demonstrated a consistent positive impact of diversity on individual-level attitudes and behaviors. Prior research still largely supports the general proposition that an individual's demographic dissimilarity to his or her work group is associated with unfavorable individual-level work-related attitudes and behaviors.

A MODEL OF RELATIONAL DEMOGRAPHY THROUGH
THE LENS OF DISCRIMINATION

This review of the literature of relational demography through the lens of discrimination is depicted in Fig. 3.1. This model does not attempt to capture the potential positive effects of being in the minority in a work group; rather the figure consolidates the research and theory on relational demography as it relates to the negative effects of discrimination.

Several interesting issues become apparent in viewing the relational demography research from a discrimination perspective:

1. Relational demography research has typically focused on the perspective of the individual in the minority and his/her reactions to being different; relational demography research has not focused on those in the majority and their reactions to and treatment of the person that is different.
2. Relational demography research has tended to take a singular approach to diversity, examining one characteristic (e.g., race) at a time, or has simply aggregated two or more dimensions of diversity (e.g., Chatman & Flynn, 2001), failing to fully account for group members' multiple characteristics or identities, the combinations of which likely impact work group processes and group member experiences.
3. The majority of relational demography research has focused on secondary or more distal outcomes, such as the job satisfaction and organizational commitment of the person that is different, rather than examining more proximal outcomes such as perceptions of discrimination, perceptions of unfair treatment, and so forth.
4. Future research on relational demography needs to incorporate contextual and personal factors as moderators.

View from Minority and Majority Perspective

As depicted in this model, it is important to note that relational demography should be viewed from how the minority and majority work group members react to the work environment, including how those in the majority treat those in the minority. That is, recognizing the majority's cognitive reactions and behavioral manifestations toward those that are demographically dissimilar deepens explanations for why individuals may react negatively when they are demographically dissimilar. In Fig. 3.1, we suggest that the cognitive reactions of majority members are a powerful influence over their behavioral treatment of those who are demographically

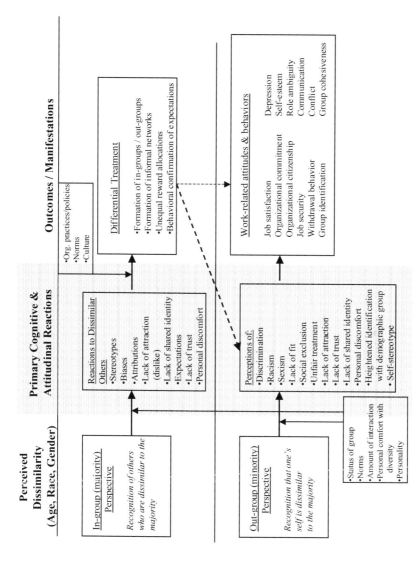

FIG. 3.1. Relational demography through the lens of discrimination.

49

dissimilar (Brewer & Kramer, 1985). This treatment by majority members, in turn, will influence the cognitive reactions of the demographically dissimilar individual, which ultimately impacts his/her work attitudes and behaviors.

For example, research has shown that members of the majority group may hold negative stereotypes of the minority group (Devine, 1989; Livingston & Brewer, 2002). Stereotypes can lead to self-fulfilling prophecies via majority group members' expectations that the minority group member will exhibit certain behaviors; majority group members behave such that they illicit expectancy confirming behavior from the target/minority member (Word, Zanna, & Cooper, 1974; Zamarripa & Krieger, 1983, p. 205). In an objective sense, the member of the minority group acts in a way that appears to validate the original expectations, though the other group members actively contributed to what was observed (cf. Cox, 1993).

A related phenomenon is often referred to as "stereotype-threat," wherein individuals behave or react according to stereotypes perceived as relevant (contextually) to a salient ingroup. In a series of experiments, Steele and Aronson (1995; cf. Steele, 1997) found that African American students performed more poorly than White students on a verbal test when they were asked to identify their race on the test form. Simply asking for race on the test form evoked negative ingroup or self-relevant stereotypes for the African American students. Similarly, female college students performed poorly compared to male students on a math test when the students were told that gender differences in scores had previously been found on the test. Research on relational demography has not directly assessed the impact of self- and other-stereotyping as an immediate outcome of being demographically dissimilar to one's group. This is a fruitful avenue for future research.

Future studies might also examine the nature of the networks that exist within a group and their impact on dissimilar individuals' perceptions of discrimination, exclusion, and so forth. Are the quality and type of network relationships stronger for demographically similar members than for demographically dissimilar members, and do these relationships (e.g., ingroups/outgroups) impact the work-related attitudes and behaviors of both groups? Similarly, as noted earlier, an important principle of social identity and self-categorization theories is that individuals will see themselves and similar others as comprising the "ingroup," and they will categorize dissimilar others into an "out-group." Future research should look at whether both majority and minority group members perceive the same ingroups/outgroups and how each relates to actual and perceived differential treatment.

Researchers may also examine the impact of the majority members' personal comfort with diversity on the minority members' work-related attitudes and behaviors. That is, if majority group members are less person-ally comfortable with diversity, will the discomfort of majority members impact minority group members' perceptions of discrimination and their work attitudes and behaviors? These are just a few examples of how future research might consider the minority and majority members' perspective of or reactions to "others who are different" in the theories and tests of relational demography.

Examine Multiple Demographic Characteristics at the Same Time

In their recent review of the organizational diversity literature, Jackson, Joshi, and Erhardt (2003) found that less than 5% of studies between 1997 and 2002 ($n = 63$; did not include laboratory experiments with un-dergraduates) addressed the question of whether the influence of a par-ticular dimension of diversity depended on the presence or absence of another dimension. Much of the relational demography research has tended to examine dimensions of diversity independent of each other (i.e., Chattopadhyay, 1999) or has aggregated indicators of multiple dimensions of diversity (e.g., Chatman & Flynn, 2001; Jehn et al., 1999). Although this research is valuable, it does not truly capture individuals' demographic complexity.

To aid in considering the multiple identities or category memberships of each workgroup member, Lau and Murnighan (1998) introduced the concept of *faultlines*, which divide work group members on the basis of one or more attributes. For example, age faultlines divide groups into rel-atively young and old subgroups. Group faultlines increase in strength as more attributes are highly correlated, reducing the number and increasing the homogeneity of the resulting subgroups. For example, a group com-posed of three young, White, male entry-level auditors who had worked for a company for less than a year and three middle-aged, Black female vice-presidents who had been with the company for 20 years or more would have a strong faultline because all of the listed characteristics are perfectly correlated, which facilitates social identification processes among subgroup members (Tajfel & Turner, 1979).

This should result in an increased likelihood of conflict over a wide array of issues with "highly predictable memberships in two subgroups" (Lau & Murnighan, 1998, p. 328). When potential subgroup members are similar in one attribute (i.e., sex) but differ in others (i.e., race and age), group members are less likely to expect similarity in attitudes, expectations, and behavioral scripts, leading to weaker faultlines or subgroups.

Applying these analyses to the question of discrimination in work-groups, minimum and maximum levels of diversity should lead to little or no discrimination, as subgroups will either not exist (minimum or zero diversity) or, in the case of maximum diversity, will be smaller and fragmented with weaker faultlines, as subgroup members will have disparate subgroup memberships. In this case, social identification processes should be weaker, and subgroups should be less motivated and able to impose themselves or desired norms on other subgroups or members. When diversity is sparse or "moderate," meaning there are a limited variety of demographic attributes among group members, the likelihood of subgroup formation with strong faultlines is increased. Under these conditions, one or a very few members belong to a small, distinct, and homogeneous subgroup, increasing the likelihood of social identification processes among majority group members and competitive/discriminatory behavior toward the minority/outgroup members.

Future research should examine the nature of group faultlines in an attempt to identify likely potential forms of discrimination given a group's particular composition. For example, research has determined that demographic identities have "master status," such that they are nearly always the basis for categorization by others (cf. Chatman et al., 1998; Cox, 1993), which would suggest attention to these faultlines when constructing groups and considering or monitoring potential discrimination. However, as established by Harrison and colleagues (1998, 2002), the negative impact of some demographic diversity can dissipate over time with regard to group performance; does the likelihood, occurrence, and/or perception of discrimination along these faultiness also diminish? Further, within a workgroup, members of a given demographic group (e.g., women) can differ along other contextually relevant dimensions such as functional area or tenure. If, for example, function or seniority is a more important or powerful subgroup relative to the subgroup "women," identification with the higher status subgroup may facilitate discriminatory behavior by women in the high status seniority ingroup toward women in the low status (newcomer) outgroup.

Along these lines, some relational demography research has begun to explore the influence of contextual power and minority/majority status. Both Chattopadhyay (1999) and Riordan (2000) observed that there is strong theortical and empirical support to incorporate asymmetrical predictions for the effects of demographic dissimilarity. Simply, the experience of being in the "minority" is likely not the same for all groups in similar contexts. For example, it may be that White females, White males, Black females, and Black males all experience being in the race and gender minorities in very different ways. As such, future theory and empirical tests need to look at a blend of demographic dimensions and make differential predictions for the effects of demography.

Expand the Outcomes of Relational Demography

In Table 3.1, we organize the dependent variables from the current set of relational demography studies into six dimensions: behavioral outcomes, attitudes/psychological adjustment, job design outcomes, workgroup outcomes, reward and career outcomes, and social support outcomes. In total, 41 different dependent variables have been examined as outcomes of relational dissimilarity.

All together, the studies from this literature review examined 145 separate relationships between a demographic dissimilarity measure and a specified work-related outcome. In an attempt to organize the collective set of findings, each of these relationships was coded as either: (a) statistically significant, and supporting the basic premises of relational demography (i.e., a negative association between dissimilarity and some favorable outcome); (b) not statistically significant; or (c) statistically significant, but in an opposite direction of that prescribed by relational demography theory.

The results of this analysis revealed that 78 relationships (54%) were consistent with relational demography theory, 47 relationships (32%) were not statistically significant, and 20 relationships (14%) were significant, but in the opposite direction of that hypothesized. Table 3.1 shows that relational demography predictions have been supported most often when the outcomes of interest were related to workgroup processes or perceptions (70%). This may be due to the fact that relational demography in groups, by definition, is theoretically based in the dynamics of workgroup functioning.

In this respect, it seems that an appropriate goal for future research is to identify outcomes that are proximal in nature to relational dissimilarity. Many of the outcomes used in prior research appear to have a more distal association with the processes associated with dissimilarity, and so it is not surprising that inconsistent support has been obtained for hypothesized relationships.

It is often theorized that demographic dissimilarity leads to ingroup/outgroup categorizations, promoting ingroup favoritism and outgroup discrimination. Yet, little research has examined the proximal outcome areas of perceived discrimination and exclusionary treatment. In an exception, Ragins and Cornwell (2001) examined both the antecedents and consequences of perceived discrimination among gay and lesbian employees. They found that when gay and lesbian employees were in primarily heterosexual groups (relational dissimilarity), they were more likely to report (perceive) discrimination. Similarly, perceptions of discrimination were less likely when a gay employee had a gay supervisor. While Ragins and Cornwell (2001) examined sexual orientation similarity, they did

TABLE 3.1

Relational Demography Results by Outcomes

Behavioral Outcomes	*37 relationships*
Group & Individual performance	
Absenteeism	19 (51%) statistically significant—support
Organizational citizenship	Relational Demography
behaviors	14 (38%) not significant
Turnover intentions, turnover	4 (11%) statistically significant—opposite
	of Relational Demography
Attitudes/Psychological Adjustment	*41 relationships*
Organizational commitment	
Work group commitment	
Union commitment	
Job satisfaction	25 (61%) statistically significant—support
Organizational attachment	Relational Demography
Organizational inclusion	10 (24%) not significant
Depression	6 (15%) statistically significant—opposite
Self-esteem	of Relational Demography
Preferences for working with	
others	
Job Design Outcomes	*6 relationships*
Role ambiguity	4 (67%) statistically significant—support
Job fit	Relational Demography
Job challenge	1 (16%) not significant
	1 (0%) statistically significant—opposite
	of Relational Demography
Work Group Outcomes	*34 relationships*
Group identification	
Group cohesiveness	
Intergroup interactions	
Cooperative behavior & norms	
Competitive behavior	
Communication	24 (70%) statistically significant—support
Work group fit	Relational Demography
Conflict	8 (24%) not significant
Liking	2 (6%) statistically significant—opposite
Impressions of others	of Relational Demography
Perceptions of outlook similarity	
Peer relations	

(cont.)

TABLE 3.1

(cont.)

Reward and Career Outcomes	*20 relationships*	
Job security		
Compensation		
Advancement opportunities	4 (20%)	statistically significant—support Relational Demography
Mentor		
Recognition	9 (45%)	not significant
Career future	7 (35%)	statistically significant—opposite of Relational Demography
Social Support Outcomes	*7 relationships*	
Social isolation		
Supervisor support	2 (29%)	statistically significant—support Relational Demography
Peer support		
Participation/involvement	5 (71%)	not significant
	0 (0%)	statistically significant—opposite of Relational Demography
Total	*145 relationships*	
	78 (54%)	statistically significant—support Relational Demography
	47 (32%)	not significant
	20 (14%)	statistically significant—opposite of Relational Demography

Note: Support for relational demography theory indicates a negative association between dissimilarity and some favorable outcome.

not examine similarity based on other demographic characteristics, such as age, race, gender, tenure, an/or education. In fact, we found no field studies to date that have done this.

It is important for future research to examine these types of outcomes because increased discrimination and ingroup favoritism resulting from diversity and difference is a primary premise of relational demography theory. For example, Riordan's (2000) model of relational demography positions stereotyping and bias as proximal outcomes of dissimilarity. Williams and O'Reilly (1998) similarly proposed that demographic diversity and dissimilarity, which are bases for social categorization, are likely to result in increased factionalism, ingroup/outgroup biases, and stereotyping. In their review of the diversity literature, Milliken and Martins (1996) asserted that "Diversity in observable attributes has consistently been found to have negative effects on affective outcomes...suggesting the possibility that deep-seated prejudices some people hold against people who are different from themselves on race and gender (and other attributes) may be adding to the difficulty of interaction for these groups" (pp. 414–415). Finally, Brickson (2000), in her review of identity orientations, suggested that the activation of one's personal and social identities brings about mechanisms that can lead to prejudice and discrimination. Together, these works support the idea that employees who are demographically dissimilar to other workgroup members will feel the effects of outgroup bias and discrimination.

Previous research has also shown that perceived discrimination is antecedent to a number of important work-related outcomes. Many of these outcomes have been used as dependent variables in relational demography research. For example, studies have shown that employees' beliefs about discrimination, whether they are accurate or not, can affect psychological and physical health and adjustment (Barak, Cherin, & Berkman, 1998; Eisenberger, Fasolo, & Davis-LaMastro, 1990; Ensher, Grant-Vallone, & Donaldson, 2001); job involvement, career satisfaction, and career prospects (e.g., Foley & Kidder, 2002; Perry, Hendricks, & Broadbent, 2000; Sanchez & Brock, 1996; Shaffer, Joplin, Bell, Lau, & Oguz, 2000; Valentine, Silver, & Twigg, 1999); work conflict, lower feelings of power, and job prestige (Gutek, Cohen, & Tsui, 1996); turnover intentions (Shaffer et al., 2000); and organizational citizenship behaviors (Ensher et al., 2001). In short, discrimination-type outcomes may act as mediators between demographic dissimilarity and some of the more traditional outcomes of relational demography. Future research should explore these linkages.

Contextual and Personal Factors as Moderators

As depicted in Fig. 3.1, future research on relational demography needs to explore the role of moderators or the conditions under which the relationships between demographic dissimilarity and the outcomes are the strongest/weakest. Earlier studies have not supported the moderating effects of minority status (Jackson et al., 1991; Kirchmeyer, 1995). Recently, Flynn et al. (2001) found that dissimilarity in citizenship, race, and gender was related to individuals forming more negative impressions of others. However, this relationship was mitigated or buffered when dissimilar individuals were more extraverted or when they were higher self-monitors. In this case, extraversion and self-monitoring were contextual variables (moderators) in the design.

The use of theoretically relevant moderators appears to provide additional information to the interpretation of observed results, and future studies in relational demography should therefore continue to incorporate such variables as part of their overall research designs. For example, as depicted in Figure 3.1, the majority group's reactions to dissimilar others could easily be tempered by the organizational practices, diversity culture, or norms, as suggested by Ely and Thomas (2001; Jackson et al., 2003). One might expect more negative reactions to demographic dissimilarity in organizations with weak diversity climates than in organizations with strong diversity climates (Ely & Thomas, 2001), or in organizations with more individualistic rather than collectivist cultures (Chatman et al., 1998). The presence or absence of organizational practices and policies for diversity might moderate the outward display of behaviors by majority members toward demographically dissimilar others.

There are also other potential moderators from the minority perspective that need to be tested. If an individual is demographically dissimilar to his/her workgroup, but that workgroup is high status, the demographic dissimilarity might not have the same negative effects as when the individual is demographically dissimilar and in a low-status workgroup (cf. Chattopadhyay, 1999; Elvira & Cohen, 2001; Ely, 1994). In a similar fashion, greater interdependence or interaction between diverse individuals will reduce conflict, prejudice, and negative stereotyping and will increase feelings of interpersonal attraction, familiarity, and group cohesion (Ellison & Powers, 1994; Sigelman & Welch, 1993). As a consequence, interdependence and interaction appear to reduce the negative impact of being demographically dissimilar in surface-level characteristics such as age and gender (Chatman & Flynn, 2001; Harrison et al., 1998, 2002; Vecchio & Bullis, 2001). Finally, future research might further examine the role of personality or dispositional variables such as personal comfort with diversity. For example, it may be that for individuals with a low personal comfort with diversity, being in a demographically dissimilar workgroup will lead to greater feelings of discrimination and more negative attitudes about the workgroup than for individuals with a high personal comfort with diversity.

SUMMARY

The proposed model attempts to provide an integrative view of relational demography through the lens of discrimination. It is obvious that future research needs to examine the impact of the majority's reactions/behaviors/characteristics on the outcomes for the individuals who are demographically dissimilar; examine multiple demographic characteristics at the same time; expand the view of relational demography to include more proximal outcomes related to discrimination; and heavily explore the role of personal and contextual variables as moderators.

REFERENCES

Ancona, D. G., & Caldwell, D. F. (1992). Demography and design: Predictors of new product team performance. *Organization Science, 3*, 321–341.

Ashforth, B. E., & Mael, F. (1989). Social identity theory and the organization. *Academy of Management Review, 14*, 20–39.

Barak, M. E. M., Cherin, D. A., & Berkman, S. (1998). Organizational and personal dimensions in diversity climate: Ethnic and gender differences in employee perceptions. *Journal of Applied Behavioral Science, 34*, 82–104.

Baskett, G. D. (1973). Interview decisions as determined by competency and attitude similarity. *Journal of Applied Psychology, 57*, 343–345.

Brewer, M. B., & Kramer, R. M. (1985). The psychology of intergroup attitudes and behavior. *Annual Review of Psychology, 36*, 219–243.

Brickson, S. (2000). The impact of identity orientation on individual and organizational outcomes in demographically diverse settings. *Academy of Management Review, 25*, 82–101.

Byrne, D. (1961). Interpersonal attraction and attitude similarity. *Journal of Abnormal and Social Psychology, 62*, 713–715.

Byrne, D. (1971). *The attraction paradigm.* New York: Academic Press.

Chatman, J. A., & Flynn, F. J. (2001). The influence of demographic heterogeneity on the emergence and consequences of cooperative norms in work teams. *Academy of Management Journal, 44*, 956–974.

Chatman, J. A., & Polzer, J. T., Barsade, S. G., & Neale, M. A. (1998). Being different yet feeling similar: The influence of demographic composition and organizational culture on work processes and outcomes. *Administrative Science Quarterly, 43*, 749–780.

Chattopadhyay, P. (1999). Beyond direct and symmetrical effects: The influence of demographic dissimilarity on organizational citizenship behavior. *Academy of Management Journal, 42*, 273–287.

Cox, T., Jr. (1993). *Cultural diversity in organizations: Theory, research and practice.* San Francisco: Berrett-Koehler.

Cox, T., Lobel, S., & McLeod, P. (1991). Effects of ethnic group cultural differences on cooperative and competitive behavior on a group task. *Academy of Management Journal, 34*, 827–847.

Devine, P. G. (1989). Stereotypes and prejudice: Their automatic and controlled components. *Journal of Personality and Social Psychology, 56*, 5–18.

Eisenberger, R., Fasolo, P., & Davis-LaMastro, V. (1990). Perceived organizational support and employee diligence, commitment, and innovation. *Journal of Applied Psychology, 75*, 51–59.

Ellison, C. G., & Powers, D. A. (1994). The contact hypothesis and racial attitudes among Black Americans. *Social Science Quarterly, 75*, 385–400.

Elvira, M. M., & Cohen, L. E. (2001). Location matters: A cross-level analysis of the effects of organizational sex composition on turnover. *Academy of Management Journal, 44*, 591–605.

Ely, R. J. (1994). The effects of organizational demographics and social identity on relationships among professional women. *Administrative Science Quarterly, 39*, 203–238.

Ely, R. J., & Thomas, D. A. (2001). Cultural diversity at work: The effects of diversity perspectives on work group processes and outcomes. *Administrative Science Quarterly, 46*, 229–273.

Ensher, E. A., Grant-Vallone, E. J., & Donaldson, S. I. (2001). Effects of perceived discrimination on job satisfaction, organizational commitment, organizational citizenship behavior, and grievances. *Human Resource Development Quarterly, 12*, 53–72.

Festinger, L. (1954). A theory of social comparison processes. *Human Relations, 7*, 117–140.

Flynn, F. J., Chatman, J. A., & Spataro, S. E. (2001). Getting to know you: The influence of personality on impressions and performance of demographically different people in organizations. *Administrative Science Quarterly, 46,* 414–442.

Foley, S., & Kidder, D. L. (2002). Hispanic law students' perceptions of discrimination, justice, and career prospects. *Hispanic Journal of Behavioral Sciences, 24,* 23–37.

Golightly, C., Huffman, D. M., & Byrne, D. (1972). Liking and loaning. *Journal of Applied Psychology, 56,* 521–523.

Granovetter, M. S. (1973). The strength of weak ties. *American Journal of Sociology, 78,* 1360–1380.

Granovetter, M. S. (1982). The strength of weak ties: A network theory revisited. In P. V. Marsden & N. Lin (Eds.), *Social structure and network analysis* (pp. 105–130). Beverly Hills, CA: Sage.

Gutek, B. A., Cohen, A. G., & Tsui, A. (1996). Reactions to perceived sex discrimination. *Human Relations, 49,* 791–813.

Harrison, D. A., Price, K. H., & Bell, M. P. (1998). Beyond relational demography: Time and the effects of surface- and deep-level diversity on work group cohesion. *Academy of Management Journal, 41,* 96–107.

Harrison, D. A., Price, K. H., Gavin, J. H., & Florey, A. T. (2002). Time, teams and task performance: Changing effects of surface- and deep- level diversity on group functioning. *Academy of Management Journal, 45,* 1029–1045.

Hinds, P. J., Carley, K. M., Krackhardt, D., & Wholey, D. (2000). Choosing work group members: Balancing similarity, competence, and familiarity. *Organizational Behavior and Human Decision Processes, 81,* 226–251.

Hogg, M. A., & Terry, D. J. (2000). Social identity and self-categorization processes in organizational contexts. *Academy of Management Review, 25,* 121–140.

Ibarra, H. (1995). Race, opportunity, and diversity of social circles in managerial networks. *Academy of Management Journal, 38,* 673–703.

Jackson, P. B., Thoits, P. A., & Taylor, H. F. (1995). Composition of the workplace and psychological well-being: The effects of tokenism on America's Black elite. *Social Forces, 74,* 543–557.

Jackson, S. E., Brett, J. F., Sessa, V. I., Cooper, D. M., Julin, J. A., & Peyronnin, K. (1991). Some differences make a difference: Individual dissimilarity and group heterogeneity as correlates of recruitment, promotions, and turnover. *Journal of Applied Psychology, 76,* 675–689.

Jackson, S. E., Joshi, A., & Erhardt, N. L. (2003). Recent research on team and organizational diversity: SWOT analysis and implications. *Journal of Management, 29,* 801–830.

Jehn, K. A., Northcraft, G. B., & Neale, M. A. (1999). Why differences make a difference: A field study of diversity, conflict, and performance in work groups. *Administrative Science Quarterly, 44,* 741–763.

Kanter, R. M. (1977). *Men and women of the corporation.* New York: Basic Books.

Katz, R. (1982). Project communication and performance: An investigation into the effects of group longevity. *Administrative Science Quarterly, 29,* 81–104.

Kirchmeyer, C. (1995). Demographic similarity to the work group: A longitudinal study of managers at the early career stage. *Journal of Organizational Behavior, 16,* 67–83.

Kirchmeyer, C., & Cohen, A. (1992). Multicultural groups: Their performance and reactions with constructive conflict. *Group and Organization Management, 17,* 153–170.

Lau, D. C., & Murnighan, J. K. (1998). Demographic diversity and faultlines: The compositional dynamics of organizational groups. *Academy of Management Review, 23,* 325–340.

Lazarsfeld, P. F., & Merton, R. K. (1954). Friendship as a social process: A substantive and methodological analysis. In M. Berger, T. Abel, & C. H. Page (Eds.), *Freedom and control in modern society.* New York: Van Nostrand.

Li, J. (1994). Demographic diversity, tokenism, and their effect on individuals' behavior in group process. In D. P. Moore (Ed.), *Academy of Management Best Paper Proceedings.*

Livingston, R. W., & Brewer, M. B. (2002). What are we really priming? Cue-based versus category-based processing of facial stimuli. *Journal of Personality and Social Psychology, 82,* 5–18.

Milliken, F. J., & Martins, L. L. (1996). Searching for common threads: Understanding the multiple effects of diversity in organizational groups. *Academy of Management Review, 21,* 402–433.

Newcomb, T. M. (1961). *The Acquaintance Process.* New York: Holt, Rinehart & Winston.

O'Reilly, C. A., Snyder, R. C., & Boothe, J. N. (1993). Effects of executive team demography on organizational change. In G. P. Huber & W. H. Glick (Eds.), Organizational Change and Redesign (pp. 147–175). New York: Oxford University Press.

Pelled, L. H. (1996). Relational demography and perceptions of group conflict and performance: A field investigation. *The International Journal of Conflict Management, 7,* 230–246.

Perry, E. L., Hendricks, W., & Broadbent, E. (2000). An exploration of access and treatment discrimination and job satisfaction among college graduates with and without physical disabilities. *Human Relations, 53,* 923–955.

Pulakos, E. D., & Wexley, K. N. (1983). The relationship among perceptual similarity, sex, and performance ratings in manger-subordinate dyads. *Academy of Management Journal, 26,* 129–139.

Ragins, B. R. (1997). Antecedents of diversified mentoring relationships. *Journal of Vocational Behavior, 51,* 90–109.

Ragins, B. R. (1999). Gender and mentoring relationships: A review and research agenda for the next decade. In G. N. Powell (Ed.), *Handbook of gender and work* (pp. 347–370). Thousand Oaks, CA: Sage.

Ragins, B. R., & Cornwell, J. M. (2001). Pink triangles: Antecedents and consequences of perceived workplace discrimination against gay and lesbian employees. *Journal of Applied Psychology, 86,* 1244–1261.

Rand, T. M., & Wexley, K. N. (1975). Demonstration of the effect, "similar to me," in simulated employment interviews. *Psychological Reports, 36,* 535–544.

Riordan, C. M., & Shore, L. M. (1997). Demographic diversity and employee attitudes: An empirical examination of relational demography within work units. *Journal of Applied Psychology, 82,* 342–358.

Riordan, C. M., & Weatherly, E. W. (1999). *Relational demography within groups: An empirical test of a theoretical model.* Paper presented at the annual meeting of the Academy of Management, Chicago.

Riordan, C. M. (2000). Relational demography within groups: Past developments, contradictions, and new directions. *Research in Personnel and Human Resources Management, 19,* 131–173.

Sanchez, J. I., & Brock, P. (1996). Outcomes of perceived discrimination among Hispanic employees: Is diversity management a luxury or a necessity? *Academy of Management Journal, 39,* 704–719.

Schneider, B. (1987). The people make the place. *Personnel Psychology, 40,* 437–453.

Sigelman, L., & Welch, S. (1993). The contact hypothesis revisited: Black-white interaction and positive racial attitudes. *Social Forces, 71,* 781–795.

Shaffer, M. A., Joplin, J. R. W., Bell, M. P., Lau, T., & Oguz, C. (2000). Gender discrimination and job-related outcomes: A cross-cultural comparison of working women in the United States and China. *Journal of Vocational Behavior, 57,* 395–427.

Spangler, E., Gordon, M., & Pipkin, R. (1978). Token women: An empirical test of Kanter's hypothesis. *American Journal of Sociology, 28,* 960–971.

Steele, C. M. (1997). A threat in the air: How stereotypes shape intellectual identity and performance. *American Psychologist, 52,* 613–629.

Steele, C. M., & Aronson, J. (1995). Stereotype threat and the intellectual test performance of African Americans. *Journal of Personality and Social Psychology, 69,* 797–811.

Tajfel, H., & Turner, J. (1979). An integrative theory of intergroup conflict. In W. G. Austin & S. Worchel (Eds.), *The social psychology of intergroup relations* (pp. 33–47). Monterey, CA: Brooks/Cole.

Thomas, D. A. (2001). The truth about mentoring minorities: Race matters. *Harvard Business Review, 79,* 98–107.

Tsui, A. S., & O'Reilly, C. A. (1989). Beyond simple demographic effects: The importance of relational demography in superior–subordinate dyads. *Academy of Management Journal, 32,* 402–423.

Tsui, A. S., Egan, T. D., & O'Reilly, C. A. (1992). Being different: Relational demography and organizational attachment. *Administrative Science Quarterly, 37,* 547–579.

Turner, J. C., Brown, R. J., & Tajfel, H. (1979). Social comparison and group interest in in-group favouritism. *European Journal of Social Psychology, 9,* 187–204.

Valentine, S., Silver, L., & Twigg, N. (1999). Locus of control, job satisfaction and job complexity: The role of perceived race discrimination. *Psychological Reports, 84,* 1267–1273.

Vecchio, R. P., & Bullis, R. C. (2001). Moderators of the influence of supervisor–subordinate similarity on subordinate outcomes. *Journal of Applied Psychology, 86,* 884–896.

Wagner, W. G., Pfeffer, J., & O'Reilly, C. A. (1984). Organizational demography and turnover in top-management teams. *Administrative Science Quarterly, 29,* 74–92.

Watson, W. E., Kumar, K., & Michaelsen, L. K. (1993). Cultural diversity's impact on interaction process and performance: comparing homogeneous and diverse task groups. *Academy of Management Journal, 36,* 590–602.

Williams, K. Y., & O'Reilly, C. A. (1998). Demography and diversity in organizations: A review of 40 years of research. *Research in Organizational Behavior, 20,* 77–140.

Word, C. O., Zanna, M. P., & Cooper, J. (1974). The nonverbal mediation of self-fulfilling prophecies in interracial interaction. *Journal of Experimental Social Psychology, 10,* 109–120.

Young, J. L., & James, E. H. (2001). Token majority: The work attitudes of male flight attendants. *Sex Roles, 45,* 299–319.

Zenger, T., & Lawrence, B. (1989). Organizational demography: The differential effects of age and tenure distributions on technical communication. *Academy of Management Journal, 32,* 353–376.

Zamarripa, P. O., & Krueger, D. L. (1983). Implicit contracts regulating small group leadership: The influence of culture. *Small Group Behavior, 14,* 187–210.

4

Group-Level Explanations of Workplace Discrimination

Kecia M. Thomas
University of Georgia

Donna Chrobot-Mason
University of Colorado at Denver

Companies evaluate potential employees' education and experiences in order to make sound predictions regarding who will perform best in their organization. Yet employees do not enter the organization with only their knowledge, skill, ability, and experience. Employees, new and old, enter organizations daily with a group or social identity and a personal identity. Often our social identities motivate how others will respond to us both inside and outside of the workplace. Differences in social identity predispose us to be biased toward people similar to ourselves and biased against those who we identify as being somehow different. This chapter focuses on the salience of group identity, especially resulting from race, gender, and sexuality, and how multiple group identities can create opportunities for discrimination and conflict in the workplace. We also discuss the impact of group representation on workgroup dynamics and outcomes and the consequence of group identity on both individual and organizational behavior. Finally, the chapter concludes with a discussion of avoiding group-based discrimination in the workplace.

WHY GROUP MEMBERSHIP MATTERS

Organizations select employees based upon applicants' knowledge, skill, and ability, so why should your group identity, such as your race, gender, or your sexuality impact how you are treated by your peers or your leaders at work? There are a variety of ways in which to explain why such arbitrary characteristics and differences seem to matter in organizations. Both social identity theory and social categorization theory illustrate how group membership differences can create opportunities for discrimination. Social marking explanations of group-based discrimination in organizations aid in conveying the importance of social power in the determination of which differences matter and the consequences of those differences for the dominant group's identities and self worth. Social marking also explains how mere differences can serve as a justification for mistreatment and discrimination. Finally, we examine the relevance of privilege to discussions of group-based discrimination in organizations and how privilege and social dominance helps to further illustrate social identity, social categorization, and social marking explanations of group-based discrimination.

Social identity theory (Tajfel & Turner, 1986) suggests that as individuals we are motivated to feel positively about ourselves. To acquire a positive sense of self, we view other people as either members of our ingroup or outgroup, and we compare ourselves favorably relative to outgroup members. Members of our ingroup are those with whom we presume to share common characteristics. Despite our sense of kinship with ingroup members, we also appreciate the diversity within our ingroup (the ingroup differentiation effect). That is, a female executive may identify other women in her organization as part of her ingroup, yet still appreciate that these women differ in regard to their talents, racial background, and age.

In contrast, members of our outgroups are those with whom we presume we share little in common. We also lack an appreciation of our outgroups' diversity (the outgroup homogeneity effect). If we refer back to the female executive, she may identify men, as members of the outgroup, as all being the same, and therefore she may not be able to as easily appreciate the significance of their differences in regards to their talents, race, and age.

It is not at all uncommon for race, gender, and even sexuality to be used as determinants of who is (or is not) a member of our ingroup. Tajfel (1982) argued that the need to divide the world into ingroups and outgroups is a cognitive process that enables the mind to simplify an increasingly complex world. Certainly diversity is part of that complexity. Numerous studies using the "minimal group paradigm," (a technique in which researchers divide their participant sample into subgroups based upon an arbitrary criteria), demonstrate that the mere division of a group by some arbitrary characteristic is enough to ignite discrimination (Bourhis, Sachdev, & Gagnon, 1994). Categorization is a normal activity that likely initiates the "us vs. them" mentality that often precedes prejudice and discrimination.

The simplistic division of the world into ingroups and outgroups satisfies our own needs for identity and for a sense of worth. Ingroups provide a sense of identity in that they enable us to learn from others similar to ourselves, even if what we learn is stereotypical. According to the similarity-attraction effect (Byrne, 1971), we are attracted to those people we presume to be like ourselves. In addition, surrounding ourselves with members of our identified ingroup provides consensual validation (Bochner, 1994). That is, by surrounding ourselves with people we perceive to be similar to ourselves, we avoid challenges to our beliefs, values, and worldview. The similarity in beliefs, values, and worldviews offered by members of our ingroup is validating and helps us to feel secure. The ingroup becomes a source of reinforcement as well as pride. Outgroups help cement identity through the contrast they present; they inform us of who we are not. Likewise, they facilitate our sense of worth through comparison because in essence we typically see ourselves as superior or better than members of our outgroups.

Self-categorization theory (SCT; Tajfel, 1982), an extension of social identity theory, stresses the cognitive function that drives social identity theory. SCT's contribution to our understanding of group membership and discrimination is that individuals enact a personal or social identity at different times. In fact, SCT suggests that we each have different group memberships that we may call on and that these group memberships differ in their level of inclusiveness. For example, employees within an organization may see themselves as (a) members of humanity (the superordinate level), (b) members of their organization (the intermediate level), or (c) simply as unique individuals (the subordinate level). We have a choice of which identity to enact at any given time, but our environment, including the workplace, may drive which identity is most salient. Some identities, such as a racial group identity, are more noticeable and accessible than other group identities, such as one's professional identity. Therefore, being a numeric minority because of some noticeable characteristics such as race or gender may facilitate the choice of one's group identity over any other identity available.

In organizations, social identity has consequences for members of organizations through its effects on issues such as organizational socialization and intergroup relations (Ashforth & Mael, 1989). For example, Mehra, Kilduff, and Brass (1998) examined networking and friendship patterns within an MBA program. Both women and racial minorities were underrepresented in the program. Yet despite both groups having a minority status, only ethnic minorities were motivated to form ingroup friendships. Women established relationships more broadly than their ethnic minority counterparts. The researchers suggest that differences in the friendship formation patterns between women and minorities in this study may be in part the result of differences in the stereotype and marks attached to each group.

For example, Asian Americans and African Americans may both have low levels of representation within a particular work setting. Yet if the mark (or status) of being Asian within that setting is less negative than the mark (or status) of being Black, Asian Americans will likely have an easier time forming relationships and networks with non-Asian Americans, compared to the opportunities that Blacks may have for building relationships with Whites. Given this example, we may expect that Blacks in this environment may be very motivated to form a strong network with other members of their racial ingroup.

What are the consequences of this natural tendency to divide ourselves into ingroups and outgroups as the world increasingly becomes more complex due to diversity? Do we find new ways in which to construct ingroups and outgroups, for example, turning away from race but instead embracing a national identity due to globalization? Further, how does this "new" identity dimension influence our ability to work globally? Perhaps as diversity increases, instead of embracing new identity dimensions, individuals hold more tightly to the most salient identities. In fact, Maume (1999) found that increasing racial and gender diversity seemed to benefit White men's career mobility (the glass escalator) as compared to the career mobility of women and men of color. Perhaps decision makers embrace the "known" in times of demographic uncertainty and rely upon ingroup favoritism rather than risk promoting an "unknown."

Social Marking

Sampson (1999) discussed the importance of group distinction for social marking. The differences that are most salient in our society and in organizations, such as race and gender, are a result of the emphasis placed by dominant social groups on those categories so that members of the dominant group can distinguish themselves from others. This counters an essentialist model Grillo and Wildman (1996) of difference, which suggests that the major categories by which we organize our world and society are somehow natural and essential to defining others. Marking is a result of a history of social relations between groups; it is not a quick and immediate process. The differences that are important and those that are ignored reflect a choice made by dominant social groups that occupy positions of power. Finally, the differences that become most salient within a particular society provide dominant group members not only a sense of identity, but also a positive sense of self.

For example, West (1993) suggested that without Blacks, European Americans would have no sense of what it means to be White in America today. Instead their identity would be largely shaped by other characteristics that may reflect previous struggles over resources such as national origin. Socially dominant groups achieve a sense of their own identity by highlighting the differences between themselves and others. These differences are also used to justify attitudes and negative behaviors toward disempowered others, thus securing the dominant person's positive sense of self and own self-interests.

In a related vein, Cox (1994) identified macro and micro legacy effects that demonstrate how a history of social marking is embedded in modern personal and professional relationships. Macro legacy effects involve how individuals enact relationships with members of other social groups based upon their shared (likely negative) history. For example, the history of enslavement of Africans by Europeans and European Americans, not only creates tension between modern day Blacks and Whites, but also reinforces the identities of the groups. Whites are seen as powerful and controlling, and Blacks are seen as weak yet needing to be controlled. Micro legacy effects reflect the extent to which one's personal (rather than social group) history with a member of one's outgroup affects other subsequent relationships. For example, if a Latino student has a negative experience with a White teacher, that student may become distrusting and antagonistic toward other White teachers and authority figures. Therefore, both macro and micro legacy effects interfere with employees' abilities to initiate and develop productive relationships with outgroup members.

Privilege

Another way to think about the importance of social group membership in organizations is to consider how demographic characteristics can afford or deny one's privilege.

Wildman (1996) defines privilege as the

"... systemic conferral of benefit and advantage. Members of a privileged group gain this status by affiliation, conscious or not and chosen or not, to the dominant side of a power system ... Affiliation with the dominant side of the power line is often defined as merit and worthiness. Characteristics and behaviors shared by those on the dominant side of the power line often delineate the societal norm." (p. 29)

McIntosh (1993) provides several examples of workplace privileges based upon White skin color such as "I can be pretty sure that if I ask to talk to the person in charge, I will be facing a person of my race," and "I can go home from most meetings of organizations I belong to feeling somewhat tied in, rather than isolated, out-of-place, outnumbered, unheard, held at a distance, or feared" (p. 33).

Social group membership matters because it is often an indicator of privilege. Privilege is not unique to organizations, but instead it is an attribute that employees bring into the workplace. Privilege represents dominance because of one's social identity (McIntosh, 1993). McIntosh (1988) described privilege as an invisible knapsack of provisions that one counts on each day but that are largely invisible and unacknowledged. Those most aware of privilege are those who may lack privilege. For example, African Americans are likely more aware of how Whiteness provides privileges in our society and in our workplaces, whereas members of the gay and lesbian population are aware of the many ways in which heterosexuality is privileged. Characteristics of privilege are largely invisible and normalized, that those holding privilege have the opportunity to confront or ignore (Wildman & Davis, 1996).

Maier (1997) listed his privileges as someone who is both male and White. Among the list of privileges that he acknowledges are, "I am not likely to be restricted from business-related networking opportunities because of my gender (or my race)" and "As a man, at social functions involving partners of organization members; I am not likely to be mistaken for 'just a spouse' (and possibly ignored) (pp. 31–32)." An example of a privilege based upon heterosexuality includes, "Most people I meet will see my marital arrangements as an asset to my life or as a favorable comment on my liability, my competence, or my mental health" (McIntosh, 1993, p. 37).

Privilege provides the member of a majority group with resources in organizations that minority group members may not have access to themselves. Privileged personnel in organizations are never considered "different," but they instead represent what is perceived as normal. It is *normal* for high-level executives to be White, male, and middle-class. Privileged employees have the opportunity to network and develop productive relationships with one another without the barriers that may be presented when differences in race, gender, culture, or sexuality are introduced. Likewise, privileged employees, because of their attraction to other privileged employees, are likely to distance themselves from those who do not have the privilege of being a part of the status quo. Wildman (1996) commented, "Systems of privilege and power, by privileging those with certain characteristics or behaviors, are 'limiting' individuals who lack those characteristics and behaviors" (p. 33).

Allowing unearned privilege to persist in organizations not only reinforces a system of domination and institutional discrimination, but also may also reinforce interpersonal discrimination. Because differences such as race and gender have been socially constructed to be meaningful in relationship to other attributes such as competence or worth, our group identities not only can become opportunities for privilege, but also cues for interpersonal discrimination. Interpersonal discrimination reflects one-on-one discrimination that involves avoidance, distancing, and exclusion based upon a person's group identity (Lott & Maluso, 1995). Social distancing on the part of employees in positions of power toward minority or female targets, likely deny and limit minority and female employees' access to mentors and to networks that are critical for professional and career development. For example, Dreher and Cox (1996) found that *not* having a White male mentor significantly cost potential protégés (especially people of color) financially in terms of lost income. In fact, having a low-status mentor, such as a person of color, was financially the same as having no mentor at all.

The examination of privilege holds promise for future research on group-level explanations of workplace prejudice and discrimination. Those with privilege and those who lack privilege likely have very different perceptions of the extent to which one's demographic membership affords certain advantages. How do these differences in perceptions of privilege and advantage affect broad diversity efforts and interpersonal relationships across demographic groups? For example, having race-based privilege likely results in a failure to see race as a critical issue within one's organization.

Another frontier issue involves the extent to which we all have multiple group identities, some of which afford us privilege and others that deny access to privilege. For example White women may be afforded race privilege but denied gender privilege. Is there a dominant identity lens or perspective that these women use to understand their place in the organization and their relationships with members of other groups, such as Black women. If White women are most connected to their White privilege, they may be unlikely to see racism in their organizations and unsympathetic to the racism that other women may encounter. Yet White women who feel denied privilege because of gender, and who view the organization from that perspective, may feel a kinship to Black women because of their shared perception of sexism within their organization. How individuals negotiate multiples identities and the privilege (or the lack thereof) likely is context dependent. Some identities become more salient given the demographic composition of one's workgroup, which we will discuss in the next section. In a group of women, gender is unlikely to be salient, but race may become more visible.

Summary

Why does group membership matter in organizations? The answer is complex. Social and cognitive psychology theories such as social identity theory and social categorization illustrate that as individuals, we are naturally predisposed to favor people similar to ourselves, and we are naturally biased against those we perceive as different. However, why do some differences matter and others do not? The social marking explanation suggests that those differences that matter reflect a history of social relationships among groups, and that the differences identified by society as significant are those that have been chosen by groups in power to (a) help dominant groups members distinguish themselves from other groups so that they can develop a sense of their own identity; and (b) enable dominant groups to justify their attitudes toward and treatment of others so that they can protect their own self interests. Similarly, a privilege explanation reinforces the idea that some group memberships afford hidden and subtle advantages whereas others do not.

What are the consequences for having a workplace in which some groups are "marked" and others achieve social dominance and privilege? The demographic composition of workgroups in organizations can make more salient the marks and privileges that individuals bring to their workgroup. The following sections will review the literature that examines the role of group composition on minority success and group dynamics such as conflict.

GROUP COMPOSITION

One possible explanation for discrimination in the workplace comes from research on group composition. In essence, this body of research suggests that the relative proportion or composition of social identity groups can affect differences in the experience of organizational members (Konrad & Gutek, 1987). Generally, research has shown that as minority numbers increase in the workplace, majority member satisfaction decreases (e.g., Tsui, Egan, & O'Reilly, 1992) and minority satisfaction and performance increase (e.g., Niemann & Dovidio, 1998; Schmitt & Noe, 1986). Discrimination against minority group members may fluctuate with changes in minority representation in the workplace for two primary reasons: (a) increasing numbers of minority group members present a perceived threat to the existing power structure, and (b) minority group member distinctiveness creates a situation in which minority members become highly visible and group membership becomes particularly salient.

Minority Representation Threatens Status-Quo

Social dominance theory suggests that all human social systems, including organizations, involve a caste system with a hegemonic group at the top and a negative reference group at the bottom (Sidanius, Devereux, & Pratto, 2001). The dominant or hegemonic group at the top is motivated to maintain its status and power as the socially dominant group and accomplishes this goal in part through aggregated institutional discrimination. The U.S. Commission on Civil Rights (1981) defined institutional discrimination in the organizational context as well-established rules, policies, and practices that favor the dominant group and serve to protect and promote the status quo that arose from the racism and sexism of the past. Such organizational practices have an adverse effect on minorities and women, even when there is no conscious intent on the part of individuals to affect minorities or women adversely. Examples of institutional discrimination in organizations include: (a) height and weight requirements geared unnecessarily toward the physical proportions of White males that tend to exclude females from jobs, and (b) seniority rules stating that the "last hired, are the first fired," leaving minorities and females more subject to layoffs and less eligible for advancement in jobs historically held by White males.

When minority group representation begins to increase and traditional policies and practices in the workplace begin to change as a result, the dominant group will likely feel that the status quo is threatened and react negatively toward diversity initiatives (Konrad & Gutek, 1987; Milliken & Martins, 1996) and perhaps even negatively toward minority group members who are the perceived beneficiaries of such initiatives (see chapter 15 in this volume). For example, Tsui et al. (1992) found that in comparison to non-White individuals, White individuals reported lower levels of organizational commitment, more absences, and a lower intent to stay when workgroup racial heterogeneity increased.

Minority Distinctiveness

Another possible explanation for discrimination based on or exacerbated by group composition is the subjective experience of distinctiveness that minority members may perceive in the work context. In their review of the literature, Milliken and Martins (1996) concluded that "group heterogeneity, thus, may have a negative impact on individuals' feelings of satisfaction through decreasing individuals' sense of identification or social integration within the group" (p. 415). Minority perceptions of distinctiveness and social isolation in the workplace was first examined by Rosabeth

Kanter (1977). Kanter collected qualitative data in a field study of working women in which they comprised only 10% of the total workforce. She identified different groups based on the proportional representation of males versus females, defining skewed groups as those in which the sex ratio involved a preponderance of men over women (e.g., 85:15). Women in these groups were defined as "tokens," and she found them to be treated as representatives of their category, and as symbols of their group rather than individuals. In some situations, she found that women were "solos" or the only one of their kind. She labeled a second type of group, those with ratios of 65:35 for example, as "tilted," representing less extreme distributions in which dominants are the majority and tokens become a minority. In such situations, minority members have the potential to find allies among each other, form coalitions, and affect the culture of the group. Since Kanter's original work, a number of researchers have found support for the notion that gender composition of workgroups significantly impacts women's social integration, performance, and overall success in the workplace (Riordan, 2000; Ragins & Sundstrom, 1989). For example, Sackett and colleagues (1991) found that when women formed less than 20% of the group, they received lower performance ratings than men, but when their proportion was greater than 50%, they were rated higher than men. It should be noted that Kanter's theory has generally been supported when studying women as the minority, but the same results are not found when men are in the minority (see review by Riordan, 2000).

Other researchers have also found support for the importance of solo and token status for racial and ethnic minorities. Pettigrew and Martin (1987) argued that African Americans face significant barriers during the recruitment, entry, and promotional stages of their careers as a result of being a solo or token member of the organization. Solos are often met with very low expectations from their supervisor and coworkers. These low expectations are insulting to the minority member, may result in less challenging work assignments, and may affect performance as Blacks internalize the low expectations and begin to expect less of themselves. Research by Taylor, Fiske, Close, Anderson, and Ruderman (1977) showed that compared to nonsolos, solos were rated by others as more prominent (i.e., talking more, making a stronger impression, and more confident and assertive). This prominence, however, was not found to be a positive advantage for solos. Instead, their contributions were rated as less creative and effective when making the same contribution as a nonsolo. In rare instances, solo status may be met with very high expectations, but such expectations may be unrealistically high, setting the stage for eventual failure. Pettigrew and Martin (1987) suggested that "either a solo is 'golden' and can do no wrong, or else the solo is a hopeless case who is doomed to failure" (p. 57). Token status implies preferential treatment, which also may lead to negative consequences and stereotyping of the minority employee. Like solos, tokens are often assumed to be incompetent (see chapter 15) and experience exclusion and isolation in the workplace. Some minority members unfortunately face the negative implications of both solo and token status. Pettigrew and Martin (1987) concluded that a critical mass constitutes roughly 20% and that organizations dealing with small numbers of minority employees should cluster rather than scatter minorities throughout, in order to lessen the negative impact of isolation and exclusion often experienced by women and people of color at work.

More recently, Niemann and Dovidio (1998) studied the relationship between solo status for racial and ethnic minorities and feelings of distinctiveness and job dissatisfaction. The authors defined distinctiveness as feelings of high visibility, encapsulation in one's role, feeling highly contrasted from other workgroup members, and being stereotyped and viewed primarily in terms of category membership. They hypothesized that feelings of distinctiveness would be closely associated with awareness of stigmatization and feelings of vulnerability, which in turn would adversely affect job satisfaction. They also argued that solo status and feelings of distinctiveness could heighten the salience of negative stereotypic expectancies, a phenomena known as stereotype threat (Steele, 1997). Research on stereotype threat has shown that when minority group members are made aware of existing negative stereotypes toward their group, the threat of possibly behaving in such a manner as to confirm existing stereotypes is enough to impede performance (Steele & Aronson, 1995). As predicted, Niemann and Dovidio (1998) found that minority faculty members with solo status within their departments felt more distinctive and were less satisfied with their jobs. More specifically, their results suggest that "the daily experiences of minority faculty in predominantly White institutions, in which African Americans and Hispanics represent less than 3% of faculty, may be affected by stereotypic biases and feelings of vulnerability" (p. 66).

Effects of Composition on Minority Success   In situations where minority group members represent a very small percentage of the workforce, group status becomes exaggerated. Stereotypes and group bias likely become exaggerated as well, particularly when minority members are perceived as a threat to the status quo. Under such conditions, minority members are faced with unrealistically high or low expectations, are highly scrutinized and criticized, and experience feelings of distinctiveness, isolation, exclusion, and stereotype threat. All of these feelings may negatively affect work relationships, performance, and organizational commitment.

Other significant barriers to success when minority group representation is low include perceived limits to upward mobility and the lack of opportunities to develop mentoring relationships. Interpersonal discrimination disadvantages minority and female employees when race and gender are used as cues for distancing, avoidance, and exclusion Lott and Maluso (1995). Ragins and Sundstrom (1989) argued that women enter the organization at lower-ranking positions, have less position power, are highly underrepresented in top ranking positions, and occupy departments with less influence than men. For all these reasons, women and minorities lack power in organizations, and we may conclude that career advancement is unlikely for members of their group. Underrepresentation may also lead to increased competition for power in organizations. For example, Ely (1994, 1995) studied the effects of female representation on professional relationships. She found that in firms with low proportions of women, sex roles were more stereotypical. Moreover, women in these situations were less likely to perceive senior women as role models with legitimate authority and were more likely to perceive competition in relationships with women peers.

Ibarra (1993, 1997) suggests that women and racial minority group members lack informal support and resources provided by networking relationships in organizations. Because minorities are highly underrepresented in organizations, it is difficult to consult with members of one's own group to seek friendship, support, feedback, and role models. Additionally, Ibarra (1992) has shown that the homophily bias exists with respect to network relationships. The preference to interact with people who are similar in terms of background socioeconomic status, race, attitudes, and so forth, is known as the homophily bias and has been widely supported in the literature (Konrad & Gutek, 1987). The implications of this for minority members in networking relationships is that (a) there are fewer opportunities to establish homophilous network relationships, (b) minority members must develop diverse interpersonal networks that include relationships with the dominant group to provide instrumental support (meeting job demands) and relationships with minorities for psychosocial support (enhancing the employee's sense of competence and identity), and (c) minorities view networking relationships as less beneficial than Whites (Ibarra, 1995). Although Ibarra's work suggested that minority members who develop a diverse set of network ties are likely to reap professional benefits from such relationships, there seems to be a limit to such benefits. For example, Ibarra reported that the network resources reached through women's ties were relatively poor and that women were more likely to benefit from developing ties to male colleagues than to female colleagues (Ibarra, 1992). However, these homophilous ties did serve an important function in the development of women's careers by providing a source of advice from others who have faced similar obstacles (Ibarra, 1997).

In summary, research suggests that group composition can play a significant role in either increasing or decreasing the barriers that women and minorities face in the workplace as a result of stereotyping, discrimination, and bias. The results of studies that suggest that majority dominance, minority distinctiveness, and limited access to organizational power and resources all contribute to individual and institutional discrimination may help to explain the detrimental and cumulative negative impact discrimination can have on minority satisfaction and success. Continued research in this area may help us to better understand why there are consistent findings in the organizational literature that report that minorities are less satisfied with their jobs, receive lower performance ratings, and demonstrate slower promotion rates (see review by Cox, Welsch, & Nkomo, 2001). Future research on the effects of group composition on group dynamics and perceived threat will continue to become more complicated as workforce demographics continue to shift and in many regions of the country, Whites become the minority group, and Hispanics become the majority group. Additionally, researchers are just beginning to examine the impact of group-based discrimination and injustice on the individual as chronic stressors that can have long-term psychological and physical health outcomes for the individual employee (e.g., Clark, Anderson, Clark, & Williams, 1999). Another source of workplace stress and possible explanation for the prevalence of group-based discrimination in the workplace is conflict both between and among identity groups. Research and theory on group conflict is presented in the next section.

Intra- and Intergroup Conflict

Conflict between members of different social identity groups and between social identity groups themselves is likely to emerge within a multicultural workplace and may have a negative effect on work process variables and ultimately impede overall team performance (De Dreu & Van Vianen, 2001). Campbell (1965) theorized that social identity groups must compete for scarce resources (e.g., power, status, and opportunities in the workplace) and as a result, groups are engaged in very real conflicts involving high stakes for both the winner and the loser. Realistic group conflict theory (Campbell, 1965) suggests that when groups must compete for scarce resources, discrimination, bias, hostility, and prejudice against the outgroup is likely to occur.

In a now-famous study of the theory of realistic group conflict, Sherif and his colleagues (Sherif, Harvey, White, Hood, & Sherif, 1961) conducted an experiment at a summer boys' camp. The boys were assigned to two groups (the Eagles and the Rattlers) and competed against each other in a series of sporting events. Over time, the researchers observed evidence of prejudice and discrimination against the outgroup and positive bias toward ingroup members. For example, when asked who their friends were, the boys listed only ingroup members as friends. Although the researchers attempted to reduce prejudice through increased contact among group members (they were forced to sit together in the camp cafeteria), the results backfired and food fights erupted between the two groups. It was only when the researchers introduced a problem requiring both groups to work together toward a common goal that conflict between the two groups subsided.

Other researchers have demonstrated the extent to which animosity among group members can emerge even when the groups are temporary and unimportant. As previously discussed, Tajfel and his colleagues (e.g., Tajfel, Flament, Billig, & Bundy, 1971) demonstrated that ingroup/outgroup categorization and competition among groups occurs even when research participants are arbitrarily assigned to groups. Brewer and Brown (1998) conclude that after two decades of research on this topic, there is sufficient evidence to suggest that "any salient and situationally meaningful ingroup–outgroup, we–they distinction is sufficient to activate differential responses to others on the basis of ingroup or outgroup membership" (p. 559). In other words, it is the mere presence of group differences that can be enough to evoke ingroup/outgroup categorization and competition.

Identity-Based Conflicts

Although conflict between any groups may emerge as a result of actual or perceived competition for scarce resources, conflict is more likely to erupt and is more likely to be characterized as intransigent when there is conflict among members of social identity groups that have historically been in competition with each other. Northrup (1989) argued that when a conflict between parties involves a core sense of identity, the conflict will likely be intractable. When derogatory comments or discriminatory actions are directed toward an individual or group because of one's social identity, group identity becomes highly salient, and under some situations, will supercede personal identity. This serves to heighten the importance of maintaining and protecting one's social identity (particularly ethnicity, nationality, race, gender, and religion) and results in protective responses. Research based on terror management theory has shown that after people are reminded of their mortality, they are especially likely to defend beliefs of groups with which they identify and that such defenses serve to protect the individual from the threat of death by providing a sense of security and safety as a member of a larger culture (Greenberg, Solomon, & Pyszczynski, 1997).

An experienced or perceived threat to one's social group will often result in intractable conflicts in which both parties believe their own existence is threatened by the mere existence of the other, and psychic or even physical annihilation will seem imminent (Northrup, 1989). "Identity-driven conflicts are rooted in the articulation of, and the threats or frustrations to, people's collective need for dignity, recognition, safety, control, purpose, and efficacy" (Rothman, 1997, p. 7). Because group members' existential needs and values are at stake, intractable or identity-based conflicts are often viewed from a win–lose perspective in which compromise is not possible (Rothman, 1997).

In the workplace, conflict between social identity groups may become salient, intense, and perhaps intractable when the organization experiences shifts in minority/majority group representation, power, and status. Such shifts are likely to result in perceived or actual threats to scarce organizational resources such as decision-making authority, opportunities for advancement, access to information, and even survival. Viewing resistance to diversity from the perspective of group conflict theory may help to explain employee attitudes, reactions, and backlash to diversity initiatives discussed in other chapters throughout this book. For example, some researchers suggest that negative attitudes toward affirmative action on the part of Whites may be the result not of negative feelings toward minority group members, but rather the result of an exaggerated belief that one's existence in the organization is at risk or a fear of losing status and power within the organization (Crosby, 2004).

Positive versus Negative Conflict

Although conflict in the workplace is generally assumed to be a hindrance to organizational performance, there is some evidence to suggest that certain types of conflict can actually facilitate performance. Researchers have attempted to distinguish between two types of conflict: relational and task. Relationship conflict is the result of interpersonal differences such as values, personality, political beliefs, and social identity group membership. Task conflict involves disagreement because of differences in the recognition of and solution to a task-related problem (Rahim, 2001). In a series of studies, Jehn (1994, 1995, 1997) showed that relationship or emotional conflict is detrimental to workgroup performance, satisfaction, and survival, whereas task conflict is positively associated with group performance. Research suggests that relational conflict likely impedes group performance because it causes distress and animosity among team members, limits the information processing ability and cognitive functioning of workgroup members, and diminishes group loyalty and satisfaction (De Dreu & Van

Vianen, 2001; Jehn, 1995; Rahim, 2001). Alternatively, task conflict may improve workgroup performance because it encourages a broader understanding of the issues and exploration of alternative solutions (Jehn, 1997; Pelled, Eisenhardt, & Xin, 1999).

Conflict Triggers Researchers are really just beginning to theorize about and examine the complex nature of identity-based conflicts in organizations. Proudford and Smith (2003) proposed that both interpersonal and intergroup interactions create complex dynamics in the workplace, involving multiple layers of difference that exist among organizational members. Furthermore, they suggest that conflicts among heterogeneous groups must be viewed as dynamic rather than static, as group and personal identities become more or less salient and the focus of the conflict shifts. Identity-based conflict may emerge when some organizational event or issue serves to trigger a conflict and polarize members along group lines including gender, race, ethnic, religious, or function, as examples.

Lau and Murnighan (1998) drew an analogy between geological faultlines in the Earth's crust and social identity faultlines that exist in the organizational context that may become activated and trigger otherwise dormant intergroup conflict. They defined group faultlines as "hypothetical dividing lines that may split a group into subgroups based on one or more attributes" (Lau & Murnighan, 1998, p. 328). The importance of such attributes may go unnoticed until some external force reveals their importance and relevance to understanding and interpreting a specific event or workplace issue. For example, a gender faultline may divide an organizational group based on male and female subgroups. The salience of gender as a subgroup may be minimal until the issue of sexual harassment emerges and serves to activate group membership along gender lines and create a visible "crack" or fissure within the workgroup. Conditions for prejudice may flourish when group composition serves to activate faultlines or when social/demographic categorizations equate to organizational subcategories. For example, Brewer (1995) argued that discrimination may be exacerbated in organizations when executives are White males, clerical staff are females, and assembly line workers are Black.

The Cycle of Conflict Among Groups

Intergroup conflict based on social identity membership will likely result in prejudice, discrimination, and bias in the workplace. Likewise, stereotypes and prejudicial attitudes formed outside of the organizational context are likely to emerge and fuel intergroup conflicts within the workplace. Thus, group conflict and discrimination may both be viewed as cause and consequence. The cyclical nature of this interaction has been discussed within the context of the theory of intergroup anxiety. Stephan and Stephan (1985) presented a model of intergroup anxiety in which they argue that prior relations between groups and preconceived expectations of outgroup members can influence anxiety toward intergroup interactions, which in turn may have a negative impact on interaction between group members. For example, when contact between groups has been minimal or prior relations have been characterized by conflict, then intergroup anxiety will be high. When intergroup anxiety is high, normative response patterns will be amplified. A dominant response to many forms of anxiety is avoidance or suspicion. Another common reaction to anxiety may be to exaggerate behavioral norms such as politeness or interest in the individual to the point that it is perceived as ingenuine or condescending. Still another consequence of high intergroup anxiety involves information processing biases. Anxious individuals are more likely to attend to information that confirms existing stereotypes rather than information that disconfirms stereotypes (Fiske & Neuberg, 1990). Intergroup anxiety may explain research that has shown that White interviewers spent less time with, demonstrated greater interpersonal distance from, and exhibited less eye contact with Black applicants than with White applicants (Word, Zanna, & Cooper, 1974) and that African Americans received less feedback about their performance because managers felt uncomfortable providing corrective feedback to minority members (Blank & Slipp, 1994).

Intergroup anxiety can thus negatively influence both current and future intergroup interactions. Biased information processing, such as attending to stereotype confirming information, can serve to escalate intergroup conflict as people attribute negative attributions and motives to the other person or group. Pettigrew (1979) referred to the "ultimate attribution error" as a common phenomena in which people explain the actions of their own group as a response to situational or external demands, but view the actions of enemies as internally based and therefore "evil." For example, researchers have shown that Americans view military actions of their own nation as morally correct and necessary, but view similar military actions performed by other nations as aggressive and diabolically evil (Oskamp, 1965; Sande, Goethals, Ferrari, & Worth, 1989). As the image of the group as an evil other strengthens, the cycle of conflict progresses. Northrup (1989) defined three stages that tend to characterize identity-based, intractable conflicts. In the first stage of conflict, labeled as threat, an event occurs in which one or more parties perceive the situation as invalidating its core sense of identity and thus experiences significant threat. The second stage, distortion, is characterized by the groups' attempt to deal with the threat of invalidation by distorting or misperceiving incoming information to maintain the core sense of identity. In stage three, rigidification, threatened groups develop increasingly rigid interpretations of the world and seek to separate ingroup and outgroup members. Northrup (1989) suggested that rigidification occurs to protect one's self and one's group, and it is during this stage that communication shuts down and the group is construed as an evil other. In stage four, collusion, maintaining the conflict becomes more important than resolving the conflict, because the conflict itself has now become a part of the group's identity. Northrup (1989) noted that each stage contributes to the creation of the next stage, and as the conflict moves from one stage to the next, deescalation becomes less and less likely.

This cycle of miscommunication and misattribution may help to explain why discrimination and bias continue to create problems in organizations. Devine, Evett, and Vasquez-Suson (1996) suggested that individuals who lack experience with dissimilar others may be considered intergroup-unskilled and may experience high anxiety during intergroup interactions. Their anxiety is manifested in avoidant nonverbal behaviors (such as lack of eye contact in an interview situation), which is likely interpreted by the minority member not as anxiety, but rather as prejudice. In response then, the minority member is likely to withdraw or respond with hostility, which in turn may be perceived by the majority member not as a response to prejudice, but rather prejudice toward the majority. Thus, this cycle of misattribution can result in confirmed expectations and increased intergroup anxiety that consequently influences future intergroup interactions. Furthermore, there is some evidence to suggest that intergroup anxiety and the suppression of stereotypes can be quite taxing and requires a significant amount of cognitive capacity that may impair performance on other cognitively complex tasks (Richeson & Shelton, 2003). Thus, organizational members who are prejudiced or lack experience with dissimilar others and who find themselves in a diverse workplace may experience cognitive overload as they attempt to monitor their behavior and simultaneously engage in complex work tasks.

Future research in this area will likely focus on trying to better understand complex intra- and intergroup dynamics that involve multiple social identities and how and when various identities become salient within the work context. We still know very little about what kinds of organizational rhetoric, policies, or practices serve as triggers for the eruption of social identity-based conflicts and perhaps more importantly about what organizations and leaders may do to prevent, mitigate, and resolve such types of conflict.

AVOIDING GROUP-BASED DISCRIMINATION IN ORGANIZATIONS

There is a natural tendency to notice individual differences such as race and gender. Furthermore, acknowledgment of these differences often causes employees and those outside of organizations as well to divide humanity into "us" and "them." This simplistic dichotomy can lead to both subtle and overt bias and discrimination as well as intergroup conflict that can interfere with an organization's ability to establish a productive climate where individuals can focus on the work at hand. Despite the natural inclination to notice differences and to order our worlds according to these distinctions, the distinctions themselves are artificial. In no way are we born knowing that race and gender matter and that one's identity in reference to these designations affords one status and privilege. Our understanding of the meaning of being White or of being female, in and outside of organizations, is socially constructed and passed down in organizations through its history, its human resource system, its leadership, and its culture. Therefore, in order for organizations to avoid group-based discrimination and its high financial and productivity costs, companies must construct new identities for its members, or at a minimum, find ways to allow multiple identities to constructively coexist.

Developing New Organizationally Relevant Identities

The intergroup approach to prejudice reduction identifies three alternatives for eliminating group based bias: decategorization, recategorization, and subcategorization (Brewer & Miller, 1996). Decategorization involves personalizing interactions between members of different groups; helping employees see one another as individuals rather than simply members of groups. The focus is to minimize social identity while maximizing personal identity (Sampson, 1999). For example, one decategorization strategy would be to avoid assigning workgroups or teams based upon demographic group membership. Recategorization tolerates the existence of multiple social identities but also encourages individuals to develop a superordinate identity that is motivated by having a superordinate goal. The "us" versus "them" that is so prevalent as a result of our natural inclination to attend to social identities is replaced with a "we" identity when an important and common goal is introduced. This was demonstrated in the Sherif camp study mentioned previously in which feuding camps were forced to "come together" to solve a common problem. The common superordinate goal allows individuals to recategorize their memberships and identities so that they belong to a single inclusive group (Sampson, 1999).

Although social identities can be an impetus for prejudice, as mentioned earlier, the social groups to which we belong often provide us with a sense of self worth or at a minimum a sense of identity. Both decategorization and recategorization downplay that aspect of one's self that may be quite important, and which in an increasingly diverse society, many people may not want to deny (Cox, 1994; Sampson, 1999). In addition, being blind to social and group identities may promote prejudice rather than discourage it. Konrad & Linnehan (1995) found organizations with identity-blind selection procedures were less effective in their diversity efforts than those organizations with diversity conscious strategies, whereas organizations with identity-conscious structures had minority groups with lower employment status (Konrad & Linnehan, 1995). The authors conclude "... that identity-conscious structures are needed to ameliorate the biases of decision makers and reward systems in order to foster improvement in employment statistics" (p. 807). In addition, these researchers found that organizations with poor employment statistics for people of color were most likely to undergo EEO-AA related lawsuits (Konrad & Linnehan, 1995). In addition to reinforcing the inherent group-based bias that employees bring into their organization, an organizational ideal of color-blindness can also foster group-based discrimination (Schofield, 1986).

Color-blindness is a myth; it is impossible not to notice another person's race or gender, especially when they are in the numeric minority (Kanter, 1977). Rather than creating a context of fairness and equality, the American myth of color-blindness makes race a taboo thus discouraging dialogues about how the intersection of race (and other sources of difference such as gender) and power in organizations disadvantage some groups. Color-blind ideals also help to create work environments in which one has the individual freedom to engage in group-based discrimination without fear of being suspected of prejudice or punished (Thomas, Mack, Montagliani, 2004). For example, in two experiments, Brief, Dietz, Cohen, Pugh, & Vaslow (2000) found that modern racists feel free to discriminate against Blacks when those in authority provide them with an acceptable forum for doing so. Unlike previous forms of overt and hostile prejudice, modern racism (McConahay, 1986) refers to subtle acts of prejudice that are shaped by a modern societal value system in which overt forms of racism are viewed as bad. Modern racists therefore require a justification, such as orders from one's superior, to act upon their negative racial attitudes.

In these ways, recategorization may perpetuate the myth of color-blindness and its negative consequences. Brewer & Miller (1996) also cautioned that the adoption of a superordinate identity is likely only a short-term solution for intergroup tensions. Subcategorization involves creating a context of cooperation in which multiple social identities can coexist constructively. To create this context, ground rules for social interaction that preserve social identities while encouraging cooperation must be established. The development of an organizational culture that values diversity and that views it as a strategic opportunity is a subcategorization strategy. Kelman's (1997) Israeli and Palestinian problem-solving workshops involved strict adherence to ground rules that include focusing on problems analytically rather than argumentatively and keeping workshop conversations private and confidential, while trained facilitators help to keep the attendees' work on target.

Creating a Context to Support Multiple Group Identities

Shaping an organizational context that supports and values diversity appears to be key in avoiding group-based discrimination. McDaniel & Walls (1997) discussed how group-based conflict in organizations should be seen as an opportunity for effectiveness rather than as a barrier. In order for diverse groups to be effective, they cannot rely upon implicit norms and assumptions that may have been functional in a more homogeneous past. In modern diverse groups, those norms must be broken and communication needs to be more explicit and old assumptions openly challenged.

Williams & O'Reilly (1998) suggested that demographic diversity can benefit groups in organizations when companies take advantage of the idea generation and creativity that diversity offers while avoiding the emotional conflict brought about by diversity that can impede a group's ability to carry out group-based innovation. Those cognitive processes that are responsible for the preoccupation with differences can also be used to help employees define inclusive categories that will accommodate diversity (Williams & O'Reilly, 1998). They also suggested making employees aware of their own discriminatory tendencies so that they can avoid acting upon them.

Groups that leverage their diversity as an opportunity for success are able to manage conflict, establish increased cooperation, and create collective norms and cultures that help develop a superordinate identity for group members (Williams & O'Reilly, 1998). Likewise, Thomas & Ely (1998) argued that an organization's diversity orientation may assist companies in avoiding group-based biases and discrimination and enable them to reap the benefits of diversity rather that spend valuable resources defending themselves against claims of harassment and discrimination. Organizations with a learning and effectiveness orientation use diversity and group differences as opportunities for employee and organizational learning, rather than an opportunity to discriminate. Richard (2000) found that diversity has a positive impact on bottom line indicators of financial success when the organization's strategy is growth oriented. That is, corporate strategy seemed to moderate the diversity-effectiveness relationship such that the organization's perspective regarding its market could deny or support a positive relationship between diversity and effectiveness.

CONCLUSION

In this chapter, we have provided a number of possible group-level explanations for discrimination in the workplace. One explanation includes the notion that group identities provide individuals with a sense of self and worth, but can prompt ingroup/outgroup categorization that disconnects members of one group from members of other groups perceived to be different. Additionally, we discussed group identity as a socially constructed phenomena in which some groups become "marked" as subordinate and less powerful, whereas others are perceived to be dominant and experience privilege as a result. As minority group members begin to challenge the status quo and seek to gain power, status, and credibility within the organization, discrimination and intergroup conflict are likely to increase. Although we are just beginning to examine strategies for avoiding and/or reducing group-based discrimination in organizations, some researchers suggest the need to create a superordinate category (i.e., the organization or workgroup itself) in which members of various identity groups can identify strongly with and feel committed to its goals and mission. In addition, it seems critical to establish ways in which subgroup identities, such as race and gender, can still be valued and maintained within the organizational context. For example, Aronson (1990) adopted a "jigsaw classroom" approach to attempting to resolve interracial conflict in a desegregated school system, in which each child was able to bring a unique contribution to the class project (i.e., each student represented a piece of the jigsaw puzzle). Cooperation and respect among the students increased as each child became a valued and important contributor to the class assignment. It seems then that this is the primary challenge that both practitioners and researchers will face in the future, as the workplace continues to diversify and the possible incidence of group-based discrimination increases, to create a shared and common identity so that employees may work effectively together to accomplish work goals, but yet still allow organizational members to derive a sense of self-worth and value from their own unique social identities.

REFERENCES

Aronson, E. (1990). Applying social psychology to desegregation and energy conservation. *Personality and Social Psychology Bulletin, 16,* 118–132.

Ashforth, B. E., & Mael, F. (1989). Social identity theory and the organization. *Academy of Management Review, 14,* 20–39.

Blank, R., & Slipp, S. (1994). *Voices of diversity: Real people talk about problems and solutions in a workplace where everyone is not alike.* New York: American Management Association.

Bochner, S. (1994). Culture shock. In W. J. Lonner & R. S. Malpass's (Eds.), *Psychology and culture* (pp. 245–252). Needham Heights, MA: Allyn & Bacon.

Bourhis, R. Y., Sachdev, I., & Gagnon, A. (1994). Intergroup research with the Tajfel matricies: Methodological notes. In M. P. Zanna & J. M. Olson (Eds.), *The psychology of prejudice: The Ontario symposium: Vol. 7* (pp. 209–232). Hillsdale, NJ: Lawrence Erlbaum Associates.

Brewer, M. B. (1995). Managing diversity: The role of social identities. In S. E. Jackson & M. N. Ruderman (Eds.), *Diversity in work teams* (pp. 47–68). Washington, DC: American Psychological Association.

Brewer, M. B., & Brown, R. J. (1998). Intergroup relations. In D. T. Gilbert, S. T. Fiske, & G. Lindzey (Eds.), *The handbook of social psychology, Vol. 2* (4th ed., pp. 554–495). New York: McGraw-Hill.

Brewer, M. B., & Miller, N. (1996). *Intergroup relations.* Pacific Grove, CA: Brooks/Cole.

Brief, A. P., Dietz, J., Cohen, R. R., Pugh, S. D., & Vaslow, J. B. (2000). Just doing business: Modern racism and obedience to authority as explanations for employment discrimination. *Organizational Behavior and Human Decision Processes, 81,* 72–97.

Byrne, D. (1971). *The Attraction Paradigm.* New York: Academic Press.

Campbell, D. T. (1965). Ethnocentric and other altruistic motives. In D. Levine (Ed.), *Nebraska Symposium on Motivation* (pp. 283–311). Lincoln: University of Nebraska Press.

Clark, R., Anderson, N. B., Clark, V. R., & Williams, D. R. (1999). Racism as a stressor for African Americans: A biopsychosocial model. *American Psychologist, 54*(10), 805–816.

Cox, T., Jr. (1994). *Cultural diversity in organizations.* San Francisco: Berrett-Kohler.

Cox, T., Jr., Welch, J., & Nkomo, S. M. (2001). Research on race and ethnicity: An update and analysis. In R. T. Golembiewski (Ed.), *Handbook of organizational behavior* (pp. 255–286). New York: Marcel Dekker, Inc.

Crosby, F. J. (2004). *Affirmative action is dead; long live affirmative action.* New Haven, CT: Yale University Press.

De Dreu, C. K. W., & Van Vianen, A. E. M. (2001). Managing relationship conflict and the effectiveness of organizational teams. *Journal of Organizational Behavior, 22,* 309–328.

Devine, P. G., Evett, S. R., & Vasquez-Suson, K. A. (1996). Exploring the interpersonal dynamics of intergroup contact. In R. M. Sorrentino & E. T. Higgins (Eds.), *Handbook of motivation and cognition: The interpersonal context* (Vol. 3, pp. 423–464). New York: Guilford.

Dreher, G. F., & Cox, Jr., T. H. (1996). Race, gender, and opportunity: A study of compensation attainment and the establishment of mentoring relationships. *Journal of Applied Psychology, 81,* 297–308.

Ely, R. J. (1994). The effects of organizational demographics and social identity on relationships among professional women. *Administrative Science Quarterly, 39,* 203–238.

Ely, R. J. (1995). The power in demography: Women's social constructions of gender identity at work. *Academy of Management Journal, 38,* 589–634.

Fiske, S. T., & Neuberg, S. L. (1990). A continuum of impression formation, from category-based to individuating processes: Influences of information and motivation on attention and interpretation. In M. P. Zanna (Ed.), *Advances in experimental social psychology* (Vol. 23, pp. 1–74). New York: Academic Press.

Greenberg, J., Solomon, S., & Pyszczynski, T. (1997). Terror management theory of self-esteem and social behavior: Empirical assessments and conceptual refinements. In M. P. Zanna (Ed.), *Advances in experimental social psychology* (Vol. 29, pp. 61–139). New York: Academic Press.

Grillo, T., & Wildman, S. M. (1996). Obscuring the importance of race: The implication of making comparisons between racism and sexism (or other isms). In S. M. Wildman's (Ed.), *Privilege revealed: How invisible preference undermines America* (pp. 85–102). New York: New York University Press.

Ibarra, H. (1992). Homophily and differential returns: Sex differences in network structure and access in an advertising firm. *Administrative Science Quarterly, 37,* 422–447.

Ibarra, H. (1993). Personal networks of women and minorities in management: A conceptual framework. *Academy of Management Review, 18,* 56–87.

Ibarra, H. (1995). Race, opportunity, and diversity of social circles in managerial networks. *Academy of Management Journal, 38,* 673–703.

Ibarra, H. (1997). Paving an alternate route: Gender differences in managerial networks. *Social Psychology Quarterly, 60,* 91–102.

Jehn, K. A. (1994). Enhancing effectiveness: An investigation of advantages and disadvantages of value-based intragroup conflict. *The International Journal of Conflict Management, 5,* 223–238.

Jehn, K. A. (1995). A multimethod examination of the benefits and detriments of intragroup conflict. *Administrative Science Quarterly, 40,* 256–282.

Jehn, K. A. (1997). A qualitative analysis of conflict types and dimensions in organizational groups. *Administrative Science Quarterly, 42,* 530–557.

Kanter, R. M. (1977). *Men and women of the corporation.* New York: Basic Books.

Kelman, H. C. (1997). Group processes in the resolution of international conflicts: Experiences from the Israeli–Palestintian case. *American Psychologist, 52,* 212–220.

Konrad, A. M., & Gutek, B. A. (1987). Theory and research on group composition: Applications to the status of women and ethnic minorities. In S. Oskamp & S. Spacapan (Eds.), *Interpersonal processes* (pp. 85–121). Thousand Oaks, CA: Sage.

Konrad, A. M., & Linnehan, F. (1995). Formalized HRM structures: Coordinating equal employment opportunity or concealing organizational practices? *Academy of Management Journal, 38,* 787–820.

Lau, D. C., & Murnighan, J. K. (1998). Demographic diversity and faultlines: The compositional dynamics of organizational groups. *Academy of Management Review, 23,* 325–340.

Lott, B., & Maluso, D. (1995). Introduction: Framing the questions. In B. Lott & D. Maluso (Eds.), *The social psychology of interpersonal discrimination* (pp. 1–11), New York: Guilford.

Maier, M. (1997). Invisible privilege: What white males don't see. *Diversity Factor, Summer,* 28–33.

Maume, D. J. (1999). Glass ceilings and glass escalators: Occupational segregation and race and sex differences in managerial promotions. *Work and Occupations, 26,* 483–509.

Mehra, A., Kilduff, M., & Brass, D. J. (1998). At the margins: A distinctiveness approach to the social identity and social networks of underrepresented groups. *Academy of Management Journal, 41,* 441–452.

McConahay, J. B. (1986). Modern racism, ambivalence, and the modern racism scale. In J. F. Dovidio & S. L. Gaertner (Eds.), *Prejudice, discrimination, and racism* (pp. 91–125). Orlando, FL: Academic Press.

McDaniel, R. R., Jr. & Walls, M. (1997). Diversity as a management strategy for organizations: A view through the lenses of chaos and quantum theories. *Journal of Management Inquiry, 6,* 363–375.

McIntosh, P. (1993). White privilege and male privilege: A personal account of coming to see correspondences through work in women's studies. In A. Minas (Ed.), *Gender basics* (pp. 30–38). Belmont, CA: Wadsworth.

Milliken, F. J., & Martins, L. L. (1996). Searching for common threads: Understanding the multiple effects of diversity in organizational groups. *Academy of Management Review, 21,* 402–433.

Niemann, Y. F., & Dovidio, J. F. (1998). Relationship of solo status, academic rank, and perceived distinctiveness to job satisfaction of racial/ethnic minorities. *Journal of Applied Psychology, 83,* 55–71.

Northrup, T. A. (1989). The dynamic of identity in personal and social conflict. In L. Kriesberg, T. A. Northrup, and S. J. Thorson (Eds.), *Intractable conflicts and their transformation* (pp. 55–82). Syracuse, NY: Syracuse University Press.

Oskamp, S. (1965). Attitudes toward U.S. and Russian actions: A double standard. *Psychological Reports, 16,* 43–46.

Pelled, L. H., Eisenhardt, K. M., & Xin, K. R. (1999). Exploring the black box: An analysis of work group diversity, conflict, and performance. *Administrative Science Quarterly, 44,* 1–28.

Pettigrew, T. F. (1979). The ultimate attribution error: Extending Allport's cognitive analysis of prejudice. *Personality and Social Psychology Bulletin, 5,* 461–476.

Pettigrew, T. F., & Martin, J. (1987). Shaping the organizational context for Black American inclusion. *Journal of Social Issues, 43,* 41–78.

Proudford, K. L., & Smith, K. K. (2003). Group membership salience and the movement of conflict. *Group and Organization Management, 28,* 18–44.

Rahim, M. A. (2001). *Managing conflict in organizations* (3rd ed.). Westport, CT: Quorum Books.

Ragins, B. R., & Sundstrom, E. (1989). Gender and power in organizations: A longitudinal perspective. *Psychological Bulletin, 105,* 51–88.

Richard, O. C. (2000). Racial diversity, business strategy, and firm performance: A resource-based view. *Academy of Management Journal, 43,* 164–177.

Richeson, J. A., & Shelton, J. N. (2003). When prejudice does not pay: Effects of interracial contact on executive function. *Psychological Science, 14,* 287–290.

Riordan, C. M. (2000). Relational demography within groups: Past developments, contradictions, and new directions. *Research in Personnel and Human Resources Management, 19,* 131–173.

Rothman, J. (1997). *Resolving identity-based conflict in nations, organizations, and communities.* San Francisco: Jossey-Bass.

Sackett, P. R., DuBois, C. L. Z., & Noe, A. W. (1991). Tokenism in performance evaluations: The effects of work group representation on male-female and white-black differences in performance ratings. *Journal of Applied Psychology, 76,* 263–267.

Sampson, E. E. (1999). *Dealing with difference.* Fort Worth, TX: Harcourt Brace.

Sande, G. N., Goethals, G. R., Ferrari, L., & Worth, L. T. (1989). Value-guided attributions: Maintaining the moral self-image and the diabolical enemy-image. *Journal of Social Issues, 45,* 91–118.

Schmitt, N., & Noe, R. A. (1986). Personnel selection and equal employment opportunity. In C. L. Cooper & I. T. Robertson (Eds.), *International review of industrial and organizational psychology* (pp. 71–116). New York: Wiley.

Sherif, M., Harvey, O. J., White, B. J., Hood, W. R., & Sherif, C. W. (1961). Intergroup conflict and cooperation: The Robber's Cave experiment. University of Oklahoma: Institute of Group Relations.

Schofield, J. W. (1986). Causes and consequences of the colorblind perspective. In J. Dovidio & S. Gaertner (Eds.), *Prejudice, discrimination, and racism* (pp. 231–253). New York: Academic Press.

Sidanius, J., Devereux, E., & Pratto, F. (2001). A comparison of symbolic racism theory and social dominance theory as explanations for racial policy attitudes. *The Journal of Social Psychology, 132,* 377–395.

Steele, C. M. (1997). A threat in the air: How stereotypes shape intellectual identity and performance. *American Psychologist, 52,* 613–629.

Steele, C. M., & Aronson, J. (1995). Stereotype threat and the intellectual test performance of African Americans. *Journal of Personality and Social Psychology, 69,* 797–811.

Stephan, W. G., & Stephan, C. W. (1985). Intergroup anxiety. *Journal of Social Issues, 41,* 157–175.

Tajfel, H. (1982). *Social identity and intergroup relations*. Cambridge, UK: Cambridge University Press.

Tajfel, H., & Turner, J. C. (1986). The social identity theory of intergroup behaviour. In S. Worchel & W. G. Austin (Eds.), *Psychology of intergroup relations* (pp. 7–24). Chicago: Nelson.

Tajfel, H., Flament, C., Billig, K., & Bundy, R. (1971). Social categorization and intergroup behavior. *European Journal of Social Psychology, 1,* 149–175.

Taylor, S. E., Fiske, S. T., Close, M., Anderson, C., & Ruderman, A. (1977). *Solo status as a psychological variable: The power of being distinctive.* Unpublished manuscript, Harvard University.

Thomas, D. A., & Ely, R. J. (1996). Making differences matter: A new paradigm for managing diversity. *Harvard Business Review, Sept-Oct,* 79–90.

Thomas, K. M., Mack, D. A., & Montagliani, A. (2004). The arguments against diversity: Are they valid? In P. Stockdale & F. Crosby (Eds.), *The Psychology and management of diversity in organizations.* Oxford, UK: Blackwell.

Tsui, A. S., Egan, T. D., & O'Reilly, C. A., III. (1992). Being different: Relational demography and organizational attachment. *Administrative Science Quarterly, 37,* 549–579.

West, C. (1993). *Race matters.* New York: Vintage.

Wildman, S. M. (1996). Privilege in the workplace: The missing element in antidiscrimination law. In S. M. Wildman (Ed.), *Privilege revealed: How invisible preference undermines America* (pp. 25–42). New York: New York University Press.

Wildman, S. M., & Davis, A. (1996). Making systems of privilege visible. In S. M. Wildman (Ed.), *Privilege revealed: How invisible preference undermines America* (pp. 7–24). New York: New York University Press.

Williams, K. Y., & O'Reilly, III, C. A. (1998). Demography and diversity in organizations: A review of 40 years of research. *Research in Organizational Behavior, 20,* 77–140.

Word, C., Zanna, M. P., & Cooper, J. (1974). The verbal mediation of self-fulfilling prophecies in interracial interaction. *Journal of Experimental Social Psychology, 10,* 109–120.

5

Discrimination in Organizations: An Organizational-Level Systems Perspective

Michele J. Gelfand[1]
University of Maryland

Lisa H. Nishii
Cornell University

Jana L. Raver
Queen's University

Benjamin Schneider
University of Maryland and Personnel Research Associates, Inc.

It has become increasingly clear to organizational decision makers that employment discrimination is a serious and expensive problem that needs to be addressed. For instance, in 2000, Coca-Cola Co. settled a class-action racial discrimination lawsuit for $192.5 million, which was preceded by Texaco Inc.'s settlement for $176.1 million, and Shoney's Inc.'s settlement for $132 million (King & Spruell, 2001). In fact, the financial costs associated with discrimination settlements extend beyond the costs of the actual settlement to include negative stock price changes, presumably the result of investor perceptions that discriminating firms may have less talented and committed workforces, high operating costs because of turnover,

---

[1] Authorship is alphabetical because of equality of contributions.

absenteeism, and job dissatisfaction, poor reputations with diverse customers, and/or lower organizational adaptability (Wright, Ferris, Hiller, & Kroll, 1995).

At the same time, there have been some genuine advances, where traditional monolithic (unicultural) organizations have been transformed into more multicultural (Cox, 1994) environments. For instance, after Denny's parent company, Advantica Restaurant Group, Inc., settled a racial discrimination lawsuit for $54.4 million in 1994, they made organization-wide changes toward increasing diversity. By 1998, the company was listed on *Fortune* magazine's list of the best U.S. companies for Asians, African Americans, and Hispanics, and has remained near the top of that list since then (Hickman, Tkaczyk, Florian, Stemple, & Vazquez, 2003). Similarly, Coca-Cola made widespread changes immediately following the 2000 discrimination settlement and has now also been named a top U.S. company for racial minorities (Hickman et al., 2003). Although such rankings do not necessarily reflect genuine cultural changes (Prasad, Mills, Elmes, & Prasad, 1997), the apparent success of these corporations in dealing with discrimination highlights several organizational-level factors that may predict discrimination. These organizational-level antecedents to discrimination are the focus of this chapter.

In what follows we present a systems model, summarized in Fig. 5.1, of discrimination at the level of the organization. We elaborate on the model shown in Fig. 5.1 and illustrate the ways in which aspects of organizations—including formal and informal structure, organizational culture, leadership, strategy, human resource systems, and organizational climates—may contribute to or attenuate discrimination. As depicted in Fig. 5.1 and as discussed in detail in previous chapters, the relationship between these organizational-level processes and actual levels of discrimination is necessarily mediated by individual cognitions and interpersonal behaviors. Furthermore, we recognize that organizations do not exist in a vacuum but rather they exchange resources and information with the environment. To fully attend to the implications of this point, we utilize an open-systems model of organizations (Katz & Kahn, 1978) to briefly discuss inputs from the environment and organizational outputs to the environment. Thus, we begin below with a brief overview of environmental factors, such as the legal, economic, and social environment, which serve as inputs into the organization that are relevant to the phenomenon of discrimination. Then, the major section of the chapter is devoted to a detailed analysis of the existing literature on discrimination at the level of the organization. This exploration is accomplished through an examination of six different organizational throughputs: organizational structure, organizational culture, leadership, strategy, HR systems, and

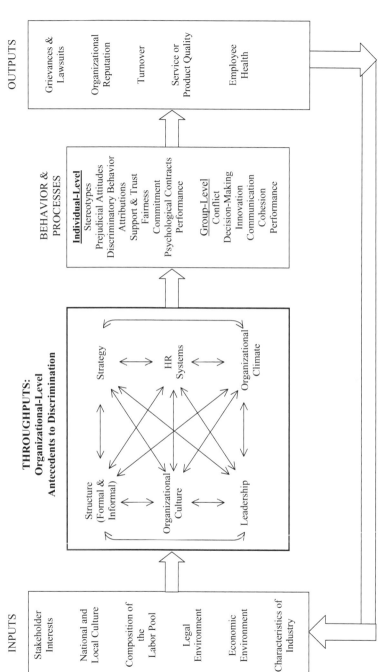

FIG. 5.1. A model of discrimination at the level of the organization.

INPUTS

Stakeholder Interests

National and Local Culture

Composition of the Labor Pool

Legal Environment

Economic Environment

Characteristics of Industry

THROUGHPUTS:
Organizational-Level
Antecedents to Discrimination

Strategy

HR Systems

Organizational Climate

Structure (Formal & Informal)

Organizational Culture

Leadership

BEHAVIOR &
PROCESSES

Individual-Level
Stereotypes
Prejudicial Attitudes
Discriminatory Behavior
Attributions
Support & Trust
Fairness
Commitment
Psychological Contracts
Performance

Group-Level
Conflict
Decision-Making
Innovation
Communication
Cohesion
Performance

OUTPUTS

Grievances & Lawsuits

Organizational Reputation

Turnover

Service or Product Quality

Employee Health

organizational climate. We then briefly discuss some of the outcomes associated with organizational discrimination and the ways in which these outputs are then fed back into the environment in which organizations function. Finally, we conclude with future directions for the study of discrimination at the organizational level.

INFLUENCE OF THE ORGANIZATION'S LARGER CONTEXT

Organizations, as systems, function within the larger context in which they exist. Environmental inputs into organizations can have a marked impact upon the types of behaviors, processes, and structures that are enacted within the organization. In this section, we briefly discuss a number of inputs from the environment into the organization system that influence the levels of discrimination that might emerge. We do not mean to suggest that these inputs from the environment of the organization always or even likely yield discrimination as we discuss it later in the chapter. However, what is important to understand is that organizations existing in specific contexts have an increased probability of engaging in discriminatory behaviors because of these contextual issues.

First, national culture influences the extent to which discrimination will occur in organizations, particularly resulting from cross-cultural variability in the extent to which discrimination against certain groups is codified in cultural norms (House, Hanges, Javidan, Dorfman, & Gupta, 2004; World Values Study Group, 1994). In addition, local norms and sociocultural legacy with respect to prejudice may influence people's propensity to discriminate within organizations in those communities (Cox, 1994). In addition, the legal environment in which organizations operate affect both experiences of discrimination and attention that is paid to discrimination-related issues by organizations and their employees. For example, the design and implementation of HR practices in U.S. companies are constrained by a variety of employment laws that collectively prohibit discrimination on the basis of race, color, religion, sex, national origin, age, and disability (Ledvinka & Scarpello, 1991), and additional employment laws in some states prohibit discrimination on the basis of sexual orientation (Jackson & Schuler, 2003).

The policies, practices, and strategies that organizations adopt are also strongly influenced by the interests of the organizations' stakeholders, which include customers, professional organizations, government agencies, labor unions, stockholders, and suppliers/vendors, among others (Donaldson & Preston, 1995). For example, pressure from professional organizations, government agencies, and union contracts tends to lower discrimination in organizations (Blum, Fields, & Goodman, 1994; Delaney & Lundy, 1996; Perry, Davis-Blake, & Kulik, 1994).

Economic conditions may influence an organization's willingness to devote attention and resources to combating discrimination (Kahn, 2001). For example, compared to conditions of low threat, under conditions of threat (e.g., recessions, downsizing), organizations are more likely to become rigid, relying on a limited set of well-learned and habituated behavioral scripts and focusing on business issues that are of core strategic importance (Staw, Sandelands, & Dutton, 1981). Moreover, the degree to which organizations feel pressured to integrate diverse workers may be influenced both by industry-based norms (i.e., the diversity-related practices of peer organizations) and by the demographic characteristics of a particular industry (DiMaggio & Powell, 1983).

THE INFLUENCE OF THE ORGANIZATION'S INTERNAL CONTEXT

The environmental factors discussed above all feed into the organization, which comprises several interdependent processes, systems, and structures. Of particular interest in this chapter are the six organizational-level antecedents to discrimination depicted in Fig. 5.1 (i.e., formal and informal structure, organizational culture, leadership, strategy, HR systems, and organizational climate). The identification of six major throughputs in no way implies that these are independent of each other. On the contrary, as Fig. 5.1 shows, these interact with each other; identifying them as separate is merely for convenience of exposition.

Structure

Formal Structure   Perhaps the most widely publicized form of discrimination in organizations is the "glass ceiling," which refers to the invisible barrier that blocks women and racial minorities from advancing to senior leadership positions in organizations (i.e., access discrimination). There is substantial evidence suggesting that women and racial minorities are underrepresented in upper management. For instance, women make up only 34% of "officials and managers" in U.S. corporations, whereas they constitute 47% of the private workforce. Also concerning are the low numbers of racial minorities in management, where only 15% of "officials and managers" are members of a minority group, yet they constitute 30% of the private U.S. workforce (U.S. Equal Employment Opportunity Commission, 2001). A study comparing data from 1995 and 2000 found that the status of women in management has not improved in recent years (U.S. General

Accounting Office, 2002), where women held a share of all management jobs proportionate to their share of the industry workforce in only half of the industries studied. These statistics are unsettling when one considers that women and minorities constituted 63% of the private U.S. labor force in 2001 (USEEOC, 2001), and that the projected rates of participation in the labor force are expected to grow three to six times as fast for racial minority groups than for White non-Hispanics (U.S. Bureau of Labor Statistics, 1999).

Structural integration, or diverse representation at senior management levels, is an important consideration not only because it is a symptom of the level of discrimination in an organization (Bennet, 2002; James, 2000) but also because it is an antecedent of further discrimination. Segregation perpetuates itself because of "homosocial reproduction," in which individuals hire and promote those who are like themselves, thereby resulting in fewer opportunities for individuals who are different from the people in power (Kanter, 1977; Perry et al., 1994; Ragins & Sundstrom, 1989). Furthermore, a lack of diverse representation at high levels makes it more likely that the organizational culture is monolithic (Cox, 1994), or defined by cultural norms associated with White, heterosexual, able-bodied males who have access to powerful others (i.e., the dominant coalition; Brass, 1985). In such organizations, nontraditional employees often feel pressure to assimilate rather than being free to be themselves. Moreover, organizations that have diverse representation at the top and throughout the organization are less likely to have employees who rely on stereotypes in their social interactions (Perry et al., 1994). This is based on the notion that such employees are able to develop more idiosyncratic schemas for other individuals because of a balanced exposure to diverse people. Of course, increasing representation above the glass ceiling is not the only goal for organizations seeking to reduce discrimination; building a critical mass of diverse workers throughout the organization can also be an effective deterrent to discrimination (Arvey, Azevedo, Ostgaard, & Raghuram, 1996).

In addition to the structural integration of racial minorities throughout an organization, other aspects of organizational structure relate to discrimination within organizations. Bureaucratic organizations characterized by formal job ladders tend to perpetuate gender discrimination because job ladders are typically segregated by gender, with women's ladders offering fewer opportunities, less visibility, and lower pay (Perry et al., 1994). Large companies may have greater levels of discrimination because of stable and unchanging employment conditions, whereas small, growing companies hire and promote with greater frequency and are in a better position to reduce access discrimination and reshape the demographic composition of their workforces (Arvey et al., 1996). Large companies also tend to have greater specialization of labor, a proliferation of titles, narrow spans of control, and lengthy chains of command. In addition to facilitating segregation, these characteristics decrease discretion by making it more likely that behaviors are closely monitored (Kelley, 1993). Deviations from the norms of the dominant coalition may be less acceptable and nonmajority group members' diverse approaches to work tasks may be less likely to be encouraged (Oerton, 1994). The existence of a formal diversity or EEO officer also has implications for discrimination. The diversity officer has an important role in reengineering HR systems to avoid discriminating against those who do not "fit" (Arvey et al., 1996). When the diversity/EEO officer is highly paid relative to other administrators, the officer is seen as powerful within the organization and employees perceive that the organization is committed to eliminating discrimination (Morrison & Von Glinow, 1990; Perry et al., 1994).

Informal Structure   The patterns of interpersonal relationships in organizations also play an important role in organizational discrimination. Racial minorities often lack access to informal social networks in organizations because participation in informal groups is influenced by sociocultural similarity or "homophily" (Ibarra, 1993). Similarly, women tend to belong to gender-segregated networks within organizations (Brass, 1985). The result of segregated networks is that women and racial minorities tend to be less central to the networks of the dominant coalition and hence receive fewer favorable organizational outcomes such as access to information about jobs, organizational status, and mobility (Ragins & Sundstrom, 1989; Seidel, Polzer, & Stewart, 2000). Moreover, because of the fact that most high-ranking positions in organizations are still held by White males, women and racial minorities are at a disadvantage when it comes to finding a mentor who can offer instrumental or career-related support and access (Burke, McKeen, & McKenna, 1993; Tsui & O'Reilly, 1989; Whitely, Dougherty, & Dreher, 1991). When women and racial minorities do find mentors, the mentor relationships tend to provide a narrower range of benefits and are more difficult to manage successfully (Kram, 1985; Thomas, 1993).

Organizational Culture

Traditional approaches to eliminating discrimination have typically focused on recruiting and hiring increased numbers of nontraditional employees (Gottfredson, 1992; Jackson, 1992), but have stopped short of emphasizing the elimination of more subtle forms of discrimination in organizations, such as in an organization's basic assumptions and values, or culture (Carnevale & Stone, 1995; Triandis, Kurowski, & Gelfand, 1994).

The concept of organizational culture has been referred to as the "personality" of an organization, which is typically defined by shared values, common understandings, and patterns of beliefs and expectations, which are often taken for granted (Gagliardi, 1986; Sathe, 1985; Schein, 1985) and manifested in many different ways, such as in actual patterns of behavior (Sathe, 1985), organizational climates (Schneider, 2000), and material artifacts such as office arrangements and dress (e.g., Peters & Waterman, 1982).

Culture Content   Organizational cultures are not neutral with regard to what types of employees fit and which employee behaviors are valued. Organizational leaders hold stereotypes with regard to which types of employees are best, and they tend to reward employees who behave most consistently with their stereotypes (Ilgen & Youtz, 1986). Such discriminatory cultural beliefs, values, and assumptions may be manifested in cultural artifacts such as behavioral norms, HR practices, and physical arrangements. Cox (1994) provided numerous examples, including the practice of scheduling 50-hour-plus workweeks and evening meetings, valuing and promoting employees with high verbal fluency (e.g., polished English in presentations, input during meetings, self-confident speech patterns), and lack of wheelchair access despite ADA regulations. In addition, discriminatory cultural assumptions may also be communicated directly through derogatory language referring to nontraditional employees (e.g., "the affirmative action hiree"; Heilman, Block, & Lucas, 1992), sexual or ethnic harassment (e.g., Schneider, Hitlan, & Radhakrishnan, 2000), inappropriate jokes (Siehl & Martin, 1988), backlash attitudes toward diversity-related programs (Morrison, 1992), or business justifications for discriminating (Brief, Dietz, Cohen, Pugh, & Vaslow, 2000).

Culture Strength   When discussing organizational culture, it is also important to address the *strength* of the culture, or the extent to which organizational members agree about the organization's values, beliefs, assumptions, and norms (Cox, 1994). In strong cultures, there tends to be a preponderance of strong situations that require members to behave according to agreed-upon standards for proper behavior by imposing sanctions if behavior deviates from those standards (Mischel, 1976). At an extreme, strong cultures could result in nontraditional employees needing to conform to the norms of the dominant coalition, and thus experiencing discrimination because their diverse approaches to work are devalued. In contrast, weak cultures are characterized by multiple sets of contrasting norms and values, thereby allowing for greater variability in the behavioral scripts that are deemed culturally appropriate (Mischel, 1976). Yet in a weak culture with no strong situational norms that prescribe how one should behave, people may be most likely to invoke their own identities in determining their behavior (Cox, 1994; Mischel, 1977), which could result in a situation in which each person is free to act based upon his or her own particular desires or prejudices without regard for organizational priorities (i.e., a fragmented culture; Martin, 2002). Thus, neither a weak nor a strong organizational culture is necessarily an antecedent to discrimination. Rather, the essential consideration is whether the values pertaining to the inclusion of all employees are strong (i.e., the cultural content about diversity and inclusion), whereas values pertaining to the range of behavioral styles and diverse approaches to work are weak. Organizations that have this particular combination of strong and weak cultural values are those that are likely to be the most successful at eradicating discrimination (Cox, 1994).

Leadership

Without the full commitment of upper-level leaders in an organization, diversity initiatives are likely to fail and thus discriminatory practices are unlikely to be eradicated (Cox & Blake, 1991). However, it is also necessary to look below the upper-most levels to examine the ways in which the behaviors and decisions of mid-level management and direct supervisors may also perpetuate discrimination.

Upper-level Management   At the highest levels of leadership in organizations, the CEO, the top management team (TMT), and the corporate board are instrumental in determining the direction that the organization will take with regard to diversity and discrimination. Leaders must first recognize the potential for discrimination in traditional organizational practices and structures and must believe in the need to value all employees and remove obstacles to their success (Stoner & Russell-Chapin, 1997). The CEO and top management team make important decisions regarding organizational strategies and resources, and they communicate the organization's priorities to all members and stakeholder groups (Yukl & Van Fleet, 1992). The extent to which leaders choose to emphasize inclusiveness in the organization's strategy and the extent to which resources (i.e., personnel, money, time) are devoted to eliminating all forms of discrimination are indicators of leaders' priorities and of which "types" of employees are valued (Loden & Rosener, 1991). Top-level leaders can also discourage discrimination by implementing systems of accountability that make rewards contingent upon meeting diversity goals (Morrison, 1992).

In the case in which the corporate board and TMT have decided to pursue an organizational change strategy to increase diverse representation and inclusiveness throughout the organization, the symbolic role of the CEO is particularly important. Cox and Blake (1991) argued that "champions for diversity" are needed to enact change—and the CEO is in a very good position to passionately pursue change, to role model the behaviors required for change, and to help the organization to move forward (Loden & Rosener, 1991). Such a leader can help to establish an inclusive organizational culture through persistent communication of and visible support for all programs and policies aimed at reducing discrimination (Stoner & Russell-Chapin, 1997). In addition, when successes occur, he or she would provide rewards and retrospective interpretations consistent with the desired values (Gagliardi, 1986; Trice & Beyer, 1991). In this manner, a CEO who demonstrates commitment to eliminating all forms of discrimination throughout the organization may play a crucial role in transforming an organization from monolithic (unicultural) to multicultural (Cox, 1994).

Mid-level Management and Direct Supervisors   Whereas top management serves a symbolic function and makes decisions that affect the organization as a whole, most employees' daily experiences with organizational leaders are with direct supervisors or mid-level departmental (unit) managers. These instrumental leaders interpret organizational strategies, policies, and practices (Zohar, 2000), and therefore act as a "lens" through which employees perceive the organization. Immediate supervisors set the tone for what behaviors are acceptable and what behaviors are not acceptable (Yukl & Van Fleet, 1992); thus when management fails to punish discriminatory behaviors, employees may assume that such discriminatory actions are acceptable, which then perpetuates such acts.

Furthermore, mid-level management and supervisors make decisions about access to organizational rewards (e.g., pay, promotions, access to training, performance appraisals), and this acts as a proximal determinant of the extent to which discrimination exists in a particular department. As will be described in more detail below, evidence suggests that because of stereotyping, prejudicial attitudes, and the similar-to-me bias, supervisors are more likely to reward those employees who are similar to themselves (Fadil, 1995; Ilgen & Youtz, 1986). If most supervisors are White, male, able-bodied, and heterosexual, these negative attitudes and the similarity-attraction effect may lead to systematic biases against those who are different. In other words, personnel decisions (i.e., selection, promotion) in a single department may not appear discriminatory, yet in the aggregate across an entire organization where this same process occurs repeatedly, the end result is organizational-level patterns of discrimination.

The quality of leader-subordinate relationships is also an important consideration for discrimination in organizations. High-quality leader-member exchanges (LMX) may be less likely to develop between leader-subordinate dyads composed of individuals who are demographically different (Hiller & Day, 2003). Yet, because LMX relationship quality is thought to be pivotal for the access that subordinates receive to resources, information, important networks, and opportunities, high-quality LMX relationships with diverse subordinates are one key to combating discrimination in organizations (Douglas, Ferris, Buckley, & Gundlach, 2003). Ultimately, those managers who establish high quality LMX relationships with *all* of their employees without discriminating against minority subordinates will be in a better position to utilize all of their human resources (Douglas et al., 2003). Indeed, recent evidence demonstrated that departments in which racial minorities reported high-quality LMX relationships with their managers had higher profits than departments where minorities reported low-quality LMX relationships (Nishii, Mayer, Goldstein, & Dotan, 2004).

Strategy

When strategies for advancing diverse employees and creating a culture of inclusiveness are embedded within an organization's strategic business plan, consequent levels of discrimination tend to be lower (Catalyst, 1993; U.S. Department of Labor, 1995). Actually including EEO as part of a company's business strategy is important because statements of nondiscrimination are a very tangible and salient sign that discrimination is not tolerated within an organization (Morrison & Von Glinow, 1990). Further, publicly stating the importance of diversity as a basis of competitive advantage and human resource quality fosters the belief that diversity represents an opportunity for the organization rather than a problem (Cox & Blake, 1991).

Although the specific business case for reducing discrimination may differ across organizations or industries, there are several business rationales for being committed to the recruitment, retention, and advancement of diverse employees. They include better customer-oriented decision making resulting from a better reflection of a company's consumer base within the company's workforce and management (Robinson & Dechant, 1997); attracting both customers and qualified applicants as a result of gaining a reputation as a good place to work for all types of employees (Cox, 1994); the full utilization of the organization's human capital (Wentling & Palmas-Rivas, 1997); lower costs because of reduced turnover, absenteeism, and discrimination lawsuits (Jackson & Alvarez, 1992); and increased workforce productivity and improved organizational health (Jackson & Alvarez, 1992).

There is also a theoretical basis for expecting that organizations that pursue an innovation strategy will be motivated to capitalize on the diversity of behavioral scripts that results from a diverse workforce (i.e., the value-in-diversity hypothesis; Cox, Lobel, & McLeod, 1991). This is based on the evidence that diverse groups are more likely to produce a diverse set of ideas compared to homogeneous groups (Milliken & Martins, 1996), and the wider set of ideas is expected to translate into better decisions (O'Reilly, Williams, & Barsade, 1998). An organization that perceives the differential competencies and experiential bases of diverse employees as a source of competitive advantage is less likely to engage in practices that discriminate against nontraditional groups.

Human Resource Systems

Human resource practices play a critical role in shaping the extent of discrimination that occurs within an organization by influencing the access that employees have to opportunities and valued rewards within the organization (access discrimination) and their treatment as organizational citizens (treatment discrimination; Levitin, Quinn, & Staines, 1971). One of the hallmarks of equitable HR systems design is the establishment of objective or formalized criteria for various HR practices, which leads to the elimination of bias and subjectivity in the implementation of HR practices (Delaney & Lundy, 1996). It is important to emphasize that HR practices work as a system in influencing the level of discrimination that is experienced within an organization—disproportionate opportunities or biased treatment in one area (e.g., access to mentoring, training) can have ripple effects in other areas of functioning (e.g., promotion) within an organization.

Recruitment and Selection   Affirmative action programs (AAPs) are aimed at eliminating employment discrimination against women and racial minorities and to redress the effects of past discrimination within an organization. In a review of the literature, Kravitz et al. (1996) concluded that white males respond more negatively to AAPs than other demographic groups, and women generally have more positive attitudes than men. In addition, reactions to AAPs are more favorable when attention to demographic status is given during recruiting stages as compared to the final stage during which selection decisions are made (Kravitz et al., 1996). Thus, while AAPs may help to alleviate initial access discrimination, they may create stigmas (Heilman et al., 1992) that exacerbate problems related to treatment discrimination. Methods of combating discriminatory perceptions that might result from AAPs involve providing justifications for the adoption of AAPs and providing clear and compelling evidence of the target members' competence (Biernat & Kobrynowicz, 1997; Kravitz et al., 1996).

The extent of discrimination that occurs during the recruiting process depends on the channels that are used to recruit applicants. The U.S. Department of Labor found that organizations that actively recruit at minority/female-oriented colleges and universities evidence lower levels of discrimination (USDOL, 1995). When engaging in such targeted recruitment strategies, organizations might consider showcasing their diversity efforts in their recruiting materials, consistent with evidence which indicates that candidates with strong ethnic identities are more attracted to organizations that explicitly make reference to their diversity initiatives than those that do not (Kim & Gelfand, 2003). In comparison to organizations that engage in targeted recruiting, organizations that rely on informal networks to fill open positions (both from internal and external labor markets) may increase the probability of discriminating against groups who often do not have equal access to the social networks that are connected to jobs (Braddock & McPartland, 1987; Ragins & Sundstrom, 1989).

With regard to selection procedures, much is known about the discriminatory impact of various selection instruments. The best way to combat discrimination in selection is to use measures that tap as many aspects of job performance as possible, to utilize different media in terms of the ways in which content is presented and responses are required (oral, video-based, and behavioral media exhibit lower adverse impact than written ones), and to use noncognitive measures such as personality and integrity tests when possible (Campion et al., 2001). In addition, interviews tend to result in lower group differences, although the structuring of interviews and interviewer training to reduce cognitive biases are both important for minimizing adverse impact (Conway, Jako, & Goodman, 1995; Hough, Oswald, & Ployhart, 2001). In sum, research on adverse impact clearly indicates that the continued use of only paper and pencil measures of cognitive ability as a basis for access decisions is unwarranted and will likely be perceived as unfair by applicants, especially when the job relevance of the measure is not transparent (Ryan & Ployhart, 2000).

Performance Management   There are two main issues involving discrimination in performance appraisal systems, namely removing bias in the evaluation process itself and ensuring that performance evaluation and reward systems reinforce the goal of managing diversity and eliminating discrimination in the workplace (Cox, 1994). Performance management systems that involve explicit performance expectations, clear performance standards, accurate measures, and reliable performance feedback, and the consistent application of these standards across ratees, help to reduce the chances of discriminatory ratings (Bernardin, Hagan, Kane, & Villanova, 1998; Klimoski & Donahue, 1997; Morrison & Von Glinow, 1990). Whereas clear expectations are important for minimizing subjectivity and the potential for discrimination within the performance management process, performance norms should permit some latitude for expressing individuality and should not be arbitrarily based on a singular cultural perspective (Delaney & Lundy, 1996). Utilizing outcome-based performance measures rather than process-based performance measures may help minimize discrimination because the former allow for equifinality in the way that tasks are accomplished on the job (Kelley, 1993), thereby reducing the probability that certain behavioral styles (that might be correlated with group membership) are preferred over others.

The unbiased implementation of performance management systems also requires that the feedback process be formalized and consistently enacted so that all employee groups receive developmental feedback. Otherwise, women might be less likely to receive critical feedback from managers who hold stereotypical beliefs about the likelihood that women might respond emotionally to critical feedback, or racial minorities might be disadvantaged by managers who are afraid of providing them with critical feedback for fear of appearing prejudiced. Receiving critical feedback and opportunities for challenging assignments are essential to performance for all employees; not receiving such opportunities can cause minority employees to lag behind White males in their career development and experience further discrimination, what Ilgen and Youtz (1986) aptly termed "the lost opportunities effect." Indeed, the differential expectations of employee ability on the part of supervisors can have pervasive effects on employee performance and thus can be an important source of discrimination in organizations. Research has shown, for example, that low leader expectations are associated with self-fulfilling prophecies and low levels of performance (the "Golem effect," Davidson & Eden, 2000), while high expectations are associated with enhanced performance (Pygmalion effect; Dvir, Eden, & Banjo, 1995). Low expectations may be particularly problematic for employees in jobs that are incongruent with sex-role or racial stereotypes (Nieva & Gutek, 1980).

Finally, performance goals that are explicitly geared toward enhancing managerial accountability in reducing discrimination are associated with lower levels of discrimination (USDOL, 1995). Supervisor supportiveness of diversity and family issues can be assessed through the use of upward feedback mechanisms, with recognition provided to managers who provide creative and sensitive solutions to managing diversity (Lobel & Kossek, 1996).

Training   There are two forms of training that are important to discuss here: diversity training and competency training. The primary objectives of most diversity training programs are to increase awareness of diversity issues, to reduce stereotypes and biases about the suitability of diverse workers for career success, and to provide employees and managers with the skills necessary to interact effectively with diverse others (Hanover & Cellar, 1998; Wentling & Palmas-Rivas, 1997). In addition to diversity-specific training, the availability of career development training for diverse employees is an important antecedent of discrimination in that it influences the effectiveness with which diverse employees can compete for promotions within organizations. Organizations that institute succession planning or fast-track development programs, in which qualified employees with management potential are identified and properly trained, exhibit lower levels of discrimination (USDOL, 1995). These programs are most effective in reducing discrimination when they are designed to specifically enhance the competencies and thus the potential promotion of disadvantaged groups to line management positions.

Benefits The elimination of institutional biases is facilitated by making it easier for employees to balance work and family role demands. Family-friendly benefits include time-based strategies such as flextime, telecommuting and leave policies; information-based strategies such as referral programs, child and elder care support groups, and help with retirement planning; money-based strategies such as flexible benefits, tuition reimbursement, and benefits for spouses, domestic partners, and dependents; and direct services such as on-site day care and legal and psychological counseling (Button, 2001; Lobel & Kossek, 1996; Mills, 2000). In addition, policies for scheduling and holidays communicate the extent to which an organization values different religions, and the breadth of accommodation policies for employees with disabilities are critical antecedents of discrimination against disabled workers (Roberts, 1996). It is important to recognize that by addressing only the most visible problems of employees—such as child care—organizations risk discriminating against childless employees or against people with less visible problems such as alcoholism. Therefore, programs that incorporate all kinds of diversity and lifestyles are the most effective at reducing discrimination.

Grievance Procedures Despite care that is taken in the design and implementation of HR practices, employees may still perceive that they have experienced discrimination. Thus, it is important to have grievance procedures in place that give employees an opportunity to voice their concerns to the company and provide an opportunity for conflicts to be resolved internally rather than externally in the court systems (Jackson & Schuler, 2003). Indeed, the mere presence of grievance systems that overtly offer the possibility to lodge a grievance can help reduce perceptions of inequitable treatment (Gordon & Bowlby, 1988; Olson-Buchanan, 1996). However, it is important to recognize that the design of grievance systems itself may inadvertently favor certain groups and thus perpetuate discrimination in organizations. For example, Rigor (1991) notes that the use of grievance systems to report sexual harassment is extremely low because of the fact that sexual harassment policies in organizations have a gender bias and do not reflect women's perceptions of the phenomenon. To reduce discrimination and promote inclusiveness, organizations must create grievance systems that are sensitive to diverse concerns among employees, are structured to encourage diverse employees to file complaints, and provide protection and recourse to the less powerful, lest those employees be labeled "whistle-blowers."

Organizational Climate

The final organizational-level antecedent to discrimination in our model is organizational climate. Climate is most typically viewed as one manifestation of the culture (Schneider, 2000) that reflects shared perceptions of the organization's policies, practices, and procedures, as well as employees' perceptions of the kinds of behavior that management rewards, expects, and supports (Reichers & Schneider, 1990). An organization can have multiple climates, each with a particular referent (Schneider & Reichers, 1983), thus one must speak of a "climate for X" rather than simply referring to "the" organizational climate.

One important type of climate that is highly relevant for discrimination is an organization's diversity climate, for organizations with positive climates for diversity are likely to exhibit lower levels of discrimination because of their heightened sensitivity and commitment to issues having to do with managing a diverse workforce (Cox, 1994). In the present framework, we define climate for diversity (CFD) as employees' shared perceptions of the policies, practices, and procedures that implicitly and explicitly communicate the extent to which fostering and maintaining diversity and eliminating discrimination is a priority in the organization (Nishii & Raver, 2003). In practice, when organizations have a positive CFD, all employees are integrated into the fabric of the organization and are encouraged to attain their full potential unhindered by group identities. In such a climate, discrimination should be lower than when the climate for diversity is negative and HR practices are inconsistently enacted, when minorities are in segregated and nonpowerful networks, and when prejudicial organizational assumptions and values abound.

Although there has been little empirical work on diversity climates at the organizational level of analysis, a handful of studies has examined individual level perceptions of climate for diversity and its correlates. The assumption here is that there will be within-organization variability in CFD perceptions, and that it is important to understand the ways in which employees differ in their perceptions, for these perceptions are associated with differential experiences vis-à-vis discrimination in the workplace. Research has found, for example, that diversity climate perceptions vary along gender and racial lines, with women and racioethnic minorities perceiving lower levels of inclusion, bias in informal processes, lost opportunities because of bias, and insufficient attention paid to diversity (Kossek & Zonia, 1993; Mor Barak, Cherin, & Berkman, 1998). Further, differential diversity climate perceptions are important because they are related to organizational commitment, job satisfaction, and career satisfaction (Hicks-Clarke & Iles, 2000). More recently, Nishii and Raver (2003) found that the sharedness of employees' CFD perceptions is based on shared identity (e.g., race and organizational status) rather than formal organizational groupings (e.g., units/divisions) as is often the case with other types of climates (e.g., climate for service), and that clusters of employees with similar perceptions differ in their levels of job satisfaction and organizational commitment. This discussion implies that if diverse employees believe that the organization is discriminatory and report experiences that reflect bias, this is the "reality" about which the organization should be concerned, for employees behave according to their perceptions and attributions (Weick, 1995). Thus, organizational leaders should assess employees' perceptions of discrimination in organizations and pay particular attention to any group differences that arise.

ORGANIZATIONAL CONSEQUENCES OF DISCRIMINATION

In this final section, we present some outcomes that may result when organizational diversity has not been effectively managed, and thus discrimination is prevalent. At the individual level of analysis, discriminatory behaviors are the primary outcome of interest, yet at the organizational level of analysis, it is the aggregate of these discriminatory behaviors that creates serious and expensive consequences for organizations. As Fig. 5.1 illustrates, negative outcomes of discrimination feed back into the environment and subsequently influence the organizational-level throughputs in a cyclical process.

Perhaps the most tangible consequences of discrimination are the costs associated with lawsuits, grievances, and turnover. The legal costs of discrimination can be particularly high, with settlements for discrimination cases often in the tens or hundreds of millions of dollars (King & Spruell, 2001). In addition to lawsuits, investigations of employee grievances can also be costly, both in terms of personnel time and resources necessary to conduct an investigation (Hauck, 1997). Furthermore, with the high costs of recruiting, selecting, and training replacement employees, turnover associated with perceived bias and discrimination can be extremely costly for organizations (Robinson & Dechant, 1997).

In addition to these financial costs, there are other consequences of discrimination that may impair organizational effectiveness. The reputation of the organization is likely to be impaired by public awareness of discrimination in that organization (Wentling & Palmas-Rivas, 1997). An organization's reputation not only influences current employees' commitment and the perceived fulfillment of their psychological contracts, but also it influences the organization's ability to attract qualified applicants (Robinson & Dechant, 1997) and may also influence customers' willingness to purchase products and services (Pruitt & Nethercutt, 2002). Discrimination may also have implications for the overall quality of the product or service being produced (e.g., Eisenberger, Fasolo, & Davis-LaMastro, 1990). Employees in service organizations tend to treat customers consistently with how they are treated (Schneider, White, & Paul, 1998), thus employees who are mistreated through discriminatory behaviors may be likely to provide poor customer service. Finally, researchers have proposed and found a link between experiences of discrimination and employees' levels of stress and strain (Gee, 2002; Shaffer, Joplin, Bell, Lau, & Oguz, 2000; Waldo, 1999), which may increase organizations' costs through worker's compensation claims, health insurance, and disability leave (Northwestern National Life Insurance Company, 1991).

FRONTIERS OF RESEARCH ON ORGANIZATIONAL DISCRIMINATION

We have shown that organizational discrimination is the result of multiple interrelated organizational-level processes. That is, throughout our discussion, we have illustrated how organizational structure, culture, leadership, strategy, HR systems, and climate all work together as organizational throughputs to create an environment in which discrimination is either prohibited and sanctioned or subtly tolerated. In this final section, we highlight a number of critical areas for future research on organizational discrimination.

The Importance of Alignment

In this chapter, we have discussed organizational-level antecedents to discrimination as if they were largely independent. This was done, in part, for ease of presentation. However, existing research on discrimination has, in fact, tended to examine sources of discrimination in isolation of each other.

Future research is needed to examine the consequences that the alignment among organizational processes and structures (Delery, 1998) has for levels of organizational discrimination. This is critical because an intervention into a single process or structure is unlikely to effectively reduce organizational discrimination. For example, if top management leaders adopt a strategic business plan that explicitly involves reducing discrimination, but fail to also build a culture of inclusion, to show leadership support and accountability for the initiative, and to design HR systems that actively seek to promote access and treatment inclusion at all levels, their efforts are likely to be ineffective. Indeed, research may show that the misalignment of organizational processes and structures with respect to discrimination actually produces *more* discrimination and mistreatment of employees. For example, we would predict that when harassment training is implemented in an organization that has a strong climate that permits harassment, there could be backlash effects, and ultimately higher levels of harassment (Raver & Gelfand, 2003). Along these lines, it would be useful to examine how individuals *perceive* the alignment of organizational processes and structures vis-à-vis issues of discrimination, and the consequences that such perceptions have for organizations. To the extent that managers perceive that discrimination issues are dealt with idiosyncratically across organizational systems, they will likely feel less accountable and motivated to behave in ways that combat discrimination. Likewise, minorities who perceive that practices are not aligned may be reluctant to use grievance systems to report discrimination for fear of backlash, even if such systems are technically in place. More generally, research needs to take a systems approach to discrimination wherein the interrelationship between processes and structures is considered to be as important as documenting their independent influence on discrimination.

Cross-Level Research

Throughout this chapter, we have presented evidence that organizational processes and structures impact discrimination in organizations. Future research is needed to develop multilevel models that illustrate how such macro-level factors affect lower-level phenomena in organizations. Perry et al. (1994) argued that the organizational demography of top management teams as well as aspects of organizational structure affect lower level employees' cognition in ways that can result in discriminatory hiring decisions on the part of those employees; yet there is a dearth of research on such cross-level processes in the field. For example, a lack of structural integration and a climate that permits discrimination is likely to have implications for minorities' cognitive processes and their sensemaking of everyday ambiguous events. As compared to organizations that have a diverse representation of top managers and a climate for inclusiveness, minorities are likely to feel more "stereotype threat" (Steele, 1997) on a daily basis and thus may tend to interpret ambiguous events as discriminatory in nature (Leslie & Gelfand, 2004). Discriminatory organizational processes and structures are also likely to affect the dynamics of teams. For example, Martins, Milliken, Wiesenfeld, & Salgado (2003) found that in organizations that are highly homogeneous, teams were much more likely to pay attention to racioethnic category differences, as compared to teams in more heterogeneous organizations. It is even conceivable that macro-level organizational processes may filter down to how customers behave toward minorities in organizations, particularly in service firms in which employees and customers are involved in the coproduction of the service. Given that climate experiences reported by employees are accurately perceived by customers (Schneider, Bowen, Ehrhart, & Holcombe, 2000), it is possible that a climate for discrimination within an organization, as perceived by the customers served by that organization, may increase the perceived permissiveness of discriminatory behavior on the part of customers toward boundary role employees. In support of this notion, Gettman, Gelfand, Leslie, Schneider, and Salvaggio (2004) found that departments that have high levels of sexual harassment also tend to have high levels of customer harassment of employees. Although the causal direction of such relationships remains to be examined, it is important that research examine discrimination that is perpetrated by individuals outside of organizational boundaries.

The Organization Embedded in Context

Taking an open-systems perspective, we have argued that the external contexts in which organizations are embedded also affect the dynamics of discrimination in organizations. We briefly discussed a number of environmental inputs into organizations—such as the local context, the political and legal context, and the larger cultural context—that can affect levels of discrimination in organizations. Much research, however, is needed to explore how such extra-organizational forces affect discrimination in organizations. For example, much of the research in this chapter focused on U.S.-based organizations, and our discussion implicitly assumed that organizational boundaries were *within* the United States. Yet with the era of globalization, many U.S. companies now operate globally and are characterized by complex organizations that cross national borders in the form of multinational companies, international mergers and acquisitions, joint ventures, and international alliances. Accordingly, there is a critical need for research on discrimination in organizations to move beyond the domestic context to incorporate the global context of organizations.

Moving beyond domestic boundaries presents a number of cultural and legal complexities in dealing with discrimination. For example, we previously discussed the importance of building an organizational climate and culture that is intolerant of discrimination, of designing HR systems to reflect values for inclusiveness, and of the importance of top management support for a zero-tolerance policy on discrimination. Yet a key question is how organizations can create and sustain such processes and structures when operating on foreign soil where there may be different cultural practices, values, and norms regarding discrimination that conflict with those in the United States. As noted by Cava and Mayer (1993), multinational organizations often feel pressure to follow local norms in the host country in which they are operating, in order to gain a competitive advantage. Many companies may simply "take the line of least resistance" (Hutchings, 1998), causing multinationals to be reluctant to transfer their own practices regarding discrimination to the host country. A critical question, then, is how U.S. companies that are attempting to create a global organizational culture attempt to "negotiate" the culture for intolerance of discrimination that is derived from Westerns practices, values, and laws, with those of other cultures. In some countries, legal restrictions prevent women in the local context from occupying particular jobs (Cava & Mayer, 1993)—and, in effect, contrary to the U.S. civil rights act, gender can be considered a bona fide occupational qualificiation (BFOQ). Relatedly, whereas U.S.-based employees operating on foreign soil are still technically protected by the Civil Rights Act (Caligiuri & Cascio, 1998), women and minorities may still face overt and covert discrimination in other cultures. Research has shown that U.S. female expatriates, for example, experience overt prejudice and discrimination from host nationals (Izraeli, Banai, & Zeira, 1980; Stone, 1991). At the same time, it is also important to examine how cultural constructions of what constitutes discriminatory behavior may vary across cultures. For example, perceptions of what is considered sexual harassment can vary across cultural boundaries (Pryer et al., 1997), as can cultural norms for coping with harassment (Wasti & Cortina, 2002). A critical agenda for discrimination research, therefore, is to understand how to best protect diverse employees operating in discriminatory environments abroad, while at the same time, being culturally sensitive to local definitions and practices.

CONCLUSION

In this chapter, we have argued that discrimination in organizations is a complex, multi-determined phenomenon. We emphasized that organizations need to critically analyze how organizational structures, processes, and practices separately and collectively serve to perpetuate discrimination in organizations, and need to understand how the contexts in which organizations are embedded serve as critical inputs that affect levels of discrimination. It is only by making concerted efforts targeted across the great variety of issues we have identified and by taking a truly systems approach that organizations can best eliminate discrimination.

AUTHORS' NOTE

We thank the editors of this volume for their very helpful suggestions and insights.

REFERENCES

Arvey, R. D., Azevedo, R. E., Ostgaard, D. J., & Raghuram, S. (1996). The implications of a diverse labor market on human resource planning. In E. E. Kossek & S. A. Lobel (Eds.), *Managing diversity: Human resource strategies for transforming the workplace* (pp. 51–73). Cambridge, MA: Blackwell.

Bennett, R. J. (2002). Cracking the glass ceiling: Factors affecting women's advancement into upper management. *Academy of Management Executive, 16,* 157–159.

Bernardin, H. J., Hagan, C. M., Kane, J. S., & Villanova, P. (1998). Effective performance management: A focus on precision, customers, and situational constraints. In J. W. Smither (Ed.), *Performance appraisal: State of the art in practice* (pp. 3–48). San Francisco: Jossey-Bass.

Biernat, M., & Kobrynowicz, D. (1997). Gender and race-based standards of competence: Lower minimum standards but higher ability standards for devalued groups. *Journal of Personality and Social Psychology, 72,* 544–557.

Blum, T. C., Fields, D. L., & Goodman, J. S. (1994). Organizational-level determinants of women in management. *Academy of Management Journal, 37,* 241–268.

Braddock, J. H., III, & McPartland, J. M. (1987). How minorities continue to be excluded from equal employment opportunities: Research on labor market and institutional barriers. *Journal of Social Issues, 43,* 5–39.

Brass, D. J. (1985). Men's and women's networks: A study of interaction patterns and influence in an organization. *Academy of Management Journal, 28,* 327–343.

Brief, A. P., Dietz, J., Cohen, R. R., Pugh, S. D., & Vaslow, J. B. (2000). Just doing business: Modern racism and obedience to authority as explanations for employment discrimination. *Organizational Behavior and Human Decision Processes, 81,* 72–97.

Burke, R. J., McKeen, C. A., & McKenna, C. (1993). Correlates of mentoring in organizations: The mentor's perspective. *Psychological Reports, 72,* 883–896.

Button, S. B. (2001). Organizational efforts to affirm sexual diversity: A cross-level examination. *Journal of Applied Psychology, 86,* 17–26.

Caligiuri, P. M., & Cascio, W. F. (1998). Can we send her there? Maximizing the success of Western women on global assignments. *Journal of World Business, 33,* 394–417.

Campion, M. A., Outtz, J. L., Zedeck, S., Schmidt, F., Kehoe, J. F., Murphy, K. R., & Guion, R. M. (2001). The controversy over score banding in personnel selection: Answers to 10 key questions. *Personnel Psychology, 54,* 149–185.

Carnevale, A. P., & Stone, S. C. (1995). Diversity beyond the golden rule. *Training & Development, 48,* 22–37.

Cava, A., & Mayer, D. (1993). Gender discrimination abroad. *Business and Economic Review, 40,* 13–16.

Catalyst. (1993). *Successful initiatives for breaking the glass ceiling to upward mobility for minorities and women.* New York: Author.

Conway, J. M., Jako, R. A., & Goodman, D. F. (1995). A meta-analysis of interrater and internal consistency reliability of selection interviews. *Journal of Applied Psychology, 80,* 565–579.

Cox, T., Jr. (1994). *Cultural diversity in organizations: Theory, research, and practice.* San Francisco: Berrett-Koehler.

Cox, T. H., & Blake, S. (1991). Managing cultural diversity: Implications for organizational competitiveness. *Academy of Management Executive, 5,* 45–56.

Cox, T. H., Lobel, S., & McLeod, P. (1991). Effects of ethnic group cultural difference on cooperative versus competitive behavior in a group task. *Academy of Management Journal, 34,* 827–847.

Davidson, O. B., & Eden, D. (2000). Remedial self-fulfilling prophecy: Two field experiments to prevent Golem effects among disadvantaged women. *Journal of Applied Psychology, 85,* 386–398.

Delaney, J. T., & Lundy, M. C. (1996). Unions, collective bargaining, and the diversity paradox. In E. E. Kossek & S. A. Lobel (Eds.), *Managing diversity: Human resource strategies for transforming the workplace* (pp. 245–272). Cambridge, MA: Blackwell.

Delery, J. E. (1998). Issues of fit in strategic human resource management: Implications for research. *Human Resource Management Review, 8,* 289–310.

DiMaggio, P. J., and Powell, W. W. (1983). The iron cage revisited: Institutional isomorphism and collective rationality in organizational fields. *American Sociological Review, 48,* 147–160.

Donaldson, T., & Preston, L. E. (1995). The stakeholder theory of the corporation: Concepts, evidence and implications. *Academy of Management Review, 20,* 65–91.

Douglas, C., Ferris, G. R., Buckley, M. R., & Gundlach, M. J. (2003). Organizational and social influences on leader-member exchange processes: Implications for the management of diversity. In G. B. Graen (Ed.), *Dealing with diversity.* Greenwich, CT: Information Age Publishing.

Dvir, T., Eden, D., & Banjo, M. L. (1995). Self-fulfilling prophecy and gender: Can women be Pygmalion and Galatea? *Journal of Applied Psychology, 80,* 253–270.

Eisenberger, R., Fasolo, P., & Davis-LaMastro, V. (1990). Perceived organizational support and employee diligence, commitment, and innovation. *Journal of Applied Psychology, 75,* 51–59.

Fadil, P. A. (1995). The effects of cultural stereotypes on leader attributions of minority subordinates. *Journal of Managerial Issues, 7,* 193–208.

Gagliardi, P. (1986). The creation and change of organizational cultures: A conceptual framework. *Organization Studies, 7,* 117–134.

Gee, G. C. (2002). A multilevel analysis of the relationship between institutional and individual racial discrimination and health status. *American Journal of Public Health, 92,* 615–623.

Gettman, H., Gelfand, M. J., Leslie, L., Schneider, B., & Salvaggio, A. N. (2004). The effects of manager practices and service climate on sexual harassment: An integrated model. Paper presented at the annual meeting of the Academy of Management, New Orleans, LA.

Gordon, M. E., & Bowlby, R. L. (1988). Propositions about grievance settlements: Finally, consultation with grievants. *Personnel Psychology, 41,* 107–123.

Gottfredson, L. S. (1992). Dilemmas in developing diversity programs. In S. E. Jackson & Associates (Eds.), *Diversity in the workplace* (pp. 279–305). New York: Guilford.

Hanover, J. M. B., & Cellar, D. G. (1998). Environmental factors and the effectiveness of workforce diversity training. *Human Resource Development Quarterly, 9,* 105–125.

Hauck, V. E. (1997). *Arbitrating race, religion, and national origin discrimination grievances.* Westport, CN: Quorum Books.

Heilman, M. E., Block, C. J., & Lucas, J. A. (1992). Presumed incompetent? Stigmatization and affirmative action efforts. *Journal of Applied Psychology, 77,* 536–544.

Hickman, J., Tkaczyk, C., Florian, E., Stemple, J. , & Vazquez, D. (2003). 50 best companies for minorities. *Fortune, 148,* 103–109.

Hicks-Clarke, D., & Iles, P. (2000). Climate for diversity and its effects on career and organizational attitudes and perceptions. *Personnel Review, 29,* 324–346.

Hiller, N. J., & Day, D. V. (2003). LMX and teamwork: The challenges and apportunities of diversity. In G. B. Graen (Ed.), *Dealing with diversity.* Greenwich, CT: Information Age Publishing.

Hough, L. M., Oswald, F. L., & Ployhart, R. E. (2001). Determinants, detection and amelioration of adverse impact in personnel selection procedures: Issues, evidence and lessons learned. *International Journal of Selection and Assessment, 9,* 152–194.

House, R. J., Hanges, P. J., Javidan, M., Dorfman, P. W., & Gupta, V. (2004). *Culture, leadership, and organizations: The GLOBE study of 62 cultures.* Thousand Oaks, CA: Sage.

Hutchings, K. (1998). Good corporate citizens or perpetrators of social stratification? International business in Malaysia. In R. M. Afzalur & R. T. Golembiewski (Eds.) *Current topics in management* (Vol. 3, pp. 345–364). Stamford, CT: JAI.

Ibarra, H. (1993). Personal networks of women and minorities in management: A conceptual framework. *Academy of Management Review, 18,* 56–87.

Ilgen, D. R., & Youtz, M. A. (1986). Factors affecting the evaluation and development of minorities in organizations. *Research in Personnel and Human Resources Management, 4,* 307–337.

Izraeli, D. N., Banai, M., & Zeira, Y. (1980). Women executives in MNC subsidiaries. *California Management Review, 23,* 53–63.

Jackson, S. E. (1992). Preview of the road to be traveled. In S. E. Jackson & Associates (Eds.), *Diversity in the Workplace* (pp. 3–12). New York: Guilford.

Jackson, S. E., & Alvarez, E. B. (1992). Working through diversity as a strategic imperative. In S. E. Jackson & Associates (Eds.), *Diversity in the workplace* (pp. 13–29). New York: Guilford.

Jackson, S. E., & Schuler, R. S. (2003). *Managing human resources through strategic partnerships* (8th ed.). Cincinnati: South-Western College Publishing.

James, E. H. (2000). Race-related differences in promotions and support: Underlying effects of human and social capital. *Organization Science, 11,* 493–508.

Joplin, J. R. W., & Daus, C. S. (1997). Challenges of leading a diverse workforce. *Academy of Management Executive, 11,* 32–47.

Kahn, J. (2001). Diversity trumps the downturn. *Fortune, 144,* 114.

Kanter, R. M. (1977). *Men and women of the corporation.* New York: Basic Books.

Katz, D., & Kahn, R. L. (1978). *The social psychology of organizations* (2nd ed.). New York: Wiley.

Kelley, S. W. (1993). Discretion and the service employee. *Journal of Retailing, 69,* 104–126.

Kim, S. S., & Gelfand, M. J. (2003). The influence of ethnic identity on perceptions of organizational recruitment. *Journal of Vocational Behavior, 63,* 396–416.

King, A. G., & Spruell, S. P. (2001). Coca-Cola takes the high road. *Black Enterprise, 31*(7), 29.

Klimoski, R., & Donahue, L. (1997). HR strategies for integrating individuals with disabilities into the work place. *Human Resource Management Review, 7,* 109–138.

Kossek, E. E., & Zonia, S. C. (1993). Assessing diversity climate: A field study of reactions to employer efforts to promote diversity.*Journal of Organizational Behavior, 14,* 61–81.

Kram, K. E. (1985). *Mentoring at work: Developmental relationships in organizational life.* Glenview, IL: Scott, Foresman.

Kravitz, D. A., Harrison, D. A., Turner, M. E., Levine, E. L., Chaves, W., Brannick, M. T., Denning, D. L., Russell, C. J., & Conard, M. A. (1996). *Affirmative action: A review of psychological and behavioral research.* Bowling Green, OH: Society for Industrial and Organizational Psychology.

Ledvinka, J., & Scarpello, V. G. (1991). *Federal regulation of personnel and human resource management (Kent human resource management series).* Boston: PWS Publishing Co.

Leslie, L., & Gelfand, M. J. (2004). Climate for discrimination and the attribution to discrimination process. Paper presented at the Annual Conference of the Society for Industrial and Organizational Psychology, Chicago, IL, April.

Levitin, T., Quinn, R. P., & Staines, G. L. (1971). Sex discrimination against the American working women. *American Behavioral Scientist, 15,* 238–254.

Lobel, S. A., & Kossek, E. E. (1996). Human resource strategies to support diversity in work and personal lifestyles: Beyond the "family-friendly" organization. In E. E. Kossek & S. A. Lobel (Eds.), *Managing diversity: Human resource strategies for transforming the workplace* (pp. 221–244). Cambridge, MA: Blackwell.

Loden, M., & Rosener, J. B. (1991). *Workforce America! Managing employee diversity as a vital resource.* Homewood, IL: Business One Irwin.

Martin, J. (2002). *Organizational culture: Mapping the terrain.* Thousand Oaks, CA: Sage.

Martins, L. L., Milliken, F. J., Wiesenfeld, B. M., & Salgado, S. R. (2003). Racioethnic diversity and group members' experiences; the role of the racioethnic diversity of the organizational context. *Group and Organization Management, 28,* 75–106.

Milliken, F. J., & Martins, L. L. (1996). Searching for common threads: Understanding the multiple effects of diversity in organizational groups. *Academy of Management Review, 21,* 402–433.

Mills, K. I. (2000). GLBT employees make gains in workplaces nationwide. *Diversity Factor, 9,* 8–11.

Mischel, W. (1976). Towards a cognitive social model learning reconceptualization of personality. In N. S. Endler & D. Magnusson (Eds.), *Interactional psychology and personality* (pp. 166–207). New York: Wiley.

Mischel, W. (1977). The interaction of person and situation. In E. Magnusson & N. S. Endler (Eds.), *Personality at the crossroads.* Hillsdale, NJ: Lawrence Erlbaum Associates.

Mor Barak, M. E., Cherin, D. A., & Berkman, S. (1998). Organizational and personal dimensions of diversity climate: Ethnic and gender differences in employee perceptions. *Journal of Applied Behavioral Sciences, 31,* 82–104.

Morrison, A. M. (1992). *The new leaders: Guidelines on leadership diversity in America.* San Francisco: Jossey-Bass.

Morrison, A. M., & Von Glinow, M. A. (1990). Women and minorities in management. *American Psychologist, 45,* 200–208.

Nieva, V. F., & Gutek, B. A. (1980). Sex effects on evaluation. *Academy of Management Review, 5,* 267–276.

Nishii, L. H., Mayer, D., Goldstein, H., & Dotan, O. (2004). *Diversity and bottom-line performance: The moderating role of leader-member exchange.* Paper presented at the annual conference of the Society for Industrial and Organizational Psychology, Chicago, IL.

Nishii, L. H., & Raver, J. L. (2003). *Collective climates for diversity: Evidence from a field study.* Paper presented at the annual conference of Society for Industrial and Organizational Psychology, Orlando, FL.

Northwestern National Life Insurance Company. (1991). *Employee burnout: America's newest epidemic.* Minneapolis, MN: Author.

Oerton, S. (1994). Exploring women workers' motives for employment in cooperatives and collectives. *Journal of Gender Studies, 3,* 289–297.

Olson-Buchanan, J. B. (1996). Voicing discontent: What happens to the grievance filer after the grievance? *Journal of Applied Psychology, 81,* 52–63.

O'Reilly, C. A., Williams, K. Y., & Barsade, S. (1998). Group demography and innovation: Does diversity help? *Research on Managing Groups and Teams, 1,* 183–207.

Perry, E. L., Davis-Blake, A., & Kulik, C. T. (1994). Explaining gender-based selection decisions: A synthesis of contextual and cognitive approaches. *Academy of Management Review, 19,* 786–820.

Peters, T. J., & Waterman, Jr., R. H. (1982). *In search of excellence: Lessons from America's best-run companies.* New York: Harper & Row.

Prasad, P., Mills, A. J., Elmes, M., & Prasad, A. (1997). *Managing the organizational melting pot: Dilemmas of organizational diversity.* Thousand Oaks, CA: Sage.

Pruitt, S. W., & Nethercutt, L. L. (2002). The Texaco racial discrimination case and shareholder wealth. *Journal of Labor Research, 13,* 685–693.

Pryer, J., DeSouza, E. R., Fitness, J., Hutz, C., Kumpf, M., Lubbert, K., Pesonen, O., & Erber, M. W. (1997). Gender differences in the interpretation of social-sexual behavior: A cross-cultural perspective on sexual harassment, *Journal of Cross-Cultural Psychology, 28,* 509–534.

Ragins, B. R., & Cornwell, J. M. (2001). Pink triangles: Antecedents and consequences of perceived workplace discrimination against gay and lesbian employees. *Journal of Applied Psychology, 86,* 1244–1261.

Ragins, B. R., & Sundstrom, E. (1989). Gender and power in organizations: A longitudinal perspective. *Psychological Bulletin, 105,* 51–88.

Raver, J. L., & Gelfand, M. J. (2003). *Beyond the individual victim: The impact of sexual harassment on team processes and performance.* Paper presented at the annual conference of the Academy of Management, Seattle, WA.

Reichers, A. E., & Schneider, B. (1990). Climate and cultures: An evolution of constructs. In B. Schneider (Ed.), *Organizational Climate and Culture* (pp. 5–39). San Francisco: Jossey-Bass.

Riger, S. (1991). Gender dilemmas in sexual harassment policies and procedures. *American Psychologist, 46,* 497–505.

Roberts, K. (1996). Managing disability-based diversity. In E. E. Kossek & S. A. Lobel (Eds.), *Managing diversity: Human resource strategies for transforming the workplace* (pp. 310–331). Cambridge, MA: Blackwell.

Robinson, G., & Dechant, K. (1997). Building a business case for diversity. *Academy of Management Executive, 11,* 21–31.

Ryan, A. M., & Ployhart, R. E. (2000). Applicants' perceptions of selection procedures and decisions: A critical review and agenda for the future. *Journal of Management, 26,* 565–606.

Sathe, V. (1985). How to decipher and change corporate culture. In R. H. Kilmann, M. J. Saxton, R. Serpa, & Associates (Eds.), *Gaining Control of the Corporate Culture* (pp. 230–261). San Francisco: Jossey-Bass.

Schein, E. H. (1971). The individual, the organization and the career: A conceptual scheme. *Journal of Applied Behavioral Science, 7,* 401–426.

Schein, E. H. (1985). *Organizational culture and leadership.* San Francisco: Jossey-Bass.

Schneider, B. (2000). The psychological life of organizations. In N. M. Ashkanasy, C. P. M. Wilderom, & M. F. Peterson (Eds.), *Handbook of organizational culture and climate* (pp. xvii–xxii). Thousand Oaks, CA: Sage.

Schneider, B., Bowen, D. E., Ehrhart, M. G., & Holcombe, K. M. (2000). The climate for service: Evolution of a construct. In N. M. Ashkanasy, C. P. M. Wilderom, & M. F. Peterson (Eds.) *Handbook of organizational culture and climate* (pp. 21–36). Thousand Oaks, CA: Sage.

Schneider, B., & Reichers, A. E. (1983). On the etiology of climates. *Personnel Psychology, 36,* 19–39.

Schneider, B., White, S., & Paul, M. C. (1998). Linking service climate and customer perceptions of service quality: Test of a causal model. *Journal of Applied Psychology, 83*, 150–163.

Schneider, K. T., Hitlan, R. T., & Radhakrishnan, P. (2000). An examination of the nature and correlates of ethnic harassment experiences in multiple contexts. *Journal of Applied Psychology, 85*, 3–12.

Seidel, M. L., Polzer, J. T., & Stewart, K. J. (2000). Friends in high places: The effects of social networks on discrimination in salary negotiations. *Administrative Science Quarterly, 45*, 1–24.

Shaffer, M. A., Joplin, J. R. W., Bell, M. P., Lau, T., & Oguz, C. (2000). Gender discrimination and job-related outcomes: A cross-cultural comparison of working women in the United States and China. *Journal of Vocational Behavior, 57*, 395–427.

Siehl, C., & Martin, J. (1988). Measuring organizational culture: Mixing qualitative and quantitative methods. In M. Jones, M. Moore, & R. Snyder (Eds.), *Inside organizations: Understanding the human dimension* (pp. 79–104). Newbury Park, CA: Sage.

Staw, B. M., Sandelands, L. E., & Dutton, J. E. (1981). Threat-rigidity effects in organizational behavior: A multilevel analysis. *Administrative Science Quarterly, 26*, 501–524.

Steele, C. M. (1997). A threat in the air: How stereotypes shape intellectual identity and performance. *American Psychologist, 52*, 613–629.

Stone, R. (1991). Expatriate selection and failure. *Human Resource Planning, 14*, 9–18.

Stoner, C. R., & Russell-Chapin, L. A. (1997). Creating a culture of diversity management: Moving from awareness to action. *Business Forum, 22(2/3)*, 6–12.

Thomas, D. A. (1993). Racial dynamics in cross-race developmental relationships. *Administrative Science Quarterly, 38*, 169–194.

Triandis, H. C., Kurowski, L. L., & Gelfand, M. J. (1994). Workplace diversity. In H. C. Triandis, M. D. Dunnette, & L. M. Hough (Eds.), *Handbook of industrial and organizational psychology, Vol. 4* (2nd ed., pp. 769–827). Palo Alto, CA: Consulting Psychologists Press.

Trice, H. M., & Beyer, J. M. (1991). Cultural leadership in organizations. *Organization Science, 2*, 149–169.

Tsui, A. S., & O'Reilly, C. A. (1989). Beyond simple demographic effects: The importance of relational demography in superior-subordinate dyads. *Academy of Management Journal, 32*, 402–423.

U.S. Bureau of Labor Statistics (1999). *BLS releases new 1998-2008 employment projections, News release USDL-99-339* [On-line]. Available: http://www.bls.gov/opub/working/sources.htm.

U.S. Department of Labor, Office of Federal Contract Compliance Programs (1995). *OFCCP glass ceiling initiative: Are there cracks in the ceiling?* Washington, DC: Office of Federal Contract Compliance Programs, U.S. Department of Labor.

U.S. Equal Employment Opportunity Commission (2001). *Job patterns for minorities and women in private industry (EEO-1)* [On-line]. Available: http://www.eeoc.gov/stats/jobpat/2001/national.html

U.S. General Accounting Office (2002). *A new look through the glass ceiling: Where are the women?* [On-line]. Available: http://www.house.gov/dingell/dingellmaloneyreport.pdf

Waldo, C. R. (1999). Working in a majority context: A structural model of heterosexism as minority stress in the workplace. *Journal of Counseling Psychology, 46*, 218–232.

Wasti, A., & Cortina, L. (2002). Coping in context: Sociocultural determinants of responses to sexual harassment. *Journal of Personality and Social Psychology, 83*, 394–405.

Weick, K. E. (1995). *Sensemaking in Organizations.* Thousand Oaks, CA: Sage.

Wentling, R. M., & Palma-Rivas, N. (1997). *Diversity in the workforce: A literature review (MDS-934).* Berkeley, CA: National Center for Research in Vocational Education.

Whitely, W., Dougherty, T. W., & Dreher, G. F. (1991). Relationship of career mentoring and socioeconomic origin to manager's and professionals' early career progress. *Academy of Management Journal, 34,* 331–351.

World Values Study Group. (1994). *World values survey.* Ann Arbor, MI: Inter-University Consortium for Political and Social Research.

Wright, P., Ferris, S. P., Hiller, J. S., & Kroll, M. (1995). Competitiveness through management of diversity: Effects on stock price valuation. *Academy of Management Journal, 38,* 272–287.

Yukl, G., & Van Fleet, D. D. (1992). Theory and research on leadership in organizations. In M. D. Dunnette & L. M. Hough (Eds.), *Handbook of industrial and organizational psychology, Vol. 3* (2nd ed., pp. 147–197). Palo Alto, CA: Consulting Psychologists Press.

Zohar, D. (2000). A group-level model of safety climate: Testing the effect of group climate on microaccidents in manufacturing jobs. *Journal of Applied Psychology, 85,* 587–596.

II

Understanding Discrimination
Against Specific Groups

6

Organizations as Reflections of Their Environments: The Case of Race Composition

Arthur P. Brief
Rebecca M. Butz
Elizabeth A. Deitch
Tulane University

We are not sure how comfortable organizational psychologists will be with this chapter because much of the analyses presented will be sociological. The central thesis advanced is that organizations are reflections of the environments in which they are embedded [see, for example, Pfeffer and Salancik (1978) for an analogous idea]. Of course, such an assertion is only part of the story. Also part of the tale, one we will detail for it is where our potential contribution lies, is the role psychological processes play in transmitting environmental influences. That is, we will argue that the thoughts, feelings, and actions of organizational members mediate the influence of environmental elements, such as customers/clients, suppliers, and regulatory groups (e.g., Dill, 1958; Thompson, 1967), on the look of an organization.

The story to be told has a distinct purpose, perhaps even a moral. That aim is to explain the race composition of organizations, more specifically, to help us understand better the representation and distribution (horizontally and vertically) of Blacks in American work organizations. We begin by addressing why this problem was chosen as the focus of attention and its multiple facets. Next, we outline a very crude theory of environmental influences on race composition by specifying a small, exemplary set of environmental attributes for consideration. For each attribute, we will attempt to trace how it might affect matters of race in organizations (e.g., how the race composition of an organization's customer base might affect the practices it uses to recruit and select customer service personnel). After presenting our theoretical ideas, some of the methodological challenges they pose for organizational psychologists are raised. The chapter closes with the assertion that the theoretical lens we brought to bear on discrimination against Blacks in American organizations is applicable to other stigmatized groups (e.g., women and foreign workers) in other settings (e.g., Asia and Europe).

WHY THE ISSUE OF RACE?

We take on the sticky issue of race in organizations because there is a clear need. In a study of urban inequality in Los Angeles, almost 60% of Black respondents reported experiencing some form of work-related discrimination (in comparison, only 25% of Whites reported discrimination) (Bobo & Suh, 2000). Take these numbers to the national level, and it is not surprising that in fiscal year 2002, almost 30,000 allegations of racial discrimination were filed with the EEOC against private sector employers (U.S. Equal Employment Opportunity Commission, April 7, 2002). This being said, however, we do acknowledge that conditions in the labor market and workplace have dramatically improved in the last 50 years. Prior to the Civil Rights Act of 1964, it was legal in much of the United States to use race or sex to recruit, hire, and assign jobs (Reskin, 1998). The Civil Rights Act and subsequent antidiscrimination legislation in the 1960s and 1970s made these practices illegal and spurred decreases in racial disparity, for example, a significant narrowing of the Black–White earnings gap (e.g., see Alexis, 1998; Couch & Daly, 2002).

Despite progress, however, there is still widespread evidence that racial disparities persist in America's workplaces (Reskin, 1998). For instance, although the earnings gap has narrowed, America's Black workers are still grossly underpaid relative to their White counterparts (Neumark, 1999). In 2002, among full-time wage and salary workers, the median weekly earnings of Blacks ($498) was much lower than those of Whites ($624); and the earnings gap was especially pronounced for Black males whose median was a mere 74.5% of that of White males (U.S. Dept. of Labor, 2002). Furthermore, although jobless rates declined dramatically between

1992 and 2001, Blacks in America continue to be more than twice as likely as their White counterparts to be unemployed (U.S. Dept. of Labor, 2002). Indeed, as we highlight below, there is evidence that Black workers face disparities in treatment and opportunity at every step of the employment process, from recruitment and hiring, to mentoring and day-to-day life within organizations.

Differences in treatment and opportunities between Blacks and Whites begin even before applicants appear at the organization's door. Interviews with employers indicate that they commonly recruit applicants by word-of-mouth referrals or by targeting advertising of job openings to particular neighborhoods, often avoiding inner city or predominately Black neighborhoods (Kirschenman & Neckerman, 1991). Because word-of-mouth referrals travel through employees' social networks, they tend to produce applicants similar to those employees already in place. This can mean that, at the outset, Blacks and Whites have different levels of knowledge and awareness of job openings. Moreover, studies show that equally qualified Black and White applicants have different experiences during the selection process. A series of clever studies, called "audit studies," examined the differential outcomes of Black and White job applicants who were matched in qualifications, credentials, and interviewing skills (e.g., Bendick, Jackson, & Reinoso, 1994; Turner, Fix, & Struyk, 1991; see also Bendick, 1998). Because the pairs of individuals in these studies were so matched, any differences in their treatment was attributed to race (for a critique of the audit study method, however, see Heckman, 1998). Studies of this sort conducted by the Urban Institute in Chicago and Washington D.C. found that Black males were three times as likely to be turned down for a job as White males (Mincy, 1993). Similarly, audit studies conducted by the Fair Employment Council of Greater Washington, Inc., showed that White applicants were almost 10% more likely to receive interviews than were Black applicants (Bendick et al., 1994). Overall, the Fair Employment Council studies found that over 20% of employers treated Black applicants less favorably than White applicants. Finally, a more recent study that manipulated names (Black-sounding versus White-sounding) of job applicants on matched resumes found that applicants with White-sounding names were 50% more likely to be called for interviews than were those with Black-sounding names (Bertrand & Mullainathan, 2003).

These kinds of disparities in recruitment and selection processes likely are responsible, in part, for differential Black and White representation across occupations. United States Department of Labor statistics show that Blacks are severely underrepresented in some occupations and overrepresented in others, often those with lower status. For example, in 2001, Blacks made up only 10% of management and executive ranks, while making up more than 21% of service occupations (U.S. Department of Labor, 2001). Further, even within single industries, horizontal segregation by race is strikingly common. For instance, 35.5% of postal clerks are Black, but only 14.9% of mail carriers are Black; 17.4% of restaurant cooks are Black, whereas Blacks make up less than 6% of wait staffs (U.S. Bureau of the Census, 2002a). In essence, although the American population has become more diverse racially and ethnically (Whites now account for only 75% of the population; U.S. Bureau of the Census, 2000), the above statistics suggest that racial composition within and across organizations does not parallel or reflect the increase in demographic diversity (Operario & Fiske, 2001).

Once in the organization, Blacks continue to receive differential treatment. For instance, evidence suggests that Blacks are paid less and are pigeon-holed into jobs with lower status and shorter career ladders. In a review of the audit studies mentioned above, Bendick et al. (1994) found that once a job offer was made, there was an overall 17% chance that White applicants were offered a higher starting salary than Blacks. In addition, Whites were steered into jobs that were below their qualifications 37% less than were their Black counterparts. In a study of wage differentials in Atlanta, Boston, Detroit, and Los Angeles, Neumark (1999) compared the starting wages of Blacks and Whites who later came to perform equally well on the job (i.e., starting wages were regressed on performance that was measured some time after the beginning of employment). His overall finding was that Blacks were paid lower starting wages than Whites with the same eventual performance. Although such wage differentials can be explained partially by differences in education, human capital, and job experience, a significant portion of the wage gap remains unexplained, raising the possibility of race as a cause (Cohn, 2000; Couch & Daly, 2002; Gill, 1989). For instance, Cawley, Heckman, and Vytlacil (1999) examined wages and ability and found that cognitive ability and human capital measures combined explained less than a third of the variance in Black–White wage differentials. These authors concluded that the wage return to ability is not uniform across races—what one earns on the job does depend on race.

In addition to pay, Black–White differences can be seen in job placements and promotions. Research indicates that when Black employees are promoted, they are often promoted into jobs with less power and responsibility than Whites and are relegated to stereotypical jobs—for example, those dealing with "minority issues" (Collins, 1989; Mueller, Parcel, & Kazuko, 1989). Also, studies have shown that shortly after entry into an organization, Blacks are more likely to be assigned to a Black supervisor than are their White counterparts (Lefkowitz, 1994). This type of assignment based on race helps ensure that Black employees continue in the same career paths and ladders as those who have come before them. Unfortunately, computer simulations of the impact of these types of decisions have shown that even miniscule differences at the lower levels of an organization's hierarchy can produce wide disparity at the top levels (Martell, Lane, & Emrich, 1996). The above evidence suggests that even if Blacks are hired by firms in relatively large numbers (for example, in response to pressure to comply with Affirmative Action or Equal Employment Opportunity directives), Black–White disparities often emerge in other areas such as pay, placement, and opportunities to advance (Mitra, 1999).

Finally, there is some evidence of Black–White differences in informal day-to-day interaction in the workplace. Research has indicated that Black employees often face a less welcoming workplace than Whites that may include fewer mentors to sponsor and guide them, greater social isolation from important informal networks (Reskin, 1998), greater supervisory control of their work (Sidanius & Pratto, 1999), and more everyday incidents of devaluation and exclusion (Deitch et al., 2002; Essed, 1991). Compared to their White counterparts, Blacks in the workplace more often hold what Kanter (1977) has called "token" status, where they are treated like symbols or representatives of a category rather than as individuals. Having token status can result in being held to a different or higher standard (Cox & Nkomo, 1986). So, for example, Black employees might be evaluated not only on how well they perform their job, but also on how well they represent (or do not represent) their minority category (Kanter, 1977).

We have offered the above evidence of Black–White disparities in the American labor market and workplace because, by and large, a perusal of the organizational literature might lead one to think that organizations are largely race neutral (Brief, 1998; Cox & Nkomo, 1990). Organizations are *not* race neutral; Blacks face less chance of being hired as well as, once in the door, lower income, prestige, opportunity and increased performance pressure. Indeed:

> Despite protestations to the contrary, there is widespread and convincing evidence that [minority group members] face a rather daunting situation in the labor market. The level of stress this situation is likely to produce may even interfere with the way in which they perform their jobs and result in things like higher levels of job alienation and less commitment to their employers (Sidanius & Pratto, 1999, p. 175).

It is for these reasons that we feel the need *and* the responsibility to better understand how race composition in organizations is impacted by the larger organizational environment.

OUTSIDE THE BOX

We were very pleased, and also a bit embarrassed, to have discovered an impressive body of literature in sociology concerned with the factors affecting sex and race compositions of organizations (e.g., Reskin, McBrier, & Kmec, 1999). The pleasure stemmed from our interest in understanding how racial prejudice plays out in organizational settings (e.g., Brief, Dietz, Cohen, Pugh, & Vaslow, 2000). As will be demonstrated, the discovered sociological literature taught us that we had been approaching the problem of racial discrimination in organizations too narrowly and that a fuller explanation of the problem (and consideration of its tentative solutions) requires one to look outside *and* inside organizations. Discipline-wise, this necessitates building bridges between organizational sociology and organizational psychology that likely and naturally will be constructed from ideas evident in social psychology. These bridges, however, are more the subject matter of the next section of this chapter than this one.

The embarrassment associated with our sociological discovery is a function of timing; as serious students of employment discrimination, we should have found the body of work considerably earlier than we did. It clearly would have enriched our research. Although we were aware of an occasional sociological study on the race and sex compositions of organizations, not until we read Reskin et al. (1999), who pulled much of the available research together, did we recognize that sociology had so much to offer in regard to what we had been studying psychologically for several years. The only explanation (not justification) for our oversight stems from our "micro" organizational behavior view of the world. Like most organizational psychologists, we look to people and organizations to understand whatever phenomenon intrigues us. Here, we intend to show that it is time to step out of that box and embrace organizational sociology as an *essential* source of knowledge for understanding what goes on in organizations. As it is clearly time to abandon a micro–macro distinction, we now turn to the organizational sociology literature to attempt to aid other organizational psychologists concerned with employment discrimination discover what is outside the box.

According to Reskin et al. (1999), the literature on workplace sex and race composition emerged following Baron and Bielby's (1980) appeal to those studying stratification and inequality in labor markets to "bring the firm back in" (p. 760). Reskin et al. (1999) also observed that this growing body of scholarship had been guided by Baron and Bielby's own empirical research (e.g., Baron & Bielby, 1985) and by ideas evident in the organizational demography literature (e.g., Pfeffer, 1983) and in Blau (1977) and Kanter (1977).

The slice of the pertinent literature we have chosen to highlight emphasizes the importance of the environments in which organizations are embedded as determinants of sex and race composition. We have not given much attention here to attributes of organizations per se (e.g., their size) as determinants of composition or the consequences of composition (e.g., the stresses that may be experienced by minority workers). In addition, whereas the focus of this chapter is on race, the composition literature focuses on sex, as is also the case with the organizational psychology literature (e.g., Brief & Hayes, 1997; Cox & Nkomo, 1990). Consequently, our assertions about race often will be based upon findings regarding sex.

The Most Obvious

Although not of particular theoretical concern here, it is important to note, at least briefly, the most obvious: The racial composition of the labor pools available to an organization should influence its race composition (e.g., Holzer, 1998). (Please note the term "available" refers to those whom an organization could recruit, not necessarily to those whom it does recruit.) Moreover, across jobs, the racial composition of labor pools varies, with pools for those jobs requiring higher levels of skills comprising relatively fewer Blacks. This is so, in part, because the educational attainment of Blacks continues to lag behind that of Whites, even though the gap has narrowed over time (e.g., Mare, 1995; Neal & Johnson, 1996; U.S. Bureau of the Census, 2002b). Thus, the race composition of available labor pools should influence both the representation and distribution of Blacks in an organization (i.e., who is hired and where they are placed).

The Less Obvious

The race composition of the labor pools available to an organization can be taken as an aspect of the social structure of the organization's environment, and, as such, it gains in theoretical import. If, in available labor markets, Blacks were found to be proportionally overrepresented in the pools for low-skill, low-wage level jobs and underrepresented in those pools for high-skill, high-wage level jobs, then, as indicated above, one would expect a similar representation in jobs occupied. In fact, this is so as was hinted at earlier. For example, although Blacks comprise 11.3% of the total civilian labor force in the United States, they make up only 3.1% of architects; 5.5% of engineers; 5.6% of physicians; 5.6% of pharmacists; and 5.1% of lawyers (U.S. Bureau of the Census, 2002a). Alternatively, Blacks comprise 22.4% of mail clerks (except postal service); 25.6% of guards; 32.7% of nursing aides, orderlies, and attendants; 21.9% of maids and housemen; 23.6% of barbers; and 29% of pressing machine operators (U.S. Bureau of the Census, 2002a).

This inequality in the structure of labor markets is problematic for several reasons. Principal among them for our purposes are the relationships between social structure and stereotypes. People tend to infer stereotypes from social structure, (i.e., from the roles they see members of groups playing in society; e.g., Bayton, McAlister, & Hamer, 1956; Hoffman & Hurst, 1990; Jost & Banaji, 1994). More specifically, Eagly and her colleagues showed that stereotypes emerge as explanations (or justifications) for existing divisions of labor (e.g., Eagly, 1987, 1995; Eagly & Steffen, 1986; also see, for example, Hoffman & Hurst, 1990; Skrypnek & Snyder, 1982). Highly skewed sex or race composition in the occupational marketplace is likely to activate stereotypes automatically (e.g., Heilman, 1995) and, perhaps, without the observer's awareness (e.g., Fiske, 1998), and, as discussed in more detail later, these stereotypes affect organizational decision makers. So, for instance, if one were to observe relatively few Blacks in a job requiring considerable training and skill (e.g., registered nurse) and relatively many Blacks occupying a job requiring little training and skill (e.g., orderly), this could evoke and reinforce a negative stereotype of Blacks as not very smart and/or not very motivated. Obviously, such beliefs likely would not bode well for Black job applicants.

Thus, a vicious cycle exists: Social structure, in the form of occupational roles, evokes negative stereotypes about Blacks, which, when acted upon by organizational decision makers (consciously or unconsciously), serves to maintain the existing social structure. Such stereotypes have been described as "relatively enduring cultural phenomena" (Brief, 1998, p. 123; also see, for example, Stroebe & Insko, 1989). As such, the stereotypes of Blacks in America can be thought of as a cultural stereotype that persists and whose content is known widely by both prejudiced and nonprejudiced individuals (e.g., Devine, 1989).

In summary, social structure matters. How Blacks are distributed across occupations in the environment in which an organization is embedded (e.g., city, industry, or nation) could evoke negative stereotypes of Blacks; and, those stereotypes could influence the personnel decisions made in the organization.

Attitudinal Baggage

This exemplary environmental influence, although evident in the sociology literature in general, is least explored in terms of its potential influence on the race composition of organizations. Scott (1987, p. 19) observed "employees come to the organization with heavy cultural and social baggage obtained from interactions in other social contexts." In the same vein, but more narrowly, Brief (1998) addressed the "attitudinal baggage" people bring to work, particularly their "excess baggage" in the form of negative racial attitudes. It is this excess baggage that is the next environmental influence to be examined.

Earlier, it was asserted that the negative stereotype of Blacks in America can be thought of as a "cultural stereotype," one whose content is known widely. As we proceed, it is important to recognize that mere knowledge of this stereotype does *not* equal endorsement (e.g., Bettelheim & Janowitz, 1964; Devine, 1989; but see Crosby, Bromley, & Saxe, 1980). Knowledge of a negative stereotype translates into prejudice *only* when that knowledge also represents the personal beliefs of the individual. For now, we are concerned with prejudice (i.e., negative attitudes toward Blacks) and not stereotypes per se.

What might produce differences in racial attitudes across communities? Why, for example, might the attitudes of Whites be more negative toward Blacks in Detroit than they are in Minneapolis? An answer may be the local Black population share is larger in Detroit (81.6%) than in Minneapolis (18.0%). The idea that sizeable minority populations increase White hostility is not new (e.g., Allport, 1954). Blumer (1958) argued that racial antagonism arises in defense of a group's position. So, as the proportion of Blacks increases in a community, they are more likely to be seen by Whites as competitors for scarce economic and/or political resources, and, such competition is at the heart of realistic group conflict theory (e.g., Sherif, 1967). This theory postulates that real, direct competition for valuable but limited resources (or the false perception of it) breeds hostility between groups (LeVine & Campbell, 1972). [Also see Giles and Evans' (1986) power theory.] Nagel (1995), in summarizing various theoretical approaches to the influence of resource competition on ethnic relations, observed that increased interethnic contact, when resource competition is present, increases the likelihood of racial prejudice.

Taylor (1998) reviewed a variety of indirect sources of empirical evidence pertaining to the notion that, as the proportion of the Black population increases, prejudice among Whites increases. Generally, she found links between local racial composition and "racial inequality in income, jobs, education, and housing; school and residential segregation; lynching and incarceration of Blacks; mobilization of Whites against desegregation; and political party registration and voting among Whites" (p. 514). More specifically, for example, she noted the following findings: (a) metropolitan concentrations of Blacks were associated with occupational inequality in the South (Wilcox & Roof, 1978; also see Burr, Galle, & Fossett, 1991); (b) in Southwestern metropolitan areas, a high percentage of minorities was associated with greater occupational inequality between minorities and non-Hispanic Anglos, whether the minority population was Mexican American or Black (Frisbie & Neidert, 1977); (c) and, when the local labor market area contained a high proportion of Blacks, all groups of minority men lost earnings and White men gained them (Tienda & Lii, 1987).

Considerably less and somewhat more mixed direct attitudinal evidence is available based upon Taylor's (1998) review (e.g., Giles & Evans, 1985; Glaser, 1994). Particular findings reported by Taylor (1998) included, for instance: Pettigrew's (1959) finding that prejudice among White southerners was greater in localities in which the Black population share was large; Fossett and Kiecolt's (1989) results indicating that perceived threat and opposition to integration increased among Whites as the proportion of local Blacks increased; and Quillian's (1996) findings that regional Black population share (construed of, along with per capita income, as indicating group threat) was associated positively with traditional prejudice and opposition to race targeting among Whites.

Research results reported by Taylor (1998) herself showed that as the proportion of the Black population increases, prejudice among Whites increases. She found the local percentage of Blacks to influence adversely traditional prejudice, opposition to race-targeting, and policy-related beliefs among Whites. Moreover, Taylor observed that the independent effect of percent Blacks is stronger than the net effect of Southern location, with the South generally having a nonsignificant influence on White racial views when percent Blacks is controlled (also see Lieberson, 1980). However, the South appeared to moderate the relationship between local percent Blacks and traditional prejudice (but not opposition to race-targeting or policy related beliefs), with the impact of percent Black evident only outside the South. [For more on South/non-South differences in racism, see, for example, Emerson (1994); Firebaugh and Davis (1988); and Wilcox and Roof (1978).]

In summary, the prevailing attitudes of Whites toward Blacks do seem to vary across communities, and, in part, such variance appears to be attributable to the local Black population share. Later, we will attend to how attitudes that are brought to work as excess baggage may manifest themselves in organizations to influence their race composition.

The Markets for Goods and Services

The race of customers and clients matters for the racial composition of organizations. Before turning to the sociological literature to address this claim, we will examine management practice and education by telling a tale that has been told before by Brief (1998). In late 1992, Shoney's agreed to pay $132.5 million in response to allegations that the restaurant company discriminated against its Black employees. A former vice-president of the company stated that the firm's discriminatory practices were the result of the CEO's unwritten policy that "Blacks should not be employed in any position where they would be seen by customers" (Watkins, 1993, p. 424). The CEO himself admitted:

> In looking for anything to identify why is this unit under-performing, in some cases, I would probably have said this is a neighborhood of predominantly White neighbors, and we have a considerable amount of Black employees and this might be a problem. (p. 427)

At lower levels of the organization such analyses by the CEO translated into some managers feeling they needed to "lighten-up" their restaurants—a company euphemism for reducing the number of Black employees—and to hire "attractive White girls" instead (p. 424).

Shoney's CEO reasoned that a restaurant's performance was affected positively if the racial makeup of the unit's customer contact personnel *matched* the customer population served. Brief (1998) asserted that the reasoning of Shoney's CEO reflects a bottom-line business perspective that is seen as plausible and nonprejudicial to many managers and is commonplace in business organizations. The idea of a business justification to discriminate, at first glance, may seem farfetched. It is not. Prior to the civil rights movement, these justifications were explicitly part of the content of management education. Take, for instance, the lessons taught by Chester I. Barnard (1938) in his classic *The Functions of the Executive*. He described the informal executive organization whose purpose is to communicate "intangible facts, opinions, suggestions, suspicions, that cannot pass through formal channels" (p. 225). For this informal organization to operate effectively, Barnard prescribed selecting and promoting people to executive positions who *match* those already in place. He stated:

> Perhaps often and certainly occasionally men cannot be promoted or selected, or even must be relieved, because they cannot function, because they "do not fit" where there is no question of formal competence. This question of "fitness" involves such matters as education, experience, age, sex, personal distinctions, prestige, race. (p. 224)

More than three decades after the publication of Barnard's advice to executives, a Black manager wrote, "I believe that many of the problems I encountered were of fit. . . . I was out of the 'place' normally filled by Black people in the company" (Jones, 1973, p. 114).

Today, "race matching rules" have not disappeared from the management literature. Using the same business logic as Shoney's CEO, however, these rules are advanced by those advocating racial integration (e.g., Cox, 1993). The president of Avon Corporation, for example, concluded that his company's inner-city markets became significantly more profitable when additional Black and Hispanic customer contact personnel were placed in them, because newly placed personnel were uniquely qualified to understand certain aspects of the worldview of the minority populations in the inner city (Cox & Blake, 1991). Brief (1998) contended that it is naïve to believe that if an organization uses a matching rule to include Blacks, the use of the same sort of rule to exclude Blacks will be precluded. Although the staffing consequences of the two forms of the rule are different, they both rest on the same business logic—race matching enhances organizational effectiveness.

What do the sociology (and economics) literatures say about the veracity of Brief's (1998) tale? Research shows the hiring of Blacks is lower in those organizations with many White customers (e.g., Holzer, 1998; Holzer & Ihlanfeldt, 1998). In the sociology literature, such results have been interpreted as an organization's customers creating race-specific demands for workers, especially in organizations in which employees interact with customers (e.g., retail and service-sector firms; e.g., Mittman, 1992). These demands result in an emphasis on personality and appearance as job qualifications, leading to the exclusion of Blacks from retail and service organizations, particularly Black men (e.g., Moss & Tilly, 1996). So, it seems that firms, in fact, do seek to match the race of their customer service personnel to the race of their customers. It appears they may do so in the belief that this is what their customers desire, but, actual motivation within the firm for such discrimination remains an open empirical question.

What are the implications of race matching? To us, perhaps the most serious is that Blacks, relative to Whites, will tend to populate the lowest paying sales and service positions because these involve servicing those customers with the least economic resources. According to the U.S. Bureau of the Census (2000), 12.7% of Black households earned $75,000 or more in 1999, whereas for Whites the percentage was 25.0; and, at the other end of the continuum, 28.5% of Black households earned less than $15,000, whereas for Whites the percentage was only 14.0. Thus, one would expect Blacks to be represented more in the presumably lower paying customer contact workforce of a discount store than they would be in the corresponding workforce of an up-scale department store. In total, therefore, markets for goods and services seem to matter for the race composition of organizations, across industries (e.g., retailing versus manufacturing) and within industry (e.g., up-scale versus discount retailing).

The Law and Its Enforcement

In theory, since the passage of Title VII of the 1964 Civil Rights Act, which prohibited, among others, sex and race discrimination in establishments with at least 15 workers, it should have been costly to engage in such discrimination. However, because of legal ambiguities about what constitutes compliance and spotty enforcement (e.g., Donohue & Siegelman, 1991; Edelman, 1992; Leonard, 1989), organizations can choose to "take substantive action or merely comply symbolically" (Bielby, 2000, p. 125; see also, Edelman & Petterson, 1999). Organizations subjected to stronger enforcement pressures (e.g., federal contractors) are more open to minorities than those who are not (e.g., Brown, 1982; Holzer, 1998; Leonard, 1984).

One can think of equal employment opportunity (EEO) legislation and administrative orders (e.g., Executive Order 11246) as having generated what Konrad and Linnehan (1995) called "formalized human resource management (HRM) structures" within organizations. These structures refer to formal rules, procedures, programs, and positions that influence personnel decisions. As noted above, these formalized structures merely may be symbolic (e.g., Edelman, 1992), intended to do little to improve the employment status of protected groups. A more favorable view is that these structures are ineffective because they are intended to be "identity-blind" (Konrad & Linnehan, 1995) or to function under "a veil of ignorance as to group identification" (Glazer, 1988, p. 32) thereby supposedly eliminating discrimination based on group membership. However, Konrad and Linnehan reasoned that the impact of identity-blind structures is limited, for they do not adequately control biases against members of protected groups. Alternatively, they argue that "identity-conscious" or "race-conscious" (e.g., Glasser, 1988) structures, which include demographic group identity in HRM decision-making processes, are more effective. This is so because personnel decisions are monitored more closely and, thus, the numbers, experiences, and outcomes of protected group members are attended to more closely, with special efforts made to employ and promote them.

Empirically, Konrad and Linnehan (1995) observed, among the organizations they studied, that identity-conscious but not identity-blind HRM structures were associated positively with indicators of the employment status of people of color. Therefore, it seems vigorous law enforcement matters, likely by promoting HRM policies, practices, and procedures that are race sensitive. Weak law enforcement, on the other hand, likely promotes ineffective or simply symbolic gestures on the part of organizations subjected to them. These conclusions were drawn based upon research addressing the enforcement of federal law. However, state and local laws and the enforcement of them may matter too; only future research will tell.

Summary

We noted that the racial composition of the labor pools available to an organization is the most obvious environmental influence on its racial composition. Other environmental attributes that likely influence the race composition of organizations include: (a) the *social structure* surrounding an organization, which was argued to prime stereotypes that organizational members may use when making hiring and placement decisions; (b) the *Black population share* of the area where an organization is located, which was argued to increase negative racial attitudes brought to work as excess baggage; (c) the *customer base* of an organization, whose race composition organizational decision makers may seek to mirror among sales and service personnel; and (d) the *legal environment* of an organization, which may promote internal HRM policies, practices, and procedures that are race sensitive and effective or merely ineffective symbolic gestures toward equal opportunity. Clearly, the environment in which an organization is embedded can influence its race composition; and, it likely does so, for example, by affecting the stereotypes and prejudices of organizational decision makers and the organization's HRM climate. These mediating factors are addressed in the next section.

If we have created the impression that organizations somehow are at the mercy of their environments, it is important to correct such before moving on. Although it is the case, as stated by Scott (1998, p. 144), that "there is little doubt that environments profoundly shape organizations—their structures, their performances, their outcomes," it also is clear that "managers construct, rearrange, single out, and demolish many 'objective' features of their surroundings" (Weick, 1979, p. 164). That is, organizations and their environments are related reciprocally, and here, only the influence of environments on organizations has been considered. But of course, organizations often, for instance, do choose where they locate, the customers they target, and the labor markets from which they recruit.

INSIDE THE BOX

The environments in which organizations are embedded appear to influence their race composition. What processes, stimulated by environmental conditions, unfold inside the box (the organization) and affect race composition? In this section, we attempt to describe further some of the mechanisms linking the environment to race composition. In approaching what goes on inside the box, the term "decision" will be used frequently and very loosely; it will be taken to include implicit choices and judgments, such as letting the status quo stand. Organizational practices and policies, once in place, become institutionalized and rarely change without substantial pressure (e.g., Stinchcombe, 1965; Hannan & Freeman, 1984). This inertia, often adversely affects the representation of minorities (e.g., Bielby, 2000; Cohen, Broschak, & Haveman, 1998; Reskin, 1998). For instance, recruiting through informal networks commonly is the status quo (e.g., Marsden, 1994; Miller & Rosenbaum, 1997) and tends to reproduce the existing, and often segregated, organizational composition (Braddock & McPartland, 1987; Kalleberg, Knoke, Marsden, & Spaeth, 1996; Kasinitz & Rosenberg, 1996). (A segregated organization essentially can be composed of a race or races separated horizontally, vertically, or both.)

In addition to such important implicit decisions as maintaining the status quo, explicit HRM decisions, such as those regarding selection, placement, and recruitment, can constitute significant barriers to racial integration within organizations (e.g., Braddock & McPartland, 1987). We begin below by examining how the decision processes that link the environment to race composition may be influenced by stereotypes and prejudice.

Stereotypes and Prejudice

Recall, negative stereotypes of Blacks and prejudice toward them principally were seen as arising from the environments in which organizations are embedded rather than from the organizations themselves. Also recall that a distinction was made between negative stereotypes (cognitions) and prejudice (an attitude; e.g., Mackie & Smith, 1998). Here, because of the voluminous literature pertaining to each of these constructs and the limited space available to us, the discussion that follows necessarily will be somewhat superficial. For much more general and thorough treatments of stereotypes and prejudice, see, for example, Brief (1998), Brewer and Brown (1998), and Fiske (1998).

A *stereotype* is a set of beliefs about the personal attributes of a group of people (e.g., Hilton & von Hippel, 1996). This set of beliefs is not necessarily negative in nature; but, stereotypes of outgroups typically have more negative connotations than those of ingroups (e.g., Esses, Haddock, & Zanna, 1993). The cultural stereotypes of Blacks in America are decidedly negative, containing the beliefs that they, for example, are lazy, ignorant, and dirty (Stephan & Rosenfield, 1982). As argued earlier, knowledge or awareness of this stereotype does not equal endorsement of or belief in it. That is, we imagine most readers know that Blacks commonly are stereotyped as lazy, but, we suspect that many who are aware of this do not personally believe Blacks, in fact, are lazy. Moreover and very importantly, Bargh, Chen, and Burrows (1996) have demonstrated that negative reactions following subliminal priming of a Black stereotype are *not* moderated by level of prejudice. For instance, therefore, assuming a Black stereotype had been primed for a nonprejudiced White interviewer, he or she might *unintentionally* react negatively to a Black job applicant [e.g., by feeling uncomfortable shaking the applicant's hand (Pettigrew, 1987).] Even though unintended, these reactions of nonprejudiced persons are problematic for race composition because they may unintentionally bias personnel decisions.

Stereotypes are more troublesome in those organizations whose HRM policies and practices allow individual managers a great deal of discretion, providing little in the way of written guidelines or effective oversight (American Psychological Association, 1991; Bielby, 2000; Mittman, 1992). Such a loose HRM system can result in personnel decisions characterized as arbitrary, allowing beliefs about the undesirable characteristics of a group (e.g., Blacks) to be applied to all its members (e.g., Braddock & McPartland, 1987; Reskin, 1998). Managers who make such ascriptions tend to disregard inconsistent information and lower their expectations for members of the negatively stereotyped group (e.g., Foschi, Lai, & Sigerson, 1994; Heilman, 1984; Nieva & Gutek, 1980), resulting, for instance, in White workers being evaluated more positively than equally performing Blacks (e.g., Greenhaus, Parasuraman, & Wormley, 1990; Kraiger & Ford, 1985; but also see Roberson & Block, 2001). In addition, it is known that biased perceivers (e.g., managers endorsing a negative stereotype of Blacks) unknowingly can elicit confirmatory behaviors from members of the stigmatized group (e.g., Black job applicants) through such very subtle cues as nonverbal displays and gestures (Operario & Fiske, 2001); and these elicited behaviors can diminish interviewee performance (e.g., Word, Zanna, & Cooper, 1974).

The picture painted above is bleak, but, how accurate is it to assert that many managers act on negative racial stereotypes unless inhibited from doing so? Generalizing from studies examining how stereotypes might affect housing segregation, it appears the problem is real (e.g., Massey & Denton, 1993). Farley, Steeh, Krysan, Jackson, and Reeves (1994), for instance, found that Whites have a strong overall aversion toward living among Blacks and "a substantial minority of Whites mention stereotypes when asked direct questions about living with Blacks on their block" (p. 776). Damning proof of the reality of the problem is supplied by several recent studies documenting that employers' stereotypes about Blacks prompt them to discriminate against Black job applicants (e.g., Kasinitz & Rosenberg, 1996; Kirschenman & Neckerman, 1991; Moss & Tilly, 1996; Neckerman & Kirschenman, 1991).

The following quotes from employers in the Chicago area exemplify the data (Wilson, 1996):

> The general manager of an inner-city hotel stated, "I see far more Blacks thinking the employer has the obligation to give him a check for doing nothing." (p. 112)

> A vice president of an offset printing firm stated, "Well, I worked with them in the military, and the first chance they get, they'll slack off, they don't want to do the job, they feel like they don't have to, they're a minority. They want to take the credit and shift the blame." (pp. 118–119)

The above statements not only depict stereotype content, but also they can be taken to indicate that those who made them endorse the negative stereotype's content and, therefore, could be labeled as blatantly racist. Such racism clearly has declined over the course of the last quarter century, with Brief and Barsky (2000) [based upon data reported by Schuman, Steeh, Bobo, and Krysan (1997)] estimating that slightly more than 10% of the United States' adult, White population still openly endorse negative stereotypes of Blacks. However, the situation in organizations may be much more problematic than a 10% estimate of blatant racists might suggest. As so aptly put by Dovidio and Gaertner (1998), racial prejudice in America is a virus that has mutated. This mutated virus is a blend of early learned racial fears and stereotypes (evident as a residue of negative racial sentiments) and such treasured American values as individualism and self-reliance (reflected in deep-seated feelings of social morality and propriety; Kinder & Sears, 1981). Those infected by this new virus [which we will call "modern racism" (McConahay, 1986)] do not necessarily show outward signs of being ill nor are they aware of their illness (see, for example, Gaertner & Dovidio, 1986; Greenwald & Banaji, 1995). Those who endorse the ideology of modern racism fail to define their beliefs and attitudes as racist and act in ways to protect a nonprejudicial, nondiscriminatory self-image. For modern racists to behave consistently with their (unconscious) negative racial attitudes requires that they have available "a plausible, nonprejudiced explanation for what might be considered prejudiced behavior" (McConahay, 1986, p. 100).

Based upon the above, the behaviors of modern racists within organizations would be expected to be no different than nonprejudiced persons unless they are embedded in an organizational context that supplies them with an appropriate (seemingly nonprejudiced) justification to discriminate against Blacks. For example, a manager may not want to place a Black applicant in the presumably awkward position as the first person of color in a socially tight all-White work team or take the risk of placing a Black person in the position of supervising a group of potentially hostile Whites.

These business related justifications, like the one evoked by Shoney's CEO, also may serve to release modern racists to act. This phenomenon has been demonstrated experimentally. Brief et al. (2000) showed that the sorts of business justifications we have identified produce a significant association between scores on a measure of modern racism and discriminatory behaviors and that this association is *not* present in conditions void of such justifications. These results suggest that modern racists in organizational settings hold themselves in check unless supplied with a business justification to discriminate. [For more on this subtle, new form of racism, see, for example, Lambert, Cronen, Chasteen, and Lickel (1996); Monteith, Deneen, and Tooman (1996); Schnake and Ruscher (1998); von Hipple, Sekaquaptewa, and Vargas (1997); and Wittenbrink, Judd, and Park (1997).]

In this section, we focused on "negative" forms of prejudice leading to discrimination and ignored "positive" forms and their consequences (Brewer and Brown, 1998). Of the material we neglected, this troubles us the most, for the consequences of "positive" prejudice likely are exceedingly common. "Positive" prejudice, at least in the form of ingroup favoritism, often entails according more positive outcomes to the members of one's ingroup than to the members of some outgroup, without treating the outgroup members negatively. For more on this phenomenon, see Brewer (1997).

In summary, negative racial stereotypes and racial prejudice imported into organizations affect personnel decisions. The function of stereotypes and prejudice in personnel decision making and subsequently, in the determination of the race composition of organizations, may be quite evident, for example, among those relatively few individuals driven by blatant racism. Alternatively, and we believe much more commonly, their role is considerably less noticeable, characterized, for instance, as subtle and rationalizable. The influence of stereotypes and this more subtle kind of prejudice likely will be more difficult to track from the environment into organizations, but, a fuller understanding of the race composition of organizations demands we give it a try.

The Role of HRM

The sociology literature tells us about the influence of environmental factors (e.g., the law and the vigor with which it is enforced) on HRM systems. HRM researchers, on the other hand, have addressed the consequences of such systems (or cluster of practices) for organizational effectiveness, defined, for instance, in terms of turnover, productivity, and profitability (e.g., Arthur, 1994; Huselid, 1995), not race composition. Moreover, based upon Becker and Gerhart's (1996) observations of the HRM-organization effectiveness literature, little or no attention has been paid to why a specific cluster of practices has the effects that it does. So, one currently cannot turn to the HRM literature to learn how or why HRM systems might influence the race composition of organizations. Clearly, there is a need for those that profess an interest in strategic human resource management (e.g., Jackson & Schuler, 1995; Lengnick-Hall & Lengnick-Hall, 1988) to consider broadening the dimensions of organizational effectiveness they attend to, emphasizing the development of process knowledge.

What do we know about the role of HRM inside the box? As noted earlier, HRM systems that provide written guidelines and effective oversight reduce managerial discretion, thereby promoting racial integration (e.g., Mittman, 1992). Moreover, if these formalized systems are identity-conscious (i.e., race-conscious), the employment status of people of color will be enhanced further (e.g., Konrad & Linnehan, 1995). Supporting the former assertions are various arguments, and considerable empirical evidence, that bureaucratizing HRM practices undermines "ascription" [allocating status, position, or opportunity based, at least in part, on an ascribed characteristic such as race (e.g., Parsons, 1964)] (e.g., Pfeffer and Cohen, 1984; Sutton, Dobbin, Meyer, and Scott, 1994; Szafran, 1982). Support for the positive consequences of identity-conscious (vs. identity-blind) formalized HRM systems is less prevalent. It is known that the sheer existence of goals for minorities' and women's representation in organizations fosters hiring members of those groups (e.g., Leonard, 1985, 1990) and that evaluating and rewarding managers on the basis of their progress toward achieving such goals also enhances representation (e.g., Reskin, 1998).

Conceptually, what might all of this mean? It may be the case that formalized HRM systems supply the tools necessary to inhibit discrimination based upon race. These tools might include posting job openings and advertising them in public media in lieu of sole reliance on word-of-mouth recruiting (e.g., Marsden, 1994), and using achievement and aptitude tests in addition to interviews (e.g., Neckerman & Kirschemman, 1991). Race-conscious goals (and the monitoring of them), based upon the ideas of Locke and Latham (1990) may (a) direct attention to goal-relevant behaviors and outcomes, (b) motivate the exertion and persistence of goal-relevant efforts, and (c) stimulate the development of strategies for goal attainment (including planning). Also drawing from Locke and Latham's ideas, the rewards/sanctions attached to goal progress may promote a determination (or commitment) to attain a goal of racial diversity. In summary, whereas formalized HRM systems may provide the means for constructing a racially integrated organization, goals can provide the incentive to do so.

In attempting to understand the processes by which HRM influences race composition, we hope researchers are intrigued by the importance we have placed on goals. We, therefore, think it is worthwhile to fuel the fire by speculating a bit more about race-conscious goals. Extrapolating from Ely and Thomas's (2001) research on cultural diversity, we see the rationale for race-conscious goals in organizations being framed in one of three ways: (a) to eliminate unjust discrimination, (b) to gain access to and legitimacy with minority markets and constituent groups, or (c) to provide a resource for learning and adaptive change. These rationales, we suspect, have long-term consequences for race composition, particularly in regard to vertical integration. For instance, given the positive influence on workgroup processes and outcomes Ely and Thomas (2001) observed for the learning/adaptive change perspective relative to the eliminate discrimination and access/legitimacy perspectives, we speculate that a learning/adaptive change rationale for race-conscious goals is more likely to yield a sustained effort to achieve racial diversity, resulting in people of color fairly represented at all levels of an organization.

Again, we have argued that environmental forces influence the existence of formalized HRM systems within organizations that, in turn, can affect positively race composition. In this section, we largely have speculated how and why those systems operate the way they do. Others relying on the same literatures may be led to alternative, even contradictory, speculations. For example, although some evidence noted above indicates that firms relying primarily on interviews to screen applicants employ fewer Blacks than those who do not (e.g., Moss & Tilley, 1995), the results of a meta-analysis of 31 studies in the applied psychology literature indicated that employment interviews as a whole do not appear to adversely affect minorities nearly as much as do ability tests (Huffcutt and Roth, 1998; but also see Roth, Van Iddekinge, Huffcutt, Eidson, and Bobko, 2002). Based upon these meta-analytic results, one might speculate that interviews in the selection process are more likely to inhibit discrimination based on race than those primarily relying on test results.

CONCLUSIONS

The take-home message of this chapter is a simple one that regrettably often has been ignored by organizational psychologists: Organizations are reflections of their environments. As we have shown in regards to matters of race, environmental conditions can generate actions within organizations as well as constrain them. Managers, therefore, should not be viewed as "free agents," able to choose the problems they tackle and the solutions they apply; rather, managers, despite their best intentions, often are presented with problems they cannot ignore and sometimes are required to impose solutions they may see as dubious. Thus, to understand how the race composition of organizations comes about requires one to look both outside (in the environment) and inside (in the organization) the box. Traditional, discipline-bound research will not work.

What might the required research look like? To provide one answer to this question, let us begin by returning to the place where Detroit and Minneapolis were used as examples. It was claimed that the attitudes of Whites in Detroit may be more negative toward Blacks than those of Whites in Minneapolis, because the local Black population share is larger in Detroit (81.6%) than in Minneapolis (18.0%). This claim was based on the idea that sizeable minority populations increase White hostility toward minorities as a result of competition among the groups. Following this line of thought, one would hypothesize that Black population shares across cities are associated positively with the negative racial attitudes of White decision makers in organizations embedded in those cities. For instance, one would expect White organizational decision makers in Detroit to be more prejudiced than those in Minneapolis. Also, based on arguments previously advanced, one would hypothesize that this prejudice would be associated negatively with the fair representation of Blacks in organizations. (One simply could not study the number of Black employees, because, as Black population share increases, the aggregate number of Black employees within an organization would be expected to increase also.) Therefore, a more complete story would go as follows: The negative association between Black population share and the fair representation of Blacks in organizations is mediated by the level of prejudice of White organizational decision makers. Relying once again on previously advanced arguments, this story easily could be complicated further. It would be reasonable to hypothesize that the negative relationship between the level of prejudice of White organizational decision makers and the fair representation of Blacks is moderated by the degree to which an organization's formalized HRM systems are race-conscious; the more race-conscious, the weaker the relationship.

Methodologically, what might be required to test these three hypotheses? One would need a sample of cities that varied by Black population share, at least one organization in each of those cities whose type (e.g., bank) is held constant, and a sample of White decision makers in each of these organizations. One also would need to develop indicator(s), for instance, of the "fair representation of Blacks in organizations" and to obtain scores on a measure of prejudice from White organizational decision makers, which, practically speaking, is a daunting task (see, for example, James, Brief, Dietz, & Cohen, 2001). Given the data needed, then come problems of aggregating individual responses to measures of racial attitudes up to the organization level of analysis and problems of conducting statistical analyses appropriately sensitive to the cross-level inferences required. Ignoring the methodological issues not raised, the picture we have painted likely would be seen as bleak by virtually any social scientist, be he or she an economist, psychologist, or sociologist.

The research we are calling for is tough stuff but absolutely necessary and achievable, either in more piecemeal or comprehensive ways. Early on in this chapter, it was demonstrated clearly that Blacks still have not been integrated fully into America's work organizations, and, we, with the tools available for doing the job, have an obligation to produce knowledge that can fuel solutions to this continuing economic and social dilemma (Brief & Hayes, 1997). Tackling the problem piecemeal obviously is the most reasonable way to proceed, but, no matter what, we see the need for sampling organizations—a research tactic not often used by organizational psychologists. An attractive, more holistic model for doing so is available: the National Organization Study (NOS) (e.g., Kalleberg et al., 1996; Spaeth & O'Rourke, 1996). The NOS, primarily funded by the National Science Foundation, consists of information obtained from a nationally representative sample of organizations. This information pertains to "multiple levels of the work establishment, the larger organizational setting (if any) of which it is a part, and the work experiences of an employee within it" (Kalleberg et al., 1996, p. 18). Research psychologists, with their bent for multiple-item measures and relatively large samples at the individual level of analysis, may not find the NOS especially attractive. That is not the point. What is important is that the NOS provides an excellent, large-scale example of a study that entailed sampling many organizations and incorporating measures of organizational and individual characteristics. It also is noteworthy that the NOS was funded by the United States government. It appears desirable that organizational psychologists put their heads together (probably with organizational sociologists) to design the sort of studies that will allow one to understand better the how and why of race composition as a reflection of an organization's environment. Once designed, the federal government ought to be lobbied to support such research.

We would like to add another practical note, this one aimed at managers and those who consult to them on diversity issues. If we are right about the importance of environments, organizational leaders need to recognize that the resources they expend on improving race relations at work should be coupled with like expenditures within the communities where their employees live. Again, "employees come to the organization with heavy cultural and social baggage" (Scott, 1987, p. 19), and, it would be naïve to assume that even if this baggage could be unloaded in the workplace that it would not be repacked the same way at home.

We close by noting that the scope of this chapter has been limited intentionally to a concern with environmental influences on the *race* composition of organizations. Given the literature from which many of our arguments were drawn (that sociological body of evidence addressing the race *and* sex composition of organizations), we are confident many of the ideas advanced also should be helpful for understanding the distribution of women across jobs in organizations. Beyond race and sex, the chapter demonstrates how the problems of employment discrimination experienced, for instance, by gays and lesbians in America or by the Turkish in Germany might be approached. Once more, our thesis is a simple one: What goes on inside organizations is influenced by what is happening outside them. So, for example, how Germans tend to stereotype the Turkish will influence the personnel decisions made in a German firm about the selection and placement of Turkish job applicants; these decisions, in turn, will help shape the Turkish composition of the organization. Only looking inside organizations severely limits the development of the knowledge needed to tackle the problem of employment discrimination experienced by so many groups of people in America and around the world.

REFERENCES

Alexis, M. (1998). Assessing 50 years of African-American economic status, 1940–1990. *The American Economic Review, 88*, 368–375.

Allport, G. W. (1954). *The nature of prejudice*. Reading, MA: Addison-Wesley.

American Psychological Association. (1991). In the Supreme Court of the United States: Price Waterhouse v. Ann B. Hopkins. Amicus Curiae Brief for the American Psychological Association. *American Psychologist, 46*, 1061–1070.

Arthur, J. B. (1994). Effects of human resource systems on manufacturing performance and turnover. *Academy of Management Journal, 37*, 670–687.

Bargh, J. A., Chen, M., & Burrows, L. (1996). Automaticity of social behavior: Direct effects of trait construct and stereotype activation on action. *Journal of Personality and Social Psychology, 71*, 230–244.

Barnard, C. (1938). *The functions of the executive*. Cambridge, MA: Harvard University Press.

Baron, J. N., & Bielby, W. T. (1980). Bringing the firm back in: Stratification, segmentation, and the organization of work. *American Sociological Review, 45*, 737–765.

Baron, J. N., & Bielby, W. T. (1985). Organizational barriers to gender equality: Sex segregation of jobs and opportunities. In A. Rossi (Ed.), *Gender and the life course* (pp. 33–47). New York: Aldline.

Bayton, J. A., McAlister, L. B., & Hamer, J. (1956). Race-class stereotypes. *Journal of Negro Education, 25*, 75–78.

Becker, B., & Gerhart, B. (1996). The impact of human resource management on organizational performance: Progress and prospects. *Academy of Management Journal, 39*, 779–801.

Bendick, M. Jr. (1998). Adding testing to the nation's portfolio of information on employment discrimination. In M. Fix and M. A. Turner (Eds.), *A national report card on discrimination: The role of testing*. Washington, DC: The Urban Institute.

Bendick, M., Jr., Jackson, C. W., & Reinoso, V. A. (1994). Measuring employment discrimination through controlled experiments. In F. L. Pincus and H. J. Ehrlich (Eds.), *Race and ethnic conflict: Contending views on prejudice, discrimination, and ethnoviolence*. Boulder, CO: Westview.

Bertrand, M., & Mullainathan, S. (2003). *Are Emily and Brendan more employable than Lakisha and Jamal? A field experiment on labor market discrimination*. Unpublished manuscript, University of Chicago GSB/MIT working paper.

Bettelheim, B., & Janowitz, M. (1964). *Social change and prejudice*. New York: The Free Press.

Bielby, W. T. (2000). Minimizing workplace gender and racial bias. *Contemporary Sociology, 29*, 120–129.

Blau, P. M. (1977). *Inequality and heterogeneity*. New York: The Free Press.

Blumer, H. (1958). Racial prejudice as a sense of group position. *Pacific Sociological Review, 1*, 3–7.

Bobo, L. D., & Suh, S. A. (2000). Surveying racial discrimination: Analyses from a multiethnic labor market. In L. D. Bobo, M. L. Oliver, J. H. Johnson, Jr., & A. Valenzeula, Jr. (Eds.), *Prismatic metropolis: Inequality in Los Angeles*. New York: Russell Sage Foundation.

Braddock, J. H., III, & McPartland, J. M. (1987). How minorities continue to be excluded from equal employment opportunities: Research on labor market and institutional barriers. *Journal of Social Issues, 43*, 5–39.

Brewer, M. B. (1997). The social psychology of intergroup relations: Can research inform practice? *Journal of Social Issues, 53*, 197–211.

Brewer, M. B., & Brown, R. J. (1998). Intergroup relations. In D. T. Gilbert, S. T. Fiske, & G. Lindzey (Eds.), *The handbook of social psychology* (Vol. 2, pp. 554–594). New York: McGraw-Hill.

Brief, A. P. (1998). *Attitudes in and around organizations*. Thousand Oaks, CA: Sage.

Brief, A. P., & Barsky, A. (2000). Establishing a climate for diversity: Inhibition of prejudice reactions in the workplace. In G. R. Ferris (Ed.), *Research in personnel and human resources management* (pp. 91–129). Greenwich, CT: JAI.

Brief, A. P., Dietz, J., Cohen, R. R., Pugh, S. D., & Vaslow, J. B. (2000). Just doing business: Modern racism and obedience to authority as explanations for employment discrimination. *Organizational Behavior and Human Decision Processes, 81*, 72–97.

Brief, A. P., & Hayes, E. L. (1997). The continuing "American dilemma": Studying racism in organizations. In C. L. Cooper & D. M. Rouseau (Eds.), *Trends in organizational behavior* (Vol. 4, pp. 89–105). Chichester, UK: Wiley.

Brown, C. (1982). The Federal attack on labor market discrimination: The mouse that roared? In R. Ehrenberg (Ed.), *Research in labor economics* (Vol. 5, pp. 33–68). Greenwich, CT: JAI.

Burr, J. A., Galle, O. R., & Fossett, M. A. (1991). Racial occupational inequality in Southern metropolitan areas, 1940–1980: Revisiting the visibility—discrimination hypothesis. *Social Forces, 69*, 831–850.

Cawley, J., Heckman, J., & Vytlacil, E. (1999). Meritocracy in America: Wages within and across occupations. *Industrial Relations, 38*, 250–296.

Cohen, Y., & Pfeffer, J. (1986). Organizational hiring standards. *Administrative Science Quarterly, 31*, 1–24.

Cohen, L. E., Broschak, J. P., & Haveman, H. A. (1998). And then there were more? The effect of organizational sex composition on the hiring and promotion of managers. *American Sociological Review, 63*, 711–727.

Cohn, S. (2000). *Race and gender discrimination at work*. Oxford: Westview Press.

Collins, S. (1989). The marginalization of Black executives. *Social Problems, 36*, 369–331.

Couch, K., & Daly, M. C. (2002). Black–White wage inequality in the 1990s: A decade of progress. *Economic Inquiry, 40*, 31–41.

Cox, T. (1993). *Cultural Diversity in organizations: Theory, research, and practice*. San Francisco: Berrett-Koehler.

Cox, T. H., Jr., & Blake, S. (1991). Managing cultural diversity: Implications for organizational competitiveness. *The Executive, 5*, 45–56.

Cox, T., Jr., & Nkomo, S. M. (1986). Differential performance appraisal criteria: A field study of Black and White managers. *Group and Organization Studies, 11*, 101–119.

Cox, T., Jr., & Nkomo, S. M. (1990). Invisible men and women: A status report on race as a variable in organization behavior research. *Journal of Organizational Behavior, 11*, 419–431.

Crosby, F., Bromley, S., & Saxe, L. (1980). Recent unobtrusive studies of Black and White discrimination and prejudice: A literature review. *Psychological Bulletin, 87*, 546–563.

Deitch, E. A., Barsky, A., Butz, R. M., Brief, A. P., Chan, S. S. Y., & Bradley, J. C. (2004). *Subtle yet significant: The existence and impact of everyday racial discrimination in the workplace*. *Human Relations, 56*, 1299–1324.

Devine, P. G. (1989). Stereotypes and prejudice: Their automatic and controlled components. *Journal of Personality and Social Psychology, 56*, 5–18.

Dill, W. R. (1958). Environment as an influence on managerial autonomy. *Administrative Science Quarterly, 2*, 409–443.

Donohue, J., & Siegelman, P. (1991). The changing nature of employment discrimination litigation. *Stanford Law Review, 43*, 983–1033.

Dovidio, J. F., & Gaertner, S. L. (1998). On the nature of contemporary prejudice: The causes, consequences, and challenges of aversive racism. In J. L. Eberhardt & S. T. Fiske (Eds.), *Confronting racism: The problem and the response* (pp. 3–32). New York: Sage.

Eagly, A. H. (1987). *Sex differences in social behavior: A social-role interpretation*. Hillsdale, NJ: Lawrence Erlbaum Associates.

Eagly, A. H. (1995). The science and politics of comparing women and men. *American Psychologist, 50*, 145–158.

Eagly, A. H., & Steffen, V. J. (1986). Gender stereotypes, occupational roles, and beliefs about part-time employees. *Psychology of Women Quarterly, 10*, 252–262.

Edelman, L. B. (1992). Legal ambiguity and symbolic structures: Organizational mediation of civil rights law. *American Journal of Sociology, 97*, 1531–1576.

Edelman, L. B., & Petterson, S. M. (1999). Symbols and substance in organizational response to civil rights law. *Research in Social Stratification and Mobility, 17*, 107–135.

Ely, R. J., & Thomas, D. A. (2001). Cultural diversity at work: The effects of diversity perspectives on work group processes. *Administrative Science Quarterly, 46*, 229–273.

Emerson, M. O. (1994). Is it different in dixie? Percent Black and residential segregation in the south and non-south. *Sociological Quarterly, 35*, 571–580.

Essed, P. (1991). *Understanding everyday racism*. Newbury Park, CA: Sage.

Esses, V. M., Haddock, G., & Zanna, M. P. (1993). Values, stereotypes, and emotions as determinants of intergroup attitudes. In D. M. Mackie & D. L. Hamilton (Eds.), *Affect, cognition, and stereotyping: Interactive processes in group perception* (pp. 137–166). San Diego: Academic Press.

Farley, R., Steeh, C., Krysan, M., Jackson, T., & Reeves, K. (1994). *American Journal of Sociology, 100*, 750–780.

Firebaugh, G., & Davis, K. E. (1988). Trends in antiblack prejudice, 1972–1984: Region and cohort effects. *American Journal of Sociology, 94*, 251–272.

Fiske, S. T. (1998). Stereotyping, prejudice, and discrimination. In D. T. Gilbert, S. T. Fiske, & G. Lindzey (Eds.), *The handbook of social psychology* (Vol. 2, pp. 357–411). New York: McGraw-Hill.

Foschi, M., Lai, L., & Sigerson, K. (1994). Gender and double standards in the assessment of job applicants. *Social Psychology Quarterly, 57*, 326–339.

Fossett, M. A., & Kiecolt, K. J. (1989). The relative size of minority populations and White racial attitudes. *Social Science Quarterly, 70*, 820–835.

Frisbie, W. P., & Neidert, L. (1977). Inequality and the relative size of minority populations: A comparative analysis. *American Journal of Sociology, 82*, 1007–1030.

Gaertner, S. L., & Dovidio, J. F. (1986). The aversive form of racism. In J. F. Dovidio & S. L. Gaertner (Eds.), *Prejudice, discrimination, and racism* (pp. 61–89). New York: Academic Press.

Giles, M. W., & Evans, A. S. (1985). External threat, perceived threat, and group identity. *Social Science Quarterly, 66*, 50–66.

Giles, M. W., & Evans, A. S. (1986). The power approach to intergroup hostility. *Journal of Conflict Resolution, 30*, 469–486.

Gill, A. (1989). The role of discrimination in determining occupational structure. *Industrial and Labor Relations Review, 42*, 610–623.

Glaser, J. M. (1994). Back to the black belt: Racial environment and White racial attitudes in the South. *Journal of Politics, 56*, 21–41.

Glasser, I. (1988). Affirmative action and the legacy of racial injustice. In P. A. Katz & D. A. Taylor (Eds.), *Eliminating racism: Profiles in controversy* (pp. 341–357). New York: Plenum.

Glazer, N. (1988). The future of preferential affirmative action. In P. A. Katz & D. A. Taylor (Eds.), *Eliminating racism: Profiles in controversy* (pp. 329–339). New York: Plenum.

Greenhaus, J. H., Parasuraman, S., & Wormley, W. M. (1990). Effects of race on organizational experiences, job performance evaluations, and career outcomes. *Academy of Management Journal, 33*, 64–86.

Greenwald, A. G., & Banaji, M. R. (1995). Implicit social cognition: Attitudes, self-esteem, and stereotypes. *Psychological Review, 102*, 4–27.

Hannan, M. T., & Freeman, J. (1984). Structural inertia and organizational change. *American Sociological Review, 49*, 149–164.

Heckman, J. J. (1998). Detecting discrimination. *Journal of Economic Perspectives, 12*, 101–116.

Heilman, M. E. (1984). Information as a deterrent against sex discrimination: The effects of applicant sex and information type on preliminary employment decisions. *Organizational Behavior and Human Decision Processes, 33*, 174–186.

Heilman, M. E. (1995). Sex stereotypes and their effects in the workplace: What we know and what we don't know. *Journal of Social Behavior and Personality, 10*, 3–26.

Hilton, J. L., & von Hippel, W. (1996). Stereotypes. *Annual Review of Psychology, 47*, 237–271.

Hoffman, C., & Hurst, N. (1990). Gender stereotypes: Perception or rationalization? *Journal of Personality and Social Psychology, 58*, 197–208.

Holzer, H. J. (1998). Employer skill demands and labor market outcomes of blacks and women. *Industrial and Labor Relations Review, 52*, 82–98.

Holzer, H. J., & Ihlanfeldt, K. R. (1998). Customer discrimination and employment outcomes for minority workers. *Quarterly Journal of Economics, 113*, 835–867.

Huffcut, A. I., & Roth, P. L. (1998). Racial group differences in employment interview evaluations. *Journal of Applied Psychology, 83*, 179–189.

Huselid, M. A. (1995). The impact of human resource management practices on turnover, productivity, and corporate financial performance. *Academy of Management Journal, 38*, 635–672.

Jackson, S. E., & Schuler, R. S. (1995). Understanding human resource management in the context of organizations and their environments. *Annual Review of Psychology, 46,* 237–264.

James, E. H., Brief, A. P., Dietz, J., & Cohen, R. R. (2001). Prejudice matters: Understanding the reactions of Whites to affirmative action programs targeted to benefit Blacks. *Journal of Applied Psychology, 86,* 1120–1128.

Jones, E. W. (1973, July). What it's like to be a black manager. *Harvard Business Review, 51,* 114.

Jost, J. T., & Banaji, M. R. (1994). The role of stereotyping in system-justification and the production of false consciousness. *British Journal of Social Psychology, 33,* 1–27.

Kalleberg, A. L., Knoke, D., Marsden, P. V., & Spaeth, J. L. (1996). *Organizations in America: Analyzing their structures and human resource practices.* Newbury Park, CA: Sage.

Kanter, R. M. (1977). *Men and women of the corporation.* New York: Basic Books.

Kasinitz, P., & Rosenberg, J. (1996). Missing the connection: Social isolation and employment on the Brooklyn waterfront. *Social Problems, 43,* 180–196.

Kinder, D. R., & Sears, D. O. (1981). Prejudice and politics: Symbolic racism versus racial threats to the good life. *Journal of Personality and Social Psychology, 40,* 414–431.

Kirschenman, J., & Neckerman, K. M. (1991). "We'd love to hire them, but…": The meaning of race for employers. In C. Jencks & P. E. Peterson (Eds.), *The urban underclass.* Washington, DC: The Brookings Institution.

Konrad, A. M., & Linnehan, F. (1995). Formalized HRM structures: Coordinating equal employment opportunity or concealing organizational practices? *Academy of Management Journal, 38,* 787–820.

Kraiger, K., & Ford, J. K. (1985). A meta-analysis of ratee race effects in performance ratings. *Journal of Applied Psychology, 70,* 56–65.

Lambert, A. J., Cronen, S., Chasteen, A. L., & Lickel, B. (1996). Private vs public expressions of racial prejudice. *Journal of Experimental Social Psychology, 32,* 437–459.

Lefkowitz, J. (1994). Race as a factor in job placement: Serendipitous findings of "ethnic drift." *Personnel Psychology, 47,* 497–513.

Lengnick-Hall, C. A., & Lengnick-Hall, M. L. (1988). Strategic human resources management: A review of the literature and a proposed typology. *Academy of Management Review, 13,* 454–470.

Leonard, J. S. (1984). Employment and occupations advance under affirmative action. *Review of Economics and Statistics, 66,* 377–385.

Leonard, J. S. (1985). The effect of unions on the employment of blacks, hispanics, and women. *Industrial and Labor Relations Review, 39,* 115–132.

Leonard, J. S. (1989). The changing face of employees and employment regulation. *California Management Review, 31,* 29–38.

Leonard, J. S. (1990). The impact of affirmative action regulation and equal opportunity law on black employment. *Journal of Economic Perspectives, 4,* 47–63.

LeVine, R. A., & Campbell, D. T. (1972). *Ethnocentrism: Theories of conflict, ethnic attitudes, and group behavior.* New York: Wiley.

Lieberson, S. (1980). The interpretation of net migration rates. *Sociological Methodology, 11,* 176–190.

Locke, E. A., & Latham, G. P. (1990). Work motivation and satisfaction: Light at the end of the tunnel. *Psychological Science, 1,* 240–246.

Mackie, D. M., & Smith, E. R. (1998). Intergroup relations: Insights from a theoretically integrative approach. *Psychological Review, 105,* 499–529.

Mare, R. D. (1995). Changes in educational attainment and school enrollment. In R. Farley (Ed.), *State of the union: America in the 1990s* (Vol. 1, pp. 155–214). New York: Russell Sage Foundation.

Marsden, P. V. (1994). Selection methods in US establishments. *Acta Sociologica, 37,* 287–301.

Martell, R. F., Lane, D. M., & Emrich, C. (1996). Male-female differences: A computer simulation. *American Psychologist, 51*, 157–158.

Massey, D. S., & Denton, N. A. (1993). Racial identity and the spatial assimilation of Mexicans in the United States. *Social Science Research, 21*, 235–260.

McConahay, J. B. (1986). Modern racism, ambivalence, and the Modern Racism Scale. In J. F. Dovidio & S. L. Gaertner (Eds.), *Prejudice, discrimination, and racism* (pp. 91–125). New York: Academic Press.

Miller, S. R., & Rosenbaum, J. (1997). Hiring in a Hobbesian world: Social infrastructure and employers' use of information. *Work and Occupations, 24*, 498–523.

Mincy, R. B. (1993). The Urban Institute audit studies: Their research and policy context. In M. Fix & R. J. Struyk (Eds.), *Clear and convincing evidence: Measurement of discrimination in America*. Washington, DC: The Urban Institute Press.

Mitra, A. (1999). The allocation of Blacks in large firms and establishments and Black–White wage inequality in the U.S. economy. *Sociological Inquiry, 69*, 382–403.

Mittman, B. S. (1992). Theoretical and methodological issues in the study of organizational demography and demographic change. *Research in the Sociology of Organizations, 10*, 3–53.

Monteith, M. J., Deneen, N. E., & Tooman, G. D. (1996). The effect of social norm activation on the expression of opinions concerning gay men and Blacks. *Basic and Applied Social Psychology, 18*, 267–288.

Moss, P., & Tilly, C. (1995). Skills and race in hiring: Quantitative findings from face-to-face interviews. *Eastern Economic Journal, 21*, 357–374.

Moss, P., & Tilly, C. (1996). "Soft" skills and race: An investigation of Black men's employment problems. *Work and Occupations, 23*, 252–276.

Mueller, C. W., Parcel, T. L., & Kazuko, T. (1989). Particularism in authority outcomes of Black and White supervisors. *Social Science Research, 18*, 1–20.

Nagel, J. (1995). Resource competition theories. *American Behavioral Scientist, 38*, 442–458.

Neal, D. A., & Johnson, W. R. (1996). The role of pre-market factors in Black-White wage differences. *Journal of Political Economy, 104*, 869–895.

Neckerman, K. M., & Kirschenman, J. (1991). Hiring strategies, racial bias, and inner-city workers. *Social Problems, 38*, 433–447.

Neumark, D. (1999). Wage differentials by race and sex: The roles of taste discrimination and labor market information. *Industrial Relations, 38*, 414–445.

Nieva, V. F., & Gutek, B. A. (1980). Sex effects on evaluation. *Academy of Management Review, 5*, 267–276.

Operario, D., & Fiske, S. T. (2001). Causes and consequences of stereotypes in organizations. In M. London (Ed.), *How people evaluate others in organizations: Applied in psychology*. Mahwah, NJ: Lawrence Erlbaum Associates.

Parsons, T. (1964). *Essays in sociological theory*. Glencoe, IL: The Free Press.

Pettigrew, A. M. (1987). Context and action in the transformation of the firm. *Journal of Management Studies, 24*, 649–670.

Pettigrew, T. F. (1959). Regional differences in anti-Negro prejudice. *Journal of Abnormal and Social Psychology, 59*, 28–36.

Pfeffer, J. (1983). Organizational demography. In L. L. Cummings & B. M. Staw (Eds.), *Research in organizational behavior* (Vol. 5, pp. 299–357). Greenwich, CT: JAI.

Pfeffer, J., & Salancik, G. (1978). *The external control of organizations: A resource dependence perspective*. New York: Harper & Row.

Pfeffer, J., & Cohen, Y. (1984). Determinants of internal labor markets in organizations. *Administrative Science Quarterly, 29*, 550–572.

Quillian, L. (1996). Group threat and regional change in attitudes toward African-Americans. *American Journal of Sociology, 102*, 816–860.

Reskin, B. F. (1998). *The realities of affirmative action in employment.* Washington, DC: American Sociological Association.

Reskin, B. F., McBrier, D. B., & Kmec, J. A. (1999). The determinants and consequences of workplace sex and race composition. *Annual Review of Sociology, 25,* 335–361.

Roberson, L., & Block, C. J. (2001). Racioethnicity and job performance: A review and critique of theoretical perspectives on the causes of group differences. *Research in Organizational Behavior, 23,* 247–326.

Roth, P. L., Van Iddekinge, C. H., Huffcutt, A. I., Eidson, C. E., Jr, & Bobko, P. (2002). Corrections for range restriction in structured interview ethnic group differences: The values may be larger than researchers thought. *Journal of Applied Psychology, 87,* 369–376.

Schnake, S. B., & Ruscher, J. B. (1998). Modern racism as a predictor of the linguistic intergroup bias. *Journal of Language and Social Psychology, 17,* 484–491.

Schuman, H., Steeh, C., Bobo, L., & Krysan, M. (1997). *Racial attitudes in America: Trends and interpretations, revised edition.* Cambridge, MA: Harvard University Press.

Scott, W. R. (1987). *Organizations: Rational, natural and open systems* (2nd ed.). Englewood Cliffs, NJ: Prentice-Hall.

Scott, W. R. (1998). *Organizations: Rational, natural and open systems* (4th ed.). Upper Saddle River, NJ: Prentice-Hall.

Sherif, M. (1967). *Social interaction: Process and products.* Chicago: Aldine-Atherton.

Sidanius, J., & Pratto, F. (1999). *Social dominance: An intergroup theory of social hierarchy and oppression.* Cambridge, MA: Cambridge University Press.

Skrypnek, B. J., & Snyder, N. (1982). On the self-perpetuating nature of stereotypes about women and men. *Journal of Experimental Social Psychology, 18,* 277–291.

Spaeth, J. L., & O'Rourke, D. P. (1996). Design of the National Organizations Study. In A. L. Kalleberg, D. Knoke, P. V. Marsden, & J. L. Spaeth (Eds.), *Organizations in America: Analyzing their structures and human resource practices* (pp. 23–39). Thousand Oaks, CA: Sage.

Stephan, W., & Rosenfield, D. (1982). Racial and ethnic stereotypes. In A. Miller (Ed.), *The eye of the beholder: Contemporary issues in stereotyping* (pp. 112–148). New York: Praeger.

Stinchcombe, A. L. (1965). Social structure and organizations. In J. G. March (Ed.), *Handbook of organizations* (pp. 142–193). Chicago: Rand McNally.

Stroebe, W., & Insko, C. A. (1989). Stereotype, prejudice, and discrimination: Changing conceptions in theory and research. In D. Bar-Tal, C. F. Graumann, A. W. Kruglanski, & W. Stroebe (Eds.) *Stereotyping and prejudice: Changing conceptions* (pp. 3–34). Berlin: Springer.

Sutton, J. R., Dobbin, F., Meyer, J. W., & Scott, W. R. (1994). The legalization of the workplace. *American Journal of Sociology, 99,* 944–971.

Szafran, R. F. (1982). What kinds of firms hire and promote women and Blacks? A review of the literature. *Sociological Quarterly, 23,* 171–190.

Taylor, M. C. (1998). How White attitudes vary with the racial composition of local populations: Numbers count. *American Sociological Review, 63,* 512–535.

Thompson, J. D. (1967). *Organizations in action.* New York: McGrawHill.

Tienda, M., & Lii, D. (1987). Minority concentration and earnings inequality: Blacks, Hispanics, and Asians compared. *American Journal of Sociology, 93,* 141–165.

Turner, M. A., Fix, M., & Struyk, R. J. (1991). Hiring discrimination against Black men. *The Urban Institute Policy and Research Report, Summer,* 4–5.

U.S. Bureau of the Census (2000). *Overview of race and Hispanic origin.* Washington DC: U.S. Government Printing Office.

U.S. Bureau of the Census (2002a). *Statistical abstract of the United States: 2000* (120th ed.). Washington, DC: U.S. Government Printing Office.

U.S. Bureau of the Census (2002b). *Educational attainment in the United States: March 2002 Detailed Tables.* [On-line]. http://www.census.gov/population/socdemo/education.

U.S. Department of Labor, Bureau of Labor Statistics (2001). *Report on the American Workforce.* Washington, DC: U.S. Government Printing Office.

U.S. Department of Labor, Bureau of Labor Statistics (2002). *Report on the American Workforce.* Washington, DC: U.S. Government Printing Office.

U.S. Equal Employment Opportunity Commission, (April 7, 2002). Charge Statistics FY 1992 through FY 2001. [On-line]. Available: http://www.eeoc.gov/stat/charges.html.

von Hippel, W., Sekaquaptewa, D., & Vargas, P. (1997). The linguistic intergroup bias as an implicit indicator of prejudice. *Journal of Experimental Social Psychology, 33*, 490–509.

Word, C. O., Zanna, M. P., & Cooper, J. (1974). The nonverbal mediation of self-fulfilling prophecies in interracial interaction. *Journal of Experimental Social Psychology, 10*, 109–120.

Watkins, S. (1993). Racism du jour at Shoney's. *The Nation, October 18*, 424–427.

Weick, K. E. (1979). *The social psychology of organizing.* Reading, MA: Addison-Wesley.

Wilcox, J., & Roof, W. C. (1978). Percent black and black-white status inequality: Southern versus nonsouthern patterns. *Social Science Quarterly, 59*, 421–434.

Wilson, W. J. (1996). *When work disappears.* New York: Knopf.

Wittenbrink, B., Judd, C., & Park, B. (1997). Evidence for racial prejudice at the implicit level and its relationship with questionnaire measures. *Journal of Personality and Social Psychology, 72*, 262–74.

7

Gender Discrimination in Organizations

Jeanette N. Cleveland
Theresa K. Vescio
Pennsylvania State University

Janet L. Barnes-Farrell
University of Connecticut

Women and men are treated differently in the workplace. Sometimes, women are treated less favorably than men. Other times women are treated more favorably than men. Although male and female employees may come to the workplace with some preexisting gender differences that provide reasonable explanations for the differential treatment they receive, often differences in the treatment of men and women are linked to the inaccurate perception of differences (Cleveland, Stockdale, & Murphy, 2000). For this reason, it is important to document the kinds of gender discrimination that occur in the workplace and the kinds of psychological processes that contribute to gender discrimination at work. However, it is also our contention that a narrow focus on documenting gender bias and gender discrimination process strictly within the temporal, physical, and social confines of the workplace masks some important differences in the way men and women experience work. It leaves us wanting with respect to explanations and solutions for well-documented differences between men and women on important work outcomes, such as compensation. Understanding variations in the experiences and outcomes of men and women at work requires that we look beyond the immediate work environment to the societal and cultural context in which work takes place and to the developmental history that people bring with them to work. We believe that a broader perspective on the antecedents of gender discrimination and the outcomes of workplace gender discrimination will provide industrial/organizational psychologists with a richer understanding of the phenomenon of workplace gender discrimination and with insights into the kinds of interventions that may address injustices that discrimination creates.

In this chapter, we first summarize findings of gender bias in decisions and outcomes at work, followed by a description of the individual-based and situational antecedents involved in gender discrimination. We then introduce a broader discussion of discrimination and equality at the societal, institutional, and organizational levels drawing on a number of literatures including careers, sociology, economics, and work and family. By broadening the conceptualization of discrimination, we are able to identify some antecedent conditions that set the stage for discrimination, which we hope will encourage a more comprehensive consideration of the consequences of gender discrimination. Our broad definition of discrimination is followed by a brief description of the seriousness and pervasiveness of gender discrimination, which illustrates major gaps in existing research and important methodological issues for future consideration to research theorizing about gender discrimination. Finally, we conclude our chapter with a discussion of how organizations can be a tool for change and for activism in reducing gender discrimination.

GENDER DISCRIMINATION IN WORK EXPERIENCES AND OUTCOMES

What kinds of evidence exist for gender discrimination in the workplace? Traditional definitions of gender discrimination in the workplace emphasize legal approaches to sex discrimination. In the United States, two basic kinds of evidence define gender discrimination. The first, known as disparate treatment, occurs when individuals are intentionally treated differently by virtue of their group membership. Examples of disparate treatment include unwillingness to hire a woman because of her gender, reluctance to place a woman in career-track positions, asking a woman questions during an interview that are different from those asked of male applicants, and offering a lower starting salary because the recruit is a woman. A somewhat broader definition of gender discrimination (disparate impact) is represented by evidence that members of a particular group are adversely affected by the procedures used to make workplace decisions and by workplace practices. Even though these practices may not be intended to discriminate between men and women, they have the impact of providing proportionately fewer opportunities to women than to men. If job-related reasons (such as differences in job qualifications) cannot account for gender differences in outcomes, the most viable explanation for those differences is gender discrimination.

Most studies that provide evidence regarding gender discrimination in the workplace approach the problem in one of two ways:

1. By examining decisions made about job candidates or workers who are alike in all respects except their gender. The behavior of decision makers toward male and female workers is compared for evidence that they are treated differently in ways that disadvantage women (in most cases).
2. Important organizational outcomes are compared for women and men; when gender differences are observed, it is recognized that such differences could be artifacts of other preexisting differences between the groups that represent job-related explanations for these decisions. (These might include differences in qualifications, education, work experience, career aspirations, and so forth that arise for a variety of reasons discussed elsewhere in this chapter.)

When such alternative explanations for gender differences in outcomes are statistically controlled, any remaining differences between the two groups are taken as evidence of gender bias produced by differential treatment of men and women.

In addition, women's perceptions that they have been denied work and career opportunities on the basis of their gender or have been required to endure work conditions that were more stressful or unpleasant than those of comparably qualified male coworkers represent a third type of evidence regarding the prevalence and impact of gender discrimination.

Regardless of the way in which gender discrimination is assessed in the workplace, there is ample evidence that men and women have different experiences and different outcomes in work settings. These differences can be seen on "objective" indicators of worth such as pay and salary and are reflected in many personnel practices and in the perceptions of those who are the presumed targets of gender discrimination.

Differences in Organizational Access

Gender bias in recruitment, selection, and development opportunities is a critical predecessor to gender differences in access to many other types of organization outcomes (e.g., salary, promotion). Field and laboratory experiments report contradictory findings regarding gender discrimination in recruitment and selection. A meta-analysis conducted in the 1980s found that evidence for gender discrimination in selection was strongest when decision makers had only minimal information about applicants other than their gender (Tosi & Einbender, 1985). More recent evidence focusing specifically on selection interviews also provides ambiguous results regarding gender bias in interview evaluations. Several studies have reported small to negligible sex differences in interview outcomes (e.g., Graves, 1999) whereas others studies find that both the interview process and interview outcomes are biased against women (e.g., Silvester, 1996). It is possible that job type moderates sex effects in interviews; women applying for jobs that are typically held by men may be more likely to experience discrimination in interviews (Davison & Burke, 2000). There is also some evidence that physical characteristics (e.g., emphasis on attractiveness) influence interview evaluations and put women at a disadvantage (Graves, 1999).

With respect to development opportunities, a study of American federal civil service employees reported that, even after controlling for education, experience, and job level, men were more likely than women to receive management training (Smithey & Lewis, 1998). However, contrary to popular belief, the same study found no evidence of differential access to mentoring based on protégé gender. In fact, among professionals and administrators, women were more likely than men to report being mentored.

Differences in Evaluations of Performance

The most notable illustration that some of the critical judgments and decisions made in organizations are *not* systematically biased against women comes from research on performance appraisal. There are many good reasons to believe that the performance appraisals received by men and women *should* systematically differ (e.g., most supervisors are male, stereotypes of jobs usually fit men better than women; Murphy & Cleveland, 1995). It is clear, however, that gender does not have a strong or systematic effect on performance evaluations (Bartol, 1999; Pulakos, White, Oppler, & Borman, 1989). Performance ratings received by men are highly similar to those received by women. Similarly, male supervisors tend to assign similar evaluations to those given by female supervisors. However, as we will discuss in a later section, the few systematic differences that have been reported may still reflect underlying prejudice and a propensity to discriminate against women in decisions that have long-term individual and organizational significance (Crandall & Eshleman, 2003). It is also important to keep in mind that women often perceive and report prejudice in evaluations, something that can coexist with a lack of bias in ratings.

Differences in Advancement and Pay

Women hold less prestigious and influential jobs, advance more slowly in organizations, receive lower starting pay, and are less likely to benefit from transfers and job changes than men (Brett & Stroh, 1997; Reskin & Ross, 1995; Valian, 1998). Differences in the jobs, occupations, and careers held by men and women, in turn, contribute to (but do not fully explain) differences in their pay and rewards.

The most consistent findings of differences in opportunities and outcomes for men and women are found in the area of compensation. The gap in wages earned by men and women is substantial, and it shows little sign of closing in the near future. In 2001, women employed full-time earned a median weekly salary of $511 compared to the median weekly salary of $672 per week that men earned (U.S. Department of Labor, 2002). Importantly, a substantial wage gap remains when men and women within the same occupation are compared (Budig, 2002) and when controlling for qualifications, training, and experience (Ostroff & Atwater, 2002).

Differences in Perceived Treatment

Studies that have examined perceptions of gender-based discrimination at work indicate that a disturbing proportion (approximately 10%) of employed women report having experienced some form of sex discrimination at work (e.g., hiring, pay, promotions; Neumark & McLennan, 1995). Furthermore, in a study of business school alumni, both men and women perceived discrimination against women, with bias against women believed to be stronger at the top of organizations (Trentham & Larwood, 1998). It also appears that different political and cultural environments may affect the incidence and perception of gender discrimination. Shaffer, Joplin, Bell, Lau, & Oguz (1999) reported that national differences in education level, equal employment legislation, and equal employment enforcement that are likely to affect the sensitivity of workers to incidents of gender discrimination were reflected in differential perceptions of the extent to which gender affected various decisions at work.

Differences in the Experience of Work

There is little doubt that men and women have different experiences in the workplace. One of the most widely discussed differences in the experiences of men and women at work is the sexualization of work environments or sexual harassment. Sexual harassment is generally categorized into three major forms of harassment: verbal requests (e.g., sexual and relational advances/pressures), verbal comments (e.g., personal remarks, objectification), and nonverbal displays (e.g., sexual assault, sexual posturing). Estimates of the prevalence of sexual harassment vary, depending on the precise definition of harassment and the methods used in specific surveys (Cleveland et al., 2000). However, virtually all large-scale studies of sexual harassment (cf. Schneider, Swan, & Fitzgerald, 1997; United States Merit Systems Protection Board, 1995) have reached the same conclusion, i.e., a large proportion of women experience some form of sexual harassment at work. The prevalence of such experiences is important because sexual harassment is associated with a wide range of adverse employment effects, including decreased productivity, diminished opportunities for advancement, job loss, decreased morale, absenteeism, and job dissatisfaction (Pryor, 1995). In fact, it is estimated that sexual harassment costs organizations hundreds of millions in dollars a year in lost productivity, health care costs, and decreased efficiency (Faley, Knapp, Kustis, & DuBois, 1994). Sexual harassment has also been associated with adverse psychological outcomes, including stress, sleep and eating disorders, nausea and crying spells (Loy & Stewart, 1984).

In summary, bias against women in work settings is not universal. For example, gender does not appear to be a significant predictor of performance appraisals. One implication is that when we look for explanations of differences in men's and women's employment opportunities and advancement, it is unlikely that the evaluations commonly carried out in organizations will explain a significant proportion of the variance at a given point in time (Cleveland et al., 2000). Rather we need to look to broader societal processes to understand the differences in the working lives of women and men.

UNDERSTANDING STEREOTYPES, PREJUDICE, AND DISCRIMINATION

A consideration of the antecedents of organizational discrimination requires attention to both the intrapersonal processes involved in the perception of people who belong to stereotyped groups (e.g., stereotyping and prejudice processes that operate within individuals) and situational characteristics (e.g., power relations, contextual norms, situational goals). We begin with a discussion of the intrapersonal cognitive processes, noting the consequences of stereotype-based judgments for behavior. We then turn attention to prejudice, noting how individual differences in prejudice may exacerbate or attenuate stereotype-based judgments and behaviors and also noting how prejudice toward women is unique. Then we conclude with a consideration of situational factors that influence the magnitude of gender discrimination effects.

The perception of others in terms of visually apparent and socially meaningful categories, such as sex, is presumed to happen immediately and outside of awareness. More specifically, stereotypes provide perceivers with expectations about the kinds attributes and ranges of behaviors that members of a particular group will exhibit, influencing judgment in one of two ways (Biernat & Vescio, 2002). First, stereotype-based expectations can serve as interpretive frames that guide the encoding and processing of information, resulting in assimilative (or stereotype consistent) judgments of individuals who belong to stereotyped groups (e.g., women are judged less competent than men; Heilman, 1984). Second, stereotype-based expectations sometimes provide standards against which members of a given group are compared and contrasted (e.g., Vescio & Biernat, 1999). When stereotype-based expectations are low, as for negatively stereotyped groups, comparison of an individual to the stereotype of the group to which one belongs often results in counter-stereotypic appraisals of the individual (e.g., a woman judged more favorably than a similar man). This represents a sort of "wow" effect, or a demonstration surprise that a woman, for example, has surpassed low stereotype-based performance expectations. Therefore, such judgments have an implicit qualifier: "She's great—*for a woman.*"

Being "excellent for a woman," however, is not the same as being "excellent." Such gender-based evaluations have an implicit qualifier (e.g., "excellent for a woman"), send mixed messages, and can contribute to the negative work environments many women experience. The "wow" response women sometimes receive from important others when they perform up to the standards expected for their male colleagues is patronizing in nature (p. 195) and may marginalize high-performing females (Foschi, 1992). In other words, the positive evaluations given to women who surpass expectations about how women should perform represent the perception that this woman is performing well for a woman, rather than performing well by common standards applied to set of actors, both men and women.

Prejudice toward women also differs from prejudice toward racial outgroups in ways that may exacerbate the patronizing nature of behaviors in stereotypically masculine work environments. First, most "new racism" models of racial prejudice assume both that White Americans (a) sympathize with Black Americans as victims of injustices (e.g., Katz & Hass,

1988) and (b) are motivated to preserve an egalitarian or nonprejudiced self-image (e.g., Gaertner & Dovidio, 1986). Therefore, subtle racists (e.g., aversive racists, Gaertner & Dovidio, 1986; ambivalent racists, Katz & Hass, 1988; modern racists, McConahay, Hardee, & Batts, 1981) are motivated to behave in a nonracist manner and are responsive to situational cues about appropriate interracial behavior. When it is clear that race is a component of an interaction (even as indicated by subtle situational cues; Biernat & Vescio, 1993), subtle racists alter their behavior and control prejudiced responses (e.g., Gaertner & Dovidio, 1986).

Subtle or modern sexism, however, takes a different form. Rather than sympathizing with women as victims of discrimination, inequity, and injustice, modern sexists (Swim, Aiken, Hall, & Hunter, 1995) deny that sexism is a problem in contemporary society. In fact, Swim et al.'s modern sexism scale comprises two kinds of items. Half of the items tap denial that sexism is a problem in contemporary society. The other half tap anger toward those who suggest sexism is a problem. Furthermore, although subtle racists are particularly attentive to cues as guides for behavior in interracial contexts, recent findings show that modern sexists are less able to identify instances of sexist behavior, even when given instructions about what they are looking for (e.g., sexist language). The inability of modern sexists to identify sexist behavior as such likely exacerbates women's experiences of patronizing behaviors.

Prejudice toward women is also different from racial prejudice, in that there is typically a great deal of positive affect associated with the opposite sex. According to Fiske and her colleagues (Fiske, Cuddy, Glick, & Xu, 2002), stereotype content is derived from perceptions of the extent that members of a particular group are perceived as threatening and in competition with the ingroup. In this view, groups get what they deserve. They get the status they deserve by virtue of their competence and they get the relationship to the ingroup they deserve by virtue of their warmth. The crossing of competence and warmth results in four cases of prejudice. Groups are perceived as (a) warm and competent, (b) warm, but incompetent, (c) not warm, but competent, and (d) neither warm nor competent.

The first and the fourth situations depict the prejudice in evaluations of members of ingroups and outgroups. Ingroups are positively stereotyped, reflecting both respect for and warmth toward the ingroup. Outgroups are perceived in terms that reflect both disrespect and dislike (or lack of human qualities); they are low status outgroups that are perceived as draining resources from the ingroup (e.g., people on welfare, poor people, homeless people). The other two cases represent ambivalent perceptions of outgroups. First, there are envied outgroups, who are stereotyped in terms that imply competence, but that lack important human qualities (e.g., Asians,

Jewish people). There are also pitied outgroups, or unsuccessful, nonthreatening outgroups (e.g., elderly and mentally or physically handicapped). These groups are disrespected because of their low status, but liked for their human qualities. As a result, such groups are stereotyped in terms that reflect the disrespect and warmth of the dominant group.

In this typology, women fall into one of the two ambivalent groups. Within the ambivalent sexism framework (Glick & Fiske, 2002), benevolent sexism treats women as warm but incompetent. Traditional women are here held up as exemplars of the desirable human quality (e.g., gentle, loving, nurturing), but perceived as incompetent and disrespected. Relations between dominant male groups and the female subgroups to which they feel benevolent sexism are characterized by paternalistic relations, in which heterosexist gender roles are respected and women are perceived as nonthreatening (i.e., not in competition with men). Alternatively, women who are viewed as not warm, but respected, are subjected to hostile sexism. These are the women respected for their high status and, in turn, perceived as competent, but disliked for their lack of human qualities. In other words, different kinds of prejudice turn against these different types of women; hostility is directed toward nontraditional women and paternalistic benevolence toward traditional women (Glick, Diebold, Bailey-Werner, & Zhu, 1997).

In both cases, however, stereotyping is a means of system justification; high status groups that hold power stereotype low status groups in a way that reinforce and maintain the status quo, which is a feature of both hostile and benevolent sexist responding. For example, the Ambivalent Sexism Inventory (Glick & Fiske, 1996) conceptualizes hostile sexism as involving dominating power relations, competition across gender roles, and tension over heterosexual control. Nontraditional women are perceived as challenging men's societal and cultural power along each dimension, and are therefore stereotyped in negative trait terms. Whereas benevolent sexism is also associated with the ascription of positive stereotypic traits to women, it also is associated with heterosexist power dynamics. Benevolent sexism entails paternalistic power relations, cooperation around complementary gender roles, and idealized heterosexual intimacy.

SITUATIONAL FACTORS THAT INFLUENCE DISCRIMINATION

Social psychologists have suggested that the default perceptual tendency is to judge others in terms of the social categories to which they belong. In other words, it has been assumed that perceivers automatically interpret and make sense of information about others with reference to their beliefs about groups to which those individuals belong (e.g., gender stereotypes) unless perceivers are sufficiently motivated to individuate others (e.g., Fiske & Neuberg, 1990). There are, however, factors that both exacerbate and attenuate this tendency.

Power

It has been suggested that the tendency to stereotype others increases with power. Following from the assumption that people will stereotype unless sufficiently motivated to do otherwise, low power individuals should be highly motivated to individuate high power people who have control over them. In contrast, powerful people are likely stereotype low power people either because the powerful are motivated to preserve power differentials or because they are unmotivated to process information more carefully (for a review of related findings, see Keltner, Gruenfeld, & Anderson, 2003). Importantly, the stereotyping tendencies of the powerful are particularly problematic in traditional achievement domains, where success requires attributes stereotypically associated with men (e.g., logic, strategic, and competitive skills), but not women (who are stereotyped as illogical, emotional, and weak). In such situations, men are more likely than women to hold positions of power and findings show that perceivers have less complex and varied stereotypes of gender outgroups than gender ingroups (Park & Judd, 1990). This suggests that low power women are likely to be the recipients of the gender-based discrimination of powerful men, which may take different forms depending on the degree to which women are threatening. As noted above, women are more likely to belong to outgroups toward which powerful men have ambivalent perceptions (Fiske et al., 2002). Therefore, nontraditional women who are perceived as competent but not warm may be treated in hostile sexist manners, whereas traditional women who are perceived as incompetent but warm may be treated in benevolent sexist manners.

Female Underrepresentation

Stereotyping may also be particularly strong in situations where women are underrepresented (or skewed environments; Kanter, 1977). When extremely underrepresented, Kanter (1977) suggested that women come to hold a token status; their numeric infrequency makes their gender highly salient, such that women come to be viewed as representatives of their gender. Additionally, in such situations Kanter suggested that women are constrained to gender-relevant roles and may be the recipients of various types of gender-based behaviors depending on the degree that the role to which they are constrained is threatening to or supportive of traditional gender roles. Integrating this suggestion with our previous review of the content of gender stereotypes, for example, "iron maidens" (Kanter, 1977), who are respected for their competence but disliked because of their lack of human qualities, may be subjected to hostile sexism (Fiske et al., 2002).

Powerful Men and the Construal of Their Goals

Whereas power, masculine contexts, and female underrepresentation enhance the degree that women are stereotyped in work environments, Vescio and her colleagues (Vescio, Snyder, & Butz, 2003; Vescio, Gervais, Snyder, & Hoover, 2004) recently demonstrated that powerful men may be encouraged to construe goals and ideas about subordinates' ability to enhance goal strivings in ways that eliminate stereotyping tendencies. Traditionally masculine domains often encourage adversarial processes that focus attention toward the weaknesses that employees may possess, which may impair goal strivings (e.g., the so-called corporate "up or out" policy). In such situations, gender stereotypes provide information of relevance, or point out the dimensions along which women have critical shortcomings (e.g., illogical, irrational, weak) and low power women are treated in patronizing ways (e.g., receive fewer valued resources, but are praised more) and exhibit performance decrements (e.g., Vescio et al., 2004). However, stereotypes of women are uninformative when powerful men are encouraged to construe goals in approach-related terms and to attend to those strengths that subordinates have that may enhance goal strivings. Stereotypes of women provide information about the attributes that women possess (e.g., caring, nurturing), but these attributes are irrelevant to masculine domains and do not inform the goal striving of strength-focused powerful men (i.e., did not provide information about how subordinate women would enhance goal strivings). Importantly, stereotyping does not occur in such situations. Therefore, when workers belong to negatively stereotyped groups, stereotyping can be eliminated by having those in positions of authority seek information about workers in attempts to address the question of whether a given subordinate possesses strengths or skills that will enhance, rather than weaknesses that will inhibit, goal strivings.

A PERSON X SITUATION APPROACH
TO UNDERSTANDING DISCRIMINATION

Integrating the above considerations, we suggest that gender stereotyping should occur in organizations when cultural stereotypes of women are (a) endorsed and internalized by decision makers, (b) contextually relevant (i.e., provide information of relevance to the judgment tasks at hand), and (c) inform the strategies that people in positions of power adopt in attempts to exert power over, or influence, lesser power others. Factors that limit the likelihood that one of these three propositions will hold, should temper the magnitude of the gender-based stereotyping and discrimination that occurs in organizations. For example, situational manipulations of "appropriate" ways to construe goals (strength or weakness focused) may exacerbate or eliminate gender discrimination, as recent findings suggest (see Vescio, Snyder, & Butz, 2003; Vescio et al., 2004). Likewise, successful interventions that challenge the endorsement of gender stereotypes, or perceived relevance of gender stereotypes to contexts, should also decrease the magnitude of gender stereotyping and effectively temper the patronizing behaviors exhibited toward women. However, attempts in the latter regard require a broader consideration of gender stereotypes in society and a reconceptualization of the social role of organizations in personal development and socialization more generally.

AN INTEGRATIVE APPROACH TO WORKPLACE DISCRIMINATION

Although the psychological and management literatures have documented the differences in treatment and organizational outcomes among men and women, they provide only partial illumination of the portrait of gender discrimination in our society because they fail to recognize the larger developmental and societal context in which workplace discrimination is embedded. In this section we draw from developmental, cultural, sociological, economic, and feminist research on gender discrimination in order to understand that even prior to entering organizational settings, women are systematically at a disadvantage to their male counterparts.

Developmental Perspective

We use the term "developmental perspective on discrimination" to refer to a lifetime process of the acquisition and socialization of gender roles, views on gender, values placed on paid work, perspectives on child rearing, and beliefs about the respective roles of men and women. A developmental perspective on discrimination includes beliefs about gender in work and nonwork settings, including the beliefs about gender that we bring with us when we first enter work organizations. Importantly, a developmental perspective on discrimination stresses that beliefs and attitudes about the relevance of gender to behavior in work settings does not stop when individuals enter work organizations, but rather continues to unfold over time and throughout one's career. In other words, attitudes, beliefs, and behaviors continue to develop and to be reinforced (or challenged) when one relocates to another organization, shifts to a new career, takes on a new project, or moves within an organizational career path.

Research on discrimination has traditionally focused on differences between people (e.g., differences between high- and low-prejudiced individuals have been studied extensively). The developmental perspective pays attention to within-individual differences or changes across time. Individuals' beliefs and behaviors fostering discrimination in the workplace are not cast in stone, and they can be influenced by workplace interventions. Individuals may differ in their propensity for development or change (i.e., the attitudes, beliefs, and behaviors of some individuals may be more resistant to change); these differences may have implications for both the timing of interventions and the contexts in which discrimination-reduction interventions are most likely to succeed. A developmental view is also important because it conveys more clearly the nature of the discrimination process—small but consistent differences in the treatment of men and women in the workplace (e.g., small decrements in pay, conditions of work, and so forth) can have large cumulative effects over time (Martell, Lane, & Emrich, 1996; Valian, 1998).

Cultural Gendering   According to sociologists Padavic & Reskin (2002), societies produce, reinforce, and maintain gender differences through processes of socialization, the actions of social institutions, and interactions among people. Together, the processes, actions, and interactions that produce and reinforce gender differences have been referred to as *gendering*. Thus, gender is more than biology—it is a system of social relations that is embedded in the way major institutions (including the workplace) are organized (Acker, 1990; Lorber, 1992, p. 748). Sociological research on gendering helps us to examine the ways that social institutions embrace gendered arrangements and thus, create and maintain differences in the behavior and expectations of a society's male and female members (Padavic & Reskin, 2002).

Why does gendering exist? According to Acker (1990), Padavic and Reskin (2002), and others, a primary reason for gendering is to maintain male advantage. Gender roles and gendered organizations institutionalize the favored position of men as a group. In our society, organizations play a fundamental role in establishing a gender hierarchy that tends to favor men over women. Although many men may not be aware of the benefits they derive on the basis of their gender, these benefits are real and meaningful. Two institutions that are particularly important to most adults are work and family, both characterized by strong sets of assumptions about the differences in the roles of men and women (Padavic & Reskin, 2002).

Furthermore, the strong gendering of family roles reinforces the gendering of work roles, and vice versa. For example, it is often assumed that women will have less commitment to the work role because of the concomitant assumption that women have stronger commitments to family roles. The interplay of gendered assumptions about work and about family show up most strongly in research on work–family conflicts and on sex segregation in occupational choice.

Gendered Work: Occupational Sex Segregation   Goldin (2002) reviews evidence suggesting that the gendering of work roles in the United States may be a fairly recent phenomenon that started in the early 1900s. Although some have argued that gendered roles date back to hunting vs. foraging and childcare of earliest man, Goldin's analysis suggests that the development of strong links between perceptions of work roles and perceptions of gender roles in organized work settings became especially prominent during the time when the concept of "white collar" work was starting to develop. Historically, women have been concentrated in a relatively small number of occupations, particularly in service sector work, clerical work, and retail sales, a category of occupations often referred to as "pink-collar" jobs (a label consistent with the distinction between "white collar" jobs and "blue collar" jobs occupied primarily by men).

A number of indices of gender segregation in the workplace exist, but they all tell essentially the same story. A woman entering the workforce is very likely to be found in an occupation where the majority of workers are women. About half of all working women are employed in occupations that are more than 75% female (Cleveland et al., 2000).

Sex-segregation in occupations provides the most obvious piece of evidence of the gendered nature of work. There are entire categories of jobs that are implicitly defined as women's work (e.g., cashiers, librarians, daycare workers) and others that are implicitly defined as men's jobs (automobile mechanic, garbage truck driver, football coach), and although many individuals cross these implicit gender boundaries (e.g., male nurses, female judges), associations between gender and occupations are often strong. There is also considerable sex segregation within occupations. That is, women and men within the same occupational category often perform different jobs for the same employer. Therefore, data reflecting people's occupations can often underestimate the amount of sex segregation in the workplace.

Although the gendering of occupations does not necessarily imply that women will be disadvantaged by this situation, jobs that are held primarily by women tend to involve lower levels of technical skill and responsibility than jobs held primarily by men and these jobs are generally not as highly valued by organizations. In fact, one of the best predictors of the status and pay level of a job is the proportion of women holding that job (England, Herbert, Kilbourne, Reid, & Medgal, 1994). The more women found in a particular job, the lower the average pay, the lower its status (Rantalaiho, Heiskanen, Korvajarvi, & Vehvilainen, 1997), and the lower the mobility prospects to mid- and upper-level leadership positions (cf. Martin & Harkreader, 1993).

Occupational sex segregation is increasingly obvious the higher in the organization one goes. Women are particularly underrepresented in top management positions (Powell, 1999). For example, women only make up 12.4% of Fortune 500 board directors. When representation in the seven highest corporate titles (e.g., chief executive officer, president, senior executive vice-president) is scrutinized, women merely occupied 7.9% of these positions as of 1999 (Catalyst, 2002). Furthermore, the Federal Glass Ceiling Commission concluded that equally qualified women are being denied advancement to top levels in organizations on the basis of gender (Cotter, Hermsen, Ovadia, & Vanneman, 2001). The roots of occupational segregation are likely to be linked both directly and indirectly to societal definitions of sex roles. Boys and girls (and later men and women) are bombarded with messages from numerous sources that define the behaviors that are valued and expected of men and women. These messages influence choices made early in one's working life, and even choices before one enters the workforce (e.g., the decision to take or avoid math classes in high school) that can in turn affect a wide range of work outcomes. Differences in men's and women's educational backgrounds, aspirations, and accomplishments may substantially affect their later occupational choices (McCall, 2001).

Structures of Work and Structures of Family Consistent with the notion of a gendered workplace is the idea that the normative structure of work may have differential implications for men and women. For example, face time is an important part of work. Even with technology that allows telecommuting, it is still important to be seen at one's workplace. This creates problems for those (predominantly women) who telecommute in order to care for young children in their homes. Furthermore, technology has been instrumental in nurturing consumers' expectations for immediate turnaround for information, which results is an increasingly 24/7 society and economy (Presser, 2000). For this reason, many emerging jobs require nontraditional work hours or shift work. Many of these jobs involve lower pay and are often held by women. Likewise, the overwhelming majority of part-time work is carried out by women. Nontraditional hours and part-time work have significant and less positive career implications for incumbents, including the lack of benefits (e.g., no family leaves, lack of medical coverage, absence of retirement benefits). Further, the normative expectation of a gendered work environment is that workforce members will have continuous employment; those with gaps or "interruptions" in employment tend to be less valued and less rewarded, which immediately places many women at a disadvantage.

Finally, despite a general awareness that family structures have changed, most work is still structured with the implicit assumption that the prevailing family structure includes one earner and one stay-at-home person. Today's family structures are diverse, yet one fact is clear: The single-earner, stay-at-home wife is the *minority* type of family structure. In traditional married families, often both adults work, not by choice but by economic necessity; dual earners frequently must juggle taking care of young children. In addition, a sizable proportion of families are permanent single parent families and an even larger segment are single parent families for some period of time. The normative structures of work ignore the reality of these family structures. Further, the division of labor within households is not taken into consideration in typical work structures. As discussed in the next section, women in paid employment continue to put greater numbers of hours in both childcare *and* household chores than men (Crouter, Bumpus, Head, & McHale, 2001). In dual-earner families, men may increase their time with their children (compared to single-earner families), but their time spent on household chores is roughly the same as single-earner families. It is difficult to obtain an accurate picture of gender discrimination *at* work until we understand the "tilted" playing field that exists within families.

Gendered Family Work: Family and Workplace Discrimination   Work roles and family roles often place competing demands on an individual's time and attention. There is substantial evidence that when the demands of work and family come into conflict, women are much more likely to reduce or adjust their work roles than men (Crouter et al., 2001). Women still provide considerably more childcare and housework, even when they are part of the paid labor force (Bianchi, 2000). However, one U.S. study demonstrated that husbands' participation in family work reflected their wives' employment level, such that husbands completed a more equal share of housework when their wives had a career as opposed to a job (Dancer & Gilbert, 1993). In both U.S. and European samples, it has been shown that the addition of a child increases the total amount of work (the combination of paid work and unpaid housework) for mothers, more so than fathers (Sanchez & Thomson, 1997). Women also shoulder a greater proportion of the responsibility for tasks associated with care of elderly parents (their own and their spouse's), indicating that the disproportionately increased workload does not appear to be limited to women of child-bearing age.

This is significant because when the total workload becomes work "overload," it should be expected that the kinds of negative consequences

regularly associated with work overload in the occupational stress literature are likely to ensue (e.g., experienced stress, decreased performance,
decreased well-being). Studies of work overload that focus only on paid
work consistently report that men, on average, work longer hours and thus
are at greater risk of experiencing the strains of work overload. However,
when we take the broader perspective and recognize that an individual's
workload encompasses both paid and unpaid work, women appear to be
at increased risk of these consequences.

Rethinking "Work"

Work has traditionally been a male domain. Our definitions of what sort of
work is valuable, the relative importance of work and nonwork roles, the
sorts of behaviors that contribute to or detract from organizations, and so
forth, all reflect a male-oriented perspective. The assumption that supervising 10 subordinates is more valuable and more important than teaching
10 children (pay differentials for managers and teachers are substantial)
reflects the values of the dominant culture—in this case the male culture.
Our assumptions about what "work" means in our lives, how, when, and
where people should work, how organizations should be structured, and
how conflicts between work and nonwork roles should be juggled tend
to reflect and reinforce a particular perspective on the world that seems
more compatible with male sex roles than with female sex roles. On the
whole, the world of work seems friendlier and more comfortable to men
than to women, which should come as no surprise. Feminist scholars argue
that the world of work was designed by and for men, and that efforts to
improve the fit between people and work must not be limited to changing sex roles, but must also include a reconsideration of fundamental assumptions that we make about work itself (Kessler-Harris, 1985; Lorber,
1986).

IMPLICATIONS OF AN INTEGRATIVE APPROACH
TO WORKPLACE DISCRIMINATION

In our discussion of workplace gender discrimination, we have attempted
to demonstrate that in order to understand women's and men's experiences of work, one also must understand the context and developmental
processes outside of work that occur during the years prior to and following the entrance into the workplace. Discrimination may reflect disparate
treatment between men and women or differential impact of decisions or
evaluations made within the workplace. Yet even when the same treatment

at work is provided, there may be discrimination. The very practice that is similarly implemented for men and women may put women at a disadvantage because the conditions of *nonwork* differ dramatically for men and women. For example, a seemingly harmless and neutral practice of scheduling a critical meeting for 4:00 pm may differentially affect male and female employees with caregiving responsibilities. Women are more likely to take responsibility for their children's after-school care and will be disadvantaged by that practice. In this final section of the chapter, we point out some important implications of recognizing the broader context in which gender discrimination resides. In particular, we will focus on the implications of this approach for (a) less often considered indicators of unfair bias, (b) the seriousness of sex discrimination, and (c) methodological issues and gaps in current research in industrial and organizational psychology and applied psychology.

Alternative Indicators of Discriminatory Workplaces

The developmental, sociological, and feminist literatures allow us to construct alternative lenses from which to view the workplace. Through these lenses, we can identify a number of features of the work and nonwork place that have been researched but not in relation to gender discrimination. These include more general issues of definitions of success or performance at work (e.g., criterion deficiency), less visible forms of potential discrimination (including the influence of language and humor/joking), workplace exclusion, the structure of work, and family structure. Each of these issues is briefly discussed below.

What is Success? Criterion Deficiency in Our Assessments   In industrial and organizational psychology, more attention has been given to such predictors of performance as cognitive ability tests and personality tests than to the performance construct itself (Campbell, 1990). How has success been defined? Historically, work psychologists have defined *job* success as the extent to which an employee successfully performs the core tasks in the job—namely the required aspects of the job including production, problem solving, organizing activities, and so forth. It is only within the last 15 years that another facet of job success has been recognized, variously known as contextual performance (CP) or organizational citizenship behavior (OCB). CP (and OCB) represents behaviors that create and maintain a context in which people can work together and cooperate in production. Work occurs in social settings and maintenance of the social fabric of work is every bit as important as maintaining the machines and grounds. Good performance, in terms of CP, involves helping coworkers, being considerate, paying attention to other other's needs and so forth.

A key issue is: How and why has performance been defined in this manner and by whom? Does operationalization of success in terms of task or contextual performance place men at an advantage over women? For example, when work performance was defined strictly in terms of task performance, there was evidence during the 1970s that women performed less well at certain tasks than men including leadership, problem solving, and risk taking (cf. Rice, Bender, & Vitters, 1980). However, more recent evidence shows few differences between men and women on these core task areas (Pulakos et al., 1989). Interestingly, CP (or OCB) has been defined as helping others and has been considered to be necessary once one's own tasks are completed; picking up another person's responsibilities if needed, staying longer hours at work, and so forth. Yet it may be that some employees are constrained by nonwork circumstances that make it more difficult to work extra hours or to take on the tasks of another employee. In other words, the shift to CP as an important facet of our criteria for success will primarily benefit those who have the opportunity to engage in those behaviors. Workers (both men and women) who shoulder family care responsibilities may find that they are perceived as competent at their jobs but "unwilling to go the extra mile" and are not seen as team players.

Career success, or the succession of (usually) related positions or roles one holds through paid employment, is another important issue. Attention has been given to what a successful career looks like, but I/O psychologists have not paid sufficient attention to the relationship between careers and the rest of one's life. Career success has often been defined in a way that implies that family is less important than work (e.g., "successful" careers often involve substantial time commitments). Rigid definitions of career success may disproportionately affect the career success of women for reasons described earlier in this chapter, related to their relatively larger time obligations to nonwork responsibilities and the sometimes "interrupted" nature of their job sequences.

Finally, if we turn to a consideration of appropriate criteria of *organizational* success, we note that surprisingly little attention has been given to the role of work organizations in society and how they should be evaluated (Murphy, 1998). During the 1990s, there was significant downsizing activity among U.S. organizations with the intent of maximizing bottom-line profits and short-term investor returns. However, there is evidence that organizational gains from such detrimental human resource practices exist only in the short term (cf., Cascio, 1998). Huselid's (1995) work on organizations with strong, well-developed human resource practices finds that, in the long term, organizations that value employees and devote resources to select, develop, and evaluate their human resources tend to have greater reported profitability (see also Huselid, Jackson, & Schuler,

1997). For example, Cascio's (2003) work on the utility of work and family benefits on organizational performance reinforces these findings and suggests that organizations benefit substantially from family-friendly policies. Work by Cascio and others is critical as it includes financial organizational level criteria and crosses disciplinary boundaries by using utility. Yet these techniques may not go far enough; factors such as employee divorce rates, children's school performance, and physical and mental well-being are often not included in such estimates.

Subtle and Covert Sexism   Both subtle and covert sexism refer to "unequal and harmful treatment of women that is typically less visible" (Benokratis, 1997, p. 11). Subtle sexism is less obvious than blatant sexual discrimination because most individuals have internalized it as "normal" or "acceptable" behavior, which can be seen as well meaning, unintentional, and nonmalicious. Covert sexism, in contrast, is purposeful and often maliciously motivated as well as hidden. The presence of either or both of these forms of sexism in the workplace results in different workplace experiences for men and women. Also, although Benokratis (1997) described these forms of discrimination as subtle or covert, they may seem fairly blatant to individuals (especially women) who experience them at work on a daily basis.

For example, humor, jokes, and more general work language often reinforce and perpetuate discrimination in socially acceptable ways. Furthermore, when women do not laugh at "stupid, harmless" jokes, they are often accused of not having a sense of humor—adding insult to injury (Benokratis, 1997). Additionally, when humor is of a sexual nature, it often expresses male dominance over women with the consequence of negating or silencing women. Sexual humor is therefore experienced as demeaning and aggressive, particularly when such jokes are specifically targeted toward women in powerful positions of authority.

Other forms of subtle or covert sexism include exclusion and "liberated sexism." Exclusion can be both physical and linguistic, including, for example, informal lunches, pickup basketball games, urinal conversations, or discussion of work issues and strategies using sports, cars, sexual or war analogies and metaphors. On the other hand, liberated sexism exists when women are welcomed into the workplace to compete with men (and others) for valued rewards, but only so long as they continue to perform their gender role responsibilities such as childcare, housework, and so forth.

Gender Discrimination Beyond the Boundaries of Professional and Managerial Work

Much of the research reported here is based on literature on White men and women in managerial or professional occupations (Powell, 1999). Yet, little research in the applied work psychology or management literatures has addressed the plights of women of color or the situations of older, poor, or rural women. Although there are good reasons to think that gender differences in the experience of work may be affected by ethnicity (cf. Mellor, Barnes-Farrell, & Stanton, 1999), the intersection of ethnicity and gender is not well understood. Likewise, the dearth of research that examines how gender affects the experiences of men and women in low-income and noncareer-oriented jobs leaves significant gaps in our knowledge of gender discrimination at work.

In many cases, the working poor are single women with children or women in part-time or multiple part-time employment involving minimum wages. The need to understand this growing segment of workers is increasingly critical because the welfare to work programs of the 1990s are now having an impact on the working poor and their children. Further, it is our contention that the most blatant, serious forms of gender discrimination are likely to occur in part-time jobs occupied largely by women, where equal pay for full-time equal work is nonexistent, and where most women hold minimum wage jobs, and nonmanagerial jobs.

We also need to address women's work cycles, careers, and work–nonwork interfaces. For example, one way that women have attempted to balance work and family needs is to take time off from work briefly when starting a family. Although this may not be an option for many women (for economic reasons), some dual-earner families make great sacrifices to make this possible. However, there is both sociological and economic evidence that once this brief gap occurs, a woman's income never catches up to her female peers (Budig & England, 2001; Waldfogel, 1998).

In addition, there is little research with older women on important work outcomes such as job performance, organizational commitment, or organizational citizenship. We know little about the preretirement behavior of older women or the extent to which discrimination occurs in retirement outcomes. It may be that although *some* women have employment gaps in order to adapt to incredibly rigid work structures for family care, women in general may continue to work longer and more productively than their male counterparts, with greater physical and mental health.

Methodological Considerations

The methodological limitations of research on gender discrimination mirror the issues that we have raised with respect to our knowledge of gender discrimination outside the professional and managerial ranks. First, more research that examines gender discrimination by race, ethnicity, culture, socioeconomic status, and family structure is needed. Our current discussion is woefully biased toward samples comparing White males and

White females. More multiple demographic groups need to be investigated: Hispanic, Black, Asian, and White women in professional, managerial, clerical, part-time, and full-time work who are married, cohabitating, single, with younger and with grown children.

A second limiting assumption of our research and our everyday lives is that discrimination exists only where there are large gender differences: that small, isolated differences in pay, informal comments about the high performance of a male employee (without mention of the female employee), dismissive or condescending gestures, gendered language, the relative size of supervisory budgets, number of subordinates, developmental assignments, and so forth are not a big deal. It is our contention, as well as the contention of others (Valian, 1998; Martell, Lane, & Emrich, 1996), that small seemingly insignificant differences or even slights between men and women can accrue over time. Within a short period of time, women find themselves hopelessly at a disadvantage to their male counterparts. The assumption that small differences can be disregarded has permeated the gender discrimination literature and is inextricably linked with the cross-sectional research design that typifies our research. The need for longitudinal, interdisciplinary research focused on gender discrimination is imperative in order to recognize when apparently trivial differences are likely to accumulate into lasting and important disadvantages.

Finally, as industrial and organizational psychologists, we have yet to tap all we have to offer in terms of understanding discrimination at work. Historically, we have focused on examining gender or ethnic differences on predictor variables or comparing differences on job attitudes and a narrow range of work outcomes. However, we have unquestioningly accepted job performance, promotions, salary, job title, organizational level, and so forth as encompassing the domain of success. We have both implicitly and explicitly ignored the permeability of the boundary between work and nonwork domains in our definitions of "success." Instead we have rigidly held to the belief that marital and family well-being do not fall within the purview of responsible organizations. This flies in the face of evidence that many employees place family as their number one priority (Lewis & Cooper, 1999) and the wealth of evidence that employees' work demands regularly interfere with their ability to meet family demands and (to a lesser degree) employees' family demands interfere with their ability to carry out work demands (cf. Greenhaus & Parasuraman, 1999). Our current criteria for success (and theories of performance) are deficient because we know little about the facets and structures of work that affect meaningful nonwork areas of our lives. To rectify this situation, it is critical that industrial and organizational psychologists, experts in work psychology and behavior, address criterion deficiency by tapping previously ignored or taboo sources of work performance information. These might include, for example, spousal ratings and children's reactions to the effects of parental work on family interactions. In addition to expanding the source of criterion information, these sources expand the content of success to include marital health and functioning, individual and family stress, children's physical health, educational development, and mental and social well-being.

CONCLUDING REMARKS: ROLE OF THE ORGANIZATION AS A TOOL FOR ACTIVISM AND CHANGE

Two key terms reflect the major themes in our conclusions: multidisciplinary and partnerships. These themes are not mutually exclusive. However, thus far, the skeptical organizational manager might read this chapter and respond with frustration, "Great, no matter what we do, discrimination is locked in before employees even enter the organization, so we should not be held accountable." Not so fast—our chapter is intended to point out alternative organizational partnerships in addition to both EEOC and affirmative action strategies. As this chapter suggests, discrimination is developmental in nature. Therefore, one way that organizations can address issues of gender discrimination is by developing partnerships with schools (especially at primary levels) to discuss work settings, fairness issues, working in diverse teams, and conflict resolution across cultures. Organizations can also partner with educational institutions and community child-care programs to enrich after-school care activities and develop age-appropriate diversity programs—both by reducing costs of such programs and enhancing quality. Organizations can partner with community mental health providers to increase accessible positive parenting programs and affordable, quality marital and healthy relationship counseling, including steps to wise decision making and constructive conflict resolutions. Organizations can work together through organizational coalitions (e.g., Corporate Voices) to identify common workforce needs and can work to lobby for congressional support for either federal funding or corporate incentives for the above partnerships.

Academic researchers can develop multidisciplinary teams to address the multiple causes and consequences of gender discrimination. It is critical that senior scholars educate students in their own specific disciplines to understand and embrace their unique contributions to the study of a problem (e.g., gender discrimination), while simultaneously stressing the value added by the contributions of other disciplines. To give an example, a recent article (Brett & Stroh, 2003) showed that managers who worked longer hours reported greater levels of job involvement and job satisfaction. Yet we know little from this article about whether this relationship holds for both men and women who work on average 40 hours, 60 hours, or 80 hours. There is evidence from the family and marriage literature (e.g., Crouter, et al, 2001) that employees who work over a certain number of hours show detrimental effects on family functioning. It would be interesting to know whether or not spouses and the children of these managers who worked long hours would have had similar positive responses to their parents' work hours (Crouter, Bumpus, Maguire, & McHale, 1999).

In conclusion, in order to fully understand, predict, and address gender discrimination in organizations, it is necessary to appreciate the reciprocal relationships between work and nonwork and to recognize the larger developmental and cultural context in which work behaviors unfold. Furthermore, to provide a *level* playing field for all employees within organizations, it is critical to recognize that there may be a *tilted* playing field outside the workplace.

REFERENCES

Acker, J. (1990). Hierarchies, jobs, bodies: A theory of gendered organizations. *Gender and Society, 4*, 139–158.

Bartol, K. (1999). Gender influences on performance evaluations. In G. Powell (Ed.), *Handbook of gender and work* (pp. 95–123). Thousand Oaks, CA: Sage.

Benokratis, N. V. (1997) *Subtle sexism: Current practices and perspectives for change.* Thousand Oaks, CA: Sage.

Bianchi, S. M. (2000). Maternal employment and time with children: Dramatic change or surprising continuity. *Demography, 37*, 401–414.

Biernat, M., & Vescio, T. K. (1993). Categorization and stereotyping: Effects of group context on memory and social judgment. *Journal of Experimental Social Psychology, 29*, 166–202.

Biernat, M., & Vescio, T. K. (2002). She swings, she hits, she's great, she's benched: Shifting judgment standards and behavior. *Personality and Social Psychology Bulletin, 28*, 66–76.

Brett, J., & Stroh, L. K. (1997). Jumping ship: Who benefits from an external labor market strategy? *Journal of Applied Psychology, 82*, 331–341.

Brett, J., & Stroh, L. K. (2003). Working 61 plus hours a week: Why do managers do it? *Journal of Applied Psychology, 88*, 67–78.

Budig, M. J. (2002). Male advantage and the gender composition of jobs: Who rides the glass escalator. *Social Problems, 49*, 258–277.

Budig, M. J., & England, P. (2001). The wage penalty for motherhood. *American Sociological Review, 66*, 204–225.

Campbell, J. P. (1990). Modeling the performance prediction problem in industrial and organizational psychology. In M. D. Dunnette & L. M. Hough (Eds.), *Handbook of industrial and organizational psychology* (Vol. 1, 2nd ed., pp. 687–732). Palo Alto, CA: Consulting Psychologists Press.

Cascio, W. F. (1998). Learning from outcomes: financial experiences of 311 firms that have downsized. In M. K. Gowing, J. D. Kraft, & J. C. Quick (Eds.), *The new organizational reality: Downsizing, restructuring, and revitalization* (pp. 55–70). Washington, DC: American Psychological Association.

Cascio, W. F., & Young, C. E. (2003, February). *Work-family balance: Does the market reward firms that respect it?* Paper presented at Claremont Institute Conference, Claremont, CA.

Catalyst. (2002). *2002 Catalyst census of women corporate officers and top earners in the Fortune 500.* New York: Catalyst.

Cleveland, J., Stockdale, M., & Murphy, K. (2000). *Women and men in organizations.* Mahwah, NJ: Lawrence Erlbaum Associates.

Cotter, D. A., Hermsen, J. M., Ovadia, S., & Vanneman, R. (2001). The glass ceiling effect. *Social Forces, 80*, 655–681.

Crandall, C. S., & Eshleman, A. (2003). A justification-suppression model of the expression and experience of prejudice. *Psychological Bulletin, 129, 3*, 414–447.

Crouter, A., Bumpus, M., Head, M., & McHale, S. (2001). Implications of overwork and overload for the quallity of men's family relationships. *Journal of Marriage and Family, 63*, 404–416.

Crouter, A., Bumpus, M., Maguire, M., & McHale, S. (1999). Linking parents' work pressure and adolescents' well-being: Insights into dynamics in dual-earner families. *Developmental Psychology, 35*, 1453–1461.

Crull, P. (1982). Stress effects of sexual harassment on the job: Implications for counseling. *American Journal of Orthopsychiatry, 52*, 539–544.

Dancer, L. S., & Gilbert, L. A. (1993). Spouses' family work participation and its delation to wives' occupational level. *Sex Roles, 28*, 127–145.

Davison, H. K., & Burke, M. J. (2000). Sex discrimination in simulated employment contexts: A meta-analytic investigation. *Journal of Vocational Behavior, 56*, 225–248.

Darley, J. M., & Gross, P. H. (1983). A hypothesis-confirming bias in labeling effects. *Journal of Personality and Social Psychology, 44*, 20–33.

England, P., Herbert, M. S., Kilbourne, B. S., Reid, L. L., & Hedgal, L. M. (1994). The gendered valuations of occupations and skills: Earnings in 1980 census occupations. *Social Forces, 73*, 65–99.

Faley, R. H., Knapp, D. E., Kustis, G. A., & Dubois, C. L. Z. (1994, May). *Organizational cost of sexual harassment in the workplace.* Paper presented at the Ninth Annual Conference of the Society for Industrial and Organizational Psychology, Nashville, TN.

Fiske, S. T. (1993). Controlling other people: The impact of power on stereotyping. *American Psychologist, 48*, 621–628.

Fiske, S. T. (2001). Effects of power on bias: Power explains and maintains individual, group, and societal disparities. In A. Y. Lee-Chai & J. A. Bargh (Eds.), *The use and abuse of power: Multiple perspectives on the causes of corruption* (pp. 181–194). Philadelphia: Academic Press.

Fiske, S. T., Cuddy, A., Glick, P., & Xu, J. (2002). A model of (often mixed) stereotype content: Competence and warmth respectively follow from perceived status and competition. *Journal of Personality and Social Psychology, 82*, 878–902.

Fiske, S. T., & Neuberg, S. L. (1990). A continuum of impression formation, from category-based to individuating processes: Influences of information and motivation on attention and interpretation. In M. Zanna (Ed.), *Advances in experimental social psychology* (Vol. 23, pp. 1–74). New York: Academic Press.

Foschi, M. (1992). Gender and double standards for competence. In C. L. Ridgeway (Ed.), *Gender, interaction, and inequality* (pp. 181–207). New York: Springer-Verlag.

Gaertner, S. L., & Dovidio, J. F. (1986). The aversive form of racism. In J. F. Dovidio & S. L. Gaertner (Eds.), *Prejudice, discrimination, and racism* (pp. 61–90). Orlando, FL: Academic Press.

Glick, P., Diebold, J., Bailey-Warner, B., & Zhu, L. (1997). The two faces of Adam: Ambivalent sexism and polarized attitudes toward women. *Personality and Social Psychology Bulletin, 23,* 1323–1334.

Glick, P., & Fiske, S. T. (1996). The ambivalent sexism inventory: Differentiating hostile and benevolent sexism. *Journal of Personality and Social Psychology, 70,* 481–512.

Glick, P., & Fiske, S. T. (2002). Ambivalent Responses. *American Psychologist, 57,* 444–446.

Goldin, C. (2002). The rising and then declining significance of gender. Working paper 8915, Cambridge, MA: National Bureau of Economic Research.

Graves, L. (1999). Gender bias in interviewers evaluations of applicants. In G. Powell (Ed.), *Handbook of gender and work* (pp. 145–164). Thousand Oaks, CA: Sage.

Greenhaus, J., & Parasuraman, S. (1999). Research on work, family and gender: Current status and guture directions. In G. N. Powell (Ed.), *Handbook of gender and work* (pp. 391–412). Thousand Oaks, CA: Sage.

Heilman, M. E. (1984). Information as a deterrent against sex discrimination: the effects of applicant sex and information type on preliminary employment decisions. *Organizational Behavior and Human Decision Processes, 33,* 174–186.

Huselid, M. A. (1995). The impact of human resource management practices on turnover, productivity, and corporate financial performance. *Academy of Management Journal, 38,* 635–672.

Huselid, M. A., Jackson, S. E., & Schuler, R. S. (1997). Technical and strategic management effectiveness as determinants of firm performance. *Academy of Management Journal, 40,* 171–188.

Katz, I., & Hass, R. G. (1988). Racial ambivalence and American value conflict: Correlational and priming studies of dual cognitive structures. *Journal of Personality and Social Psychology, 55,* 7893–7905.

Kanter, R. M. (1977). Some effects of proportions on group life: Skewed sex ratios and responses to token women. *American Journal of Sociology, 82,* 965–990.

Keltner, C., Gruenfeld, D. H., & Anderson, C. (2003). Power, approach, and inhibition. *Psychological Review, 110,* 265–284.

Kessler-Harris, A. (1985). The debate over equality for women in the workplace: Recognizing differences. In L. Larwood, A. Stromberg, & B. Gutek (Eds.), *Women and work: An annual review* (Vol. 1, pp 141–161). Beverly Hills, CA: Sage.

Lewis, S., & Cooper, C. L. (1999). The work-family research agenda in changing contexts. *Journal of Occupational Health Psychology, 4,* 382–393.

Lorber, J. (1986). Dismantling Noah's Ark. *Sex Roles, 14,* 567–580.

Lorber, J. (1992). Gender. In Edgar F. Borgatta & Marie L. Borgatta (Eds.), *Encyclopedia of Sociology, 2,* 748–765. NY: Macmillan.

Loy, P. H., & Stewart, L. P. (1984). The extent and effects of the sexual harassment of working women. *Sociological Focus, 17,* 31–43.

Martell, R. F., Lane, D. M., & Emrich, C. (1996). Male-female differences: A computer simulation. *American Psychologist, 51,* 157–158.

Martin, P., & Harkreader, S. (1993). Multiple gender contexts and employee rewards. *Work and Occupations, 20,* 296–336.

McCall, L. (2001). *Complex inequality: Gender, class and race in the new economy.* New York: Routledge.

McConahay, J. B., Hardee, B. B., & Batts, V. (1981). Has racism declined in America? It depends on who is asking and what is asked. *Journal of Conflict Resolution, 25,* 563–579.

Mellor, S., Barnes-Farrell, J., & Stanton, J. (1999). Unions as justice-promoting organizations: The interactive effect of ethnicity, gender, and perceived union effectiveness. *Sex Roles, 40,* 331–346.

Murphy, K. R. (1998). *In search of success: Everyone's criterion problem.* SIOP Presidential Address at the Annual Conference for Industrial and Organizational Psychology, Dallas, TX.

Murphy, K., & Cleveland, J. (1999). *Understanding performance appraisal: Social, organizational and goal-oriented perspectives.* Newbury Park, CA: Sage.

Neumark, D., & McLennan, M. (1995). Sex discrimination and women's labor market outcomes. *Journal of Human Resources, 30,* 713–740.

Ostroff, C., & Atwater, L. E. (2002). *Male or female, young or old: Does who you work with influence your pay or performance rating?* Paper presented at the Annual Conference of the Academy of Management, Denver, CO.

Padavic, I., & Reskin, B. (2002). *Women and men at work.* Thousand Oaks, CA: Pine Force Press.

Park, B., & Judd, C. M. (1990). Measures and models of perceived variability. *Journal of Personality and Social Psychology, 59,* 173–191.

Powell, G. N. (1999). Reflections on the glass ceiling: Recent trends and future prospects. In G. N. Powell (Ed.), *Handbook of gender and work* (pp. 325–346). Thousand Oaks, CA: Sage.

Presser, H. B. (1999). Toward a 24-7 economy. *Science, 284*(Issue No. 5421), 1778–1779.

Pryor, J. B. (1995). The psychosocial impact of sexual harassment on women in the U.S. military. *Journal of Social Issues, 17,* 581–604.

Pulakos, E. D., White, L. A., Oppler, S. H., & Borman, W. C. (1989). Examination of race and sex effects on performance ratings. *Journal of Applied Psychology, 74,* 770–780.

Rantalaiho, L., Heiskanen, T., Korvajarvi, P., & Vehvilainen, M. (1997). Studying gendered practices. In L. Rantalaiho and T. Heiskanen (Eds.), *Gendered practices in working life* (pp. 3–15). New York: St. Martin's Press.

Reskin, B. F., & Ross, C. E. (1995). Jobs, authority and earnings among managers: The continuing significance of sex. In J. Jacobs (Ed.), *Gender inequality at work* (pp. 127–151). Thousand Oaks, CA: Sage.

Rice, R. W., Bender, R. L., & Vitters, A. G. (1980). Leader sex, follower attitudes toward women and leadership effectiveness: A laboratory experiment. *Organizational Behavior and Human Performance, 25,* 46–78.

Sanchez, L., & Thomson, E. (1997). Becoming mothers and fathers: Parenthood, gender, and the division of labor. *Gender and Society, 11,* 742–772.

Schneider, K. T., Swan, S., & Fitzgerald, L. F. (1997). Job-related and psychological effects of sexual harassment in the workplace: Empirical evidence from two organizations. *Journal of Applied Psychology, 82,* 401–415.

Shaffer, M. A., Joplin, J., Bell, M., Lau, R., & Oguz, C. (1999). Gender discrimination and job-related outcomes: A cross-cultural comparison of working women in the United States and China. *Journal of Vocational Behavior, 57,* 395–427.

Silvester, J. (1996). Questioning discrimination in the selection interview: A case for more field research: Commentary. *Feminism and Psychology, 6,* 574–578.

Smithey, P. N., & Lewis, G. B. (1998). Gender, race and training in the federal civil service. *Public Administration Quarterly, 22*(2), 204–228.

Swim, J. K., Aiken, K. J., Hall, W. S., & Hunter, B. A. (1995). Sexism and racism: Old-fashioned and modern prejudices. *Journal of Personality and Social Psychology, 68,* 199–214.

Taylor, S. E., Fiske, S. T., Etcoff, N., & Ruderman, A. (1978). The categorical and contextual bases of person memory and stereotyping. *Journal of Personality and Social Psychology, 36,* 78–793.

Thompson, C. A., Beauvais, L. L., & Lyness, K. S. (1999). When work-family benefits are not enough: The influence of work-family culture on benefit utilization, organizational attachment, and work-family conflict. *Journal of Vocational Behavior, 54,* 392–415.

Tosi, H. L., & Einbender, S. W. (1985). The effects of the type and amount of information in sex discrimination research: A meta-analysis. *Academy of Management Journal, 28,* 712–723.

Trentham, S., & Larwood, L. (1998). Gender discrimination and the workplace: An examination of rational bias theory. *Sex Roles, 38,* 1–28.

United States Department of Labor (2001). *Highlights of women's earnings.* Washington, DC: U.S. Department of Labor. [On-line]. Available: http://www.bls.gov/cps/cpswom2000.pdf.

United States Department of Labor (2002). *Highlights of women's earnings.* Washington, DC: U.S. Department of Labor. [On-line]. Available: http://www.bls.gov/cps/cpswom2001.pdf.

United States Merit Systems Protection Board (1995). *Sexual harassment in the Federal workplace: Trends, progress, and continuing challenges.* Washington, DC: U. S. Government Printing Office.

Valian, V. (1998). *Why so slow?* Cambridge, MA: MIT Press.

Vescio, T. K., & Biernat, M. (1999). When stereotype-based expectancies impair performance: The effect of prejudice, race, and target quality on judgments and perceiver performance. *European Journal of Social Psychology, 29,* 961–969.

Vescio, T. K., Gervais, S., Snyder, M., & Hoover, A. (2004). *Power and the creation of patronizing environments: The stereotype-based behavior of the powerful and their consequences for female performance in masculine domains.* Manuscript submitted for publication.

Vescio, T. K., Snyder, M., & Butz, D. A. (2003). Power in stereotypically masculine domains: A social influence strategy X stereotype match model. *Journal of Personality and Social Psychology, 85,* 1062–1078.

Waldfogel, J. (1998). Understanding the "family gap" in pay for women with children. *Journal of Economic Perspectives, 12,* 137–156.

8

Understanding Heterosexism at Work: The Straight Problem

Belle Rose Ragins
University of Wisconsin, Milwaukee

Carolyn Wiethoff
Indiana University, Bloomington

Gay and lesbian employees constitute between 4% and 17% of the U.S. workforce (Gonsiorek & Weinrich, 1991), a larger proportion than many other minority groups. However, unlike racism and sexism in organizations, relatively little attention has been paid to *heterosexism*, or the anti-gay attitudes, prejudice, and discrimination encountered by gay men and lesbians in the workplace (Sears, 1997). Gay and lesbian employees face unique challenges that have no real parallel in other minority groups (Ragins, 2004; Ragins, Cornwell, & Miller, 2003). Most notably, discrimination against gay and lesbian employees, or even those who appear to be gay or lesbian, is legal in most workplaces in the United States (Herrschaft & Mills, 2002). Between 25% and 66% of gay and lesbian employees experience workplace discrimination, including losing their jobs because of their sexual orientation (see review by Croteau, 1996). This represents a conservative estimate because most gay and lesbian employees do not fully reveal their sexual identity at work (Badgett, 1996; Ragins & Cornwell, 2001a). Moreover, unlike race and gender, sexual orientation is generally invisible. This complicates the study of both heterosexism and the workplace experiences of gay and lesbian employees. Finally, there is an affective component of heterosexism, *homophobia*, that has no counterpart in racism or sexism.

As these differences suggest, existing models and theories of race and gender discrimination may have limited applicability to the study of sexual orientation-based discrimination. We need to chart a separate, though related, course of study that examines the unique workplace experiences of this understudied population. The purpose of this chapter is to guide future research by illuminating the complexities, issues, and dilemmas in the study of sexual orientation in the workplace. We start by defining sexual orientation, heterosexism, and homophobia and by reviewing distinctions between gays and lesbians and other identity groups. Next, we provide a brief review of the antecedents and consequences of heterosexism in the workplace. We then examine methodological issues involved with identifying and surveying gay and lesbian employees in organizational research. Finally, we provide a brief overview of biases that can hinder research on sexual orientation in the workplace and identify areas for future research.

DEFINING THE CONSTRUCTS

Sexual Orientation

For 50 years, researchers have struggled with the complexities involved in defining sexual orientation. Early research used a simple bipolar behavioral perspective: Individuals were viewed as either heterosexual or homosexual based on whether they engaged in sexual relations with someone of the same biological sex (Kinsey, Pomeroy, & Martin, 1948; Kinsey, Pomeroy, Martin, & Gebhard, 1953). Garnets and Kimmel (1993) identified three limitations associated with this simple dichotomy. First, individuals may engage in homosexual behaviors without viewing themselves as gay or lesbian. This is particularly significant when studying adolescents engaging in sexual experimentation and individuals in cultures that do not view same-sex sexual contact as homosexuality (Schmitt & Sofer, 1992). Second, like heterosexuals, gay men and lesbians may self-identify as gay, but choose to be celibate. The decision to engage in same-sex sexual behaviors is complex and may follow or precede the development of a gay or lesbian identity (Rivers, 1997). Third, this simple dichotomy views bisexuality as falling midway on a single dimension between homosexuality and heterosexuality. This ignores the complexity of a bisexual identity and excludes those who are transgendered and transsexual (cf., Horowitz & Newcomb, 2001).

Recognizing these limitations, researchers began to define sexual orientation more precisely (Coleman, 1987; Garnets & Kimmel, 1993). Three main distinctions emerged. First, instead of viewing sexual orientation as a single dimension, sexual orientation was viewed as falling along two continuous scales of homosexuality and heterosexuality. This view allowed for a more accurate assessment of bisexuals (i.e., those with high scores on both the heterosexual and homosexual dimensions) and also addressed the construct of asexuality (i.e., those with low scores on both dimensions.) Second, a distinction was made between behavioral preference, based on physical actions, and affectional preference, based on feelings and emotions (Shively & DeCecco, 1977). This distinction allowed for the scenario in which an individual is physically attracted to one sex, but emotionally attracted to another. Third, sexual identity was conceptualized as involving four factors: (a) biological sex; (b) gender identity, which is the individual's sense of being male or female; (c) social sex role, which involves the display of characteristics that are culturally stereotyped as masculine or feminine, and (d) sexual orientation, which involves both behavioral and affectional dimensions. These four components may not be congruent. For example, a biological woman with a male gender identity may be in a same-gender relationship but self-identity as heterosexual because of her gender identity.

Heterosexism and Homophobia

Heterosexuals' negative attitudes toward gay men and lesbians have been given a number of different names. In 1972, Weinberg coined the phrase *homophobia* to describe the dread of being in close quarters with gay men (Weinberg, 1972). Although this term was intended to capture the personal discomfort and fear, often at phobic levels, that some heterosexuals feel when associating with gay men and lesbians (Herek, 1984), it is often inappropriately used to describe all negative attitudes toward lesbians and gay men (Logan, 1996). Phobic reactions include emotional responses of anger and anxiety that are not typically present in prejudice toward lesbians and gays (Berkman & Zinberg, 1997). Indeed, overusing the term homophobia, as is done when all prejudice toward lesbians and gays is described in this manner, may be counterproductive in that true cases of homophobia could be left untreated (Haaga, 1991).

Research suggests that most prejudiced reactions to lesbians and gays are best conceived of as just that—prejudice—rather than phobias (Logan, 1996). A more appropriate term to describe negative attitudes toward gays and lesbians is *heterosexism*. This term reflects the belief that heterosexuality is the only legitimate sexual orientation, such that alternatives to it need not be acknowledged (Simoni & Walters, 2001). Heterosexism is defined as "an ideological system that denies, denigrates, and stigmatizes any non-heterosexual form of behavior, identity, relationship, or community" (Herek, 1993, p. 89).

Armed with an understanding of the terms and constructs central to understanding prejudice against lesbians and gay men, we now examine the qualities of sexual orientation that make lesbians, gay men, and bisexual and transgendered men and women unique from other minority groups.

UNDERSTANDING THE UNIQUE EXPERIENCES OF GAY EMPLOYEES

Invisible Group Membership

The invisibility of sexual orientation sets gay men and lesbians apart from most other marginalized groups (Ragins, 2004). For the most part, the sexual orientation of gay and lesbian employees becomes visible only when they communicate it, a process known as "coming out." Coming out is an ongoing process, and the decision to disclose sexual orientation must be made with every new person a gay man or lesbian meets (Appleby, 2001). Consequently, gay and lesbian employees face an ongoing and often challenging process of negotiating their invisible identity in the workplace (cf., Creed & Scully, 2000; Johnson, 1997; Ragins, 2004).

Gay and lesbian employees use various strategies to manage disclosure of their sexual identity. Woods (1993) identified three tactics used in the workplace. Individuals can: (a) "counterfeit" or construct a heterosexual identity; (b) use an avoidance strategy in which they evade the issue, maintain a social distance, and appear to be asexual; and (c) use an integration strategy and openly disclose their sexual identity to others at work. Woods (1993) found that nearly all of the 70 gay male professional workers under study sought to avoid discrimination by posing as a heterosexual at some point in their careers (see also Badgett, 1996). Existing research indicates that gay and lesbian employees' attitudes towards identifying with gay groups, as well as the organizational context, predict the use of various identity management strategies (Button, 2001; Chrobot-Mason, Button, & DiClementi, 2001; Ragins & Cornwell, 2001b).

Most gay and lesbian employees report that they limit the disclosure of their sexual identity to a select group of trustworthy coworkers (c.f., reviews by Croteau, 1996; Ragins, 2004). For example, a recent national study of 534 gay men and lesbians revealed that 12% of the sample were out to no one at work, 37% were out to some people, 24% were out to most people, and 27% reported that they were out to everyone at work (Ragins & Cornwell, 2001a). Coming out to some coworkers, but not all, can create considerable ambiguity as to "who knows and who does not."

Research on the work and individual outcomes associated with disclosure yields inconsistent findings. Some researchers found that gay and lesbian employees who disclosed their sexual orientation to more people at work had less general anxiety (Jordan & Deluty, 1998), greater job satisfaction, and less job anxiety (Griffith & Hebl, 2002) than those who did not disclose. However, other researchers found no relationship between disclosure and work attitudes, psychological strain, or occupational coping (Croteau & Lark, 1995; Driscoll, Kelley, & Fassinger, 1996). In fact, some studies found that gay and lesbian employees who disclosed to more people at work had lower continuance organizational commitment (Day & Schoenrade, 1997), earned less compensation (Ellis & Riggle, 1995; Schneider, 1987), and had less pay satisfaction (Ellis & Riggle, 1995) than those who concealed their sexual identity from others in the workplace. One reason for these inconsistent findings may be that the actual decision to disclose at work, although important and complex, has less of an impact than the immediate fears preceding this decision. In fact, Ragins and Cornwell (2001b) found that the fear of negative consequences of disclosure had a greater impact on work attitudes and psychological strain than the actual disclosure decision, which brought a sense of relief to gay and lesbian employees. This suggests that the organization's climate is a key factor to consider when examining outcomes associated with disclosure; staying in the closet may be an optimal survival strategy for gay and lesbian employees in hostile organizational climates. However, when gay and lesbian workers feel free to "be their true selves" in the workplace, the organization may also benefit. For example, Creed and Scully (2000) observed that disclosure of a gay or lesbian identity in the workplace is a tool for positive change, as it can heighten others' awareness of the potential for heterosexism and discrimination.

Support for Identity

Gay and lesbian employees get little support in managing their sexual identities, and the coming out process is usually a difficult and isolating experience (c.f. Garnets & Kimmel, 1993; Rivers, 1997). Because families of lesbians and gay men are typically heterosexual, they often cannot provide adult gay children with role models or coping mechanisms to address heterosexism. Whereas the family unit is a source of support for many people of color, families are often disrupted, and even lost, when adult gay children come out to their families. Similarly, close friends can be alienated or lost during the coming out process. Supportive relationships in the workplace may also be disrupted; gay and lesbian employees who disclose at work may lose mentors, role models, and important peer relationships. Similarly, gay and lesbian employees who hide their sexual identity may need to keep a social distance that precludes the development of supportive work relationships. Finally, unlike that of other racial and ethnic groups, gay history is rarely taught in school and is not passed on through family traditions, thus limiting the sense of gay pride and community. Consequently, many lesbian and gay employees face isolation and limited support for their sexual identity both in and out of the workplace.

Compounding the lack of support for gays' and lesbians' sexual identities are the negative reactions they may receive from coworkers. As previously noted, the invisibility of sexual orientation fuels the paranoia of homophobia and has no parallel in race or gender. In addition, the invisibility of sexual orientation amplifies "courtesy stigmas" (Goffman, 1963; Herek & Capitanio, 1996). Heterosexuals may avoid associating with gay and lesbian coworkers because they fear that they will be perceived as being gay if they simply extend the "courtesy" of socializing with gay colleagues. This outcome of stigma does not occur on the basis of gender and rarely on the basis of race. In summary, these processes create a unique sense of isolation among gay and lesbian employees.

Understanding the unique challenges faced by lesbians and gay men at work is a prerequisite for appreciating the reasons for prejudice toward them. In the next section, we first provide an overview of the extent of sexual orientation discrimination. We then explore the antecedents and consequences of heterosexism in the workplace.

THE NATURE AND CONSEQUENCES OF HETEROSEXISM IN THE WORKPLACE

Extent of Discrimination and Societal Sanctions

Heterosexism, and the discrimination it engenders, is well documented in the United States. Survey research indicates that nine out of ten gay men and lesbians have faced verbal abuse or threats, and more than one in five have been physically assaulted because of their sexual orientation (Elliott, 2000). In fact, gays and lesbians are more likely to be victims of hate crimes in the United States than are members of many other social groups (Nelson & Krieger, 1997). Some of the stigma that continues to be associated with homosexuals, particularly gay men, is related to the AIDS epidemic: about 40% of the American population holds the outdated belief that AIDS is spread primarily through homosexual behavior (Herek & Capitanio, 1999). Studies of prejudice and discrimination toward gays and lesbians in countries other than the United States have produced similar findings. Heterosexism and the resulting negative treatment of lesbians and gays has been documented in Canada (Mallon, 2001), Britain (Ellis & Fox, 2001), Israel (Ben-Ari, 2001), New Zealand (Appleby, 2001), and India (Bhugra, 1997). Heterosexism is particularly prevalent in countries where conservative religious beliefs shape social mores, such as strongly Islamic countries in the Middle East (Schmitt & Sofer, 1992).

Although relatively little research has examined the nature and effects of workplace discrimination toward gay men and lesbians (Croteau, 1996), existing reports indicate this discrimination is fierce (Van Den Bergh, 1999). Research indicates that more than half of those who disclose their sexual orientations at work experience discrimination on the job (Croteau, 1996; Ragins & Cornwell, 2001a), including termination of employment (Croteau, 1996).

One reason for this continued discrimination is its legality. Internationally, gays and lesbians are not protected by the United Nation's Universal Declaration of Human Rights (Wetzel, 2001) and the United States lacks federal legislation prohibiting sexual orientation discrimination. At this writing, only 14 states, the District of Columbia, 119 cities, and 23 counties in the United States have passed ordinances banning sexual orientation discrimination in employment, and it is estimated that only one-fifth of gay and lesbian Americans live in areas that offer this protection (Herrschaft & Mills, 2002).

The absence of legislation prohibiting sexual orientation discrimination in the workplace is an important antecedent of discrimination. A recent study found that gay and lesbian employees in organizations covered by protective legislation reported significantly less heterosexism in the workplace than did employees in organizations not covered by protective legislation (Ragins & Cornwell, 2001a). Still, discrimination against employees who are gay or lesbian (or are merely perceived to be) is legal in most workplaces.

Organizational Antecedents of Heterosexism

A key factor in reducing heterosexism in the workplace is the presence of "gay-friendly" organizational policies and practices. These range from policies that prohibit sexual orientation discrimination to practices that create a more inclusive workplace climate (Button, 2001; Ragins & Cornwell,

2001a). Companies that lack protective policies and practices may foster a climate of heterosexism in the workplace (Button, 2001). For example, Ragins and Cornwell (2001a) found that gay and lesbian employees were less likely to report sexual orientation discrimination in organizations that (a) had written policies forbidding it, (b) included sexual orientation discrimination in their definition of diversity, or (c) offered same-sex domestic partner benefits. In fact, although the presence of protective legislation and gay coworkers were significantly related to reduced reports of discrimination, the overriding variable affecting reported discrimination was the presence of gay-friendly organizational policies and practices. A particularly interesting finding was that of all the gay-friendly practices and policies examined, inviting same-sex partners to company social events had the strongest relationship to reduced reports of workplace discrimination. This practice reflects a climate that is not only inclusive of gay employees, but also promotes and reflects a high comfort level in social interactions with them. Work climate is clearly a key predictor of workplace heterosexism (Button, 2001; Driscoll, Kelley, & Fassinger, 1996), and other research indicates that heterosexism is positively related to perceptions that the employer lacks antidiscrimination policies, does not take such policies seriously, and will permit the open expression of heterosexist attitudes in the workplace (Monteith, 1996; Waldo, 1999).

Group Level Antecedents

Heterosexism in the workplace may be affected by a number of group-level factors. First, we can examine the influence of the group's relational demography on individual and group outcomes. Relational demography theory is based on the principle that the more similar the individual is to the work group, the more positive will be the individual's work attitudes and behaviors (Riordan, 2000). In support of relational demography predictions, Ragins, Cornwell & Miller (2003) found that gay and lesbian employees with gay supervisors or primarily gay work groups were more likely to be out at work and reported less heterosexism than those who worked in mostly heterosexual work teams. In addition, gay and lesbian employees were more likely to disclose their sexual identity when they had supervisors of the same race or ethnicity, regardless of the supervisor's sexual orientation. However, no support was found for demography predictions regarding gender similarity, perhaps because these predictions assume that gender similarity dispels underlying sexual tensions or other relational difficulties, which may not be the case for gay and lesbian employees.

The demography of the workgroup may not be as important as the attitudes held by group members and the degree to which gay employees receive support from their coworkers. For example, in one study, even when holding the sexual orientation of the group constant, gay and lesbian employees with supportive coworkers and supervisors reported less fear of disclosure and were more likely to be out at work than those lacking a supportive work group (Ragins & Cornwell, 2001b). This suggests that the presence of supportive heterosexual coworkers also allows gay and lesbian employees to bring their true identity to work.

In summary, this research suggests that, when individuals within a work group have heterosexist attitudes, gay and lesbian employees are likely to feel threatened, resulting in less group cohesion and, potentially, more group conflict. On the other hand, when group members have tolerant and/or positive attitudes toward homosexuality, lesbians and gays can be open and productive members of the team.

Individual Level Antecedents

In addition to examining organizational- and group-level predictors, researchers have tried to determine personal aspects of heterosexuals that correlate with heterosexism. Although no studies support the claim that individual traits cause heterosexism, they do create a general profile of heterosexuals who are most likely to hold these attitudes. For example, some research indicates that race and ethnicity may affect attitudes toward gays and lesbians; both Asians (Lippincott, Wlazelek, & Schumacher, 2000) and African Americans (Herek & Capitanio, 1999) were found to harbor more heterosexism than their Caucasian counterparts. Results of this work also indicated that heterosexual men are typically less tolerant of gays and lesbians, particularly gay men, than are heterosexual women (Moss, 2001). Additionally, antigay prejudice is stronger among men and women who strongly adhere to traditional gender roles (Kite & Whitley, 1998). This may be related to a more general finding that people who support rigid social rules, such as those who adhere to right-wing authoritarianism (Whitley & Lee, 2000) and socially conservative philosophies (Heaven & Oxman, 1999) are also likely to harbor negative attitudes toward lesbians and gays. Similarly, individuals who hold traditional and conservative religious values are often opposed to homosexuality on religious grounds (Hunter, 1991). Existing research indicates more negative attitudes toward homosexuality among individuals with fundamentalist Christian religious orientations (Kirkpatrick, 1993), and those from conservative non-Christian religions, such as Muslims (Beck, 1999). Finally, researchers have found links between heterosexist attitudes and (a) sexist attitudes in general (Stevenson & Medler, 1995), (b) personal contact with gay men and lesbians (Horvath & Ryan, 2003) and (c) the belief that homosexuality is a choice rather than a biological orientation (King, 2001).

Consequences of Discrimination

Now that we understand the antecedents of heterosexism, we can begin to examine some of the outcomes associated with its practice. Research in this area addresses two basic questions. First, what are the behavioral consequences of heterosexism? And second, how do gays and lesbians react to this treatment? This section will explore each of these questions in turn.

Heterosexism prompts heterosexuals to engage in a variety of negative behaviors toward lesbians and gay men in the workplace. At best, these behaviors can be described as "avoidance"; at worst, they represent overt and aggressive forms of discrimination and physical harassment (Bernat, Calhoun, Adams, & Zeichner, 2001). A national study of 534 gay and lesbian professionals revealed that over a third had been physically or verbally harassed in prior positions because of their sexual orientation, 37% faced discrimination because others suspected or assumed that they were gay or lesbian, and 12% left their last job because of sexual orientation discrimination (Ragins & Cornwell, 2001b). Swim and her colleagues found that heterosexual women made public statements to distance themselves from attitudes and opinions held by a lesbian (Swim, Ferguson & Hyers, 1999). Other studies indicate that individuals who hold heterosexist beliefs help gays and lesbians far less than do those without this prejudice (Ellis & Fox, 2001). Similarly, Kite and Deaux (1986) found less information-seeking behaviors and more guarded self-presentation among heterosexual males interacting with a gay man. Participants in other research experiments were found to speak more quickly and abruptly to people believed to be gay (Cuenot & Fugita, 1982) and to label gay men as less preferred work partners, regardless of the quality of their work (Karr, 1978). Moreover, although many heterosexuals recognize that overt discrimination is unacceptable or illegal in some locales, more subtle forms of interpersonal discrimination emerge. For example, one study found that while job applicants who posed as gay men and lesbians did not face overt workplace discrimination, they still were subject to interpersonal biases that resulted in shorter job interviews, less eye contact, and more negative and truncated communication interactions (Hebl, Foster, Mannix, & Dovidio, 2002). This suggests that even in the presence of formal organizational policies and legislation that prohibit discrimination more subtle, even unconscious, forms of discrimination can persist.

This research suggests that prejudiced heterosexuals can make work life difficult to intolerable for lesbian and gay colleagues. At best, gay and lesbian workers are avoided; at worst, they face overt job discrimination or even physical assault. To date, very few studies have directly investigated the effects of workplace heterosexist behaviors on lesbians and gays, but the existing research provides some insight. First, heterosexism thwarts career progression for many lesbians and gay men (Friskopp & Silverstein, 1996). For example, one study found that lesbians limited their job and career choices to avoid heterosexist work environments (Fassinger, 1996). Gay male workers have been found to earn significantly less compensation than their heterosexual counterparts, although this finding was not replicated for lesbians (Badgett, 1995, 2001; Black, Makar, Sanders, & Taylor, 2003; Clain & Leppel, 2001). Other studies confirm that heterosexism has a negative effect on lesbians' and gays' workplace productivity (Powers, 1996). Additionally, the Ragins and Cornwell (2001a) study cited earlier found that greater reports of workplace heterosexism were associated with fewer promotions over a 10-year period. In this investigation, reports of heterosexism also had a negative relationship with job satisfaction, organizational commitment, career commitment, organization-based self-esteem, and satisfaction with opportunities for promotion, and a positive relationship with intentions to leave the job. Moreover, repeated discriminatory treatment takes its toll on lesbian and gay workers. Research documents the stress gay men and lesbians experience as a result of the discrimination they encounter both on and off the job (e.g., Bosanok, 1995; Waldo, 1999). The health hazards associated with this stress include drug and alcohol abuse (Appleby, 2001), mental health problems (Garnets, Herek, & Levy, 1992), and diminished physical health and well being (DiPlacido, 1998).

Research into the antecedents and consequences of heterosexism has unique methodological and conceptual challenges. We now turn to examining some of these dilemmas.

METHODOLOGICAL AND CONCEPTUAL ISSUES IN STUDYING HETEROSEXISM IN THE WORKPLACE

In this section we review some of the key conceptual and methodological challenges confronting research on heterosexism in the workplace. These include the measurement of sexual orientation and workplace

discrimination, the disclosure of sexual identity, and practical issues relating to obtaining a representative sample of gay and lesbian respondents.

Operationalizing Sexual Orientation

One key methodological issue is the operationalization of sexual orientation; findings may well vary as a function of the way it is operationalized
(Black, Gates, Sanders, & Taylor, 2000; Herek, Kimmel, Amaro & Melton,
1991). The two primary methods are behavioral reports and self-labeling.
There are limitations to each of these methods (Martin & Knox, 2000). Behavioral reports exclude individuals who self-identify as gay but have not
acted on their feelings because of choice or opportunity. They also may
eliminate those in early stages of sexual identity development (Troiden,
1989) and those who are celibate. Behavioral reports may also misclassify
people who have same-sex relations but maintain a heterosexual identity,
such as those who engage in same-sex behaviors while in married heterosexual relationships.

Self-labeling eliminates some of these problems, but also brings a unique
set of limitations. Gay men and lesbians may choose not to label themselves as such for a number of reasons. To start, they may be hesitant to
openly assume an identity that can make them targets of discrimination
(Herek, 1991). Respondents may view themselves as gay or lesbian, but
checking the "gay" option on a survey or sharing this information in an
interview may be a self-defining act that elicits discomfort or anxiety. In
addition, sexual identity is often experienced as a fluid and changing state
that varies by time, place, and person (e.g., Horowitz & Newcomb, 2001);
a cross-sectional approach to self-identification is limited in this regard.
In short, although many respondents may have little difficulty checking
survey boxes that indicate their race or gender, sexual identity is quite a
different matter.

Another limitation of the self-labeling approach is that sexual identity
may vary by age and geographic location (Martin & Knox, 2000). Older
gay men and lesbians, and those living in areas with highly visible gay
populations, may be more likely to self-identify than are young people
who have just come to terms with their sexual identity or those living
in locations with a less visible gay community. Self-labeling may also be
affected by the gender of the respondent (Martin & Knox, 2000). Garnets
and Kimmel (1993) observed that lesbians were often more delayed in
their sexual identity development than were gay men, and thus were more
likely to deny same-sex attraction and enter heterosexual relationships
because of social pressures. Because of the limitations involved with both

self-labeling and behavioral reports of sexual orientation, Martin and Knox (2000) advised that studies provide respondents with a host of options to describe their sexual identity. In particular, respondents should be allowed to indicate same-gender attraction, sexual and affectional behaviors, and to report if they have gay identities.

Measuring Direct and Indirect Discrimination

Another important issue is the distinction between direct and indirect forms of workplace discrimination (Ragins, 2004). Direct forms of discrimination are overt (i.e., denial of a promotion because an employee is gay or lesbian). However, because most gay employees do not disclose their sexual identity to everyone in their workplace (Badgett, 1996), they may avoid being targets for direct discrimination. Although closeted gay and lesbian employees may experience less direct discrimination, they may still experience indirect discrimination by watching negative treatment of other openly gay and lesbian coworkers or hearing heterosexist comments and jokes. Indirect discrimination is undoubtedly stressful for gay and lesbian employees, who may retreat further into the closet after hearing heterosexist comments or observing discriminatory treatment of gay coworkers.

Experiences of indirect discrimination may also affect gay and lesbian employees' perceptions and attributions about direct discrimination. For example, a gay employee may be more likely to assume that the loss of a promotion is due to his sexual identity if he overheard his supervisor making an anti-gay comment. A key issue here is the degree to which the gay employee is out at work. Because the supervisor's actions may in fact be driven by knowledge of the employee's sexual orientation, the degree of disclosure is an important variable to both study and control for in investigations of heterosexism in the workplace.

Examining the Relationship Between Disclosure and Discrimination

Disclosure of sexual identity in the workplace is intricately linked to experiences of heterosexism in the workplace and presents its own quagmire of methodological challenges. Let us relay a few scenarios that capture some of these complexities. Consider a lesbian employee who believes that no one at work knows she is gay, although many of her coworkers have known or suspected for some time. Or, perhaps she disclosed her sexual identity to a few trusted coworkers, but unbeknownst to her, word has spread to everyone else in the organization. Finally, consider the scenario where she makes no attempt to hide her sexual orientation, but coworkers are simply oblivious to her gay identity. These scenarios illustrate both that self-reports of disclosure may not reflect the actual degree of disclosure and that coworker's reports of sexual orientation are fallible.

There are a number of potential outcomes associated with these scenarios. One is that gay and lesbian employees may experience discrimination based on their sexual orientation, but may not perceive or report it because they believe that no one knows they are gay. Another outcome is that gay and lesbian employees mistakenly believe that their sexual identity is known to all and therefore misattribute negative work outcomes to heterosexism. Reports and attributions of heterosexism may become even more complex for gay and lesbian people of color, who may question whether a negative work outcome was due to their sexual orientation, gender, race, or just their work performance. Finally, heterosexual employees who are assumed to be gay may encounter sexual orientation discrimination, but may not perceive or report it because they are unaware of these perceptions. These outcomes also point to a much broader issue: the distinction between reported and actual discrimination. Self-reports of discrimination reflect perceptions that may over- or under-estimate actual discrimination. Although this is an issue in the study of workplace discrimination for all groups (cf. Ruggiero & Taylor, 1995), the variability in the visibility of sexual orientation, and the uncertainty as to "who knows and who does not," makes this a critical issue in the study of gay men and lesbians in the workplace. However, even though self-reports may or may not reflect actual discrimination, perceived discrimination is the employee's reality and most certainly affects his or her work attitudes, behavior, and psychological stress.

To more accurately assess heterosexism in the workplace, it is useful to examine both heterosexual and gay employees' perceptions. A good example of this was a study of 71,570 service members on 38 military bases and 11 navel vessels (Myers, 2000). Recognizing that the military's "don't ask, don't tell" policy would bias reports of heterosexism, the researchers did not ask respondents to reveal their sexual orientation and instead simply asked about the work climate for gay military personnel. They found that, in the past year, 80% of the respondents had heard offensive speech, derogatory names, jokes, or remarks about gays, and 37% had witnessed or experienced an incident of harassment based on perceived homosexuality. More than half of these incidents involved threats, unfair discipline, or discrimination in training or career opportunities. This study provides a good example of an alternative method of assessing heterosexism in the workplace.

In summary, it is important to study both direct and indirect forms of sexual orientation discrimination from the perspective of gay and lesbian employees and their heterosexual coworkers. A key factor in these investigations is disclosure in the workplace, which can also be measured using multiple perspectives. This multisource approach will help disentangle the perceptual and attributional processes that permeate reports of heterosexism in the workplace. We now turn to some practical issues involved with identifying a sample of gay and lesbian employees.

Identifying Target Populations

A key challenge in the study of sexual orientation in the workplace is obtaining a representative sample of gay or lesbian respondents. Although the routine practice of surveying members of organizations is effective for studying race and gender, this practice has limitations for gay and lesbian employees. Those who are not out at work may be reluctant to participate in a study of heterosexism in the workplace. They may not return surveys or even could report that they are heterosexual, thus jeopardizing the key variable in the study. In addition to creating unknown error variance, this method may also introduce a response bias in that gay and lesbian employees may be more likely to return a survey on sexual orientation if they are out at work. Because of these issues and limitations, studies of heterosexism in the workplace often rely on nonprobability samples, such as using members of gay or lesbian organizations, or rely on snowballing sampling techniques. These samples avoid some of the problems discussed above, but face limitations to the generalizability of findings. Herek and his colleagues (Herek et al., 1991) point out that these limitations can be reduced by targeting participants from a variety of settings (i.e., gay coffeehouses, political or religious organizations, community centers, bookstores, social clubs, parenting groups, and student organizations). In addition, respondents can be recruited through electronic or paper advertisements in gay publications and through exit polls at voting sites in primarily gay neighborhoods.

There are other issues involved with sampling gay and lesbian employees. Because most gay and lesbian employees conceal their sexual identity to some degree at work, privacy and confidentiality become critical issues. Martin and Knox (2000) note that gay and lesbian employees may feel uncomfortable disclosing their sexual identity to researchers for fear that word will spread and result in discrimination, retaliation, or even physical harm. These fears are well grounded because it is legal in most states to terminate an employee simply for being gay or lesbian (Herrschaft & Mills, 2002).

Now that we have reviewed some methodological and conceptual issues in studying heterosexism, we turn to an examination of some heterosexist biases that pervade research on sexual orientation and diversity in the workplace.

HETEROSEXIST BIASES IN RESEARCH

A number of potential biases hinder effective research on sexual orientation in the workplace, as well as more general research on diversity in organizations. In this section, we examine some of these potential biases and their associated limitations.

Biases in Research on Sexual Orientation in the Workplace

Herek and his colleagues (Herek et al., 1991) identified a number of specific biases present in research on gay men and lesbians. First, they observed that lesbians and gay men are often viewed as a single homogeneous group, thus masking significant gender differences between them. Garnets and Kimmel (1993) emphasized the limitations involved in grouping gay men and lesbians together, and contend that: "Gender is a powerful organizer of sexual behavior, identity, and relationship patterns. In general, gay men are more similar to heterosexual men, and lesbian women are more similar to heterosexual women, than to each other" (p. 25).

Second, researchers failed to examine the mediating influences of race, ethnicity, class, age, and other social group memberships (Herek et al., 1991). Such research not only fails to examine the effects of multiple group memberships on workplace experiences of gay men and lesbians, but also does not recognize that gay people of color may experience racism within the gay community. Gender, race, and sexual orientation may have cumulative or independent effects on experiences of heterosexism and other forms of workplace discrimination. Significant gender and race effects were in fact found in a recent study of 534 gay and lesbian employees, 162 of whom were gay employees of color (Ragins et al., 2003). Specifically, lesbians in male-dominated environments reported more heterosexism than did gay men. In addition, gay employees of color were less likely to disclose their sexual identity at work than their White counterparts, which is supported by other research indicating that gay men of color are more frequent targets of workplace discrimination than other groups (Crow, Fok, & Hartman, 1998).

A third limitation is that research on sexual orientation usually fails to analyze transgendered and bisexual people (Herek et al., 1991). In the few instances where they are studied, these individuals are most often grouped with gay men and lesbians, offering little information or insight into their unique workplace experiences.

There are other more subtle biases in research on sexual orientation in the workplace. Most studies focus exclusively on gay employees, thus assuming that only gay men and lesbians have a sexual orientation. Research on sexual orientation in the workplace essentially becomes a study of the "other" and fails to examine the cumulative effects of heterosexuality on workplace policies and norms. A poststructuralist queer theory approach to this issue (i.e., Namaste, 1996) would entail an examination of how heterosexuality is infused into workplace cultures, norms, policies, and practices. An example of the pervasiveness of heterosexist norms on workplace culture is the concept of "family-friendly workplaces." Family is defined as heterosexual in both implicit and explicit ways. Even in many family-friendly organizations, gay and lesbian employees are denied health care benefits for their partners. Display of family pictures is accepted and even implicitly encouraged for heterosexuals, but gay employees who display pictures of their partners meet with a quite different reaction (Herek, 1996).

A final limitation is that research on sexual orientation has often relied on person-centered variables, ignoring the influence of group and organizational level variables. Martin and Knox (2000) point out that researchers often rely on person-centered variables because they are easier to measure and are less complex. However, a focus on person-centered variables may lead to an inadvertent blaming of gay men and lesbians for their own predicament, or of labeling particular groups as "heterosexist," rather than examining the environmental and cultural factors that affect workplace discrimination.

Heterosexist Biases and Assumptions in Diversity Research

It is telling that although researchers have been studying diversity in organizations for the past 15 years, only a handful of very recent publications examine sexual identity in the workplace. Current definitions of diversity often omit sexual orientation; Ragins and Gonzalez (2003) point out that there is little reason to assume that diversity researchers are somehow immune from the subtle, and sometimes subconscious, effects of stereotyping, prejudice, and discomfort with those who are different. In addition to the overall stigma associated with sexual orientation and the religious conflicts that are sometimes raised in discussions of homosexuality, scholars who study sexual orientation are susceptible to courtesy stigma effects (Goffman, 1963), in which others assume that they are gay simply because they study gay people. These factors, combined with the methodological and sampling challenges discussed earlier, may contribute to the lack of research on sexual identity in the workplace.

The stigma associated with homosexuality, combined with its invisibility, may lead to other biases in the literature. Apart from research on sexual orientation, one would be hard-pressed to find even a single study that reports the sexual orientation of its sample, even when the research is focused on diversity. Some researchers contend that asking respondents about their sexual orientation may be an invasion of privacy. However, not asking about it not only assumes a heterosexual sample, but also sends the implicit message that sexual orientation should remain invisible, best kept in the closet.

Assumptions of heterosexuality underlie many emerging theories and research on diversity in organizations. For example, relational demography theory predicts that individuals with same-gender managers and teams will form closer work relationships than those in dissimilar work groups (Riordan, 2000). These predictions are based on the assumption that same-gender work environments evoke "similar to me" reactions that increase comfort and security. However, this gender similarity prediction may be reversed for gay and lesbian employees and may be entirely meaningless for transgendered employees (Ragins et al., 2003). Other theoretical perspectives used to understand diversity in organizations also have limited applicability for gay men and lesbians. For example, social identity theory addresses the degree to which individuals identify with social groups and the role of context in social identification (Tajfel & Turner, 1986). It holds that individuals categorize themselves and others into social categories and that personal identity is driven in part from identification with other social groups. However, applications of social identity theory to the workplace often assume that group membership is visible and that personal identities are stable (Ashforth & Mael, 1989). This has limited applicability to gay men and lesbians, who are usually not visible in organizations and who may have fluid identities that develop and change over time.

Other constructs in the diversity literature may also reflect heterosexist biases. As discussed earlier, the concept of "family" assumes heterosexuality. As a consequence, we know little about gay and lesbian families and the unique issues they face in the workplace. In addition, whereas studies have documented the relationship between family-friendly workplace policies and employee work attitudes, little attention has been placed on the effects of these policies on gay employees (Ragins & Cornwell, 2002).

We have provided an initial exploration into some of the more visible heterosexist biases and limitations that underlie theory and research on diversity in organizations. It is clear that researchers need to more thoroughly examine the similarities and differences between heterosexism and other forms of social prejudice.

CONCLUSION AND ROADMAP FOR FUTURE RESEARCH

It is clear that researchers face a number of conceptual and methodological challenges while studying sexual orientation in the workplace. This chapter identified dilemmas and complexities in constructing, operationalizing, measuring, and studying sexual orientation in the workplace. We also highlighted the concern that many existing theories and models of workplace diversity have limited applicability to gay, lesbian, bisexual, and transgendered employees.

Although the study of sexual orientation in the workplace presents unique challenges, it also represents an incredible opportunity for meaningful and important research on a vastly understudied topic. As a starting point, we pose the following research questions for future consideration:

What individual, interpersonal and organizational factors are associated with heterosexism and the disclosure of a gay identity at work? This chapter highlighted the sparse research at these three levels of analysis, but we need a better assessment of how these levels interact to affect workplace experiences for lesbians, gay men, bisexuals, and transgendered employees. Multiple levels of analysis are necessary to capture the full experiences of gay and lesbian employees. For example, what are the individual, group, and organizational outcomes associated with heterosexism, and what factors predict outcomes at each level of analysis?

What are the effects of individual and multiple identities on heterosexism and the decision to come out at work? Emerging research often views "gay employees" as a monolithic group, thus ignoring important differences based on biological gender, race, ethnicity, class, and other group memberships. To start, we need to explore similarities and differences in the workplace experiences of lesbians and gay men, and whether these relationships vary by race and ethnicity. We need to delve into the interactive and additive effects of race, sexual orientation, and biological gender on workplace discrimination and disclosure decisions. We need to analyze the similarities and differences between heterosexism, racism, sexism, and other forms of social prejudice (see discussion by Ragins et al., 2003). Along parallel lines, we need to understand how the multiple identities of heterosexual employees combine to affect their interactions with gay and lesbian coworkers. For example, what factors affect the reaction of heterosexual employees to gay coworkers? This leads to a larger issue: We need a more thorough understanding of the overarching effects of sexual identity in the workplace, and we need to not limit our study of sexual identity to investigations of homosexuality.

How does sexual identity become constructed in the workplace? Using a queer theory perspective (Namaste, 1996), we need to examine how assumptions of heterosexuality infuse the very fabric of organizational culture, practices, and everyday social interactions. Similar to the idea that the study of gender is not the study of women, and the study of race is not limited to the study of people of color, so must the study of sexual identity not be constrained to the study of gay men and lesbians. Of course we need to understand their unique experiences, but we also need to take a broader perspective in deconstructing sexual identity and in understanding how the dominant paradigm of heterosexuality affects organizational culture, processes, and practices.

What are the workplace experiences of bisexual and transgendered employees? To our knowledge, there is no research that examines the workplace experiences of bisexual and transgendered employees. In fact, discussions of sexual orientation in the workplace often do not even mention these groups. We need to understand the similarities and differences in workplace experiences among gay, bisexual, and transgendered men and women. It is reasonable to expect that the nature, form, and consequences of heterosexism may differ for these groups.

How do the antecedents and consequences of direct and indirect forms of discrimination differ? Although we are encouraged by the recent surge of companies adopting antidiscrimination policies, we know that this alone will not lessen heterosexism in the workplace. Like racism and sexism, heterosexism takes subtle and even subconscious forms. For example, heterosexuals may be uncomfortable interacting with gay and lesbian colleagues, and this may result in social distance, more formal interactions, and avoiding developmental and close work relationships. We need to examine the processes involved with subtle and aversive heterosexism (Ragins et al., 2003).

What are the processes underlying the management of hidden stigmatized identities in the workplace? We need to understand the similar and different experiences of individuals with various hidden stigmatized identities. For example, gay men and lesbians may share similar experiences with other individuals with invisible stigmas, such as those in the religious minority, those with invisible disabilities, and some multiracial individuals, but there are also unique attributes of various hidden identities that create unique workplace experiences. We need both research and theory that examines the similarities and differences in the management of hidden stigmatized identities at work.

In summary, the horizon for future research on sexual identity in the workplace is truly vast. We hope we have provided an initial road map for future research in this exciting and provocative field of research.

REFERENCES

Appleby, G. A. (2001). Ethnographic study of gay and bisexual working-class men in the United States. *Journal of Gay & Lesbian Social Services: Issues in Practice, Policy, and Research, 12*, 51–62.

Ashforth, B. E., & Mael F. (1989). Social identity theory and the organization. *Academy of Management Review 14*, 20–39.

Badgett, L. (1995). The wage effects of sexual orientation discrimination. *Industrial and Labor Relations Review, 48*, 726–739.

Badgett, L. (1996). Employment and sexual orientation: Disclosure and discrimination in the workplace. *Journal of Gay and Lesbian Social Services, 4*, 29–52.

Badgett, L. (2001). *Money, myths and change: The economic lives of lesbians and gay men.* Chicago: University of Chicago Press.

Beck, J. (1999). Should homosexuality be taught as an acceptable alternative lifestyle? A Muslim perspective: A response to Halstead and Lewicka. *Cambridge Journal of Education, 29*, 121–130.

Ben-Ari, A. T. (2001). Homosexuality and heterosexism: Views from academics in the helping professions. *British Journal of Social Work, 31*, 119–131.

Berkman, C. S., & Zinberg, G. (1997). Homophobia and heterosexism in social workers. *Social Work, 42*, 319–332.

Bernat, J. A., Calhoun, K. S., Adams, H. E., & Zeichner, A. (2001). Homophobia and physical aggression toward homosexual and heterosexual individuals. *Journal of Abnormal Psychology, 110*, 179–187.

Bhugra, D. (1997). Experiences of being a gay man in urban India: A descriptive study. *Sexual & Marital Therapy, 12*, 371–375.

Black, D., Gates, G., Sanders, S., & Taylor, L. (2000). Demographics of the gay and lesbian population in the United States: Evidence from available systematic data sources. *Demography, 37*, 139–154.

Black, D., Makar, H., Sanders, S., & Taylor, L. (2003). The earnings effect of sexual orientation. *Industrial and Labor Relations Review, 56*, 449–469.

Bosanok, D. (1995). Stress and the gay life. *American Demographics, 17*, 23–36.

Button, S. B. (2001). Organizational efforts to affirm sexual diversity: A cross-level examination. *Journal of Applied Psychology, 86*, 17–28.

Chrobot-Mason, D., Button, S. B., & DiClementi, J. D. (2001). Sexual identity management strategies: An exploration of antecedents and consequences. *Sex Roles, 45*, 321–336.

Clain, S. H., & Leppel, K. (2001). An investigation into sexual orientation discrimination as an explanation for wage differences. *Applied Economics, 33*, 37–47.

Coleman, E. (1987). Assessment of sexual orientation. *Journal of Homosexuality, 14*, 9–24.

Creed, W. E. D., & Scully, M. A. (2000). Songs of ourselves: Employees' deployment of social identity in workplace encounters. *Journal of Management Inquiry, 9*, 391–413.

Croteau, J. M. (1996). Research on the work experiences of lesbian, gay and bisexual people: An integrative review of methodology and findings. *Journal of Vocational Behavior, 48*, 195–209.

Croteau, J. M., & Lark, J. S. (1995). On being lesbian, gay, or bisexual in student affairs: A national survey of experiences on the job. *NASPA Journal, 32*, 189–197.

Crow, S. M., Fok, L. Y., & Hartman, S. J. (1998). Who is at greatest risk of work-related discrimination—Women, blacks or homosexuals? *Employee Responsibilities and Rights Journal, 11,* 15–26.

Cuenot, R. G., & Fugita, S. S. (1982). Perceived homosexuality: Measuring heterosexual attitudinal and nonverbal reactions. *Personality and Social Psychology Bulletin, 8,* 100–106.

Day, N. E., & Schoenrade, P. (1997). Staying in the closet versus coming out: relationships between communication about sexual orientation and work attitudes. *Personnel Psychology, 50,* 147–163.

DiPlacido, J. (1998). Minority stress among lesbians, gay men, and bisexuals: A consequence of heterosexism, homophobia, and stigmatization. In G. M. Herek (Ed.), *Stigma and sexual orientation: Understanding prejudice against lesbians, gay men, and bisexuals* (pp. 138–159). Thousand Oaks, CA: Sage.

Driscoll, J. M., Kelley, F. A., & Fassinger, R. E. (1996). Lesbian identity and disclosure in the workplace: Relation to occupational stress and satisfaction. *Journal of Vocational Behavior, 48,* 229–242.

Elliott, D. (2000, January 3). Nondiscrimination laws now cover 60 million Americans, new report finds. Press release. National Gay and Lesbian Task Force. [Online.] Available: http://www.ngltf.org (Accessed January 4, 2000).

Ellis, J., & Fox, P. (2001). The effect of self-identified sexual orientation on helping behavior in a British sample: Are lesbians and gay men treated differently? *Journal of Applied Social Psychology, 31,* 1238–1247.

Ellis, A. L., & Riggle, E. D. B. (1995). The relation of job satisfaction and degree of openness about one's sexual orientation for lesbians and gay men. *Journal of Homosexuality, 30,* 75–85.

Fassinger, R. E. (1996). Notes from the margins: Integrating lesbian experience into the vocational psychology of women. *Journal of Vocational Behavior, 48,* 160–175.

Friskopp, A., & Silverstein, S. (1996). *Straight jobs, gay lives: Gay and lesbian professionals, the Harvard Business School, and the American workplace.* New York: Touchstone/ Simon & Schuster.

Garnets, L., Herek, G. M., & Levy, B. (1992). Violence and victimization of lesbians and gay men: Mental health consequences. In G. M. Herek & K. T. Berrill (Eds.), *Hate crimes: Confronting violence against lesbians and gay men* (pp. 207–226). Thousand Oaks, CA: Sage.

Garnets, L. D., & Kimmel, D. C. (1993). Introduction: Lesbian and gay male dimensions in the psychological study of human diversity. In L. D. Garnets & D. C. Kimmel (Eds.), *Psychological perspectives on lesbian and gay male experiences* (pp. 1–51). New York: Columbia University Press.

Goffman, E. (1963). *Stigma: Notes on the management of spoiled identity.* New York: Simon & Schuster.

Gonsiorek, J. C., & Weinrich, J. D. (1991). The definition and scope of sexual orientation. In J. C. Gonsiorek and J. D. Weinrich (Eds.), *Homosexuality: Research implications for public policy* (pp. 1–12). Newbury Park: Sage.

Griffith, K. H., & Hebl, M. R. (2002). The disclosure dilemma for gay men and lesbians: "Coming Out" at work. *Journal of Applied Psychology, 87,* 1191–1199.

Haaga, D. A. (1991). "Homophobia?" *Journal of Social Behavior and Personality, 6,* 171–174.

Heaven, P. C. L., & Oxman, L. N. (1999). Human values, conservatism, and stereotypes of homosexuals. *Personality and Individual Differences, 27,* 109–118.

Hebl, M. R., Foster, J. B., Mannix, L. M., & Dovidio, J. F. (2002). Formal and interpersonal discrimination: A field study of bias toward homosexual applicants. *Personality and Social Psychology Bulletin, 28,* 815–825.

Herek, G. M. (1984). Beyond "homophobia": A social psychological perspective on attitudes towards lesbians and gay men. *Journal of Homosexuality, 10,* 1–21.

Herek, G. M. (1991). Stigma, prejudice, and violence against lesbians and gay men. In J. C. Gonsiorek and J. D. Weinrich (Eds.), Homosexuality: Research implications for public policy (pp. 60–80). Newbury Park: Sage.

Herek, G. M. (1993). The context of anti-gay violence: Notes on cultural and psychological heterosexism. In L. D. Farnets & D. C. Kimmel (Eds.), *Psychological perspectives on lesbian and gay male experiences* (pp. 89–107). New York: Columbia University Press.

Herek, G. M. (1996). Why tell if you're not asked? Self-disclosure, intergroup contact, and heterosexuals' attitudes towards lesbians and gay men. In G. M. Herek, J. B. Jobe, and R. M. Carney (Eds.), *Coming out in force: Sexual orientation and the military* (pp. 197–225). Chicago: University of Chicago Press.

Herek, G. M., & Capitanio, J. P. (1996). "Some of my best friends": Intergroup contact, concealable stigma, and heterosexuals' attitudes toward gay men and lesbians. *Personality & Social Psychology Bulletin, 22,* 412–424.

Herek, G. M., & Capitanio, J. P. (1999). AIDS stigma and sexual prejudice. *American Behavioral Scientist, 42,* 1130–1147.

Herek, G. M., Kimmel, D. C., Amaro, H., & Melton, G.B. (1991). Avoiding heterosexist bias in psychological research. *American Psychologist, 46,* 957–963.

Herrschaft, D., & Mills, K. I. (2002). *The state of the workplace for lesbian, gay, bisexual and transgender Americans 2002.* Washington, DC: Human Rights Campaign.

Horowitz, J. L., & Newcomb, M. D. (2001). A multidimensional approach to homosexual identity. *Journal of Homosexuality, 42,* 1–19.

Horvath, M., & Ryan, A. (2003). Antecedents and potential moderators of the relationship between attitudes and hiring discrimination on the basis of sexual orientation. *Sex Roles, 48,* 115–130.

Hunter, J. D. (1991). *Culture wars: The struggle to define America.* New York: Basic Books/Harper Collins.

Johnson, B. K. (1997). *Coming out every day.* Oakland, CA: New Harbinger.

Jordan, K. M., & Deluty, R. H. (1998). Coming out for lesbian women: Its relation to anxiety, positive affectivity, self-esteem, and social support. *Journal of Homosexuality, 35,* 41–63.

Karr, R. G. (1978). Homosexual labeling and the male role. *Journal of Social Issues, 34,* 73–83.

King, B. R. (2001). Ranking of stigmatization toward lesbians and their children and the influence of perceptions of controllability of homosexuality. *Journal of Homosexuality, 41,* 77–97.

Kinsey, A. C., Pomeroy, W. B., & Martin, C. E. (1948). *Sexual behavior in the human male.* Philadelphia: Saunders.

Kinsey, A. C., Pomeroy, W. B., Martin, C. E., & Gebhard, P. H. (1953). *Sexual behavior in the human female.* Philadelphia: Saunders.

Kirkpatrick, L. A. (1993). Fundamentalism, Christian orthodoxy, and intrinsic religious orientation as predictors of discriminatory attitudes. *Journal for the Scientific Study of Religion, 32,* 256–268.

Kite, M. E., & Deaux, K. (1986). Attitudes towards homosexuality: Assessment and behavioral consequences. *Basic and Applied Social Psychology, 7,* 137–162.

Kite, M. E., & Whitley, B. E., Jr. (1998). Do heterosexual women and men differ in their attitudes toward homosexuality? A conceptual and methodological analysis. In G. M. Herek (Ed.), *Stigma and sexual orientation: Understanding prejudice against lesbians, gay men, and bisexuals* (pp. 39–61). Thousand Oaks, CA: Sage.

Lippincott, J. A., Wlazelek, B., & Schumacher, L. J. (2000). Comparison: Attitudes toward homosexuality of international and American college students. *Psychological Reports, 87,* 1053–1056.

Logan, C. R. (1996). Homophobia? No, homoprejudice. *Journal of Homosexuality, 31*, 31–53.

Mallon, G. P. (2001). Oh, Canada: The experience of working-class gay men in Toronto. *Journal of Gay & Lesbian Social Services, 12*, 103–117.

Martin, J. I., & Knox, J. (2000). Methodological and ethical issues in research on lesbians and gay men. *Social Work Research, 24*, 51–59.

Monteith, M. J. (1996). Affective reactions to prejudice-related discrepant responses: The impact of standard salience. *Personality & Social Psychology Bulletin, 22*, 48–59.

Moss, D. (2001). On hating in the first person plural: Thinking psychoanalytically about racism, homophobia, and misogyny. *Journal of the American Psychoanalytic Association, 49*, 1315–1334.

Myers, S. L. (2000, March 25). Survey of troops finds antigay bias common in service. *New York Times*, pp. A1, A10.

Namaste, K. (1996). The politics of inside/out: Queer theory, poststructuralism, and a sociological approach to sexuality. In S. Seidman, (Ed.), *Queer theory/sociology* (pp. 194–212). Cambridge, MA: Blackwell.

Nelson, E. S., & Kreiger, S. L. (1997). Changes in attitudes toward homosexuality in college students: Implementation of a gay men and lesbian peer panel. *Journal of Homosexuality, 33*, 63–81.

Powers, B. (1996). The impact of gay, lesbian, and bisexual workplace issues on productivity. *Journal of Gay and Lesbian Social Services, 4*, 79–90.

Ragins, B. R. (2004). Sexual orientation in the workplace: The unique work and career experiences of gay, lesbian and bisexual workers. *Research in Personnel and Human Resources Management, 23*, 37–122.

Ragins, B. R., & Cornwell, J. M. (2001a). Pink triangles: Antecedents and consequences of perceived workplace discrimination against gay and lesbian employees. *Journal of Applied Psychology, 86*, 1244–1261.

Ragins, B. R., & Cornwell, J. M. (2001b). Walking the line: Fear and disclosure of sexual orientation in the workplace. Paper presented at the National Academy of Management Meeting, Washington, DC.

Ragins, B. R., & Cornwell, J. M. (2002). Valuing all of your employees: The impact of domestic partner benefits on gay employees' work attitudes. In A. Sagie & M. Stasiak (Eds.), *Proceedings for the 8th Annual Conference on Work Values and Behavior* (pp. 354–360). Lodz, Poland: Academy of Humanities and Economics.

Ragins, B. R., Cornwell, J. M., & Miller, J. S. (2003). Heterosexism in the workplace: Do race and gender matter? *Group & Organization Management, 28*, 45–74.

Ragins, B. R., & Gonzalez, J. A. (2003). Understanding diversity in organizations: Getting a grip on a slippery construct. In J. Greenberg (Ed.), *Organizational behavior: The state of the science* (2nd ed., pp. 125–163). Mahwah, NJ: Lawrence Erlbaum Associates.

Riordan, C. M. (2000). Relational demography within groups: Past developments, contradictions, and new directions. *Research in Personnel and Human Resource Management. 19*, 131–173.

Rivers, I. (1997). Lesbian, gay and bisexual development: Theory, research and social issues. *Journal of Community & Applied Social Psychology, 7*, 329–343.

Ruggiero, K. M., & Taylor, D. M. (1995). Coping with discrimination: How disadvantaged group members perceive the discrimination that confronts them. *Journal of Personality and Social Psychology, 68*, 826–838.

Schmitt, A., & Sofer, J. (1992). *Sexuality and eroticism among males in Moslem societies*. New York: Haworth Press.

Schneider, B. E. (1987). Coming out at work: Bridging the private/public gap. *Work and Occupations, 13*, 463–487.

Sears, J. T. (1997). Thinking critically/intervening effectively about homophobia and heterosexism. In J. T. Sears & W. L. Williams (Eds.), *Overcoming heterosexism and homophobia: Strategies that work* (pp. 13–48). New York: Columbia University Press.

Shively, M. G., & DeCecco, J. P. (1977). Components of sexual identity. *Journal of Homosexuality, 3*, 31–48.

Simoni, J. M., & Walters, K. L. (2001). Heterosexual identity and heterosexism: Recognizing privilege to reduce prejudice. *Journal of Homosexuality, 41*, 157–172.

Stevenson, M. R., & Medler, B. R. (1995). Is homophobia a weapon of sexism? *Journal of Men's Studies, 4*, 1–8.

Swim, J. K., Ferguson, M. J., & Hyers, L. L. (1999). Avoiding stigma by association: Subtle prejudice against lesbians in the form of social distancing. *Basic & Applied Social Psychology, 21*, 61–68.

Tajfel, H., & Turner, J. C. (1986). The social identity theory of intergroup behavior. In S. Worchel & W. G. Austin (Eds.), *The psychology of intergroup relations* (2nd ed., pp. 7–24). Chicago: Nelson-Hall.

Troiden, R. R. (1989). The formation of homosexual identities. *Journal of Homosexuality, 17*, 43–73.

Van Den Bergh, N. (1999). Workplace problems and needs for lesbian and gay male employees: Implications for EAPs. *Employee Assistance Quarterly, 15*, 21–60.

Waldo, C. R. (1999). Working in a majority context: A structural model of heterosexism as minority stress in the workplace. *Journal of Counseling Psychology, 46*, 218–232.

Weinberg, G. (1972). *Society and the healthy homosexual.* New York: St. Martin's Press.

Wetzel, J. W. (2001). Human rights in the 20th century: Weren't lesbians and gays human? In M. E. Swigonski & R. S. Mama (Eds.), *From hate crimes to human rights: A tribute to Matthew Shepard* (pp. 15–31). New York: Haworth Press.

Whitley, B. E., Jr., & Lee, S. E. (2000). The relationship of authoritarianism and related constructs to attitudes toward homosexuality. *Journal of Applied Social Psychology, 30*, 144–170.

Woods, J. D. (1993). The corporate closet: The professional lives of gay men in America. New York: The Free Press.

9

Age Discrimination in the Workplace

Lynn M. Shore[1]
San Diego State University

Caren B. Goldberg
The George Washington University

> Our preoccupation with youthfulness has tended to undermine the importance and wealth of experience offered by our senior members. Indeed, Golda Meir became prime minister at age seventy-one. The New York Mets hired Casey Stengel as their manager when he was seventy five. Not to be forgotten are Benjamin Franklin who worked on the U.S. Constitution at eighty-one, and Milton Petrie, who at ninety, still presides over Petrie Stores.
>
> —Paul and Townsend (1993, p. 67)

With the aging of the U.S. work force (U.S. Department of Labor, 2002), and evidence that age discrimination can lead to feelings of uselessness, powerlessness, and lower self-esteem (Butler, 1969; Cowgill, 1974; Hassell & Perrewe, 1993), it is important that we continue to explore issues pertaining to age discrimination. In addition to demographic trends, there are several

---

[1] This chapter was prepared while Lynn Shore was a visiting professor at the Graduate School of Management, University of California, Irvine.

other societal changes that make the study of aging at work particularly important. Organizations have been laying off employees in record numbers for the last 15 years (Cascio, 2002), challenging assumptions of job security for loyalty and hard work (Rousseau, 1995). Such changes may be particularly likely to adversely affect middle-aged and older workers who may have significant financial responsibilities, yet many more problems than younger workers getting re-employed (Bureau of Labor Statistics, 2002). Additionally, with decreasing management layers in organizations, fewer promotional opportunities are available for employees. Such restructuring may exacerbate career progression problems faced by older workers, particularly during this period of rapid technological changes when older workers are assumed to be less trainable (Maurer, 2001), and evidence of age norms that suggest older workers will be judged less favorably when compared with their younger counterparts (Lawrence, 1987, 1988). Furthermore, a recent survey of 340 executives showed that 61% believe that age discrimination is a greater problem today than it was just one year ago, and 35% reported encountering age discrimination in their most recent job search (ExecuNet, 2002).

In this chapter, we first discuss alternative causes of age discrimination, including stereotyping, relational demography, career timetables, and prototype matching. Second, we present a model of age discrimination. Third, we present summaries of the research on the effects of age discrimination on organizational entry, experiences in organizations, and organizational exit. Finally, we suggest an agenda for future research.

VIEWS OF AGE DISCRIMINATION

Stereotyping

In the early 1950s, Kirchner and his colleagues found that hourly employees had more positive attitudes toward older workers than did their supervisors (Kirchner & Dunnette, 1954; Kirchner, Lindbom, & Paterson, 1952). These results were duplicated by Bird and Fisher 30 years later (1986), suggesting the continued importance of exploring reasons for differential attitudes toward older workers. One potential explanation is that of negative stereotypes of older workers. Stereotypes of older people include views that they are less productive, less flexible, less creative, less ambitious, harder to train (Kulik, Perry, & Bourhis, 2000; Ringenbach & Jacobs, 1994; Sonnenfeld, 1978), and less economically beneficial (Finkelstein & Burke, 1998). Craft, Doctors, Shkop, and Benecki (1979) found that older job candidates were more likely than young candidates to be viewed as opinionated, lacking in physical strength, and less serious and ambitious. Bassili and Reil (1981) concluded that older people were viewed as conservative, traditional, present-oriented, and moral. Rosen and Jerdee (1976a) found that younger employees are seen as being more productive, efficient, motivated, capable of working under pressure, innovative, creative, and logical than older employees. Additional studies (Rosen & Jerdee, 1976b, 1977) using hypothetical incidents of younger and older employees depicted in identical circumstances found:

1. Older workers were seen as more rigid and resistant to change and thus were provided with less feedback and given less opportunity to improve their substandard performance.
2. Older workers were seen as less interested in keeping up with technological change and were less likely to be supported in a request for training funds.
3. When an older worker's skills had grown obsolete, respondents were much less likely to endorse sending the older employee to a company-sponsored retraining course.

Recent research by Fiske, Cuddy, Glick, & Xu (2002) showed that compared to other groups (e.g., southerners, rich, Asians), older people were viewed as high on warmth (tolerant, good natured, and sincere) and low on competence (confident, independent, competitive, and intelligent). Although perceptions of warmth may be an asset, the incompetence stereotype suggests that older workers are likely to be denied workplace opportunities.

Relational Demography

Relational demography suggests that similarity to referent others results in favorable outcomes, whereas dissimilarity results in unfavorable outcomes. This literature is based on the similarity-attraction paradigm (Byrne, 1971; Riordan & Shore, 1997) and social identity theory (Riordan, 2000). The similarity-attraction paradigm argues that individuals who are similar will like each other, and hence, be more likely to treat each other in a favorable manner. Social identity theory is based on the notion that individuals classify themselves into social categories in ways that allow them to maintain positive self-identities. One means of doing this is by favoring similar others (Lemyre & Smith, 1985). Thus, old workers in old workgroups and young workers in young workgroups should experience more positive work outcomes than individuals in workgroups that are dissimilar in age to the target employee.

A number of studies that have examined employee age relative to the workgroup have supported relational demography theory. Dissimilarity in age between an individual and his/her workgroup was shown to be positively related to turnover intentions (Tsui, Egan, & O'Reilly, 1992), turnover (O'Reilly, Caldwell, & Barnett, 1989; Wagner, Pfeffer, & O'Reilly, 1984), and negatively related to social integration (O'Reilly, Caldwell, & Barnett, 1989), identification, organizational commitment, group performance, and group citizenship behaviors (Riordan & Weatherly, cited in Riordan, 2000), and communication among members (Zenger & Lawrence, 1989). Less support was found for relational demography theory in research that has focused on age similarity in manager–employee dyads (Epitropaki & Martin, 1999; Liden, Stilwell, & Ferris, 1996; Shore, Cleveland, & Goldberg, 2003; Tsui & O'Reilly, 1989).

Career Timetables

Whereas relational demography assumes that matches result in more favorable outcomes than do mismatches, Lawrence's (1984, 1987, 1988) notion of career timetables posits that some age differences have positive effects and some have negative effects. Her research suggests that there are clear norms regarding where one should be on the organizational chart at a given age. Individuals who are promoted at a rate consistent with their peer group (based on age similarity) are viewed as "on schedule," those who are promoted more quickly than their peer group are considered "ahead of schedule," and those who are promoted less often than their peer group are considered "behind schedule." Although the latter two groups both represent target-referent mismatches, the career timetable approach makes very different predictions about these two groups. For example, Lawrence (1984) found that managers who see themselves as "behind schedule" (10 or more years behind the typical age) have lower work satisfaction and work orientation than other managers do. A subsequent study (Lawrence, 1988) showed that "ahead of schedule" managers received the highest performance ratings whereas "behind schedule" managers received the lowest performance ratings.

A number of other studies suggest the value of treating different age mismatches differently. Cleveland, Montgomery, and Festa (1984) found that the proportion of older workers in a workgroup influenced decisions about older workers. Similarly, Cleveland, Festa, and Montgomery (1988) found that as the number of older applicants in an applicant pool increased, an older applicant received more favorable ratings of job suitability and potential for advancement. Field studies have shown that age relative to the workgroup significantly impacts performance ratings, attitudes, and development opportunities (Cleveland & Shore, 1992; Ferris, Judge, Chachere, & Liden, 1991).

Whereas Lawrence's (1984, 1987, 1988) work focused on the work group as a referent, Shore et al. (2003) argued that it is likely that the presence of a young manager may contribute to the perception of an older employee as being behind time. When employees are older than their managers, they may perceive that their situation violates the career timetable associated with managerial positions (Perry, Kulik, & Zhou, 1999). However, Perry et al.'s study (1999) found little support for the impact of employee age relative to the manager on self-rated citizenship, self-rated work change, and absenteeism. In contrast, Shore et al. (2003) found some support: (a) the fewest development opportunities were reported when the employee was older and the manager was younger, and (b) older employees with younger managers received the lowest potential and promotability ratings. Furthermore, Tsui, Porter, & Egan (2002) found that subordinates who were older than their supervisors were rated lower on performance than employees who were younger than or similar in age to the supervisor. These studies suggest that employees who are older than their managers may receive lower performance ratings and fewer career-enhancing opportunities than employees who are younger than their managers, because the former situation represents a violation of age norms.

Although there is support for the career timetable perspective, future research should integrate more contextual information into these studies. In particular, occupational and organizational norms should be examined. For example, occupational norms may enhance opportunities for the young in areas such as technology where rapid change favors those who are most recently educated (usually younger people). Other occupations that require knowledge and skill development that come primarily through experience may have norms that favor career opportunities for older workers. Likewise, Lawrence's (1984, 1987, 1988) conceptualization argues for the importance of organizational age norms, and subsequent research would benefit from the incorporation of her ideas.

Prototype Matching

The prototype matching approach involves comparing an individual's age relative to the age of the prototypical incumbent for a given job. Perry (1994, 1997) and Perry and Finkelstein (1999) suggested a cognitive matching process in which greater matches between target age and job age prototype result in more favorable selection outcomes and greater mismatches result in less favorable selection outcomes. A number of studies suggest support for the existence of job and occupational age prototypes. Perry and Bourhis

(1998) found that individuals deem some features to be central to their perceptions of the typical jobholder for young-typed jobs (e.g., "energetic," "efficient," and "able to handle multiple tasks"). Warr and Pennington (1994) concluded that (a) nonmanagerial jobs defined as mainly for older employees were perceived to make fewer demands on cognitive resources than younger people's jobs, and (b) work for younger employees was seen as calling for greater expenditure of energy and more rapid pacing. Cleveland and Berman (1987) and Cleveland and Landy (1987) found convergence among managers and between students and managers on age stereotypes of jobs.

Much of the empirical research on prototype matching has studied its impact on selection. Perry (1994) found that a matching process operates for applicant age and the age-type of jobs. Cleveland and Landy (1983) showed that older and younger applicants were not evaluated significantly differently for different age-typed jobs, but that age-typed behaviors influenced perceived suitability for age-typed jobs. Perry, Kulik, and Bourhis (1996) found that older applicants were evaluated more negatively for young-typed jobs, but that younger and older applicants were evaluated similarly for old-typed jobs.

Prototype-matching may play a role in other work decisions as well. Goldberg, Finkelstein, Perry, and Konrad (2001) found that women whose age matched the perceived industry age received more promotions than did women whose age did not match the perceived industry age. However, an opposite effect was found for men's promotions, whereby young men in old-typed industries (e.g., government, aerospace, industrial/construction equipment) received considerably more promotions than did any other group of men. In summary, these studies provide mixed support for age prototype job matching, suggesting that other contextual variables (e.g., workgroup composition, industry) may also influence matching processes.

A MODEL OF AGE DISCRIMINATION

A number of themes are apparent in the literature: (a) age is most meaningful when considered in context, such that the employee's age is compared with multiple social referents, (b) the age comparisons that take place in organizations influence employment opportunities for individuals, and (c) there are forces both inside and outside the organization that influence employment opportunities of older workers. In Fig. 9.1, we present our model of age discrimination and discuss each of the elements in the model.

Many studies have suggested the role of social comparison processes by individuals in evaluating their work experiences (i.e., people compare

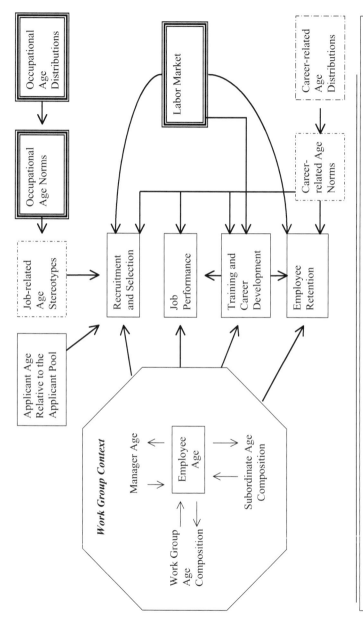

FIG. 9.1. Age discrimination in the workplace.

Note: Single lined boxes (——) represent processes that are internal to the organization, dashed boxes (⁃⁃⁃⁃) are processes that are both internal to and external to the organization, and double lined boxes (▰▰) are external to the organizations.

209

themselves with others). It is also clear that social comparisons are used to make many personnel decisions (e.g., who is the best candidate in an applicant pool). In terms of employee age, several comparisons are likely. First, the immediate work context (department or team) is one source of comparison. The age of the manager (Liden et al., 1996; Shore et al., 2003; Tsui, Xin, & Egan, 1995; Tsui et al., 2002), and of coworkers (Cleveland & Holmann, 1990; Cleveland & Shore, 1992; Cleveland, Shore, & Murphy, 1997; O'Reilly et al., 1989; Riordan, 2000; Tsui et al., 1992; Wagner et al., 1984; Zenger & Lawrence, 1989) relative to the employee have been shown to impact many personnel decisions, including supervisor performance evaluations, training and development opportunities, and turnover. Although it has not been researched, we included subordinate age composition in our model, because this may be a social referent for many managers. Finally, the age composition of the applicant pool may influence hiring decisions (Finkelstein, Burke, & Raju, 1995).

Second, career-related age norms have been shown to influence employee attitudes and performance ratings (Lawrence, 1984, 1988), such that being older ("behind schedule") than others at the same job level in the organization has negative consequences. Although it is not clear whether career-related age norms operate outside the organization as well, the greater difficulty of obtaining employment with increasing age suggests that they do (Bureau of Labor Statistics, 2002). Career-related age norms may be particularly important in occupations and professions with strong external labor markets. Older individuals who explore jobs outside of their current organization may discover that age norms contribute to a lack of upward mobility.

Third, there is some evidence that job-related age stereotypes operate in determining recruitment and selection decisions (Perry, 1994, 1997; Perry & Finkelstein, 1999), such that older workers fare better in old-type jobs, and younger workers in young-type jobs. A final variable that is included in our model is the labor market, because a tight labor market may increase opportunities for older workers by increasing their value both inside and outside their organizations.

In the following section, we summarize research linking age with entry into employment, experiences in organizations, and exiting the organization. Extensive research exists in all three categories, with several themes apparent: (a) evidence linking age and decisions by organizational agents is inconsistent, (b) contextual issues, such as the social and technological context, appear to be important in determining if and when older workers are discriminated against, and (c) no single paradigm for explaining links between age and employment opportunities applies across all situations or decisions.

ENTRY INTO EMPLOYMENT

Job Search and Unemployment

According to the Bureau of Labor Statistics, for the period January 2002 to November 2002, employers initiated 17,799 mass layoff incidents, resulting in nearly 2 million claims for unemployment compensation insurance. Although these data show the greatest level of unemployment for those in the 25–44 year age range, the length of time until reemployment is longest for older Americans. Specifically, the mean duration for 25 to 35 year olds is 12.7 weeks, whereas the mean for those over age 54 is 18 weeks. The U.S. Bureau of the Census (1993) showed that whereas 49.6% of displaced workers between the ages of 55 and 64 found other employment, 65–70% of workers under age 55 were reemployed. In addition, a recent meta-analysis (Kanfer, Wanberg, & Kantrowitz, 2001) showed that younger people reported a greater likelihood of becoming employed; however, the authors suggested that there was under-sampling of people over the age of 55. Although this body of research suggests that younger workers are more easily reemployed than older workers, more research is needed that studies job search activities and the criteria used for evaluating jobs by the old and the young. There are likely elements of discrimination at play, but there may also be differences in the activities and expectations of unemployed workers depending on their age, which influence opportunities.

Selection

Finkelstein et al. (1995) conducted a meta-analysis of laboratory studies of age and selection and found no significant age effects when raters evaluated either a younger or an older applicant. However, they did find a significant age effect when raters evaluated both younger and older applicants, such that young applicants were rated as more qualified than were old applicants. This suggests that the ages of other applicants may play an important role in understanding how target age impacts selection.

Three field studies also show inconsistent results. Arvey, Miller, Gould, & Burch (1987) found that age was positively related to hireability, Goldberg and Shore (2003) found no significant age effects, and Raza and Carpenter (1987) found a negative relationship. In all three studies, applicants had a median age in their twenties or early thirties, raising questions as to the generalizability of these results.

Even though research results linking age and selection are inconsistent, court judgments in age discrimination cases suggest this is an important issue. Miller, Kaspin, and Schuster (1990) found that plaintiff age is the best predictor of a court's judgment in ADEA cases. In *O'Connor v. Consolidated Coin Caterers Corp.*, 56 F. 3d 542 (4th Cir. 1995), the court ruled that the issue is not whether the favored applicant falls within the statutory threshold of age 40, but rather whether the favored person is *substantially* younger than the rejected older applicant. In *Hartley v. Wisconsin Bell, Inc.*, 124 F. 3d 887 (7th Cir. 1997), the court held that a 10-year age difference between the plaintiff and the replacement is presumptively substantial. These cases suggest that age differences play a critical role in court judgments.

EXPERIENCES IN ORGANIZATIONS

Job Performance

Meta-analytic studies concerning the effects of employee age on job performance ratings have shown weak support (Avolio, Waldman, & McDaniel, 1990; McEvoy & Cascio, 1989; Waldman & Avolio, 1986). Waldman and Avolio (1993) cited a number of problems with the research linking age and job performance: (a) few studies have included workers older than 60 years of age; (b) much of the research is cross-sectional; (c) longitudinal research suggests a nonlinear relationship with age; and (d) age-performance relationships are influenced by occupation. Salthouse and Maurer (1996) also point to some additional serious limitations, including (a) there have been relatively few studies; (b) the small sample sizes of most studies may have led to weak power to detect performance differences that may exist; and (c) most studies have had restricted age ranges, with under-sampling of older workers. Thus, conclusions about the relationship between age and performance ratings should be viewed with caution.

Despite the lack of consistent empirical evidence, there continues to be an assumption among many managers that performance declines with age (Prenda & Stahl, 2001). Although there are age-related changes in certain abilities, including sensory functioning, strength and endurance, response speed, and cognitive processes, the decline in these abilities is almost always gradual, and most older adults remain healthy and functionally able until very late in life (Czaja, 1995). In fact, Avolio et al.'s (1990) meta-analysis showed that job experience was a better predictor than age of performance such that experience leads to better performance ratings. Landy, Shankster-Cawley, & Moran (1995) argued that "there is little credible evidence to suggest any substantial reduction in abilities (cognitive or physical) as a result of age, *per se*" (p. 276). This suggests the influence of age stereotypes, but many questions remain as to when such stereotypes play a role in evaluations of older workers (Landy et al., 1995).

Avolio (1992) points out that most research on age and performance has not described contextual issues, such as opportunities for retraining, which may influence this relationship. Other aspects of the social context, including age norms (Lawrence, 1988), the manager's age (Shore et al., 2003; Tsui et al., 2002), and ages of workgroup members (Cleveland & Shore, 1992; Ferris et al., 1991; Perry et al., 1999) have been studied. This research provides some evidence that performance ratings may be influenced by the social context, such that older employees are less likely to be evaluated highly when compared with younger referents.

Another contextual factor is the availability of objective information for evaluating performance. Liden et al. (1996) found that for a sample of sales representatives, employee age was positively related to both objective and supervisor-rated performance. They suggested that when objective performance data are available, any supplemental subjective performance ratings will not be unfairly biased against older workers. However, meta-analytic evidence of the moderating impact of rating type on the age-performance relationship has been mixed (McEvoy & Cascio, 1989; Waldman & Avolio, 1986). A final contextual factor that may be important for influencing the link between age and performance is the actual job requirements (Avolio & Waldman, 1989).

Older employees may behave differently toward their managers than do younger employees, in ways that affect how their manager evaluates performance. Research on influence tactics suggests that employees use influence tactics to build relationships with the manager, and the manager in turn rates the employee more highly (Wayne & Liden, 1995). Interestingly, Ferris and King (1992) found that older nurses were less likely to engage in ingratiation, which was associated with less liking by the supervisor and subsequently lower performance ratings. In short, although there is little evidence of a significant relationship between age and actual work performance, there is evidence that nonwork factors, such as managers' stereotypes and employees' use of impression management may result in managers providing lower ratings to older workers than to younger workers.

Absenteeism

Recent information from the Bureau of Labor Statistics (2001) shows very little actual difference between older and younger workers in terms of total absence rate. Although the link between age and absenteeism has been well studied, it is rather poorly understood. It appears that differences in findings across studies may be attributable to two major factors; raters' stereotypes about older workers (stability versus declining health), and the type of indices of absenteeism studied.

A host of studies provided evidence that older workers are perceived as more reliable, stable, and dependable (c.f., Crew, 1983; Ringenbach & Jacobs, 1994; Rosen & Jerdee, 1976a) than are younger workers. On the other hand, stereotypes abound that older workers are expected to have higher absence rates because of poor health (Prenda & Stahl, 2001). In light of these conflicting stereotypes, it is not surprising that the conceptual (Rhodes, 1983) and empirical (Hackett, 1990; Martocchio, 1990) reviews of the age-absenteeism relationship have produced mixed results.

Goldberg and Waldman (2000) provided evidence that the predictors of absenteeism vary as a function of the type of absence measure studied. Martocchio (1989) included indices of absence frequency and of time-lost in his meta-analytic review of age and absenteeism. Although a stronger negative relationship was observed between age and absence frequency than between age and time-lost, both effects were statistically significant. Hackett (1990) divided absence measures into classifications of avoidable (snow days) and unavoidable (sickness) in his meta-analysis and found the negative relationship between age and absenteeism exists only for avoidable absenteeism. Thus, the notion that older employees ought to be absent more than younger employees because of age-related health problems appears to be unfounded.

Training and Development

With increasing changes in technology in the workplace and reorganizations that require employees to take on new tasks, the ability of employees to learn new skills has become paramount. At the same time, there is evidence that information processing speed declines with age (Salthouse, 1985), as does working memory (Baddeley, 1986), and attentional abilities (Craik & McDowd, 1987). In contrast, there is also evidence that intellectual abilities that involve verbal skills do not change with age (Botwinick, 1967, 1977). Likewise, crystallized intelligence tends to decline at a much later age than fluid intelligence does (Schaie, 1989). Taken together, these results do not suggest that older workers are less able to learn; rather, they underscore the need for organizations to consider different training and development approaches as people age in order to optimize learning.

Sandra Timmerman of the Mature Market Institute argues (Wellner, p. 32, March, 2002), "People learn differently as they age. Because your reaction time is slower, it's more difficult to learn things by rote memory." She contends that older workers perform better in self-paced learning environments that are pressure-free. Likewise, Maurer, Wrenn, and Weiss (2001) note that self-paced learning, allowing plenty of time, having plenty of help available, and reducing stress associated with training will all enhance the learning of older employees in a training and development context. A recent meta-analysis supports these contentions, showing training performance was particularly enhanced for older learners when self-pacing was used (Scully, Kiker, & Cross, in press).

Another training issue for older workers is stereotypes regarding both their motivation and ability to learn. Prior research on stereotypes of older workers suggests that they are viewed as having low potential for development (Rosen and Jerdee, 1976a), as having less ability to understand new ideas than younger workers (Perry & Varney, 1978), and as less interested in keeping up with technological change (Rosen & Jerdee, 1976b). Furthermore, Avolio and Waldman (1989) found that technical skills were rated as less important for older job incumbents, and Dedrick and Dobbins (1991) found that managers were more likely to recommend job simplification for poorly performing older subordinates and training for poorly performing younger subordinates.

Although negative age stereotypes pertaining to training and learning abound, Sara Rix, senior policy advisor at the AARP Public Policy Institute notes "Research shows that the ability to learn continues well into older age, and older workers can and do learn new technologies" (Wellner, p. 31, March 2002). Nonetheless, McCann and Giles (2001) point out that the technology lawsuits are on the rise. They say, "given widely held perceptions that older workers struggle with new technology, it comes as no surprise that the courts are beginning to hear increasing numbers of 'new technology' age discrimination cases. For example, in Ryther v. KARE (1997), a supervisor told his 53-year-old sportscaster that he 'had bags under his eyes,' was 'an old fart,' 'wasn't able to grasp the new computer system,' and 'couldn't handle the new technology'" (p. 183).

Whereas evidence as to whether older trainees lack motivation and ability to learn relative to their younger counterparts has been mixed (Salthouse & Maurer, 1996; Warr & Bruce, 1995), evidence regarding age-related differences in training opportunities is quite consistent. The Department of Labor found that 55- to 60-year-olds were much less likely to receive training than 35- to 44-year-olds (cited in Maurer & Rafuse, 2001). Further, Heywood, Ho, and Wei (1999) found a greater willingness among firms to invest in training for younger workers. Other studies suggest that older workers receive fewer training and development experiences than do younger workers, particularly when they are older than their workgroup (Cleveland & Shore, 1992) or manager (Shore et al., 2003). To the extent that training and development affect subsequent pay and promotion decisions, organizations would be wise to make these opportunities available to both younger and older employees (*Mitchell v. Sisters of Charity of Incarnate Word*, 1996).

Given the increasing numbers of older workers, it is critical that organizations understand how older employees learn best, and factors in the work context, including age discrimination and lack of technical support, that may prevent learning and developmental opportunities for older workers. As stated by Maurer and Rafuse (2001), "an over-arching recommendation is to treat all workers, regardless of age, on an individual basis, taking into consideration their own performance and capabilities, and not to treat individuals simply as members of an age group" (p. 119).

Careers

Career opportunities are important to workers of all ages. Cleveland and Shore (1992) found younger workers were more likely than older workers to receive career counseling with the supervisor. Salthouse and Maurer (1996) describe some other potential impediments to the career development of older employees, including lower communication levels in age-diverse workgroups, assignment to more routine jobs, and lower likelihood of being selected for training and retraining experiences. In addition, Ohlott and Eastman (1994) found that older managers reported fewer task-related challenges than younger managers.

The trend from a single career in one organization to a "protean" career that can involve many organizations and career shifts has presented some significant challenges for older employees (Hall & Mirvis, 1995). Older workers may be less likely to engage in continuous learning critical to a protean career because of their own tendency to approach training and development with caution and because of age discrimination that leads to more investment in younger workers (Maurer & Barbeite, 2001). Rosen and Jerdee (1988) recommended that organizations experiment with new career management strategies for older workers, such as formalizing new mentoring and consulting roles for senior employees, allowing for part-time work and short sabbaticals, and providing frequent training and development opportunities. They argued that these strategies would be beneficial for both older individuals and for the organizations that employ them.

Finkelstein, Allen, and Rhoton (2000) studied age and mentoring and reported that the mentoring literature discussed the "ideal" mentoring relationship as one in which the protégé is at least 8 to 15 years younger than the mentor. They found that younger protégés reported receiving more frequent career-related mentoring, and that mentors reported spending fewer hours per week with their protégé as protégé age increased. Unexpectedly, older protégés reported higher relationship quality than did younger protégés. Interestingly, when asked about the potential disadvantages of mentoring someone older, the mentors in their study cited the lack of credibility or respect that might be afforded to a younger mentor, whereas the protégés stated concerns about the younger mentor's knowledge and experience. This study suggests the importance of greater understanding of the mentoring relationship in relation to age and underscores the importance of future investigations of younger employees serving as mentors for older employees. As an example, younger employees may have knowledge (e.g., pertaining to technology) that they can impart to older protégés whose skills are not as up-to-date.

Upward mobility has been found to decrease with age (Lawrence, 1984; Cox & Nkomo, 1992). Cox and Nkomo suggest this may be due to the favoring of younger candidates because of the longer available time to work for the organization than older candidates. Lawrence (1990) studied managerial perceptions of career progress and concluded that "managers' assumptions about individual attainment may be violated when, in lower levels, promotions are too fast or too slow, and in upper levels, when managers are too young or too old" (p. 81). Thus, she argues that age bias is more likely to occur at higher levels of career progression. Shore et al. (2003) found that employee age was negatively related to promotability, but that this relationship was moderated by manager age such that young managers were much more likely than old managers to favor young employees. Cleveland and Shore (1992) also found a negative relationship between age and promotability, and showed that employees who were older than their work group were less likely to be viewed as promotable.

EXITING THE ORGANIZATION

Although logically it seems that older workers would be less likely to quit their jobs, research suggests that age is not a significant predictor of voluntary turnover (Healy, Lehman, McDaniel, 1995). Cohen (1993) found that unlike for younger workers, commitment is not a good predictor of turnover for older workers and suggested that this may occur because, even when older employees have low organizational commitment, they may not quit because of structural bonds (e.g., benefits), few employment alternatives, and a desire for stability.

Downsizing and restructuring continue to be popular business strategies for improving firm performance (Cascio, 2002). The emphasis on cost reduction results in older workers being targeted in downsizing efforts, as they typically represent greater costs to the organization. For example, in *Marks v. Loral* (1997), the court ruled that using salary as a basis for layoff decisions was acceptable, even though it disparately impacts older workers. The aging of the workforce along with the trend toward early retirement may represent a large loss in human capital that may be difficult for organizations to replace. A study done by the Conference Board (reported in Estabrook, 1993) based on interviews with 400 senior human resource executives showed that 40% of companies have offered early retirement incentives as part of downsizing. By the year 2005, one out of every seven workers will be age 55 or older (Estabrook, 1993), suggesting potential problems with labor shortages. Thus, it behooves organizations and society more generally to consider ways to keep people in the labor force.

CONCLUSIONS

There are a number of implications of our review and model. One implication is that many forces are at work when considering the opportunities of older workers. However, it is clear that being older than others, whether relative to the immediate manager, the workgroup, or job level, works to the disadvantage of individuals for most employment opportunities. In addition, although there is limited evidence that age stereotypes have direct effects on employment opportunities, more work clearly needs to be done in this area, particularly in light of the strong and consistent effects involving age comparisons. That is, research needs to further explore the cognitive mechanisms that underlie age comparisons, including the potential role of age stereotypes. Finally, more research needs to examine ways in which older workers themselves may contribute to employment opportunities. Maurer (2001) has suggested self-efficacy for learning as one potential influence on training opportunities for older workers. There may be other factors, especially when one considers that the ageism inherent in many aspects of western culture may negatively affect employee self-perceptions. Older employees may be given subtle cues about their limited value to the organization creating a self-fulfilling prophecy for these individuals.

Based on the perspective that social comparison plays a major role in age discrimination, Figure 9.2 is a model depicting some of the elements that are likely important in evaluations of employees. Building on Mussweiler's (2003) ideas, Fig. 9.2 contains three key steps in evaluation of employees based on age comparisons. Step 1 involves the selection of the standard used for comparison purposes. We have discussed the potential importance of the many different standards of age comparison that are available when evaluating the employee, including occupational, organizational, industrial, workgroup (coworkers and subordinates), and societal norms. Although we suspect that the direct manager's age may most likely

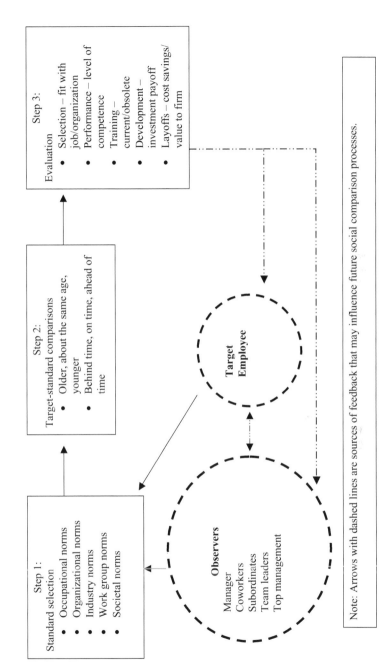

Note: Arrows with dashed lines are sources of feedback that may influence future social comparison processes.

FIG. 9.2. Social comparison in age discrimination.

219

invoke societal norms (i.e., employees are supposed to be younger than their managers), such norms may be superceded by occupational, organizational, or industrial norms. Whereas different standards of comparison have been used across different conceptual models and empirical studies, as yet there has been little exploration of why a particular age standard is chosen or how each may operate to influence decisions about employees. Step 2 consists of target-standard comparisons in which a determination is made on the particular features of the standard and target the comparison is to be based. If a hiring manager uses the workgroup norms for comparative purposes, then age and its associated meaning (e.g., "behind time") must be identified as a feature that will be used in the comparison process. If the employee is much older or younger than current employees, then age and its associated meaning is likely to become a salient feature for comparison purposes. Step 3 involves using the information generated in step 2 for evaluation purposes. In the example above, the hiring manager may decide that the applicant who is substantially older than current employees is "behind time" and is thus a poor fit with the job.

In Fig. 9.2, the target employee and observers are both sources of social comparison. That is, the individual is compared with others, but also compares him or herself with others. In fact, employees through their behavior and communication (e.g., discussions of retirement plans with coworkers) may influence observers' perceptions and choice of standard used for comparison purposes. Likewise, observers may influence self-assessments through decisions and treatment of employees. For example, subordinates who jokingly call their manager "the old man" may cause the manager to think of himself as old.

Clearly, despite the extensive literature on aging at work, there are many questions that remain unanswered. Of particular importance is to understand more clearly the cognitive processes that contribute to age discrimination. Also, additional work is needed on the ways in which organizations can improve opportunities for older workers. As the work force becomes older, it is in the best interests of both employees and organizations to contribute to improved opportunities for the development, performance, and retention of older workers.

REFERENCES

Arvey, R. D., Miller, H. E., Gould, R., & Burch, P. (1987). Interview validity for selecting sales clerks. *Personnel Psychology, 40*, 1–12.

Avolio, B. (1992). A levels of analysis perspective of aging and work research. In K. W. Schaie and M. P. Lawton (Eds.) *Annual Review of Gerontology and Geriatrics* (pp. 239–260). New York: Springer.

Avolio, B., & Waldman, D. (1989). Ratings of managerial skill requirements: Comparison of age- and job-related factors. *Psychology and Aging, 4*, 464–470.

Avolio, B., Waldman, D., & McDaniel, M. A. (1990). Age and work performance in non-managerial jobs: The effects of experience and occupational type. *Academy of Management Journal, 33*, 407–422.

Baddeley, A. (1986). *Working Memory.* Oxford, UK: Clarendon Press.

Bassili, J. N., & Reil, J. E. (1981). On the dominance of old age stereotypes. *Journal of Gerontology, 36*, 682–688.

Bird, C. P., & Fisher, T. D. (1986). Thirty years later: Attitudes toward the employment of older workers. *Journal of Applied Psychology, 71*, 515–517.

Botwinick, J. (1967). *Cognitive processes in maturity and old age.* New York: Springer.

Botwinick, J. (1977). Intellectual abilities. In J. E. Birren & K. W. Schaie (Eds.), *Handbook of the psychology of aging.* New York: Van Nostrand Reinhold.

Bureau of Labor Statistics (2001). U.S. Department of Labor, *Employment and Earnings,* Washington, DC.

Bureau of Labor Statistics (2002). U.S. Department of Labor, *Employment and Earnings,* Washington, DC.

Butler, R. (1969). Ageism: Another form of bigotry. *The Gerontologist, 9,* 243–246.

Byrne, D. E. (1971). *The attraction paradigm.* New York: Academic Press.

Cascio, W. F. (2002). Strategies for responsible restructuring. *Academy of Management Executive, 16,* 80–91.

Cleveland, J. N., & Berman, A. H. (1987). Age perceptions of jobs: Agreement between samples of students and managers. *Psychological Reports, 61,* 565–566.

Cleveland, J. N., Festa, R. M., & Montgomery, L. (1988). Applicant pool composition and job perceptions: Impact on decisions regarding an older applicant. *Journal of Vocational Behavior, 32,* 112–125.

Cleveland, J. N., & Hollman, G. (1990). The effects of the age-type of tasks and incumbent age and composition on job perceptions. *Journal of Vocational Behavior, 36,* 181–194.

Cleveland, J. N., & Landy, F. J. (1983). The effects of person and job stereotypes on two personnel decisions. *Personnel Psychology, 34,* 19–29.

Cleveland, J. N., & Landy, F. J. (1987). Age perceptions of jobs: Convergence of two questionnaires. *Psychological Reports, 60,* 1075–1081.

Cleveland, J.N., Montgomery, L., & Festa, R. M. (1984). *Group composition and job perceptions: Impact on decisions about suitability of applicants for group membership.* Unpublished manuscript, Department of Psychology, Baruch College, City University of New York.

Cleveland, J. N., & Shore, L. M. (1992). Self- and supervisory perspectives on age and work attitudes and performance. *Journal of Applied Psychology, 77,* 469–484.

Cleveland, J. N., Shore, L. M., & Murphy, K. R. (1997). Person- and context-oriented perceptual age measures: Additional evidence of distinctiveness and usefulness. *Journal of Organizational Behavior, 18,* 239–251.

Cohen, A. (1993). Organizational commitment and turnover: A meta-analysis. *Academy of Management Journal, 36,* 1140–1157.

Cowgill, D. I. (1974). The aging of population and societies. *Annals of the American Academy of Political and Social Science, 415,* 1–18.

Cox, T., & Nkomo, S. M. (1992). Candidate age as a factor in promotability ratings. *Public Personnel Management, 21,* 197–210.

Craft, J. A., Doctors, S. I., Shkop, Y. M., & Benecki, T. J. (1979). Simulated management perceptions, hiring decisions and age. *Aging and Work, 2,* 95–102.

Craik, F. I., & McDowd, J. M. (1987). Age differences in recall and recognition. *Journal of Experimental Psychology: Learning, Memory, and Cognition, 13,* 474–480.

Crew, J. C. (1983). Age stereotypes as a function of sex, race, and vocational preference. *Psychology: A Quarterly Journal of Human Behavior, 20,* 25–33.

Czaja, S. J. (1995). Aging and work performance. *Review of Public Personnel Administration Sprin, 8,* 46–61.

Dedrick, E. J., & Dobbins, G. H. (1991). The influence of subordinate age on managerial actions: An attributional analysis. *Journal of Organizational Behavior, 12,* 367–377.

Epitropaki, O., & Martin, R. (1999). The impact of relational demography on the quality of leader-member exchanges and employees' work attitudes and well being. *Journal of Occupational and Organizational Psychology, 72,* 237–240.

Estabrook, M. A. (1993). False economies: Downsizing as cure costs valuable older workers. *Pension World,* 10–12.

ExecuNet (2002). Age discrimination on the rise (News Release). Norwalk, CT: Author.

Ferris, G. R., Judge, T. A., Chachere, J. G., & Liden, R. C. (1991). The age context of performance-evaluation decisions. *Psychology and Aging, 6,* 616–622.

Ferris, G. R., & King, T. R. (1992). The politics of age discrimination in organizations. *Journal of Business Ethics, 11,* 341–350.

Finkelstein, L. M., Allen, T. D., & Rhoton, L. (2000). *An examination of the effects of age diversity in mentoring relationships.* Paper presented at meeting of the Society for Industrial and Organizational Psychology, New Orleans.

Finkelstein, L. M., & Burke, M. J. (1998). Age stereotyping at work: The role of rater and contextual factors on evaluations of job applicants. *Journal of General Psychology, 125,* 317–345.

Finkelstein, L. M., Burke, M. J., & Raju, N. S. (1995). Age discrimination in simulated employment contexts: An integrative analysis. *Journal of Applied Psychology, 80,* 40–45.

Fiske, S. T., Cuddy, A. J. C., Glick, P., & Xu, J. (2002). A model of (often mixed) stereotype content: Competence and warmth respectively follow from perceived status and competition. *Journal of Personality and Social Psychology, 82,* 878–902.

Goldberg, C. B., Finkelstein, L. M., Perry, E. L., & Konrad, A. M. (2001). *Age, gender, and career progress: Tests of simple and moderated effects.* Paper presented at the Academy of Management Conference, Washington, DC.

Goldberg, C. B., & Shore, L. M. (2003). The impact of age of applicants and of referent others on recruiters' assessments: a study of young and middle-aged job seekers. *Representative Research in Social Psychology, 27,* 11–22.

Goldberg, C. B., & Waldman, D. A. (2000). Modeling employee absenteeism: Testing alternative measures and mediated effects based on job satisfaction. *Journal of Organizational Behavior, 21,* 665–676.

Hackett, R. D. (1990). Age, tenure, and employee absenteeism. *Human Relations, 43,* 601–619.

Hall, D. T., & Mirvis, P. H. (1995). The new career contract: Developing the whole person at midlife and beyond. *Journal of Vocational Behavior, 47,* 269–289.

Hartley v. Wisconsin Bell, Inc., 124 F. 3d 887 (7th Cir. 1997).

Hassell, B. L., & Perrewe, P. L. (1993). An examination of the relationship between older workers' perceptions of age discrimination and employee psychological states. *Journal of Management Issues, 5,* 109–120.

Healy, M. C., Lehman, M., & McDaniel, M. A. (1995). Age and voluntary turnover: A quantitative review. *Personnel Psychology, 48,* 335–345.

Heywood, J. S., Ho, L., & Wei, X. (1999). The determinants of hiring older workers: Evidence from Hong Kong. *Industrial and Labor Relations Review, 52,* 444–459.

Kanfer, R., Wanberg, C. R., & Kantrowitz, T. M. (2001). Job search and employment: A personality-motivational analysis and meta-analytic review. *Journal of Applied Psychology, 86,* 837–855.

Kirchner, W. K., & Dunnette, M. D. (1954). Attitudes towards older workers. *Personnel Psychology, 7*, 257–265.

Kirchner, W. K., Lindbom, T., & Paterson, D. G. (1952). Attitudes toward the employment of older people. *Personnel Psychology, 36*, 154–156.

Kulik, C. T., Perry, E. L., & Bourhis, A. C. (2000). Ironic evaluation processes: Effects of thought suppression on evaluations of older job applicants. *Journal of Organizational Behavior, 21*, 689–711.

Landy, F. J., Shankster-Cawley, L., & Moran, S. K. (1995). Advancing personnel selection and placement methods. In A. Howard (Ed.), *The changing nature of work* (pp. 252–289). San Francisco: Jossey-Bass.

Lawrence, B. S. (1984). Age grading: The implicit organizational timetable. *Journal of Occupational Behavior, 13*, 181–191.

Lawrence, B. S. (1987). An organizational theory of age effects. In S. Bacharach & N. DiTomaso (Eds.), *Research in the Sociology of Organizations* (Vol. 5, pp. 37–71). Greenwich, CT: JAI.

Lawrence, B. S. (1988). New wrinkles in the theory of age: Demography, norms, and performance ratings. *Academy of Management Journal, 31*, 309–337.

Lawrence, B. S. (1990). At the crossroads: A multiple-level explanation of individual attachment. *Organization Science, 1*, 65–85.

Lemyre, L., & Smith, P. M. (1985). Intergroup discrimination and self-esteem in the minimal group paradigm. *Journal of Personality and Social Psychology, 49*, 660–670.

Liden, R. C., Stilwell, D., & Ferris, G. R. (1996). The effects of supervisor and subordinate age on objective performance and subjective performance ratings. *Human Relations, 49*, 327–347.

Marks v. Loral Corporation, 57 Cal. App. 4th 30 (1997).

Martocchio, J. J. (1989). Age-related differences in employee absenteeism: A meta-analysis. *Psychology and Aging, 4*, 409–414.

Martocchio, J. J. (1993). Employee decisions to enroll in microcomputer training. *Human Resource Development Quarterly, 4*, 51–69.

Maurer, T. J. (2001). Career-relevant learning and development, worker age, and beliefs about self-efficacy for development. *Journal of Management, 27*, 123–140.

Maurer, T. J. & Barbeite, F. G. (2001). Job performance and the aging worker. In D. Ekerdt (Ed.), *Encyclopedia of aging*. New York: Macmillan Reference USA.

Maurer, T. J., & Rafuse, N. E. (2001). Learning, not litigating: Managing employee development and avoiding claims of age discrimination. *Academy of Management Executive, 15*, 110–121.

Maurer, T. J., Wrenn, K. A., & Weiss, E. M. (2001). *Toward understanding and managing stereotypical beliefs about older worker's ability and desire for learning and development.* Paper presented at the meeting of the Academy of Management, Washington DC.

McEvoy, G. M., & Cascio, W. F. (1989). Cumulative evidence of the relationship between employee age and job performance. *Journal of Applied Psychology, 74*, 11–17.

McCann, R., & Giles, H. (2002). Ageism in the workplace: A communication perspective. In T. Nelson (ed). *Ageism: Stereotyping and prejudice against older persons* (pp. 163–199). Cambridge, MA: MIT Press.

Meisenheimer, J. R., & Iig, R. E. (2000). Looking for a 'better' job: Job-search activity of the employed. *Monthly Labor Review*, September 2000, 3–14.

Miller, C. S., Kaspin, J. A., & Schuster, M. H. (1990). The impact of performance appraisal methods on age discrimination in Employment Act cases. *Personnel Psychology, 29*, 11–27.

Mitchell v. Sisters of Charity of Incarnate Word, 924 F. Supp. 793 (1996).

Musswiler, T. (2003). Comparison processes in social judgment: Mechanisms and consequences. *Psychological Review, 110*, 472–489.

O'Connor v. Consolidated Coin Caterers Corp., 56 F. 3d 542 (4th Cir. 1995).

Ohlott, P. J., & Eastman, L. J. (1994). Age differences in developmental job experiences: Evidence of a gray ceiling? Paper presented at the meeting of the Academy of Management, Dallas, TX.

O'Reilly, C. A., Caldwell, D. F., & Barnett, W. P. (1989). Work group demography, social integration, and turnover. *Administrative Science Quarterly, 34*, 21–37.

Paul, R. J., & Townsend, J. B. (1993). Managing the older worker—Don't just rinse away the gray. *Academy of Management Executive, 7*, 67–70.

Perry, E. L. (1994). A prototype matching approach to understanding the role of applicant gender and age in the evaluation of job applicants. *Journal of Applied Social Psychology, 24*, 1433–1473.

Perry, E. L. (1997). A cognitive approach to understanding discrimination: A closer look at applicant gender and age. In G. R. Ferris (Ed.), Research in personnel and human resources management (Vol. 15, pp. 175–240). Greenwich, CT: JAI.

Perry, E. L., & Bourhis, A. C. (1998). A closer look at the role of applicant age in selection decisions. *Journal of Applied Social Psychology, 28*, 16–30.

Perry, E. L., & Finkelstein, L. M. (1999). Toward a broader view of age discrimination in employment-related decisions: A joint consideration of organizational factors and cognitive processes. *Human Resource Management Review, 9*, 21–49.

Perry, E. L., Kulik, C. T., & Bourhis, A. C. (1996). Moderating effects of personal and contextual factors in age discrimination. *Journal of Applied Psychology, 81*, 628–647.

Perry, E. L., Kulik, C. T., & Zhou, J. (1999). A closer look at the effects of subordinate supervisor age differences. *Journal of Organizational Behavior, 20*, 341–357.

Perry, J. S., & Varney, T. L. (1978). College students' attitudes toward workers' competence and age. *Psychological Reports, 42*, 1319–1322.

Prenda, K. M., & Stahl, S. M. (2001). The truth about older workers. *Business and Health*, 30–37.

Raza, S. M., & Carpenter, B. (1987). A model of hiring decisions in real employment interviews. *Journal of Applied Psychology, 72*, 596–603.

Rhodes, S. (1983). Age-related differences in work attitudes and behavior. *Psychological Bulletin, 93*, 328–367.

Ringenbach, K. L., & Jacobs, R. R. (1994). *Development of age stereotypes in the workplace scale.* Paper presented at the Society of Industrial and Organizational Psychologists Conference, Nashville, TN.

Riordan, C. M. (2000). Relational demography within groups: Past developments, contradictions, and new directions. In G. Ferris (Ed.), *Research in personnel and human resource management* (Vol. 19). Greenwich, CT: JAI.

Riordan, C. M., & Shore, L. M. (1997). Demographic diversity and employee attitudes: An empirical examination of relational demography within work units. *Journal of Applied Psychology, 82*, 342–358.

Rosen, B., & Jerdee, T. H. (1976a). The influence of age stereotypes on managerial decisions. *Journal of Applied Psychology, 62*, 428–432.

Rosen, B., & Jerdee, T. H. (1976b). The nature of job-related age stereotypes. *Journal of Applied Psychology, 62*, 180–183.

Rosen, B., & Jerdee, T. H. (1977). Too old or not too old. *Harvard Business Review, 55*, 97–106.

Rosen, B., & Jerdee, T. H. (1988). Managing older workers' careers. In G. R. Ferris & K. M. Rowland (Eds.), *Research in Personnel and Human Resources Management, 6*, 37–74. Greenwich, CT: JAI Press.

Rousseau, D. M. (1995). *Psychological Contracts in Organizations. Understanding Written and Unwritten Agreements.* Thousand Oaks, CA: Sage.

Salthouse, T. A. (1985). Speed of behavior and its implications for cognition. In J. E. Birren and K. W. Schaie (Eds.), *Handbook of the Psychology of Aging* (2nd ed., pp. 400–426). New York: Van Nostrand Reinhold.

Salthouse, T. A. (1990). Influence of experience on age differences in cognitive functioning. *Human Factors, 32,* 551–569.

Salthouse, T. A., & Maurer, T. J. (1996). Aging and work. In J. E. Birren & K. W. Schaie (Eds.), *Handbook of the Psychology of Aging* (4th ed., pp. 353–364). San Diego: Academic Press.

Schaie, K. W. (1989). The hazards of cognitive aging. *The Gerontologist, 29,* 484–493.

Scully, J., Kiker, S., & Cross, T. (in press). Does method matter?: A meta analysis of the effects of training method on older learner training performance. *Journal of Management.*

Shore, L. M., Cleveland, J. N., & Goldberg, C. (2003). Work Attitudes and Decisions as a Function of Manager Age and Employee Age. *Journal of Applied Psychology, 88,* 529–537.

Sonnenfeld, J. (1978). Dealing with the aging work force. *Harvard Business Review, 78,* 81–92.

Tsui, A. S., Egan, T. D., & O'Reilly, C. (1992). Being different: Relational demography and organizational attachment. *Administrative Science Quarterly, 37,* 549–579.

Tsui A. S., & O'Reilly, C. A. (1989). Beyond simple demographic effects: The importance of relational demography in superior-subordinate dyads. *Academy of Management Journal, 32,* 402–423.

Tsui, A. S., Porter, L. W., & Egan, T. D. (2002). When both similarities and dissimilarities matter: Extending the concept of relational demography. *Human Relations, 55,* 899–929.

Tsui, A. S., Xin, K. R., & Egan, T. D. (1995). Relational demography: The missing link in vertical dyad linkage. In S. E. Jackson & M. N. Ruderman (Eds.), *Diversity in work teams: Research paradigms for a changing workplace* (pp. 97–129). Washington, DC: American Psychological Association.

U.S. Bureau of the Consus. (1993). Statistical abstracts of the United States (113 ed.). Washington, DC: US Government Printing Office.

Wagner, W. G., Pfeffer, J., & O'Reilly, C. A. (1984). Organizational demography and turnover in top-management groups. *Administrative Science Quarterly, 29,* 74–92.

Waldman, D., & Avolio, B. (1986). A meta-analysis of age differences in job performance. *Journal of Applied Psychology, 71,* 33–38.

Waldman, D. A., & Avolio, B. J. (1993). Aging and work performance in perspective: Contextual and developmental considerations. In G. R. Ferris (Ed.), *Research in Personnel and Human Resources Management, 11,* 133–162. Greenwich, CT: JAI Press.

Warr, P., & Bunce, D. (1995). Trainee characteristics and the outcomes of open learning. *Personnel Psychology, 48,* 347–375.

Warr, P., & Pennington, J. (1994). Occupational age-grading: Jobs for older and younger non-managerial employees. *Journal of Vocational Behavior, 45,* 328–346.

Wayne, S. J., & Liden, R. C. (1995). Effects of impression management on performance ratings. *Academy of Management Journal, 38,* 232–260.

Wellner, A. S. (March, 2002). Tapping a silver mine. *HR Magazine, 47,* 26–32.

Zenger, T. R., & Lawrence, B. S. (1989). Organizational demography: The differential effects of age and tenure distributions on technical communication. *Academy of Management Journal, 32,* 353–376.

10

Workplace Discrimination Toward Persons with Disabilities: A Call for Some New Research Directions

Adrienne Colella
Texas A&M University

Dianna L. Stone
University of Central Florida

The issue of workplace discrimination resulting from disability has not received nearly as much attention in the psychological literature as other forms of discrimination. There are many reasons for this lack of attention ranging from the recency of the Americans with Disabilities Act (1990) compared to other civil rights legislation, to problems with defining what actually constitutes a disability in both the legal and behavioral sense. However, it is particularly imperative that we work to better understand disability discrimination in the workplace given what little change there has been in the employment status of persons with disabilities since the advent of the ADA (Wells, 2001). In this chapter we examine what work has been done and what major issues still remain to be addressed in future research. Behavioral research on disability discrimination has grown since the passage of the ADA, has become more systematic, and is more relevant to employment issues. Yet, our review underscores the point that there is still a long way to go until we can gain a workable understanding of the psychological aspects of disability discrimination in the workplace. The purpose of this chapter is to help guide that research.

We begin by briefly describing research that has been done examining disability discrimination. We divide this research into nonpsychological research and, the subject of this chapter, psychologically based research. As our brief review shows, this literature is somewhat scattered and inconclusive. We then move to a discussion of issues that need to be addressed before we can have a better understanding of the psychological processes underlying discrimination against people with disabilities.

LITERATURE REVIEW

The purpose of this literature review is to give the reader an understanding of the current state and findings of disability employment discrimination research, rather than to provide a comprehensive review of all studies. We devote the most attention to the empirical psychologically based research because it serves as the background to our suggestions for where this area of research needs to go in the future to advance our understanding of the psychological bases of workplace discrimination against people with disabilities.

Nonpsychological Research

Labor economists, rehabilitation psychologists, and general surveys of managers and the public have all examined the issue of disability treatment in the workplace. Labor statistics indicate that people with disabilities are more likely to be unemployed and paid less than people who do not have disabilities. Recent data from the Harris Poll organization (Taylor, 2000) indicated that only 31% of all people with disabilities are employed full or part time, and 56% of people with disabilities who report that they are able to work, do so. This is compared to 81% of the total U.S. population. One should not interpret these results as indicating that persons with disabilities do not want to work. A recent Harris Poll (Taylor, 1998) reported that 72% of people with disabilities who were not working wanted to work. Current census data present very similar results (McNeil, 2000). Also, recent census reports indicate that people with disabilities earn less ($33,109 annually in 2000) compared to individuals without disabilities ($43,269; U.S. Census Bureau, 2002). Indeed, these numbers have changed little since the ADA was enacted in 1992 (see National Council on Disability, 2002), indicating that employment discrimination exists. Furthermore, the extent to which employment and wage differentials exist varies by disability

(Baldwin, 1999) and is larger for women (Baldwin, Zeager, & Flacco, 1999). This line of research clearly indicates that there is employment discrimination (see Schall, 1998), however, it offers little explanation for why this discrimination exists.

Another area of literature that examines the issue of disability and work is that from the rehabilitation field. This body of work is extensive, but does not tend to address discrimination directly. Rehabilitation research typically examines personal factors that are likely to be related to employment outcomes (e.g., Butterworth & Staruch, 1994; Meuller, Wilgosh, & Dennis, 1987); examines workplace factors associated with integration (e.g., Gates, 1993); evaluates rehabilitation programs (e.g., Gatti, 1991); develops rehabilitation practices, policies, and programs (e.g., Gates, Akabas, & Oran-Sabia, 1998); and presents many small sample qualitative studies of employee experiences at work (e.g., Chima, 1998; Crudden & McBroom, 1999; Duckett, 2000; Gillies, Knight, & Baglioni, 1998). The goal of this research is to examine what can be done to better integrate persons with disabilities into the workforce. However, this literature has been criticized for ignoring problems associated with the negative attitudes of others and the environment (Hahn, 1996). Thus, it offers little in guiding our understanding of discrimination against persons with disabilities. There is some research in this area that directly addresses discrimination from a psychological perspective. This work is included in our discussion below.

Although labor statistics indicate that employment discrimination exists against persons with disabilities, surveys of the public and of employers (e.g., Callahan, 1994; B. Cooper, 1991; M. Cooper, 1995) generally report more positive responses toward employing persons with disabilities, although responses vary by industry (Diska & Rogers, 1996). For example, a survey of the general public found that between 85% and 95% supported the basic employment provisions of the ADA (Taylor, 1999). A survey of over 1,200 private and public organizations (Bruyere, 2000) found that employer groups were responsive to disability issues in the workplace and were attempting to make accommodations. Another line of research that surveyed managers aimed to determine the effectiveness of different policies and employment procedures in affecting employees with disabilities (e.g., Berkowitz & O'Leary, 2000). However, there has been very little of this research done in a systematic fashion. Therefore, we do not know what policies and procedures work, or if they do, why (Berkowitz & O'Leary, 2000).

However, these positive management findings should not be given too much weight in assessing the extent of and mechanisms underlying disability discrimination. First of all, this research is subjected to a great deal of social desirability bias (Stone, Stone, & Dipboye, 1992). It has been suggested that managers' stated attitudes do not reflect their hiring behavior (Wilgosh & Meuller, 1989). Second, overwhelmingly positive statements can be read as a sign of paternalism—an issue that we discuss later. Third, reports from people with disabilities contradict these findings (e.g., Crudden & McBroom, 1999). Finally, most respondents to these surveys are human resource managers who may have more positive attitudes than other people in general. This is supported by the finding that the one of the biggest problems reported by manager surveys is the way coworkers (not human resource managers) react to persons with disabilities (Bruyere, 2000; Greenwood, Shiner, & Johnson, 1991; Hahn, 1996; McFarlin, Song, & Sonntag, 1991).

Psychologically Based Disability Discrimination Research

In an extensive review of the impact of disability on personnel decisions, we uncovered 37 published studies (a summary of these studies is available from the first author) that allowed one to assess whether there was discrimination. In order to assess workplace discrimination, a study must include a nondisabled control group, hold performance constant, and measure a work-related dependent variable (e.g., hiring decision, performance evaluation). We found several studies that examined discrimination between different types of disabilities, but did not have a nondisabled control group (e.g., Bordieri & Drehmer, 1987; Gouvier, Steiner, Jackson, Schlater, & Rain, 1991; Jones & Stone, 1995; Koser, Matsuyama, & Kopelman, 1999). Most of the included studies focused on selection or interviewing (24). The reminder focused on performance evaluations and/or employee interactions, acceptance, and inclusion. One other note of interest is that the number of studies doubled since 1990, the year that the ADA was passed.

Our review indicates that this research is inconclusive, sometimes finding that disability results in overly negative (discriminatory) evaluations and decisions (11 studies), overly positive evaluations (5), no effect for disability on personnel decisions (6), or mixed results depending on the disability or dependent variable (15). For this line of research to advance, we believe that several issues ranging from the methodological to the conceptual need to be addressed in future research. These issues are study context, generalizing across disabilities, expanding the range of behaviors studied, and conceptual considerations.

Study Context. The overwhelming majority of these studies (30) were conducted in the laboratory using student or MBA manager subjects. It is easy to say that more fieldwork needs to be done, but it is particularly difficult to study disability discrimination in the workplace. First, very few people with disabilities disclose to the organization. If disclosure takes place, it is just usually to the supervisor. Thus, there is no centralized knowledge of who has a disability, which makes it difficult to locate respondents. Second, as any discrimination researcher knows, it is often difficult to get past the legal department when conducting this type of research. However, researchers need to overcome these difficulties.

Our review indicated that all seven studies conducted in field settings (Bowman, 1987; Colella & Varma, 2001 (study 1); Farina, Felner, & Boudreau, 1973; Johnson & Heal, 1976; Millington, Szymanski, & Hanley-Maxwell, 1994; Ravaud, Madiot, & Ville, 1992; and Schloss & Soda, 1989) found negative discriminatory effects on at least some dependent measures. When results were mixed, there was either no effect or a negative effect. In other words, positive effects (i.e., evaluations that are overly positive for applicants or employees with disabilities) were only found in the lab.

Researchers using student respondents often justify this choice by citing research that shows that students do not vary in their attitudes toward people with disabilities compared to managers. This may indeed be the case, however, we suggest that this is not the problem. Rather the problem lies in conducting research in a context where there are no personal consequences to respondents.

Many have argued (see Stone et al., 1992 with respect to disabilities) that social desirability effects rule out the expression of negative bias when the interaction situation is of little consequence to respondents. Indeed, several studies have demonstrated that when the situation matters to respondents (Colella, DeNisi, & Varma, 1998; Gibbons, Stephan, Stephanson, & Petty, 1980; Piner & Kahle, 1984; Stone & Michaels, 1993, 1994), subjects are much more likely to discriminate against people with disabilities. Colella et al. (1998) used social adaptation theory (Piner & Kahle, 1984) to explain this effect.

The point is that we need to stop conducting the modal disability discrimination study whereby respondents react to a paper person or a videotape in a situation that is of no personal consequence and conduct research in settings where the interaction is of real consequence to respondents. This means that laboratory research needs to be more carefully designed, and research in the field needs to be conducted. There are many ways to make the situation of consequence to respondents such as interdependence of tasks, competition for a valued reward, or real-life, real-time work relationships (or the anticipation of such).

Generalizing Across Disabilities   It is safe to conclude that people do not respond to all disabilities in the same manner. Indeed there is a line of research which illustrates that there is a hierarchy of disabilities in terms of how negatively nondisabled people respond to them (e.g., Bowman,

1987; Jones & Stone, 1995; Tringo, 1970). In our review, six out of the eight studies reporting positive effects used a target person in a wheelchair or on crutches. This actually corresponds to the "disability discrimination" hierarchy research that shows that people respond most favorably to people with physical disabilities compared to those with sensory or, especially, mental disabilities.

Paraplegia, a wheel chair, or leg braces and crutches were used as a disability manipulation in 21 out of 37 studies. Thus, it possible that we are paying the most attention to a disability that evokes less negative responses than other disabilities or else elicits stronger social desirability bias. This is not to say that we shouldn't study discrimination against persons with paraplegia, but rather we should be careful about generalizing across disabilities.

It is not useful to treat discrimination as a special case for each type of existing disability. A framework (Stone & Colella, 1996) has been put forth for examining those characteristics of disability that do lead to certain reactions that can be used to make generalizations. Stone & Colella (1996), based on the work of Jones et al. (1984) posited that it is the following features of disability that relate to negative reactions: aesthetic qualities, danger or peril, course, origin, concealability, and disruptiveness. None of these characteristics has received systematic research in a discrimination study. One characteristic associated with disability that has been systematically studied is the perceived cause or blame for the disability. Bordieri, Drehmer, and their colleagues (Bordieri & Drehmer, 1986, 1987, 1988; Bordieri, Drehmer, & Comninel, 1988; Bordieri, Drehmer, & Taricone, 1990) have conducted research that has consistently found that the extent to which respondents blame the target person for his or her disability moderates the impact of disability on workplace evaluations. Based on these findings we can conclude that to the extent that a person is perceived as personally responsible for his or her disability, the worse reactions will be toward that person. Systematic research of this sort needs to be conducted on the other characteristics mentioned above.

Another issue that makes it difficult to generalize findings across disabilities is that characteristic of "disability" is not only ambiguous from a legal perspective, but also from a psychological perspective (on both the part of observers and actors). The ADA (1990) defines an individual with a disability as a person who has a physical or mental impairment that substantially limits one or more major life activities, has a record of such an impairment, or is regarded as having such an impairment. Major life activities are activities that an average person can perform with little or no difficulty such as walking, breathing, seeing, hearing, speaking, learning, and working. This is a very broad and general definition. When the

ADA was first enacted, employers were very fearful that the definition was too broad and would cover almost anyone. In the past decade, however, court rulings have narrowed the legal definition of disability considerably so that if one has a disability that is not severe enough to prevent working (Hahn, 2000) or has a disability that is correctable (e.g., with glasses or a hearing aid; *Albertsons v. Kirkingburg*, 1999; *Murphy v. UPS*, 1999; *Sutton v. United Airlines*, 1999), then that person is not considered disabled. Indeed, the primary reason that plaintiffs lose ADA cases is that they are determined not to have a disability (Lee, 1998), and therefore, not covered by the ADA (1990). This is simply not an issue with other civil rights legislation—everyone has a sex, race, ethnicity, and so forth, and is therefore protected on these characteristics. Apart from legal definitions, there is also the issue of how people, both actors and observers, define disabilities.

The ADA (1990) acknowledges the importance of the perceptual process involved in defining persons with disabilities by stating that one is covered by the law if he or she is "regarded" as having an impairment. Furthermore, Stone and Colella (1996) in their model of how employees with disabilities are treated at work argue that a critical process is that a person be categorized by the observer as "disabled." We know relatively little about this process or what features people use to personally define "disability." If there is legal ambiguity about what constitutes a disability, then certainly individuals vary in how they define the construct. One could argue that there are some disabilities that most people would consider as disabilities (e.g., paraplegia, blindness, and deafness); however, there are others that may not be so uniformly categorized (e.g., mental illness, back pain, and recovering addict). This issue is complicated by the findings that show that people react differently to different disabilities (e.g., Bowman, 1987; Jones & Stone, 1995; Tringo, 1970) and that reactions to specific disabilities can vary by the context in which the social interaction is taking place (Christman & Slaten, 1991; Grand, Bernier, & Strohmer, 1982; Strohmer, Grand, & Purcell, 1984). These issues indicate that in comparison to other discrimination research, disability research needs to (a) understand whether observers consider the target to be "disabled"; (b) take context into consideration; and (c) deal with generalizing findings across disabilities.

Finally, any discussion of the definition of disability must consider a person's own self-concept of being disabled (Colella & DeNisi, 1994). The disability literature has been criticized for making the assumption that persons with disabilities define themselves in terms of that disability (Fine & Asch, 1988). Indeed, clinical and rehabilitation psychology researchers (e.g., Krauss, Mehnert, Nadler, & Greenberg, 1993) have studied the self-identity as "disabled" of individuals with known disabilities and found that individuals with the same physical impairment vary greatly in their self-conceptualizations. This impacts greatly on research because many people who have impairments and may be considered by others to have a disability do not report that they are disabled. Recent census data collection has found that people unreliably report over time their disability status (McNeil, 2000). In order to determine one's disability status, it is best to ask about specific impairments than to ask about disability in general (McNeil, 2000). This is in contrast to other types of discrimination research where most respondents can very clearly, reliably, and unambiguously self-classify into a category such as sex or race. This makes taking a group-identity or relational demography approach to the study of disability discrimination difficult.

Evaluation Type As previously noted, the vast majority of studies examined selection decision using either paper credentials, videotaped interviews, or both. Given the inconclusive results of this research, we are not going to suggest a moratorium on such research, but rather that researchers broaden their choice of reactions. One such reaction is inclusion into workgroups.

There exists in the rehabilitation literature several studies that examine the factors affecting and the extent to which people with disabilities are included in their workgroups. However, most of this research is qualitative, focuses on people with mental retardation, and focuses on the skills and behaviors of persons with disabilities (not the work environment). Recently, a few studies in the management literature have studied inclusion into workgroups (Colella & Varma, 1999; Stone & Michaels, 1993, 1994), but there is still quite a bit to be done in this arena. Colella (1996) developed a conceptual model for the socialization of people with disabilities in the workplace that has yet to be tested. Because any bias in selecting people with disabilities may be tempered by tax incentives or by EEOC concerns, it is worthwhile to study how people with disabilities are actually treated in the workplace.

A second issue that has been somewhat ignored in the I/O psychology literature is that of accommodation. The ADA (1990) requires "reasonable accommodation" so that a person with a disability can apply for a job, perform a job, or enjoy benefits equal to those of other employees (EEOC ADA handbook, 2003). This notion is different from that of equal treatment specified by other civil rights legislation (Colella, 2001). Failure to provide a needed accommodation, which is of reasonable cost, to a qualified individual with a disability can legally be viewed as discrimination and should therefore be studied as a form of discrimination. There are three outcomes associated with accommodation that need to be addressed by empirical research: (a) coworkers' reactions, (b) supervisors' reactions and willingness to accommodate, and (c) persons with disabilities' willingness to request an accommodation.

Theoretical models have been posited for each of these outcomes. Colella and her colleagues have applied an organizational justice framework to examine coworkers' reactions to accommodation (Colella, 2001; Colella, Paetzold, & Belliveau, 2004). There have also been conceptual models put forth regarding whether or not an organization or manager will grant an accommodation (Cleveland, Barnes-Farrell, & Ratz, 1997; Florey & Harrison, 1998). Finally, Baldridge and Veiga (2001) developed a model concerning what will influence whether or not a person requests an accommodation. However, empirical research on these three issues is sorely lacking, despite sound theoretical frameworks for guiding it.

Conceptual Underpinnings of Disability Discrimination Research   There is a great deal of theory that explains discrimination against persons with disabilities. Indeed, the empirical work on workplace discrimination lags behind the theoretical work. Rather than describe every conceptual reason for disability discrimination, we draw attention to concepts that have been relatively ignored. Most research on disability discrimination has taken a cognitive approach, focusing on stereotypes, expectations, and stigmas (Stone & Colella, 1996; Stone, Stone, & Dipboye, 1992), and this issue is treated in detail elsewhere in this volume, as well as in Stone & Colella's (1996) model. We focus here on two other explanations for disability discrimination that have received very little attention in the work discrimination literature: emotional responses and the notion of paternalism.

Emotional Responses   One factor that distinguishes disability discrimination from other types of discrimination is that anyone can become disabled at any time. Recent census data report that nearly one in five people in the United States report having some disability (U.S. Census Bureau, 2001), and this number is expected to grow given the aging population. People do not usually switch categories on other demographic characteristics—thus, this fact introduces different dynamics into the disability discrimination process. Livneh (1982) argued that one of the bases for discrimination against persons with disabilities results from the existential anxiety that occurs when a nondisabled person identifies with a person with a disability and consequently fears becoming disabled him or herself. Thus, we argue that because of this, emotion plays a significant role in disability discrimination, and as discuss below, there is an emotional component to many disability discrimination theories. Yet, little empirical research has focused on emotional or "gut level" reactions. Examining disability discrimination from an emotional perspective may lead, as we propose, to more effective means for overcoming disability discrimination.

According to Lazarus and Lazarus (1994), emotions are defined as "Complex reactions that engage both our minds and bodies. These reactions include a subjective mental state such as feelings of anger, anxiety, and profound changes in the body such as an increase in heart rate or blood pressure" (p. 3). It has long been argued that some disabilities evoke primitive affective responses in others. For example, Goffman's (1963) seminal work on stigmas argued that abominations of the body, especially facial deformities and amputations, elicit feelings of disgust or revulsion in others. Furthermore, other authors (Jones et al., 1984) maintained that emotional reactions to disabilities are determined by cognitive appraisal and cultural norms. For example, stigmas based on what could be considered by some as blemishes of character (Goffman, 1963), such as obesity or drug addictions, are often determined by the extant norms in the culture. In particular, in modern American culture obesity is considered a stigma because it is attributed to a lack of willpower or a character flaw (Pingatore, Bernard, Tindale, & Spring, 1994), and individuals who are obese receive lower wages and are assigned to less challenging jobs than those who are not overweight (Roehling, 1999). The primary reason for this is that willpower and self-control are highly valued in modern society; however, in Renaissance times a high level of body fat was considered a sign of beauty because it was a symbol of wealth and status. Thus, cultural norms and values may, in part, dictate how individuals should emotionally react to varying disabilities.

Despite the intriguing arguments just noted, little empirical research has focused directly on emotional reactions to disabilities (cf. Colella, 1996; Jones et al., 1984; Stone & Colella, 1996). One reason for this is that there has been considerable controversy in psychology about whether emotions are automatic or require cognitive appraisal. Some theorists argue that emotional reactions are automatic and innate, (Zajonc, 1980), and aversion to anomalies is a response that ensures survival of the fittest of the species. It follows that if emotions are innate, they will be highly resilient and difficult to change. However, other theorists (Lazarus, Kanner, & Folkman, 1980) contend that emotions require cognitions in the form of appraisals. For example, Lazarus and his colleagues (1980) argue that there are two forms of appraisal, primary and secondary. In particular, primary appraisal poses the question "What are the implications of the stimulus (e.g., disability) for the person's well-being?" For instance, a person may react more negatively to working with a person with AIDS than one with paraplegia because AIDS is perceived as contagious whereas paraplegia is not (Vest, Vest, Perry, & O'Brien, 1995). Furthermore, secondary appraisal addresses the issue of "How can the person cope with the stimulus (e.g., disability) or prevent harm to himself or herself?" Using the same example, one means of coping with a coworker with AIDS is to avoid the person or ask for a transfer to another unit. However, another strategy for coping is to alter one's cognitive beliefs so that the stimulus is perceived as less threatening or harmful (e.g., a person may learn that AIDS is not contagious through casual contact). Interestingly, although we have presented two opposing views of emotions we believe that both theories may be correct, and emotional responses may depend on the type of disability and cultural norms. As noted previously, emotional responses to some types of disability may be automatic (e.g., facial deformities), but reactions to other disabilities may be influenced by the degree to which the disability is perceived as contagious or terminal (e.g., cancer, AIDS).

As noted previously, we believe, as do others (Jones et al., 1984), that cultural values affect individuals' emotional responses to disabilities in several ways. First, culture influences the cognitive appraisal of disabilities by defining the significance of the disability for the observer's well-being (Lazarus et al., 1980). For example, in U.S. culture many diseases that were once contagious are controlled and no longer pose severe risks to those near the person (e.g., tuberculosis, polio, and smallpox). However, in some less developed cultures these diseases have yet to be controlled, and individuals may perceive they will be harmed if they are exposed to someone with the diseases just noted. As a result, individuals in one culture may react more negatively to individuals with illnesses than those in other cultures. Second, culture influences emotions by informing individuals on how emotional responses to disabilities should be controlled or expressed. For example, in the U.S. culture the norm to treat the person with a disability with kindness converts revulsion into compassion (Stone et al., 1992). However, in the same culture the norms associated with equity and self-reliance may mean that coworkers will react negatively when individuals with disabilities are given special accommodation in the workplace (Colella, 2001).

Although there are a number of emotional reactions that may lead to unfair discrimination in the workplace, we consider three key emotions (i.e., pity, anxiety, and resentment) in the sections that follow, and we discuss strategies for overcoming the negative consequences associated with these emotions in work-related settings.

Compassion and Pity Individuals often experience compassion at the sight of someone with a disability, and the emotion may become particularly pronounced when they are aware that the person is suffering or in distress. For example, individuals often experience compassion when they observe someone with a physical disability who is confined to a wheelchair.

Compassion can be defined as a sympathetic consciousness of another's distress coupled with the desire to help (Lazarus & Lazarus, 1994). Some synonyms for compassion include sympathy, empathy, and pity. Sympathy is expressed as concern, understanding, or appreciation for the person with the disability, whereas empathy is actually experiencing the same emotion as the other. However, pity is often defined as feeling sorry for the person with the disability. Interestingly, pity is a more condescending or disdainful feeling than compassion or empathy and is often coupled with a view the person with the disability is inferior. Thus, people with disabilities may be more likely to experience unfair discrimination in the workplace when others view them with pity rather than with compassion. Furthermore, pity is typically considered less acceptable in the American culture than the other emotions of compassion, sympathy, or empathy.

Research has shown that individuals rationalize feelings of pity for persons with disabilities in two ways. In particular, considerable research suggests that when observers experience feelings of discomfort they avoid contact and distance themselves from people with disabilities (cf. Stone & Colella, 1996). In addition, observers distance themselves emotionally from individuals with disabilities by dehumanizing the person (Stone et al., 1992). For instance, when individuals observe unmerited or needless suffering, it threatens their beliefs in a just world, and they infer that the individual must be responsible for his or her problems (Lerner, 1980). It merits noting that this rationalization process has been labeled the "just world hypothesis" and suggests that suffering is always based on one's conduct (Lerner, 1980). Not surprisingly, considerable research has shown that observers react more negatively to persons with disabilities when they perceive that the person caused the disability (e.g., paraplegia as a result of a motorcycle accident) than when they did not (e.g., Bordieri & Drehmer, 1987; Bordieri, Drehmer, & Cominel, 1988).

Although little research has focused on the emotional responses of compassion and pity and treatment of people with disabilities, some research has suggested that people vary in terms of empathy, and individuals higher in empathy levels may feel more discomfort working with people with disabilities than those lower in empathy levels (Cesare, Tannenbaum, & Delessio, 1990). Furthermore, it has long been known that health care workers distance themselves from patients' illnesses, but help them at same time (Lazarus et al., 1980). Thus, the ability to distance oneself emotionally from a disability may require both sensitivity and self-control and may be an important determinant of reactions to persons with disabilities in the workplace. As a result, organizations may want to train supervisors and coworkers to distance themselves emotionally from an employee's disability and focus on the individuals' abilities rather than their ability limitations. Likewise, organization might select supervisors who can form effective working relationships with employees with disabilities rather than those who empathize with their subordinates' problems (Colella & Varma, 2001). Given that little research has examined strategies for overcoming empathy and pity as emotional responses to coworkers and disabilities, additional research is needed on the topic.

Anxiety As noted previously, observers often experience anxiety and discomfort when interacting with persons with disabilities (Stone & Colella, 1996). Furthermore, anxiety is often considered an existential emotion because it is based on personal security, concerns about life and death, or quality of life (Lazarus et al., 1980). For example, encounters with individuals with cancer may remind us of our own vulnerability or the inevitability of death, and encounters with individuals with AIDS may evoke danger because it is potentially contagious (Vest et al., 1995). Furthermore, anxiety may stem from uncertainty or the inability to predict another's behavior (Stone & Colella, 1996). As a result, observers often react quite negatively to persons with mental illness or neurological problems (e.g., epilepsy) because the observers are unable to predict the person's behavior and fear they will experience harm. Given that some disabilities evoke feelings of anxiety in others, it is likely that the higher others' anxiety levels, the more the person with the disability will relegated to experience unfair discrimination in the workplace. To our knowledge, no research has directly assessed this proposition, and additional research is needed.

Interestingly, the cognitive appraisal view of emotions (Lazarus & Lazarus, 1994) suggests two important strategies that might be used to overcome anxiety associated with disabilities, including emotion-centered and problem-solving coping. Emotion-centered coping often involves avoiding or distancing oneself from the person, but also involves reappraising the encounter in less threatening ways. For example, although one may experience anxiety when interacting with a person with cancer, the same person may reappraise the situation by noting that individuals are less likely to die from cancer today than in years past. Problem-solving coping typically involves changing others thoughts and actions and may use training or knowledge gathering as a means of reducing the anxiety associated with disabilities. For instance, training or knowledge about AIDS may reduce the anxiety of interacting with a coworker with AIDS. Although these two strategies seem plausible, to our knowledge, no research has directly examined the degree to which emotion-centered or problem-centered coping reduce feelings of anxiety associated with working with people with disabilities. Thus, additional research is needed to assess the effectiveness of these strategies.

Resentment   Apart from the emotions just noted, individuals often experience resentment when working with someone with a disability. One reason for this is that work-related settings typically require some levels of interdependence among coworkers, and working with a person with a disability can have a negative impact on coworkers' outcomes. For example, a person's ability limitations can increase the workload for others, decrease coworkers' status, and increase the awkwardness of interactions (cf. Stone & Colella, 1996). Furthermore, accommodations or the differential treatment of persons with disabilities can also evoke resentment in the workplace especially when the accommodation violates equity norms (e.g., coworkers perceive that the individual with a disability is receiving the same level of outcomes without providing the same inputs; see Colella, 2001 for a review). In addition, Colella (2001) maintained that coworkers often resent accommodations for employees with disabilities when the accommodation is requested for utilitarian motives or when the disability is invisible or perceived to be self-caused. This feeling of resentment toward people with disabilities may also be a potential cause of the backlash against the ADA (1990).

Consistent with the arguments noted above (Jones et al., 1984; Lazarus et al., 1980) cultural norms may influence the extent to which coworkers experience resentment when working with people with disabilities. For example, the U.S. culture espouses humanitarian values, but places particular emphasis on self-reliance, rugged individualism, and equity allocation systems (Trice & Beyer, 1993). As a result, some anthropologists (Hsu, 1961, cited in Trice & Beyer, 1993) contend that one of the greatest fears in American life is dependence on others, and the fear of dependence is so great that an individual who is not self-reliant is an objective of hostility and is stigmatization. Furthermore, cultural norms in the United States suggest that organizational systems should be standardized or applied to everyone equally, and policies should be impersonal. Thus, coworkers are likely to resent and react negatively to individuals with disabilities when they ask for special treatment (or accommodation) because such a request violates cultural norms about fairness (Colella, 2001). Interestingly, some research supports this argument and has shown that asking for a reasonable accommodation lowered suitability ratings for job applicants with disabilities (Hazer & Bedell, 2000). Similarly, research by Florey and Harrsion (2000) found that reactions to a request for accommodation were dependent on the person's past performance level, the magnitude of the accommodation request, and the controllability of the disability's onset.

Given that coworkers may experience resentment when working with individuals with disabilities, it is important to identify strategies that might be used to decrease resentment and increase the inclusion of people with disabilities. Interestingly, some authors (Stone & Stone-Romero, 2002) argued that organizational policies, especially the use of competitive reward systems and adherence to inflexible policies, may be important sources of the problem. In particular, when competitive reward systems are used only a few people can get the most desired outcomes, and individuals may resent working with a coworker with a disability because it decreases their chances of receiving valuable outcomes (Stone & Stone-Romero, 2002). Interestingly, some research suggests that interdependent or competitive reward systems decrease the selection of persons with disabilities as coworkers (Colella, DeNisi, & Varma, 1998; Stone & Michaels, 1994). Thus, we believe that one strategy for overcoming resentment toward people with disabilities is to increase the use of cooperative reward systems in organizations.

In addition, we believe that the use of impersonal standardized policies may put people with disabilities and others who have special needs (e.g., employees with children or older parents) at a disadvantage in organizations. Thus, we believe that the use of flexible or need-based systems may be useful in organizations especially when the policies are applied to everyone, not just those disabilities. Finally, to reduce anxiety associated with working with people with disabilities, team members and workers with disabilities should be trained to reduce interpersonal anxiety and focus on increasing team effectiveness. Research, however, is needed to assess the effectiveness of these strategies.

In summary, in the preceding section we argue that emotional reactions may affect reactions to people with disabilities and may be an important cause of unfair discrimination in organizations. Research, however, is needed to understand these emotional reactions and to develop strategies for decreasing negative reactions to persons with disabilities in work settings.

Paternalism Legal and political science scholars have often adopted the view that the courts and medical and rehabilitation professions treat persons with disabilities in a paternalistic fashion (Hahn, 1996). Indeed interviews with people with disabilities suggest that one of the major social problems they face is that of patronization from nondisabled people (Fox, 1994) or that people use the same behavioral scripts as they would use in interacting with a child (Jones et al., 1984). Behaviorally, this response is similar to the pity response discussed above; however, the reasoning behind paternalistic behavior differs.

One reason often given for paternalistic behavior toward persons with disabilities is that nondisabled people often desire to show that they are kind and caring toward persons with disabilities in order to foster their self-beliefs about "being a good person" (Katz & Glass, 1979; Weinberg, 1983).

Another explanation is one that focuses on intergroup relations by describing paternalization as one way of demonstrating that one is higher on the social hierarchy (e.g. Fox & Giles, 1996a, 1996b) than the other person. Finally, Hastorf, Northcraft, & Picciotto (1979) introduced the notion of the "norm to be kind," arguing that persons with disabilities are often treated better than others because there is a societal norm to be kind to the "disadvantaged." Whatever the reason paternalization exists, it can have severely negative consequences on the integration of persons with disabilities in the workforce. Thus, paternalization needs to be studied as a form of discrimination.

To our knowledge, there has been no direct examination of paternalization as a form of disability discrimination. In our review, the number of studies finding positive disability effects (8 out of 37) suggests that paternalization may indeed take place and manifest itself in terms of inflated evaluations and personnel decisions (Bailey, 1991; Christman & Branson, 1990; Christman & Slaten, 1991; Czajka & DeNisi, 1988; Nordstrom, Huffaker, & Williams, 1998; Rose & Brief, 1979; Tagallakis, Amsel, & Fichten, 1988) and unrealistic feedback (Hastorf et al., 1979). These findings are usually attributed to the "norm to be kind" or to be thought as arising from initially low expectations that were exceeded by the performance of the person with a disability. Generally, this research concludes that these effects are positive indications of how people react to those with disabilities. However, if one considers that these inflated evaluations are indications of paternalism, then these results are not so encouraging.

Research on social interaction between people with disabilities and nondisabled people shows that nondisabled people ask people with disabilities to do useless tasks to make the "person feel useful" (Fichten & Bourden, 1986) or they communicate using "baby talk," condescending language, depersonalizing language, or ignoring the disabled person by talking to a third party (Fox, 1994). Furthermore, others may perceive the recipient of patronization as being more weak and passive (Fox & Giles, 1996b). In workplace scenarios, this can translate into giving people easier work assignments, holding lower expectations, treatment as a lower status group member, and the perception of people with disabilities as child-like, helpless, or passive. Patronizing behavior can also serve to threaten the positive self-identity of persons with disabilities (Fox & Giles, 1996b). This is evidenced by accounts from people with disabilities who are made to feel incompetent at work because coworkers are overzealous in their attempts to "help" them (Ainsley, 1988; Schneider, 1988). Colella (1996), using an organizational socialization perspective, argued that paternalization can have long-lasting career effects. However, again, there has been no research that directly examines patronization as a cause or form of workplace discrimination against persons with disabilities.

Examining disability discrimination as resulting from paternalism brings up several important issues. The first is getting at the underlying cause of the paternalism. This obviously has implications for how to eradicate discrimination. Earlier we mentioned several motives for paternalization. One group concerns good, if misplaced, intentions. In this case, nondisabled people want to be nice or are following "norm to be kind" scripts. If this is the motive underlying paternalization, then education whereby coworkers are made aware of paternalization and the negative consequences it may have should go far in helping people to overcome this tendency. Furthermore, education that focuses on the reality and experiences of persons with disabilities can be used to enlighten others about how paternalistic behavior may be perceived by the target.

On the other hand, there are other positive motives underlying paternalistic behaviors, having to do with intergroup relations (Fox & Giles, 1996a, 1996b). Paternalism can be used as a way in which to communicate the lower status of the target. Instead of paternalism resulting from a desire to help, it results from a desire to degrade. This view is consistent with Lerner's "just world hypothesis." In this case, it would be expected that education alone would not be enough to ameliorate paternalistic behavior, and that the problem needs to be approached as an intergroup problem.

Another issue arising from considering disability discrimination from a paternalism framework is that we need to develop a conceptual framework that allows us to predict and understand when paternalism will occur. Throughout this paper, we have mentioned several factors that tend to be related to inflated evaluations, such as the disability is physical (rather than mental or sensory) and the situation is of little consequence to the actor. However, these observations are post hoc; no integrated conceptual framework exists. Most conceptual treatments of disability discrimination (see Stone & Colella, 1996) focus on predicting and explaining outright negative reactions. One outcome of this is that we tend to dismiss inflated evaluations and overly positive responses to persons with disabilities, rather than studying the phenomena in its own right. We only reviewed published articles. We wonder how common this phenomenon is in "file drawer" research that hypothesized negative disability effects, but found positive effects instead.

A final issue is that we need to examine the impact of paternalization on the target. Most research on this topic appears in the communication or rehabilitation literature and focuses primarily on qualitative assessments. Empirical work in this area is necessary if we are to understand disability discrimination. Heilman's (Heilman, Block, & Lucas, 1992) work on targets' reactions to affirmative action can provide a model of how to go about conducting this research.

In conclusion, we agree with Hahn (1996, p. 42) who wrote "...paternalistic sentiments about disability may actually tend to dilute the effectiveness of antidiscrimination laws." Writing from a political science and legal perspective, he notes that people rarely display the outward hostility and bigotry toward disability policy issues that is displayed toward policies concerning other minority groups. Rather, the public and courts seem to take a paternalistic stance toward disability issues and therefore feel that stringent legal protection from discrimination is not really necessary. We believe that by ignoring the issue of paternalism in workplace discrimination, we may be ignoring one of the major roadblocks to successful integration of people with disabilities into the workforce.

SUMMARY AND CONCLUSION

Data from labor economists clearly indicate that discrimination against people with disabilities in the workplace still exists and has not been greatly ameliorated since the ADA (1990). Yet we know relatively little about how this discrimination manifests itself, what causes it, and consequently, how we can reduce it. Psychological literature aimed at understanding these issues is still in its infancy. As indicated in our review above, what research has been published is inconclusive and somewhat scattered, focuses mainly on selection decisions, relies heavily on laboratory studies with student respondents, and focuses primarily on cognitive explanations for disability discrimination, which may not be the most useful paradigm to follow. Recently, research has begun to go beyond these limitations (cf., Colella & Varma, 2001). However, there is still quite a way to go.

Examining disability discrimination poses some unique challenges in comparison to other types of discrimination. As discussed earlier, one such issue focuses on defining disability from both the observers' and actors' perspective. Different disabilities may result in differential level of discrimination, different responses (e.g., empathy versus anxiety), and have effects that vary by context and culture.

Second, we believe that additional research is needed to examine disability issues from a multiple stakeholder point of view including the perspectives of (a) individuals with disabilities, (b) coworkers and supervisors, (c) organizations, and (d) the larger society or community. Most research in this area has focused on how coworkers and supervisors react to people with disabilities, ignoring the role of people with disabilities in their own interactions and organizational and cultural norms.

Research is sorely needed to understand the self-identities of employees with disabilities. In comparison to work on ethnic and gender identities, there is relatively little research on "disability" identity. One notable exception is some recent research on the coping styles and personalities of polio survivors (Maynard & Roller cited in Polio Post News, 2000). Results of this research suggested that individuals who have had polio use one of three strategies for coping with chronic illness including passing, minimizing, and identifying (cf. Maynard & Roller, cited in Post Polio News, 2000). Passers often have minimal or hidden disabilities and typically do not view themselves as disabled. Minimizers are moderately disabled and are typically high achievers who pursue intellectual vocations, push themselves to the limit, and develop good interpersonal skills to ensure that others focus on their abilities not disabilities. Identifiers have obvious disabilities and usually use assistive devices to facilitate mobility and other life functions (e.g., wheelchairs). In addition, identifiers more fully integrate disability in their self-images and often take an active role in the disability rights movement or promoting environmental change.

Although the categories just noted may be a gross simplification, the research does suggest that a chronic illness or disability may influence an individual's coping strategies and personality. Furthermore, the person's personality and survival strategy may affect the extent to which he or she experiences unfair discrimination in the workplace. For example, if an individual who is obviously disabled attempts to use a "passing" strategy, then an employer may question the person's maturity and suitability for jobs. Alternatively, if the person minimizes the disability by emphasizing good interpersonal skills and high levels of achievement, employers may be more motivated to focus on the individual's abilities rather than the disability. Thus, the coping strategies used by persons with disabilities may influence the degree to which employers look for individuating information or focus on the individual's disability. Thus, research is needed to understand the influence that disabilities may have on self-identity, coping strategies, and the degree to which these factors affect discrimination against persons with disabilities.

Apart from the research just noted, in the past several years, there has been a rise in the political coalescence of persons with disabilities (Hahn, 1996), and perhaps this development has changed the self-identity of many persons with disabilities. Thus, the use of intergroup and identity theories to explore disability discrimination may be more useful in the future.

In terms of understanding coworker and supervisor reactions, we suggested earlier that emotions and paternalism need to be better understood as concepts underlying disability discrimination. Furthermore, additional research is needed to examine interpersonal interactions in organizations and to develop strategies for increasing the effectiveness of these interactions.

At the organization and societal levels, research is needed to examine the effectiveness of changes in organizational culture and policies and the practices on the inclusion of persons with disabilities. Previous research has shown that competitive or interdependent reward systems (Colella et al., 1998; Stone & Michaels, 1994) has a negative impact on the acceptance of people with disabilities. Also, some research has shown that community-based awards for employing people with disabilities can alter employers' beliefs about hiring people with disabilities (Stone, Williams, Lukaszewski, & Feigelson, 1998).

More research of this type is warranted, because it directly addresses the issue of how to eliminate disability discrimination. For example, researchers might examine the business case for hiring employees with disabilities including the extent to which employing people with disabilities has a positive effect on organizational image or customer satisfaction levels. Interestingly, some European countries (e.g., Germany) are quite willing to make continued employment of persons with disabilities a major employment policy, and in those countries men with disabilities receive 93% of the wage rates for those who are not disabled (Burkhauser & Daly, 1994). As a result, although the United States has developed some key disability policies, research is needed to compare the effectiveness of U.S. employment policies with those of other nations.

A third issue that makes disability discrimination unique is that people with disabilities have impairments, which is not true about other discrimination characteristics. This makes studying disability discrimination difficult because it is not easy to determine if unequal treatment or benefits are due to discriminatory behavior or actually result from decreased functioning due to the impairment. Critiques of the legal system and rehabilitation fields (Hahn, 1988, 1996, 2000) argue that too much attention is placed on the impact of impairments, so that it disguises discrimination resulting from attitudes and stigmatization. For example, one can argue that someone is denied a promotion because her depression makes her "unstable" and that this is due to the impairment rather than erroneous beliefs or stereotypes. We have both experienced reviewer comments that strongly argued that discrimination results found in our research were because of the impairment of the actor with a disability, not discriminatory beliefs—even when behavior and performance were tightly controlled and comparable to the comparison nondisabled actor. One implication of this is that disability discrimination research needs to carefully control for impairment effects to get a better understanding of what dynamics underlie discrimination. It also may mean that it is easier to conceal disability discrimination behind the guise of blaming unfavorable evaluations or decisions on one's impairment.

We are optimistic about the future progression of research on disability discrimination. In the eight years since our last review of this literature (Stone & Colella, 1996), there has been a steady stream of research that has taken off in new directions including fieldwork, understanding interaction dynamics, examining the accommodation scenario, and examining ways in which disability discrimination may be eliminated. We expect this research to continue and hope that our suggestions and observations here serve to fuel that research.

REFERENCES

Ainsley, S. C. (1988). Aging and new vision loss: Disruptions here and now. *Journal of Social Issues, 44*, 79–94.

Alberstons Inc. v. Kirkingburg, 1999. 143 F.32 1228, 119 S. Ct. 2162.

Americans with Disabilities Act of 1990, Pub. L. No. 101-336, 42 U.S.C. 12101 *et seq.* (1990).

Bailey, J. W. (1984). Evaluation of a task partner who does or does not have a physical disability: Response amplification or sympathy effect? *Rehabilitation Psychology, 36*, 99–110.

Baldridge, D. C., & Veiga, J. F. (2001). Toward a greater understanding of the willingness to request an accommodation: Can requesters' beliefs disable the Americans with Disabilities Act? *The Academy of Management Review, 26*, 85–99.

Baldwin, M. L. (1999). The effects of impairments on employment and wages: Estimates from the 1984 and 1990 SIPP. *Behavioral Sciences and the Law, 17*, 7–27.

Baldwin, M. L., Zeager, L. A., & Flacco, P. R. (1993). Gender differences in wage losses from impairments. *The Journal of Human Resources, 29*, 865–887.

Benson v. Northwest Airlines. 62 F.3d 1108, 1114 (8th Circuit, 1995).

Berkowitz, M., & O'Leary, P. K. (2000). Persons with disabilities at work. The Atlantic City gaming casinos. *Journal of Disability Policy Studies, 11*, 152–160.

Blalock, J. W. (1981). Persistent problems and concerns of young adults with learning disabilities. In W. Cruickshank & A. Silver (Eds.), *Bridges to tomorrow: Vol. 2. The best of ACLD* (pp. 35–55). Syracuse, NY: Syracuse University Press.

Blanck, P. D. (1997). The economics of employment provisions of the American with Disabilities Act: Part I—Workplace accommodations. *DePaul Law Review, 46*, 877–914.

Bordieri, J. E., & Drehmer, D. E. (1986). Hiring decisions for disabled workers: looking at the cause. *Journal of Applied Social Psychology, 16*, 197–208.

Bordieri, J. E., & Drehmer, D. E. (1987). Attribution of responsibility and predicted social acceptance of disabled workers. *Rehabilitation Counseling Bulletin, 30*, 218–226.

Bordieri, J. E., & Drehmer, D. E. (1988). Causal attribution and hiring recommendations for job applicants with lower back pain. *Rehabilitation Counseling Bulletin, 32*, 140–148.

Bordieri, J. E., Drehmer, D. E., & Cominel, M. E. (1988). Attribution of responsibility and hiring recommendations for disabled job applicants. *Rehabilitation Psychology, 30*, 218–226.

Bordieri, J. E., Drehmer, D. E., & Taricone, P. F. (1990). Personnel selection bias for job applicants with cancer. *Journal of Applied Social Psychology, 20*, 244–253.

Bowman, J. T. (1987). Attitudes towards disabled persons: Social distance and work competence. *Journal of Rehabilitation, 53*, 41–44.

Braddock, D., & Bachelder, L. (1994). *The glass ceiling and persons with disabilities.* Washington, DC: U.S. Department of Labor, Glass Ceiling Commission.

Bruyere, S. M. (2000). *Disability employment policies and practices in private and federal sector organizations.* Ithaca, NY: Cornell University, School of Industrial and Labor Relations.

Burkhauser, R. V., & Daly, M. C. (1994). The economic consequences of disability: A comparison of German and American people with disabilities. *Journal of Disability Policy Studies, 5,* 25–52.

Butterworth, J., & Strauch J. (1994). The relationship between social competence and success in the competitive work place for persons with mental retardation. *Education and Training in Mental Retardation, 29,* 118–133.

Callahan, T. J. (1994). Managers beliefs about and attitudes toward the American with Disabilities Act of 1990. *Applied H.R.M. Research, 5,* 28–43.

Cesare, S. J., Tannenbaum, R. J., & Delessio, A. (1990). Interviewers' decisions related to applicant handicap type and rater empathy. *Human Performance, 3,* 151–171.

Chima, F. O. (1998). Workplace and disabilities: Opinions on work, interpersonal, and intrapersonal factors. *Journal of Applied Rehabilitation Counseling, 29,* 31–37.

Chirikos, T. N. (1999). Will the costs of accommodating workers with disabilities remain low? *Behavioral Sciences and the Law, 17,* 93–106.

Christman, L. A., & Branson, D. H. (1990). Influence of physical disability and dress of female job applicant on interviewers. *Clothing and Textiles Research Journal, 8,* 51–57.

Christman, L. A., & Slaten, B. L. (1991). Attitudes towards people with disabilities and judgments of employment potential. *Perceptual and Motor Skills, 72,* 467–475.

Cleveland, J. N., Barnes-Farrell, J., & Huestis, J. (1996). *Reactions to requests for accommodations from disabled and nondisabled applicants.* Paper presented at the annual conference of the Society for Industrial and Organizational Psychology, San Diego, CA.

Cleveland, J. N., Barnes-Farrell, J., & Ratz, J. M. (1997). Accommodation in the workplace. *Human Resource Management Review, 7,* 77–108.

Colella, A. (1996). The organizational socialization of employees with disabilities: Theory and research. In G. R. Ferris (Ed.), *Research in personnel and human resources management* (Vol. 14, pp. 351–417). Greenwich, CT: JAI.

Colella, A. (2001). Coworker distributive fairness judgments of the workplace accommodation of employees with disabilities. *Academy of Management Review, 26,* 100–116.

Colella, A., & DeNisi, A. S. (1994). *Conducting research on persons with disabilities at work: Problems and future needs.* Paper presented at the Ninth Annual Conference of the Society for Industrial and Organizational Psychology, Nashville, TN.

Colella, A., DeNisi, A. S., & Varma, A. (1998). The impact of ratee's disability on performance judgments and choice as partner: The role of disability-job fit stereotypes and interdependence of rewards. *Journal of Applied Psychology, 83,* 102–111.

Colella, A., & Paetzold, R., and Belliveau, M. (2004). Factors affecting coworkers' procedural justice inferences of the workplace accommodation of employees with disabilities. *Personnel Psychology, 57,* 1–23.

Colella, A., & Varma, A. (1999). Disability-job fit stereotypes and evaluations of persons with disabilities at work. *Journal of Occupational Rehabilitation, 9,* 79–95.

Colella, A., & Varma, A. (2001). The impact of subordinate disability on leader-member exchange relationships. *Academy of Management Journal, 44,* 304–316.

Combs, I. J., & Omvig, C. P. (1986). Accommodation of disabled people into employment: Perceptions of employers. *Journal of Rehabilitation, 52,* 42–45.

Cooper, B. M. (1991). Employment potential of persons with mild intellectual impairments. *Canadian Journal of Rehabilitation, 5,* 81–92.

Cooper, M. (1995). Epilepsy and employment-employers' attitudes. *Seizure, 4,* 193–199.

Crudden, A., & McBroom, L. W. (1999). Barriers to employment: A survey of employed persons who are visually impaired, *Journal of Visual Impairment & Blindness, rest of cite*

Czajka, J. M., & DeNisi, A. S. (1988). Effects of emotional disability and clear performance standards on performance ratings. *Academy of Management Journal, 31*, 394–404.

Dipboye, R. L., Fromkin, H. L., & Wibak, K. (1975). Relative importance of applicant sex, attractiveness, and scholastic standing in the evaluation of job applicant resumes. *Journal of Applied Psychology, 60*, 39–43.

Diska, E., & Rogers, E. S. (1996). Employer concerns about hiring persons with psychiatric disability: Results of the employer attitude questionnaire. *Rehabilitation Counseling Bulletin, 40*, 31–44.

Duckett, P. S. (2000). Disabling employment interviews: Warfare to work. *Disability & Society, 15*, 1019–1039.

EEOC ADA handbook, (2003). [On-line]. Available: http://www.eeoc.qov.

Farina, A., Felner, R. D., & Boudreau, L. A. (1973). Reactions of workers to male and female mental patient job applicants. *Journal of Consulting and Clinical Psychology, 41*, 363–372.

Fichten, C. S., & Amstel, R. (1986). Trait attributions about college students with a physical disability: Circumplex analyses and methodological issues. *Journal of Applied Social Psychology, 16*, 47–51.

Fichten, C. S., & Bourden, C. V. (1986). Social skill deficit or response inhibition: Interaction between disabled and non-disabled college students. *Journal of College Student Personnel, 27*, 326–333.

Fine, M., & Asch, A. (1988). Disability beyond stigma: Social interactions, discrimination, and activism. *Journal of Social Issues, 44*, 3–21.

Florey, A. (1998). *Factors affecting a disabled employee's decision to make an accommodation request: Test of a comprehensive framework.* Unpublished manuscript, University of Texas at Arlington.

Florey, A. T., & Harrison, D. A. (1998). *The managerial perspective: Supervisor reactions to formal and informal accommodation requests.* Paper presented at the meetings of Annual Academy of Management, San Diego, CA.

Florey, A., & Harrison, D. (2000). Responses to informal accommodation requests from employees with disabilities: Multistudy evidence on willingness to comply. *Academy of Management Journal, 43*, 224–233.

Fox, S. A. (1994). *Patronizing others in intergroup encounters: The experiences and evaluations of people in interability situations.* Unpublished doctoral dissertation, University of California, Santa Barbara.

Fox, S. A., & Giles, H. (1996a). "Let the wheelchair through!": An intergroup approach to interability communication. In W. P. Robertson (Ed.), *Social groups and identity: The developing legacy of Henri Tajfel* (pp. 215–248). Amsterdam: Elsevier.

Fox, S. A., & Giles, H. (1996b). Interability communication: Evaluating patronizing encounters. *Journal of Language and Social Psychology, 15*, 265–290.

Fuqua, D. R., Rathbun, M., & Gade, E. M. (1984). A comparison of employer attitudes toward the worker problems of eight types of disabled workers. *Journal of Applied Rehabilitation Counseling, 15*, 40–43.

Gates, L. B. (1993). The role of supervisor in successful adjustment to work with a disabling condition: Issues for disability policy and practice. *Journal of Occupational Rehabilitation, 3*, 179–194.

Gates, L. B., Akabas, S. H., & Oran-Sabia, V. (1998). Relationship accommodations involving the work group: Improving work prognosis for persons with mental health conditions. *Psychiatric Rehabilitation Journal, 21*, 264–272.

Gatti, D. (1991). A supported employment enclave model for the psychiatrically challenged: A program critique. *Work, 1,* 19–27.

Gibbons, F. X., Stephan, W. G., Stephenson, B., & Petty, R. C. (1980). Reactions to stigmatized others: Response amplification vs. sympathy. *Journal of Experimental Social Psychology, 16,* 591–605.

Gillies, R. M., Knight, K., & Baglioni, A. J., Jr. (1998). World of work: perceptions of people who are blind or vision impaired. *International Journal of Disability, Development and Education, 45,* 397–409.

Goffman, E. (1963). *Stigma: Notes on the management of spoiled identity.* Englewood Cliffs, NJ: Prentice-Hall.

Gouvier, W. D., Steiner, D. D., Jackson, W. T., Schlater, D., & Rain, J. S. (1991). Employment discrimination against handicapped job candidates: An analog study of the effects of neurological causation, visibility of handicap, and public contact. *Rehabilitation Psychology, 36,* 121–129.

Grand, S. A., Bernier, J. E., & Strohmer, D. C. (1982). Attitudes toward disabled persons as a function of social context and specific disability. *Rehabilitation Psychology, 27,* 165–174.

Greenwood, R., Shiner, K. F., & Johnson, V. A. (1991). Employer concerns regarding workers with disabilities and the business-rehabilitation partnership: The PWI practitioners' perspective. *Journal of Rehabilitation, 57,* 21–25.

Hahn, H. (1988). The politics of physical differences: Disability and discrimination. *Journal of Social Issues, 44,* 39–47.

Hahn, H. (1996). Antidiscrimination laws and social research on disability: The minority group perspective. *Behavioral Sciences and the Law, 14,* 41–59.

Hahn, H. (2000). Accommodations and the ADA: Unreasonable bias or biased reasoning. *Berkeley Journal of Employment and Labor Law, 21,* 166–192.

Harasymiw, S. J., Horne, M. D., & Lewis, S. C. (1976). A longitudinal study of disability group acceptance. *Rehabilitation Literature, 37,* 98–102.

Harlan, S. L., & Robert, P. M. (1998). The social construction of disability in organizations: Why employers resist reasonable accommodation. *Work and Occupations, 25,* 397–435.

Harris, L., & Associates (1987). *The ICD survey II: Employing disabled Americans.* New York: Louis Harris and Associates, Inc.

Hastorf, A. H., Northcraft, G. B., & Picciotto, S. R. (1979). Helping the handicapped: How realistic is the performance feedback received by the physically handicapped. *Personality and Social Psychology Bulletin, 5,* 373–376.

Hazer, J. T., & Bedell, K. V. (2000). Effects of seeking accommodation and disability on pre-employment evaluations. *Journal of Applied Social Psychology, 30,* 1201–1223.

Heilman, M. E., Block, C. J., & Lucas, J. A. (1992). Presumed incompetent? Stigmatization and affirmative action efforts. *Journal of Applied Psychology, 77,* 536–544.

Johnson, R., & Heal, L. (1976). Private employment agency responses to the physically handicapped applicant in a wheelchair. *Journal of Rehabilitation Counseling, 7,* 12–21.

Jones, E. E., Farina, A., Hastorf, A. H., Markus, H., Miller, D. T., & Scott, R. A. (1984). *Social stigma: The psychology of marked relationships.* San Francisco: Freeman.

Jones, G. E., & Stone, D. L. (1995). Perceived discomfort associated with working with persons with varying disabilities. *Perceptual and Motor Skills, 81,* 911–919.

Katz, I. (1981). *Stigma: A social psychological analysis.* Hillsdale, NJ: Lawrence Erlbaum Associates.

Katz, I., & Glass, D. C. (1979). An ambivalence amplification theory of behavior toward the stigmatized. In W. Austin & S. Worchel (Eds.), *The social psychology of intergroup relations* (pp. 55–70). Monterey, CA: Brooks/Cole.

Klimoski, R., & Donahue, L. (1997). HR strategies for integrating individuals with disabilities into the workplace. *Human Resource Management Review, 7,* 109–138.

Knox, M., & Parmenter, T. (1993). Social networks and support mechanisms for people with mild intellectual disabilities in competitive employment. *International Journal of Rehabilitation Research, 16,* 1–12.

Koser, D. A., Matsuyama, M., & Kopelman, R. E. (1999). Comparison of a physical and a mental disability in employee selection: An experimental examination of direct and moderated effects. *North American Journal of Psychology, 1,* 213–222.

Kralik v. Durbin. 97-3089 (U.S. Court of Appeals, 3rd Cir., 1997).

Krauss, H. K., Mehnert, T., Nadler, R., & Greenberg, R. H. (1993). Perceiving oneself as "disabled" or having a "disabling condition": A discriminant function analysis. *International Journal of Rehabilitation Research, 16,* 119–131.

Krefting, L., & Brief, A. (1976). The impact of applicant disability on evaluative judgments in the selection process. *Academy of Management Journal, 19,* 675–680.

Lazarus, R. S., Kanner, A. D., & Folkman, S. (1980). Emotions: A cognitive phenomenological analysis. In R. Plutchik & H. Kellerman (Eds.). *Emotion: Theory, research and experience* (Vol. 1, pp. 199–214). New York: Academic Press.

Lazarus, R. S., & Lazarus, B. N. (1994). *Passion and reason: Making sense of emotions.* New York: Oxford University Press.

Lee, B. A. (1996). Legal requirements and employer responses to accommodating employees with disabilities. *Human Resource Management Review, 6,* 231–251.

Lee, B. A. (1998). *A review of ADA jurisprudence in who should be accommodated.* Paper presented at the annual meeting of the Academy of Management, San Diego, CA.

Lee, B. A., & Thompson, R. J. (1997). Reducing the consequences of disability: Policies to reduce discrimination against disabled workers. In T. Thomason, D. Hyatt, & J. Burton (Eds.), *New Approaches to disability in the workplace.* IRRA.

Lerner, M. J. (1980). *The belief in a just world: A fundamental delusion.* New York: Plenum.

Livneh, H. (1982). On the origins of negative attitudes toward people with disabilities. *Rehabilitation Literature, 43,* 338–347.

Makas, E. (1988). Positive attitudes toward disabled people: Disabled and nondisabled persons' perspectives. *Journal of Social Issues, 44,* 49–61.

McFarlin, D. B., Song, J., & Sonntag, M. (1991). Integrating the disabled into the work force: A survey of Fortune 500 company attitudes and practices. *Employee Responsibilities and Rights Journal, 4,* 107–122.

McNeil, J. M. (2000). *Employment, earnings, and disability.* Paper presented at the 75th Annual Conference of the Western Economic Association International, Vancouver, British Columbia.

Miller, M. (1992). *The effects of disability-related information on employment decisions regarding persons with disabilities.* Unpublished doctoral dissertation, University of Oregon, Eugene, OR.

Millington, M. J., Szymanski, E. M., & Hanley-Maxwell, C. (1994). Effect of the label of mental retardation on employer concerns and selection. *Rehabilitation Counseling Bulletin, 38,* 27–43.

Mueller, H. H., Wilgosh, L., & Dennis, S. (1987). Employment survival skills: What vocational rehabilitation professionals believe to be most important. *The Mental Retardation & Learning Disabilities Bulletin, 15,* 7–20.

Murphy v. United Parcel 1999. Service 141 F.3d 1185, 119 S.Ct. 1331.

National Council on Disability (July 26, 2002). National disability policy: A progress report. [On-line]. Available: http://www.ncd.gov/newsroom/publications/progressreport_07-26-02.html.

Nordstrom, C. R., Huffaker, B. J., & Williams, K. B. (1998). When physical disabilities are not liabilities: The role of applicant and interviewer characteristics on employment interview outcomes. *Journal of Applied Social Psychology, 28,* 283–306.

Piner, K. E., & Kahle, L. R. (1984). Adapting to the stigmatizing label of mental illness: Foregone but not forgotten. *Journal of Personality and Social Psychology, 47,* 805–811.

Pingotore, R., Bernard., L. D., Tindale, R. S., & Spring, B. (1994). Bias against overweight job applicants in a simulated employment interview. *Journal of Applied Psychology, 79,* 909–917.

Polio Post News (2000). Coping styles and personal perspectives of polio survivors. Dunellon, FL: North Central Florida Post-Polio Support Group.

Ravaud, J., Madiot, B., & Ville, I. (1992). Discrimination towards disabled people seeking employment. *Social Science & Medicine, 35,* 951–958.

Robinson, S. L. (1995). The effects of wanted and unwanted help on recipients with developmental disabilities. *Developmental Disabilities Bulletin, 23,* 58–68.

Roehling, M. (1999). Weight-based discrimination in employment: Psychological and legal aspects. *Personnel Psychology, 52,* 969–1016.

Rose, G. L., & Brief, A. P. (1979). Effects of handicap and job characteristics on selection evaluations. *Personnel Psychology, 32,* 385–398.

Russell, D., Lenel, J. C., Spicer, C., Miller, J., Albrecht, J., & Rose, J. (1985). Evaluating the physically disabled: An attributional analysis. *Personality and Social Psychology Bulletin, 11,* 23–31.

Schall, C. M. (1998). The Americans with Disabilities Act—Are we keeping our promise? An analysis of the effect of the ADA on the employment of persons with disabilities. *Journal of Vocational Rehabilitation, 10,* 191–203.

Schloss, P. J., & Soda, S. L. (1989). Employer attitudes concerning training time and on the job success of mentally handicapped in low and high employment areas. *Vocational Evaluation and work adjustment Bulletin, 22,* 129–132.

Schneider, J. W. (1988). Disability as a moral experience: Epilepsy and self in routine relationships. *Journal of Social Issues, 44,* 63–78.

Schneider, C. R., & Anderson, W. (1980). Attitudes toward the stigmatized: Some insights from recent research. *Rehabilitation Counseling Bulletin, 23,* 299–313.

Scotch, R. K. (1988). Disability as a basis for social movement: Advocacy and politics of definition. *Journal of Social Issues, 44,* 159–172.

Snyder, M. L., Kleck, R. E., Strenta, A., & Mentzer, S. J. (1979). Avoidance of the handicapped: An attributional ambiguity analysis. *Journal of Personality and Social Psychology, 37,* 2297–2306.

Smith, J. L. (1992). Accommodating the American Disabilities Act to collective bargaining obligations under the NLRA. *Employee Relations Law Journal, 18,* 273–285.

Sowa, P. A., & Cutter, H. S. (1974). Attitudes of hospital staff toward alcoholics and drug addicts. *Quarterly Journal of Studies on Alcohol, 35,* 210–214.

Stone, D. L., & Colella, A. (1996). A model of factors affecting the treatment of disabled individuals in organizations. *Academy of Management Review, 21,* 352–401.

Stone, D. L., & Michaels, C. (1993). *Factors affecting the acceptance of disabled individuals in organizations.* Paper presented at the meeting of the Academy of Management, Atlanta, GA.

Stone, D. L., & Michaels, C. (1994). *Effects of nature of the disability and competitiveness of the reward system on selection of disabled team members.* Paper presented at the meeting of the Academy of Management, Dallas, TX.

Stone, D. L., & Stone-Romero, E. F. (2002). The religious underpinnings of social justice conceptions. In S. Gilliland, D. Steiner, & D. Skarlicki (Eds.), *Emerging perspectives on managing organizational justice* (pp. 35–76). Greenwich, CT: Information Age Publishing.

Stone, E. F., Stone, D. L., & Dipboye, R. L. (1992). Stigmas in organizations: Race, handicaps, and physical unattractiveness. In K. Kelley (Ed.), *Issues, theory, and research in industrial and organizational psychology* (pp. 385–457). New York: Elsevier.

Stone, D. L., Williams, K., Lukaszewski, K., & Feigelson, M. (1998, August). *An evaluation of a community-based intervention designed to increase the employment of persons with disabilities.* Paper presented at the meeting of the Academy of Management, San Diego, CA.

Strohmer, D. C., Grand, S. A., & Purcell, M. J. (1984). Attitudes towards persons with a disability: An examination of demographic factors, social context, and specific disability. *Rehabilitation Psychology, 29,* 131–145.

Sutton v. United Airlines (1999). 130 F.3d 893, 119S. Ct. 2139.

Tagallakis, V., Amsel, R., & Fichten, C. S. (1988). Job interview strategies for people with a visible disability. *Journal of Applied Social Psychology, 18,* 520–532.

Taylor, H. (October 14, 1998). Americans with disabilities still persuasively disadvantaged on a broad range of key indicators. *The Harris Poll, 56.* [On-line]. Available: http://www.louisharris.com?harris_poll/index.asp?PID=152.

Taylor, H. (May 12, 1999). Overwhelming majority of Americans continue to support the Americans with Disabilities Act. *The Harris Poll, 306.* [On-line]. Available: http://www.louisharris.com?harris_poll/index.asp?PID=63.

Taylor, H. (October 7, 2000). Conflicting trends in employment of people with disabilities 1986–2000. *The Harris Poll, 59.* [On-line]. Available: http://www.louisharris.com?harris_poll/index.asp?PID=121.

Trice, H., & Beyer, J. (1993). The cultures of work organizations. Englewood Cliffs, NJ: Prentice-Hall.

Tringo, J. L. (1970). The hierarchy of preference toward disability groups. *The Journal of Special Education, 4,* 295–306.

U.S. Census Bureau (March 16, 2001). Press Release: Nearly 1 in 5 Americans has some level of disability, U.S. Census Bureau Reports. [On-line]. Available: http://www.census.gov/Press-Release/www/2001/cb01-46.html.

U.S. Census Bureau (July 12, 2002). Press Release: 12th anniversary of Americans with Disabilities Act (July 26). [On-line]. Available: http://www.census.gov/Press-Release/www/2002/cb02ff11.html.

Vest, J. M., Vest, M. J., Perry, S. J., & O'Brien, P. P. (1995). Factors influencing managerial disclosure of AIDS health information to coworkers. *Journal of Applied Social Psychology, 12,* 1043–1057.

Weinberg, N. (1983). Social equity and the physically disabled. *Social Work, 28,* 365–369.

Weiner, B., Perry R., & Magnusson, J. (1988). An attributional analysis of reactions to stigmas. *Journal of Personality and Social Psychology, 55,* 738–748.

Wells, S. J. (2001). Is the ADA working? *HR Magazine, 46,* 38–47.

West, M. S., & Cardy, R. L. (1997). Accommodating claims of disability: The potential impact of abuses. *Human Resource Management Review, 7,* 233–246.

Wilgosh, L., & Mueller, H. H. (1989). Employer attitudes toward hiring individuals with mental disabilities. *Canadian Journal of Rehabilitation, 3,* 43–47.

Wooten v. Farmland Foods. (1995). 58 F.3d 382, 386 (8th Cir., 1995).

Zajonc, R. B. (1980). Feeling and thinking: Preferences need no inferences. *American Psychologist, 38,* 151–175.

11

Personality-Based Stigmas and Unfair Discrimination in Work Organizations

Eugene F. Stone-Romero
University of Central Florida

Individuals who bear various types of stigmas (Goffman, 1963) are often the target of unfair discrimination in work organizations (Stone, Stone, & Dipboye, 1992). This discrimination results when decision makers use data from invalid measures (e.g., preemployment tests) or observations (e.g., age, attractiveness, disability, race, and sex) as a basis for making decisions about who will and will not be offered one or more desirable outcomes (e.g., jobs, training, mentoring, promotions). This type of discrimination is extremely important because a considerable body of research shows that individuals in various social categories (e.g., racial minorities, females, disabled, unattractive, homosexual) experience a host of problems in the workplace that are unrelated to their actual or predicted job performance (Stone et al., 1992). In view of the potential for stigmatized individuals to experience unfair discrimination in work organizations, this chapter focuses on one type of stigma that may serve as the basis for such discrimination, i.e., formal or informal measures of personality "traits." Among the important issues surrounding personality-based unfair discrimination that are considered in the chapter are (a) the notion of unfair discrimination in organizational contexts, (b) the stigma concept and the stigmatization process, (c) the social–psychological processes associated with stigmatization,

(d) the consequences of stigmatization, (e) the personality construct, (f) personality measures in organizational contexts, (g) the negative affectivity construct, (h) construct validity problems with measures of negative affectivity, (i) social causation models of well-being, (j) the criterion-related validity of personality measures, and (k) several conclusions concerning the use of personality measures as predictors of various criteria.

UNFAIR DISCRIMINATION IN THE WORKPLACE

Measures that discriminate have the capacity to differentiate between the attributes of measured entities (e.g., people). The better the measure, the greater its capacity to discriminate and provide information about the degree to which measured entities differ from one another. For example, a meter stick that is calibrated in millimeter units has a greater capacity to discriminate among the heights of individuals than one that is calibrated in centimeter units. In addition, all else constant, a test of job-related ability with 50 items has greater capacity to discriminate among test takers than a test with 10 items. The longer test would have greater reliability and, thus, greater ability to discriminate.

Fair Discrimination

There is nothing wrong (vis-a-vis either psychometric or ethical perspectives) with measures that are valid and, thus, discriminate fairly. For example, there would be no problem with an organization using a highly discriminating, construct valid (i.e., highly reliable and unbiased) measure of job aptitude for the purpose of personnel selection. In fact, all else constant, the greater the capacity of such a measure to discriminate, the more effective it would be in predicting job performance. However, a biased measure would present both operational and ethical problems. More specifically, because of the fact that it lacked construct validity, it would discriminate unfairly.

Unfair Discrimination

In organizational contexts, *unfair discrimination* can result from the use of invalid (biased) measures of both predictors and criteria. For example, a preemployment test that measured factors that were not predictive of actual job performance (e.g., previous membership in college fraternities or sororities) would discriminate unfairly among job applicants. In addition, a measure of job performance would discriminate unfairly against job incumbents to the extent that its variance was a function of factors other than their actual performance (e.g., their race, age, or sex). It deserves adding that when measures of both predictors and criteria share the same bias, there can be a very strong, but highly *spurious* relationship between scores on such measures, leading to the erroneous conclusion that the predictor has criterion-related validity.

Bases for Unfair Discrimination in the Workplace

Unfair discrimination in the workplace can stem from a number of factors, including measures of job aptitude, job ability, or job performance that focus on such abstract properties of individuals as their race, sex, religion, or sexual orientation. In cases in which selection systems discriminate unfairly in terms of these and other criteria, individuals (also referred to hereinafter as targets) who are harmed by the systems have the potential to seek redress through the legal system. Unfortunately, however, there is no redress for individuals who experience unfair discrimination on the basis of many other variables. Of particular relevance to this chapter is unfair discrimination based on personality. This issue is important for two reasons. First, individuals who experience unfair personality-based discrimination typically are afforded little or no protection by existing laws governing the employment relationship (e.g., Civil Rights Act of 1991). Second, decision makers often have little or no compunction over the use of such measures in selecting individuals for jobs or other types of "treatments" (e.g., training, promotion, mentoring).

STIGMAS

Individuals are stigmatized (i.e., bear stigmas or marks) to the extent that there is a negative (discrediting) discrepancy between their virtual social identity and their actual social identity (Goffman, 1963; Jones et al., 1984). A *virtual social identity* is a perceiver's conception (e.g., prototype, stereotype) of what a target should be like in terms of a host of factors, including race, physical appearance, moral character, religious beliefs, sexual orientation, nationality, and personality. It generally reflects what the perceiver considers to be acceptable, normal, or desirable.

In contrast to a virtual social identity, an *actual social identity* is a perceiver's views about a target's actual characteristics, which may be real (i.e., verifiable) or assumed (i.e., inferred by the perceiver). Thus, for example, because Blacks (as a group) are often perceived to be less intelligent than Whites (as a group), any given Black person may bear the "low intelligence" stigma, irrespective of his or her actual level of cognitive ability.

Individuals may be marked or stigmatized on the basis of a large number of characteristics, including race, skin color, height, weight, unattractiveness, foreign accents, social class, intelligence, and personality (Goffman, 1963; Jones et al., 1984). All of these characteristics are special cases of what Goffman (1963) viewed as three general bases for stigmatization: (a) abominations of the body (e.g., unattractiveness, deformities), (b) blemishes of character (e.g., mental illness, bizarre sexual proclivities, homosexuality, criminality, drug and alcohol addictions, and radical political views), and (c) tribal stigmas (e.g., race, nationality, and religion). Although Goffman (1963) considered these to be conceptually distinct types of stigmas, information about one type frequently serves as a basis for inferences about other types. For example, upon encountering a Black male, a White racist may view the target as being both unattractive and prone to criminal behavior.

SOCIAL PSYCHOLOGICAL PROCESSES ASSOCIATED WITH STIGMATIZATION

Because stigmatization results from a comparison of actual and virtual social identities, the psychological processes associated with it deserve consideration. Of particular relevance to the stigmatization process are the roles that categorization, stereotyping, expectation effects, and illusory correlation play in the inferences that observers make about targets (Fiske & Taylor, 1991; Jones et al., 1984). Research in the field of social cognition is concerned with the way in which information about a target is acquired, processed, organized, stored, and retrieved (Hamilton, 1976, 1981a; Hamilton & Sherman, 1994; Higgins & Bargh, 1987; Sherman, Judd, & Park, 1989).

Categorization plays a central role in the inferences that observers make about a target (e.g., his or her traits). More specifically, when an observer encounters a target, a cursory consideration of his or her salient attributes (e.g., skin color, foreign accent, behavior) leads the observer to view the target as a member of a specific social group (e.g., neurotics). Interestingly, the categorization of the target is often based upon a consideration of only a few of his or her attributes.

Stereotypes are beliefs and expectancies about members of social groups. They are often widely shared, overgeneralized, and typically not valid as concerns any specific member of a group (Ashmore & Del Boca, 1981; Brewer & Kramer, 1985; Hamilton, 1976, 1981a, 1981b; Hamilton & Sherman, 1994; Jones et al., 1984; Miller & Turnbull, 1986). Regrettably, stereotypes are often highly negative in nature (Katz & Braly, 1933; Plous & Williams, 1995; Stone-Romero, Stone, & Hartman, 2002). In addition, they often are a function of *illusory correlation*, i.e., unfounded beliefs about the degree of association between the attributes of category members (Brewer & Kramer, 1985; Hamilton, 1981b). Once a target has been categorized in terms of one or more attributes, the observer generates inferences about his or her standing on a host of other attributes. These inferences are typically based on beliefs about the characteristics that are common to category members; that is, they stem from stereotypes about category members. For example, because a person manifests anxiety during a job interview, the interviewer may infer that he or she lacks emotionally stability, is prone to depression, has low self-esteem, and has low job-related ability. Note that illusory correlation-based inferences about individuals can lead to a number of problems, several of which are considered below.

Closely related to stereotypes are *expectation effects* (Hamilton, 1976, 1981a; Higgins & Bargh, 1987; Jones et al., 1984; Miller & Turnbull, 1986). More specifically, once individuals have been categorized, observers may generate a host of stereotype-consistent expectations about them, including their behaviors, behavioral tendencies, and abilities. For example, an interviewer may assume that because a job applicant seemed anxious during a job interview, he or she was not suitable for a job.

The expectations that observers have about targets bias the way that targets are treated by the observers and others. Regrettably, when expectations about a target are negative, the consequences for him or her can often be quite damaging. For instance, negative expectations about an applicant's ability to perform suitably on a job may lead a decision maker (e.g., job interviewer) to not offer him or her a job. Moreover, even if he or she were offered a job and accepted it, negative expectations about the applicant's performance may lead to a number of undesirable consequences. For example, the target may be placed on a job that the decision maker believes to be "appropriate for a person with his or her abilities and traits" (e.g., personality). Unfortunately, the same job may be less desirable than others on which the individual might have been placed.

In addition, note that the observer's expectations about the target may lead to behaviors on the part of the target that serve to confirm the same expectations (Jones et al., 1984; Merton, 1948; Miller & Turnbull, 1986; Rosenthal & Jacobson, 1968). For example, to the degree that a supervisor viewed a job incumbent as emotionally unstable, his or her interactions with the incumbent might be strained. This might lead the incumbent to believe that he or she was not well-regarded by the supervisor and others (e.g., coworkers) and would be treated poorly by them. And to the extent that the incumbent had such beliefs, his or her interactions with the supervisor and others might be strained. As a result, the incumbent might avoid contact with others and might manifest anxiety in interactions with them. As a consequence, the incumbent's standing in the eyes of others may turn even more negative. This could have very important consequences in organizational contexts. More specifically, stigmatized job incumbents might shy away from involvements and activities that would serve to improve their position in both the organization and the world of work.

SOME IMPORTANT CONSEQUENCES OF STIGMATIZATION

Stigmatization can lead to a number of negative consequences, several of which were alluded to above. Thus, this section considers four issues: (a) the relation between unfair discrimination and justice (fairness), (b) access discrimination, (c) treatment discrimination, and (d) the affective reactions that observers have to stigmatized individuals.

Unfair Discrimination and Organizational Justice

Relative to individuals who control various types of resources in organizational settings (i.e., ingroup members), stigmatized people are often viewed as being members of outgroups. As such, they face three general types of injustice in such settings (Stone-Romero & Stone, 2004). First, in spite of their inputs or contributions, stigmatized individuals may get lower levels of outcomes than they deserve, resulting in *distributive injustice*. Second, the procedures used to allocate outcomes to stigmatized individuals may be less fair than those used to allocate outcomes to nonstigmatized individuals, leading to *procedural injustice*. Third, and finally, stigmatized individuals may be accorded less considerate interpersonal treatment than nonstigmatized individuals, causing *interpersonal injustice* Examples of various types of injustice are considered below.

Access Discrimination

To the degree that individuals (targets) are stigmatized, they have lowered odds of being selected for jobs. There are at least two reasons for this. One reason is that to the extent that targets feel stigmatized, they may view the odds of being hired for a job as very low, and, as a result of the stigma's "chilling effect" may not even apply. The other reason is that individuals who make hiring decisions may not respond favorably to the employment applications of stigmatized individuals. Among the many reasons for this is that, as noted above, decision makers may have low expectations about the ability of stigmatized individuals to succeed on the job. These expectations would be quite problematic when the stigma was based on a factor that was unrelated to job performance or some other legitimate criterion. Denying a stigmatized person a job who was actually qualified for it would be an instance of distributive injustice.

Treatment Discrimination

Assuming that a stigmatized person was actually hired, their stigma could affect the way he or she was treated on the job. Relative to nonstigmatized individuals, those who are stigmatized might experience (a) less desirable job assignments, (b) lower levels of mentoring, (c) decreased odds of being promoted, (d) lesser levels of training and development, (e) lower performance ratings, (f) physical segregation from coworkers, and (g) strained interpersonal relations with supervisors and peers. The stigmatized individual would suffer distributive injustice, for example, if he or she were given an unfavorable job assignment. In addition, he or she would experience interpersonal injustice if supervisors and peers treated him or her in an uncaring and impolite manner. Taken together, these and other forms of unfair treatment might serve to significantly lower the job and/or career success of stigmatized individuals. In addition, the unfair treatment would likely have a negative impact of the psychological well-being of such individuals.

Affective Reactions to Stigmatized Individuals

Many types of stigmas have the capacity to evoke strong negative affective responses in observers (Bodenhausen, 1993; Hosoda, Stone-Romero, & Stone, 2003; Stone et al., 1992; Stone & Colella, 1996). This is especially true for marks that (a) are considered to be disruptive (e.g., person is considered to be emotionally unstable), (b) have to do with aesthetic factors (e.g., gross physical deformities, severe skin problems), or (c) pose a threat to the well-being of others (e.g., leprosy, psychopathy, AIDS). Especially important here are personality-based stigmas. Individuals with such stigmas may be viewed as having the potential to be disruptive (e.g., to have low levels of sociability) and to threaten the welfare of others (e.g., to have low levels of emotional stability). As a result, they may be the targets of both access and treatment discrimination in work organizations.

It deserves adding that research suggests that negative affective reactions to stigmatized individuals are often automatic in nature (Bodenhuasen, 1993; Hosoda et al., 2003; Stone & Colella, 1996). One important implication of this is that cognitively-oriented interventions that are designed to alter such reactions may meet with little or no success.

PERSONALITY

In view of this chapter's focus on the stigmatizing consequences of personality, this section considers two major issues. First, a working definition of personality is presented. Second, a popular typology of personality is described.

The Personality Construct

Personality is often viewed from two perspectives: (a) the person's *social reputation* in terms of the way that he or she is viewed by others with respect to such traits as dominance, agreeableness, extroversion, and risk-taking propensity, and (b) the person's *inner nature* in terms of "the structures, dynamics, processes, and propensities inside a person that explain why he or she behaves in a characteristic way" (Hogan, 1991, p. 875). In accordance with the social reputation perspective, many theorists and researchers argue that traits are central to the structure of personality and its measurement (e.g., Wiggins & Pincus, 1992). Thus, this chapter focuses largely on the trait perspective.

Major Dimensions of Personality

In recent years, the approach to conceptualizing and measuring personality traits that has attracted the most attention among industrial and organizational psychologists is the Big Five model (Digman, 1990). It posits the existence of five major dimensions of personality: (a) neuroticism or emotional stability, (b) extraversion or surgency, (c) intelectance or openness to experience, (d) agreeableness or likability, and (e) conscientiousness or conformity. Of these factors, the construct that is of greatest interest here is neuroticism or emotional stability, which has also been labeled negative affectivity (Watson & Clark, 1984). One important reason for this focus is that being labeled as emotionally unstable or neurotic can be especially stigmatizing and harmful to either job applicants or job incumbents.

PERSONALITY MEASUREMENT IN ORGANIZATIONS

In view of this chapter's focus on the stigmatizing effects of formal and informal assessments of personality, this section consider two issues surrounding such assessments in work organizations. First, some views on the use of personality measures for personnel selection purposes are presented.

Second, brief descriptions are provided of a number of uses of such measures for personnel-related purposes.

Views on the Use of Personality Measures for Selection Purposes

Years ago, Guion and Gottier (1965) cautioned against the use of personality measures for personnel selection purposes, arguing that "it is difficult in the face of this summary to advocate with a clear conscience the use of personality measures in most situations as a basis for making employment decisions" (p. 160). More recently, Guion (1991) noted that much of the evidence on the use of personality measures for selection purposes was seriously flawed, that the evidence came from concurrent as opposed to predictive validation studies, and that studies often lacked replication. As a result, he argued that "the evidence does not exist to justify the use of personality measures, without specific research for specific purposes, as the basis for employment decisions" (p. 343). In spite of these and other concerns, in the past 20 years, there has been considerable interest in the use of personality measures for personnel selection and other purposes. In contrast to the views of Guion (Guion, 1991; Guion & Gottier, 1965) and others (e.g., Stone-Romero, 1994), the developers of some such measures (e.g., Hogan, 1991) argue that not only are they quite useful in work organizations, but also that the validity problems cited by Ghiselli (1973) and Guion and Gottier (1965) are mythical and unfounded. In addition, several recent meta-analyses (e.g., Barrick & Mount, 1991; Tett, Jackson, & Rothstein, 1991) have been conducted in the hopes of documenting the validity of such measures for predicting job performance and other types of criteria. Regrettably, as is demonstrated below, optimistic views of the value of personality measures for various organizational purposes seem quite inconsistent with the extant evidence on their validity.

Uses of Personality Measures in Organizations

A review of the literature in industrial and organizational psychology and allied fields (e.g., human resources management) shows that personality measures are being used widely for a number of purposes. The sections that follow consider several such purposes.

Individual Assessment   Personality measures often play a key role in individual assessment efforts, in which a psychologist evaluates an individual for the purpose of an important personnel decision (e.g., hiring, promotion, and development). For example, in a recent study, Ryan and Sackett (1987) asked members of the Society for Industrial and Organizational

Psychology who performed individual assessments to report on the methods they used. Results showed that 84.7% of the respondents reported using personality inventories for selection purposes.

Person–Organization Fit   The degree of fit between people and their employing organizations (P-O fit) has been the focus of a considerable amount of theoretical and empirical work. A major theme in this body of literature is that enhancing the degree of P-O fit can yield a number of benefits (e.g., greater job satisfaction, improved performance, decreased turnover, enhanced organizational commitment). Of considerable relevance to the P-O fit issue is Schneider's (1987) ASA (attraction-selection-attrition) model. It suggests that organizations operate so as to (a) attract and select individuals who fit (e.g., in terms of their personality), and (b) encourage the attrition of people who don't fit. Unfortunately, even though the maximization of P-O fit may lead to a number of positive outcomes, it can also prove quite dysfunctional in terms of several criteria, one of which is the capacity of the organization to adapt to changing internal and external conditions and ultimately to survive (Katz & Kahn, 1978; Schneider, 1987; Stone & Stone-Romero, 2004; Stone-Romero, Stone, & Salas, 2003).

Team Formation   There are several ways in which personality may be taken into account in team formation efforts. For example, the logic of the ASA model (Schneider, 1987) suggests that in forming teams, there may be overt efforts to maximize the degree of fit among team members in terms of personality variables. However, this may not be wise because in forming teams, it is important to have individuals with compatible, as opposed to similar, personalities (in terms of their need orientations; Schutz, 1958). Whatever the strategy used in forming teams, it is clear that personality variables are often considered implicitly or explicitly It also is clear that team members who have personalities that differ from extant prototypes of the ideal team member can experience a host of role-related problems (Stone & Stone-Romero 2004; Stone-Romero et al., 2003).

360 Degree Feedback   Unlike traditional performance appraisal in which a supervisor provides ratings of the performance of his or her subordinates, in 360 degree feedback the target receives feedback from superiors, peers, and subordinates. The dimensions along which 360 feedback is given often extend far beyond job performance itself. Thus, targets may receive feedback from others on their personality, interpersonal style, and a host of other variables. Unfortunately, when feedback about personality is provided to targets, it is often based upon unsophisticated assessments by feedback agents. As such, the same feedback is likely to be invalid. To the degree that it is invalid, it may have a number of negative consequences for targets (e.g., lead to losses in self-esteem and motivation to perform).

THE NEGATIVE AFFECTIVITY CONSTRUCT

As noted above, a major focus of this chapter is on the stigmatizing effects of negative affectivity in organizational contexts. Conceptually, negative affectivity (NA) has been viewed as a mood-dispositional dimension "that reflects pervasive individual differences in negative emotionality and self-concept. High-NA individuals tend to be distressed and upset and have a negative view of [the] self, whereas those low on the dimension are relatively content and secure and satisfied with themselves" (Watson & Clark, 1984, p. 465). In addition, as Watson and Clark contend, "the negative mood states experienced by persons high in NA include subjective feelings of nervousness, tension, and worry" (p. 465). As a result, they regard the trait of anxiety as one of the central features of NA. Moreover, they argue that NA is conceptually equivalent to the constructs of negative emotionality and neuroticism.

Operational Definitions of Negative Affectivity

Operationally, NA has been indexed by measures of manifest anxiety, anxiety, trait anxiety, psychoneurosis, neuroticism, defensiveness, depression, and ego strength. As documented by Watson and Clark (1984), these measures tend to correlate highly with one another. For example, the Eysenck and Eysenck (1968) Neuroticism Scale correlates .81 with a commonly used measure of anxiety, and .65 or above with a host of other measures of NA, including depression, psychoneurosis, trait anxiety, subjective distress, and defensiveness.

The Supposed Trait Nature of Negative Affectivity

It is critical to add that Watson and Clark (1984) and researchers concerned with the use of NA in the prediction of various criteria in the context of work organizations (e.g., Brief, Burke, George, Robinson, & Webster, 1988) argue that NA is a *trait*. As such, they contend, it remains stable across a wide variety of contexts. For example, Watson and Clark (1984) argued that "NA primarily reflects individual differences in negative emotionality that are maintained under all conditions, even in the absence of external stress" (p. 475). This is a *critical point* because it suggests that the variance in various measures of NA (e.g., anxiety) is a function of stable individual differences, *not* the nature of environments in which individuals are found. The speciousness of this trait perspective is considered below.

CONSTRUCT VALIDITY PROBLEMS IN MEASURES
OF NEGATIVE AFFECTIVITY

The use of measures of NA for various organizational purposes would not be problematic if such measures had substantial levels of construct validity. However, as is detailed below, there are serious construct validity problems with such measures.

Uses of the Negative Affectivity Construct in Organizational Research

Taken at face value, the arguments in support of the trait nature of NA seem compelling. So much so, it appears, that entire programs of research in industrial and organizational psychology and related fields have been devoted to demonstrating the value of NA for predicting a host of variables that are of relevance to work organizations (e.g., Brief et al., 1988; Burke, Brief, & George, 1993; Levin & Stokes, 1989). In addition, as noted above, two major meta-analytic reviews have considered the criterion-related validity of emotional stability (equivalent to NA) for predicting such criteria as job performance, tenure, promotions and other status changes, and salary (Barrick & Mount, 1991; Tett et al., 1991). As a consequence of research on NA, several publications have presented overly optimistic and highly misleading views of its value in predicting and/or explaining organizationally relevant variables. For example, George and Jones (2004) wrote that "Individuals who are high on neuroticism [or NA] are more likely to experience negative moods at work, feel stressed, and have a negative orientation to the work situations" (p. 9). In addition, DuBrin (2004) argued that "People with negative affectivity are often distressed even when working under conditions that coworkers perceive as interesting and challenging" (p. 164). Moreover, Cascio (1998) stated that "the evidence now indicates that scores on well-developed measures of normal personality (1) are stable over reasonably long periods of time, (2) predict important occupational outcomes, ... [and] ... (3) do not discriminate unfairly against any ethnic or national group" (p. 228). As is demonstrated below, there are very serious construct validity problems with many of the studies that have dealt with relations between NA and various outcomes. Thus, the validity of the just-noted arguments (Cascio, 1998; DuBrin, 2004; George & Jones, 2004) is highly debatable.

Confounding of Measures of Negative Affectivity

A review of many popular measures of NA (and of such related constructs as neuroticism, anxiety, and depression) reveals a very serious construct validity problem. As Stone-Romero (1994) demonstrated, many measures of NA have items that deal with stressor-induced psychological and physical strain. Strain is "a set of psychological and physiological responses to stressors, including long-term problems with physical and mental well-being" (Stone-Romero, 1994, p. 460).

One of the many examples of an NA measure that has considerable strain content is Taylor's (1953) Manifest Anxiety Scale. Samples of items in this measure are "I have diarrhea once a month or more," "I work under a great deal of tension," "I have a great deal of stomach trouble," and "Life is a strain for me much of the time." Items such as these overlap considerably with items in measures of role-related stress and strain (e.g., the measures of Caplan, Tripathi, & Naidu, 1985; House & Rizzo, 1972; Karasek, 1979; Patchen, 1970). Thus, it is clear that many measures that purport to index NA have suspect construct validity because they include items that index stress and/or strain. To the extent that they actually index strain, the use of such measures for selection purposes would appear to violate the spirit, if not the letter, of the Americans with Disabilities Act.

Interestingly, some researchers have noted that responses to a host of measures typically used to index psychopathology may represent nothing more than the presence of what Frank (1973) called demoralization, defined as a set of psychological symptoms that develop when individuals find themselves in environments that are stressful and that cannot be escaped (Dohrenwend & Dohrenwend, 1981). The importance of this is that strain is a consequence of exposure to stressors, as opposed to an immutable trait (Stone-Romero, 1994). In support of this argument, the next section considers literature that is relevant to the view that strain is a *consequence* of exposure to stressors, not an unchangeable property of individuals. In addition, it demonstrates how the use of personality measures for selection purposes may lead to unfair discrimination.

SOCIAL CAUSATION MODELS OF WELL-BEING

A rather large body of literature exists on the social causation perspective on mental health or psychological well-being (Dohrenwend, 1975; Dohrenwend & Dohrenwend, 1974; Taylor, Repetti, & Seeman, 1997). It argues that the chronic stress and strain that is experienced by many individuals is, in large measure, a function of the characteristics of their environments (eg., work, home, community; see Dohrenwend, 1975; Dohrenwend & Dohrenwend, 1974, 1981; Kessler, 1979; Link, Dohrenwend, & Skodol, 1986; Link, Lennon, & Dohrenwend, 1993; Taylor et al., 1997; Williams & Collins, 1995; Yu & Williams, 1999). This is a crucial issue because of relations among race, socioeconomic status (SES), and exposure to stressors.

Race and Socioeconomic Status

There is strong and consistent evidence that Blacks and individuals from selected other "minority" groups (e.g., Mexican Americans, American Indians) have much lower SES than do Whites (Abelda, Drago, & Shulman, 1997; Cohn, 2000; Kerbo, 1983; Williams & Williams-Morris, 2000; Yu & Williams, 1999). For example, 2000 U.S. Census Bureau data reveal that the percentages of individuals living below the poverty level were 9.1 for Whites, 24.9 for Blacks, 22.6 for Hispanics or Latinos, and 25.7 for American Indians (Bishaw & Iceland, 2003). The relation between race and SES is important because, as is demonstrated below, SES is strongly related to both exposure to stressors and the physical and psychological strain that results from such exposure. Thus, because race appears to have direct effects on SES, it will also have *indirect* effects on physical and psychological strain.

Race and Occupational Attainment

One of the major indices of SES is occupation. Because of this, it is important to consider the relation between race and occupational attainment. Research shows clear evidence of a strong relation between these two variables (Kerbo, 1983). For instance, 2001 U.S. Census data show that relative to Whites, Blacks and Hispanics tend to be grossly underrepresented in high occupational status jobs (e.g., managerial, professional) and overrepresented in jobs at the lower end of the occupational status hierarchy (e.g., laborer, service occupations). This is important because it is generally the case that the lower an individual's occupational status, the greater the degree to which he or she will be exposed to aversive work conditions (e.g., high levels of noise, heat, vibration, chemical toxins) and will manifest signs of physical illness and psychological strain (Williams & Collins, 1995).

Socioeconomic Status, Exposure to Stressors, and Strain

There is strong and compelling evidence that the lower a person's SES, the greater the degree to which he or she will be chronically exposed to environmental stressors, including unemployment, poverty, ethnic prejudice and discrimination, crime, residential congestion and crowding, aversive or undesirable work environments, and barriers to occupational attainment

(Dohrenwend et al., 1992; Kessler, 1979; Kessler, Price, & Wortman, 1985; Link et al., 1986, 1993; Taylor et al., 1997; Williams, 1990, 1999; Williams & Collins, 1995; Williams & Rucker, 1996; Williams & Williams-Morris, 2000; Yu & Williams, 1999). In addition, exposure to such stressors leads not only to poor physical health (Taylor et al., 1997; Williams & Collins, 1995), but also to psychological strain (Dohrenwend, 1975, 2000; Dohrenwend & Dohrenwend, 1981; Holzer et al., 1986; Johnson, Cohen, Dohrenwend, Link, & Brook, 1999; Kessler et al.,1985; Stone-Romero, 1994). For example, results of the Epidemiologic Catchment Area Study, the largest study of psychiatric disorders ever conducted in the United States, found that the lower the level of SES, the greater the rates of a broad range of psychiatric conditions (Holzer et al., 1986; Robbins & Regier, 1990). One factor that may contribute to this strain is that the lower the SES of individuals, the lesser their access to such "treatments" (e.g., social support and organizational support) that may serve to buffer the effects of stressors and stress (Williams, 1990; Williams & Rucker, 1996).

In the world of work, research shows that psychological strain (e.g., anxiety, depression) is especially high among workers who have low-level jobs, characterized by low levels of self-direction, planning, and control (Link et al., 1993). In addition, Kohn and Schooler (1983) argued that personality variables are influenced by the social and occupational conditions that workers face. These findings are especially important in that they suggest that high scores on measures of psychological strain (e.g., NA and related variables) may reflect the *effects of adversity* rather than the immutable dispositions of individuals.

Race, Exposure to Stressors, and Strain

Because of the relations among race, SES, and strain, relative to Whites, individuals in several ethnic groups (e.g., Blacks, American Indians) will have greater exposure to environmental stressors and, as a result, will manifest poorer levels of physical health and psychological well-being. In this regard, a growing body of research shows links between ethnic minority status and low levels of both physical and mental health (Contrada et al., 2000; Crocker, Major, & Steele, 1998; Kessler, 1979; Kessler & Neighbors, 1986; Taylor et al., 1997; Warheit, Holzer, & Arey, 1975; Williams, 1990, 1999). For example, Crocker et al. (1998) reported that depression was more prevalent in African Americans than European Americans. In addition, research by Kessler (1979) involving a large sample of adults in the New Haven, Connecticut area, revealed that compared to Whites, non-Whites (Blacks and Puerto Ricans) were twice as likely to report extreme levels of psychological distress (i.e., depression and anxiety). Moreover,

Kessler and Neighbors (1986) wrote that "Since the late 1950s, when large-scale surveys were first used to study the distribution of mental health problems in the general population, it has been known that Blacks in the United States have higher levels of psychological distress than Whites" (p. 107). Indeed, their research, involving the analysis of data from eight separate studies, showed that Blacks had higher levels of depressed mood than Whites, and that race and income interactively predicted depressed mood. The nature of the interaction was that the lower the level of income, the stronger the relation between race and depression. Overall, these results suggest that studies that assess the main effects of race on psychological strain may yield *underestimates* of race effects and overestimates of SES effects.

Racism, Stress, and Strain

There is clear and convincing evidence that members of various ethnic minority groups perceive unfair discrimination in various contexts, including work organizations. In addition, there is a strong link between self-reported levels of ethnic discrimination and stress. Moreover, research results are consistent with the view that racism has effects on physical health and psychological strain because it indirectly influences the socioeconomic attainment of minority group members and directly affects environmental conditions that influence health (Williams, 1999; Williams & Collins, 1995; Williams & Williams-Morris, 2000). With regard to workplace discrimination, for example, results of a national survey by Joyner (2002) showed that whereas personal workplace discrimination was reported by 28% of Blacks and 22% of Hispanic respondents, only 13% of Whites reported such discrimination. Also, with respect to the negative outcomes of discrimination, research by Sanchez and Brock (1996) revealed that perceived discrimination was related to a host of negative outcomes, including stress, tension, and dissatisfaction. Moreover, the results of 15 empirical studies reviewed by Williams and Williams-Morris (2000) showed a clear relation between experienced racial discrimination and psychological distress.

Availability of Stress Buffers

Interestingly, the lower the SES of individuals, the lesser the degree to which they have access to social support and other factors that may serve as buffers of stress (Dohrenwend & Dohrenwend, 1970; Kessler, 1979; Kessler et al., 1985; Taylor et al.,1997; Williams & Rucker, 1996). Because of this, relative to Whites, members of various minority groups (e.g., Blacks, Native Americans) have fewer functional mechanisms for coping with environmental stressors and stress. As a result, such stressors will have a more negative impact on members of many minority groups than on members of more advantaged groups (e.g., Whites).

Confounding of the Race-Strain Relation

Several studies have shown that when SES effects are held constant statistically, the magnitude of the relation between race and psychological strain (e.g., anxiety, depression) drops markedly. Thus, some have argued that race is *not* an independent determinant of psychological distress. Rather, it serves as a proxy for SES.

On its face, evidence of a decrease in the magnitude of the relation between race and psychological strain when SES is controlled might be interpreted as meaning that Blacks and other minorities are no worse off in terms of psychological strain than are Whites. However, because race and SES are related, strain is far more common among Blacks and other minorities than it is among Whites. Moreover, it merits noting that the stronger the correlation between predictor variables, the lesser the ability of multiple regression or any other statistical technique to determine the relative importance of such variables for predicting any given outcome (Darlington, 1968; Stone-Romero & Rosopa, 2004). Because of this, nonexperimental research aimed at determining the relationship between race and stress, controlling for SES, has little or no capacity to provide convincing and credible evidence on the relative importance of race and SES as determinants of strain.

Interestingly, however, research shows that even when SES is controlled, minority group status is negatively related to psychological well-being. For example, research by Dohrenwend (1975) demonstrated that Puerto Ricans have higher levels of psychiatric disorder than do non-Puerto Ricans. In addition, other research shows evidence of interactions between race and SES in predicting psychological health. For instance, a study by Kessler and Neighbors (1986) showed that at low levels of SES, African Americans had higher rates of psychological distress than did Whites. Thus, as a result of exposure to a host of environmental stressors, members of several minority groups manifest greater levels of stress and psychological strain (e.g., anxiety, depression, and low self-esteem) than do Whites. Therefore, the typical minority group member will *appear* to have higher NA than will the typical White person. The very important implication of this is that researchers and practitioners who subscribe to the view that NA is a *trait* (e.g., Brief et al., 1988; Burke et al., 1993; Watson & Clark, 1984) will erroneously regard signs of strain as attributable to the stable characteristic of individuals, rather than the result of environmental stressors.

The Correspondence Bias in Person Perception

Research in social cognition shows evidence of a *correspondence bias* in perceptions of targets. More specifically, on the basis of their observations of
targets, observers will infer that targets have traits or dispositions, even
when the behavior of the targets was a function of or was constrained by
situational factors (Hamilton & Sherman, 1994). For example, observers are
likely to attribute signs of stress or strain that are observed in targets to underlying dispositions, as opposed to the effects of environmental stressors.
To the degree that dispositional inferences are made about targets, they are
likely to suffer both access and treatment discrimination. Thus, not only
will targets suffer harm from a host of other environmental factors (e.g.,
stressful jobs, poor housing), but also they will further be harmed by the
correspondence biases of observers.

Unfair Discrimination on the Basis of Strain-Confounded Measures

Because of the above-noted relations among race, SES, exposure to stressors, and strain, to the extent that measures of psychological strain (e.g.,
neuroticism, NA, emotional stability) are used in personnel selection, individuals who have elevated scores on such measures may suffer both
access and treatment discrimination. More specifically, the use of such measures for selection purposes may lead to indirect race-based discrimination
against members of several minority groups (eg., African Americans, Mexican Americans, American Indians). In addition, if such measures are applied to existing employees, those who have elevated scores on them may
suffer various types of treatment discrimination. Overall, therefore, it appears *highly inappropriate* to use measures of psychological strain (e.g.,
many popular measures of NA) for most personnel decision-making purposes. However, there is one important exception to this. More specifically,
it is acceptable to use information from such measures for making decisions
about providing individuals with access to employee assistance programs
(e.g., stress reduction programs).

Although there is considerable evidence of relations among SES, race
and psychological strain, some research suggests that the use of measures
of personality for selection purposes generally does *not* result in adverse
impact. More specifically, based upon the analysis of data derived from empirical studies of several other researchers, Hough, Oswald, and Ployhart
(2001) reported that there were very small difference between Blacks and
Whites on measures of adjustment (standardized mean score difference, *d*
less than .05). Interestingly, however, relative to Whites (a) Blacks had lower
scores on measures of affiliation, dependability, openness to experience,

and managerial potential, (b) Hispanics had lower scores on measures of dependability, agreeableness, and openness to experience, (c) American Indians had lower scores on measures of extraversion, surgency, dependability, and agreeableness, and (d) Asian Americans had lower scores on measures of extraversion, dependability, and openness to experience. It deserves adding that in highly competitive hiring situations, even small differences on personality measures can have a large impact on the likelihood of an offer being made to a job applicant.

Note moreover that Hough et al.'s (2001) results for measures of adjustment are *inconsistent* with a great deal of research on race-psychological strain relations. Thus, the same results may be a function of the samples that were included in their study. More specifically, individuals with high levels of strain may have self-selected out of applicant pools or have been screened out through organizational selection practices. Both such processes would serve to decrease the difference between Blacks and Whites on adjustment measures.

Unfair Discrimination on the Basis of Other Measures of Personality

Although the foregoing discussion focused on problems with NA measures, problems also may stem from the use of other measures of personality for selection and most other personnel purposes. Consider, for example, the Big Five dimension of extroversion. The major problem associated with the use of extraversion in selection is that there are well-established cultural differences in this variable among members of several ethnic groups. More specifically, because of socialization, Asians and Native Americans typically have lower levels of extroversion than do Anglo Americans (Iwawaki, Eysenck, & Eysenck, 1980; Leighton & Kluckholn, 1947; Loo & Shiomi, 1982). Thus, to the degree that personnel decisions are based on measures of extroversion, there may very well be unfair discrimination against such groups as Native Americans and Asian Americans.

General Conclusion

Overall, therefore, consistent with earlier admonitions (e.g., Guion, 1991; Stone-Romero, 1994), the findings of the above-noted studies suggest that personality measures should *not* be used for selection and many other personnel purposes unless there is (a) a sound theory tying a personality trait to one or more important criterion measures, and (b) convincing evidence that the supposed trait measure does *not* correlate with such characteristics of individuals as their race, sex, and age.

THE CRITERION-RELATED VALIDITY
OF PERSONALITY MEASURES

There is yet another important reason to eschew the use of many types of personality measures for selection and many other personnel decision-making purposes. More specifically, the extant evidence (e.g., Barrick & Mount, 1991; Tett et al., 1991) shows that they explain only *trivial* amounts of variance in various criterion measures. For example, Barrick and Mount's (1991) meta-analysis revealed that measures of emotional stability had an average observed correlation of .05 with a number of performance measures. A subsequent meta-analysis by Tett et al. (1991) was alleged to be superior to that of Barrick and Mount (1991) because it dealt with theory-relevant (confirmatory) predictions between personality measures and various outcomes. It showed an average correlation of $-.15$ between neuroticism and various criteria. Finally, a recent meta-analysis by Bobko, Roth, and Potosky (1999) showed that measures of conscientiousness had an average validity of only .18 with job performance.

Taken together, the just-noted meta-analytic studies paint a *very dismal* picture of the value of using measures of NA or other dimensions of personality for personnel selection purposes. Thus, selection should be based upon predictors that have lesser potential for unfair discrimination than do measures of personality. One alternative is work samples. Research shows that they have *much* higher criterion-related validity than do personality measures (Hunter & Hunter, 1984). In addition, they often have lower levels of adverse impact than do traditional preemployment tests (Schmitt & Mills, 2001). However, it is important to note that in some circumstances, work samples may have fairly high levels of adverse impact. For example, this would be true in situations in which they called for applicants to exhibit technical skills and knowledge that were not critical to job success *at the time of hire*, because all persons hired would receive the training needed to develop the same skills and abilities.

CONCLUSIONS CONCERNING THE USE OF PERSONALITY
PREDICTORS OF VARIOUS CRITERIA

As the foregoing clearly shows, there are serious construct validity problems with many measures of so-called personality traits (e.g., emotional stability, NA, extraversion). In addition, the use of such measures for selection purposes appears to open the door to indirect forms of unfair discrimination against both minority group members and majority group members who have scores on personality measures that differ from organizational ideals. Finally, there is often no sound theory linking many personality measures to job performance. Thus, it appears unwise to use such measures for personnel selection and most other decision-making purposes.

Stigmas based upon personality can lead to unfair discrimination against both job applicants and incumbents. This flies in the face of widely expressed beliefs about the importance of treating job applicants and incumbents in a fair and ethical manner. For this and other reasons, organizations must take steps to reduce (or eliminate) the unfair treatment of job applicants and incumbents stemming from the use of personality measures. Among these are (a) developing and using selection systems that have maximum criterion-related validity and minimum bias, (b) developing and using criterion measures that are highly valid and minimally biased, (c) affording legal remedies to individuals who have been discriminated against unfairly on the basis of selection systems that use predictor measures that are biased or have low criterion-related validity, and (d) training organizational decision makers to minimize the degree to which personnel decisions are affected by impressionistic data about the personality of job applicants or job incumbents.

Eliminating biases against those who fail to conform to extant personality standards is likely to involve more than simply educating personnel decision makers on the biasing effects of personality measures. More specifically, it will often require changing organizational norms about the types of individuals who are most likely to fit with given roles. In addition, it may require that organizational members modify patterns of behavior that perpetuate personality-based biases. These efforts will not be easy. One reason for this is that personality biases in interactions with others frequently emerge in the form of psychological processes that are effortless, unconscious, and uncontrolled (Hamilton & Sherman, 1994). Another reason is that because of the drive to maximize P-O fit and the effects of similarity on interpersonal attraction, individuals who have personality profiles that differ from extant standards will continue to face unfair discrimination in organizational contexts. Nevertheless, it is critical that personnel decisions be based upon valid data about individuals. As such, it appears quite imprudent to use personality measures for personnel selection and a host of other purposes.

AUTHOR NOTES

I thank Robert L. Dipboye for very helpful comments on an earlier version of this chapter. Correspondence concerning this chapter should be addressed to Eugene F. Stone, Department of Psychology, University of

Central Florida, Orlando, FL 32816-1390. Electronic mail may be sent to estone@pegasus.cc.ucf.edu.

REFERENCES

Albelda, R., Drago, R., & Shulman, S. (1997). *Unlevel playing fields: Understanding wage inequality and discrimination.* New York: McGraw-Hill.

Ashmore, R. D., & Del Boca, F. K. (1976). Psychological approaches to understanding intergroup conflicts. In P. A. Katz (Ed.), *Towards the elimination of racism* (pp. 73–123). New York, NY: Pergamon.

Barrick, M., & Mount, M. (1991). The Big Five personality dimensions and job performance: A meta-analysis. *Personnel Psychology, 44,* 1–26.

Bishaw, A., & Iceland, J. *Poverty: 1999, Census 2000 Brief (C2KBR-19).* Washington, DC: U.S. Department of Commerce, U.S. Census Bureau.

Bobko, P., Roth, P. L., & Potosky, D. (1999). Derivation and implications of a meta-analytic matrix incorporating cognitive ability, alternative predictors, and job performance. *Personnel Psychology, 52,* 561–589.

Bodenhausen, G. V. (1993). Emotions, arousal, and stereotypic judgements: A heuristic model of affect and stereotyping. In D. M. Mackie & D. L. Hamilton (Eds.), *Affect, cognition, and stereotyping: Interactive processes in group perception* (pp. 13–37). San Diego: Academic Press.

Brewer, M. B., & Kramer, R. M. (1985). The psychology of intergroup attitudes and behavior. *Annual Review of Psychology, 36,* 219–243.

Brief, A. P., Burke, M. J., George, J. M., Robinson, B. S., & Webster, J. (1988). Should negative affectivity remain an unmeasured variable in the study of job stress? *Journal of Applied Psychology, 73,* 193–198.

Burke, M. J., Brief, A. P., & George, J. M. (1993). The role of negative affectivity in understanding relations between self-reports of stressors and strains: A comment on the applied psychology literature. *Journal of Applied Psychology, 78,* 402–412.

Caplan, R. D., Tripathi, R. C., & Naidu, R. K. (1985). Subjective past present, and future fit: Effects on anxiety, depression, and other indicators of well being. *Journal of Personality and Social Psychology, 48,* 180–197.

Cascio, W. F. (1998). *Applied psychology in human resource management* (5th ed.). Upper Saddle River, NJ: Prentice Hall.

Civil Rights Act of 1991, Public Law No. 102-66, 105 Stat. 1071 (1991). Codified as amended at 42 U.S.C., Section 1981, 2000e *et seq.*

Cohn, S. (2000). *Race and gender discrimination at work.* Boulder, CO: Westview Press.

Contrada, R. J., Ashmore, R. D., Gary, M. L, Coups, E., Egeth, J. D., Sewell, A., Ewell, K., Goyal, T. M., & Chasse, V. (2000). Ethnicity-related sources of stress and their effects on well-being. *Current Directions in Psychological Science, 9,* 136–139.

Crocker, J., Major, B., & Steele, C. (1998). Social stigma. In D. T. Gilbert, S. T. Fiske, & G. Lindzey (Eds.), *The handbook of social psychology* (4th ed., Vol. 2, pp. 504–553). Boston: McGraw-Hill.

Darlington, R. B. (1968). Multiple regression in psychological research and practice. *Psychological Bulletin, 69,* 161–182.

Digman, J. M. (1990). Personality structure: Emergence of the five-factor model. *Annual Review of Psychology, 41,* 417–440.

Dohrenwend, B. P. (1975). Sociocultural and social-psychological factors in the genesis of mental disorders. *Journal of Health and Social Behavior, 16,* 365–392.

Dohrenwend, B. P. (2000). The role of adversity and stress in psychopathology: Some evidence and its implications for theory and research. *Journal of Health and Social Behavior, 41* (March), 1–19.

Dohrenwend, B. P., & Dohrenwend, B. S. (1970). Class and race as status-related sources of stress. In S. Levine & N. A. Scotch (Eds.), *Social stress* (pp. 111–140). Chicago: Aldine-Atherton.

Dohrenwend, B. P., & Dohrenwend, B. S. (1974). Social and cultural influences on psychopathology. *Annual Review of Psychology, 25*, 417–452.

Dohrenwend, B. P., & Dohrenwend, B. S. (1981). The 1980 Division 27 Award for Distinguished Contributions to Community Psychology and Mental Health. *American Journal of Community Psychology, 9*, 123–164.

Dohrenwend, B. P., Levav, I., Shrout, P. E., Schwartz, S., Naveh, G., Link, B. G., Skodol, A. E., & Stueve, A. (1992). Socioeconomic status and psychiatric disorders: The causation-selection issue. *Science, 255*, 946–952.

DuBrin, A. J. (2004). *Applying psychology: Individual and organizational effectiveness* (6th ed.). Upper Saddle River, NJ: Prentice-Hall.

Eysenck, H. J., & Eysenck, S. B. G. (1968). *Manual for the Eysenck Personality Inventory.* San Diego, CA: Educational and Industrial Testing Service.

Fiske, S. T., & Taylor, S. E. (1991). *Social cognition* (2nd ed.). New York: McGraw-Hill.

Frank, J. D. (1973). *Persuasion and healing.* Baltimore: Johns Hopkins University Press.

George, J. M., & Jones, G. R. (2004). Individual differences: Personality and ability. In B. M. Staw (Ed.), *Psychological dimensions of organizational behavior* (3rd ed., pp. 3–23). Upper Saddle River, NJ: Prentice-Hall.

Ghiselli, E. E. (1973). The validity of occupational aptitude tests in personnel selection. *Personnel Psychology, 26*, 461–477.

Goffman, E. (1963). *Stigma: Notes on the management of spoiled identity.* Englewood Cliffs, NJ: Prentice-Hall.

Guion, R. M. (1991). Personnel assessment, selection, and placement. In M. D. Dunnette & L. M. Hough (Eds.), *Handbook of industrial and organizational psychology* (2nd ed., Vol. 2, pp. 327–397). Palo Alto, CA: Consulting Psychologists Press.

Guion, R. M., & Gottier, R. F. (1965). Validity of personality measures in personnel selection. *Personnel Psychology, 18*, 135–164.

Hamilton, D. L. (1976). Cognitive biases in the perception of social groups. In J. S. Carroll & J. W. Payne (Eds.), *Cognition and social behavior* (pp. 81–93). Hillsdale, NJ: Lawrence Erlbaum Associates.

Hamilton, D. L. (1981a). *Cognitive processes in stereotyping and intergroup behavior.* Hillsdale, NJ: Lawrence Erlbaum Associates.

Hamilton, D. L. (1981b). Illusory correlation as a basis for stereotyping. In D. L. Hamilton (Ed.), *Cognitive processes in stereotyping and intergroup behavior* (pp. 115–144). Hillsdale, NJ: Lawrence Erlbaum Associates.

Hamilton, D. L., & Sherman, J. W. (1994). Stereotypes. In R. S. Wyer & T. K. Srull (Eds.), *Handbook of social cognition* (2nd ed., Vol. 2, pp. 1–68). Hillsdale, NJ: Lawrence Erlbaum Associates.

Higgins, E. T., & Bargh, J. A. (1987). Social cognition and social perception. *Annual Review of Psychology, 38*, 369–425.

Hogan, R. T. (1991). Personality and personality measurement. In M. D. Dunnette, & L. M. Hough (Eds.), *Handbook of industrial and organizational psychology* (2nd ed., Vol. 2, pp. 873–919). Palo Alto, CA: Consulting Psychologists Press.

Holzer, C., Shea, B., Swanson, J. Leaf, P., Myers, J., George, L., Weissman, M., & Bednarski, P. (1986). The increased risk for specific psychiatric disorders among persons of low socioeconomic status. *American Journal of Social Psychiatry, 6,* 259–271.

Hosoda, M., Stone-Romero, E. F., & Stone, D. L. (2003). The effects of co-worker race and task demand on task-related outcomes as mediated by evoked affect. *Journal of Applied Social Psychology, 33,* 145–178.

Hough, L. M., Oswald, F. L., & Ployhart, R. E. (2001). Determinants, detection and amelioration of adverse impact in personnel selection procedures: Issues, evidence, and lessons learned. *International Journal of Selection and Assessment, 9,* 152–194.

House, R. J., & Rizzo, A. (1972). Role conflict and role ambiguity as critical variables in a model of organizational behavior. *Organizational Behavior and Human Performance, 7,* 467–505.

Hunter, J. E., & Hunter, R. F. (1984). Validity and utility of alternative predictors of job performance. *Psychological Bulletin, 96,* 72–98.

Iwawaki, S., Eysenck, S. B., & Eysenck, H. J. (1980). Japanese and English personality structure: A cross-cultural study. *Psychologia: An International Journal of Psychology in the Orient, 23,* 195–205.

Johnson, J. G., Cohen, P. Dohrenwend, B. P., Link, B. G., & Brook, J. S. (1999). A longitudinal investigation of social causation and social selection processes involved in the association between socioeconomic status and psychiatric disorders. *Journal of Abnormal Psychology, 108,* 490–499.

Jones, E. E., Farina, A., Hastorf, A. H., Markus, H., Miller, D. T., Scott, R. A., & de French, R. (1984). *Social stigma: The psychology of marked relationships.* San Francisco: Freeman.

Joyner, T. (2002, January 18). A divided workplace. *The Atlanta Journal-Constitution,* p. C.1.

Karasek, R. A. (1979). Job demands, job decision latitude, and mental strain: Implications for job redesign. *Administrative Science Quarterly, 24,* 295–308.

Katz, D., & Braly, K. N. (1933). Verbal stereotypes and prejudice. *Journal of Abnormal and Social Psychology, 133,* 280–292.

Katz, D., & Kahn, R. L. (1978). *The social psychology of organizations* (2nd ed.). New York: Wiley.

Kerbo, H. R. (1983). *Social stratification and inequality: Class conflict in the United States.* New York: McGraw-Hill.

Kessler, R. C. (1979). Stress, social status, and psychological distress. *Journal of Health and Social Behavior, 20,* 259–272.

Kessler, R. C., & Neighbors, H. W. (1986). A new perspective on the relationships among race, social class, and psychological distress. *Journal of Health and Social Behavior, 27,* 107–115.

Kessler, R. C., Price, R. H., & Wortman, C. B. (1985). Social factors in psychopathology: Stress, social support, and coping processes. *Annual Review of Psychology, 36,* 531–572.

Kohn, M., & Schooler, C. (1983). *Work and personality: An inquiry into the impact of social stratification.* Norwood, NJ: Ablex.

Larsen, R. J., Diener, E., & Cropanzano, R. S. (1987). Cognitive operations associated with individual differences in affect intensity. *Journal of Personality and Social Psychology, 53,* 767–774.

Leighton, D., & Kluckholn, C. (1947). *Children of the people.* Cambridge, MA: Harvard University Press.

Levin, I., & Stokes, J. P. (1989). Dispositional approach to job satisfaction: Role of negative affectivity. *Journal of Applied Psychology, 74,* 752–758.

Link, B. G., Dohrenwend, B. P., & Skodol, A. E. (1986). Socio-economic status and schizophrenia: Noisome occupational characteristics as a risk factor. *American Sociological Review, 51,* 242–258.

Link, B. G., Lennon, M. C., & Dohrenwend, B. P. (1993). Socioeconomic status and depression: The role of occupations involving direction, control, and planning. *American Journal of Sociology, 98,* 1351–1387.

Loo, R., & Shiomi, K. (1982). The Eysenck personality scores of Japanese and Canadian undergraduates. *Journal of Social Psychology, 118*, 3–9.

Merton, R. K. (1948). The self-fulfilling prophecy. *Antioch Review, 8*, 193–210.

Miller, D. T., & Turnbull, W. (1986). Expectancies and interpersonal processes. *Annual Review of Psychology, 37*, 233–256.

Patchen, M. (1970). *Participation, achievement, and involvement on the job.* Englewood Cliffs, NJ: Prentice-Hall

Plous, S., & Williams, T. (1995). Racial stereotypes from the days of American slavery: A continuing legacy. *Journal of Applied Social Psychology, 25*, 461–476.

Robbins, L., & Regier, D. A. (1990). *Psychiatric disorders in America.* New York: Free Press.

Rosenthal, R., & Jacobson, L. (1968). *Pygmalion in the classroom.* New York: Holt, Rinehart & Winston.

Ryan, A. M., & Sackett, P. R. (1987). A survey of individual assessment practices by I/O psychologists. *Personnel Psychology, 40*, 455–488.

Sanchez, J. L., & Brock, P. (1996). Outcomes of perceived discrimination among Hispanic employees: Is diversity management a luxury or a necessity? *Academy of Management Journal, 39*, 704–719.

Schmitt, N., & Mills, A. (2001). Traditional tests and job simulations: Minority and majority performance and test validities. *Journal of Applied Psychology, 86*, 451–458.

Schneider, B. (1987). The people make the place. *Personnel Psychology, 40*, 437–453.

Schutz, W. C. (1958). *FIRO: A three-dimensional theory of interpersonal behavior.* New York: Rinehart.

Sherman, S. J., Judd, C. M., & Park, B. (1989). Social cognition. *Annual Review of Psychology, 40*, 281–326.

Stone, D. L., & Colella, A. (1996). A model of factors affecting the treatment of disabled individuals in organizations. *Academy of Management Review, 21*, 352–401.

Stone, D. L., & Stone-Romero, E. F. (2004). The influence of culture on role-taking in culturally diverse organizations. In M. S. Stockdale & F. J. Crosby (Eds.), *The psychology and management of workplace diversity* (pp. 78–99). Malden, MA: Blackwell.

Stone, E. F., Stone, D. L., & Dipboye, R. L. (1992). Stigmas in organizations: Race, handicaps, and physical attractiveness. In K. Kelley (Ed.), *Issues, theory, and research in industrial/organizational psychology* (pp. 385–457). Amsterdam: Elsevier.

Stone-Romero, E. F. (1994). Construct validity issues in organizational behavior research. In J. Greenberg (Ed.), *Organizational behavior: The state of the science* (pp. 155–179) Hillsdale, NJ: Lawrence Erlbaum Associates.

Stone-Romero, E. F., & Rosopa, P. L. (2004). Inference problems with the hierarchical multiple regression strategy used in testing for mediating effects. In J. J. Martocchio (Ed.), *Research in Personnel and Human Resources Management, 23*, 249–290.

Stone-Romero, E. F., & Stone, D. L. (2004, April). *Effects of ingroup versus outgroup status on unfair treatment in organizations.* Paper presented at the meeting of the Society for Industrial and Organizational Psychology, Chicago, IL.

Stone-Romero, E. F., Stone, D. L., & Hartman, M. (2002, April). *Stereotypes of ethnic groups: Own views versus assumed views of others.* Paper presented at the meeting of the Society for Industrial and Organizational Psychology, Toronto, Canada.

Stone-Romero, E. F., Stone, D. L., & Salas, E. (2003). The influence of culture on role conceptions and role behavior in organizations. *Applied Psychology: An International Review, 52*, 328–362.

Taylor, J. A. (1953). A personality scale of manifest anxiety. *Journal of Abnormal and Social Psychology, 29*, 285–290.

Taylor, S. E., Repetti, R. L., & Seeman, T. (1997). Health psychology: What is an unhealthy environment and how does it get under the skin? *Annual Review of Psychology, 48*, 411–447.

Tett, R., Jackson, D., & Rothstein, M. (1991). Personality measures as predictors of performance: A meta-analytic review. *Personnel Psychology, 44,* 703–742.

Warheit, G., Holzer, C. E., & Arey, S. S. (1975). Race and mental illness: An epidemiologic update. *Journal of Health and Social Behavior, 16,* 243–256.

Watson, D., & Clark, L. A. (1984). Negative affectivity: The disposition to experience aversive emotional states. *Psychological Bulletin, 96,* 465–490.

Wiggins, J. S., & Pincus, A. L. (1992). Personality: Structure and assessment. *Annual Review of Psychology, 43,* 473–504.

Williams, D. R. (1990). Socioeconomic differentials in health: A review and redirection. *Social Psychology Quarterly, 53,* 81–99.

Williams, D. R. (1999). Race, socioeconomic status, and health: The added effects of racism and discrimination. *Annals of the New York Academy of Sciences, 896,* 173–188.

Williams, D. R., & Collins, C. (1995). US socioeconomic and racial differences in health: Patterns and explanations. *Annual Review of Sociology, 21,* 349–386.

Williams, D. R., & Rucker, T. (1996). Socioeconomic status and the health of racial minority populations. In P. M. Kato and T. Mann (Eds.), *Handbook of diversity issues in health psychology* (pp. 407–423). New York: Plenum.

Williams, D. R., & Williams-Morris, R. (2000). Racism and mental health: The African American experience. *Ethnicity & Health, 5,* 243–268.

Yu, Y., & Williams, D. R. (1999). Socioeconomic status and mental health. In C. S. Aneshensel, & J. C. Phelan (Eds.), *Handbook of the sociology of mental health* (pp. 151–166). New York: Plenum.

12

Looking the Part: Bias Against the Physically Unattractive as a Discrimination Issue

Robert L. Dipboye
University of Central Florida

The ideal public and private organization for the 1990s has been described as multicultural in that it not only tolerates but openly embraces differences among employees (Cox, 1991; Cox & Blake, 1991). This chapter focuses on a barrier to achieving the multicultural ideal that has been largely ignored in these discussions—bias on the basis of appearance and in particular against the physically unattractive. At first glance, this may seem peripheral to the issue of workplace discrimination. Yet, appearance standards and norms in organizations can have the effect of favoring the White, the young, and the physically unimpaired. Those who violate these norms can be subjected to severe sanctions. Take, for example, the following incidents.

> A TV anchor on a local station is fired because she is "too old, too ugly, unfeminine, and didn't dress right."
>
> A black employee of a national pizza chain, cannot shave because of a skin disorder that is more common among Blacks than Whites. Nevertheless, he is fired for wearing a beard in violation of the corporate dress code.
>
> A manager of a car rental agency is dismissed from his job for being obese, despite receiving high performance ratings and eight commendations over a five-year period.

A female employee has the best record in securing contracts for her accounting firm, but her candidacy for partner is deferred largely on the basis of her
appearance. She is advised to "wear make-up, have her hair styled, and wear
jewelry."

Evaluating employees on the basis of their looks is not always inappropriate, but incidents such as these are common and can easily undermine
efforts to foster a fair and just workplace. Moreover, appearance standards
and the rejection of those who are "physically unattractive" can undercut
diversity by rationalizing racism, sexism, ageism, and other forms of prejudice. Consequently, efforts to encourage organizational diversity need to
take into account physical appearance biases and the other stigmas that are
normally addressed in such efforts. In examining this issue, I first review
the research demonstrating a bias against physical unattractive persons
and consider whether this is a trivial effect that deserves our attention.
Some of the alternative sources of this bias are then explored, along with
implications for the management of appearance in organizations.

EVIDENCE OF BIAS AGAINST THE PHYSICALLY UNATTRACTIVE

"Attractive persons" is used to refer to those who conform to norms for
attractiveness on both mutable facets of appearance, such as dress and
grooming, and relatively immutable facets, such as facial features, bodily
weight, and stature. "Unattractive persons" are those who deviate from
these norms. From a humanistic perspective, one could legitimately argue
that everyone is beautiful, but the harsh reality is that there are widely
held standards of attractiveness (Berry & McArthur, 1985, 1986; Cunningham, 1986). Jackson (1992) concluded that ". . . contrary to folk wisdom that
'beauty is in the eye of the beholder,' there is remarkable consensus in people's ratings of others' attractiveness. Consensus has been observed across
a variety of rater characteristics—such as sex, race, age, and socioeconomic
status—and across cultural backgrounds" (p. 4). Similar conclusions were
reached in an exhaustive meta-analysis (Langlois et al., 2000). The authors
found agreement among raters on attractiveness across both ethnic and
cultural groups. Additionally, attractive children and adults are evaluated
more positively and treated more favorably than those who are unattractive regardless of their familiarity with the rater.

Not only do people appear to agree in their judgments of attractiveness,
but also, not surprisingly, people are personally attracted to those who
conform to conventional standards of physical attractiveness and tend to

reject those who do not conform to these norms (Hatfield & Sprecher, 1986; Jackson, 1992). More surprising is the research showing that the physically attractive appear to have advantages over the less attractive in the world of work. For example, research has shown that attractiveness is related to general occupational success (Langlois et al., 2000) and to biases in selection, appraisal, and promotion judgments (e.g., Hosoda, Stone-Romero, & Stone, 2003; Stone, Stone, & Dipboye, 1992).

The Relationship of Physical Attractiveness to Occupational Success

In their meta-analysis, Langlois et al. (2000) calculated an average weighted effect size (d) of .76 (p < .05) that showed that attractive persons were more successful than unattractive persons. This was the largest effect found for adults with the only larger effect found for popularity ratings of children (d = .77). It is instructive to examine in more detail two of the studies in the Langlois et al. (2000) meta-analysis that examined physical attractiveness as a predictor of career success. In a survey of 3,692 persons, Umberson and Hughes (1987) found that ratings of attractiveness were positively related to education, occupational status, and life satisfaction. Roszell, Kennedy, and Grabb (1989) examined the relationship of attractiveness to income attainment for 1,062 Canadians. In the 1979 wave of interviews, the physical attractiveness of the respondents was measured on a 5-point scale that ranged from "strikingly handsome or beautiful," to "homely." A statistically significant effect of physical attractiveness was found in which annual 1981 income increased by $1,046 for every unit increase in attractiveness rating. This effect held even after controlling for income in 1979, the gender composition of the job, and gender of the respondent. The effect was moderated, however, by both age and sex. Attractiveness had more of an effect in the evaluation of men than women, and for those above the age of 30 than for those below the age of 30. The authors speculate from these results that "individuals for whom attractiveness is a commonly occurring attribute (women, those in female-dominated jobs, and the young) receive little direct economic return from the attribute. However, among those where attractiveness is a more scarce resource, its 'market value' was more readily apparent and more directly realized" (p. 558).

In a study not included in the Langlois et al. (2000) meta-analysis, Frieze, Olson, and Russell (1991) asked a group of people with corporate management experience to rate on a 5-point scale the physical attractiveness of 737 MBA graduates who graduated between 1973 and 1982. Starting salaries of the graduates were regressed on facial attractiveness, which was found to predict a man's but not a woman's starting salary. When 1983 salaries were regressed on attractiveness, a strong effect was found for both men and women in which every unit increase in attractiveness yielded an increase of $2,600 in the men's salary and an increase of $2,100 a year in the women's salary.

In addition to general physical attractiveness, there are specific physical appearance factors, often related to attractiveness, that have been shown to be related to occupational success. At least two surveys have shown a relationship of height and weight to occupational success. Quinn (1978) used data from national surveys at the University of Michigan and found that taller men earned more money and held more prestigious jobs than shorter men. Also, men and women who were underweight and overweight earned less than those who were average in weight. Frieze, Olson, and Good (1990) surveyed 859 male MBAs and 355 female MBAs who graduated from the University of Pittsburgh between 1973 and 1982. Weight and height were particularly important correlates of salary for the male MBAs, with the salary differences between overweight and normal weight employees increasing over time.

Physical Attractiveness as a Factor in Selection Judgments

A possible reason for the greater occupational success of physically attractive persons is that they are given advantages in the initial screening and selection into jobs. In support of this hypothesis, research suggests that the appearance of the applicant seems to influence the interviewer's selection decisions at all phases of the selection process (Carlson, 1967; Carroll, 1966; Kinicki & Lockwood, 1985; Raza & Carpenter, 1987; Rynes & Gerhart, 1990; Springbett, 1958).

In one of the first field demonstrations of attractiveness effects, Carroll (1966) examined the relationship of attractiveness to the success of graduating business students in finding employment. Handsomeness of the applicant was rated by three judges from photographs. Of 19 characteristics used as predictors in this study (e.g., age, grades, major), only appearance, marital status, and work experience were related to success in job-hunting; the strongest relationship was for appearance. The more handsome the applicant, the more visit offers received, the higher the job-visit ratio, and the higher the score on a composite criterion of job-hunting success.

More recently, Rynes and Gerhart (1990) examined evaluations of MBA graduates by recruiters. Recruiters rated the applicants on three kinds of measures: (a) trait scales (e.g., general knowledge, leadership), (b) overall employability, and (c) employability in your firm. Two placement officials independently rated each applicant's physical attractiveness and height on a 3-point scale (average, significantly above, significantly below average).

Attractiveness was a stronger correlate of recruiter evaluations of firm-specific fit than were objective characteristics of the applicants such as GPA, sex, business experience, major and extracurricular activities.

A limitation of much of the field research showing a relationship of attractiveness to selection outcomes is that it is open to alternative interpretations such as the possibility that attractive applicants have higher objective qualifications or greater social skill (Goldman & Lewis, 1977; Reingen, Gresham, & Kernan, 1980). Indeed, Langlois et al. (2000) concluded that beauty is more than skin deep. They found that attractiveness is positively related to a variety of attributes in adults including physical health, extraversion, traditional attitudes, self-esteem, social skills, mental health, and intelligence. These effects were larger when the attractiveness measure included the face plus other cues than when the measure was based on face only.

Showing that bias against unattractive persons is independent of these attributes requires research in which attractive and unattractive persons are judged who have the same objective qualifications. Experimental research providing such control has consistently has shown a bias against unattractive persons among both college student subjects and organizational gatekeepers such as recruiters (Hosoda et al., 2003). A limitation of much of this experimental research is its obtrusiveness, i.e., it is obvious to participants that they are subjects in research. However, the bias against unattractive persons has been found in the few unobtrusive field experiments that have been conducted. Benson, Severs, Tagenhorst, & Loddengaard (1980) sent a cover letter and resumé of a fictitious applicant to 70 male public health administrators who were unaware of the bogus nature of the inquiry. In the letter accompanying the resumé, the applicant requested career guidance. Weight of the person was manipulated by including a picture that depicted the applicant as either normal in weight or overweight (her clothing was padded). Only 27% of the inquiries in the overweight condition received a reply, compared to 57% in the normal weight condition. When the nature of the response was examined, only 29% of the respondents in the overweight condition conveyed optimism about employment prospects of the applicant compared to 81% in the normal weight condition.

Physical Attractiveness in Performance Appraisal and Promotions

The greater occupational success of attractive employees relative to unattractive employees could also reflect biases in performance appraisal and promotion. In complex jobs where decision makers may have difficulty in reaching consensus as to what should or should not be important, physical appearance may be one of the few attributes on which decision makers agree. The importance of appearance in determining appraisals and promotions was demonstrated by Nykodym and Simonetti (1987) in a survey of managers from Fortune 500 companies. Personal appearance was ranked eighth in importance for surviving and succeeding in organizations, below items such as excellent performance record, personality, communication skills, technical skills, human relations skills, work experience, and ability to stay cool, but above items such as your health and energy, ability to judge people, power, a sponsor, an MBA degree, willingness to relocate, high identity organizational activities, and working long days.

Consistent with survey results, field studies have also have shown a small to moderate bias in appraisals and promotions against unattractive employees (Bentz, 1985; Dickey-Bryant, Lautenschlager, Mendoza, & Abrahams, 1986; Ross & Ferris, 1981). Ross and Ferris (1981) rated the facial attractiveness of male employees in two public accounting firms from photographs. They then regressed salary, performance evaluations, and likelihood of making partner on ratings of attractiveness and also weight, tenure, academic training, marital status, rated motivation, attitudes, and height. Weight was strongly related to "relative performance" (i.e., rated performance relative to their cohort). The heavier the employees relative to their height, the more negative the ratings of their performance. Both height and facial attractiveness were positively related to the rated likelihood of making partner, but failed to predict salary, achieved performance appraisals, or ratings of relative performance.

Further support of the notion that appearance influences appraisal comes from a validation of selection procedures at Sears (Bentz, 1985). Potential candidates for managerial training were invited to participate in a mini-assessment center where they were subjected to structured interviews. One of the dimensions on which applicants were evaluated was their appearance ("the physical equipment they possess"). This proved to be the strongest and most consistent predictor of performance on the job, with significant correlations ($p < .05$) found between appearance and 23 of the 26 criterion ratings. In a follow-up study, appearance again emerged as the strongest correlate of on-the-job performance.

Most studies found at least some evidence of bias against unattractive persons (Hosoda et al., 2003) and the few failures to show the effect seem attributable to weak manipulations (Greenwald, 1981; Jackson, 1983a, 1983b). The findings of research on work-related judgments are consistent with the conclusions of a recent meta-analysis of the social psychological research (Eagly, Ashmore, Makhijani, & Longo, 1991), which found a bias in favor of the attractive target person in 92% of the studies reviewed.

UNRESOLVED ISSUES IN THE RESEARCH
ON ATTRACTIVENESS BIASES

Although a main effect for attractiveness is frequently found, there are several unresolved issues that need to be addressed in future research. First, it is unclear whether attractiveness biases reflect a rejection of the highly unattractive, a preference for the highly attractive, or both. There is some indication that there is a strong rejection of highly unattractive persons and very little difference in the rating of the highly and moderately attractive persons (Hatfield & Sprecher, 1986), but few studies have included a moderate level of attractiveness. Also, the sampling of stimuli used in the manipulation of attractiveness is often inadequate (Guion & Gibson, 1988), with most studies using static displays of facial attraction to the neglect of other physical cues such as nonverbal behavior (Raines, Hechtman, & Rosenthal, 1990) and vocal quality (Zuckerman, Hodgins, & Miyako, 1990). A more serious problem is that the sample of stimuli used in the manipulation of attractiveness is often small (typically one to four photographs) and unrepresentative (Fontenelle, Peek-Phillips, & Lane, 1985).

Another unresolved issue is whether the target person's sex moderates the effects of attractiveness. Contrary to the common belief that physical attractiveness is unimportant for men, attractive men are consistently preferred over unattractive men. A possible manifestation of the importance of looks to men is the increasing frequency with which men are undergoing cosmetic surgery to enhance their careers ("Men try to put a new face on careers," *Wall Street Journal*, August 28, 1991; "Workplace edge: plastic surgery." Journal of Commerce, August 23, 1999; "Leaders: The right to be beautiful," The Economist May 24, 2003). The effect of attractiveness for women is much less clear. Although most studies seem to show that attractive women are preferred over unattractive women, a few studies show that attractive women are disadvantaged in traditionally male jobs (Heilman & Saruwatari, 1979; Heilman & Stopeck, 1985a, 1985b). However, this "beauty is beastly" effect is possibly the result of the idiosyncratic characteristics of the photographs used in the manipulation of attractiveness, and research is needed with broader samples of stimuli to see if the effect generalizes across target persons (Bieber & Dipboye, 1989). In a recent experiment using a sample of 100 male and 100 female pictures and over 30 occupations, evidence was found for a bias against attractive females but only in a few extremely sex-typed occupations (Podratz & Dipboye, 2002; Maccarone, 2003).

Still another issue is that the typical experiment places subjects in the role of passive observers who judge resumés or videotapes on the basis of information that is provided to them by the experimenter. Participants perform the task as isolated individuals with no opportunity to interact with others in the session. Finally, subjects are not emotionally involved and can assume a detached role in judging the target person. The passive-observer procedures used in research are ideal for exploring information processing, but they do not allow exploration of the complex mix of cognitive, affective, behavioral, and social factors that account for attractiveness bias in organizations. The first step in improving research on this topic is to develop more comprehensive models to guide these efforts and to conduct research involving actually interaction of the perceiver and the target of perception.

HOW IMPORTANT IS THE BIAS AGAINST UNATTRACTIVE PERSONS?

The consistency with which an attractiveness bias is found is impressive, but doubts have been raised as to the importance of the effect. One argument is that the attractiveness bias is trivial because it typically accounts for a smaller amount of variance than grades, past performance, and other "objective" qualifications. When effect sizes are measured with r^2, eta, and omega, the amount of variance attributable to attractiveness is often only between 1 and 5%. The reliance on effect size measures as an indicator of importance seems misguided, however, and ignores the fact that small statistical effects can still have important practical consequences (Abelson, 1982; Rosenthal, 1990). For instance, Rosenthal (1990) observed that only 5.4% of the variance was accounted for in research showing the inhibiting effects of AZT on AIDS, only 3.6% in research on the effects of cyclosporine on rejection of organ transplants, and only .11% in research showing the relationship of aspirin to heart failure. Martell, Lane, and Willis (1992) recently found in a computer simulation that rating biases against women 4% or smaller could result in marked violations of the 4/5ths rule of the EEOC and skewed sex composition at the higher levels of the organization. More research is needed on the issue, but it seems clear on the basis of existing research that small effect sizes can translate into major consequences. This seems particularly true when many people are competing for relatively few positions or scarce resources and when the biases have an opportunity to accumulate as the result of repeated judgments.

A second argument against taking attractiveness effects seriously is that unlike biases based on race, sex, age, and disability, most discrimination against unattractive individuals is legal. Although one could interpret some existing civil rights laws as covering discrimination against the unattractive (c.f., Anonymous, 1987), there is little indication that legal remedies are forthcoming. Requirements of homogeneous appearance standards seem most vulnerable to litigation where they discriminate against women, but the courts generally have given employers considerable discretion in setting appearance standards (Mapes-Riordan, 1991; Matusewitch, 1989). Even if biases against unattractive persons are not protected by law, however, one could argue that they are worthy of consideration because they are inconsistent with the concept of a multicultural organization and play an important role in discrimination against groups that *are* protected under the law. As stated earlier, the prototypic attractive person is White, middle-class, young, and physically unimpaired, and this prototype seems to be at the core of a variety of biases. Disabilities involving facial deformities are subject to greater rejection than disabilities not having facial deformities (Giancoli & Neimeyer, 1983; Richardson, Goodman, Hastorf, & Dornbusch, 1961). Prejudice against Blacks, Hispanics, and Asians is stronger to the extent that their appearance violates White, middle-class norms for "attractive" appearance (Bernstein, Lin, & McClelland, 1981; Cross & Cross, 1971; Hernandez, 1981; Hill, 1994; Langlois & Stephan, 1977; Martin, 1964). Younger faces are judged more attractive than older faces, suggesting that bias against older employees is greater to the extent that they appear unattractive (Deutsch, Zalenski, & Clark, 1986; Jackson, 1992; O'Connell & Rotter, 1979, pp. 60–61). Gender related stereotypes (e.g., bimbo, lesbian, castrating female) can be instantiated and intensified as a consequence of physical attractiveness cues (Bieber & Dipboye, 1988; Heilman & Saruwatari, 1979). Even the labeling of "homosexuality" has been shown related to unattractive facial features (Dew, 1985; Dunkie & Francis, 1990; Unger, Hilderbrand, & Madar, 1982). Raza and Carpenter (1987) went so far as to hypothesize that the bias against minorities, women, and older employees in interviews is mediated by perceptions of physical attractiveness.

SOURCES OF ATTRACTIVENESS BIASES

As is the case with other types of discrimination, the underlying reasons for biases against unattractive persons in organizational settings are complex in that they involve a variety of causes with the relative importance of these causes varying with the situation. The efforts to tease apart the antecedents of attractiveness bias have only begun, but the findings of research conducted so far suggest a rich mixture of cognitive, affective, social, and behavioral factors.

Cognitive Sources of Attractiveness Bias

The bias against unattractive persons reflects in part the ignorance of the perceiver insofar as it originates from faulty information processing. In other words, perceivers misjudge and mistreat unattractive employees because of the information they notice, encode, organize, and retrieve on the unattractive person. In judging another person, the data that are available almost always exceed the information processing capabilities of the perceiver. Consequently, perceivers simplify by determining how the individual stimulus person compares to categories of others. Once categorized, the stimulus person is assigned attributes prototypical of the category. The subsequent search for and processing of information on the stimulus person is initially guided by an attempt to confirm this category. If information is encountered that contradicts the initial categorization, the perceiver attempts to account for this discrepancy and recategorize. If disconfirmation continues, then the perceiver may eventually rely more on individual information regarding the unique attributes of the target person and less on categories.

Appearance is especially important in determining which cognitive categories are activated. Not only is appearance salient, novel, and the first information obtained (McArthur, 1982), but also research shows that appearance is among the first items mentioned when describing others (Fiske & Cox, 1979). Attractiveness of appearance is a basis for categorization that seems to play an especially important role in encoding and organizing memories of others' behavior (Miller, 1988). The face is probably the most important of the visual cues of attractiveness (Jackson, 1992, p. 3).

Once a category is activated or instantiated, the label associated with this category can lead to the inference of a variety of attributes associated with the prototypical member of the category. Implicit theories guide these inferences. One view is that broad generalizations of positive traits are made from physically attractive appearances (the beauty-is-good hypothesis). According to Hatfield and Sprecher (1986), "People believe good-looking people possess almost all the virtues known to humankind" (p. xix). Similarly, attractiveness has been presented as a diffuse status characteristic that along with sex, race, and age implies the possession of many different positive attributes (Kalick, 1988; Morrow, 1990; Webster & Driskell, 1983). Partial support for these views was recently found in a meta-analysis of the social psychological research (Eagly et al., 1991). This study found that attractive persons are more likely to be seen as socially competent, powerful, adjusted, and intellectually competent than unattractive persons, but no more socially sensitive or honest. A slight tendency was found for attractive persons to be seen as more vain than unattractive persons.

A crucial cognitive factor in determining reactions to the physically attractive or unattractive are the causal attributions that perceivers make for the appearance of these individuals. To the extent that perceivers see unattractiveness as something under the control of the other, then negative stereotyping of that person is much more severe (Jones et al., 1984). For instance, the traits attributed to obese individuals are usually quite negative because their weight is seen as something that is their doing (DeJong & Kleck, 1986; Maddox, Back, & Liederman, 1968).

The end result of biases in information processing is that persons tend to perceive the attractive individual as providing a better fit to the organization and the job (Heilman, 1983). Two processes seem to be involved here. Evaluators attribute characteristics to the attractive and unattractive ratees on the basis of their categorizations of these individuals. They then assess the degree to which the stimulus person possesses the characteristics associated with the stereotype of the ideal person in the job or organization. Attractive persons tend to be seen as possessing more of the attributes required in the job and are consequently evaluated more positively than the unattractive ratee. Raters are biased, but for what they think are the best of reasons.

Affective Sources of Attractiveness Bias

Attractiveness bias can result not only from what is *known* about the attractive and the unattractive person but also from the way the perceiver *feels* about the person. Thus, attractiveness biases are mediated not only by cognitive processes but also by emotional responses that the perceiver may be unaware of and unable to control. Zajonc (1980, 1984) argues that sensory input of the person's appearance directly evokes affect, without the involvement of mediating mental processes. The importance of affective responses reflects the fact that "Before we evolved language and our cognitive capacities, which are so deeply dependent on language, it was the affective system alone upon which the organism relied for its adaptation" (p. 170). Possibly indicative of an affective basis for appearance bias, infants as young as three months old prefer female faces judged as attractive more than faces judged as unattractive (Jackson, 1992; Langlois, Ritter, Roggman, & Vaughn, 1991; Langlois, Roggman, Casey, & Ritter, 1987). Simply showing pictures of physically attractive and unattractive people induces affective states that have important behavioral and attitudinal consequences (Larsen, Diener, & Cropanzano, 1987). Also, the presentation of deformed faces has been shown to evoke strong autonomic responses (Aamot, 1978).

Negative responses to unattractive persons also may reflect the violation of unconscious psychological needs. Just as racial discrimination or sexism can serve an ego-defensive function, rejection of the unattractive may be a way of protecting self-esteem. Research on the belief in a just world suggests another possible motivational mechanism. People have a fundamental need to believe that people receive what they deserve (Lerner, 1980). An unattractive person threatens this need and the observer attributes moral failure to the unattractive person as a means of coping with the subsequent anxiety. In support of this view, Dion and Dion (1987) found that those who have a strong belief in a just world showed more pronounced differences in the attribution of socially desirable personality characteristics to attractive and unattractive others than those with a lower belief in a just world.

Social and Organizational Factors in Attractiveness Bias

The discussion of the cognitive and affective approaches would suggest that bias against unattractive individuals is a reflection of the privately held beliefs and feelings of the perceiver. However, bias against unattractive individuals in organizations may reflect compliance to social norms rather than an expression of personal beliefs or feelings (Berman, O'Nan, & Floyd, 1981). The type that seems most relevant is the "identity norm," which Goffman (1963) described as images of "ideal persons, consisting of shared beliefs as to what persons should be." The ideal in the United States, according to Goffman, is "young, married, white, urban, northern, heterosexual Protestant father of college education, fully employed, of good complexion, weight, and height, and a recent record in sports" (p. 128). Also possibly indicative of the influence of normative influences is evidence that participants of individualistic cultures are more likely to stereotype on the basis of attractiveness than are participants of communal cultures (Dion, Pak & Dion, 1990).

As is the case with any norm, appearance norms serve both an informational function in helping persons to predict, control, and understand the behavior of others well as a social function in maintaining harmony among group members and aiding in the achievement of goals (Deutsch & Gerard, 1955). Moreover, norms for appearance are seen as emerging from interactions of organizational members as they attempt to understand, control, and predict organizational events (Ashforth, 1985). Kanter (1977) commented on similar functions of appearance norms in *Men and Women of the Corporation*, when she observed that "Managers at Indsco had to look the part. . . . . The norms were unmistakable, after a visitor saw enough managers, invariably white and male, with a certain shiny, clean-cut look. . . . . An inappropriate appearance could be grounds for complaint to higher management (p. 55)." Moreover, Kanter saw pressures to comply with appearance norms as an attempt to reduce uncertainty. Essentially, people who are like "us" can be better trusted than those who look different. Kanter further proposes that people who do not "fit in" are clustered in those parts of management with the least uncertainty. "They are in places where what to do and how to judge its doing tend to be more routine. They are found in increasing numbers away from the top, and they are found in staff positions where they serve as technical specialists" (p. 55).

The dominant culture in an organization uses appearance along with other cultural artifacts, such as dress, to express core values that are to be shared by organizational members. For example, Martin and Siehl (1983) described an implicit dress code in GM in the 1960s that appeared to express the core values of respecting authority, fitting in, and being loyal. As the dominant culture exerts pressure for conformity on organizational members, the organization can become increasingly homogeneous. Schneider (1987) suggests in his attraction–selection–attrition model that this homogenization of the organization occurs as the consequence of recruiting, selection, and socialization practices. Applicants are attracted to those organizations that appear to fit their values, and the organization, in turn, screens out those whose values do not appear to fit the culture. Those who do not fit are more likely to leave. Physical looks can enter into the process by serving as a signal to prospective employees of what the organization is like. In turn, recruiters and other gatekeepers prefer applicants who "look the part" over those with less desirable appearances. As present employees see fewer exceptions to the norm, the modal value becomes an ideal that further discourages the recruiting of nontraditional applicants.

Attractiveness Bias as a Behavioral Effect

In examining attractiveness biases, the most frequent approach has been to use passive-observer procedures where the judge watches and evaluates with no opportunity to interact with the ratee. One might expect that when the perceiver and the perceived can interact, this would provide an opportunity for the perceiver to overcome his or her biases. This would suggest that attractiveness biases are attenuated in situations in which there is interaction and an opportunity to become familiar with the target person (Jones et al., 1984). However, it is also possible that interaction can perpetuate or even magnify these biases as the result of self-fulfilling prophecies (Snyder, Tanke, & Berscheid, 1977). Prior expectations for how persons of different appearance will behave can shape how these persons are treated and differences in treatment can evoke responses that fulfill the original expectations. Clearly, future research needs to examine the effects of attractiveness on sexual harassment, supervision, mentoring, feedback, goal setting, and other varieties of treatment in the workplace. Except for one study examining the relationship of attractiveness to sexual harassment (Ellis, Barak, & Pinto, 1991), these behavioral manifestations of attractiveness bias have been ignored. Just as the perceiver's expectations can influence treatment of the target, the expectations of the target can influence how that individual acts with regard to the perceiver. A person who expects to be discriminated against acts in a way that fulfills this expectation. Thus, future research also needs to examine the behavior of the target person and its role in perpetuating and reversing attractiveness biases.

IMPLICATIONS FOR CHANGE

The cognitive, affective, behavioral, and social antecedents each suggest an intervention to eliminate appearance bias. To the extent that these biases are based on cognitive conceptions, then it may be sufficient to individuate the target person by providing specific information. Consistent with this possibility, Eagly et al. (1991) found that the strength of the attractiveness stereotype was weakened when specific data were provided on the characteristics and qualifications of the person. Similarly, Watkins and Johnston (2000) found that bias against unattractive applicants was most pronounced when the applicants had mediocre qualifications but not when they had clear high qualifications. Another suggestion is to change the cognitive structures of the rater or judge. Along these lines, Bartunek, Gordon, and Weathersby (1983) propose strategies for developing "complicated" understanding in administrators that include requiring that they take the role of others, surfacing and challenging their assumptions, and requiring them to work on ill-structured problems. Similarly, Wagner and Schonbach (1984) hypothesized that cognitive complexity is a mediator of the decrease in stereotyping of outgroups that commonly results from increases in education.

To the extent that the bias against unattractive persons reflects social pressures, elimination of this bias requires interventions to change the norms and the culture of the group and organization. The first step is to make organizational members aware of the core values of the organization and to decouple appearance norms from these values. Organizational members need to be shown how persons who differ in marked ways can still share the values that really count. Changing norms also may mean changing dress and appearance codes and modifying or eliminating appearance ratings in selection interviews and performance appraisals.

The existence of behavioral biases suggests that training is needed to impart social skills in interacting with persons of different appearance. Training of this nature could include not only those who are the perpetrators of the discrimination but also those who are the targets. Both those who are the perpetrators and the victims can be instructed in how deal with the "awkward moments" that can occur in interactions with persons of different appearance and how to put others at ease in interactions (Hebl, Tickle, & Heatherton, 2000). These awkward moments constitute behavioral episodes that are crucial in shaping a relationship. Identifying and attempting to impart specific behavioral strategies have considerable potential in helping to lessen appearance biases.

If affective responses are an element of the bias against unattractive persons, then interventions to eliminate this bias may require efforts to reduce the anxiety and other negative emotion associated with appearance. Along these lines, desensitization therapy has been used to reduce racial bias by having persons visualize increasingly threatening racial situations while undergoing relaxation (Sappington, 1976). Although it is doubtful that organizations will (or should) submit employees to psychotherapy to eliminate appearance bias, the irrational, even unconscious, emotions that can motivate these biases need to be acknowledged. A more likely intervention is to increase self-awareness of the bias and provide insight into the underlying dynamics.

As part of the efforts to make employees more open to diversity, workshops and seminars on the topic should attempt to increase awareness of attractiveness bias and its effect on judgments and behavior. Such efforts may not succeed, however, unless there are also changes in personnel policies and procedures. In particular, appearance should be deemphasized as a factor in selection and appraisal systems except for those aspects of appearance that are clearly shown to be related to performance of the job. Explicit appearance ratings are frequently used in the evaluation of applicants and employees, but can serve as a surrogate for all sorts of biases. If appearance is shown to be job-related, then behaviorally specific scales should be developed to conduct appearance ratings. A careful study is likely to reveal that some appearance standards are justifiable, such as a prohibition against beards for employees who must wear safety masks. In other cases, appearance standards are unrelated to success in the job, such as might be the case with weight requirements for a clerical worker. Some standards may be harder to call, particularly those based on customer preferences. For instance, if we find physical attractiveness to be related to success in sales, should we then use this in the selection and appraisal of salespeople? While attractiveness may seem necessary in a service-oriented, customer driven market, achieving diversity may require educating customers rather than simply accepting their values as givens.

In summary, eliminating bias against unattractive persons is likely to involve more than educating employees, but will often require changing the norms of the organization, modifying behavioral patterns that perpetuate the bias, and helping people deal with the strong feelings evoked by stigmas. These efforts will not be easy. As stated in the discussion of antecedents, appearance bias frequently emerges as an effortless response that is unconscious and uncontrolled.

CONCLUSIONS

Both access and treatment bias have been found against persons who violate norms for physical attractiveness. Although the effects are typically small, I believe that these effects are more important than indicated in the effect sizes (Stone et al., 1992). Although appearance standards are sometimes needed, the standards used in many organizations appear unduly restrictive and serve to encourage unfair discrimination against groups such as racial minorities, people who are disabled, and older employees. Perhaps Thomas (1992) best expressed what needs to be done when he stated that "Diversity does not mean that anything goes or that no assimilation will be required; instead, it calls for assimilation only where absolutely necessary... The trick becomes that of identifying requirements as opposed to preferences, conveniences, or traditions" (p. 310). We suspect that many physical appearance standards are mere "preferences, conveniences, and traditions," that can be eliminated at little cost to performance.

REFERENCES

Aamot, S. (1978). Reactions to facial deformities: Autonomic and social psychological. *European Journal of Social Psychology, 8*, 315–333.

Abelson, R. (1985). A variance explanation paradox: When a little is a lot. *Psychological Bulletin, 97*, 129–133.

Anonymous. (1987). Facial discrimination: Extending handicap law to employment discrimination on the basis of physical appearance. *Harvard Law Review, 100*, 2035–2053.

Ashforth, B. E. (1985). Climate formation: Issues and extensions. *Academy of Management Review, 10*, 837–847.

Bartunek, J. M., Gordon, J. R., & Weathersby, R. P. (1983). Developing "complicated" understanding in administrators. *Academy of Management Review, 8*, 273–284.

Benson, P. L., Severs, D., Tagenhorst, J., & Loddengaard, N. (1980). The social costs of obesity: A non-reactive field study. *Social Behavior and Personality, 8*, 91–96.

Bentz, B. J. (1985). Research findings from personality assessment of executives. In H. J. Bernardin & D. A. Bownas (Eds.), *Personality assessment in organizations* (pp. 82–145). New York: Praeger.

Berman, P. W., O'Nan, B. A., & Floyd, W. (1981). The double standard of aging and the social situation: Judgments of attractiveness of the middle-aged woman. *Sex Roles, 7*, 87–96.

Bernstein, I. H., Lin, T. D., & McClellan, P. (1981). Cross- vs. within-racial judgments of attractiveness. *Perception and Psychophysics, 32*, 495–503.

Berry, D. S., & McArthur, L. Z. (1985). Some components and consequences of a babyface. *Journal of Personality and Social Psychology, 48*, 312–324.

Berry, D. S., & McArthur, L. Z. (1986). Perceiving character in faces: The impact of age-related craniofacial changes on social perception. *Psychological Bulletin, 100*, 3–18.

Bieber, L., & Dipboye, R. L. (April, 1988). *Biases in evaluating managerial job applicants: the effects of gender and physical attractiveness.* Paper presented at the meeting of the Society of Industrial and Organizational Psychology, Dallas, TX.

Bull, R., & Rumsey, N. (1988). *The social psychology of facial appearance.* London: Springer-Verlag.

Carlson, R. (1967). Evaluating interview and employment application data. *Personnel Psychology, 20*, 441–460.

Carroll, S. J., Jr. (1966). Relationship of various college graduate characteristics to recruiting decisions. *Journal of Applied Psychology, 50*, 421–423.

Cash, T. F., Gillen, B., & Burns, D. S. (1977). Sexism and 'beautyism' in personnel consultant decision making. *Journal of Applied Psychology, 62*, 301–310.

Cash, T. F., & Kilcullen, H. L. (1985). The eye of the beholder: Susceptibility to sexism and beautyism in evaluation of managerial applicants. *Journal of Applied Social Psychology, 15*, 591–605.

Cox, T. H. (1991). The multicultural organization. *Academy of Management Executive, 5*, 34–47.

Cox, T. H., & Blake, S. (1991). Managing cultural diversity: implications for organizational competitiveness. *Academy of Management Executive, 5*, 45–56.

Cross, J. F., & Cross, J. (1971). Age, sex, race, and the perception of facial beauty. *Developmental Psychology, 5*, 433–439.

Cunningham, M. R. (1986). Measuring the physical in physical attractiveness: Quasi-experiments on the sociobiology of female facial beauty. *Journal of Personality and Social Psychology, 50*, 925–935.

DeJong, W., & Kleck, R. E. (1986). The social psychological effects of overweight. In C. P. Herman, M. P. Zanna, & E. T. Higgins (Eds.), *Physical appearance, stigma, and social behavior* (pp. 65–87). Hillsdale, NJ: Lawrence Erlbaum Associates.

Deutsch, M., & Gerard, H. B. (1955). A study of normative and informational social influences upon individual judgment. *Journal of Abnormal and Social Psychology, 51*, 629–636.

Deutsch, F. M., Zalenski, C. M., & Clark, M. E. (1986). Is there a double standard of aging? *Journal of Applied Social Psychology, 16*, 771–785.

Dew, M. A. (1985). The effect of attitudes on inferences of homosexuality and perceived attractiveness in women. *Sex Roles, 12*, 143–155.

Dickey-Bryant, L., Lautenschlager, G. J., & Mendoza, J. L., & Abrahams, N. (1986). Facial attractiveness and its relation to occupational success. *Journal of Applied Psychology, 71*, 16–19.

Dion, K. L., & Dion, K. K. (1987). Belief in a just world and physical attractiveness stereotyping. *Journal of Personality and Social Psychology, 52*, 775–780.

Dion, K. K., Pak, A. W., & Dion, K. L. (1990). Stereotyping physical attractiveness. *Journal of Cross-Cultural Psychology, 21*, 158–179.

Dunkie, J. H., & Francis, P. L. (1990). The role of facial masculinity/femininity in the attribution of homosexuality. *Sex Roles, 23*, 157–167.

Eagly, A., Ashmore, R. D., Makhijani, M. G., & Longo, L. C. (1991). What is beautiful is good, but....: A meta-analytic review of research on the physical attractiveness stereotype. *Psychological Bulletin, 110,* 109–128.

Ellis, S., Barak, A., & Pinto, A. (1991). Moderating effects of personal cognitions on experienced and perceived sexual harassment of women at the workplace. *Journal of Applied Social Psychology, 21,* 1320–1337.

Fiske, S. T., & Cox, M. G. (1979). Person concepts: The effect of target familiarity and descriptive purpose on the process of describing others. *Journal of Personality, 47,* 136–161.

Fontenelle, G. A., Peek-Phillips, A., & Lane, D. M. (1985). Generalizing across stimuli as well as subjects. A neglected aspect of external validity. *Journal of Applied Psychology, 70,* 101–107.

Frieze, I. H., Olson, J. E., & Good, D. C. (1990). Perceived and actual discrimination in the salaries of male and female managers. *Journal of Applied Social Psychology, 20,* 46–67.

Frieze, I. H., Olson, J. E., & Russell, J. (1991). Attractiveness and income for men and women in management. *Journal of Applied Social Psychology, 21,* 1039–1057.

Giancoli, D. L., & Neimeyer, G. J. (1983). Liking preferences toward handicapped persons. *Perceptual and Motor Skills, 57,* 1005–1006.

Goffman, E. (1963). *Stigma: Notes on the management of spoiled identity.* Englewood Cliffs, NJ: Prentice-Hall.

Goldman, W., & Lewis, P. (1977). Beautiful is good: Evidence that the physically attractive are more socially skillful. *Journal of Experimental Social Psychology, 13,* 125–130.

Greenwald, M. (1981). The effects of physical attractiveness, experience, and social performance on employee decision making in job interviews. *Behavioral Counseling Quarterly, 1,* 275–287.

Guion, R. M., & Gibson, W. M. (1988). Personnel selection and placement. In M. R. Rosenzweig, & L. W. Porter (Eds.), *Annual Review of Psychology, 62,* 199–202.

Hatfield, E., & Sprecher, S. (1986). *Mirror, mirror....* New York: State University of New York Press.

Hebl, M. R., Tickle, J., & Heatherton, T. F. (2000). Awkward moments in interactions between nonstigmatized and stigmatized individuals. In T. F. Heatherton, Robert F. Kleck, M. R. Hebl, & J. G. Hull (Eds.), *The social psychology of stigma* (pp. 275–306). New York: Guilford.

Heilman, M. E. (1983). Sex bias in work settings: The lack of fit model. In B. M. Staw & L. L. Cummings (Eds.), *Research in organizational behavior* (Vol. 5). Greenwich, CT: JAI.

Heilman, M. E., & Saruwatari, L. R. (1979). When beauty is beastly: The effects of appearance and sex on evaluations of job applicants for managerial and nonmanagerial jobs. *Organizational Behavior and Human Performance, 23,* 360–372.

Heilman, M. E., & Stopeck, M. H. (1985a). Being attractive, advantage or disadvantage? Performance based evaluations and recommended personnel actions as a function of appearance, sex, and job type. *Organizational Behavior and Human Performance, 35,* 202–215.

Heilman, M. E., & Stopeck, M. H. (1985b). Attractiveness and corporate success: Different causal attributions for males and females. *Journal of Applied Psychology, 70,* 379–388.

Hernandez, O. A. (1981). *A cross-cultural comparison of adults' perceptions of infant sex and physical attractiveness.* Unpublished doctoral dissertation, Michigan State University, East Lansing, MI.

Hill, M. C. (1994). Social status and physical appearance among Negro adolescents. *Social Forces, 22,* 443–448.

Hosoda, M., Stone-Romero, E. F., & Coats, G. (2003). The effects of physical attractiveness on job-related outcomes: A meta-analysis of experimental studies. *Personnel Psychology, 56,* 431–462.

Hosoda, M., Stone-Romero, E. F., & Stone, D. L. (2003). The effects of co-worker race and task demand on task-related outcomes as mediated by evoked affect.*Journal of Applied Social Psychology, 33*, 145–178.

Jackson, L. A. (1983a). The influence of sex, physical attractiveness, sex role, and occupational sex-linkage on perceptions of occupational suitability. *Journal of Applied Social Psychology, 13*, 31–44.

Jackson, L. A. (1983b). Gender, physical attractiveness, and sex role in occupational treatment discrimination: The influence of trait and role assumptions. *Journal of Applied Social Psychology, 13*, 443–458.

Jackson, L. A. (1992). *Physical Appearance and Gender: Sociobiological and Sociocultural Perspectives.* Albany: State University of New York Press.

Jones, E. E., Farina, A., Hastorf, A. H., Markus, H., Miller, D., T., Scott, R. A., & de Sales-French, R. (1984). *Social stigma: The psychology of marked relationships.* San Francisco: Freeman.

Joyner, T. (2002, January 18). A divided workplace. *The Atlanta Journal—Constitution,* p. C.1.

Kalick, S. M. (1988). Physical attractiveness as a status cue. *Journal of Experimental Social Psychology, 24*, 469–489.

Kanter, R. M. (1977). *Men and women of the corporation.* New York: Basic Books.

Kinicki, A. J., & Lockwood, C. A. (1985). The interview process: An examination of factors recruiters use in evaluating job applicants. *Journal of Vocational Behavior, 26*, 116–125.

Langlois, J. H., Kalakanis, L., Rubenstein, A. J., Larson, A., Hallam, M., & Smoot, M. (2000). Maximx or myths of beauty? A meta-analytic and theoretical review. *Psychological Bulletin, 126*, 390–423.

Langlois, J. H., & Stephan, C. W. (1977). The effects of physical attractiveness and ethnicity on children's behavioral attributions and peer preferences. *Child Development, 4*, 1694–1698.

Langlois, J. H., Roggman, L. A., Casey, R. J., & Ritter, J. M. (1987). Infant preferences for attractive faces: Rudiments of a stereotype. *Developmental Psychology, 23*, 363–369.

Langlois, J. H., Ritter, J. M., Roggman, L. A., & Vaughn, L. S. (1991). Facial diversity and infant preferences for attractive faces. *Developmental Psychology, 27*, 79–84.

Larsen, R. J., Diener, E., & Cropanzano, R. S. (1987). Cognitive operations associated with individual differences in affect intensity. *Journal of Personality and Social Psychology, 53*, 767–774.

Lerner, M. (1980). *The belief in a just world.* New York: Plenum.

Maccarone, D. (Jan/Feb, 2003). Affirmative action for the attractive? *Psychology Today, 36*, 18.

Maddox, G. L., Back, K. W., & Linderman, V. R. (1968). Overweight as social deviance and disability. *Journal of Health and Social Behavior, 9*, 298.

Mapes-Riordan, L. D. (1991). Sex discrimination and employer weight and appearance standards. *Employee Relations Law Journal, 16*, 493–505.

Martell, R. F., Lane, D. M., & Willis, C. E. (1992). *Demonstrating the danger of using "variance explained" to assess the practical significance of research findings: A little sex bias can hurt women a lot.* Unpublished manuscript, Rice University.

Martin, J. G. (1964). Racial ethnocentrism and judgment of beauty. *Journal of Social Psychology, 63*, 59–63.

Martin, J., & Siehl, C. (1983). Organizational culture and counterculture: An uneasy symbiosis. *Organizational Dynamics, 12*, 52–64.

Matusewitch, E. (1989). Tailor your dress codes. *Personnel Journal, 68*, 86–91.

McArthur, L. Z. (1982). Judging a book by its cover: A cognitive analysis of the relationship between physical appearance and stereotyping. In A. Hastorf & A. Isen (Eds.), *Cognitive social psychology.* New York: Elsevier-North Holland.

Miller, C. T. (1988). Categorization and the physical attractiveness stereotype. *Social Cognition, 6*, 231–251.

Morrow, P. C. (1990). Physical attractiveness and selection decision making. *Journal of Management, 16,* 45–60.

Nykodym, P. C., & Simonetti, J. L. (1987). Personal appearance: Is attractiveness a factor in organizational survival and success? *Journal of Employment Counseling, 24,* 69–78.

O'Connell, A. N., & Rotter, N. G. (1979). The influence of stimulus age and sex on person perception. *Journal of Gerontology, 34,* 220–228.

Podratz, K., & Dipboye, R. L. (April 2002). *In search of the 'beauty is beastly' effect.* A poster session presented at the 17th Annual Conference of the Society for Industrial and Organizational Psychology, Toronto, Ontario, Canada.

Qunin, R. P. (1978). Psysical deviance and occupational mistreatment: The short, the fat, and the ugly. Unpublished master's thesis. Ann Arbor: University of Michigan, Survey Research Center.

Raines, R. S., Hechtman, S. B., & Rosenthal, R. (1990). Nonverbal behavior and gender as determinants of physical attractiveness. *Journal of Nonverbal Behavior, 14,* 253–267.

Raza, S. M., & Carpenter, B. N. (1987). A model of hiring decisions in real employment interviews. *Journal of Applied Psychology, 72,* 596–603.

Reingen, P. H., Gresham, L. G., & Kernan, J. B. (1980). Behavioral consequences of the physical attractiveness stereotype in personal selling. In R. P. Bagozzi, K. L. Bernhardt, P. S. Busch, D. W. Cravens, J. Fittair, & C. A. Scott (Eds.), *Marketing in the 80's* (pp. 109–113). Chicago: American Marketing Association.

Richardson, D. S., Goodman, N., Hastorf, A. H., & Dornbusch, S. M. (1961). Cultural uniformity in reaction to physical disabilities. *American Sociological Review, 26,* 241–247.

Rosenthal, R. (1990). How are we doing in soft psychology? *American Psychologist, 45,* 775–777.

Ross, J., & Ferris, K. R. (1981). Interpersonal attraction and organizational outcomes: A field examination. *Administrative Science Quarterly, 26,* 617–632.

Roszell, P., Kennedy, D., & Grabb, E. (1989). Physical attractiveness and attainment among Canadians. *Journal of Psychology, 123,* 547–559.

Rynes, S., & Gerhart, B. (1990). Interviewer assessments of applicant 'fit': An exploratory investigation. *Personnel Psychology, 43,* 13–35.

Sappington, A. A. (1976). Effects of desensitization of prejudiced Whites to Blacks upon subjects' stereotypes of Blacks. *Perceptual and Motor Skills, 43,* 938.

Schneider, B. (1987). The people make the place. *Personnel Psychology, 40,* 437–453.

Snyder, M. E., Tanke, D., & Berscheid, E. (1977). Social perception and interpersonal behavior: On the self-fulfilling nature of social stereotypes. *Journal of Personality and Social Psychology, 35,* 656–666.

Springbett, B. (1958). Factors affecting the final decision in the employment interview. *Canadian Journal of Psychology, 12,* 13–22.

Stone, E. F., Stone, D. L., & Dipboye, R. L. (1992). Stigmas in organizations: Race, handicaps, and physical attractiveness. In K. Kelley (Ed.), *Issues, theory, and research in industrial/organizational psychology* (pp. 385–457). Amsterdam, Netherlands: Elsevier.

Thomas, R. Roosevelt, Jr. (1992). Managing diversity: A conceptual framework. In S. E. Jackson & Associates (Eds.), *Diversity in the workplace: Human resources initiatives* (pp. 306–317). New York: Guilford.

Umberson, D., & Hughes, M. (1987). The impact of physical attractiveness on achievement and psychological well-being. *Social Psychology Quarterly, 50,* 227–236.

Unger, R. K., Hildebrand, M., & Madar, T. (1982). Physical attractiveness and assumptions about social deviance: Some sex-by-sex comparisons. *Personality and Social Psychology Bulletin, 8,* 293–301.

Wagner, V., & Schonbach, P. (1984). Links between educational status and prejudice: Ethnic attitudes in West Germany. In N. Miller & M. B. Brewer (Eds.), *Groups in contact: The Psychology of desegregation* (pp. 11–27). Orlando, FL: Academic Press, Inc.

Watkins, L. M., & Johnston, L. (2000). Screening job applicants: The impact of physical attractiveness and application quality. *International Journal of Selection and Assessment, 8,* 76–84.

Webster , M. Jr., & Driskel, J. E., Jr. (1983). Beauty as status. *American Journal of Sociology, 89,* 140–165.

Zajonc, R. B. (1980). Feeling and thinking: Preferences need no inferences. *American Psychologist, 35,* 151–175.

Zajonc, R. B. (1984). On the primacy of affect. *American Psychologist, 39,* 117–123.

Zuckerman, M., Hodgins, H., & Miyako, K. (1990). The vocal attractiveness stereotype: Replication and elaboration. *Journal of Nonverbal Behavior, 14,* 97–112.

III

Implications for Practice, Policy, and the Law

13

Achieving Diversity and Reducing Discrimination in the Workplace Through Human Resource Management Practices: Implications of Research and Theory for Staffing, Training, and Rewarding Performance

Winfred Arthur, Jr.
Texas A&M University

Dennis Doverspike
University of Akron

INTRODUCTION

Can human resource (HR) practices be used to reduce discrimination and achieve diversity in organizations? In addressing this issue, we acknowledge that discrimination and diversity are distinct concepts. Thus, achieving diversity does not necessarily involve reductions in discriminatory behavior, and the elimination of discrimination does not necessarily ensure diversity. Still, in the context of this distinction, one could view discrimination as one barrier to diversity such that its reduction and elimination can be considered as one means of increasing diversity. In this chapter, we explore the implications of research and theory on common HR practices as they relate to the topics of reducing discrimination and increasing diversity in organizations. In order to do this, we have identified two major approaches by which organizations can change their practices in order to reduce discrimination and increase diversity.

First, as discussed in previous chapters in this volume, HR practices can result in adverse impact for underrepresented groups (e.g., women and racial minorities). In some cases, this adverse impact can be fairly substantial. Consequently, the question arises as to whether HR practices can be altered or improved in ways that lead to reductions in adverse impact and, subsequently, to increases in the representation of members of affected groups in organizations. However within this context, we also recognize that adverse impact does not necessarily reflect the presence of unfair discrimination.

The second issue pertains to altering the behavior of majority group employees in the workforce to reduce discriminatory behavior and increase diversity and multiculturalism. Thus, for instance, one might consider the possibility of selecting employees who are less likely to show discrimination in the workplace. Relatedly, one could also consider interventions such as diversity training or changes in compensation systems in an effort to alter the behavior of majority group members. Regardless of the approach or perspective, the fundamental question is whether HR practices can be used to alter the potentially discriminatory behaviors of majority group members in ways that are practical, legal, and ethical. Although not a major focus of the present chapter, one could also consider interventions aimed at changing the behavior of the minority group members. For instance, one could provide interviewing training, career coaching, test preparation courses, realistic job previews, and training in how to cope with discrimination with these interventions targeted at specified groups such as women, racial minorities, and older workers.

HR practices can include a wide variety of initiatives or programs. We have chosen to focus on three traditional areas of HR practice—staffing, human resource development, and performance management. Although we present each of these practice areas as separate topics, in reality they are best conceptualized as interrelated parts of a system. Thus, changes in one part of the system will have implications for other parts of the system.

Discrimination can be directed toward a wide range of target groups. With regard to our choice of terminology in this chapter, we use the term "minority" to refer to any target or underrepresented group. Thus, the term is used in a very broad sense to refer to any group that might be victimized by discrimination. However, most of the research discussed in this chapter deals with minority groups defined in terms of race, sex, or age.

STAFFING

Staffing refers to a set of activities that are used to accomplish the ultimate goal of filling positions in the organization and includes both recruitment and selection. Although there are broader definitions of recruitment (e.g., Doverspike, Taylor, Shultz, & McKay, 2000), we use a narrower definition of *recruitment* that refers to the initial stages of generating and attracting applicants and also the initial exchange of information between the applicant and the organization. *Selection*, on the other hand, refers to the set of practices and activities that are deployed after the recruitment process, resulting in the final decision to hire or reject the applicant.

Recruitment

Reducing the Negative Effects of Recruitment An emphasis on diversity in recruitment is obviously critical to achieving adequate minority representation. If there are insufficient numbers of qualified minority applicants in the recruited pool, then it is highly unlikely that subsequent selection procedures will result in a balanced or representative workforce. Thus, targeted minority recruitment can be an effective strategy for diversity enhancement because it allows organizations to attract the most talented applicants.

In this section, we will discuss methods that can be used to increase the representation of racial minorities, women, and older workers in the applicant pool. We will first discuss general principles that apply across groups and will then discuss some group-specific issues. Researchers have outlined three major issues in the attraction and recruitment of potential minority employees (Doverspike, Taylor, Shultz et al., 2000). They are (a) using proper communication media and messages, (b) increasing job seekers' perceived fit between themselves and the job or organization, and (c) maintaining the job seekers' motivation to apply and remain during the selection process.

The first step in attracting sufficient numbers of minorities involves the placement, nature, and content of advertising materials and other organizational communications (AARP, 1993; Doverspike, Taylor, Shultz et al., 2000). However, the messages and media that work with White males may not be equally effective with members of minority groups and can only be successful if they reach the minority audience. When faced with potentially small numbers of minority applicants, organizations should engage in cooperative efforts with educational institutions and training centers in order to develop their own pool of potential applicants. This includes sponsoring special classes, mentoring programs, or apprenticeship programs in order to develop a skilled pool of applicants.

The advertising message should create a sincere impression that minorities are valued by the organization. Using minority images as part of the recruitment package may help in building an organization's reputation as having a minority-friendly workplace. Studies suggest that recruitment advertisements that include minority workers (e.g., African American, female) create positive organizational images among minorities (Avery, 2003; Perkins, Thomas, & Taylor, 2000). Also, using minority recruiters tends to increase the interest of minority applicants (Thomas & Wise, 1999). The presence of successful minority employees sends a signal to applicants that the organization is committed to diversifying its workforce, that potential role models exist within the organization, and that minorities have a strong likelihood of success.

Individuals are likely to apply to an organization if it is viewed as socially responsible (Turban & Greening, 1997). However, the effects of advertising an affirmative action policy on the recruitment of minorities are less clear and given that one of the main goals of any affirmative action program is to increase the recruitment of minorities, it is somewhat surprising that relatively little research attention has been directed toward the question of the effects of affirmative action policies on the attraction of applicants to an organization (Doverspike, Taylor, & Arthur, 2000). In order to successfully recruit applicants, affirmative action procedures must be perceived as both fair and emphasizing merit. Thus, communications regarding affirmative action should emphasize that affirmative action is a means for decreasing discriminatory barriers (Slaughter, Sinar, & Bachiochi, 2002; Stanush, Arthur, & Doverspike, 1998). Minorities are more likely to respond in a positive manner to an affirmative action program in which the emphasis is on creating a climate of achievement in which all individuals can compete fairly.

Once the organization has attracted the applicant and demonstrated the potential match between the applicant and the organization, it must then maintain the motivation and interest of the applicant during the initial exchanges of information and throughout a sometimes lengthy selection process. Because applicants use information about and from the selection process to make inferences about organizational attributes (Rynes, 1991), it is important to communicate to applicants that minorities are valued by the organization and that the selection procedures are fair and reflect merit. Furthermore, specific characteristics of the selection procedure such as time lags between selection procedures (Arvey, Gordon, Massengill, &

Mussio, 1975), perceived content validity (Rynes & Connerley, 1993), and perceived job-relatedness (Smither, Reilly, Millsap, Pearlman, & Stoffey, 1993) may influence minority applicants' decisions to remain or withdraw from the selection process.

In spite of higher unemployment rates for racial minorities, attempts to target recruitment toward racial minorities have produced mixed results. The research literature suggests that the recruitment of racial minorities is affected by several perceptual factors including reactions to advertising, affirmative action policies, and the fairness of selection methods and processes (e.g., Ryan, Sacco, McFarland, & Kriska, 2000; Rynes & Connerley, 1993; Smither et al., 1993). Women applicants tend to be attracted to family-friendly organizations that emphasize the availability of benefits such as flexible work arrangements, eldercare (Poe, 1989), and childcare (Van den Bergh, 1991). Also, women job seekers tend to respond more favorably to equal employment opportunity policies than do men (Doverspike & Arthur, 1995; Doverspike, Taylor, & Arthur, 2000). Finally, the job search behavior of older workers is often shaped by their health, finances, and education. In addition to health care provisions and salary, the older worker is particularly likely to be influenced by flexibility in work options and the availability of retirement programs (Sterns & Miklos, 1995).

Altering the Behavior of Majority Group Employees Through Recruitment In theory, if one could identify the characteristics associated with prodiversity attitudes or orientations in majority group employees, organizations could then attempt to target individuals with such characteristics in their recruitment efforts. This approach does not change the behavior of specific individuals but instead, the process of recruitment attracts people who are already open, tolerant, and/or nonprejudiced with the end result that at the organizational level, there is a preponderance of individuals with prodiversity attitudes or orientations. So this approach requires that one accurately identify such individuals and then develop methods for targeting recruitment toward them. Although in theory such targeted recruitment might work, through for example, the identification of colleges or universities with uniquely cosmopolitan (Doverspike, Arthur, Struchul, & Taylor, 2000) populations of students, it would seem that such an effort would have to be based more on art than on any specific scientific basis because the scientific evidence to support this approach is lacking.

Selection

Reducing the Negative Effects of Traditional Tests and Selection Devices As previously noted, although the selection process can be separated from recruitment, in reality, the two are intertwined. However, from an HR perspective, the process of selection begins once the applicant is successfully attracted to the organization, that is, they submit an application or otherwise formally indicate an interest or desire to seek employment with the organization. Next, some evaluative tool, usually a test (defined here to include any assessment tool used in selection-related decision making) is used to assist in selecting individuals from the pool of applicants. In the testing and personnel selection literature, cognitively loaded paper-and-pencil tests of knowledge, skill, and ability have been shown to be the most valid predictors of job performance (Schmidt & Hunter, 1998). However, it has also been extensively documented that paper-and-pencil tests of cognitive ability generally display large racial subgroup differences with a widely cited one standard deviation difference in African American/White performance. What remains unclear is whether the observed differences are due to the construct being assessed (cognitive ability) or the method of testing (multiple-choice paper-and-pencil tests; Arthur, Day, McNelly, & Edens, 2003; Arthur, Edwards, & Barrett, 2002; Hough, Oswald & Ployhart, 2001; Schmitt, Clause, & Pulakos, 1996).

In addition, some aptitude tests, such as those of mechanical aptitude, may result in substantial adverse impact as a function of sex. Paper-and-pencil tests may also result in adverse impact toward older test takers. The end result is that cognitively loaded paper-and-pencil tests of knowledge, skill, ability, and aptitude, supposedly neutral devices, may in fact represent a substantial barrier to the adequate representation of minorities in organizations. This has resulted in a search for ways of reducing the adverse impact associated with many traditional tests used in high-stakes testing.

Since the ban on subgroup norming and other adjustments to test scores on the basis of protected class status (Civil Rights Act, 1991), attempts to reduce adverse impact have focused on a number of approaches including (a) identifying and removing internal bias; (b) increasing test taking motivation; (c) altering the selection criteria (weighting of tests, random selection, race-based selection, banding); (d) changing the construct (the use of nonability-based constructs including personality variables, information processing skills and abilities, emotional intelligence, tacit knowledge); and (e) changing the method or using alternative test formats (in an attempt to alter test perceptions and attitudes and reduce nonjob-related reading demands).

Identifying and Removing Internal Bias   Identifying and removing internal bias from selection tests is predicated on the frequent critique that ability tests are culturally biased. For about the past 40 years, psychologists have been trying to identify and eliminate biased items in an attempt to improve tests. The techniques employed were at one time referred to as "internal item bias analysis methods." However, because of the tendency of the public to associate bias with discrimination, such techniques are now often referred to as methods for estimating measurement equivalence or "differential item functioning (DIF)." Common methods (Crocker & Algina, 1986; Raju, Laffitte, & Byrne, 2002) for investigating DIF include (a) differences in means after controlling for the total score (the ANOVA technique), (b) differences in item-total correlations, (c) differences in item characteristic curves as identified through item response theory, (d) differences in the proportion of correct responses after controlling for the total score (chi-square methods including the Mantel–Haenszel technique), and (e) differences in factor structures as identified through exploratory or confirmatory factor analysis. To date, there have been a number of problems with the application of internal bias analysis techniques. First, the use of different methods may not always lead to the identification of the same items as biased. Second, it is often difficult to determine why a particular item is identified as biased. Third, given the limited number of items identified as biased on current tests, the removal of biased items has only a small effect, if any, on subgroup differences.

Test Taking Motivation   The focus on test taking motivation is based on the premise that minorities' less favorable test perceptions such as perceived unfairness, perceived low face validity, perceived low job relatedness, test anxiety, and stereotype threat (Arvey, Strickland, Drauden, & Martin, 1990; Chan & Schmitt, 1997; Chan, Schmitt, DeShon, Clause, & Delbridge, 1997; Edwards & Arthur, 2004; Hough et al., 2001; McKay & Doverspike, 2001; Ryan, 2001; Steele, 1997) translates into lower motivation, which subsequently partially accounts for the observed subgroup differences. Research such as that cited above tends to support the view that differences in test-taking motivation can lead to test score differences. Although the amount of variance explained is typically small, these differences can translate into important consequences, especially when the selection ratios are very low.

The possibility that differences in test-taking motivation explains minority–majority test score differences leads to the practical possibility that changes in test-taking motivation could reduce adverse impact. Attempts to address these perceptual and motivational issues have been made through the use of various types of training programs including test-taking skills training, which should (a) encourage an overall positive attitude toward the testing process; (b) include some type of training on handling test anxiety (Goldstein, Yusko, Braverman, Smith, & Chung, 1998); and (c) attempt to increase participant motivation.

Altering the Selection Criteria   Altering the selection criteria in an attempt to reduce subgroup differences and adverse impact has had several foci including altering test weights, random selection after a specified cut score, race-based selection, and banding. The literature on altering test weights suggests that this may reduce the degree of adverse impact in selection systems caused by cognitive ability tests. However, the differences in weights must be fairly substantial to result in a practical difference in adverse impact (Doverspike, Winter, Healy, & Barrett, 1996). Random selection after a specified cutoff and banding are relatively effective methods of reducing adverse impact, but the greatest reduction in adverse impact occurs when race-based selection is used after banding or after setting cutoffs (Sackett & Roth, 1991). Unfortunately, in addition to questions concerning the lost utility of the test, there are legal, political, and ethical ramifications involved in the use of race-based selection (Barrett, Doverspike, & Arthur, 1995; Campion et al., 2001).

Use of Nonability Constructs   The use of nonability constructs has been considered as an approach to reducing subgroup differences. Common nonability constructs that have been investigated in attempts to reduce adverse impact include personality variables (Hogan, Hogan, & Roberts, 1996) such as conscientiousness (Schmitt et al., 1996) and integrity (Sackett & Wanek, 1996). Although subgroup differences have been shown to be lower on some of these constructs (e.g., personality variables; Hogan et al., 1996; Hough et al., 2001), the use of nonability predictor constructs in reducing adverse impact has not been very successful (Ryan, Ployhart, & Friedal, 1998), and the lower validity resulting from the use of these constructs may result in a considerable reduction in utility (Schmitt, Rogers, Chan, Sheppard, & Jennings, 1997).

Combine Cognitive Ability with Other Predictors   A variation of the construct change approach has been to combine cognitive ability with other predictors—either constructs (e.g., personality variables, integrity) or methods (e.g., structured interviews, performance tests). Although the additional predictors add incremental validity beyond cognitive ability, the empirical evidence suggests that combining cognitive ability with these alternative predictors does not necessarily eliminate subgroup differences for a wide range of selection ratios (Sackett & Ellingson, 1997; Schmitt et al., 1997).

Changing the Test Method   Another approach to reducing subgroup differences and adverse impact is to change the test method with the intention of altering test perceptions and attitudes, and also of reducing nonjob-related reading demands. This approach to reducing adverse impact recognizes that cognitively loaded paper-and-pencil tests of knowledge, skill, ability, and aptitude are the most valid predictors of job performance but posits that subgroup differences on cognitive ability may partially arise from the mode or method of testing—specifically, paper-and-pencil multiple-choice tests—instead of the construct. The mechanism of these effects is via processes of test perception, namely differences in test anxiety and stereotype threat, perceived fairness, perceived low face validity or job relatedness, and lack of motivation (Chan & Schmitt, 1997; Chan et al., 1997; Hough et al., 2001; McKay & Doverspike, 2001; Ryan, 2001; Steele, 1997). To reduce adverse impact, alternative test formats have been used, including performance tests (e.g., Chan & Schmitt, 1997), assessment centers (e.g., Goldstein et al., 1998), video-based tests with an oral presentation of test items only (e.g., Chan & Schmitt, 1997; Weekley & Jones, 1999), oral presentation of both items and responses (e.g., Rand, 1987; Schmitt & Mills, 2001), and constructed response tests (e.g., Arthur et al., 2002). In addition to engendering more favorable attitudes and perceptions, the use of these nonmultiple-choice test formats also minimizes the nonjob-related reading demands (Arthur et al., 2002). At the present time, alternative formats do appear to be a practical method of reducing adverse impact. However, empirical research delineating the psychological mechanisms responsible for these reductions is needed. Furthermore, in many real-world situations, alternative formats may not be practical.

In spite of its potential advantages, a major limitation of the method-change approach has been the confounding of method (techniques or procedures) and content (constructs, Arthur et al., 2002; Schmitt et al., 1996). For instance, if the levels of adverse impact for performance tests and paper-and-pencil multiple-choice tests are to be compared, then to obtain interpretable results, both test formats should be measuring the same construct or content. Another limitation with the preceding body of research is that there is a glaring absence of criterion-related validity data. Thus, it is still unclear whether the reductions in subgroup differences associated with alternative methods are associated with lower or higher criterion-related validity (cf. Edwards & Arthur, 2004).

A variation of the method-change approach is to use design techniques to minimize the inherent subjectivity and potential for bias and discriminatory behaviors associated with some test methods such as interviews. Specifically, in the case of interviews, which are one of the most widely used selection tools (Dipboye, 1997), they could be so highly structured as to completely eliminate any discretionary input on the part of the interviewer and consequently also eliminate the potential for subjective bias on the part of the interviewer or rater. This level of structure is what Huffcutt and Arthur (1994) designate as Level 4 structure in which all candidates are asked the exact same questions in the exact same order with no choice or follow-up, and each individual response to each question is evaluated according to preestablished answers. At this level, the interview functionally operates like an orally administered and scored objective test. This level of structure is not commonly used in practice (van der Zee, Bakker, & Bakker, 2002) but less restrictive levels of structure (e.g., Level 3, Huffcutt & Arthur, 1994) can be used with the same objective of minimizing internal bias. The use of high structure interviews can and should also be coupled with interviewer training interventions such as frame-of-reference training (Woehr & Huffcutt, 1994).

In summary, organizations should strive to maximize the perceived fairness and the validity of selection systems. Minority test-takers view cognitive ability tests with suspicion, yet respond positively to face valid tests (Chan & Schmitt, 1997; Chan et al., 1997). Hence, it is suggested that employers use valid, job-relevant tests and attempt to maximize the face validity of these tests. By doing so, not only is the process perceived as being more equitable and merit-based, but also the test-taking motivation of minority applicants is likely to be increased. In addition, beyond the legal stipulations, research suggests that the use of fair selection procedures aids minority recruitment efforts.

Altering the Behavior of Majority Group Members Through Selection

Can selection and employment testing be used to identify majority group members who will be less likely to engage in discrimination and also more likely to participate in diversity programs (i.e., pro-diversity majority group members)? In theory, yes—if there are characteristics associated with pro-diversity attitudes and behaviors, then tests can be used to select for these characteristics. The question then is what characteristics might be associated with pro-diversity orientations and attitudes in majority group members?

An individual difference variable explored in a number of studies is racism (Jacobson, 1985; Sidanius, Pratto, & Bobo, 1996). For example, Kravitz (1995) found that racism was associated with opposition to affirmative action in general, and toward specific affirmative action plans. Overall, racism appears to be related to pro-diversity attitudes with correlations ranging from .19 for classic racism and opposition to affirmative action (Sidanius, Pratto, & Bobo, 1996) to −.38 for modern racism and support for affirmative action (Jacobson, 1985). Similarly, modern sexism was found to be related to attitudes toward affirmative action (Tougas, Brown, Beaton, & Joly, 1995; Tougas, Crosby, Joly, & Pelchat, 1995).

Given that personality traits are thought to be an influential source of individual differences, coupled with the ubiquity of the five-factor model (FFM) of personality (Digman, 1990), it is surprising that individual differences in the FFM personality factors have not received greater attention as predictors of pro-diversity attitudes (cf. Douthitt, Eby, & Simon, 1999). Not only would one expect the FFM personality factors in general to be related to attitudes toward affirmative action, in particular, but also one would expect that openness would be related to judgments of racism, sexism, and reactions to affirmative action.

We have previously proposed the existence of a *cosmopolitan* personality profile (Doverspike, Arthur, Struchul et al., 2000), which is a combined knowledge structure-personality profile that has the effect of making a person more open to the acceptance of diversity programs, including affirmative action. That is, a person is more likely to be accepting of programs such as affirmative action, which benefit cultural groups other than their own, if the individual has both a culturally open personality profile and sufficient experience with a variety of cultures so as to have had the opportunity to develop multicultural knowledge. In spite of its theoretical and conceptual merit, it is questionable whether it would be practical to use standard, straightforward self-report paper-and-pencil measures of prejudice, racism, or openness in selection contexts because of the fakability of such measures and their tendency to measure expressed instead of genuine prejudice. Although there are alternatives to paper-and-pencil measures such as reaction time (Fazio, 1990, 1995) that indirectly measure implicit cognitions and thus reveal suppressed prejudice and stereotypical beliefs, Crandall and Eshleman (2003) note that they "are less sanguine about the probability that implicit measures reflect unadulterated genuine prejudice" and "suggest that genuine prejudice and implicit attitudes are related, but they are not the same concept" (p. 435). It would also seem more difficult to argue for the face validity of such reaction time measures.

HUMAN RESOURCE DEVELOPMENT

In this section, we consider discrimination-related issues in the context of both training interventions and career development. We define *training* as individual instructional activities designed to assist employees in acquiring specific skills, behaviors, or attitudes. *Career development* is defined here as set of activities aimed at general competencies designed to assist employees in progressing through a series of career stages. Despite their separate definitions, it is often very difficult to distinguish between what constitutes training and what constitutes career development and any attempt to differentiate the two is likely to seem highly artificial. Therefore, we have combined our discussion of these two methods under the single general heading of training. As with the other HR functions discussed in this chapter, conceptually, specific steps could be taken to reduce the negative effects associated with human resource development-related decisions. In addition, one could also use human resource development to alter the behavior of others in an attempt to reduce discriminatory behaviors.

Training

Reducing the Negative Effects Associated with Training   The direct relationship between training and development and adverse impact is somewhat unclear (Delahoussaye, 2001; Morrison & Von Glinow, 1990). However, if access or selection into training is based on performance appraisals or tests, then the selection methods may result in adverse impact. Thus, organizations should perform regular audits of access to training in order to ensure that minorities do not face unfair barriers that limit their participation in training programs.

The question of the adequacy of access to training programs is especially complex when the protected group is older workers. In the United States, employees over the age of 40 are protected from discrimination by the Age Discrimination in Employment Act of 1967 (as amended in 1986). However, older workers often face situational, dispositional, and institutional obstacles to their full participation in training programs (Sterns, Junkins, & Bayer, 2001). Such obstacles can be overcome by educating managers and also providing appropriate rewards to older workers participating in training programs (Sterns & Doverspike, 1989; Sterns et al., 2001).

Altering the Behavior of Majority Group Members Through Training
How can employers use training programs to alter the discriminatory behaviors of organizational members? The obvious answer is by directing training programs toward changing attitudes and stereotypes and also by designing training programs that replace discriminatory behaviors with more effective behaviors. The associated training programs can be designed to be either fairly narrow, as for example those programs aimed at eliminating the use of stereotypes and similar-to-me effects in the employment interview, or broad, as best exemplified by diversity training. In this section, we will look at one type of narrow training, sexual harassment training, and the broad approach offered by general diversity training.

Sexual Harassment Training   Sexual harassment training is a very specific type of training aimed at altering behavior. Sexual harassment training is usually directed at either antecedents or outcomes (Fitzgerald, Hulin, & Drasgow, 1995). Thus, antecedent-oriented training attempts to reduce sexual harassment by changing the organizational climate, individual attitudes, or job-sex stereotypes. Outcome-based training attempts to reduce the negative effects of sexual harassment (Barak, 1994). For example, a training objective might be teaching women how to identify and respond to sexual harassment, or training may offer coping strategies for victims of sexual harassment.

Methods used in sexual harassment training include lectures, behavior modeling, role plays, board games, group discussions, video-based training, internet-based training, and sensitivity training (Wexley & Latham, 2002). There have been relatively few studies evaluating the effectiveness of sexual harassment training or comparing the effectiveness of different training methods (Fitzgerald & Schullman, 1993; Wexley & Latham, 2002). However, regardless of the training delivery method, it appears that sexual harassment training is most effective when (a) all employees are trained, not just victims or perpetrators (Glomb et al., 1997); (b) harassing behavior is clearly defined, including legal definitions (Wexley & Latham, 2002; Zachary, 1996); (c) methods for preventing sexual harassment and altering behaviors are clearly presented (Wexley & Latham, 2002); (d) the training program is designed to fit the organizational climate (Zachary, 1996); and (e) the trainer is professional, establishes rapport with the group, and modifies the training to fit the organizational culture (Risser, 1999).

Diversity Management Diversity management incorporates a range of human resource practices including recruitment, retention, selection, performance appraisal, and compensation. However, diversity programs are often discussed as a type of training, so we have chosen to include a discussion of diversity programs in this section. Diversity training programs are offered by a variety of consultants and trainers using a wide range of training media aimed at accomplishing a variety of objectives. Some diversity training goals include changing individual attitudes, eliminating subconscious stereotypes, increasing sensitivity to minority issues and diversity concerns, and informing on legal and policy issues (Bendick, Egan & Lofhjelm, 2001; Noe, 2002; Rynes & Rosen, 1995).

Although training is often identified as one of the best ways to ensure diversity (Wentling & Palma-Rivas, 1998), there are too few rigorous evaluations of diversity training to draw conclusions as to their effectiveness (Noe, 2002; Rynes & Rosen, 1995). There is also the contrarian view that diversity training does more harm than good in many cases (Caudron, 1993). Although there is no clear consensus on the effectiveness of diversity training, based on our review and evaluation of its effectiveness, we identified a number of important elements for success. These are (a) avoid ironic reversal by training to dispel rather than avoid stereotypes (Kulik, Perry, & Bourhis, 2000); (b) incorporate action steps for translating changes in attitudes into changes in behavior (Caudron, 1993; Zhu & Kleiner, 2000); (c) provide sufficient time for training (Von Bergen, Soper, & Foster, 2002); (d) ensure that training is not simply an expression of the trainer's own values or agenda (Von Bergen et al., 2002); (e) avoid training that comes across as simply political correctness (Von Bergen et al., 2002); (f) define the goal of diversity training clearly (Rynes & Rosen, 1995; Von Bergen et al., 2002); (g) ensure top management and supervisor support (Rynes & Rosen, 1995); and (h) integrate diversity training with affirmative action efforts, while also differentiating the goals of diversity training from the goals of affirmative action (Doverspike, Taylor, & Arthur, 2002; Von Bergen et al., 2002).

PERFORMANCE MANAGEMENT

Performance management is used here to encompass the major areas of performance appraisal and compensation. The former refers to the measurement and evaluation of performance and the latter refers to the rewarding of performance using various means of compensation. The interrelatedness of these facets of performance management is highlighted by the fact that compensation, specifically pay, may be linked to performance appraisal.

Performance Appraisal

Performance appraisal can be conceptualized as a systematic description of an individual's job-relevant strengths and weaknesses, that is their job performance. Although job performance data can be obtained either objectively (hard criteria) or judgmentally (soft criteria), the term "performance appraisal" is typically used in the context of, albeit not limited to, the latter. From the perspective of the present chapter, appraisals are problematic if they are influenced by employee characteristics such as race, sex, and age.

Reducing the Negative Effects of Performance Appraisal   Performance evaluations can result in discriminatory outcomes via two mechanisms, (a) poor or ineffective appraisal or rating practices and (b) intentional distortion resulting from motivational and political factors. Concerning the former, two strategies have traditionally been advocated to address the problems with judgmentally based performance data: rating scale development and rater training. The results of rating scale comparisons indicate that format modification alone does not result in much improvement in performance evaluations (cf. Woehr & Miller, 1997). However, frame-of-reference training, which emerged from the social cognitive approach to performance appraisal, appears to be quite effective as a rater training approach to increasing the accuracy of ratings (Woehr & Huffcutt, 1994). In addition to rater training, job analysis should serve as the basis for constructing the appraisal instrument and the appraisal process so that employees are evaluated only on job-related factors.

Rater training is based on the premise of providing raters with the skills, tools, and information needed to accurately evaluate performance. However, it is also acknowledged that evaluations can reflect not the inability or limitations in raters' capacity to evaluate accurately, but instead, specific strategic decisions by raters about the sorts of evaluations they should record (Murphy & Cleveland, 1995). Although previous research has indicated the effects of employee race, sex, and age on performance evaluations, Latham and Wexley (1994) in a review of the extant literature concluded that "it would appear that when employees make their work visible to appraisers, when appraisers and appraisees together clarify objectives and task responsibilities, and when the appraiser uses behaviorally based appraisal scales, ratee characteristics, such as age, race, and sex, have a negligible effect on the resulting performance appraisal" (p. 152).

Nevertheless, under some conditions, it is easily conceivable that motivational, political, and interpersonal factors could result in performance evaluations that systematically discriminate against members of specified groups (Oppler, Campbell, Pulakos, & Borman, 1992; Sackett, DuBois, & Noe, 1991). Such intentional, politically driven evaluation distortions can be best addressed by organizational performance appraisal practices and policies that alter discriminatory behaviors. Some of these are briefly discussed below.

Altering Discriminatory Behavior Through Performance Appraisal Practices Using performance appraisals to alter discriminatory behaviors requires a fairly intensive set of activities. These include (a) using more than one rater, (b) having raters provide written justifications (Latham & Latham, 2000) or otherwise being demonstrable accountable for their evaluations (Villanova & Bernardin, 1991), and (c) making diversity a performance standard for raters; valued rewards could also be linked to performance appraisal accuracy (Murphy & Cleveland, 1995). We acknowledge that some of these recommendations may be controversial. Nevertheless, these approaches require a focus on contextual factors that have more to do with raters' willingness to accurately evaluate performance and less with their ability to make accurate judgments. Consequently, as postulated by rational bias theory (Larwood, Gutek, & Gattiker, 1984), if discrimination is a result of contextual and environmental factors, then we must change these factors to alter or eliminate discriminatory behaviors by the majority group members. For instance, Longenecker, Sims, and Gioia (1987) suggested that executive managers who viewed appraisal as a sincere and serious process were more likely to enact organizational cultures that inhibited deliberate rating distortions.

Compensation

Through the use of compensation practices, organizations attempt to both reward and motivate various types of behavior. Compensation practices include pay and benefits, and modern total compensation approaches extend the definition of compensation to include a variety of favorable outcomes experienced by the employee (Milkovich & Newman, 2002). Because of the importance of pay to employees, compensation and benefit programs can serve as a major indicator of possible discrimination in the organization. However, pay policies can also be used to reduce discriminatory behavior and encourage diversity.

Reducing the Negative Effects of Compensation Practices Although potential race and age discrimination in compensation is an important concern, most of the applied and research attention has been directed at sex-related issues, especially comparable worth and pay equity (Blumrosen, 1979; Treiman & Hartman, 1981). Organizations can reduce the negative effects of their compensation practices by auditing their policies and then, based on the results of the audits, refine their procedures to eliminate bias, and where necessary, adjust the pay of minority group members. The type of audits that organizations can engage in will correspond to the three major theories, approaches, or techniques used in defining pay discrimination. The three major approaches or types of audit are (a) an equal pay audit, (b) a pay equity audit, and (c) an analysis of across-the-board problems.

Equal Pay Analysis In the first type of audit, an organization should consider performing an equal pay analysis. According to an equal pay approach to studying wage discrimination, jobs that involve the same or highly similar tasks and knowledge, skills, and abilities should be paid the same regardless of the sex (or race, age, or other protected class status) of the incumbent. In the United States, this definition of discrimination was operationalized through the Equal Pay Act of 1963. The provisions of this Act were also incorporated into the Civil Rights Act of 1964. Although, today, most organizations appear to be in compliance with equal pay provisions, employers should pay careful attention to policies that may lead to the appearance of violations of equal pay. Two major potential problem areas for organizations are (a) paying relatively large differentials for small differences in jobs, such as paying men substantially more than women because the job occupied by men involves a lifting component not found on the female sex-typed job (Milkovich & Newman, 2002; *Shultz v. Wheaton Glass Co.*, 1970); and, (b) paying large differentials for training programs, such as paying a man more for performing the job of teller in a bank because he is considered to be in a managerial training program (Milkovich & Newman, 2002). An equal pay audit will point to areas of potential discrimination involving individuals. Where examples of unequal pay based upon sex, race, or other factors, are identified, appropriate adjustments should be made to the affected employees' salaries.

Pay Equity Audit The pay equity audit is very similar to the older term "comparable worth." According to this approach, organizations should pay equal compensation to jobs of equal worth. "Worth" can be determined using a job evaluation system or through an analysis of unbiased market rates. Proponents of pay equity argue that discrimination in pay occurs because jobs are segregated based upon sex and also race (Blumrosen, 1979). Thus, the first step in a pay equity audit is determining if sex- or race-segregated jobs exist. If sex- or race-based segregation exists, then organizations should study the causes of this segregation and determine whether organizational interventions can be aimed at reducing any identified causes.

In addition, proponents of pay equity have argued that the job evaluation system must be shown to be unbiased (Doverspike & Barrett, 1984; Treiman & Hartmann, 1981) by (a) ensuring that job analyses are conducted in an objective, fair manner; (b) ensuring that raters are selected from a range of backgrounds, are adequately trained, and provide ratings in a bias-free manner, if a job evaluation committee is used; and (c) using a bias-free job evaluation instrument. Once an unbiased job evaluation system is in place, the employer can then conduct a study to determine if female-dominated or minority-dominated jobs are underpaid, compared to the proposed salary line. If jobs are underpaid, then the pay of those jobs can be raised to an appropriate level. The topic of how best to accomplish this adjustment has been the subject of much debate (Treiman & Hartmann, 1981).

Across-the-Board Audit The basic philosophy underlying the across-the-board audit is that current pay can reflect a host of prior discriminatory behaviors in such areas as promotion, selection, and training. Thus, absent group-based discrimination, current pay should be a function of merit and should not reflect sex or race. An example of the across-the-board approach is the glass ceiling analysis in which statistical studies of pay are conducted within job grades.

A compensation factor that can negatively affect all workers, but in particular older workers, is salary compression. Salary compression occurs when the market causes entry-level pay to rise faster than merit pay (Griffeth & Horn, 2001). As a result, new employees may have to be hired at salary levels equal to or higher than that earned by experienced, older employees.

As discussed in the recruitment section, benefit programs can be tailored to enhance the attraction of minority group members. In addition to pay, benefit programs should be audited in order to identify any possible areas where discrimination may be present. Benefit practices should also be reviewed in order to ensure that the packages offered are attractive to minority groups and thereby serve as an incentive during recruitment. For older workers in particular, retirement programs, including retirement planning and alternative work arrangements, are an important benefit that influences both recruitment and retention.

Altering Discriminatory Behavior of Majority Group Members Through Compensation Practices Because total compensation can be used as both a reward and a motivator, an organization can use its pay policies to reward nondiscriminatory behaviors and punish discriminatory behaviors (Noe, 2002). Given the global focus of many organizations, employers have revised their performance appraisal systems to include ratings of competencies related to diversity. If an organization ties compensation to performance, then the ultimate result is that those employees who engage in nondisciminatory behaviors are rewarded (e.g., supervisors and managers who effectively meet specific diversity goals in hiring and retention). As with majority group members, organizations can also tailor performance appraisal and compensation systems to reward minority group members whose performance contributes to organizational diversity.

SUMMARY

The objective of this chapter has been to review and discuss HR practices that can be used to achieve diversity in organizations. Practices pertaining to staffing, human resource development, and performance management were discussed in terms of reducing negative effects resulting from these practices and altering the behaviors of organizational members via these practices to minimize discrimination and increase diversity. Where available, we have relied on the extant theory and research. However, some of our recommendations are speculative and primarily conceptual because of the limited or in some instances, complete absence of any empirical research that speaks to the specified issue. We hope that in these instances our speculative extrapolation serves as an impetus for future theory and research.

REFERENCES

AARP (1993). *How to recruit older workers*. Washington, DC: Author.

Age Discrimination in Employment Act of 1967 (ADEA) (part of the Fair Labor Standards Act of 1938), (Pub. L. 90-202), 29 U.S.C. §621 et seq.; 29 C.F.R. Part 1625.1 et seq.

Arthur, W. Jr., Day, E. A., McNelly, T. L., & Edens, P., S. (2003). Meta-analysis of the criterion-related validity of assessment center dimensions. *Personnel Psychology, 56*, 125–154.

Arthur, W. Jr., Edwards, B. D., & Barrett, G. V. (2002). Multiple-choice and constructed response tests of ability: Race-based subgroup performance differences on alternative paper-and-pencil test formats. *Personnel Psychology, 55*, 985–1008.

Avery, D. R. (2003). Reactions to diversity in recruiting advertising—Are differences Black and White? *Journal of Applied Psychology, 88,* 672–679.

Arvey, R. D., Gordon, M. E., Massengill, D. P., & Mussio, S. J. (1975). Differential dropout rates of minority job candidates due to "time lags" between selection procedures. *Personnel Psychology, 28,* 175–180.

Arvey, R. D., Strickland, W., Drauden, G., & Martin, C. (1990). Motivational components of test taking. *Personnel Psychology, 43,* 695–716.

Barak, A. (1994). A cognitive–behavioral educational workshop to combat sexual harassment in the workplace. *Journal of Counseling and Development, 72,* 595–602.

Barrett, G. V., Doverspike, D., & Arthur, W. Jr. (1995). The current status of the judicial review of banding: A clarification. *The Industrial–Organizational Psychologist, 33,* 39–41.

Bendick, M., Egan, M. L., & Lofhjelm, S. M. (2001). Workforce diversity training: From anti-discrimination compliance to organizational development. *Human Resource Planning, 24,* 10–25.

Blumrosen, R. G. (1979). Wage discrimination, job segregation, and Title VII of the Civil Rights Act of 1964. *University of Michigan Journal of Law Reform, 12,* 397–502.

Campion, M. A., Outtz, J. L., Zedeck, S., Schmidt, F. L., Kehoe, J. F., Murphy, K. R., & Guion, R. M. (2001). The controversy over score banding in personnel selection: Answers to 10 key questions. *Personnel Psychology, 54,* 149–185.

Caudron, S. (1993). Training can damage diversity efforts. *Personnel Journal, 72,* 50–55.

Chan, D., & Schmitt, N. (1997). Video-based versus paper-and-pencil method of assessment in situational judgment tests: Subgroup differences in test performance and face validity perceptions. *Journal of Applied Psychology, 82,* 143–159.

Chan, D., Schmitt, N., DeShon, P., Clause, C. S., & Delbridge, K. (1997). Reactions to cognitive ability tests: The relationship between race, test performance, face validity perceptions, and test-taking motivation. *Journal of Applied Psychology, 82,* 300–310.

Civil Rights Act of 1964, (Pub. L. 88-352), U.S.C. §2000d et seq.; 28 C.F.R. §42.101 et seq., 34 C.F.R. §100.1 et seq., and 45 C.F.R. §80.1 et seq.

Civil Rights Act of 1991, Pub. L. No. 102-166, 105 Stat. 1071 (Nov. 21, 1991).

Crandall, C. S., & Eshleman, A. (2003). A justification–suppression model of the expression and experience of prejudice. *Psychological Bulletin, 129,* 414–446.

Crocker, L., & Algina, J. (1986). *Introduction to classical and modern test theory.* New York: Holt, Rinehart and Winston.

Delahoussaye, M. (2001). Leadership in the 21st century. *Training, 38,* 50–59.

Digman, J. M. (1990). Personality structure: Emergence of the five-factor model. *Annual Review of Psychology, 41,* 417–440.

Dipboye, R. L. (1997). Structured selection interviews: Why do they work? Why are they underutilized? In N. Anderson & P. Herriot (Eds.), *International handbook of selection and assessment* (pp. 455–473). New York: Wiley.

Douthitt, S. S., Eby, L. T., & Simon. S. A. (1999). Diversity of life experiences: The development and validation of a biographical measure of receptiveness to dissimilar others. *International Journal of Selection and Assessment, 7,* 112–125.

Doverspike, D., & Arthur, W. Jr. (1995). Race and sex differences in the reactions to simulated selection decisions based on affirmative action. *Journal of Black Psychology, 21,* 181–200.

Doverspike, D., Arthur, W. Jr., Struchul, A., & Taylor, M. A. (2000). The cosmopolitan personality. In D. D. Kravitz (Chair), *Individual differences and reactions to affirmative action.* Symposium presented at the 15th Annual Conference of the Society for Industrial and Organizational Psychology, New Orleans, LA.

Doverspike, D., & Barrett, G. V. (1984). An internal bias analysis of a job evaluation instrument. *Journal of Applied Psychology, 69,* 648–662.

Doverspike, D., Taylor, M. A., & Arthur, W. Jr. (2000). *Affirmative action: A psychological perspective*. Commack, NY: Nova Scientific Publishing.

Doverspike, D., Taylor, M. A., Shultz, K. S., & McKay, P. F. (2000). Responding to the challenge of a changing workforce: Recruiting nontraditional demographic groups. *Public Personnel Management, 29*, 445–460.

Doverspike, D., Winter, J. L., Healy, M. C., & Barrett, G V. (1996). Simulations as a method of illustrating the impact of differential weights on personnel selection outcomes. *Human Performance, 9*, 259–273.

Edwards, B. D., & Arthur, W. Jr. (2004). *Race-based subgroup differences on a constructed response paper-and-pencil test*. Paper presented at the 19th Annual Conference of the Society for Industrial and Organizational Psychology, Chicago, IL.

Equal Pay Act of 1963, (Pub. L. 88-38), 29 U.S.C. §206(d); 29 C.F.R. Part 1620.1 et seq.

Fazio, R. H. (1990). A practical guide to the use of response latency in social psychological research. In C. Hendrick & M. S. Clark (Eds.), *Research methods in personality and social psychology* (pp. 74–97). Newbury Park, CA: Sage.

Fazio, R. H. (1995). Attitudes as object–evaluation associations: Determinants, consequences, and correlates of attitude accessibility. In R. E. Petty & J. A. Krosnick (Eds.), *Attitude strength: Antecedents and consequences* (pp. 247–282). Mahwah, NJ: Lawrence Erlbaum Associates.

Fitzgerald, L. F., Hulin, C. L., & Drasgow, F. (1995). The antecedents and consequences of sexual harassment in organizations. In G. Keita & J. Hurrell, Jr. (Eds.), *Job stress in a changing workforce: Investigating gender, diversity, and family issues* (pp. 55–73). Washington, DC: American Psychological Association.

Fitzgerald, L. F., & Shullman, S. L. (1993). Sexual harassment: A research analysis and agenda for the 1990s. *Journal of Vocational Behavior, 42*, 5–27.

Glomb, T. M., Richman, W. L., Hulin, C. L., Drasgow, F., Schneider, K. T., & Fitzgerald, L. F. (1997). Ambient sexual harassment: An integrated model of antecedents and consequences. *Organizational Behavior and Human Decision Processes, 71*, 309–328.

Goldstein, H. W., Yusko, K. P., Braverman, E. P., Smith, D. B., & Chung, B. (1998). The role of cognitive ability in the subgroup differences and incremental validity of assessment center exercises. *Personnel Psychology, 51*, 357–374.

Griffeth, R. W., & Horn, P. W. (2001). *Retaining valued employees*. Thousand Oaks, CA: Sage.

Hogan, R., Hogan, J., & Roberts, B. W. (1996). Personality measurement and employment decisions. *American Psychologist, 51*, 469–477.

Hough, L. M., Oswald, F. L., & Ployhart, R. E. (2001). Determinants, detection and amelioration of adverse impact in personnel selection procedures: Issues, evidence and lessons learned. *International Journal of Selection and Assessment, 9*, 152–194.

Huffcutt, A. I., & Arthur, W. Jr. (1994). Hunter and Hunter (1984) revisited: Interview validity for entry-level jobs. *Journal of Applied Psychology, 79*, 184–190.

Jacobson, C. K. (1985). Resistance to affirmative action. *Journal of Conflict Resolution, 29*, 306–329.

Kravitz, D. A. (1995). Attitudes toward affirmative action plans directed at Blacks: Effects of plan and individual differences. *Journal of Applied Social Psychology, 25*, 2192–2220.

Kulik, C. T., Perry, E. L., & Bourhis, A. C. (2000). Ironic evaluation processes: Effects of thought suppression on evaluations of older job applicants. *Journal of Organizational Behavior, 21*, 689–711.

Larwood, L., Gutek, B., & Gattiker, U. E. (1984). Perspectives on institutional discrimination and resistance to change. *Group and Organization Studies, 9*, 333–352.

Latham, G. P., & Latham, S. D. (2000). Overlooking theory and research in performance appraisal at one's peril: Much done, more to do. In C. L. Cooper & E. A. Locke (Eds.),

Industrial and organizational psychology: Linking theory with practice (pp. 199–215). Oxford: Blackwell.

Latham, G. P., & Wexley, K. N. (1994). *Increasing productivity through performance appraisal* (2nd ed.). New York: Addison-Wesley.

Longenecker, C. O., Sims, H. P., & Gioia, D. A. (1987). Behind the mask: The politics of employee appraisal. *Academy of Management Executive, 1*, 183–193.

McKay, P. F., & Doverspike, D. (2001). African-Americans' test taking attitudes and their effect on cognitive ability test performance: Implications for public personnel management selection practice. *Public Personnel Management, 30*, 67–75.

Milkovich, G. T., & Newman, J. M. (2002). Compensation (7th ed.). Boston, MA: McGraw-Hill.

Morrison, A. M., & von Glinow, M. (1990). Women and minorities in management. *American Psychologist, 45*, 200–208.

Murphy, K. R., & Cleveland, J. N. (1995). *Understanding performance appraisal.* Thousand Oaks, CA: Sage.

Noe, R. A. (2002). *Employee training and development* (2nd ed.). Boston, MA: McGraw-Hill.

Oppler, S. H., Campbell, J. P., Pulakos, E. D., & Borman, W. C. (1992). Three approaches to the investigation of subgroup bias in performance measurement: Review, results, and conclusions. *Journal of Applied Psychology, 77*, 201–217.

Perkins, L. A., Thomas, K. M., & Taylor, G. A. (2000). Advertising and recruitment: Marketing to minorities. *Psychology and Marketing, 17*, 235–255.

Poe, C. (1989). The new work force. *Employee Assistance Quarterly, 3*, 23–50.

Rand, R. (1987). Behavioral police assessment device: The development and validation of an interactive preemployment job-related video psychological test (Doctoral dissertation, University of San Francisco, 1987). *Dissertation Abstracts International, 48*, 610–611.

Raju, N. S., Laffitte, L. J., & Byrne, B. M. (2002). Measurement equivalence: A comparison of methods based on confirmatory factor analysis and item response theory. *Journal of Applied Psychology, 87*, 517–529.

Risser, R. (1999). Sexual harassment training: Truth and consequences. *Training and Development, 53*, 21–23.

Ryan, A. M. (2001). Explaining the Black–White test score gap: The role of test perceptions. *Human Performance, 14*, 45–75.

Ryan, A. M., Ployhart, R. E., & Friedal, L. A. (1998). Using personality testing to reduce adverse impact: A cautionary note. *Journal of Applied Psychology, 83*, 298–307.

Ryan, A. M., Sacco, J. M., McFarland, L. A., & Kriska, S. D. (2000). Applicant self-selection: Correlates of withdrawal from a multiple hurdle process. *Journal of Applied Psychology, 85*, 163–179.

Rynes, S. L. (1991). Recruitment, job choice, and post–hire consequences: A call for new research directions. In M. D. Dunnette & L. M. Hough (Eds.), *Handbook of industrial and organizational psychology* (2nd ed., Vol. 2, pp. 399–444). Palo Alto, CA: Consulting Psychologists Press.

Rynes, S. L., & Connerley, M. R. (1993). Applicant reactions to alternative selection procedures. *Journal of Business and Psychology, 7*, 261–277.

Rynes, S., & Rosen, B. (1995). A field survey of factors affecting the adoption and perceived success of diversity training. *Personnel Psychology, 48*, 247–270.

Sackett, P. R., DuBois, C. L. Z., & Noe, A. W. (1991). Tokenism in performance evaluation: The effects of work group representation on the male–female and White–Black differences in performance ratings. *Journal of Applied Psychology, 76*, 263–267.

Sackett, P. R., & Ellingson, J. E. (1997). The effects of forming multi-predictor composites on group differences and adverse impact. *Personnel Psychology, 50*, 707–721.

Sackett, P. R., & Roth, L. (1991). A Monte Carlo examination of banding and rank order methods of test score use in personnel selection. *Human Performance, 4,* 279–295.

Sackett, P. R., & Wanek, J. E. (1996). New developments in the use of measures of honesty, integrity, conscientiousness, dependability, trustworthiness, and reliability for personnel selection. *Personnel Psychology, 49,* 787–829.

Schmidt, F. L., & Hunter, J. E. (1998). The validity and utility of selection methods in personnel psychology: Practical and theoretical implications of 85 years of research findings. *Psychological Bulletin, 124,* 262–273.

Schmitt, N., Clause, C. S., & Pulakos, E. D. (1996). Subgroup differences associated with different measures of some common job relevant constructs. *International Review of Industrial and Organizational Psychology, 11,* 115–139.

Schmitt, N., & Mills, A. E. (2001). Traditional tests and job simulations: Minority and majority performance and test validities. *Journal of Applied Psychology, 86,* 451–458.

Schmitt, N., Rogers, W., Chan, D., Sheppard, L., & Jennings, D. (1997). Adverse impact and predictive efficiency of various predictor combinations. *Journal of Applied Psychology, 82,* 719–730.

Shultz v. Wheaton Glass Co, 421 F.2d 259 (3rd Cir. 1970).

Sidanius, J., Pratto, F., & Bobo, L. (1996). Racism, conservatism, affirmative action, and intellectual sophistication: A matter of principled conservatism or group dominance? *Journal of Personality and Social Psychology, 70,* 476–490.

Slaughter, J. E., Sinar, E. F., & Bachiochi, P. D. (2002). Black applicants' reactions to affirmative action plans: Effects of plan content and previous experience with discrimination. *Journal of Applied Psychology, 87,* 333–344.

Smither, J. W., Reilly, R. R., Millsap, R. E., Pearlman, K., & Stoffey, R. W. (1993). Applicant reactions to selection procedures. *Personnel Psychology, 46,* 49–76.

Stanush, P. L., Arthur, W., Jr., & Doverspike, D. (1998). Hispanic and African American reactions to a simulated race–based affirmative action scenario. *Hispanic Journal of Behavioral Sciences, 20,* 3–16.

Steele, C. M. (1997). A threat in the air: How stereotypes shape intellectual identity and performance. *American Psychologist, 52,* 613–629.

Sterns, H., & Doverspike, D. (1989). Aging and the training and learning process. In I. Goldstein (Ed.), *Training and development in organizations* (pp. 299–332). San Francisco: Jossey-Bass.

Sterns, H. L., Junkins, M. P., & Bayer, J. (2001). Work and retirement. In B. R. Bonder & M. B. Wagner (Eds.), *Functional performance in older adults* (pp. 179–195). Philadelphia: Davis.

Sterns, H. L., & Miklos, S. M. (1995). The aging worker in a changing environment: Organizational and individual issues. *Journal of Vocational Behavior, 47,* 248–268.

Thomas, K. M., & Wise, P. G. (1999). Organizational attractiveness and individual differences: Are diverse applicants attracted by different factors? *Journal of Business and Psychology, 13,* 375–390.

Tougas, F., Brown, R., Beaton, A. M., & Joly, S. (1995). Neosexism: Plus ca change, plus c'est pareil. *Personality and Social Psychology Bulletin, 21,* 842–849.

Tougas, F., Crosby, F., Joly, S., & Pelchat, D. (1995). Men's attitudes toward affirmative action: Justice and intergroup relations at the crossroads. *Social Justice Research, 8,* 57–71.

Treiman, D. J., & Hartman, H. I. (1981, Eds), *Women, work and wages: Equal pay for jobs of equal value.* Washington, DC: National Academy Press.

Turban, D. B., & Greening, D. W. (1997). Corporate social performance and organizational attractiveness to prospective employees. *Academy of Management Journal, 40,* 658–672.

Van den Bergh, N. (1991). Workplace diversity: The challenges and opportunities for employee assistance programs. *Employee Assistance Quarterly, 6,* 41–58.

Van der Zee, K. I., Bakker, A. B., & Bakker, P. (2002). Why are structured interviews so rarely used in personnel selection? *Journal of Applied Psychology, 87*, 176–184.

Villanova, P., & Bernardin, H. J. (1991). Performance appraisal: The means, motive, and opportunity to manage impressions. In R. A. Giacalone & P. Rosenfeld (Eds.), *Applied impression management: How image making affects managerial decisions* (pp. 81–96). Thousand Oaks, CA: Sage.

Von Bergen, C. W., Soper, B., & Foster, T. (2002). Unintended negative effects of diversity management. *Public Personnel Management, 31*, 239–251.

Weekley, J. A., & Jones, C. (1999). Further studies of situational tests. *Personnel Psychology, 52*, 679–700.

Wexley, K. N., & Latham, G. P. (2002). *Developing and training human resources in organizations* (3rd ed.). Upper Saddle River, NJ: Prentice-Hall.

Wentling, R. M., & Palma-Rivas, N. (1998). Current status and future trends of diversity initiatives in the workplace: Diversity experts' perspective. *Human Resource Development Quarterly, 9*, 235–253.

Woehr, D. J., & Huffcutt, A. I. (1994). Rater training for performance appraisal: A quantitative review. *Journal of Occupational and Organizational Psychology, 67*, 189–205.

Woehr, D. J., & Miller, M. J. (1997). Distributional ratings of performance: More evidence for a new rating format. *Journal of Management, 23*, 705–720.

Zachary, M. K. (1996). Creating a sexual harassment training program. *Supervision, 18*, 12–14.

Zhu, J., & Kleimer, B. (2000). The failure of diversity training. *Nonprofit World, 18*, 12–14.

14

Using Law and Psychology to Inform Our Knowledge of Discrimination

Ramona L. Paetzold
Texas A&M University

When is discrimination illegal? This is a question with an evolving answer, changing not only as new protected classes are added, but also as time progresses. Both judicial and Congressional pronouncements have changed the face of employment discrimination law over the last 40 years, with changes occurring in the disparate treatment and disparate impact models of discrimination and the addition of the reasonable accommodation and hostile environment models of discrimination. Refinements in the law of discrimination do not necessarily reflect the current knowledge of the psychological processes underlying discrimination. Moreover, the research in I/O, HR, and other behavioral sciences is out of touch in several respects with the law. I demonstrate in this chapter that research in HR/OB and psychology has important implications for discrimination law, yielding opportunities for experts in these areas to inform the legal system on this important topic. I also note that researchers in these areas should be more mindful of legal reasoning—even statistical issues reflecting legal reasoning—so that some of their research can directly address questions of importance to the interpretation and enforcement of discrimination law.

In essence, the key issues embodied in the models of discrimination have been framed by a few essential cases upon which I will rely in my discussion. Thus, a "back-to-basics" examination of the law provides insights into how both legal thinking and the behavioral sciences can benefit from mutual consideration of each scholarly field.

The chapter unfolds as follows. First, I discuss the disparate treatment model of intentional discrimination and the ways in which the notion of "intent" fails to correspond with social psychological research on dual-processing models of cognition. Affirmative action programs are briefly discussed in this section. In the second section, I present the disparate impact model and new ways to think about it for I/O and HR researchers. Finally, the reasonable accommodation model of disability discrimination is presented along with additional research questions stemming from current research in the area. In summary, the chapter addresses three of the major models of discrimination under the law.

DISPARATE TREATMENT AND DUAL PROCESSING

The most easily understood model of discrimination, and the one that was articulated first, is the disparate treatment model, which serves to redress intentional discrimination (e.g., *McDonnell Douglas Corp. v. Green*, 1973). Under the law, *intent* is a term of art, reflecting not just a state of mind, but also a motive, something that causes an employer to act in a particular manner. Traditionally, intentional discrimination has been viewed as stemming from dislike, hostility, or animus, although today there is certainly widespread recognition that differential treatment may result even in the absence of prejudice or bias. Nonetheless, proof of intent continues to be a required aspect of a disparate treatment lawsuit, so it is important to understand its meaning.

Legal Intent, Conscious Control, and Disparate Treatment

One function of the law is to be a coercive instrument for change (e.g., Melton, 1986). When Title VII of the Civil Rights Act went into effect on July 2, 1965, Congress most certainly expected that behaviors toward the protected classes would change so that employers would avoid illegal discrimination. Title VII obviously could not prevent all forms of illegal discrimination—e.g., some behaviors would persist as long as companies could afford the penalties; some behaviors would persist until it became clear that they were illegal—but the general expectation was that discriminatory behavior would change. The legal view of intentional discrimination implies that change is within the ability of individuals who must make important employment-related decisions. Often, but not always, it is the intentional actions—choices—of biased or prejudiced persons that cause discrimination. Intentional discrimination suggests that once persons know which behaviors constitute illegal discrimination, all they must do is choose (i.e., use free will) to avoid them, even though they are prejudiced, knowing that their resulting behavior will then not be illegal discrimination. Thus, the logic behind Title VII was that employers would change their behaviors (i.e., make conscious choices not to discriminate illegally) because they would be motivated to do so.

The touchstone of the disparate treatment model of discrimination is this motivational view of behavior and intent. Individuals may be prejudiced or hostile to racial or other groups, but they can choose not to act on those behaviors. As long as they make the right choices, discrimination will not occur. Of course, implicit in this assumption is that individuals must be consciously aware of their prejudices and hostility and of the ways in which their biases would tend to influence them. Certainly no individual can act against a stereotype or prejudice unless he or she is aware of the need to engage in counteraction.

Early disparate treatment law cases sometimes included direct evidence of this *conscious* hostility or intent to discriminate. Because perceivers can never know what another person actually thinks, the determination of intent required inferences arising from the other person's behavior. For example, in the early case of *Slack v. Havens*, (1975) four Black women claimed that they were illegally discharged because of their race when they refused to perform heavy cleaning duties that were not within their job description. Another coworker, a White woman, was excused from performing these duties. Their supervisor, Pohansky, who had ordered the women to do the heavy work, was known for making statements such as "Colored people should stay in their places" and "Colored folks are hired to clean because they clean better" (pp. 1092–1093). The court noted that these statements reflected ill motives for requiring the Black plaintiffs to perform the heavy cleaning. The statements were taken as "direct evidence" of racial animus, i.e., conscious intent to discriminate on the basis of race. Under the law, "direct evidence" suggests that the commentary from Pohansky was the equivalent of Pohansky telling the women that they were discharged as a result of their being Black. In other words, he was aware of his prejudicial attitudes toward Black persons and consciously treated them differently as a result. The bad intent *caused* the illegal discrimination to occur, supporting a district court decision (later affirmed) for the plaintiffs.

If Pohansky had not made the statements attributed to him, but had instead told the plaintiffs that they were selected because he truly believed they cleaned better than the White woman (based on his own observation), would the result have been the same? He might still have been acting out of prejudice or stereotypes, known or unknown to him, but he would not have exhibited a conscious intention to discriminate. The legal outcome would not be as straightforward. When the behaviors may reflect an unconscious or ambiguous intent to discriminate, the legal system may not recognize them as constituting illegal discrimination (Krieger, 1995).

Most cases do not involve direct evidence of illegal discrimination. Because of this, in the 1970s and early 1980s (and refined in the 1990s), the courts fashioned an indirect method of proving hostility or animus: the McDonnell Douglas/Burdine/Hicks framework (*McDonnell Douglas Corp. v. Green*, 1973; *Texas Department of Community Affairs v. Burdine*, 1981; *St. Mary's Honor Center v. Hicks*, 1993). Under this method of proof, the focus shifted to causation as a proxy for identifying bad intent. The McDonnell Douglas/Burdine/Hicks framework provides a well-known, burden-shifting scheme in which the plaintiff must first establish a prima facie case, which creates a presumption of illegal discrimination (*McDonnell Douglas Corp. v. Green*, 1973). The burden then shifts to the employer to "articulate some legitimate, non-discriminatory reason" for the conduct toward the plaintiff (*McDonnell Douglas Corp. v. Green*, 1973, p. 802; *Texas Department of Community Affairs v. Burdine*, 1981). In other words, the employer ideally would reveal the rational reason for the conscious choice of behavior exhibited toward the plaintiffs. If the employer meets this burden, then the presumption is overcome and the plaintiff, by a preponderance of the evidence, must establish that discrimination was the "real" reason for his or her treatment—that the defendant's proffered reason is a pretext for discrimination (*McDonnell Douglas Corp. v. Green*, 1973). Evidence that the employer's reason is a lie, or is not the "real" reason for the behavior, may help to create the inference of illegal discrimination, but need not be sufficient (*St. Mary's Honor Center v. Hicks*, 1993). Additional evidence—typically in the form of comparative evidence—may be needed as well. Comparative evidence refers to evidence of how members of the plaintiff's protected class are treated vis-à-vis similarly situated members outside of the plaintiff's class.

Reconsider the *Slack* case. Without statements reflecting that Pohasky selected the Black women because of their race, there is no direct evidence of bad intent. This would be true regardless whether he told them he selected them based on their observed cleaning ability or if he gave them no reason at all. In this case, the plaintiffs could use the *McDonnell-Douglas/Burdine/Hicks* framework to present their disparate treatment claim, a framework that also relies heavily on the view that an employer's consciously held prejudices are recognized by him or her as prejudices and through conscious processes produced discriminatory behavior. First, they would need to establish their prima facie case of intentional discrimination in firing: (a) They were Black and qualified for the positions they held, (b) they were fired from their jobs, and (c) the jobs remained open and were not eliminated (say, because of financial reasons). Typically, this prima facie case is easily established and shifts the burden to the employer to provide a legitimate, nondiscriminatory reason for their selection as cleaners and their subsequent firings.

A plethora of potential reasons could be offered to justify the decision in this case. As suggested above, perhaps Pohansky believed, based on observation, that they were the best cleaners. This belief may or may not have been infected with prejudicial attitudes or stereotypes. If Pohansky was aware of his biases and stereotypes and admitted that they influenced the manner in which he evaluated the women's cleaning abilities, the reason would be discriminatory and so would not meet the company's burden of production. Pohansky would therefore not be expected to produce this reason. Or, maybe he really did not like working with Black employees generally, so that he held racial animus toward them. Again, this reason would not be proffered because it would be discriminatory on its face. Perhaps he just disliked these particular women, so that personal animosity was the motivating cause of his behavior. (Racial animus could be underlying the personal animosity, of course, and Pohansky may or may not be aware of it.) If the personal animosity reason were offered, it would meet the employer's burden of providing a legitimate, nondiscriminatory reason: The reason is not discriminatory on its face and the firing could reflect a legitimate means of alleviating workplace tensions.

Now the plaintiffs would need to prove, by a preponderance of the evidence, that discriminatory ill motives were the real reason for their selection and termination. Clearly, evidence to establish this would be difficult. Evidence that he held no personal animosity might be difficult to obtain, and even if obtained, would not be sufficient to demonstrate that his motives were discriminatory. Without racial commentary, there is nothing that directly suggests that the personal animosity is, at least in part, motivated by racial animus. *Indirect* or circumstantial evidence could typically be offered, if available. Here, this would be evidence that Black women were treated differently than comparably situated White women. Although this could be sufficiently suggestive of discriminatory intent, the possibility remains that it would be insufficient. There must be enough evidence to create the inference that Pohansky held personal animosity toward the White woman and still did not assign her to clean, or held conscious stereotypes about the cleaning abilities of Black women that caused him to observe them as better cleaners in order for there to be comparative evidence suggestive of discriminatory intent. Without this, no intentional discrimination can be said to have occurred and Pohansky's employer would not be viewed as having illegally discriminated. Thus, the disparate treatment model of discrimination is a simple one, representing the belief that individuals are motivated through bias, prejudice, or stereotypes to make conscious choices to engage in discriminatory behavior. It tends to work best when those biases or stereotypes are consciously held (e.g., Krieger, 1995; McGinley, 2000).

Social psychological research indicates that this is not the manner in which many behavioral choices occur. Throughout the 1980s, this research focused not only on conscious choice, but also on the extent to which some psychological phenomena are set into motion unconsciously. Models of this view of cognitive processing, called dual process models, demonstrate that psychological phenomena can be influenced simultaneously by conscious (intentional) and unconscious or nonconscious (automatic) cognitive processes. Dual processing has been shown to exist in ways that can affect discrimination: Attitudes, stereotypes, and categorizing behavior have all been demonstrated to be activated automatically (e.g., Bargh, Chaiken, Govender, & Pratto, 1992; Devine, 1989; Kawakami, Dovidio, Moll, Hermsen, & Russin, 2000). Here, automatic refers to the fact that the processes occur without effort or intention, and that they can occur without any awareness on the part of the person experiencing them. In other words, employers perhaps cannot report their actual legitimate reason(s) for the action they have taken—they are unaware of them. In addition, research shows that when explaining their behavior, people often do not or cannot examine their cognitive processes; consequently, they select from memory an explanation that seems to "make sense" after the fact. Three recent research streams have focused on the extent to which phenomena occur automatically, with conclusions that more than half of human judgment may occur without conscious control (Bargh, 1989).

Implicit Prejudice and Stereotyping

Social psychology research indicates that people may hold both explicit and implicit prejudice. Explicit bias exists at the conscious level and can be assessed directly via questionnaire methods. Implicit bias requires more sophisticated assessment techniques because it exists at a subconscious level (e.g., Greenwald, Nosek, & Banaji, 2003). Even persons who consciously hold no negative stereotypes and who endorse egalitarian values may be prejudiced (i.e., have negative affective reactions) below the level of consciousness (Brendl, Markman, & Messner, 2001; Fazio, 1990; Greenwald, McGhee, & Schwartz, 1998). Research indicates that there are implicit prejudices, measurable as individual differences in attitudes, that are not consciously accessible to the people who hold them. Implicit sexist stereotypes have also been demonstrated to exist (e.g., Banaji & Greenwald, 1995). People may be racist or sexist without being aware of their biases, which can then lead to discriminatory behaviors.

Automatic Processing and Disparate Treatment

Stereotypes can be activated automatically by exposure to the relevant features of a stereotyped individual, such as sex or gender characteristics or skin color (Devine, 1989). Devine's work makes the point that virtually everyone in society knows (even if he or she does not believe) the negative stereotypes of African Americans as lazy or women as weak. These stereotypes are activated in the mind automatically, often outside the scope of awareness, when women, African Americans, or members of other stereotyped groups are encountered. Her work also shows that the active presence of these stereotypes can affect judgments even in persons who do not consciously believe the stereotypes and the effect can occur without awareness. A White candidate may be viewed as more intelligent and hard working by a supervisor who truly believes that his or her assessments are based on judgments unrelated to race. Automatic stereotypes can also be activated by constructs that are part of the stereotype (Banaji, Hardin, & Rothman, 1993). For example, a person focusing on the concept of "caregiving" may subsequently rate a female as giving greater care than persons who do not have stereotype-related constructs presented to them.

If the perceiver could choose not to act on the stereotype, which implicitly requires that the perceiver be aware of the stereotype possibility, discrimination need not arise. If Pohansky knew that he held stereotypes about Black women that involved their ability to clean, but chose not to act on his stereotypes and instead selected the women for other reasons—say, because they were, in fact, excellent cleaners—he would not have engaged in illegal discrimination. His behavior would involve an effortful, conscious choice to overcome his stereotype.

Much research has investigated the possibility of effortful control to avoid acting upon automatically activated stereotypes. Evidence implicating the capacity of conscious effort to override automatic stereotyping was presented by Fiske, who reported that an emphasis on teamwork, on accuracy and accountability in evaluation, and on upper-level commitment to eradicating stereotypes from the workplace can eliminate the application of stereotyping (Fiske, 1989). Fiske's argument was that motivational control can affect the choice to act on stereotypes. Research also indicated that less prejudiced responses may be given when people are induced to do so, for example by strong social norms against prejudice (Gaertner & Dovidio, 1986; Monteith, Deneen, & Tooman, 1996).

These findings are controversial, however, because other work had limited success in establishing the role of conscious effort in overcoming the use of stereotypes or prejudice, once they have been activated (e.g., Neuberg, 1994). Recent work even indicated that when stereotypes or prejudice are *known* to exist to the perceiver, a motive to control them may not be successful in preventing their application. Paradoxically, trying to remove the thoughts from one's consciousness can cause them to become even more pervasive in one's mind (Wegner, 1994). Also, suppressing such thoughts has been demonstrated to lead to more negative behavior directed toward the stereotyped target (Macrae, Bodenhausen, Milne, & Jetten, 1994; Wegner, Erber, Bowman, & Shelton, 1997). Attempts to compensate for bias are not necessarily effective; individuals have difficulty assessing the presence and effect of their biases and so cannot correctly compensate for them (e.g., Wegener & Petty, 1997). Feedback on whether the attempt at correction has been successful is difficult to obtain outside of the laboratory. For example, the inherent ambiguity in subjective methods of performance appraisal cannot accurately reveal the extent to which the evaluator may have been influenced by bias.

Automatic Activation of Behaviors

Recent studies have considered yet a more troubling question for discrimination law: Is there is an automatic perception–behavior link, so that even consciously held attitudes and stereotypes do not mediate behavior? If so, then discriminatory behavior can be totally outside of an individual's control—the behavioral responses themselves would be automatically activated. For example, perceiving that a person has dark skin may automatically activate not just stereotypes, but behavior as well, behavior that is not mediated by consciously held attitudes or stereotypes at all. Current research provided strong evidence for this unmediated, automatic behavior activation model (Bargh, Chen, & Burrows, 1996). In other words, as Bargh, Chen, & Burrows (1996) put it, behavior "operates in the absence of the person's intention to engage in that behavior and even when the person is trying to avoid that behavior" (p. 232). Thus, behavioral choice need not really be a "choice" at all.

Implications for Disparate Treatment

What are the implications for disparate treatment discrimination? Because psychological and legal definitions of "intent" are not coincident, each area could benefit from consideration of the other's perspective. On the legal side, research on dual processing suggests that the disparate treatment model may require less stringent criteria if it is to eliminate more subtle forms of discrimination from American workplaces. A reexamination of the notion of intent is warranted by legal scholars. From an HR or IO perspective, researchers need to be aware of the legal standard for "intent" and incorporate it into research on workplace discrimination to better understand illegal discrimination. In addition, research is needed on the ways in which dual processing works in organizational settings if discriminatory behaviors are to be attenuated in the workplace. Field studies, not just lab studies, need to be conducted to examine whether workplace phenomena can moderate the automaticity of cognitive processing and decision making, as Fiske (1989) suggested. Are there interventions that an organization can make to reduce the likelihood of stereotype activation or diminish the effects of stereotypes once activated? Can organizations alter situational linkages so that automatic behaviors do not occur? Do self-presentation or self-regulation goals, always present in the workplace, help to ameliorate automatic evaluations or decisions? Can stereotyping "habits" be broken through organizational training? Can the setting of egalitarian goals or values for an organization help to reduce stereotypic responses? Lab work that may form the basis for field research is already underway (Kawakami et al., 2000; Monteith, 1993; Monteith, Sherman, & Devine, 1998; Moskowitz, Gollwitzer, Wasel, & Schaal, 1999). There may be ways to disrupt automatic prejudice and/or discrimination. However, even if this is so, the presence of automatically activated attitudes, stereotypes, and behaviors will always present a challenge to discrimination law. As the Supreme Court has stated:

> It may be customary and quite reasonable simply to delegate employment decisions to those employees who are most familiar with the jobs to be filled and with the candidates for those jobs. It does not mean, however, that the particular supervisors to whom this discretion is delegated always act without discriminatory intent. Furthermore, even if one assumed that any such discrimination can be adequately policed through disparate treatment analysis, the problem of subconscious stereotypes and prejudices would remain (*Watson v. Forth Worth Bank & Trust*, 1988).

Disparate Treatment and the Affirmative Action Defense

Sometimes intentional discrimination can be justified in an even broader sense. When intentional discrimination has been proven to exist, a voluntarily undertaken affirmative action plan can serve as the "legitimate, nondiscriminatory reason" to meet the employer's burden in a disparate treatment case. To win his or her case, the burden remains with the plaintiff to prove that the plan is invalid and therefore a pretext for discrimination

(*Johnson v. Transportation Agency*, 1987). One way of viewing affirmative action is that it is a way of compensating for discriminatory practices and structures that have, either intentionally or unintentionally, kept groups of people out of jobs and careers (Crosby, 1994). Clearly, affirmative action is intended to be conscious, and it is the "consciousness" of it that contributes to its lack of popularity. Justice perspectives (Greenberg, 1987; Nacoste, 1987, 1994) and basic notions of the undesirability of consciously sex- or race-based categorizations (Clayton, 1996) suggest some of the major reasons why affirmative action is viewed negatively in our society. Racism and sexism have also been linked to negative attitudes about affirmative action, in addition to contributing to the underlying problem of discrimination itself (Bobo & Kleugel, 1993; Gaertner et al., 1999; Jacobson, 1985; Swim, Aikin, Hall, & Hunter, 1995; Tougas, Brown, Beaton, & Joly, 1995).

Importantly, affirmative action has unconscious aspects to it. First, it can be viewed as an organizational or societal corrective for discrimination that is automatic and unconscious. Media and political attention focuses on the conscious aspects of affirmative action without emphasizing the continuing unconscious or automatic discrimination that occurs in American society. Affirmative action, although legally viewed as a remedy for intentional discrimination, serves a bigger social purpose of focusing on fair outcomes in a society in which intentions are sometimes good but nonetheless result in discriminatory treatment.

Second, however, the "conscious" attempt to benefit minority members espoused by affirmative action programs is also infected with unconscious bias, and this bias may not always work toward the benefit of the intended recipients. A recent U.S. Supreme Court decision has clarified an important role for subjectivity in valid affirmative action plans; the guidelines provided by the Court will be important in both the employment and educational arenas. In *Gratz v. Bollinger* (2003), the Court rejected an undergraduate admissions plan at the University of Michigan because it provided a fixed number of points for each disadvantaged minority group applicant's application score. On the same day, the Court approved the affirmative action plan designed by the University of Michigan Law School, which allowed admissions decisions to be based on subjective, individualized, "plus-factor" considerations (*Grutter v. Bollinger*, 2003).

Both cases involved challenges under the Constitution. Of great importance, the Court allowed diversity to serve as a compelling state reason for taking race into account in college admissions decisions. The difference in the cases is based on the *manner* in which race can be taken into account.

Although the former plan (*Gratz*) did not set aside any seats for minority members and so was not viewed as a quota, it nonetheless was considered too rigid by a majority of the Justices to meet the individualized consideration requirement that is the foundation of discrimination law. In particular, this plan assigned 20 points to disadvantaged minority members out of a possible 150-point scoring system (points were also assigned for grade point average, test scores, in-state residency, legacy considerations, and so forth). However, in providing quantification of qualifications, this plan provided a fair amount of objectivity to the selection process. On the other hand, the *Grutter* plan was flexible in its requirement of individual consideration of each applicant, allowing for differing input of how minority status should be considered. The subjectivity inherent in this approach potentially exposes it to greater opportunities for unconscious bias in judgment and, for some decisionmakers, imperfect attempts to correct for their bias.

This outcome highlights the role of the individual under discrimination law. Even though the purpose of affirmative action may be to benefit underrepresented *groups*, the goal must be accomplished by admitting *individuals* into university or employment positions. Discrimination law requires individualized consideration of each applicant and therefore cannot permit a point system that adds the same number of points to each individual because of his or her race. The decision indicates that race can be used as a plus-factor—i.e., it can be one of many factors considered in the overall evaluation of the individual applicant—but the judicially approved program involves only a more subjective evaluation of the candidate's race. The irony in the affirmative action plan context is that subjectivity is required to provide fairness, whereas in avoiding intentional discrimination in the first place, objectivity is generally viewed as providing greater fairness.

The impact of this decision on racial minorities is not clear. Depending on the number of points that would have been added for race, either program could have produced more admissions for Blacks (and at Michigan, the probability of a Black person being admitted was higher for the law school than for the undergraduate program, as indicated in the cases). The efficacy of a subjective program depends on the unconscious negative biases or stereotypes held by the decision makers, as well as their motivations and efforts to overcome them. Researchers in both psychology and OB/HR can now study reactions to the decisions and look at how the framing of alternative quantification methods could make such plans more palatable under the law.

REASONABLE ACCOMMODATION

With the passage of the Americans with Disabilities Act (ADA, 1990), the reasonable accommodation model emerged as a strong addition to the disparate treatment and impact models of discrimination. This model is violated when an employer fails to reasonably accommodate a person with a disability who, with or without the accommodation, can perform the essential functions of the job. The model requires different treatment (considered preferential treatment by some) for persons having recognized physical or mental impairments. Although this model relies on conscious knowledge of the disability and requires consideration of the disability in crafting accommodations and determining whether an individual who is disabled can perform the job, it suffers from some of the same defects as the other models. Knowledge of a person's disability can automatically and unknowingly alter perceptions of the disabled person's ability to perform a job, with or without accommodation. In this manner, unconscious prejudice and stereotyping can affect the judgments or behaviors of the employer. Both conscious and unconscious beliefs about the amount of effort a person who is disabled will expend, for example, may cause an employer to determine that there are no accommodations that will allow a worker or applicant who is disabled to perform the job satisfactorily. Because the reasonable accommodation model does not demand that persons who are disabled be hired, only that they be treated equally with nondisabled persons after reasonable accommodation is considered and/or granted, the model may fail to produce the effect of helping persons who are disabled move into the workplace. The efficacy of the model has not yet been determined. OB/HR and behavioral science research generally should thoroughly study the role that bias and stereotypes play in decision making about and evaluation of persons with disabilities in the workplace.

Research conducted in the rehabilitation field needs to be extended to the organizational setting to understand the fate of employees who are disabled in American workplaces. For example, what factors account for how employees who are disabled are treated by supervisors and coworkers? Does ingroup–outgroup analysis apply in the same way to persons with disabilities as it does to other protected groups? What role does stigmatization concerning disabilities play in the workplace and does it differ for physical, sensory, and cognitive/mental disabilities? In particular, it appears that persons in wheelchairs are viewed much more sympathetically than are persons having other disabilities (Colella, Paetzold, & Ren, 2003). And which is more stigmatizing, the disability itself or the accommodation for the disability? Social science knowledge pertaining to these questions could add more nuanced understandings to the legal system's view that hiring and accommodating persons who are disabled will provide them with the same opportunities as others to be good workers (ADA, 1990). Although as productive as nondisabled employees when proper accommodation is granted (Baldwin & Johnson, 1998), employees who are disabled may encounter a variety of problems associated with unconscious and automatic discrimination that affect their ability to succeed.

Researchers have begun to focus on factors affecting the likelihood of a person with a disability requesting a workplace accommodation (Florey & Harrison, 2000) and coworkers' reactions when workplace accommodations are made (Colella, 2001; Paetzold, Colella, Garcia, & Simnons, 2003). Justice research needs to be extended to reveal what happens when coworkers experience negative justice perceptions toward workers with a disability who are given accommodations. Equity theory would suggest, for example, that to reestablish a balance in proportion of rewards to inputs, coworkers might engage in subversive efforts to reduce the rewards to workers with disabilities who are accommodated (Adams, 1965). These rewards could be the accommodations themselves or rewards given for performance. Alternatively, unions could be used to assist all workers in obtaining the same reward level (or the same perceived performance level) so that everyone in the workplace benefits—and persons with disabilities could be perceived as receiving no preferential treatment at all. These outcomes would be important because they could suggest "undue hardship" rationales for the employer to avoid accommodation (ADA, 1990) and such rationales would tend to undermine the goals of the ADA. Field studies are needed to determine actual outcomes for workers who are disabled and ways of compensating for them so that they enjoy the same opportunities to work as those who are not currently disabled.

Because justice theory also helps to explain opposition to affirmative action, and because the reasonable accommodation model is akin to affirmative action in the sense that the protected class characteristics are taken into account in decision making, it would be expected that parallels between affirmative action and reasonable accommodation would exist. For example, do coworkers (or the public) view disability as a "plus factor" that is taken into account when a worker who is disabled is hired? Do coworkers and/or the public tend to view employees with disabilities as unqualified? If so, does this lead to the same sense of violation of entitlement in affirmative action and disability hiring?

A relative dearth of research relating to disabilities, accommodations, and resulting workplace issues exists in psychological and organizational literature, thereby providing many research opportunities for new and established scientists in these areas. Social science research could inform the law as to difficulties employees or applicants may have in asking for accommodation—an important legal prerequisite to accommodation—in addition to the ways in which bias and perceptions of unfairness may affect employer and coworker reactions to accommodations.

DISPARATE IMPACT AND CONTEMPORARY PRACTICES

Intentional discrimination is not the only form of discrimination that has contributed to differential outcomes for protected groups. The disparate impact model, which requires no proof of intent to discriminate, is used to challenge employment practices or policies that are facially neutral but that have an adverse impact on a protected group. In this section, I first focus on statistical issues that reflect the individual nature of the disparate impact model (counter to common conceptions among I/O and HR researchers). Second, I briefly address growing concerns about the focus on "fit" in organizational research and potential conflicts under the disparate impact model of discrimination.

Multiple Screens and Heterogeneity

The disparate impact model has played a significant role in eliminating discrimination that appears to be unintentional, at least on its face. Although theoretical justifications for this model vary, making it a rather controversial model at law (Caldwell, 1985; Chamallas, 1983; Fiss, 1971; Paetzold & Willborn, 1996; Perry, 1977; Rutherglen, 1987), it is well-established and well-recognized among the I/O and HR communities. Causation is central to this model. To establish a prima facie case of disparate impact, a plaintiff must demonstrate that that an employer "uses *a particular employment practice that causes* a disparate impact on the basis of race, color, religion, sex, or national origin" (Title VII, 1993, emphasis added). [Because this language does not appear in other antidiscrimination statutes, such as the Age Discrimination in Employment Act (1985), its existence for proving other types of discrimination is unclear (e.g., *Hazen v. Biggins*, 1993).] If the plaintiff establishes the prima facie case—typically by using either the four-fifths rule or other statistical evidence—then the burden of proof shifts to the employer to prove business necessity or job-relatedness (*Griggs v. Duke Power Company*, 1971).

The causation element in disparate impact analysis is a complex one, as has been argued by Paetzold & Willborn (1996, 2002). Obviously, the model does not require proof that the cause of the discrimination is the result of bad motives; in addition, it does not account for the fact that there are always multiple causes why a particular employment screen would tend to have an adverse impact on a protected group. Among others, social and/or psychological causes contribute to all disparate impacts. For example, word-of-mouth recruiting may tend to replicate a predominantly White work force because of "similar-to-me" biases in who receives the "word of mouth" (see, e.g., Rand & Wexley, 1975, for a discussion of the bias) and because relevant neighborhoods may be predominantly White. These causes may even evince an unconscious prejudice against members of a protected class, but because intent is irrelevant to a showing of disparate impact, such issues are irrelevant in disparate impact cases. The disparate impact model therefore does not provide a way for unconscious intent to be considered in employment discrimination, either as a plaintiff sword or as an employer shield. It is concerned only with the consequences of certain employment practices on protected classes and seeks to eliminate "artificial, arbitrary, and unnecessary barriers to employment when the barriers operate invidiously to discriminate" (*Griggs v. Duke Power Co.*, 1971, p. 431).

The disparate impact model acts in mysterious ways, as can easily be seen by examining some statistical issues regarding it. A nonobvious characteristic of the disparate impact model is that it does not require proof that an employer's screening mechanism has an *actual* impact on the workplace (nor is absence of actual impact an employer defense (*Connecticut v. Teal*, 1982)). Most organizations rely on the use of multiple screening mechanisms, particularly for hiring decisions. Because there can be redundancy in the use of multiple screens, no one screen may be the actual cause of the impact. The plaintiffs only have to prove that the screen would have had a disproportionate impact on the members of the plaintiff's class if it were applied *independently* of any other screens used in the selection process in order to establish their prima facie case, however. For example, if word-of-mouth recruiting would have screened the same individuals as a required test, then the use of the word-of-mouth recruiting would have been redundant and the disparate impact could have been "caused" by the test. The net effect of the recruiting method would be zero. However, a challenge to the recruiting method could lead to its removal if it could not be business justified. Thus, the disparate impact model provides the somewhat counterintuitive result that a screening method can be viewed as having an adverse impact even though it has no actual (net) impact on any members of the protected class in the employer's work force. The employer's liability in the form of make-whole remedy (e.g., backpay), however, would extend only to those members of the workforce who experienced an actual effect, which in this case would be no one (Paetzold & Willborn, 1996).

The situation can become even more complicated by a further examination of the redundancy of screens. For example, it is easy to demonstrate that an employment screen can have a disparate impact on a protected group even though it has the net actual effect of benefiting the group. Consider the example in Table 14.1. The word-of-mouth recruiting approach yields a selection rate of .49 for Black persons and .70 for White

TABLE 14.1

Disparate Impact With Net Benefits to the Protected Class

	Word-of-Mouth Recruiting	
	Pass	*Don't Pass*
Pass	Black 49	Black 1
	White 70	White 10
Tests		
Don't Pass	Black 0	Black 50
	White 0	White 20

Adapted from Paetzold, R. L., & Willborn, S. L. (1996). Deconstructing disparate impact: A view of the model through new lenses. *North Carolina Law Review, 74,* 325–399.

persons, thus leading to a selection ratio of .70 (which is less than .80). Thus, an adverse impact exists on Black persons, and the one Black person who didn't "pass" through the word-of-mouth recruiting would be entitled to relief. This is true even though the net affect of the word-of-mouth recruiting operates to favor Black people as a group. In other words, only one of 100 Black persons is actually adversely affected by the selection mechanism, compared to 10 of 100 White persons. In fact, the word-of-mouth recruiting mechanism increases the proportion of Black persons in the pool available for hire from .385 to .412 vis-à-vis White persons (i.e., without the requirement, 50 Black and 80 White persons pass and are available for hire, but with the requirement, 49 Black and 70 White persons pass and are available for hire). Thus, as a group Black people should prefer that the word-of-mouth recruiting be left in place, but the one Black person who is disadvantaged would be motivated to bring (and could win, if no business necessity exists) a disparate impact lawsuit (Paetzold & Willborn, 1996, p. 362). The example demonstrates the *individual* nature of the disparate impact model, which is counter to traditional I/O or HR understanding of the model, e.g., "[D]isparate impact discrimination occurs when an apparently neutral employment practice disproportionately *excludes a protected group* from employment opportunities" (DeNisi & Griffin, 2001, p. 74, emphasis added); "[A]dverse impact...occurs when the same standard is applied to all applicants or employees, but that standard *affects a protected class more negatively* (adversely)" (Gomez-Mejia, Balkin, & Cardy, 1998, p. 91, emphasis added). It is certain members of a group who may suffer an adverse impact; the group may not suffer at all.

This line of argument suggests that employers should think carefully about the potential redundancy of their employment screens—not just in terms of their validity for predicting performance (the typical I/O or HR concern), but also in terms of their actual impact. An in-basket exercise, for example, may have some predictive validity beyond that provided by an interview, but unless the predictive validity of the exercise is substantial enough to demonstrate business necessity, it could produce disparate impact problems that the employer might rather avoid.

Yet another problematic aspect of disparate impact analysis arises when the employer uses an employment practice to screen a population that is heterogeneous along a key dimension. Factors other than the employment practice may be associated both with the pass rate and with the protected group status. For example, a recruiting technique that has a disparate impact on Black persons may have differential pass rates depending on the socioeconomic status or education level of the persons it is applied to. Suppose that education level is associated with race in the sense that persons of a given race with differing educational levels tend to have different outcomes from the recruiting technique. Because of aggregation paradoxes, it is possible that within each educational level, there is no disparate impact of the recruiting technique on Black persons—or perhaps there is even an advantage to Black persons. Traditional disparate impact analysis would ignore these latter possibilities—i.e., the Black plaintiffs could establish a disparate impact for the one selection mechanism— yet the stratification by educational level would seem to shed statistical doubt on that finding. Statistical inferences based on the initial aggregation across educational level is misleading in either of these two cases, because educational level confounds the relationship between race and recruiting pass rate. Because the recruiting technique is the only selection mechanism used by the employer (i.e., educational level is not a selection criterion), it is unlikely that the employer could defend by showing that the confounding factor—educational level—eliminated the impact (see Paetzold & Willborn, 1996, who discuss the "blindness" of the disparate impact model). The relationship between recruiting method pass rate and educational level should be examined by the employer as part of the determination as to whether the recruiting method should be employed.

Obviously, not all possible dimensions of the population can be identified as being relevant and important to consider. Nonetheless, some clearly have the potential to be related to selection mechanisms and are easy enough to consider. Because employers do not want to create a situation in which they could be held liable for a disparate impact when a practice that is useful but perhaps difficult to justify as meeting business necessity is used, they should take these heterogeneous factors into account in their decision making.

The stratification problem here could go the other way as well. Just because a practice does not appear to have a disparate impact when evaluated on its own in a heterogeneous population does not guarantee that one will not appear when plaintiffs examine it across key dimensions. In other words, even if the recruiting method did not have an overall disparate impact on Black persons, it might have one for those who have particular educational levels or even at every educational level (i.e., a Simpson's paradox; see Paetzold & Willborn, 2002).

Plaintiffs are allowed to make fairly fine-tuned statistical comparisons in establishing prima facie cases (e.g., *Bazemore v. Friday*, 1986; Paetzold & Willborn, 2002), so it is arguable that plaintiffs could be successful in this instance. Assuming a finding of adverse impact, the burden of proof would shift to the employer to prove business necessity. It is unclear whether the employer could meet its burden by demonstrating a general sense of business necessity; instead, it might have to justify use of the recruiting technique within every educational level separately for which a disparate impact exists. This would obviously be a more difficult task, often requiring more validation studies.

Thus, joint and stratified effects of employment practices need to be evaluated by employers when they consider their adoption. As the statistical sophistication of the law increases, employers must be more aware of the increased demands of employment discrimination law. Practices and considerations that have worked in the past may no longer be applicable.

"Fit" and Disparate Impact

Recently, concern has been voiced by legal scholars about the trend toward work arrangements and selection mechanisms that include a subjective evaluation of "fit" (e.g., Polland, 2000, addressing self-directed work teams). "Fit" arises in a variety of HR contexts, but especially in selection. Person–job fit (PJ) is operationalized as the match between an applicant's knowledge, skills, and abilities (KSAs) and job characteristics. Typically, the KSAs can be measured in ways that are job-related and so are justifiable even in the presence of disparate impact discrimination (see below). Person–organization fit (PO), on the other hand, relies on values to determine congruence or fit, typically assessed through a subjective interview process (Adkins, Russel, & Werbel, 1994; Cable & Judge, 1996; Huffcutt, Conway, Roth, & Stone, 2001; Judge, Higgins, & Cable, 2000) and is typically measured in terms of the alignment of the personality, values, and goals of the applicant with the values, goals, and norms of the organization (e.g., Kristof, 1996). In the case of adverse impact, PO may be more difficult to defend.

Research on interviews suggests that demographic variables such as race and sex have an impact on interview outcomes (Judge et al., 2000;

Prewett-Livingston, Field, Veres, & Lewis, 1996). Constructs such as personality traits, personal interests and preferences, and physical attributes are also assessed in interviews (Huffcutt et al., 2001). Research indicates that similarity effects exist in interviews, so that greater fit is perceived for applicants who are similar to interviewers or ideal employees, even in structured interviews (Werbel & Gilliland, 1999). Thus, although PO sounds attractive and yields benefits for employees and employers (e.g., greater organizational commitment, Cable & Judge, 1996; job satisfaction, lower stress, and fewer intentions to turnover, Lovelace & Rosen, 1996), it may be quite dangerous for selection purposes under discrimination law.

Obviously, intentional discrimination can be a problem to the extent that biases or stereotypes are used to determine this fit, and the limitations of the disparate treatment model, discussed earlier, may fail to eliminate this type of discrimination. However, to the extent that the assessment of fit is a facially neutral practice, it is also subject to disparate impact challenge. Plaintiffs must first identify what aspect(s) of the selection process cause an adverse impact to establish their prima facie case. If the aspects of the process—here, the means for determining "fit"—are "incapable of separation for analysis" (Title VII, 1993), then the plaintiffs need only identify the entire process as the basis for their challenge. If PO is based on a "gestalt" or gut feeling, it is clear that plaintiffs need only identify the PO process itself as the basis for the adverse impact challenge. The Equal Employment Opportunity Commission (EEOC) Uniform Guidelines (1978) state that whenever a selection procedure results in an adverse impact based on protected group status, the organization using that procedure must demonstrate job-relatedness or business necessity. As mentioned above, PJ measurement would seem to meet this requirement. PO, however, may pose a legal risk to the organization. Although subjective judgments are not per se illegal and courts may prefer to defer to employers (who are in better positions to assess needs and qualifications than courts are), employers are at risk when they rely on such subjective decisionmaking (e.g., *Giacoletto v. Amax Zinc Co.*, 1992). HR researchers may want to examine the possibilities for making PO assessment more objective and concrete, leading to greater reliability and validity to support the job-relatedness of the measures.

Assessment of fit does not occur only at time of hire. Other selection times—promotions, formation of work teams, and appointments to leadership positions—all involve notions of fit and typically involve some degree of subjectivity. Qualifications become imprecise or vague from a legal perspective. This suggests that much of contemporary HR functioning is affected by subjectivity in evaluation and should be reexamined by researchers.

CONCLUSION

In this chapter I have surveyed three of the major models of discrimination law with an eye to presenting ways in which the law and psychological research suffer a "gap." (I have deliberately omitted the hostile environment model, which requires a major investigation of its own.) By conducting this survey, I demonstrate that current discrimination law makes rather simplistic assumptions about the nature of employment discrimination and the ways in which motivation can defeat prejudiced attitudes and biases in decision making. A greater awareness of psychological research can perhaps help the law to make existing models more sensitive to the realities of how discrimination occurs. It also becomes clear, however, that applicable behavioral science research is etiolated by failure to consider the intricacies and demands of discrimination law, so that new research questions remain to be studied. A closer marriage of law and HR-I/O-psychological research is needed if we ultimately are to grow in our understanding of discrimination and continue to develop methods for attenuating or eliminating it.

REFERENCES

Adams, J. S. (1965). Inequity in social exchange. In L. Berkowitz (Ed.), *Advances in experimental psychology* (Vol. 2, pp. 267–299). New York: Academic Press.

Adkins, C. L., Russell, C. J., & Werbel, J. D. (1994). Judgments of fit in the selection process: The role of work value congruence. *Personnel Psychology, 47,* 505–623.

Age Discrimination in Employment Act of 1985, 29 U.S.C. §§ 621–634 (1985).

Americans with Disabilities Act of 1990, 42 U.S.C. §§ 12101–12213 (1990).

Baldwin, M. L., & Johnson, W. G. (1998). Dispelling the myths about work disability. In T. Thomason & D. W. Hyatt (Eds.), *New approaches to disability in the workplace* (pp. 39–61). Madison, WI: Industrial Relations Research Association.

Banaji, M. R., & Greenwald, A. G. (1995). Implicit gender stereotyping in judgments of fame. *Journal of Personality and Social Psychology, 68,* 181–198.

Banaji, M. R., Hardin, C. D., & Rothman, A. J. (1993). Implicit stereotyping in person judgment. *Journal of Personality and Social Psychology, 65,* 272–281.

Bargh, J. A. (1989). Conditional automaticity: Varieties of automatic influence in social perception and cognition. In J. S. Uleman & J. A. Bargh (Eds.), *Unintended thought* (pp. 3–51). New York: Guilford Press.

Bargh, J. A., Chaiken, S., Govender, R., & Pratto, F. (1992). The generality of social perception: The influence of trait information presented outside of conscious awareness on impression formation. *Journal of Personality and Social Psychology, 43,* 437–449.

Bargh, J. A., Chen, M., & Burrows, L. (1996). Automaticity of social behavior: Direct effects of trait construct and stereotype activation on action. *Journal of Personality and Social Psychology, 71,* 230–244.

Bazemore v. Friday, 478 U.S. 385 (1986).

Bobo, L., & Kleugel, J. R. (1993). Opposition to race-targeting: Self-interest, stratification ideology, or racial attitudes? *American Sociological Review, 58,* 443–464.

Brendl, C. M., Markman, A. B., & Messner, C. (2001). How do indirect measures of evaluation work? Evaluating the inference of prejudice in the implicit association test. *Journal of Personality and Social Psychology, 81,* 760–773.

Cable, D. M., & Judge, T. A. (1996). Person-organization fit, job choice decisions, and organizational entry. *Organizational behavior and human decision processes, 67,* 294–311.

Caldwell, P. M. (1985). Reaffirming the disproportionate effects standard of liability in Title VII litigation. *University of Pittsburgh Law Review, 46,* 555–606.

Chamallas, M. (1983). Evolving conceptions of equality under Title VII: Disparate impact theory and the demise of the bottom line principle. *UCLA Law Review, 31,* 305–383.

Clayton, S. D. (1996). Reactions to social categorization: Evaluating one argument against affirmative action. *Journal of Applied Social Psychology, 26,* 1472–1493.

Colella, A. (2001). Coworker distributive fairness judgments of the workplace accommodation of employees with disabilities. *Academy of Management Review, 26,* 100–116.

Colella, A., Paetzold, R. L., & Ren, L. (2003). A meta-analytic review of the effects of disability on HR measures of evaluation. Manuscript in progress, available from first author.

Connecticut v. Teal, 457 U.S. 440 (1982).

Crosby, F. J. (1994). Understanding affirmative action. *Basic and Applied Social Psychology, 15,* 13–41.

DeNisi, A. S., & Griffin, R. W. (2001). *Human resource management.* Boston: Houghton Mifflin.

Devine, P. G. (1989). Stereotypes and prejudice: Their automatic and controlled components. *Journal of Personality and Social Psychology, 56,* 5–18.

EEOC Uniform Guidelines, 29 CFR §1607.14(C)(4) (1978).

Fazio, R. H. (1990). Multiple processes by which attitudes guide behavior: The MODE model as an integrative framework. In M. P. Zanna (Ed.), *Advances in experimental social psychology* (Vol. 23, pp. 75–109). New York: Academic Press.

Fiske, S. T. (1989). Examining the role of intent: Toward understanding its role in stereotyping and prejudice. In J. S. Uleman & J. A. Bargh (Eds.), *Unintended thought* (pp. 253–286). New York: Guilford Press.

Fiss, O. M. (1971). A theory of fair employment laws. *University of Chicago Law Review, 38,* 235–278.

Florey, A. T., & Harrison, D. A. (2000). Responses to informal accommodation requests from employees with disabilities: Multistudy evidence on willingness to comply. *Academy of Management Journal, 43,* 224–233.

Gaertner, S. L., & Dovidio, J. F. (1986). An aversive form of racism. In J. F. Dovidio & S. L. Gaertner (Eds.), *Prejudice, discrimination, and racism* (pp. 61–89). New York: Academic Press.

Gaertner, S. L., Dovidio, J. F., Rust, M. C., Nier, J. A., Banker, B. S., Ward, C. M., Mottola, G. R., & Houletter, M. (1999). Reducing intergroup bias: Elements of intergroup cooperation. *Journal of Personality and Social Psychology, 76,* 388–402.

Giancoletto v. Amax Zinc Co., 954 F.2d 424 (7th Cir. 1992).

Gomez-Mejia, L. R., Balkin, D. B., & Cardy, R. L. (1998). *Managing human resources.* Upper Saddle River, NJ: Prentice-Hall.

Gratz v. Bollinger, 123 S. Ct. 2411 (2003).

Greenberg, J. (1987). Reactions to procedural injustice in payment distributions: Do the means justify the ends? *Journal of Applied Psychology, 72,* 55–61.

Greenwald, A. G., McGhee, D. E., & Schwartz, J. L. K. (1998). Measuring individual differences in implicit cognition. *Journal of Personality and Social Psychology, 74,* 14645–1480.

Greenwald, A. G., Nosek, B. A., & Banaji, M. R. (2003). Understanding and using the implicit association test: I. An improved scoring algorithm. *Journal of Personality and Social Psychology, 85,* 197–216.

Griggs v. Duke Power Co., 401 U.S. 424 (1971).

Grutter v. Bollinger, 123 S. Ct. 2325 (2003).

Hazen v. Biggins, 507 U. S. 604 (1993).

Huffcutt, A. I., Conway, J. M., Roth, P. L., & Stone, N. J. (2001). Identification and meta-analytic assessment of psychological constructs measured in employment interviews. *Journal of Applied Psychology, 86,* 897–913.

Jacobson, C. K. (1985). Resistance to affirmative action: Self-interest or racism? *Journal of Conflict Resolution, 29,* 306–329.

Johnson v. Transportation Agency, 480 U.S. 616 (1987).

Judge, T. A., Higgins, C. A., & Cable, D. M. (2000). The employment interview: A review of recent research and recommendations for future research. *Human Resource Management Review, 10,* 383–406.

Kawakami, K., Dovidio, J. F., Moll, J., Hermsen, S., & Russin, A. (2000). Just say no (to stereotyping): Effects of training in the negation of stereotypic associations on stereotype activation. *Journal of Personality and Social Psychology, 78,* 871–888.

Krieger, L. H. (1995). The content of our categories: A cognitive bias approach to discrimination and equal employment opportunity. *Stanford Law Review, 47,* 1161–1248.

Kristof, A. L. (1996). Person-organization fit: An integrative review of its conceptuali-zations, measurement, and implications. *Personnel Psychology, 49,* 1–49.

Lovelace, K., & Rosen, B. (1996). Differences in achieving person-organization fit among diverse groups of managers. *Journal of Management, 22,* 703–722.

McDonnell Douglas Corp. v. Green, 411 U.S. 792 (1973).

McGinley, A. C. (2000). ¡Viva la evolucion!: Recognizing unconscious motive in Title VII. *Cornell Journal of Law & Public Policy, 9,* 415–492.

Macrae, C. N., Bodenhausen, G. V., Milne, A. B., & Jetten, J. (1994). Out of mind but back in sight: Stereotypes on the rebound. *Journal of Personality and Social Psychology, 67,* 808–817.

Melton, G. (Ed.). (1986). *The law as a behavioral instrument.* Lincoln, NE: University of Nebraska Press.

Monteith, M. J. (1993). Self-regulation of prejudiced responses: Implications for progress in prejudice-reduction efforts. *Journal of Personality and Social Psychology, 65,* 469–485.

Monteith, M. J., Deneen, N. E., & Tooman, G. (1996). The effect of social norm activation on the expression of opinions concerning gay men and Blacks. *Basic and Applied Social Psychology,* 267–288.

Monteith, M. J., Sherman, J. W., & Devine, P. G. (1998). Suppression as a stereotype control strategy. *Personality and Social Psychology Review, 2,* 63–82.

Moskowitz, G. B., Gollwitzer, P. M., Wasel, W., & Schaal, B. (1999). Preconscious control of stereotype activation through chronic egalitarian goals. *Journal of Personality and Social Psychology, 77,* 167–184.

Nacoste, R. W. (1987). But do they care about fairness? The dynamics of preferential treatment and minority interest. *Basic and Applied Social Psychology, 8,* 177–191.

Nacoste, R. W. (Barnes) (1994). If empowerment is the goal . . . : Affirmative action and social interaction. *Basic and Applied Social Psychology, 15,* 87–112.

Neuberg, S. L. (1994). Expectancy-confirmation processes in stereotype-tinged social encounters: The moderating role of social goals. In M. P. Zanna & J. M. Olson (Eds.), *The psychology of prejudice: The Ontario Symposium* (Vol. 7, pp. 103–130). Hillsdale, NJ: Lawrence Erlbaum Associates.

Paetzold, R. L., Colella, A., Garcia, M. F., & Simmons, E. (2003). *Peer perceptions of accommodation fairness: The effects of disability, accommodation, and outcome in competitive task situations.* Unpublished manuscript, Texas A & M University (under review).

Paetzold, R. L., & Willborn, S. L. (1996). Deconstructing disparate impact: A view of the model through new lenses. *North Carolina Law Review, 74,* 325–399.

Paetzold, R. L., & Willborn, S. L. (2002). *The statistics of discrimination: Using statistical evidence in discrimination cases.* Rochester, NY: Thomson West.

Perry, M. J. (1977). The disproportionate impact theory of racial discrimination. *University of Pennsylvania Law Review, 125,* 540–589.

Polland, A. (2000). The emergence of self-directed work teams and their effect on Title VII law. *University of Pennsylvania Law Review, 148,* 931–968.

Prewett-Livingston, A. J., Field, H. S., Veres, J. G., & Lewis, P. M. (1996). Effects of race on interview ratings in a situational panel interview. *Journal of Applied Psychology, 81,* 178–186.

Rand, T. M., & Wexley, K. N. (1975). Demonstration of the effect, "similar to me," in simulated employment interviews. *Psychological Reports, 36,* 535–544.

Rutherglen, G. (1987). Disparate impact under Title VII: An objective theory of discrimination. *University of Virgina Law Review, 73,* 1297–1345.

Slack v. Havens, 522 F.2d 1091 (9th Cir. 1975).

St. Mary's Honor Center v. Hicks, 509 U.S. 502 (1993).

Swim, J. K., Aikin, K. J., Hall, W. S., & Hunter, B. A. (1995). Sexism and racism: Old-fashioned and modern prejudices. *Journal of Personality and Social Psychology, 68,* 199–214.

Texas Department of Community Affairs v. Burdine, 450 U.S. 248 (1981).

Title VII of the Civil Rights Act, 42 U.S.C. §§ 2000e-20003-17. (1993 edition).

Tougas, F., Brown, R., Beaton, A., & Joly, S. (1995). Neosexism: Plus ca change, plus c'est pareil. *Personality and Social Psychology Bulletin, 21,* 842–849.

Watson v. Forth Worth Bank & Trust, 487 U.S. 977 (1988).

Wegener, D. T., & Petty, R. E. (1995). Flexible correction processes in social judgment: The role of naïve theories in corrections for perceived bias. *Journal of Personality and Social Psychology, 68,* 36–51.

Wegner, D. M. (1994). Ironic processes of mental control. *Psychological Review, 101,* 34–52.

Wegner, D. M., Erber, R., Bowman, R., & Shelton, J. N. (1997). *On trying not to be sexist.* Unpublished manuscript, University of Virginia.

Werbel, J. D., & Gilliland, S. W. (1999). Person-environment fit in the selection process. *Research in Personnel and Human Resources Management, 17,* 209–243.

15

Combating Organizational Discrimination: Some Unintended Consequences

Madeline E. Heilman
Michelle C. Haynes
New York University

As evidenced by the collection of work in this volume, discrimination on the basis of group membership clearly has been and continues to be a pressing organizational issue. Many organizations have not turned a blind eye to this problem and have implemented programs in an attempt to eliminate harmful discriminatory practices from the workplace. These efforts have taken numerous forms, varying not only in degree of formality, but also in level of organizational implementation (from recruitment to selection to promotions). Perhaps the most well known and hotly debated of these programs is couched under the policy umbrella "affirmative action." Affirmative action is intended to rectify past discrimination and prevent current discrimination. Nonetheless, there is a growing body of research that suggests that affirmative action also can have deleterious consequences for those targeted to benefit from it. This chapter explores this research and examines these hidden potential costs of affirmative action—costs that paradoxically may undermine its intended objectives.

The majority of the studies reported in this chapter focus on women beneficiaries of affirmative action. Although we do not believe the processes we identify are likely to differ for women and other affirmative action targets (and indeed the research that focuses on race bears that out), it is important to keep our focus on women in mind when reviewing the research presented here. Also, readers should recognize that the investigations presented throughout this chapter are limited to those that address the question of how individuals who are believed to have benefited from affirmative action are viewed by others. There has, however, been a great deal of work on other unintended by-products of affirmative action—particularly those that concern its effects on the self-view and the work attitudes and behavior of intended beneficiaries. Generally, this work supports the idea that association with affirmative action can negatively influence self-evaluations of ability and performance effectiveness (Heilman, Lucas, & Kaplow, 1990; Heilman, Simon, & Repper, 1987; Major, Feinstein, & Crocker, 1994; Nacoste, 1985), the choice of task difficulty (Heilman, Rivero, & Brett, 1991), actual performance effectiveness (Brown, Charnsangavej, Keough, Newman, & Rentfrow, 2000), reactions to others in the work setting (Heilman, Kaplow, Amato, & Stathatos, 1993), and assumptions about others' expectations of oneself and ensuing task decisions and self-regard (Heilman & Alcott, 2001). Because this volume is about discrimination in organizations, however, we chose not to focus on the direct impact of affirmative action on those targeted to be beneficiaries, but rather to focus on how their association with affirmative action can affect the way in which others react to them.

HISTORICAL BACKGROUND

Title VII of the Civil Rights Act of 1964 marked a critical milestone in the fight for justice and equality for women and minorities in the workplace. Specifically, Title VII prohibited discrimination on the basis of race, color, religion, national origin, and gender. In addition, Title VII specified the creation of the Equal Employment Opportunity Commission (EEOC), a government agency charged with monitoring and investigating employment practices in violation of Title VII.

By 1967, President Lyndon Johnson had issued executive orders 11246 and 11375. In tandem, these orders required organizations wishing to enter contracts with federal agencies to take "affirmative action" to ensure that all current and future potential employees were employed in fair numbers and treated fairly on the job. Furthermore, regulations set forth by the Secretary of Labor required organizations to develop internal monitoring to identify problem areas and, should underutilization be identified, required organizations to develop goals and timetables for remedying such problems. Examples of such affirmative action might include targeted recruitment, career advancement training, and validation of selection instruments (Green, 1989).

Affirmative action, as originally conceived, is a policy designed to "overcome the discriminating effect of past or present practices, policies, or other barriers to equal employment opportunity" (EEOC, 1979). More recently, the Supreme Court ruling in *Grutter v. Bollinger* (2003) additionally legitimized affirmative action as a means of realizing diversity goals. Through a variety of methods, it aims to remedy discrimination and increase representation of designated disadvantaged groups, namely women and ethnic minorities who are underrepresented in the workforce, e.g., African Americans and Latinos. However, affirmative action goes beyond adopting an equal opportunity strategy. Equal opportunity is a passive policy in which employers disregard sex and race when making employment decisions. In contrast, affirmative action specifies that active efforts be made to consider group membership and that it be explicitly taken into account in such decisions. Thus, the assumption built into this policy is that nondiscrimination alone is not sufficient to counteract the consequences of prejudice and inequality; rather, something additional is needed.

AFFIRMATIVE ACTION IN PRACTICE

As we have seen, affirmative action in its classic form is mandated for companies entering into contract with the federal agencies by executive orders 11246 and 11375. Yet the term has come to represent a much broader range of policies. Affirmative action has become a blanket term that refers to any number of active policies adopted by organizations to remedy the effects of discrimination (Clayton & Crosby, 1992; Glazer, 1988).

Oppenheimer (as cited in Tomasson, Crosby, & Herzberger, 1996) devised a typology of the various forms of affirmative action programs and identified five basic models of programs. The first type of program is "targeted hiring," in which a position is designated a priori, to be filled by a member of a particular group. In such instances only members of the designated group are considered in filling the position. Another type of program is the quota type. This refers to all programs that set specific numerical requirements for hiring members of disadvantaged groups. A third type of affirmative action involves programs that do not designate positions or set numerical requirements, but rather give special preferences to certain categories of persons. This has sometimes been referred to as a "plus factor" policy (Clayton & Crosby, 1992) as it often involves assigning applicants additional points (used to tally a final admission score) purely on the basis of group membership. There also is the self-examination type, which involves auditing the current status of minorities and women in an organization. Should inequities be detected, goals and timetables are identified in order to remedy the underrepresentation of such group members. The final type of affirmative action program can be characterized as outreach programs, in which active efforts are made in recruitment of women and minorities to positions in the workplace where they are underrepresented.

Regardless of the multiplicity of affirmative action program types, however, *the perception* of affirmative action remains relatively undifferentiated. In particular, many continue to associate affirmative action with quotas (Clayton & Crosby, 1992; Holloway, 1989; Kravitz & Platania, 1993; Northcraft & Martin, 1982). There appears to be a widespread assumption that affirmative action is little more than preferential selection based solely on demographic group membership. The fact that targeted hiring, quotas, and some types of plus factor programs have been deemed illegal seems to make little difference. Our contention is that this assumption about what affirmative action entails, even if it is not consistent with fact, is the driving force behind the negative consequences of affirmative action for its intended beneficiaries. As we hope will become clear to the reader, the deleterious consequences of affirmative action we report are not the result of the affirmative action program itself, but rather the result of how it is perceived by others.

THE STIGMA OF INCOMPETENCE

What are the negative consequences of affirmative action, and why do they occur? There appears to be a stigma of incompetence associated with affirmative action beneficiaries. This stigma has been identified and written about by members of the community who are the intended beneficiaries of affirmative action policies and programs (Wilkerson, 1991; Wycliff, 1990). Shelby Steele (1990), an often heard voice in the affirmative action debate, has written that affirmative action "tells us that racial preferences can do for us what we cannot do for ourselves" (p. 119). Similarly, Himmelfarb (1988) asserts that beneficiaries are likely to suffer the stigma of second-class citizenship, "always laboring under the presumption, warranted or not" that they were hired because of their race or gender and not based on their qualifications. More recently, Justice Clarence Thomas (*Grutter v. Bollinger*, 2003), in his dissent to the majority opinion upholding the affirmative action policy at the University of Michigan Law School, indicated that students who would have been admitted even without an affirmative action policy in place are now "tarred as undeserving" because of their implied association with affirmative action.

There is research evidence that supports the argument that stigmatization results from affirmative action efforts. Garcia, Erkine, Hawn, and Casmay (1981) found that the qualifications of minority graduate student applicants were rated less favorably when the university's affirmative action plan was highlighted, than when there was no mention of affirmative action. Similarly, Summers (1991) found that evaluations of female managers were influenced negatively when an organization was portrayed as being committed to an affirmative action policy. Northcraft and Martin (1982) found that when a Black investment banker was purported to have been an affirmative action hire, respondents were more likely to pair him with a poor resume than when evaluating Whites or Blacks not associated with affirmative action. Finally, Jacobson and Koch (1977) found that female managers were more likely to be perceived as the cause of a team's failure, yet not given credit for its success, when she had been selected because of her sex rather than her merit or because of chance.

Attribution theory, particularly Kelley's work on the discounting principle (Kelley, 1987), offers an explanation as to why being associated with affirmative action has such negative repercussions. According to Kelley, individuals use the discounting principle when faced with several possible causes for an effect. In the case of affirmative action, the mere suggestion of the policy, because it is presumed to entail preferential selection based on demographic group membership, offers an alternate, salient, and plausible reason for a person's hire, independent of his/her job qualifications. Consequently, the importance of the role of the person's qualifications in the decision process is "discounted"—the individual is thought to be hired primarily because of his/her gender or minority status, with qualifications having been only incidental to the decision-making process. Because qualifications are typically so critical to personnel decision making, the assumption that they did not play a central role is likely to lead to the further assumption that the person is not competent and would never have obtained the position without the help of affirmative action (Pettigrew & Martin, 1987). Thus, the perceived disregard of established decision criteria gives rise to inferences of incompetence.

EMPIRICAL EVIDENCE

A series of studies was conducted to directly examine whether being labeled as an affirmative action beneficiary does indeed produce a stigma of incompetence. In the first study, reported in Heilman, Block, and Lucas (1992), we sought to determine whether women associated with an affirmative action program would be viewed as less competent than men and also women not associated with an affirmative action program. Furthermore, we reasoned that if affirmative action leads to negative competence perceptions via the discounting process, these perceptions should occur regardless of whether the situation is one in which the targeted individual would have been susceptible to negative views based on ordinary stereotype based processes. Thus, we not only expected association with affirmative action to worsen an unfavorable evaluation of a woman's competence when the job was one for which she typically was viewed as suboptimally qualified, but we also expected association with affirmative action to create an unfavorable evaluation of a woman's competence when it would not otherwise have occurred.

A laboratory experiment was used in the initial test of these ideas. Both hiree (man, woman, affirmative action woman) and job sex-type (strongly male or slightly male), were systematically varied. Participants, who were male and female college undergraduates, reviewed a packet of materials concerning a person recently hired for a job. The packet included a job description in the form of a recruitment bulletin indicating job requirements and work responsibilities and an employment application containing information about educational background, work experience, and general demographic information. These were followed by a brief questionnaire containing, among other measures, several items comprising a competence scale (e.g. "How competently do you expect this individual to perform this job?" *very competently–not at all competently*; "How effective do you think this individual will be at doing the work?" *very effective–not at all effective*).

Based on information obtained from our subject population, the job of electrician was chosen to represent a strongly male sex-typed position and that of hospital laboratory technician was chosen to represent the slightly male sex-typed job. To reinforce this manipulation, the proportional representation of men and women currently employed in the position at the hiring organization was presented (electrician—92% men; lab technician—59% men). Hiree was varied using female and male names, and a photograph was included to ensure that sex, not race was the clear basis of the affirmative action initiative. In addition, on the application form, in a section labeled "for clerical purposes only," there appeared the handwritten word, "hire," accompanied by the start date. In the affirmative action condition, the parenthetical phrase "affirmative action hire" also was included.

Results revealed the pattern of data predicted. When there was no mention of affirmative action, women were evaluated less favorably than men in terms of competence in the strongly male sex-typed position (electrician), whereas they were evaluated equally favorably in the more neutral sex-typed position (lab technician). However, when associated with affirmative action, the female hiree was rated less favorably than men in both types of positions; moreover, she was rated less favorably than female hirees not associated with affirmative action. Interestingly, male and female participants did not differ in their evaluations, suggesting that the effect of the association with affirmative action on competence perceptions is not contingent on the perceiver's sex. But, most importantly, these data attested to the existence of a stigma of incompetence tainting beneficiaries of affirmative action initiatives, and they illustrated the depth of its negative consequences. As predicted, the affirmative action label was shown not only to worsen problems for women when merely being a woman was problematic because of negative stereotypical expectations, but also to *create* problems for women when their gender would not ordinarily have resulted in negative perceptions of competence.

In order to gain insight into the processes underlying the negative effects of being associated with affirmative action, we obtained information about the assumptions our participants were making about the procedures used to select affirmative action beneficiaries. Results indicated that the affirmative action hirees were thought to have been hired far less on the basis of their qualifications to do the job well than were either the female non-affirmative action hirees or the male hirees. These findings are consistent with the idea that "discounting" mediates the stigmatization process.

The results of the laboratory study provide strong support for the idea that association with affirmative action gives rise to a stigma of incompetence. Yet, despite the apparent clarity of these results, questions could and should be raised about the degree to which they reflect the attitudes and sentiments of those actually in the workplace. Indeed, the effects of affirmative action may be different in situations such as the workplace where individuals have a great deal more information about each other. To address this issue, we designed a field study (Heilman et al., 1992, Study 2) to determine if the effects found in our lab would be paralleled by those found in the field. Specifically, we were interested in exploring how beliefs about the role affirmative action policies played in hiring decisions related to competence evaluations of women and minority group members employed in nontraditional positions in actual organizations.

Respondents were recruited to complete a questionnaire in airports, train stations, and outdoor sitting areas. All were White men ranging in age from 25 to 57, currently employed in variety of industries. The cover page informed the participant that the purpose of the survey was to get a better understanding of working people's impressions of the changing American workforce. Furthermore, it instructed participants to think of a specific coworker who had joined their unit in the past few years and is a member of a group that in the past did not typically have this type of job, and to answer the questionnaire with that individual in mind. If the respondent could not think of coworker who satisfied these criteria, he returned the questionnaire.

There were two primary variables of interest: (a) presumed role of affirmative action in the hiring decision and (b) perceived competence. The first variable was assessed at the beginning of the questionnaire by asking participants: "To what extent do you think this individual was given the position because of affirmative action policies?" (*completely–not at all*). This question was embedded in several similarly structured questions about other possible reasons for hiring (e.g., work experience, educational background, and so on) in order to disguise our interest in affirmative action. Perceived competence was assessed toward the end of the questionnaire using similar items to those used in the lab study, which were combined to create a competence scale.

Correlational analyses yielded the expected pattern. There was a significant negative relationship between the extent to which an individual was presumed to be an affirmative action hiree and perceptions of competence $(r = -.72, p < 0.001)$. The greater the role affirmative action was thought to have played in a coworker's hire, the less favorably that coworker was rated in terms of his or her competence. Indeed, approximately 50% of the variance in competence ratings can be explained by the belief that affirmative action policies had an impact on the hiring decision. Furthermore, the negative correlation between presumption of affirmative action in hiring and perceptions of competence was significant whether the target person chosen by the respondent was a White woman, a Black man, or a Black woman. Thus, these data provided strong validation of the findings of the lab study.

Data collected about the assumed role of qualifications lent further support to the discounting process as the critical underlying dynamic. The greater the presumed role of affirmative action in the hiring decision, the less were qualifications to do the job well seen as the basis of the coworker's selection and, very importantly, the less likely was the coworker to be seen as qualified to do the job at the time he or she was hired. These findings support our ideas about the assumptions that are made regarding the procedures used in implementing affirmative action policies; they also support our ideas about the assumptions that are made regarding the skills and talents brought to the job by those thought to be hired on the basis of affirmative action.

THE TENACITY OF THE EFFECT

The results of the studies just described support the idea that a stigma of incompetence is associated with affirmative action. Men and women, students and working people, all drew inferences of incompetence regarding beneficiaries of affirmative action, and these inferences occurred regardless of whether the affirmative action policy was explicitly stated or was only presumed to have been utilized, and whether the beneficiaries were women or members of racial minorities. Therefore, it is clear that this phenomenon is both widespread and affects a broad range of targets in variety of situations. But what is the ultimate impact of such inferences? Do they persist when information about performance becomes available, especially information that is inconsistent with them? If inferences of incompetence arising from the affirmative action label are quickly overridden when disconfirming evidence becomes available, then they are ultimately of little importance. If these negative inferences prevail even in the face of contradictory information, however, then there is clear reason for concern. Questions such as these led us to explore the boundaries of the affirmative action induced stigma of incompetence and to attempt to identify the conditions that regulate when it does or does not occur.

There is research that suggests that having performance information may limit incompetence inferences regarding those associated with affirmative action. Many researchers have found that category-based inferences dominate impression formation only when information is otherwise minimal (Fiske, Neuberg, Beattie, & Milberg, 1987). Indeed, evidence from a variety of literatures demonstrates that individuating information about a person can weaken or override the influence of categorical information (Locksley, Hepburn, & Ortiz, 1982; Nisbitt, Zukier, & Lemley, 1981; Tosi & Einbinder, 1985). According to these findings, as performance information about a beneficiary becomes available, it should mitigate the effects of the affirmative action label.

However, there also is evidence suggesting that it is not all types information that will preclude inferences of incompetence (Heilman, 1984; Krueger & Rothbart, 1988; Kunda & Sherman-Williams, 1992). These studies make apparent that the information must not only be relevant but also clearly diagnostic if it is to have impact on that judgment. If the information is vague or equivocal, then that information can easily be distorted to conform to the categorical prototype (Nieva & Gutek, 1980).

These ideas led us to think that although information about on-the-job performance effectiveness can override the inferences of incompetence arising from the affirmative action label, this is likely to occur only when the information is clear and unambiguous in its implications— a not-so-common occurrence in work organizations in which information about performance often lacks precision and frequently cannot be attributed exclusively to one individual. We therefore decided not only to investigate the general effects of disconfirming performance information on inferences of incompetence, but also to test the persistence of the stigma of incompetence arising from affirmative action when there are differing levels of ambiguity associated with available performance information.

In the first study, the level of ambiguity was varied by the degree of precision of the performance information provided (Heilman, Block, & Stathatos, 1997). Managers from a large Northeastern insurance company participated in this study concerning "personnel selection, placement, and advancement processes" during the course of company-sponsored training sessions. Fifty-one percent of the managers were men and 49% were women, and 94% were 25 to 54 years old. The methodology employed in this study was similar to the initial laboratory study described in this chapter, the first study in Heilman et al. (1992). However, in this investigation only one job was used, that of a computer programmer. It was chosen to represent a job that was male sex-typed, but not extremely so, so that the effects of affirmative action would not be obscured by stereotype-based incompetence inferences. As in the earlier study, participants were given packets containing a job description and an employment application containing information about an employee's education and work experience. However, in this study, participants also were given a six-month job activity summary for the employee, purportedly written by the employee's supervisor. Following these materials was a questionnaire asking for reactions to the employee on several measures including perceived competence.

Once again the hiree was either male or female and, when female, either associated with affirmative action or not. This was accomplished in exactly the same manner as in the Heilman et al. (1992) study. Performance information was manipulated via the supervisor's response to a question immediately following the description of the employee's activities, "check the category which best describes this employee's performance in the past six months." The actual response and the response format were together used to vary the ambiguity of the performance information. In the success conditions, the employee was always rated in the highest category, but the range of categories differed. In clear success conditions, there were five category ratings: top 5%, top 10%, top 25%, top 50%, or bottom 50%. In ambiguous success conditions, there were only two categories: top 50% or bottom 50%. In addition, there was a condition with no information about success, in which no rating scale was presented in the materials, and a failure condition in which the employee had been placed by his supervisor in the bottom 50% in terms of performance.

Results revealed that, as in earlier studies, with no information about success affirmative action women were rated as less competent than both the women not associated with affirmative action and the men. This pattern of data persisted when information was provided about success that was ambiguous, i.e., rated to be in the top 50% rather than the bottom

50%. It was only when information about success was clear and unequivocal (rated to be in the top 5%) that the affirmative action woman was seen as equally competent to the nonaffirmative action woman or the man. Without clear information of success, ratings of affirmative action women were as negative as when no information was provided and, even more dishearteningly, as when failure information had been provided. Ratings of the appropriateness of a salary increase, which also were obtained in this study, followed exactly the same pattern as the competence ratings.

Because of the plausible confounding of clarity of success with magnitude of success in this initial study—it is conceivable that those in unambiguous conditions were seen as more successful than those in ambiguous conditions—another study was conducted operationalizing clarity of success differently. In the second study of Heilman et al. (1997), we systematically varied the attributional ambiguity of the success information. That is, although all research participants were exposed to equally highly successful employees, the information provided to them allowed for different possible interpretations of how the employee's performance success had come about. Specifically, a report that coaching by a senior coworker had been available was designed to raise questions, for those participants in the ambiguous success conditions, about the degree to which the target employee was the unique source of his/her success.

The research participants were managers in the same insurance company that served as the site for the first study, and they too were approximately half men and half women who fell into the 25 to 54 year age range. They were each asked to evaluate either a man, woman, or woman who was an affirmative action hire and were exposed to either clear or ambiguous information about performance success. As in the first study, they evaluated a hypothetical individual who ostensibly had been employed as a computer programmer.

The procedures were identical to those of the first study, except that all participants received the same favorable information about the hypothetical employee's performance success. Performance information was once again conveyed in a six-month activity summary that contained a supervisor's description of the employee's job activity as well as the supervisor's rating of the category that best described the employee's job performance during this initial six-month period. This time, however, the possible rating categories were not percentage groups as they had been in Study 1. Instead, the categories were "far exceeded expectations," "exceeded expectations," "met expectations," and "did not meet expectations." In all cases the "far exceeded expectations" category was the one designated by the supervisor; thus, all employees reviewed were depicted as highly successful.

Although the performance information provided through the performance review instrument always conveyed a high level of performance success, the clarity of the source of success differed for participants in the clear and the ambiguous success conditions. For participants in the clear success condition, the supervisor's description of the employee's job activity was the same as that used in the first study. However, for those in the ambiguous success condition, we appended the following sentences: "Throughout this period Mark (Wendy) was coached by a senior computer programmer (as are all new hires in our department). The coach was available to Mark (Wendy) on an "as needed" basis, and could be called upon to act as a consultant when problems arose."

Results indicated that despite indications of substantial success, competence ratings of affirmative action women were equal to those of nonaffirmative action women or men only when the information conveyed about success was not ambiguous. When the information conveyed created ambiguity about the source of their success, competence ratings of affirmative action women differed from ratings of both nonaffirmative action women and men. Ratings of the appropriateness of a salary increase followed a similar pattern: Only participants in unambiguous success conditions treated an employee who had benefited from affirmative action similarly to the others; when information about the source of their success was ambiguous, employees associated with affirmative action were treated more harshly in terms of salary recommendations than either the nonaffirmative action women or the men.

The findings from these two studies are consistent in their message—only success information that is unequivocal in its implications for an individual's competence negates the stigma of incompetence attached to beneficiaries of affirmative action. Evidently, ambiguity allows people to dismiss or ignore information, and the disconfirmatory potential of successful performance information can be undercut by its lack of clarity. This suggests that the negative competence inferences accompanying the affirmative action label are not easily overpowered by job performance information. People seem to resist relinquishing a negative view of those associated with affirmative action, and these individuals remain incompetent in the minds of onlookers unless they are "proved" to be competent.

These findings are particularly important because ambiguity about performance is inherent in so many typical organizational settings. The conditions necessary to counteract the affirmative action stigma often are not present either because the success of a work product cannot be objectively assessed and inference is required to evaluate it, or because the work context is such that work is performed interdependently in teams, and the unique contribution of any one individual to the team product is difficult to discern. In either of these cases, the results of these two studies suggest that the affirmative action stigma would persist regardless of an employee's success, promoting biased decision making.

REACTIONS TO DIFFERENT AFFIRMATIVE ACTION POLICIES

As we have already noted, without information to the contrary people tend to assume that affirmative action involves preferential selection of women and minorities with little regard to qualifications. In actuality, however, affirmative action is not one monolithic policy. On the contrary, there are many variants of affirmative action policies and many different forms that affirmative action practices and initiatives can take (Nacoste, 1990, 1996; Taylor Carter, Doverspike, & Cook, 1996). Because in the investigations we have reported so far the nature of the affirmative action policy was unstated, and therefore our participants' assumptions about it were allowed free reign, it is important to examine the consequences when different affirmative action policies are explicitly presented. Particularly relevant is a study done as part of a series of investigations that directly examined the effect of different affirmative action policies. Our focus here is on the study that investigated whether different affirmative action policies mitigate the stigma of incompetence associated with affirmative action beneficiaries (Heilman, Battle, Keller, & Lee, Study 2 1998).

Although affirmative action specifies that gender or minority status be taken into account in personnel decision making, it does not rule out the use of merit considerations. In fact, the law, in the form of federal regulations and court decisions, clearly rules out the use of race alone without consideration of merit. However, it is the relative weighting of group membership versus merit criteria, such as qualifications, that differentiates between the many strategies for implementing affirmative action in the workplace. Following Seligman (1973), affirmative action can be thought of as a continuum, the critical dimension being the extent to which group membership counts in decision making, with practices that focus primarily on group membership on the "hard" end and practices that use merit as the primary criterion on the "soft" end of the continuum. Given our ideas about the discounting process as the mechanism driving negative competence inferences regarding affirmative action beneficiaries, we reasoned that policies that are softer, and focus more on merit, would produce fewer negative consequences.

In order to test these ideas, our study closely followed our laboratory study documenting the stigma of incompetence associated with affirmative action, but included variations of the specific policy guiding the selection process. Participants were MBA students, half men and half women, who were asked to review information about an employee being considered for a promotion. Participants received a packet of materials including a job description in the form of a job posting describing a position for a production supervisor for the Corporate Paper Company; a page from the hiring company's policies and procedures manual; a photocopy of an employment application; and a brief questionnaire. In all conditions, the applicant was a White woman.

The manipulation of selection policies was delivered on the page from the company's policies and procedures manual. There were a total of five levels of selection policy. The first was wholly merit-based (merit), and participants were told that the company in question "is a quality employer and has a merit-based employment policy" and that it "gives primary consideration to hiring individuals with the strongest qualifications." The other four conditions were affirmative action conditions; for all, the participants were told that the company "is an equal opportunity employer and has an affirmative action employment policy" and that it is "actively seeking female and minority employees." The affirmative action conditions were: (a) group membership based, in which primary consideration was said to be given to hiring women and members of minority groups (preferential absolute); (b) minimum qualifications were used as a screen before further consideration of group membership (preferential minimum); (c) equal qualifications were required for group membership to be considered in selection (preferential equivalent); and (d) a policy in which no information other than the general statement was given about the nature of the affirmative action policy (preferential ambiguous).

Results indicated that the hiree was viewed as more competent in the merit policy condition than in the any of the conditions involving affirmative action. However, participants did make distinctions among the various affirmative action policies in making competence judgments. The hiree was viewed as more competent in the preferential equivalent condition than in each of the other preferential policy conditions (which did not differ from one another). This data pattern was repeated for projections of the hiree's career progress. The female hirees selected based on a merit policy were expected to advance in their careers far more quickly and successfully than female hirees selected based on an affirmative action policy, regardless of the nature of that policy. However, female hirees selected based on a preferential equivalent policy were rated more likely to succeed than those in the preferential absolute, preferential minimum, or the preferential ambiguous conditions.

These results demonstrate once again that a stigma of incompetence is often attached to those believed to be the beneficiary of affirmative action.

Indeed, the female hiree in each of the four conditions involving any form of affirmative action was rated less favorably in terms of competence and likely career progress than the female hired purely on the basis of merit. Evidently, even when merit criteria are prominent in the decision process, there is a distinction made between those who are selected as part of an affirmative action effort and those who are not.

Nonetheless, the data also attest to the importance of distinguishing among different forms of affirmative action policies. They demonstrate the mitigating effects on competence perceptions when it is made clear that although affirmative action has occurred, merit was a major factor in the decision. Those in preferential-equivalent conditions were rated more favorably than others selected preferentially, and prognoses for their career progress also were more optimistic. However, it is noteworthy that the minimum standard policy, which also provided some information about merit, did little to assuage the negative effects of affirmative action. It was no different in effect than a policy in which merit was not a consideration at all. So, it was not the incorporation of any type of merit information that tempered the effects of affirmative action, but only information that clearly assured that merit standards had been maintained. These findings have since been supported by the work of Evans (2003), who distinguished between "illegal" affirmative action policies (those in which unequal or unqualified candidates are chosen) and "legal" affirmative action policies (those in which equal or comparable candidates are chosen), finding that Black targets were rated more negatively in achievement-related traits than were White targets only when the policy was an "illegal" one.

It also is noteworthy that in the absence of information about the role of merit in the decision process, participants acted as if they had received information of a policy in which merit criteria had been totally disregarded. This result is consistent with the idea that, unless given reason to think otherwise, people assume that affirmative action is little more than preferential selection without regard to qualifications. This finding thus emphasizes the need not only for the inclusion of a strict merit criterion, but also for explicitly conveying this policy information, if the unintended and unwanted by-products of affirmative action initiatives are to be quelled.

WHEN AFFIRMATIVE ACTION IS INFERRED

Thus far we have presented empirical evidence that demonstrates how being associated with affirmative action can lead to perceptions of incompetence. However, in much of this work it is clearly stated that the individual in question is "an affirmative action hire." But, often, there is more ambiguity surrounding an individual's selection, and affirmative action is only inferred. Whether stated or inferred, affirmative action should have the same consequences. But when is it inferred? When is it that an individual is thought to be hired preferentially because of his or her demographic group membership?

Inferences about why someone has been selected for a position are influenced not only by the characteristics of that individual but also by the context in which the selection occurs. Attribution theory predicts that when something out of the ordinary occurs it will spark efforts to make sense of the unexpected event (Hastie, 1984; Pyszczynski & Greenberg, 1981). With respect to the work environment, such cues may include the presence of a solo female or Black employee in an otherwise all male or all White group, respectively, or the sudden hiring of large numbers of persons representative of a demographic group that was not previously represented in a particular job or industry.

Of course, there are many possible explanations for the presence of such unexpected newcomers. However, with the visibility of affirmative action policies in recent decades and the widespread belief that it is a major factor in personnel decision making (Kravitz & Platania, 1993), affirmative action is likely to be a salient as well as readily available and plausible explanation for unexpected newcomers. In addition, because it requires far less cognitive exertion than modifying group stereotypes to account for their unexpected presence, the affirmative action explanation is much more efficient and therefore more convenient to use. Therefore we suspected that when the selection of a woman or minority group member is out of the ordinary, and it provokes a search for an explanation and none is provided, there will be a predisposition toward inferring that affirmative action was involved even when there is no direct evidence for it. In other words, we expected a proclivity to attribute the out of ordinary appearance of those from societally targeted demographic groups to preferential selection when a vacuum exists about the actual basis of selection.

To test these ideas, we designed a study (Heilman & Blader, 2001) in which undergraduate participants, both male and female, were told that the research concerned decision making in graduate school admissions and that they would be reviewing the application materials of a student recently admitted to a doctoral program at their university. We expected that when the selection policy was left ambiguous, a solo woman would elicit inferences of preferential selection on the basis of sex that would be as strong as those made when an affirmative action policy was actually made explicit. This was not expected to occur when there were many other women in the cohort, and the presence of any one woman was not out of the ordinary. Perceptions of qualifications were expected to follow the same pattern as the gender-based preferential selection inferences.

The packet of materials reviewed by research participants included a description about the department of "Urban Health Sciences" (a bogus department chosen to be neutral in sex-type), including the program requirements, opportunities for financial support, admissions criteria, number of applicants, the range of their test scores and GPAs, and a listing of the current year's admittees. After reading the departmental information, participants reviewed the application of two of the year's eight admittees and responded to a brief questionnaire. The applications of the two admittees, modeled after actual graduate school application forms, were designed to be equivalent forms and were rotated between the target, who was always rated first, and the other admittee (always of the opposite sex) to ensure there were no systematic application effects.

Selection policy was manipulated by varying the information on admissions policy contained in the department information; there were three different statements. The admissions policy indicated that The Department of Urban Health Sciences: considers diversity, and women and minority applicants were to be given particular consideration (affirmative action); only considers merit, and qualifications were to be the only factor considered (merit); or considers a variety of factors . . . applicants will be reviewed on a case by case basis (ambiguous)." Information about solo or nonsolo status was manipulated by the gender composition of the incoming class. Either there was one woman and seven men, or there were four women and four men.

The data yielded the pattern of results predicted. When the admissions policy was ambiguous, there were different perceptions of the role that gender had played in the solo and nonsolo female conditions. In the solo condition, when the admission policy was ambiguous, gender was viewed as having played as important a role in selection as when affirmative action was the stated policy. This did not however occur when the admittee was not the solo woman. Furthermore, there were differences in how qualified the female admittee was thought to be. When solo (but not when nonsolo), female admittees in the ambiguous policy condition were rated as poorly in terms of qualifications as those in the affirmative action condition, and they were viewed as significantly less qualified compared to others in the merit condition.

The results of this study demonstrate that when an "unexpected" hire is made in the absence of a clearly stated selection policy, assumptions of preferential selection can occur even when there is no apparent reason for them. Thus, the problems created by affirmative action are not limited only to those who are definitively designated as affirmative action hires. This research suggests that until conceptions of affirmative action and the role it plays in selection decisions is changed, there may be a tendency to assume that affirmative action has been involved in selection, with the result being derogation of the selectee.

OTHER ORGANIZATIONAL EFFORTS: DIVERSITY PROGRAMS

Thus far this chapter has focused on the implications of affirmative action policies as a tool used to combat discrimination in the workplace. We have presented evidence that a stigma of incompetence results from association with affirmative action efforts and demonstrated that women and minorities thought to be beneficiaries of affirmative action are inferred to be less competent that those thought to be selected on a merit basis. But affirmative action programs are not the only organizational efforts directed at remedying inequities caused by discrimination. Initiatives to actively ensure and promote demographic diversity also have abounded. It is therefore important to consider whether these efforts have effects that are similar or different than affirmative action efforts.

In recent years organizations have implemented a variety of diversity management programs, estimated to exist in as many as half of the companies in the United States with more than 100 employees (Lubove, 1997). These programs are aimed at systematically recruiting, promoting, and retaining a heterogeneous array of employees throughout the ranks of the organization. Diversity programs seek to increase the presence and participation of women and minorities at all organizational levels and seek to maximize the benefits of an increasingly diverse workforce for organizational functioning (Richard & Kirby, 1998).

However, diversity programs, by their nature, may give rise to the same unintended problems as those produced by affirmative action programs. Although the goal of achieving workforce diversity often is aimed at allowing organizations to maximize their competitive advantage, it is likely to be perceived otherwise; it is likely to be seen as yet another way of giving preferential treatment to women and members of minority groups. If this is the case, then diversity programs may also cause their presumed beneficiaries to be viewed as incompetent. Kelley's discounting principle once again provides a theoretical framework for understanding these potentially deleterious consequences. Because diversity efforts draw attention to demographic group membership and place special value on that membership, they are likely to supply onlookers with a plausible and salient explanation for selection decisions independent of qualifications. As a result, the role an individual's qualifications played in the personnel decision may be discounted, with the assumption of incompetence the result.

Three experiments were recently conducted to investigate how diversity goals affect the competence perceptions of those who are likely to have been targeted by them (Heilman & Welle, 2002). In all three studies male and female undergraduate participants were informed about a newly formed five-person work team working on a group task and were given an explanation for how the work team was assembled.

In the first study, the work team was composed of both women and men. The rationale for how the group was composed was said to be either to ensure that the organization's demographic diversity was represented (diversity) or to ensure that the best resources and expertise were present (merit). We expected that women would be viewed as less competent when a diversity rationale rather than a merit rationale was given for the group's assembly. However, because diversity goals only provide a plausible explanation for personnel decision making for certain groups—those whose representation organizations are seeking to increase—we did not expect the diversity label to negatively affect ratings of male group members. In addition, the composition of the group was varied in order to examine the role of gender salience in the process. Kanter (1977) has demonstrated that the more rare a woman is in a work unit, the more salient her gender becomes. This evidence in conjunction with Sackett, DeBois, & Noe's (1991) findings that the fewer women present in a work setting, the more negative their job evaluations, prompted the prediction that inferences of incompetence regarding women in a work group assembled for diversity reasons would be particularly negative when the woman was the solo woman in the group.

Participants were told the research was concerned with the evaluation of workgroups and the individual members of those groups. They received a packet of materials that included a description of the group task on which the group they were to review was working, a group information sheet, and a questionnaire. Rationale for group assembly and proportion of women was manipulated on the group information sheet. A photograph was also included; it depicted all group members as White. Participants rated both a female and a male target.

The results supported our predictions. Women who were members of groups reportedly assembled for diversity reasons were viewed less favorably than women in parallel groups reportedly assembled on the basis of group member merit; they were seen as less competent and expected to be less influential in their groups. In addition, there was indication that women who are solos—the only female members of their groups—were the most derogated of all group members. As expected, the rationale for group assembly had no effect on ratings of male group members.

The results of this study raised important questions. Were the negative ratings of the female group members in the diversity condition unique to the diversity rationale or would any nonmerit-based criterion for group assembly have had the same consequence? Secondly, were the results found in study 1 limited to situations in which there is a single diversity dimension represented in the group? In order to address these issues, we designed a second study in which we added a random rationale for group assembly, one of scheduling time convenience, and also varied the demographic heterogeneity of the group such that there was only gender heterogeneity (four men and one White woman) or heterogeneity in both gender and race (three White men, one Black man, and one White woman). Thus, in all cases there was only one woman in the group, but the men were either heterogeneous with respect to race or were not. The procedure used was identical to that used in the first study. A photograph of the workgroup made apparent the type of demographic heterogeneity in the group.

Analyses revealed the pattern of results expected. The woman who was a member of the group assembled for reasons of ensuring diversity was rated as less competent and expected to be less influential in the group than the woman who was a member of a group assembled for either reasons of merit or for reasons of scheduling convenience. This indicates that inferences of incompetence associated with the diversity rationale are not simply a consequence of any nonmerit-based rationale for group assembly, but rather are specific to the diversity goal rationale and the salience of demographic group that it promotes. Furthermore, heterogeneity of the group did not impact the degree of stigmatization for the female target. Evidently, it matters little whether a woman is the sole potential beneficiary of diversity efforts or if she shares this status with others in the group; she is seen as equally incompetent and noninfluential.

Both of these studies that examine the consequences of being associated with a diversity initiative have focused on gender as the demographic category of interest. However, because the reach of diversity goals often extends to racial minorities, we thought it important to investigate whether non-White members of a group are similarly negatively viewed when associated with diversity goals and whether the degree of heterogeneity is a factor in how they are perceived. We therefore designed a third study that replicated study 2, except that participants rated a Black male in the group as opposed to a White female.

Analyses revealed a similar pattern of results for the Black male as for the female target in study 2. The Black man was rated as less competent and was expected to be less influential in the group when the rationale for group assembly was ensuring diversity rather than merit or scheduling convenience. Heterogeneity of the group once again had no impact on these ratings.

Taken together this series of studies demonstrates that being associated with efforts to ensure demographic diversity can have potentially harmful consequences. It seems that affirmative action programs are not unique in their ability to raise doubts regarding a beneficiary's qualifications. Other selection processes that highlight demographic group membership also run the risk of feeding inferences that its likely beneficiaries are incompetent and ill equipped to effectively perform the work required.

CONCLUSIONS

Throughout the course of this chapter we have presented research that supports the idea that affirmative action and other programs designed to reduce the incidence of discrimination in work organizations, rather than becoming part of the solution, can become part of the problem. As we have demonstrated, being associated with programs that draw attention to gender or minority status can ultimately lead to the derogation of intended beneficiaries, tainting them with a stigma of incompetence. Thus, the very individuals these programs are designed to help may instead be harmed.

One striking finding of the many studies reported here is the apparent pervasiveness of the stigma of incompetence. Whether the raters were women or men, whether they were working people or students, and whether they were old or young, they rated potential beneficiaries of affirmative action programs in the same way. Moreover, their reactions were much the same regardless of whether the potential beneficiaries were women or racial minorities, or whether the program was specifically labeled as affirmative action or was said to be focused on ensuring demographic diversity. Thus, the general tendency we uncovered in these investigations seems quite robust: programs that highlight demographic group membership as a critical feature in decision making run the risk of harming those they are designed to help.

Does everyone react equally negatively to potential beneficiaries of affirmative action? Although we have not presented it here, extensive work has been conducted examining predictors of attitudes toward affirmative action programs. Not only have numerous studies found that attitudes toward affirmative action programs are significantly affected by the structure of the affirmative action plan (Kravitz, 1995; Kravitz & Klineberg, 2000), but also individual difference variables such as race, gender, political ideology, and prejudice have been found to predict the endorsement of affirmative action policies (Kravitz et al., 1997). Racism and sexism, for example, have been linked to negative attitudes about affirmative action (Jacobson, 1985; Tougas, Brown, Beaton, & Joly, 1995). Whether these differences in attitudes toward affirmative action affect the perceptions of what affirmative action entails and/or the perceptions of those thought to have benefited from it has not been directly investigated. However, our findings indicating that actual variations in affirmative action policies have an effect on how individuals ostensibly targeted by such policies are regarded suggest that there is indeed a connection between attitudes toward affirmative action programs and perceptions of its presumed beneficiaries.

Readers are reminded that the processes that we have illustrated throughout this chapter are based on the widely shared assumption that affirmative action is a policy that weights demographic group membership far more heavily than qualifications in decision making. However, a distinction must be made between actual organizational policies and the perceptions of such policies. In fact, merit very often is the critical factor used in decisions involving affirmative action, with demography playing a far more minor role. This fact highlights two separate but related issues critical to averting the detrimental consequences of affirmative action efforts on competence perceptions. First, affirmative action policies must have a strong and well thought through merit component. This of course means that there must be a clear sense of what constitutes merit—it may well be broader than core task requirements, encompassing team performance, organizational citizenship, and the like. Secondly, management must be extremely careful in how it frames affirmative action policies. If there is a real desire to prevent the stigma that accompanies association with affirmative action, information that merit has been central in decision making must be disseminated to those throughout the organization. It is only by directly altering the perception of what affirmative action entails that the negative consequences for its intended beneficiaries are likely to be precluded.

Finally, we want to make clear that it is not the position of the authors that affirmative action is necessarily a bad thing. Certainly we concur with its aims to increase the representation of women and minorities at all levels of the organizational hierarchy and to ensure that discrimination on the basis of demographic group membership be forever banished from the organizational landscape. Moreover, we applaud the enormous benefits affirmative action has wrought, both in work organizations and in society more generally. However, we firmly believe that affirmative action, as a policy, has unintended by-products that should be uncovered and addressed. The findings presented throughout this chapter demonstrate that a stigma of incompetence results from association with affirmative action, whether this association is explicit or only inferred. Moreover, there is evidence that these incompetence inferences prevail even in the face of disconfirming evidence. Thus, paradoxically, the aims of affirmative action may well be undermined by the policy itself. Although it provides access to those who may have been otherwise blocked from entry, affirmative action may burden them with the weight of biased perceptions of their competence, ultimately precluding them from the opportunity to be equal partners in the organizational enterprise. Thus, the findings reported here should serve as a warning. Despite the desirability of eliminating discrimination in the workplace, if care is not taken the methods used to combat it can backfire, causing their own costly and undesirable consequences.

REFERENCES

Brown, R. P., Charnsangavej, T., Keough, K. A., Newman, M. L., & Rentfrow, P. J. (2000). Putting the "affirm" into affirmative action: Preferential selection and academic performance. *Journal of Personality and Social Psychology, 79*, 736–747.

Clayton, S. D., & Crosby, F. J. (1992). *Justice, gender, and affirmative action*. Ann Arbor, MI: University of Michigan Press.

Equal Employment Opportunity Commission (EEOC) (1979). *Affirmative action guidelines* (No. 44FR444). Washington, DC: U.S. Government Printing Office.

Evans, D. C. (2003). A comparison of the other-directed stigmatization produced by legal and illegal forms of affirmative action. *Journal of Applied Psychology, 88*, 121–130.

Fiske, S. T., Neuberg, S. L., Beattie, A. E., & Milberg, S. J. (1987). Category-based and attribute-based reactions to others: Some informational conditions of stereotyping and individuating processes. *Journal of Experimental Social Psychology, 23*, 399–427.

Garcia, L. T., Erskine, N., Hawn, K., & Casmay, S. R. (1981). The effect of affirmative action on attributions about minority group members. *Journal of Personality, 49*, 427–437.

Glazer, N. (1988). The future of preferential affirmative action. In P. A. Katz, & D. A. Taylor, Dalmas A. (Eds.), (1988). *Eliminating racism: Profiles in controversy. Perspectives in social psychology* (pp. 329–339). New York: Plenum Press.

Green, K. (1989). *Affirmative action and principles of justice*. New York: Greenwood.

Grutter v. Bollinger et al. No. 02-241, Argued April 2003, Decided June 23, 2003.

Hastie, R. (1984). Causes and effects of causal attribution. *Journal of Personality and Social Psychology, 46*, 44–56.

Heilman, M. E. (1984). Information as a deterrent against sex discrimination: The effects of applicant sex and information type on preliminary employment decisions. *Organizational Behavior and Human Decision Processes, 33*, 174–186.

Heilman, M. E., & Alcott, V. B. (2001). What I think you think of me: Women's reactions to being viewed as beneficiaries of preferential selection. *Journal of Applied Psychology, 86*, 574–582.

Heilman, M. E., Battle, W. S., Keller, C. E., & Lee, R. A. (1998). Type of affirmative action policy: A determinant of reactions to sex-based preferential selection? *Journal of Applied Psychology, 83*, 190–205.

Heilman, M. E., & Blader, S. L. (2001). Assuming preferential selection when the admissions policy is unknown: The effects of gender rarity. *Journal of Applied Psychology, 86*, 188–193.

Heilman, M. E., Block, C. J., & Lucas, J. A. (1992). Presumed incompetent? Stigmatization and affirmative action efforts. *Journal of Applied Psychology, 77*, 536–544.

Heilman, M. E., Block, C. J., & Stathatos, P. (1997). The affirmative action stigma of incompetence: Effects of performance information ambiguity. *Academy of Management Journal, 40,* 603–625.

Heilman, M. E., Kaplow, S. R., Amato, M. A., & Stathatos, P. (1993). When similarity is a liability: Effects of sex-based preferential selection on reactions to like-sex and different-sex others. *Journal of Applied Psychology, 78,* 917–927.

Heilman, M. E., Lucas, J. A., & Kaplow, S. R. (1990). Self-derogating consequences of sex-based preferential selection: The moderating role of initial self-confidence. *Organizational Behavior and Human Decision Processes, 46,* 202–216.

Heilman, M. E., Rivero, J. C., & Brett, J. F. (1991). Skirting the competence issue: Effects of sex-based preferential selection on task choices of women and men. *Journal of Applied Psychology, 76,* 99–105.

Heilman, M. E., Simon, M. C., & Repper, D. P. (1987). Intentionally favored, unintentionally harmed? Impact of sex-based preferential selection on self-perceptions and self-evaluations. *Journal of Applied Psychology, 72,* 62–68.

Heilman, M. E., & Welle, B. (2002). *Disadvantaged by diversity? The effects of diversity goals on competence perceptions.* Unpublished manuscript.

Himmelfarb, G. (1988, May 15). Universities creating second-class faculties: Letter to the editor. *The New York Times.*

Holloway, F. (1989). What is Affirmative Action? In F. Blanchard & F. Crosby (Eds.), *Affirmative action in perspective* (pp. 9–19). New York: Springer-Verlag.

Jacobson, C. K. (1985). Resistance to affirmative action: Self-interest or racism? *Journal of Conflict Resolution, 29,* 306–329.

Jacobson, M. B., & Kosh, W. (1977). Women as leaders: Performance evaluation as a function of methods of leader selection. *Organizational Behavior and Human Decision Processes, 20,* 149–157.

Kanter, R. M. (1977). Some effects of proportions on group life: Skewed sex ratios and responses to token women. *American Journal of Sociology, 82,* 965–990.

Kelley, H. H. (1987). Attribution in social interaction. In E. E. Jones & D. E. Kanouse (Eds.), *Attribution: Perceiving the causes of behavior* (pp. 1–26). Hillsdale, NJ, Lawrence Erlbaum Associates.

Kravitz, D. A. (1995). Attitudes toward affirmative action plans directed at Blacks: Effects of plan and individual differences. *Journal of Applied Social Psychology, 25,* 2192–2220.

Kravitz, D. A., Harrison, D. A., Turner, M. E., Levine, E. L., Chaves, W., Brannick, M. T., Demmomg, D. L., Ruddell, C. J., & Conard, M. A. (1997). *Affirmative action: A review of psychological and behavioral research.* Bowling Green, OH: Society for Industrial and Organizational Psychology.

Kravitz, D. A., & Klineberg, S. L. (2000). Reactions to two versions of affirmative action among Whites, Blacks, and Hispanics. *Journal of Applied Psychology, 85,* 597–611.

Kravitz, D. A., & Platania, J. (1993). Attitudes and beliefs about affirmative action: Effects of target and of respondent sex and ethnicity. *Journal of Applied Psychology, 78,* 928–938.

Krueger, J., & Rothbart, M. (1988). The use of categorical and individuating information in making inferences about personality. *Journal of Personality and Social Psychology, 55,* 187–195.

Kunda, Z., & Sherman-Williams, B. (1992). Stereotypes and construal of individuating information. *Personality and Social Psychology Bulletin, 19,* 90–99.

Locksley, A., Hepburn, C., & Ortiz, V. (1982). Social Stereotypes and judgment of individuals: An instance of the base-rate fallacy. *Journal of Experimental Social Psychology, 18,* 23–42.

Lubove, S. (1997). Damned if you do, damned if you don't. *Forbes, 160,* 122–134.

Major, B., Feinstein, J., & Crocker, J. (1994). Attributional ambiguity of affirmative action. *Basic and Applied Social Psychology, 15,* 113–141.

Nacoste, R. W. (1985). Selection procedure and responses to affirmative action: The case of favorable treatment. *Law and Human Behavior, 9,* 225–242.

Nacoste, R. W. (1990). Sources of stigma: Analyzing the psychology of affirmative action. *Law and Policy, 12,* 175–195.

Nacoste, R. W. (1996). Social psychology and the affirmative action debate. *Journal of Social and Clinical Psychology, 15,* 261–282.

Nieva, V. F., & Gutek, B. A. (1980). Sex effects on evaluation. *Academy of Management Review, 5,* 267–276.

Nisbitt, R. E., Zukier, H., & Lemley, R. E. (1981). The dilution effect: Nondiagnostic information weakens the implications of diagnostic information. *Cognitive Psychology, 13,* 248–277.

Northcraft, G. B., & Martin, J. (1982). Double Jeopardy: Resistance to affirmative action from potenetial beneficiaries. In B. A. Gutek (Ed.), *Sex role stereotyping and affirmative action policy* (pp. 81–130). Los Angeles: University of California, Institute of Industrial Relations.

Pettigrew, T. F., & Martin, J. (1987). Shaping the organizational context for black American inclusion. *Journal of Social Issues, 43,* 41–78.

Pyszczynkski, T. A., & Greenberg, J. (1981). Role of disconfirmed expectancies in the instigation of attributional processing. *Academy of Management Review, 19,* 786–820.

Richard, O. C., & Kirby, S. L. (1998). Women recruits' perceptions of workforce diversity program selection decisions: A procedural justice examination. *Journal of Applied Social Psychology, 28,* 183–188.

Sackett, P. R., DuBois, C. L., & Noe, A. W. (1991). Tokenism in performance evaluation: The effects of work group representation on male-female and white-black differences in performance ratings. *Journal of Applied Psychology, 78,* 928–938.

Seligman, D. (1973, March). How "equal opportunity" turned into employment quotas. *Fortune,* 158–168.

Steele, S. (1990). The content of our character: A new vision of race in America. New York: Morrow.

Summers, R. J. (1991). The influence of affirmative action on perceptions of a beneficiary's qualifications. *Journal of Applied Social Psychology, 21,* 1265–1276.

Taylor Carter, M. A., Doverspike, D., & Cook, K. D. (1996). The effects of affirmative action on the female beneficiary. *Human Resource Development Quarterly, 71,* 31–54.

Title VII of the Civil Rights Act of 1964 (Pub. L. 88-352) (Title VII), Volume 42 of the United States Code, Section 2000e.

Tomasson, R. F., Crosby, F. J., & Herzberger, S. D. (1996). *Affirmative action: The pros and cons of policy and practice.* Lanham, MD: Rowman & Littlegfeild.

Tosi, H. L., & Einbinder, S. W. (1985). The effects of the type and amount of information in sex discrimination research: A meta analysis. *Academy of Management Journal, 28,* 712–723.

Tougas, F., Brown, R., Beaton, A. M., & Joly, S. (1995). Neosexism: Plus ca change, plus c'est pareil. *Personality and Social Psychology Bulletin, 21,* 842–849.

Wilkerson, I. (1991). Remedy for racism past has new kind of shackles. *The New York Times,* p. 11. New York: East Coast.

Wycliff, D. (1990, June 10). Blacks debate the costs of affirmative action. *The New York Times,* p. 3.

16

International Employment Discrimination: A Review of Legal Issues, Human Impacts, and Organizational Implications

Georgia T. Chao
Hannah-Hanh D. Nguyen
Michigan State University

International business has proliferated to a point where most major industries and services operate on a multinational level. Global organizations encounter a wide assortment of laws, employment practices, and individual challenges as they manage human resources located in different countries and cultures. Within this global mix, local discriminatory practices may not be salient to human resource (HR) professionals from a parent organization. Furthermore, attempts to standardize or implement nondiscriminatory HR practices may be resisted or prove counterproductive. The purpose of this chapter is to provide an overview of employment discrimination across countries from a variety of geographical and cultural settings. Organizational discriminatory practices and targets of discrimination are reviewed. Legal protections against employment discrimination and the extent to which laws are enforced will be discussed. Finally, organizational initiatives to ensure fair employment practices are presented to guide future human resource management.

There are two restrictions on the scope of this chapter. First, all the other chapters in this volume address employment discrimination from an American perspective; thus, we will minimize our coverage of U.S. employment laws and practices to avoid redundancy. Second, we limit our review to employment practices in formal organizations with adults voluntarily employed. Thus, forms of contemporary slavery, illegal migrant workers, and child labor will not be discussed. Our chapter will focus on how people from diverse countries are protected from various forms of employment discrimination and how organizations can guard against this discrimination.

DEFINING EMPLOYMENT DISCRIMINATION

Global Frameworks of Rights

There are several regional and global declarations advocating fair employment practices. Table 16.1 provides excerpts from major documents from the International Labour Organisation (ILO) and the United Nations (UN) to illustrate the scope of these doctrines. The ILO international labor standards were established by eight fundamental conventions addressing four broad areas: rights to organize at work, forced labor, child labor, and discrimination in employment. The two conventions dealing with discrimination are summarized in Table 16.1. ILO member states are legally bound to a convention if they ratify it. To date, most of the 175 member states have ratified the fundamental conventions related to discrimination in employment, although there are notable exceptions (e.g., the U.S. has not ratified either convention). If a member state does not ratify a convention, it is still obligated to respect and promote the principles of that convention even though it is not legally bound to it (*Declaration on Fundamental Principles and Rights at Work*, International Labour Organization, 1998).

Similarly, the UN's Universal Declaration of Human Rights consists of globally accepted principles for human rights in general and in employment in particular (United Nations, 1948). The rights protected in this accord were made legally binding by the International Covenant on Economic, Social and Cultural Rights (United Nations, 1960) and has served as a general moral framework for internationally acceptable behaviors with respect to employment and occupation for over 50 years.

National Laws Against Discrimination

A review of current antidiscrimination employment laws and regulations showed most nations adopted or amended legislation within the past

15 years. There is a clear trend for countries to establish national laws protecting rights at work. Across these laws, there is a wide range of what constitutes employment discrimination, how laws are enforced, and what remedies are available to victims of discrimination. For instance, Denmark incorporates enforcement terms (e.g., authority, punishment) into their antidiscrimination legislation (European Employment and Industrial Relations Glossaries, 2002). Japan generally relies on noncoercive, voluntary approaches for organizational compliance (Hamaguchi, 1997), and Vietnam offers financial enticements (Diep & Ne, 2001).

It is beyond the scope of this chapter to review national antidiscrimination employment laws. A review of four major targets of workplace discrimination—gender, race/ethnicity, age, and disability—is presented to illustrate these kinds of discrimination in various countries. In addition, we review other less apparent grounds for discrimination such as sexual orientation and religion. Most of the research we reviewed was descriptive and we selected examples to represent a broad range of countries and cultures.

TARGETS OF EMPLOYMENT DISCRIMINATION

Gender

Gender inequality is generally defined as "the restrictions placed on women's choices, opportunities and participation" (United Nations Population Fund, 2000). Despite being outlawed or condemned worldwide, gender discrimination is still pervasive. In developed and developing countries alike, women have been struggling with the problems of job and pay inequalities at different employment stages. These problems have been summarized with such metaphors as the "brick wall," the "glass ceiling," and the "feminization of poverty." Furthermore, social scientists have examined some systematic causes of the problems, such as gender stereotypes, sociocultural beliefs, and economic status of a country.

A Brick Wall This metaphor refers to societal and/or systemic organizational barriers erected to prevent women from entering the workplace. For example, Chinese employers often specify a gender in their employment advertisements (e.g., asking for only male applicants; Kerr, Delahanty, & Humpage, 1996). Even if they are considered for positions, Chinese women may have to meet higher arbitrary entry requirements than male recruits because managers generally consider women workers "troublesome" (e.g., getting pregnant or taking time off to care for family; Kerr et al., 1996). French women who return to the workforce may be the last ones to be offered a job if they have to compete against current workers or even

TABLE 16.1

International Legislation Related to Employment Discrimination

Name of Legislation	Excerpts Related to Employment Discrimination
International Labor Organization (ILO) Declaration of Philadelphia (1944)	"all human beings, irrespective of race, creed or sex, have the right to pursue both their material well-being and their spiritual development in conditions of freedom and dignity, of economic security and equal opportunity"
ILO Equal Remuneration Convention (No. 100) (1951)	Article 2 states: "Each Member shall, by means appropriate to the methods in operation for determining rates of remuneration, promote and, in so far as is consistent with such methods, ensure the application to all workers of the principle of equal remuneration for men and women workers for work of equal value."
ILO Discrimination (Employment and Occupation) Convention (No. 111) (1958)	Article 1 states: "1. For the purpose of this Convention the term *discrimination* includes—(a) any distinction, exclusion or preference made on the basis of race, colour sex, religion, political opinion, national extraction or social origin, which has the effect of nullifying or impairing equality of opportunity or treatment in employment or occupation; (b) such other distinction, exclusion or preference which has the effect of nullifying or impairing equality of opportunity or treatment in employment or occupation as may be determined by the member concerned after consultation with representative employers' and workers' organizations, where such exist, and with other appropriate bodies. 2. Any distinction, exclusion or preference in respect of a particular job based on the inherent requirements thereof shall not be deemed to be discrimination. 3. For the purpose of this Convention the terms *employment* and *occupation* include access to vocational training, access to employment and to particular occupations, and terms and conditions of employment."

United Nations Universal Declaration of Human Rights (1948)	Article 2. "Everyone is entitled to all the rights and freedoms set forth in this Declaration, without distinction of any kind, such as race, colour, sex, language, religion, political or other opinion, national or social origin, property, birth or other status. Furthermore, no distinction shall be made on the basis of the political, jurisdictional or international status of the country or territory to which a person belongs, whether it be independent, trust, non-self-governing or under any other limitation of sovereignty."
	Article 23. "(1) Everyone has the right to work, to free choice of employment, to just and favourable conditions of work and to protection against unemployment.
	(2) Everyone, without any discrimination, has the right to equal pay for equal work.
	(3) Everyone who works has the right to just and favourable remuneration ensuring for himself and his family an existence worthy of human dignity, and supplemented, if necessary, by other means of social protection.
	(4) Everyone has the right to form and to join trade unions for the protection of his interests."
	Article 24. "Everyone has the right to rest and leisure, including reasonable limitation of working hours and periodic holidays with pay."
UN International Covenant on Economic, Social, & Cultural Rights (1960)	Article 7
	"The States Parties to the present Covenant recognize the right of everyone to the enjoyment of just and favourable conditions of work which ensure, in particular:
	(a) Remuneration which provides all workers, as a minimum, with: (i) Fair wages and equal remuneration for work of equal value without distinction of any kind, in particular women being guaranteed conditions of work not inferior to those enjoyed by men, with equal pay for equal work; (ii) A decent living for themselves and their families in accordance with the provisions of the present Covenant;
	(b) Safe and healthy working conditions;
	(c) Equal opportunity for everyone to be promoted in his employment to an appropriate higher level, subject to no considerations other than those of seniority and competence;
	(d) Rest, leisure and reasonable limitation of working hours and periodic holidays with pay, as well as remuneration for public holidays."

first-time applicants (Bournois, 1993). In contrast, Germany's Civil Code specifically requires employment advertisements to be gender-neutral (Sparrow & Hiltrop, 1994).

Even if women are successfully hired, their job security may not be protected well. In China, Korea, and Japan, managers would hire young, single women on short-term contracts and then discharge them or refuse to rehire them if they get married or pregnant, regardless of education or skills (Kerr et al., 1996; "Korean Women," 1999; Strober & Chan, 1999). Women in Eastern European countries face similar fates of being expendable workers (Mertus, 1998). In order not to get fired in the name of efficiency, some women have taken drastic measures such as having themselves sterilized to comply with their employers' order or subjecting themselves to sexual harassment in exchange for job security.

The "brick wall" metaphor can also be used to refer to the phenomenon of occupational segregation or the disparity between male and female representation in clusters of occupations. A cross-national study conducted with occupational data on 41 countries in several world regions (e.g., Asia/Pacific, North America, North Africa, Middle East, and Scandinavia) revealed the troubling fact that occupational segregation is prevalent in all countries studied (Anker, 1998). For example, the number of male-dominated occupations was seven times higher than female-dominated ones, and "female" occupations (e.g., clerk, teacher, agricultural laborers) were socially perceived as less valuable. Thus, female workers received lower pay, lower status, and fewer advancement opportunities. Furthermore, some cross-cultural and historical studies show occupations that are dominated by women tend to have lower salaries and status than that of their male counterparts. For example, women doctors dominate the general medical profession in Russia, but they do not experience the same relative salaries and prestige enjoyed by predominately male doctors in the United States (Goldberg & Kishkovsky, 2000). In addition, historical trends found that as the percentage of women in an occupation increases, the wage levels of these occupations decrease (Reid, 1998).

The unavailability of employment opportunities results in the low participation rate of women in many economies. For instance, women in Bangladesh occupy only 23% of professional and technical positions (Zafarullah, 2000). Zimbabwean female workers on tobacco plantations are generally found in the lowest wage groups (contract laborers), receiving no fringe benefits and being considered dispensable (Broback & Save-Soderbergh, 1996). In Greece, Belgium, and Portugal, 60% of the unemployed were female in the early 1990s (Sparrow & Hiltrop, 1994). Globally, the lowest female participation rates are observed in the Middle East and North Africa because of cultural and religious restrictions (e.g., 27.8%

in Turkey in 1997); the highest rates are in Scandinavian countries (e.g., Iceland with 68.4%) resulting from the combination of a highly educated female workforce and government policies of childcare subsidies for working mothers (Elder & Johnson, 1999).

Another related issue is the effect of protective laws limiting women's occupational choices. For example, Hong Kong, Vietnam, and Poland have protective laws that prohibit women from working in dangerous occupations (e.g., underground, in a tunnel, in contact with gene-mutable chemicals or radiation; Diep & Ne, 2001; Mertus, 1998; Singer, 2000). The intention may be benevolent but critics of such laws claim that these protections effectively pigeonhole women into low-wage "female" jobs, and encourage employers to discriminate against women (Singer, 2000). For example, Polish women are banned from 90 occupations and jobs that are usually better paid than "feminized" jobs (Mertus, 1998).

The Glass Ceiling For some women who are employed and who intend to pursue a successful career, the discrimination against them may take a more subtle form. The "glass ceiling" metaphor refers to artificial barriers blocking women's efforts to advance to high decision-making positions in an organization. The glass ceiling effect is experienced by women in both developed and developing countries. For instance, the odds of an Australian woman occupying a middle-level managerial appointment are 46% of those of a man; these odds were significantly reduced to only one-third those of a man for a woman in Sweden (Baxter & Wright, 2000). Chinese managerial women received a less positive social image than men (Verschyurr-Basse, 1996) and were systematically excluded from senior managerial positions (Meng & Miller, 1995). However, the modest 25% of all administrative and managerial positions that Chinese women hold (Kerr et al., 1996) is still an improvement compared with only 5.1% of those in Bangladesh (Zafarullah, 2000), 6.6% in Indonesia, 8.3% in Malaysia, and 15.4% in Thailand (Wright & Tellei, 1993). In Vietnam, although approximately 50% of managerial appointments in some "feminized" major industries (e.g., process, utility) are occupied by women (Hoa, 2002), these women managers are more likely to be a deputy to male top executives than top executives themselves (Anh & Hung, 2000).

Feminization of Poverty This metaphor refers to the global phenomenon of a gender-based pay gap favoring men (Hutchings, 1998). Throughout the world, employed women typically have weaker earning power than men. For example, a national study conducted in Australia found that on the average, men earned up to 26% more than women did; this gender earnings gap was reduced to 14% after taking into account major structural factors such as demographics, sector, industry, occupation, and human capital (Preston & Crockett, 1999). Similarly, on the average, full-time female workers in industry and services earned 25% less than males in the European Union in 1995. In only four countries (Belgium, Denmark, Luxembourg, and Sweden) was the average woman's wage as high as 85% of a man's wage, and it was as low as 67% in Portugal, (Clarke, 2001). After adjusting for age (as an indicator of seniority), occupation and economic activity of employers, the average proportion of the gender earnings gap was further reduced to 15% (Benassi, 1999). In practice, organizations are allowed to justify their policies of pay inequity on the grounds of differ-ential requirements for each gender. For instance, the courts in France and Switzerland ruled that the gender disparity in pay in two specific law-suits was lawful because it was based on objective factors (e.g., the men had more skills, training, and experience than the women) and not gen-der (International Labour Organisation, 1989). The French case involved 13 female workers who sued their employer for paying them at a lower rate than 3 male employees working in the same job category (Court of Cassation, 1988). The Swiss case involved a professional actress who was paid 2,500 francs for her performance whereas other actors in the same play received 4,000 francs (Federal Court, 1988).

Systematic Reasons for Discrimination Societal beliefs or cultural/religious considerations often set the stage for the prevalence of discrim-inatory attitudes and behaviors. For example, Japanese management tra-ditionally regards women as secondary and supplementary employees, calling them *shokuba no hana* ("office flowers"; Knapp, 1995) and discharg-ing them whenever there are labor downturns (Brown, Nakata, Reich, & Ulman, 1997). Such treatment is rooted in typical gender-role stereotypes in Japan's postwar economy (e.g., men are economic warriors and breadwin-ners; women are mainly responsible for household matters). In Indonesia, the responsibility of women as citizens traditionally ranks last, after *kodrat wanita* (wifely duties; Sullivan, 1983), burdening female managers with significant work–family conflicts. In terms of work-related cultural values, a typical Indonesian organization is strongly collectivistic, having high power distance, high tolerance for uncertainty, and relative low masculin-ity (Hofstede, 1979). This culture disapproves of ego motives, assertive and competitive behaviors in women, and this fact is compounded with emphasized values attached to marriage and motherhood. Therefore, In-donesian career women tend to be judged as more selfish and neglectful of family lifestyle than their male counterparts.

In Muslim countries, gender equality and equal treatment before the law are not commonly practiced. Women in Malaysia are socially, politically, and economically disadvantaged to men, generally being excluded from many areas of public and private life (Hutchings, 1998). Despite the fact that women have constitutional rights to work for pay, Yemen's governmental officials practically endorse the ideology of females staying home and doing housework; the government also refrains from encouraging female participation in the paid labor force (Riphenburg, 1999). However, being born to an elite social class and/or possessing great wealth can alleviate a woman's sociocultural constraints in some Muslim countries, such as Indonesia or Yemen (Riphenburg, 1999; Wright & Tellei, 1993).

A national economic crisis or the emergence of a capitalistic labor market often enhances the magnitude of gender-based employment discrimination. Lachaud (1996) studied gender inequality and labor market institutions in five sub-Saharan African countries that had undergone some economic reform (Burkina Faso, Cameroon, Ivory Coast, Guinea, and Mali). He found that women in these nations disproportionately participated in the labor markets in the form of marginal self-employment or unprotected wage employment, resulting in low income and low living standards for households headed by single women. This fact was the result of employers' actions and women's self-exclusion from the labor market: Organizations were less likely to offer a first job to female job-seekers and more likely to dismiss women workers than men; women were approximately four times more likely than men to be discouraged in seeking protected wage employment. Lachaud concluded that the economic crisis and drastic reforms increased competition for scarce jobs and restricted productive resources, making women more vulnerable in gaining access to employment opportunities.

Lowered trade barriers, more consumer goods, and international agendas can jeopardize women's employment rights as in the case of central and eastern European countries (Power, 2001). Mertus (1998) conducted a comparative analysis of women's employment status in 10 former socialist nations in Central and Eastern Europe (CEE; e.g., Bulgaria, Hungary, Russia, Ukraine). Under socialism and in centrally planned economies, theoretically, women did not experience discrimination in the workplace; further, they enjoyed certain protection legislation (e.g., women prohibited from holding dangerous jobs), compensatory legislation (e.g., maternity benefits, childcare), and some affirmative action practices favoring women (e.g., quotas in political participation). In spite of these legislative measures, women still had unequal access to power and resources compared with men. With the collapse of socialist regimes and the promotion of market economies in the late 1980s, gender discrimination in employment had intensified. In the transitional period of economic crises, not only did CEE women lose their job security and benefits previously guaranteed by the state, but also they were systematically excluded from new, high-paid jobs in private sector or foreign-owned companies. Organizations, including foreign ones, overtly preferred hiring, training, and promoting men over women. Chan, Law, and Kwok (1992) believed there were similar discriminatory practices in socialist China after the economic reforms in the 1980s because the government was less willing to put resources into promoting gender equality. It is now difficult for a female college graduate to find a good job in Beijing; even government departments and social organizations would give hiring preferences to male graduates instead of female graduates with higher grades. Cultural stereotypes regarding gender roles can offer resistance to efforts to promote gender equality at work.

Race

In this section, we broadly define race-based discrimination as discriminatory practices and policies against workers on grounds of skin color or ethnic origin (racism), national origin (xenophobism), and social origin (e.g., caste or birth). This definition is in accordance with the UN's international conventions against racial discrimination (e.g., International Convention on the Elimination of All Forms of Racial Discrimination, United Nations, 1969).

Race and/or Ethnicity   Racist discriminatory practices vary around the world. Extreme cases of skin color-based labor discrimination are found in West African slavery (Khatchadourian, 2002) or in former apartheid practices in South Africa. In Japan, ethnic minorities such as the Koreans or the Ainus (aboriginal people of Japan) can be easily screened out from the applicant pool based on their names or their facial features from required pictures on applications (Madison, 1997).

Empirical evidence supports the existence of direct discriminatory selection practices in organizations worldwide. For instance, in a classic economic study using the method of "correspondent testing," Jowell and Prescott-Clarke (1970) found that British employers might consciously or nonconsciously engage in racial discriminatory employment practices such as making fewer job offers or promotion offers to ethnic minority workers and justifying these practices by the issue of person–organization fit (e.g., saying that a particular person "wouldn't fit in"). The researchers mailed pairs of fictitious job applications to prospective employers in response to their job ads. These pairs of job applications had comparable credentials and qualifications but each applicant of a pair was either a White (a British or Australian) or an ethnic minority person (e.g., being of Afro-Caribbean, Indian, or Pakistani descent). The researchers found that minority applicants generally received fewer invitations for a job interview (35%) than Whites (78%). Other more recent British and Australian studies replicated this pattern of findings (see a review in Riach & Rich, 2002).

National Origin Employment discrimination on the grounds of national origin (e.g., discrimination against hiring migrant or foreign workers) follows a similar pattern to that of racial/ethnic discrimination. In New Zealand, a national survey showed that recruiters admitted they would reject applicants with a non-New Zealand accent or coming from a different culture ("Missing out," 2001). Cross-national situational studies sponsored by the International Labour Organization show a consistent pattern of employment discrimination on the grounds of national origin in Belgium, Germany, Spain, and the Netherlands (Bovenkerk, Gras, & Ramsoedh, 2000; Colectivo IOE, 2000; Goldberg & Mourinho, 2000; Smeesters, Arrijn, Feld, & Nayer, 2000). These studies showed that, after a phone contact and/or an interview, a job applicant of foreign origin (e.g., a Turk in Germany; or a Moroccan in Belgium, Spain, or the Netherlands) was rejected more often than host nationals, regardless of the origin of the employers or the countries' regions (e.g., high versus low concentration of foreign workers). Further, the rejection rate was significantly higher for migrant applicants in jobs that require visual contacts with clients (e.g. hotel assistants, sales representatives) than in those without direct contact (e.g., manual or semi-skilled jobs). Such a high rate of rejection was not significantly attributable to migrant workers' language barriers or limited educational levels; in many cases, after identifying their ethnicity by supplying their name, foreign applicants did not even have a chance to present their credentials to prospective employers. Typical reasons for rejection that the fictitious minority applicant received from organizations involved "legitimate" reasons, such as insufficient experience and under-qualification. Furthermore, some organizations claimed that the advertised position was no longer available but at the same time, these employers were arranging interviews for the hypothetical White applicant (de Beijl, 2000). The implication of such findings is that minority victims of employment discrimination may not be aware of or cannot substantiate their complaints of an unlawful hiring practice.

Besides direct racism (e.g., racist abuse and harassment), indirect, institutional racism is very much a reality in organizations, from recruitment to advancement, despite the existence of some antidiscrimination legislation. For example, in the United Kingdom, the 1976 Race Relations Act prohibits three types of racial discrimination (direct, indirect, and victimization of those who complain about racial discrimination; The UK Home Office, 2001). However, workers of South Asian origin or Blacks are significantly less likely to get hired than Whites, even though they are proportionally more educated than White workers (e.g., 21% minority employees have educational degrees compared with only 16% of Whites; Shabi, 2000). When employed, ethnic minority workers tend to occupy lower level, unskilled jobs (Carmichael & Woods, 2000); few non-White workers ever reach senior positions in professional or governmental jobs such as those in accountancy (Fisher, 2000), or police commanders (Shabi, 2000).

Social or Descent Origin   Employment discrimination on the grounds of social or descent origin is a widespread practice in parts of Asia and Africa, affecting 250 million people worldwide (Human Rights Watch, 2001a, 2001b). India's caste system is an example of labor and power division based on heredity: members of each caste are believed to be born to different occupations and, therefore, should have no occupational mobility out of their own caste (Banerjee & Knight, 1985; Fernando, 2002). Despite India's legislation, those in the lowest caste (e.g., the Dalits) are still considered "unclean" by those in upper castes, being forced to live in segregated neighborhoods and to work in poorly paid, undesirable jobs (e.g., sweeping, removing dead animals) or even unpaid agricultural work for higher caste landowners in rural villages (U.S. Department of State, 2002a). Job discrimination against those in the lower castes is less profound in urban labor markets because these caste members can conceal their social origin from job recruiters (Banerjee & Knight, 1985). For those who choose to reveal their caste status to take advantage of affirmative action programs and hiring quotas, employers often practice wage discrimination against them (e.g., paying them at a lower rate than that of others of equal efficiency from higher caste groups; U.S. Department of State, 2002a).

Another historically "unclean," segregated caste, the Burakumins in Japan are less able to hide their birth origin than the Dalits in India. The Burakumins are Japanese in appearance and traditions, but their ancestors worked in "unclean" professions (e.g., leather producers, butchers, undertakers) by Japan's religious standards in the seventeenth century (Bryan, 1991). The Burakumins were once called *eta*, meaning "filth," and forced to live separately from the rest of the population (Magagnini, 1992). Because family history must be registered with the government, prospective employers may check an applicant's ancestral address (or even changes of these addresses) to screen out the Burakumins, because a majority of Japanese still refuses to work with members of this caste (Madison, 1997).

Age

In the industrial world, the problem of age discrimination in employment, although affecting both younger and older adults, often refers to discriminatory acts against older workers at various stages of employment. Being referred to as the "Third Age," the category of older workers is generally composed of people aged 50 and over (Barber, 1998), although some employers might classify even employees in their 40s as "older workers" (Steinberg, Donald, Najman, & Skerman, 1996).

Many countries legally prohibit age-based discrimination in employment (e.g., the 1998 Irish Employment Equality Act, Republic of Ireland, 1998, or the 1967 U.S. Age Discrimination in Employment Act), although there may be exceptions. For example, the U.S. Federal Aviation Agency enforces a mandatory retirement age of 60 for commercial airline pilots (Section 121.383(c) of Title 14, Code of Federal Regulations, United States, 1978). The U.K.'s Employment Rights Act 1996 states "An employee has the right not to be unfairly dismissed by his employer" (Section 94; Employment Rights Act, 1996). However, this right does not apply to employees at a normal retiring age or age 65 (Section 109).

At the organizational level, barring older workers' access to jobs is possibly the most commonly found discriminatory practice. In the U.K., age limits are prevalent in job advertisements (Meenan, 1999). Australian employers significantly preferred recruiting 26 to 35 year-olds for most job categories, with the exception of managerial positions (over 35 being preferred), whereas those over 56 were either rarely selected by employers, or chosen for unskilled jobs only (Steinberg et al., 1996). Even in a nation with active anti-ageism provisions as New Zealand, 80% of New Zealand's job recruiters admitted in a national survey that they would be most likely to turn down older applicants regardless of merits ("Missing out," 2001). Surprisingly, younger workers (e.g., in the mid-30s) may also find themselves victims of ageism. For example, the British Civil Service Commission specifies that applicants for the position of Executive Officer, a junior administrative position, should be between the ages of 17 and 28 (Meenan, 1999).

Older workers are particularly vulnerable in organizations' downsizing plans. A Canadian company was recently found discriminating against older workers by the Ontario Board of Inquiry, because this company decided to downsize employees who did not have "career potential" ("Human rights issues," 2000). Coupled with older workers' inability to find new employment, redundancy and voluntary retirements (e.g., the policy of "golden handshakes") resulted in an estimated 1.25 million unemployed people aged 50 to 60 in the U.K. in the early 1990s (Midgley, 1996).

Age-based discrimination is presumably rooted in negative stereotypes against older employees, such as their being more expensive to employ than younger workers, less ambitious, and more resistant to cope with technological change (Barber, 1998). Even when employers acknowledge positive qualities of older employees of age 40 and over (e.g., making better decisions, being more dependable than younger workers), at the same time employers tend to embrace negative beliefs about older workers (e.g., unhealthy, lethargic, and inefficient; Steinberg et al., 1996). These stereotypes often result in a high level of tolerance of ageism in employment and in society as a whole. Advocates for anti-ageism in the workplace argue that most age-related stereotypes are unsubstantiated by empirical evidence and such age-based discriminatory practices are costly to both business and society because valuable experience and talent is lost (Midgley, 1996; "Missing out," 2001).

Disability

Many countries in the world have legislation that prohibits discrimination on the grounds of disability such as Hong Kong's 1995 Disability Discrimination Ordinance (Lau, 1996) and India's 1995 Persons with Disabilities Act (Social Welfare Department, 1996). These protection laws generally offer a definition of disability on the spectrum of physical, mental, and biological levels, such as the loss or disfigurement of a body part(s), mental instability or illness resulting in disturbed behaviors or learning deficiency, or carrying organisms capable of causing diseases or illness (Lau, 1996; Srinivasan, 2002). Some countries such as China have passed laws that require employers to improve access to employment for workers with disabilities (e.g., modifying physical facilities and/or providing transportation), sanctioning employers who do not comply (U.S. Department of State, 2002b). Thus, many workers with disabilities are legally protected from discrimination either when applying for jobs or in the course of employment.

Despite legal protection, people with disabilities are often excluded from the workforce. For example, 50% of Canadians with disabilities who could work were unemployed in 1996 (Fulton, 1996). This reality is partly a result of the ignorance or reluctance of organizations to provide work to the persons with disabilities, coupled with poor access and insufficient or ineffective protective legislation (Kitchin, Shirlow, & Shuttleworth, 1998). Goss and Goss (1998) surveyed private-sector employers in south England for their awareness of the U.K.'s Disability Discrimination Act and issues related to workers with disabilities. The researchers found that the organization's size was positively related to legal awareness, with larger companies (e.g., over 100 employees) being more aware of labor law requirements such as actively recruiting persons with disabilities, designing special training for them, and changing the work environment to provide access for people with disabilities. Furthermore, larger organizations also were more likely than smaller firms to identify benefits from employing workers with disabilities, such as fulfilling moral obligations to the community.

In terms of nonvisible disabilities such as mental illness (e.g., work-related stress and/or depression) or HIV/AIDS, most organizations are unaware of the link between these illnesses and legal provisions classifying them as disabilities or do not know how to make "reasonable adjustments" to allow employees with these specific conditions to continue to work (McCurry, 2000). A common problem that these workers may face is dismissal from their jobs on the grounds of mental illnesses or HIV-positive status. About 50% of employers surveyed in Hungary said they would dismiss workers with HIV/AIDS, compared with 20% of Indian employers (N'Daba & Hodges-Aeberhard, 1998). In the U.K. an accountant was forcibly retired from his position because he suffered from reactive depression and anxiety as the result of an increased workload (*Kapadia v. London Borough of Lambeth*, 2000). The U.K. Tribunal Court found that the employer's decision was not discriminatory because the accountant's mental disorder symptoms did not amount to a disability. This ruling was later rejected by both the U.K. Employment Appeal Tribunal and Court of Appeal, and the case was remitted to a new tribunal court for determining its merits.

In countries where legislation bans discrimination on the grounds of mental illness or HIV/AIDS, the dismissals are often framed as decisions based on economic reasons (e.g., downsizing), or employers can justify the dismissal as based on workers' "incapacity for work." For example, in Mexico, many cases of dismissals because of the employees' HIV status in reality are ostensibly the result of organizational restructuring. In Uganda, an employee with HIV/AIDS who has to take frequent sick leaves can be legally fired if the employer can prove that such absenteeism disrupts the function of business (N'Daba & Hodges-Aeberhard, 1998).

Recently, El Salvador passed an AIDS law that legalizes HIV/AIDS testing for current and prospective employees (Elton, 2002). Although the law also prohibits employment discrimination on the basis of HIV/AIDS test results, opponents of the law are concerned the new provision will facilitate covert discrimination. To date, no other country sanctions preemployment testing for HIV/AIDS.

The Severe Acute Respiratory Syndrome (SARS) epidemic in 2002–2003 highlighted discriminatory problems against employees with the illness or perceived illness. In Hong Kong, two Indonesian domestic helpers were fired by their employers because the maids had contracted the SARS virus (but had recovered) while working for their bosses ("HK employers," 2003). In Australia and New Zealand, many corporate giants forced their employees who had traveled to a SARS-affected area into quarantine periods on annual, sick, or unpaid leaves, even though the employees did not exhibit any SARS symptoms (McIntyre, 2003; Pollard, 2003). There were outcries from migrant workers or trade unions in these countries, urging authorities to take actions against employers who had used the SARS crisis to discriminate against employees.

Other Protected Groups

In addition to defining discrimination on the basis of gender, race, age and disability, some antidiscrimination legislation now encompasses sexual orientation/preference (e.g., Ireland, Denmark) and religion or politics (e.g., India, Belgium). In England, gays, lesbians, and transsexuals are termed the "invisible minority" in the workplace because they keep a low profile of their sexual orientation and because it is difficult to obtain hard evidence of workplace discrimination against them (Welch, 1996; Williams, 1996). Nevertheless, like other minority groups, they may face similar discriminatory acts at work, from alienation and harassment by colleagues to dismissal. Compared with race and gender discrimination, little research has been published on discrimination on the basis of sexual preference.

Countries differ widely on their approach toward discrimination against gays and lesbians in the military. The Dutch armed forces abolished an official ban against gays and lesbians in 1974 (Janssen, 1993) and the Israel Defense Force instituted an antidiscrimination policy in 1993 (Gamson, 1999). The United States adopted an informal "don't ask, don't tell, don't harass" policy, but offers no legal protection for gays and lesbians in the armed forces (Kozaryn & Garamone, 1999). Individuals are separated from the U.S. military if they admit they are gay or lesbian or there is evidence of homosexual conduct. This policy is defended by arguments that gays and lesbians would compromise military unit cohesion, standards of morale, and discipline (U.S. House of Representatives Office of the Law Revision Counsel, 2000). Similarly, the U.K. defended their policy against gays and lesbians in the military by citing a potential risk to combat effectiveness (Smith, 2000). However, the European Court of Human Rights (ECHR) recently ruled the British Royal Navy and Royal Air Force violated four members' right to privacy protected by the European Convention for the Protection of Human Rights and Fundamental Freedoms (*Lustig-Prean & Beckett v. United Kingdom*, 1999a; *Smith & Grady v. United Kingdom*, European Court of Human Rights, 1999b). In these cases, separate special investigations concluded the plaintiffs were gay, and they were discharged on the grounds of their sexual orientation. The Court found the government's defense of the termination policy was neither convincing nor weighty enough to justify termination solely on the basis of homosexuality. As a result, a new policy was implemented in 2000 to allow gays and lesbians to serve in the British armed forces. Furthermore, regardless of sexual orientation, an individual's personal behavior is relevant only if it impacts on that individual's service (Smith, 2000).

Unlike other grounds for employment discrimination, religion-based discrimination in the workplace is often an expression of political conflict or oppression. As a consequence, this type of discrimination is rather systematic and structural, beyond specific organizational policies in employment. Historically, some religious beliefs (e.g., Islam, Hinduism, or Shinto) have been used to sanctify the discriminatory rulings of a dominant group against another group in terms of work opportunities and mobility (e.g., women, lower castes). Conservative religious customs often supersede governmental antidiscrimination legislation in employment, if not being supported by other legal provisions. For example, India actively designs affirmative action programs and hiring quotas to assist the Dalits (members of the traditionally lowest caste) in attaining employment in nontraditional occupations. However, those who convert from Hinduism to Christianity lose their eligibility for such programs, whereas those who convert to Buddhism and Muslim do not, because Christianity historically opposes the caste system (U.S. Department of State, 2002a).

In Europe, an example of employment discrimination on the grounds of religion is found in the differential unemployment rates between Roman Catholics and Protestants in Northern Ireland (Heaton & Teague, 1997). Since the Protestant state was formed in 1921 by the British government, Catholics always have been underrepresented in professional, managerial, skilled, and security-related jobs (e.g., police, army) and overrepresented in low-paid, unskilled jobs. In the 1990s, the unemployment rate of Catholic men was twice that of Protestant men (Heaton & Teague, 1997). This fact has been attributed to the highly segregating structure in housing and education of Northern Ireland, allowing Protestant employees to easily screen out Catholic applicants based on the school they attend. It is also caused by labor law loopholes, such as the national security provisions in the 1989 Fair Employment Act (Northern Ireland), that permit employers to reject those suspected as being involved in illegal political organizations (Human Rights Watch, 1998). Ironically, this act was created by the British government specifically to address employment inequality in Northern Ireland.

PRACTICAL IMPLICATIONS FOR ORGANIZATIONS

Legal Protections

For organizations that operate internationally, compliance with host-country laws generally supersedes compliance with home-country laws, but this issue is complex and dynamic with legal interpretations and rulings that conflict with earlier decisions. This complexity is illustrated by contradictory court rulings in employment discrimination cases involving

U.S. corporations operating abroad or foreign companies operating in the United States.

For example, Section 109 of the 1991 U.S. Civil Rights Act reverses a Supreme Court ruling (*EEOC v. Arabian American Oil Co.*, 1991) and extends protection to extraterritorial American employees unless compliance with the law violates laws in the host country. Foreign companies operating in the United States are also obligated to comply with U.S. employment legislation. However, Friendship, Commerce and Navigation Treaties (FCN treaties) between the U.S. and foreign countries can contain provisions to preclude employment discrimination claims (Hoguet & Dansicker, 1996). In *Weeks v. Samsung Heavy Industries Co., Ltd.* (1997), an American alleged that the Korean company unlawfully replaced him with a Korean employee. Samsung used the 1956 FCN Treaty between the United States and Korea to successfully defend its practice because this treaty authorizes such personnel decisions for companies of either nation without invoking any national origin discrimination. Similarly, *Bennett v. Total Minatome Corp.* (1998) found the Convention of Establishment between the United States and France granted the French company the right to hire French technical experts over Americans.

Aside from complying with employment legislation, global organizations may deliberately take advantage of loopholes in a host country's antidiscrimination legislation or use sociocultural restraints to impose discriminatory practices on local workers. For example, several Japanese and Australian human resource managers of branch operations in Malaysia only offer short-term contracts with few advancement opportunities to Malaysian women (Hutchings, 1998). They justified this policy as the organizational adoption of Malaysian social practices regarding women's family responsibilities (e.g., mothers should not work). Furthermore, younger women recruits were preferred to older female workers "because they [the former] are not as aware of their rights [as the latter]," claimed a Japanese company representative in Kuala Lumpur (Hutchings, 1998).

The jurisdiction of employment antidiscrimination laws is currently shaped by court decisions. The prevalence of global organizations complicates this issue as more companies operate worldwide. Maatman (2001) described a trend for class action cases to be tried in an organization's home jurisdiction. Organizations in major commercial jurisdictions (e.g., Australia, U.K., U.S.) are more likely to have legal systems that are experienced with the complexities, and perhaps even sympathetic to, plaintiffs with employee rights disputes. In the past, organizations have invoked the doctrine of *forum non conveniens*, that an inappropriate jurisdiction was identified to litigate a dispute. However, recent court cases have ruled that *forum non conveniens* was not sufficient to remove cases from a parent organization's home jurisdiction.

The U.S. Alien Tort Claims Act (ATCA) United States House of Representatives Office of the Law Revision Counsel, 2002) has been used to establish U.S. jurisdiction for alleged human rights violations that were committed outside U.S. territories. In *Doe v. Unocal* (2003), 14 Burmese villagers filed a class action suit against U.S.-based Unocal Corporation. The suit alleges that Unocal's foreign subsidiary colluded with the Burmese military to force villagers to build a gas pipeline. Specific charges include forced labor/slavery, torture, rape, and other human rights violations. Legal experts anticipate this case ultimately will be decided by the Supreme Court (Hall, 2002; Tam, 2003). Should the plaintiffs prevail in this case, a global organization's legal liability for violations of international law would greatly increase and massive class action suits would be a likely result (Hall, 2002). At least 10 other cases similar to *Doe v. Unocal* are pending in the United States (Girion, 2002) and the U.K. (Maatman, 2001). The implications from these cases are clear. Global organizations are likely to face more legal challenges of their human resource practices, regardless of where they may be operating. Proactive monitoring and management of these practices is imperative to minimize these risks.

Organizational Initiatives to Fair Employment Practices

Aside from legal compliance with employment laws, organizations can foster fair employment practices in a number of ways. Formal methods include strong nondiscriminatory policies clearly communicated to all organizational members, training programs to ensure fair treatment across all human resource functions, and review procedures to investigate charges of discrimination. In addition to these practices that are focused on processes internal to the organization, an organization can voluntarily participate in external organizational consortia focused on employment rights. Two examples are described to illustrate how organizations can take initiatives to protect employees from unfair discrimination. Table 16.2 lists the Global Sullivan Principles (1999) and the UN's Global Compact's nine principles (The Global Compact, 1999). Both serve as models for corporate social responsibility.

In the 1970s, global attention to unfair employment practices centered on South Africa's apartheid policies. Efforts to eliminate racial segregation and to promote ethical business practices were led by Rev. Leon Sullivan, an American pastor. In 1977, the Sullivan Principles outlined basic human rights and fair treatment. American businesses in South Africa were urged to ignore apartheid laws, adopt the Sullivan Principles,

TABLE 16.2

Principles for Corporate Social Responsibility

Global Sullivan Principles	UN Global Compact—Nine Principles
1. "Express our support for universal human rights and, particularly, those of our employees, the communities within which we operate, and parties with whom we do business."	"Principle 1: Businesses should support and respect the protection of internationally proclaimed human rights within their sphere of influence; and Principle 2: make sure that they are not complicit in human rights abuses."
2. "Promote equal opportunity for our employees at all levels of the company with respect to issues such as color, race, gender, age, ethnicity or religious beliefs, and operate without unacceptable worker treatment such as the exploitation of children, physical punishment, female abuse, involuntary servitude, or other forms of abuse."	
3. "Respect our employees' voluntary freedom of association."	"Principle 3: Businesses should uphold the freedom of association and the effective recognition of the right to collective bargaining;
4. "Compensate our employees to enable them to meet at least their basic needs and provide the opportunity to improve their skill and capability in order to raise their social and economic opportunities."	Principle 4: the elimination of all forms of forced and compulsory labour; Principle 5: the effective abolition of child labour; and Principle 6: eliminate discrimination in respect of employment and occupation."
5. "Provide a safe and healthy workplace; protect human health and the environment; and promote sustainable development."	
6. "Promote fair competition including respect for intellectual and other property rights, and not offer, pay or accept bribes."	
7. "Work with governments and communities in which we do business to improve the quality of life in those communities – their educational, cultural, economic and social well being – and seek to provide training and opportunities for workers from disadvantaged backgrounds."	"Principle 7: Businesses should support a precautionary approach to environmental challenges; Principle 8: undertake initiatives to promote greater environmental responsibility; and Principle 9: encourage the development and diffusion of environmentally friendly technologies."
8. "Promote the application of these Principles by those with whom we do business."	

and manage their South African employees without racial discrimination. Many organizations did so, and the Sullivan Principles were credited as a pivotal event in the abolition of apartheid. Twenty years later, Global Sullivan Principles were launched to promote equal opportunities in employment around the world. For example, many U.S. organizations operating in Saudi Arabia do not employ women or only employ women in segregated offices (Slavin, 2002). International pressure for these organizations to promote the Global Sullivan Principles might yield progress similar to the South African case.

The year 1999 not only saw the launch of the Global Sullivan Principles, but also the release of the UN's Global Compact. These principles were drafted by private sector company representatives from around the world, to establish guides for fair employment and environmental protection. They were billed as ethics drawn up by the private sector, for the private sector. The nine principles are broader in scope than the Global Sullivan Principles and include the protection of human rights, fair labor standards, and responsibility to the environment. The Global Sullivan Principles and the UN's Global Compact are but two voluntary ethical operating principles for global organizations. Similar guides have been proposed by other international organizations (e.g., European Parliament, ILO, OECD) and by individual countries (e.g., U.S. Model Business Principles; United States Department of Commerce, n.d.). Labor law experts anticipate these codes to play important roles in future court decisions (Savage & Wenner, 2001).

Although these ethical principles are purely voluntary, there is a growing belief that global organizations must develop new mechanisms beyond country borders to ensure good business practices. The Global Reporting Initiative is an international institution affiliated with the United Nations and charged with the mission to develop reporting guidelines for an organization's triple bottom line: economic, social, and environmental performance. Most organizations are currently only required to report their financial performance to shareholders, governments, and the general public. However, the social and environmental arenas are as important as financial data in determining future earnings potential and sustainability. Thus, the triple bottom-line yields more comprehensive information about an organization and the GRI's *Sustainability Reporting Guidelines* (2000) identify specific content to help organizations prepare sustainability reports on their economic, social, and environmental performance. These guidelines identify four categories to report an organization's social performance: (1) labor practices and decent work, (2) human rights, (3) society, and (4) product responsibility. Aspects of the labor practices and decent work category include equal opportunity and affirmative action policies; aspects of the human rights category include nondiscrimination practices. GRI claims over 2,000 companies worldwide already report their economic, environmental, and social performance.

Organizational efforts to ensure fair employment practices are based on ethical leadership and commitment to business practices with social implications beyond its boundaries. Hepple (2001) applied modern regulatory theory to explain why private, self-regulatory forms of social responsibility can be more effective in changing behaviors than compliance with laws and government regulations. Thus, organizations that develop their own principles of social responsibility (e.g., McDonald's Social Responsibility; McDonald's Corp., n.d.) or those that adopt international guidelines (e.g., General Motors with the Global Sullivan Principles; Nike with the UN Global Compact) have established frameworks for conducting business without unfair discrimination. Conversely, many NGOs (non-government organizations) and academic scholars believe organizational profit motives are likely to diminish self-regulatory efforts of social responsibility. For example, Nike's endorsement of the UN Global Compact may only be an attempt to improve its public image in light of its notorious history of labor abuses (Sethi, 2003). Without some external controls and requirements for accountability, the self-regulatory forms of social responsibility may be nothing more than business ethics rhetoric.

CONCLUSIONS

Two clear trends have emerged with regard to employment discrimination around the world. First, more and more countries are enacting antidiscrimination legislation. Global corporations are challenged to understand and comply with different versions of these laws in virtually every country on Earth. Second, international organizations are playing an increasingly visible role in establishing international laws or guidelines for fair employment practices. By 2003, 159 countries have ratified the ILO Convention on Discrimination in Employment and Occupations and 161 countries have ratified the ILO Convention on Equal Remuneration, with roughly one-third of these countries doing so within the past 10 years.

ILO member countries that have not ratified these conventions are required to submit reports on how they eliminate discrimination. In addition to government statements in these reports, national trade unions or the International Confederation of Free Trade Unions (ICFTU) may submit their own observations and governments can react to these observations. We reviewed reports submitted in 2001 and 2002 for examples of the wide variety of reactions to employment discrimination (International Labour Organization, 2001, 2002). Government reports from Bahrain, Mauritania,

Myanmar, Oman, and Qatar all claimed discrimination does not exist so there are no programs to eliminate it. The Democratic Republic of the Congo and Liberia reported that their civil wars prevent any progress to eliminate discrimination. Nigeria and Pakistan reported they have no data and few resources to assess the extent of employment discrimination, although observations from the ICFTU claim widespread discrimination in these countries. Japan stated approximately 6,000 cases of unequal opportunity and treatment for men and women were reported in 2000 but only 12 of these cases were sent to the prosecutor's office. Finally, the United States reported no changes to relevant laws or practice in 2001 and 2002. The ICFTU observed that although the U.S. laws and judicial remedies for employment discrimination are generally superior to most countries, widespread racial discrimination, discrimination against migrant workers, and nonequal remuneration for men and women still exist.

The above review of ILO reports highlights the fact that many countries are unwilling or unable to effectively address employment discrimination problems. War and poverty push employment discrimination far down any list of government priorities. National politics, religion, and/or culture prevent other countries from ratifying international conventions for the elimination of discrimination or even from acknowledging the existence of such discrimination. Clearly, there are more actions many governments can take to ensure fair employment practices. At the organizational level, there are movements for organizations to voluntarily adopt practices to eliminate unfair discrimination. With an emerging trend indicating class action suits may be heard in an organization's home country, organizations are being more proactive in their own policies and reports.

Research in international employment discrimination has been mostly descriptive. Our review of the literature affirms Sethi's (2003) conclusion that there are no systematic studies examining human rights abuses in employment contexts around the world. Future research can take many directions in this relatively unexplored arena and three general directions are presented here for industrial/organizational psychology. First, basic research on antecedents for discrimination in organizational settings is needed. This line of research would identify multilevel predictors of discrimination with cultural influences at the societal, organizational, group, and individual levels (Chao, 2000). Perhaps critical combinations of these multilevel antecedents would interact to promote or discourage employment discrimination. Second, research examining effects of specific cultural values on workplace discrimination can help understand who is likely to be a target of discrimination and why. For example, cultures with high uncertainty avoidance (i.e., low tolerance for ambiguity) may favor narrow role definitions for specific people and these role expectations may promulgate discriminatory practices. Last, from an applied perspective, more research is needed to understand what organizations can do to minimize workplace discrimination effectively. Sethi (2003) content-analyzed business news reports over an eight year period and concluded most negative reports of worker abuse centered on working conditions, wages, and working hours. These issues are generally under the control of organizations. Better design and implementation of human resource practices can alleviate these types of worker abuse. Schaffer and Riordan (2003) describe best practices for organizational researchers interested in cross-cultural studies. Their review can help future researchers in international employment discrimination avoid common pitfalls associated with cross-cultural research.

Two hundred years ago, many countries did not grant citizenship or basic rights to women or members of particular racial/ethnic groups. One hundred years ago, the industrial revolution and world wars created workforce demands that have sown the seeds for diversity. Today, diverse workforces are global and workers are aware of fair employment goals practiced by some and aspired to by others. Global business has raised new challenges for countries and corporations. Most existing institutions related to workplace discrimination were born in eras that did not comprehend how organizations transcend national borders with practices that conflict with different societies, religions, and histories. As more countries adopt national and international employment laws, the global codes of social responsibility will converge. A global organization's ability to adopt these codes will contribute to its sustainability and competitive advantage. Economic progress and social justice depend on this.

REFERENCES

Anh, T. T. V., & Hung, L. N. (2000). *Women and doi moi in Vietnam*. Hanoi, Vietnam: Woman Publishing House.

Anker, R. (1998). *Gender and jobs: Sex segregation of occupations in the world*. Geneva, Switzerland: International Labour Office.

Banerjee, B., & Knight, J. B. (1985). Caste discrimination in the Indian urban labour market. *Journal of Development Economics, 17*, 277–307.

Barber, D. (1998). The dawning of "the third age." *Management, 45*(5), 46–47.

Baxter, J., & Wright, E. O. (2000). The glass ceiling hypothesis: A comparative study of the United States, Sweden, and Australia. *Gender & Society, 14*, 275–294.

Benassi, M.-P. (1999, June). Women's earning in the EU: 28% less than men. *Statistics in Focus: Population and Social Condition, Theme 3*. [On-line]. Retrieved on January 19, 2003, from http://europa.eu.int/comm/eurostat/Public/datashop/print-catalogue/EN?catalogue=Eurostat.

Bennett v. Total Minatome Corp., 138 F.3d 1053, 1060 (5th Cir. 1998).

Bournois, F. (1993). France. In C. Brewster, A. Hegewisch, J. T. Lockhart, and L. Holden (Eds.), *The European human resource management guide*. London: Academic Press.

Bovenkerk, F., Gras, M., & Ramsoedh, D. (2000). The occurrence of discrimination in the Netherlands. In R. Z. de Beijl (Ed.), *Documenting discrimination against migrant workers in the labour market: A comparative study of four European countries* (pp. 65–76). Geneva, Switzerland: International Labour Office.

Broback, U., & Save-Soderbergh, J. (1996). *Conditions for women in the Zimbabwean labour market: A case study analysis of occupational segregation and discrimination*. Lund, Sweden: Department of Economics at the University of Lund.

Brown, C., Nakata, Y., Reich, M., & Ulman, L. (1997). *International and comparative industrial relations: Work and pay in the United States and Japan*. Oxford: Oxford University Press.

Bryan, T. L. (1991). For the sake of the country, for the sake of the family: The oppressive impact of family registration on women and minorities in Japan. *UCLA Review, 39*, 109–125.

Carmichael, F., & Woods, R. (2000). Ethnic penalties in unemployment and occupational attainment: Evidence for Britain. *International Review of Applied Economics, 14*, 71–96.

Chao, G. T. (2000). Multilevel issues and culture: An integrative view. In K. J. Klein & S. W. J. Kozlowski (Eds.), *Multilevel theory, research, and methods in organizations: Foundations, extensions, and new directions*. San Francisco, CA: Jossey-Bass.

Chan, C., Law, C. K., & Kwok, R. (1992). Attitudes of women toward work in socialist and capitalist cities: A comparative study of Beijing, Guangzhou, and Hong Kong. *Canadian Journal of Community Mental Health, 11*, 187–200.

Civil Rights Act of 1991, Public Law No. 102-166, 105 Stat. 1071 (1991). Codified as amended at 42 U.S.C., Section 1981, 2000e *et seq.*

Clarke, S. (2001, May). Earning of men and women in the EU: The gap narrowing but only slowly. *Statistics in Focus: Population and Social Condition, Theme 5*. [On-line]. Retrieved on January 19, 2003, from http://europa.eu.int/comm/eurostat/Public/datashop/print-catalogue/EN?catalogue=Eurostat.

Colectivo IOE. (2000). The occurrence of discrimination in Spain. In R. Z. de Beijl (Ed.), *Documenting discrimination against migrant workers in the labour market: A comparative study of four European countries* (pp. 77–87). Geneva, Switzerland: International Labour Office.

Court of Cassation, May 31, 1988. (1988). *Cahiers Sociaux du Barreau de Paris*, pp. 9–11.

de Beijl, R. Z. (Ed.). (2000). *Documenting discrimination against migrant workers in the labour market: A comparative study of four European countries*. Geneva, Switzerland: International Labour Office.

Diep, N. N., & Ne, H. T. (2001). *Phu nu va phap luat: Hoi dap ve thoi gio lam viec, thoi gio nghi ngoi va che do lam viec doi voi lao dong nu*. [Women and Law: Q & A regarding work hours, rest, and work standards for women labor.] Ho Chi Minh City, Vietnam: Women Publishing House.

Doe v. Unocal Corp., Nos. 00-56603, 00-57197, Nos. 00-56628, 00-57195 (9th Cir. 2003).

Elder, S., & Johnson, L. J. (1999). Sex-specific labour market indicators: What they show. *International Labour Review, 138*, 447–464.

Elton, C. (2002, March 13). "AIDS Activists Challenge New Controversial Law in El Salvador." *VOA News, 19:49 UTC*.

Employment Rights Act 1996 (1996). London: The Stationery Office Limited.

Equal Employment Opportunity Commission v. Arabian American Oil Co. (89-1838), 499 U.S. 244 (1991)

European Court of Human Rights. (1999a). Lustig-Prean & Beckett v. United Kingdom (Applications nos. 31417/96 and 32377/96). Luxemburger: Carl Heymanns Verlag KG.

European Court of Human Rights. (1999b). Smith & Grady v. United Kingdom (Applications nos. 33985/96 and 33986/96). Luxemburger: Carl Heymanns Verlag KG.

European Employment and Industrial Relations Glossaries. (2002). *Denmark: Non-discrimination act.* [On-line]. Retrieved on November 17, 2002, from http://www. eurofound. eu.int/emire/DENMARK/NONDISCRIMINATIONACT-DN.html.

Federal Court (First Civil Court), June 30, 1987. (1988, January 5). *La semaine judiciaire*, pp. 1–13.

Fernando, B. (2002, November). Discrimination and toleration: An examination of caste discrimination in India. *SikhSpectrum.com Monthly.* [On-line]. Retrieved on November 19, 2002, from http://sikhspectrum.com/112002/dalit_hr.htm.

Fisher, L. (2000). Is the profession colour blind? *Accountancy, 126*(1288), 42–43.

Fulton, E. K. (1996, April 1). A diplomatic parting for an Ottawa veteran. *Maclean's, 109*(14), 24.

Gamson, J. (1999). The officer and the diva. *The Nation, 268*(24), 19–22.

Girion, L. (2002, September 19). US ruling says firms liable for abuse abroad. *Los Angeles Times,* p. A1.

Global Sullivan Principles. (1999). *Global Sullivan Principles of Social Responsibilities.* [On-line]. Retrieved on December 10, 2002, from http://globalsullivanprinciples.org/principles. htm.

The Global Compact. (1999). *The Global Compact: Corporate citizenship in the world economy.* New York: The Global Compact Office, United Nations.

Goldberg, A., & Mourinho, D. (2000). The occurrence of discrimination in Germany. In R. Z. de Beijl (Ed.), *Documenting discrimination against migrant workers in the labour market: A comparative study of four European countries* (pp. 53–63). Geneva, Switzerland: International Labour Office.

Goldberg, C., & Kishkovsky, S. (2000, December 16). Russia's doctors are beggars at work, paupers at home. *The New York Times,* p. A1.

Goss, D., & Goss, F. (1998). SMEs and the Disability Discrimination Act: A case for change? *International Small Business Journal, 17*(1), 89–95.

GRI's Sustainability Reporting Guidelines. (2000). [On-line]. Retrieved on December 10, 2002 from http://www.sustainableproducts.com/download/gri.pdf.

Hall, S. M. (2002). Multinational corporations' post-*Unocal* liabilities for violations of international law. *The George Washington International Law Review, 34*(2), 401–434.

Hamaguchi, K. (1997, September). *New Equal Opportunity Law in Japan: Extract from "News and Views from Japan."* [On-line]. Retrieved on November 17, 2002, from http://www.jmission-eu.be/interest/equalo.htm.

Heaton, N., & Teague, P. (1997). Towards fair employment in Northern Ireland? *International Review of Applied Economics, 11,* 263–285.

Hepple, B. (2001). Equality and empowerment for decent work. *International Labour Review, 140,* 5–17.

HK employers sack their Indonesian maids after they contracted SARS. (2003, May 12). *Channel NewsAsia.* [On-line]. Retrieved on June 8, 2003 from http://www.channelnewsasia. com/stories/eastasia/view/39609/1/.html.

Hoa, N. T. (2002). *Thuc trang lao dong quan ly nganh det may o TP Ho Chi Minh: Moi quan he giua su nghiep va gia dinh duoi goc do gioi.* [The reality of management in the textile industry in Ho Chi Minh City: The relation of career to family from a gender perspective.] Unpublished research report. Ho Chi Minh City, Vietnam: The HCMC Institute of Social Sciences.

Hofstede, G. (1979). *Cultural pitfalls for Dutch expatriates in Indonesia.* Deventer, the Netherlands: Twinjnstra Gudde International.

Hoguet, L. B., & Dansicker, A. M. (1996, December/January). Defending employment decisions on US soil. *International Commercial Litigation,* (Dec. 1996/Jan. 1997) 48–50.

Human rights issues facing older persons. (2000). *The Worklife Report, 12*(4), 7–8.

Human Rights Watch. (1998, April). Justice for all? An Analysis of the Human Rights Provisions of the 1998 Northern Ireland Peace Agreement. *Human Rights Watch World Report 1998: Northern Ireland.* [On-line]. Retrieved on November 17, 2002, from http://www.hrw.org/reports98/nireland/#_1_7.

Human Rights Watch. (2001a). *End global caste discrimination.* [On-line]. Retrieved on November 17, 2002, from http://www.hrw.org/press/2001/03/caste0321.htm.

Human Rights Watch. (2001b). *India: Spotlight on Caste Discrimination.* [On-line]. Retrieved on November 17, 2002, from http://www.hrw.org/press/2001/09/wcarcaste.htm.

Hutchings, K. (1998). Good corporate citizens or perpetrators of social stratification? International business in Malaysia. In M. A. Rahim, & R. T. Golembiewski (Eds.), *Current topics in management,* (Vol. 3, pp. 345–364). Stamford, CT: JAI.

International Labour Organisation. (1958). C111 Discrimination (Employment and Occupation) Convention, 1958. *International Labour Conventions and Recommendations, 1919–1995.* Geneva: ILO.

International Labour Organisation. (1989). Judicial decisions in the field of labour law. *Internaltional Labour Review, 128,* 229–248.

International Labour Organisation. (1996). C100 Equal Remuneration Convention, 1951. *International Labour Conventions and Recommendations, 1919–1995.* Geneva: ILO.

International Labour Organisation. (1996). *Declaration of Philadelphia.* [On-line]. Retrieved on February 25, 2003, from http://www.ilo.org/public/english/about/iloconst.htm#annex.

International Labour Organisation. (1998). *Declaration on Fundamental Principles and Rights at Work.* [On-line]. Retrieved on November 17, 2002 from http://www.ilo.org/public/english/standards/decl/declaration/text/index.htm.

International Labour Organization. (2001, 2002). *The Elimination of Discrimination in Respect of Employment and Occupation: Annual Reports.* [On-line]. Retrieved in February, 2003 from http://www.ilo.org/public/english/standards/decl/database/index.htm.

Janssen, R. (1993). Gays in Dutch army. *Europe, 325,* 37.

Jowell, R., & Prescott-Clarke, P. (1970). Racial discrimination and white collar workers in Britain. *Race, 11,* 397–417.

Kapadia v. London Borough of Lambeth. (2000). IRLR 699 (Court of Appeal).

Kerr, J., Delahanty, J., & Humpage, H. (1996). *Gender and jobs in China's new economy.* Ottawa, ON: The North-South Institute.

Khatchadourian, R. (2002, February 26). Beyond survival: Freed from slavery and terror, Mauritanians fight for those left behind. *Village Voice,* pp. 47–48.

Kitchin, R., Shirlow, P., & Shuttleworth, I. (1998). On the margins: Disabled people's experience of employment in Donegal, West Ireland. *Disability & Society, 13,* 785–806.

Knapp, K. K. (1995). Still office flowers: Japanese women betrayed by the Equal Employment Opportunity Law. *Harvard Women's Law Journal, 18,* 83.

Korean women want work rights. (1999, October 13). *News for You, 47*(40), 3.

Kozaryn, L. D., & Garamone, J. (1999). Cohen adds "Don't harass" to homosexual policy, says it can work. *DefenseLINK.mil (American Forces Press Service).* [On-line]. Retrieved on January 3, 2003, from http://www.defenselink.mil/news/Dec1999/n12291999_9912291.html.

Lachaud, J.-P. (1996). *Les femmes et le marche du travail urbain en Afrique Subsaharienne* [Women and the urban job market in sub-Saharan Africa]. Bordeaux, France: Universite Montesquieu-Bordeau IV (Centre d'economie du developpement).

Lau, V. (1996, June). Anti-discrimination legislation in Hong Kong. *International Commercial Litigation,* p. 38.

Maatman, G. L. Jr. (2001). Employment practices create new class action exposures. *National Underwriter, 105*(8), 21–23.

Madison, A. D. (1997). The context of employment discrimination in Japan. *University of Detroit Mercy Law Review, 74,* 187.

Magagnini, S. (1992, October 21). Japan's "invisible minority's battles age-old bias, shame. *The Sacramento Bee,* p. A1.

McCurry, P. (2000, September). Disabling depression. *Director, 54*(2), 34.

McDonald's Corp. (n.d.). *McDonald's Corporate Social Responsibility.* [On-line]. Retrieved on January 10, 2003, from http://www.mcdonalds.com/corporate/social/.

McIntyre, L. (2003, May 13). Employers acting illegally over SARS. *New Zealand Council of Trade Union.* [On-line]. Retrieved on June 8, 2003 from http://www.union.org.nz /news/146.html.

Meenan, H. (1999). Age discrimination in the United Kingdom. *International Journal of Discrimination & the Law, 3,* 227–248.

Meng, X., & Miller, P. (1995). Occupational segregation and its impact on gender wage discrimination in China's rural industrial sector. *Oxford Economic Papers, 47,* 136–155.

Mertus, J. (1998). Human rights of women in Central and Eastern Europe. *American University Journal of Gender, Social Policy & the Law, 6,* 369.

Midgley, S. (1996). Treating mid-life unemployment with tact. *People Management, 2,* 21.

Missing out on talent? (2001, March). *New Zealand Manufacturer,* p. 20.

N'Daba, L., & Hodges-Aeberhard, J. (1998). *HIV/AIDS and employment.* Geneva, Switzerland: International Labour Office.

Pollard R. (2003, May 7). Stay-home SARS rule branded as overkill. *The Sydney Morning Herald.* [On-line]. Retrieved on June 8, 2003 from http://www.smh.com.au/articles/2003/ 05/06/1051987704035.html.

Power, C. (2001, January 8). Women of the new century: For European women, globalization may be messy. But it's bringing fresh opportunities for a group of dynamic, young entrepreneurs. The workplace will never be the same again. *Newsweek,* p. 14.

Preston, A. C., & Crockett, G. V. (1999, September). *The gender earnings gap in Australia: Learning from state comparisons.* Perth, Australia: Women's Economic Policy Analysis Unit, Curtin University.

Reid, L. L. (1998). Devaluing women and minorities: The effects of race/ethnic and sex composition of occupations on wage levels. *Work and Occupations, 25,* 511–536.

Republic of Ireland. (1998). Employment Equality Act, 1998.

Riach, P. A., & Rich, J. (2002). Field experiments of discrimination in the market place. *The Economic Journal, 112,* 480–518.

Riphenburg, C. J. (1999, May/June). Gender relations and development in the Yemen: Participation and Employment. *Peacekeeping & International Relations,* pp. 5–22.

Savage, E., & Wenner, S. (2001). Impact of US Anti-Discrimination Laws on Foreign Corporations: Part 2. *Benefits and Compensation International, 31*(4), 8–12.

Schaffer, B. S., & Riordan, C. M. (2003). A review of cross-cultural methodologies for organizational research: A best-practices approach. *Organizational Research Methods, 6,* 169–215.

Sethi, S. P. (2003). *Setting Global Standards: Guidelines for Creating Codes of Conduct in Multinational Corporations.* Hoboken, NJ: Wiley.

Shabi, R. (2000, May). The business of race. *Management Accounting, 78*(5), 34–35.

Singer, A. (2000). Sex discrimination in the Hong Kong Special Administration Region: The Sex Discrimination Ordinance, the Equal Opportunities Commission, and a proposal for change. *Indiana International & Comparative Law Review,* p. 11.

Slavin, B. (2002, May 13). U.S. firms' Saudi offices face manpower isues; Several American companies employ no women in the kingdom; others maintain strict segregation by sex. Critics say system echoes apartheid. *USA Today,* p. A5.

Smeesters, B., Arrijn, P., Feld, S., & Nayer, A. (2000). The occurrence of discrimination in Belgium. In R. Z. de Beijl (Ed.), *Documenting discrimination against migrant workers in the labour market: A comparative study of four European countries* (pp. 41–52). Geneva, Switzerland: International Labour Office.

Smith, R. K. M. (2000). European Convention on Human Rights–respect for private life–prohibition on homosexuals in the British Armed Forces. *The American Journal of International Law, 94,* 382–386.

Social Welfare Department. (1996). *The Persons with Disabilities (Equal Opportunities, Protection of Rights and Full Participation) Act, 1995.* [On-line]. Retrieved on November 1, 2002, from http://socialwelfare.delhigovt.nic.in/disabilityact.htm.

Sparrow, P. R., & Hiltrop, J. -M. (1994). *European human resource management in transition.* Englewood Cliffs, NJ: Prentice-Hall.

Srinivasan, N. (2002). *Flawed law?* [On-line]. Retrieved on November 1, 2002, from http://www.indiatogether.org/health/opinions/pwd95crit.htm.

Steinberg, M., Donald, K., Najman, J., & Skerman, H. (1996). Attitudes of employees and employers towards older workers in a climate of anti-discrimination. *Australian Journal on Aging, 15*(4), 154–158.

Strober, M. H., & Chan, A. M. K. (1999). *The road winds uphill all the way: Gender, work and family in the United States and Japan.* Cambridge, MA: MIT Press.

Sullivan, N. (1983). Indonesian women in development: State theory and urban kampung practice. In L. Manderson (Ed.), *Women's work and women's roles.* Canberra: The Australian National University.

Tam, P. (2003, February 18). Appeals court to rehear ruling on Unocal Human-rights suit. *Wall Street Journal,* p. B13.

The UK Home Office. (2001, November 21). *Race Relations Act 1976.* [On-line]. Retrieved on November 21, 2002, from http://www.homeoffice.gov.uk/raceact/racerel1.htm.

United Nations. (1948). *Universal Declaration of Human Rights.* New York: Author.

United Nations. (1960). International Covenant on Economic, Social, & Cultural Rights. *United Nations Treaty Series.* New York: Author.

United Nations. (1969). International Convention on the Elimination of All Forms of Racial Discrimination. *United Nations Treaty Series.* New York: Author.

United Nations Population Fund. (2000). *State of World Population 2000, Lives Together, Worlds Apart: Men and Women in a Time of Change.* New York: Author.

United States. (1967). Age Discrimination in Employment Act of 1967 *(Pub. L. 90-2002) (ADEA).*

United States. (1978). *Code of Federal Regulations.* Washington, DC: U.S. Government Printing Office.

United States Department of Commerce. (n.d.). *Model business principles.* [On-line]. Retrieved on December 10, 2002, from http://www.itcilo.it/english/actrav/telearn/global/ilo/guide/usmodel.htm.

United States Department of State. (2002a, March 4). *Country Reports on Human Rights Practices, 2001: India.* Washington, DC: Bureau of Democracy, Human Rights, and Labor.

United States Department of State. (2002b, March 4). *Country Reports on Human Rights Practices, 2001: China (includes Hong Kong and Macau).* Washington, DC: Bureau of Democracy, Human Rights, and Labor.

United States House of Representatives, Office of the Law Revision Counsel. (2002, January). *Alien Tort Claims Act.* Title 28, Section 1350, U.S. Code. [On-line]. Retrieved on January 12, 2003, from http://uscode.house.gov/usc.htm.

United States House of Representatives, Office of the Law Revision Counsel. (2000). *United States Code, Title 10, Subtitle A, Part II, Chapter 37, Section 654: Policy concerning homosexuality in the Armed Forces.* Washington, DC: U.S. Government Printing Office.

Verschyurr-Basse, D. (1996). *Chinese women speak.* Westport, CT: Praeger.

Weeks v. Samsung Heavy Indus. Co., 126 F.3d 926. (1997).

Welch, J. (1996). The invisible minority. *People Management, 2*(19), 24–31.

Williams, A. (1996, June 13). Transsexuals and their rights in the workplace. *People Management, 2*(12), 49–50.

Wright, L., & Tellei, V. C. (1993). Gender discrimination in the British labour market: A re-assessment. *The Economic Journal, 101,* 508–522.

Zafarullah, H. (2000). Through the brick wall and the glass ceiling: Women in the civil service in Bangladesh. *Gender, Work & Organization, 7,* 197–209.

17

Doing Research on Pay Equity in Support of the Political Process: The Wyoming Experience

Martin M. Greller
John H. Jackson
University of Wyoming

This paper is a reflection on an experience. It is not intended to prove a point or test an hypothesis. Indeed, its purpose is to help raise questions. As this volume has already illustrated, industrial and organizational psychologists (and their cousins in human resource management and applied social psychology) have played an active role in understanding and addressing discrimination. For the most part, that role has taken the form of one of two models. First, researchers contribute knowledge of the phenomenon, the forces that drive it, and the approaches for remediation. This is a classic role for the social scientist, providing a factual basis for decision making. In the second model, practitioners hone techniques associated with personnel processes and decisions to detect and reduce bias, usually working within a single organization. Organizations operate within a socio/political environment and the results of such research hopefully inform and shape both the organization and the environment.

The situation we will describe is different. The Wyoming legislature asked for assistance in assessing pay equity for women and the alternative actions it could take to deal with the issue in the state. This was not primarily a request to summarize the scientific literature, but for assistance in understanding the state's specific situation. Our purpose here is not to report on the findings of the study but to discuss the process.[1]

BACKGROUND TO THE PROJECT

Data collected in 1999 and the 2000 U.S. Census showed Wyoming as the state with the greatest gap in pay between women and men. This was not necessarily viewed as a surprise in the state. It was popularly attributed to two factors: (a) the structure of the state economy including the presence of a few high paid, but typically male jobs in mining and construction, with low paid hospitality jobs typically held by women, and (b) the "macho imagery" and "cowboy" mentality attributed to the state was also believed to work to the disadvantage of women in the workforce. However, these were only suppositions.

The information from the U.S. census provided a rallying point for a number of women in government. In the years prior to the release of this information, several women in the executive and legislative branch had begun working together to foster women's economic progress in the state. Confronted with the hard data of the state's poor performance in the area of pay equity, members of this group became vocal advocates for action by the legislature.

But, what action? The common wisdom hardly provided guidance on how to change the situation, and it certainly had not led to actions previously. The situation lent itself to commissioning a study to provide a common set of facts, although the product desired and time frame were more consistent with staff work than academic research.

At the same time, the dean of the college of business in the state's only university was soliciting contracts with the state. The dean had previously served as education aide to the governor and was involved in ongoing discussions with members of both the executive and legislative branches of government on their needs. The dean floated an inquiry through the college asking who might be interested in assisting the legislature in this task. It provided an opportunity to shape the legislative mandate so that it could be completed with the staff, resources, and time available. (This was not viewed as a contract to be bid, but work being delegated to a state entity, the university.) In defining the scope of work, extensive original data

---

[1]For those who are interested, the research report is available on the Wyoming Business Council web site: http://www.wyomingbusiness.org/women/publications/index.cfm.

collection was discouraged because a tight time line was established and money to collect original data was very limited.

LEGISLATIVE MANDATE

The legislature asked five specific questions:

1. Where do wage disparities exist?
2. What are the major causes of wage and benefit disparities?
3. What is the impact of wage and benefit disparities on Wyoming's economy?
4. What are possible solutions to reduce or eliminate wage and benefit disparities?
5. What are the benefits and costs of eliminating or reducing wage and benefit disparities?

The legislator's questions were clear and possible to address. The questions focused the research but did not provide answer to the questions in the socio/political sphere. These included questions such as: How should the information be presented for best effect? How could scientific integrity be maintained in the face of advocacy pressure? And, should the researchers recommend a solution? The socio/political questions would have to be addressed by the research team if the work was to be viewed as unbiased and therefore useful for dealing with the gender wage gap issue.

ORGANIZATION FOR THE WORK

The legislation and funding were approved by the legislature in March of 2002. Work was to be completed in less than one year. This was seen as a challenging but feasible time frame. However, the funding did not go directly to the university. It was allocated as part of the Business Council's budget. The Council is a semi-autonomous authority of the state, the primary purpose of which is to facilitate economic activity and business development. The Council itself consists of 15 appointed board members from various geographic and economic sectors of the state. Although it employs a full-time staff, the staff is committed to work on economic development. So, the council appointed an ad hoc committee comprising legislators, members of the women's business network, and interested citizens. This committee would draft the actual contract, oversee the work, and receive the initial report from the university.

FIG. 17.1. Chain of reporting authority.

This may seem a cumbersome arrangement, but one needs to understand the reasons for it. The Wyoming legislature is a part-time commitment for its members, and it does not meet during most of the year. Because the legislative committee taking the action was the Joint Minerals, Business and Economic Development Committee, they delegated oversight to an agency that reported to them, hence the involvement of the Business Council. The ad hoc committee was necessary because the council did not have the resources to carry out an oversight role on its own. Members of the legislative committee and Business Council were included as members of the ad hoc committee, and they were active members. One of the lead researchers also served as a member of the Business Council's Board of Directors. On the positive side, the multiple roles fostered greater communication and made it easier to look back to the original intent of the legislature. However, the cumbersome nature of the organizational arrangement became evident in preparing a contract that would allow the university to be paid for the project. The legislature had not drafted specific contract language. This was left to the ad hoc committee with guidance from the Business Council. As Fig. 17.1 shows, the organizational arrangement was quite different than what is normally experienced with a research or consulting client.

Not unreasonably, members of the oversight committee began to engage the issues. They thought of questions, concerns, and activities that would make a contribution to addressing the problem. Examples of ideas initiated by the ad hoc committee that were taken up by the research team include definitions of what "wage disparity" really meant, other states against which to benchmark, and different ways to present alternatives.

Of course, not all the ideas were embraced. Some suggestions would have shaped a very different research project than that framed by the legislature and that the university was prepared to complete with the time and resource constraints. Such change would not necessarily be a bad thing. However, unfortunately, these discussions were occurring during late summer and early fall. Because of the limited time and the greater availability of faculty during the summer, it was imperative that work begin if the project deadline was to be respected. Recognizing this, the research team had begun work (and the university had started disbursing its own funds in advance of the contract) to keep to the schedule. So, work consistent with the earlier discussions with the legislature had already commenced. Seven months after the legislature had authorized the study, the money to pay people was finally in place. In this instance, the organization for the project worked against efficiency.

The issue of time was not due to an arbitrary deadline. Wyoming's legislature meets for three months each year. One year its primary business is budgetary. The next year it addresses other issues. The deadline would have provided a report in time for the nonbudgetary session. A delay could push action back not one year but two.

After this initial period, the role of the oversight committee dropped into the background except for an interim progress report. It became necessary to adjust the timing of the final report, and the committee was helpful in making the adjustment.

THE RESEARCH PROCESS

So, how does a social scientist respond to a state that wants to know what is going on within its boarders with regard to gender pay equity, its causes, and potential actions but has allocated limited funding to the process? It is certainly a different situation than that of an organization client, where payroll data and personnel records are available. The nature of the actions a legislature can take are different from those a company can take. The problems and solutions are less direct than, for example, when the shipping department is found not to be hiring or advancing women.

The problem also differs from a national research effort to identify the causes of pay differences. Whereas a national study identifies occupational or human capital variables to provide insight, it does not do so in sufficient specificity. If industry makes a difference, the legislature will need to know which industries in their state are high paying, which have the greatest differences in pay between men and women, and what human capital variables are most important to their labor force. Of course those specifics may differ among counties making even the state level of analysis too broad to guide action in some instances.

Research Issues

The research strategy emerged along several dimensions. First, what could the existing literature on pay equity contribute to understanding of the situation in Wyoming? A question of particular importance was which variables should be addressed in the examination of the state's situation, and the existing research was helpful for targeting variables. This led to a second question, what sources of data were available that would allow adequate examination of the variables within the state? What have other states done that the legislature might want to consider, and what were the results of these efforts? Finally, how could the points be illustrated and explained in human terms that would make them meaningful to a broad, nontechnical audience?

A first step was to find people knowledgeable of the specific areas involved who could help address these issues, but who were also able to work together as part of an interdisciplinary team. In the present case, this resulted in a team of four faculty members who served as principal investigators on the contract. One was an organizational psychologist whose primary focus was analysis of the data. Another was an attorney and sociologist, whose research centered on women's issues and whose original involvement was based on her expertise on differing state laws and initiatives. One was an economist with background in regional economic impact, whose key task would be estimating the effects of changes in gender equity on the state economy. The project leader was an expert in human resource management.[2] Whereas areas of specialization defined what unique contributions were expected, in operation each of the principals was involved in thinking through and integrating issues from all areas. Several graduate students were funded under the project and worked under the supervision of the principals depending on the most active area of work at any given moment.

Data Issues

Given that pay equity has been a concern for half a century and equal pay the law for nearly two generations, one might expect that there would be an abundance of useful data. This was not the case.

---

[2]In addition to the two authors the two principals on the University of Wyoming faculty were Anne Alexander and Catherine R. Connelly. Dr. Alexander is an economist who currently serves as Assistant Dean of the College of Business. Dr. Connolly is an attorney and Professor of Sociology who is currently Director of the Women's Studies Program.

There was very good access to information on state or provincial laws and initiatives. This was available from the states themselves and from advocacy groups that facilitated the dissemination of such information. What was often less clear was what, if any, effect these efforts have had. Thus, it was possible to say what others had done, but not much about what role these efforts played in moving toward greater equity. One would not want to simply recommend adopting whatever regulations were in place in the states with the smallest wage gaps. Situations could differ substantially from state to state, and the level of equity might not be a function of the regulations. Further, equity can be achieved in some undesirable ways (i.e., pay for women in Vermont is very close to the level of pay for women in Wyoming. However, the pay for men in Vermont is lower, producing a smaller gap. Even if it were possible to do so, reducing men's wages would not be a way any state would want to correct its pay equity situation.)

Specific data on what people are paid in conjunction with labor market, human capital, and personal information was more difficult to access. It is not that the information itself does not exist. The state labor statistics agency collects most of the facts that would be needed, but it was not possible to link data about employment experience and income (in the unemployment insurance database) to education, to employer characteristics, and so forth. Although initially the problem appeared to be one of confidentiality, further exploration suggested that even if those issues could be addressed it would be difficult to establish reliable links.

Data collected by the federal government have the right variables (i.e., sex, earnings, hours worked, family status, education, etc.) The Current Population Survey (CPS) would be a good source of data at the national level. It is one of the more commonly used sources of data for national surveys of employment, and because it is a sample survey, the issues of confidentiality are not a concern. However, the state's small size mitigates against using the national data. Approximately 1 in 400 households participate in any given administration of the CPS. Wyoming has approximately 194,000 households, leading to an expected sample of less than 500 in any given CPS, and much of the sample would be concentrated in a few counties. When industry, occupation, sex, and education are examined, it is likely that there would be a considerable number of empty cells. As the legislature's interest was in the status of pay equity in Wyoming, not in understanding its antecedents at the national level, this reduced the value of the CPS for this study. The federally sponsored longitudinal surveys suffer from the same problem: too little representation to be useful given Wyoming's small population. Although this might be written off as a problem only applicable to small states, researchers should recognize that the same problem is at work in the less populated portions of large states. Thus, New York, Texas, or California have plenty of people who participate in the CPS or national longitudinal surveys, but limited coverage of rural areas and specific subpopulations in urban areas may make these groups invisible in the final results.

The U.S. census provides essentially complete coverage of the population and most of the variables that were needed. It also was timely, having been conducted two years previously. However, as of fall 2002 no individual level data had been released. (The Census Bureau may release a 1% sample of households, which provides anonymity for the respondents but allows analysis of the variables at the individual level, but this was not available at the time of the study.)

However, "block level" data were available from the 2000 census. Census blocks are a relatively fine geographical subdivision, usually below the county level. Thus, Wyoming has 23 counties, but 127 census blocks. Block data summarize responses from within the geographical area. Thus, one knows the percent of women heading households with children under 18 and one knows the distribution of earnings for women (and for women engaged in full-time employment). Therefore, it is possible to estimate the effect of education by looking at the average level of education and correlating it with average income. Effect size would be reduced because one cannot track the higher earnings associated with individuals, but it still should provide a basis for estimation.

It should be noted that the exploration for data sources was conducted independently of the oversight committee. Although they indicated what they wanted to know, how the team obtained the answers was a matter of its own choosing. Similarly, in estimating the economic effect of increasing women's wages, there had been no discussion of the underlying assumptions. They were, of course, presented quite clearly and most of the analysis was driven by accepted approaches in regional economic modeling, but there was no certainty that nonacademics would agree with the assumptions.

To help make the information more concrete and easier for a broad audience to understand, the attorney/sociologist conducted a qualitative study, interviewing a small sample of people from each county about their experience in the workplace and observations about pay equity. The idea was to provide an independent method of observing the same effects as might be seen in the census statistics, without excessive data collection efforts but this time with more personalized individual data that could be presented in a descriptive form. Of course, the hope was that the results would be mutually supportive and provide a consistent explanation. Contradictory results would be frustrating, but important to know.

OBSERVATIONS FROM THE STUDY

Analysis of the census data showed that as in the rest of the nation, men and women work in somewhat different occupations, with the biggest differences (as popular supposition had predicted) being that men were more frequently in higher paying construction, installation and repair, and production occupations. Women were more frequently in lower paying clerical, food-related, and teaching jobs. The industries in which men and women are employed differ as well, with men more commonly employed in construction, mining, and transportation in the state. Women predominate in the education industry, administrative and support industry, and the arts.

The size of the wage disparity was increased by women working part time and the presence of children. The gap was reduced by women's employment in high paying industries, women's increased education, women's increasing experience, and more women working full time.

The results indicated that in Wyoming the following four variables accounted for much of the wage disparity between men and women.

1. Occupation: Nursing, teaching, and administrative assistant jobs remain the "pink collar ghetto" of old, with women continuing to work in these fields over other higher paying work. Change is occurring slowly but many women work at these lower paying jobs today. Economic theory would predict the "crowding" of many people into a limited number of occupations should drive down the wages in those occupations.

2. Time spent working: Nationally, 16 years after finishing school women average 50% of the work experience that men average. In Wyoming the proportion is similar. Further, in the state 22% of the women work part time while 11% of the men work part time

3. Education: Graduation rates for both high school and college are very similar for men and women. However, the choice of majors in college finds more men going into engineering and computer science and more women into education and social work.

4. Industry of employment: In Wyoming, the industries that are highest paying (i.e., mining, construction, and transportation) have not attracted a large number of women. Thirty percent of men work in those higher paying industries. Fifty-eight percent of women are found in the lowest paying industries—education, clerical, retail, and the arts.

The telephone survey of residents' opinions on the wage gap closely followed the results of the census data, confirming the findings on a more personal level. Some of the comments were especially good illustrations of the ways differences in wages are viewed by the population:

- "We live in a rural environment without much female oriented work" (woman)
- "Women choose lower paying jobs" (man)
- "Women won't do a lot of jobs men do, for example-mining" (woman)
- "Wyoming employers don't see women as long-term employees" (man)

This was a difficult data analysis exercise, particularly as the task was to integrate information and provide a coherent picture for the legislature. It was useful to have multiple approaches, particularly as the analysis of the census data presented somewhat surprising results. Some of those are probably artifacts of using block level data (e.g., in blocks in which more people are employed in high paying industries, women reported lower pay levels, possibly due to husbands participating in the higher paying industries, bringing home a larger pay check, and reducing the need for the wife to work). However, there were some results that may require re-thinking our assumptions For example, in Wyoming, women with small children appear to earn more, possibly because (as supported by the interviews) mothers of small children are faced with increased economic need and when faced with such a need they approach the labor market with far more focused goals, to deal with the income shortfall.[3]

USE OF THE STUDY

With the results in mind, it was decided to provide the legislature a list of everything that had been tried or advocated nationally to deal with the wage gap. Three of those possible solutions were subjected to a very conservative cost benefit analysis. Those three and a synopsis of their estimated impacts follow.

Changing where women work: What if more women quit working in jobs that have traditionally been "female" and worked instead in traditionally "male" jobs? This analysis projected increases in women working in those jobs at several different levels. At the most conservative level, a 10% increase in women working in "male" jobs would reduce the wage gap in the state by 3.5–6.1 points and benefits would exceed costs by half a million dollars annually.

---

[3]While women earned higher wages in census blocks where there were more children, apparently men in the same block earned more still as the wage gap was larger where there were more children.

Changing what women make where they currently work: Two occupations in Wyoming that are overwhelmingly female are nurses [90%] and public school teachers [70%], where they are paid far below the national averages. Yet wage rates are somewhat controlled by different government entities. Bringing the pay for teachers and nurses up to the national average would reduce the wage gap by 2.1–3.3 points. It is estimated that the benefits of doing so out weigh the costs by $76 million annually.

Changing how much women work: What would happen if more women were in the full time workforce? If just half of the women working part time worked 35 hours per week the wage gap would drop by 4.5 points and benefits would exceed costs by $85 million annually for the state.

The total estimated reduction in the wage gap from these three actions would be from 10.1 to 13.9 points, putting Wyoming toward the top of the 50 states with regard to pay equity.

The logic behind providing a range of alteratives was to keep the researchers from impinging upon the role of elected officials, but to provide pertinent information for those policy makers. Scientific neutrality rather than advocacy for a particular solution put the researchers in the role of information provider rather that that of defender of a solution based on a point of view.

What was to be done with the study? From the research team's perspective, the formal answer was clear. A preliminary report would be shared with the oversight committee. Subsequently, a final report would be provided to the oversight committee and be distributed to the legislative committee. The legislative committee would then have the option of calling on the researchers to participate in a public hearing to review findings and alternative actions. Those things did happen. However, the effects do not necessarily reflect the seemingly linear, logical process implied.

THIS EFFORT AS AN INTERVENTION

Consider what was done in comparison to the two other models suggested earlier. When social scientists consult to organizations, we often endeavor to have the client highly involved in the process. But who is the client here? A liaison committee might be present in more conventional interventions, but it would be comprised of people in the organization who would be involved in the adoption and implementation of the results. Here adoption means something quite different because any change will be a legislative decision. The decision-making process will be quite public, be subject to influence by a wide range of people, and be based on perceptions of the public good as much as any individual preference. In organization consulting, the report or intervention is something assumed to be close to the end of a process. Here it might be viewed as something occurring more nearly at the beginning of the process.

Certainly, this sets in place a basis for a very different set of interactions than would be the case with other interventions. The oversight committee was less involved in the execution of the work than might be the case in an organizational consultation. By presenting a complete report to the oversight committee, there is the temptation to think of it as helping them get up to speed on a project that had largely been completed in their absence. Doing so would fail to appreciate their role in the process. For the legislature, the oversight committee represents a knowledgeable group, reflecting a cross section of the constituencies that they anticipate will have an interest in the legislation that may stem from the research. The oversight committee did make a summary report that was forwarded to the legislative committee suggesting four possible state interventions. After identifying all the other possibilities, these seemed quite limited, and it would have been hard not to fret (after all most of us would like every footnote and nuance of our work to be appreciated). But such a reaction fails to recognize the role played by the oversight group. They were not a filter. The legislative committee has direct access to the report and the researchers.

One needs to understand that the members of the oversight committee may play a role after the committee itself ceases to exist. The participants included people in administrative and civil service positions whose functions could be affected by subsequent legislative decisions. People who might appear as advocates before the legislature were included, as were several legislators. So, the members of the oversight committee may be expected to reappear in different roles at a later point in the decision process. Their participation may be made more effective because of what they have learned as members of the oversight committee. Indeed, if the oversight committee was sufficiently inclusive, the interaction may provide a sense of the direction that debate will take in the legislature.

One area that presented a difficult time avoiding the appearance of advocacy was estimating the proportion of the wage gap that could be attributed to illegal discrimination against women in their wages. Some of the problem is implicit in the models used to study pay equity. Some advocates are quick to use the presence of any male–female difference in pay as proof of discrimination. Certainly, some of the difference is due to discrimination. On the other side, in an effort to defend pay practices that recognize legitimate reasons for differences in pay, there is a body of research demonstrating that much of the male–female differences in pay can be "explained" by factors such as jobs, human capital, industry, hours worked, and so forth. Such factors can be used to reduced the unexplained difference from the 30%–40% range to the 5%–10% range. The argument continues that any inappropriate differences in pay are to be found in this residual variance. For an individual employer this may be a reasonable argument, as they do not control the explanatory variables. However, when the question is raised by a state (or nation), the antecedent variables are equally interesting. What leads to differing occupational choices and decisions regarding invests in human capital? Does the educational system contribute to these differences? Do the agencies tasked with aiding in employment and training play a role in creating these differences? Further, on the opposite side, what role is played by individual preferences and ambitions? It is not the role of government to compel individuals to take the highest paid employment possible, even when that requires work that is not of intrinsic interest.

Although it is possible to note these questions, we were not in a position to make a substantive estimate of how much of the difference in pay was due to illegal discrimination. Further, the study was not funded at a level that would allow the necessary empirical research to make such an estimate with accuracy. The study notes that illegal discrimination likely exists and is a likely a factor in Wyoming's wage gap, but that the problems in identifying and quantifying it accurately are immense. A useful bit of research would identify a range of discrimination present in different employment situations (government employment vs. private, or by industry, for example) and would identify costs (and benefits) for employers of such discrimination.

THE POLITICS OF THE PROCESS AND THE REPORT

Given the considerable number of participants who have reason to take a position or may arrive with one already well established, it is tempting to look to the traditional researcher/expert role as a model. In that model the researcher acts as a fair and impartial assessor of data and existing knowledge, much the same as traditional academic researchers. However, academic researchers also generally can expect to be left alone, to develop their ideas at a pace dictated by the progress of their research, and to present their findings in an environment where debate is intended to advance knowledge or to reveal truth. These assumptions are tenuous in the politically charged climate of advocacy for political change. The milieu into which the results will enter is clearly one of advocacy and opinion, not science. Also, there is every reason to suppose that the other participants will be quick to assume that there is an element of advocacy in the researchers.

The schedule and reporting are dictated by others (although, this need not be without influence by the researchers, as was the case in the present study, where it was necessary to postpone completion by several months). Perhaps the most difficult thing for an academic researcher to recognize is that the public expects to be in contact and to have the "right" to try to influence the research. This is not to suggest that such a project will be changed based on these influence attempts. Certainly good ideas, regardless of the source, are good ideas. However, the public expects to be heard, not just through their elected representatives, but by the agents of those representatives, people doing research for the legislature as well. From the public perspective, a researcher may not be much different than a legislative staffer, who is fair game for lobbying. After each major announcement or news story, the project director would receive calls from people who had suggestions. Some were of the form "Why do you need to do research when it is perfectly obvious that the problem is . . . " Others wanted to call attention to specific facts, issues, or circumstances. For the most part, these people wanted to make sure their ideas has been heard. Certainly, given the reporting structure, they were not in a position to compel changes in the work that was done.

In preparing to meet with the legislative committee that commissioned the work, the researchers were told to expect to have half an hour (some of which would be used by the chair of the oversight committee) and to assume that no one had read the report. That was probably unfair. At least two members of the legislative committee had been on the oversight committee. However, the notion that this one report would be the sole focus of the legislative committee's attention would be fanciful. (On the same day that the report was heard, five other significant reports were also presented!) One cannot expect a great deal of information to be conveyed in such a setting. Indeed, at best one can hope to address a few major misconceptions and provide information for those with higher levels of interest to pursue after the presentation.

So, should one expect a frustrating end to the project? That depends on what constitutes the ending. When the presentation to the legislative committee was over, the researchers packed up their overheads having fulfilled their contractual obligations. There is a bound report. In that sense the project is done, but it leaves many things in an unfinished state. For example, the chairman of the legislative committee asked the researchers if they wished to make a formal recommendation for legislation based upon their research. That option is open, but would that really be the end? It is likely that the legislative process will continue and gender equity will continue to be an issue and, for some, a priority. People not directly involved in the decision-making process have requested copies of the report, and it has had circulation to surrounding states as word-of-mouth information about the research spreads. Several independent initiatives (such as fostering greater awareness of career options for girls in high school) are underway. News reports have helped to disseminate the information. The researchers have been invited to speak at various women's business forums and economic development groups around the state.

Because the upcoming legislative session is a budget session, it is unlikely there will be any efforts to take legislative action this term. However, that gives all those involved another year to decide how they want to use the information. This may be an expression of wanton optimism; however, it is also an acknowledgment that the work is now out of our hands. It is likely that we will have little influence over how it is used, perhaps even less so than in organizational consultations where the implementation process may be part of the consultation. However, in a political process, there is no special right for expertise to govern. The will of those who are governed is far more important. In agreeing to fill a supportive role, one agrees to support the process that government uses and that is quite different either from that of academic research or organizational consultation.

Does direct involvement with a legislative or executive arm of government provide a viable way to contribute? The answer is at least partially personal. What sources of satisfaction do you expect from your work? After the fact, the members of the research team realized we never actually discussed our own political views or positions with regard to pay equity. Our role required subordinating personal political views. If one finds fulfillment in advocacy, this would be a frustrating assignment.

On the other end of the continuum, the opportunity to conduct academically valued research may also have been limited. The pressures to answer a specific set of questions (with time and resource limitations) led us to manage the size and scope of the research in ways that may make it less appealing to our academic colleagues. This is not to say there will not be research that could be published nor that ideas for future projects may not be developed. However, the major focus had to be meeting the needs of the client.

For all the constraints and limitations, supporting the legislative process in one's professional capacity creates opportunities to aid in decision making and advance the nature and quality the public debate. We believe this is a contribution consistent with our professional roles. However, the limitations one accepts to make that contribution must be weighed as well.

18

The Dilemmas of Workplace Discrimination

Robert L. Dipboye
University of Central Florida

Adrienne Colella
Texas A&M University

In this concluding chapter we return to a question posed to the authors of this book: Is discrimination still a significant problem in the workplace or is it largely resolved and on the way to a solution? Based on the chapters in this book, we must conclude that workplace discrimination remains a major problem but has evolved into different forms than those dominant in the past. When the sociologist Gunnar Myrdal (1944) wrote about an "American Dilemma" he referred to the obvious inconsistencies between democratic values and the overt oppression of African Americans in the workplace and in many other social settings. In the half century that has passed since these observations, impressive progress has been made by African Americans and other minority and historically disadvantaged groups. There are now laws providing for equal opportunity. Diversity is now endorsed by most major corporations. Overt discrimination is now viewed as socially unacceptable in most circles. However, despite these signs of progress, the "dilemma" of workplace discrimination continues in forms that still harm even though they appear more complex and subtle than the old-fashioned discrimination of past years. This complexity and subtlety constitute the new dilemmas of workplace discrimination.

Compared to the rather blatant oppression that existed in the form of Jim Crow laws and apartheid prior to the 1960s, discrimination in today's workplace comes as a multifaceted and convoluted system in which it is difficult to identify or separate out the simple, primary origins of the problem. Discrimination must be defined to include not only blatant mistreatment in the workplace but also a variety of covert forms that are entangled with other more immediate causal influences and often far removed from the workplace. In its most proximal forms, discrimination occurs when members of disadvantaged groups are recruited, selected, and placed and during the appraisals, compensation, promotions, training, and day-to-day interactions on the job. In more distal forms, discrimination occurs in the organizational structures, systems, policies, and practices that can have the unintended effect of perpetuating inequalities. However, we would go even further to include among the distal forms of discrimination societal and cultural factors, such as socialization of disadvantaged groups in childhood as they learn what to expect from the world of work and form self-identities based on these expectations. In these cases, the individuals are still victims of discrimination. What we say should not be interpreted that the victim bears the responsibility or is to blame. Rather, we suggest that discrimination results from the interrelationships among many factors in a dynamic, complex system, which can become self-perpetuating and in which the victim can become a unwitting contributor to his or her own plight.

The subtlety of modern forms of discrimination poses another dilemma. We still see ugly, even violent, episodes of racism, sexism, ageism, heterosexism, and other forms of prejudice. Vivid illustrations can be found among the 84,442 complaints filed with the EEOC in 2002 (U.S. Equal Employment Opportunity Commission, 2003). Nevertheless, open bigotry is less frequent than subtle discrimination, which is harder to identify, confront, and overcome. Laws and rules can deal with blatant racism and sexism, but what can be done to deal with exclusion from informal networks, ambivalent feelings, joking, and negative nonverbal behavior? Moreover, as bigotry has become less visible, attempts to eliminate discrimination can appear unwarranted and can provoke accusations of reverse discrimination and preferential treatment. Thus, efforts to deal with discrimination can have the unfortunate and unintended consequence of worsening the problem it was intended to correct (see Heilman & Haynes, in this volume).

More subtle and complex discrimination still adversely influences the status of those who are the target of the discrimination. Gross inequalities in labor market outcomes persist in which females, minorities, people who are disabled, gays and lesbians, or older persons are disadvantaged compared to younger, White, physically and mentally unimpaired, heterosexual, or male employees (Acemoglu & Angrist, 2001; Albelda, Drago, & Schulman, 1997; Badgett, 1996; Catalyst, 2000; Scott, Berger, & Garen, 1995; Seglin, 2002; U.S. Census Bureau, 2002; U.S. Department of Labor, 2003a, 2003b). Inequalities remain even after differences in skills, education, experience, and other human capital factors are taken into account. In turn, discrepancies in workplace status and labor market outcomes are determinants of other inequalities, such as those that exist in wealth, crime, education, housing, and health. Discrimination cannot explain all of the gaps, but it remains a particularly important explanation that deserves the attention of industrial and organizational psychologists (Albelda et al., 1997; Cohn, 2000). We would further argue that it is not productive to seek or expect simple, single cause of disparities. In most cases, discrimination and inequality are complexly entwined in a pattern that has evolved over many years. They feed on each other to such an extent that it is irrelevant to even ask such questions as "How important is discrimination in accounting for the differences in the economic status of racial, gender, and other groups?" We would also suggest that the subtlety and complexity of discrimination in today's workplace makes it even more pernicious in some respects than the simple and easily identifiable discrimination of the past.

The authors of this volume examined several areas of discrimination. In this chapter we will explore possible bases for a general understanding of discrimination in the workplace. In particular we will explore the multilevel factors and general dynamics that cut across the specific types of workplace discrimination. Finally, we will examine the implications for future research and application.

THE SPECIFIC TYPES OF WORKPLACE DISCRIMINATION

The authors in this volume presented evidence of discrimination against several groups in the workplace. Social and economic inequalities in our society are most apparent along racial and ethnic lines, and for that reason, discrimination on the basis of race and ethnicity continues to attract the most attention. Physically and mentally disabled persons also suffer serious economic disadvantages compared to persons who are unimpaired, but it has only been in recent years that disabled persons have received substantial attention as victims of discrimination. The older worker is facing increasing discrimination in the workplace that seems exacerbated by the downsizing and restructuring in today's economy and the emphasis on youth. Women have made major advances in their economic status, but occupational sex segregation, the wage gap between men and women, and the gross underrepresentation of women in top executive positions persist. Discrimination based on sexual orientation is perhaps the least documented of all the areas of workplace discrimination, but here again there is evidence that gays and lesbians are disadvantaged in terms of income and employment and are also targets of discrimination. Finally, discrimination based on appearance and personality is quite common in the workplace with few legal or social restraints to discourage these forms of bias.

Research is likely to reveal unique aspects of discrimination peculiar to each specific target group. The discrimination against each target group has its own history and context and deserves separate attention. Nevertheless, a theme running through the chapters in this volume is that there are dynamics that cut across the various forms and that provide the foundation for a general understanding of workplace discrimination. We will explore these commonalities, but before doing so, we provide a quick assessment of the state of the research.

What is the State of the Research on Discrimination in the Workplace?

There is no shortage of social science research on the various types of discrimination, but how much progress has been made in our understanding of discrimination in the workplace? We would argue on the basis of the chapters in this volume that substantial progress has been made in understanding many facets of discrimination. We would also argue that even more progress is possible if attention is given in future research to the limitations imposed in previous research by the participants, settings, obtrusiveness, and degree of participant involvement.

Limited Sampling of Participants The psychological research on workplace discrimination has relied too much on college students as subjects. When nonstudent participants are sampled, they tend to be from professional, technical, and managerial occupations (Dipboye & Flanagan, 1979). As a consequence of oversampling of participants with higher education and middle-class backgrounds, we suspect that the research literature underestimates the extent of the problems of discrimination, prejudice, and stereotyping. Clearly, greater use needs to be made of nonstudent participants from a larger variety of occupational and demographic segments of the population.

Use of Laboratory Settings Much has been learned in the laboratory but too few attempts have been made to observe discrimination in the interactions that occur in field settings. More so-called "audit research" is needed in which persons from a disadvantaged group are matched with persons from a nondisadvantaged group and sent into real-world work settings

(Bendick, Jackson, & Romero, 1996; Bendick, Jackson, Reinoso, & Hodges, 1991; Siegelman, 1999). Research replicating laboratory findings in the field found stronger discrimination effects (e.g., Colella & Varma, 2001). Thus, an overreliance on laboratory settings may lead to an underestimation of discriminatory effects.

Obtrusive Research Strategies   Social desirability bias is a major problem in research that is obtrusive, i.e., where participants are aware that their behavior is subject to scrutiny (Stone, Stone, & Dipboye, 1992). Being seen as biased against persons who are female, older, disabled, gay and lesbian, or who belong to a racial minority group is aversive to one's self and others. Perhaps for that reason the research appears to show a remarkable amount of tolerance that is inconsistent with the self-reports of members of discrimination traget groups. Regardless of the participants or the setting, it is clear that more unobtrusive research is needed to avoid social desirability bias.

Paper People and Low Involvement Situations   Another potential problem is the use of research settings and methods that engender low levels of involvement on the part of the participants and that use passive observers rather than actual interactions. Although some methods are ideal for exploring some facets of discrimination, they seem inadequate for exploring others (Dipboye, 1985). For instance, a paper-and-pencil study asking people to judge scenarios might be appropriate for examining the cognitive processes, but would not be well-suited for exploring affective and behavioral elements. In calling for more unobtrusive field research with nonstudents and high involvement situations, we are not calling for a "ban" or "moratorium" on other types of research. Rather than condemning all research of a certain genre, we call for the use of a variety of settings and strategies to compensate for the weaknesses of some approaches with the strengths of other approaches (Runkel & McGrath, 1972).

The Lack of a General Model of Discrimination in Organizations   Perhaps more than any other single improvement, the research on discrimination in organizations could benefit from constructing general models of discrimination in the organization that capture the dynamics common to the various areas of discrimination. The research on discrimination is large and growing larger, but so far is a hodgepodge with little interdisciplinary cross-talk. Much of the conceptual foundation for the research in I/O psychology has come from the exhaustive storehouse of work in social psychology. The theory and research in social psychology should be used, but to properly understand discrimination in the workplace, we must also address the multilevel antecedents and consequences rather than rely solely on individual level models. In the remainder of this chapter we will examine some general dynamics to help set the stage for a coherent framework for interpreting past findings and setting the agenda for future research.

TOWARD A GENERAL MODEL OF DISCRIMINATION

We can consider the antecedents of discrimination at the levels of the individual, the group, the organization, and the environment of the organization. Variables at each level are potential determinants of discrimination. In what follows, we will attempt to summarize some of the key variables identified in the previous research and some of the unresolved issues. Our intent is to provide an agenda for future research and to lay the foundation for a multilevel model of discrimination in the workplace.

The Organizational Context as a Determinant of Discrimination

Psychologists seldom look outside the organization in attempting to understand discrimination inside the organization and leave this analysis to sociologists and economists. Several chapters in this book (c.f., Brief et al.; Gelfand et al.) considered some of the contextual influences. These include stakeholders such as customers, labor unions, stockholders, suppliers/vendors, and government agencies. The typical organization is likely faced with multiple stakeholders with competing and conflicting demands regarding discrimination and diversity. According to institutional theory, decision makers adopt organizational practices through imitation of other organizations in the same environment (e.g., DiMaggio & Powell, 1983; Scott, 1995; Tolbert & Zucker, 1983). Just as an individual may manage impressions to gain the approval of those around them, decision makers in organizations attempt to legitimize their practices to stakeholders who control important resources. These attempts to gain legitimacy can include practices that encourage discrimination in some cases and discourage discrimination in others. For instance, one study found that work–family practices were more likely to be adopted the more widespread this type of program was in the organizational environment of the organization (Goodstein, 1994). The industrial and organizational psychology literature on discrimination would benefit from broadening its focus to include the impact of these stakeholder expectations on individual, group, and organizational discrimination.

Other aspects of the context include the national and local culture that is defined by the shared values and the symbols, heroes, and rituals of those residing in the country where the organization is located. Hofstede (2001) speculated, on the basis of research and theory, on how the cultural dimensions in his model relate to various types of prejudices and biases. He suggested that national cultures defined by uncertainty avoidance and collectivism are more likely to harbor various forms of outgroup bias and racism and more likely to defend the idea that immigrants should give up their own culture and assimilate to the new culture. He further notes that those in collectivist cultures appear, according to some research, to differ in how they deal with disability—with those in collectivist communities expressing more grief, shame, and pessimism than those from individualistic cultures. He suggested that persons in cultures high on masculinity are more likely to show heterosexism, sexism, opposition to immigration, and heterosexism than those from cultures low on masculinity. Finally, he suggested that those in high-power distance cultures are more likely to believe in the legitimacy of hierarchical arrangements than those in a low-power distance cultures.

The extent of concern over fair employment and diversity is likely to vary with economic conditions. Realistic threat theories of discrimination suggest that economic conditions are a major environmental determinant of the extent of discrimination in the work place (LeVine & Campbell, 1972). In times of economic threat, the focus in organizations is more on core, strategic interests and less on social issues such as diversity, whereas in times of economic well-being, organizations broaden their concerns and take a more long-range interest in the public good (Warner & Steel, 1989; Wentling & Palma-Rivas, 1997). The labor market also dictates the extent of concern with diversity. When the market is tight and organizations are in competition for employees, employers are more open to diversity in their recruiting and hiring. On the other hand, in a loose labor market in which there is little competition among employers for employees, employers can indulge their "tastes" (Becker, 1971) by engaging in prejudice, stereotyping, and discrimination. The threat and insecurity of the competition for jobs in a loose market also can encourage discrimination among those who are competing for these jobs. Except for anecdotal accounts (Lloyd, 2003; Shea, 2003; Tamen, 2002) and a few empirical studies (Bobo & Kluegel, 1993; Henry & Sears, 2002; McConahay, 1982), there is surprisingly little research directly exploring the relation of economic conditions and discrimination.

Discrimination also appears to vary with the characteristics of the industry in which an organization is located. In part this could be explained by institutional theory in that those organizations that are the leaders in an industry can wield great influence over other organizations in that industry (DiMaggio & Powell, 1983). Brief et al. (in this volume) identify the racial composition of the community, the occupational structure, and the customer base as major influences on the racial composition of the organization. Each of these external factors is responsible for attitudes and stereotypes at the individual level. In the case of occupational structure, the larger the proportion of Blacks in lower level occupations, the more negative the stereotypes of Blacks and the less likely they are to be seen as qualified for higher level positions (Brief et al., in this volume). In the case of Black representation in the community, attitudes on the part of the White majority toward Blacks tend to be more negative the larger the Black population (Brief et al., in this volume). The effects of continuing discrimination within the organization reinforce factors at the levels of the individual (e.g., stereotypes), group (e.g., norms and roles), and organization (e.g., climate, structure), further perpetuating the problem. As the discrimination accumulates across organizations, the external factors that originally spawned the attitudes are reinforced or even amplified.

The legal environment is still another part of the organizational context. Organizations are likely to take proactive steps to avoid discrimination and increase diversity if there are laws and regulations to encourage these actions. Not surprisingly, organizations comply to avoid punishment (Baron, Mittman, & Newman, 1991; Leonard, 1984; Oliver, 1991). However, laws also define what is valued and acceptable in the culture and can influence organizations even in the absence of strict enforcement. There is evidence that firms responded to civil rights legislation in the 1960s and 1970s even when the consequences for failing to comply were neither clear nor specific (Dobbin, Sutton, Meyer & Scott, 1993; Edelman, 1990). In the long run, however, the mere existence of laws and regulations seems insufficient. A crucial factor is how these laws and regulations are enforced. Given the ambiguity of the typical law, these legal pressures are more symbolic than real if there is a failure to vigorously pursue enforcement (Edelman, 1992). Again, an important area for future research is to explore the environmental factors influencing compliance at the organizational level with fair employment laws and regulations.

Organizational Determinants of Discrimination

What goes on "within the box" (Brief et al., in this volume) is also important in shaping the extent of discrimination. Whether discrimination is encouraged, ignored, or actively opposed is a function of a variety of organizational factors including strategy, formal and informal structure, human resource practices, culture, climate, and leadership as some of the more important organizational factors determining the extent of discrimination.

The organization's culture is defined by the values and basic assumptions of organizational participants. A culture is strong if there is consensus among participants and weak if there is little agreement. The influences of culture emerge in a variety of forms, one manifestation being the organizational climate or the shared perception of how things are done in the organization. As noted by Gelfand et al. (in this volume), a climate that supports diversity would appear to go hand-in-hand with the discouragement of discrimination at the level of the individual and group.

A variety of structural factors can influence discrimination. One is the degree of representation of minorities, women, and other groups at senior management levels. To the extent that the senior management ranks are homogenous in demographic characteristics, one can expect greater recruiting, hiring, placement, and promotion of those who are similar to the existing senior management. This homosocial reproduction can occur and perpetuate the status quo (Kanter, 1977; Perry & Davis-Blake, 1994; Ragins & Sundstrom, 1989). Perry and Davis-Blake (1994) present evidence that gender segregation increases with the increased number of men in traditional male positions, job titles, and formal job ladders. Social dominance theory (Sidanius & Pratto, 1999) would suggest that a hierarchical structure encourages group dominance. Once some are placed in superordinate positions, justifications emerge to justify the hierarchical arrangement. Similar to this reasoning, Korman (1976) hypothesized that hierarchical control and routinization in the workplace lead to beliefs that people are undesirable and must be controlled. In turn, these beliefs will lead to negative attitudes toward racial and sexual integration in work and nonwork settings. The relation of discrimination in organizations to structural features of these organizations is a research question that deserves much more attention than it has received so far in the I/O literature.

In addition to the formal organizational structure, the informal structures that emerge in the organization are also important to consider. For instance, informal social networks tend to exclude those who differ from the majority group in race and gender (Ibarra, 1993). Women and racial minorities tend to be located in less central positions in the networks and consequently have less access to resources and information. Seidel, Polzer, and Stewart (2000) found from an analysis of over 3,000 salary negotiation outcomes that racial minorities negotiated lower increases primarily because of the lack of social ties in the organization.

The strategies and policies of the organization are obvious potential antecedents of discrimination but also have been relatively ignored in the research. Although it would seem clear that formal statements by top management convey in a tangible way that discrimination is unacceptable and that diversity is a potential strength, in some cases strategies and policies that are intended to increase diversity may actually encourage discrimination. An example would be a customer orientation that fosters matching of employees to customers on their race, gender, and other demographic characteristics. It is also possible that assertions of equal opportunity and nondiscrimination in mission statements serve as substitutes for action unless backed by deeds. A dramatic declaration of support for diversity and zero tolerance for discrimination could delude employees into believing that there are no problems of discrimination in the workplace (Darley,

2001). Such declarations can also provide a psychological license to discriminate. In a laboratory demonstration of the latter, Monin and Miller (2001) found that participants who were given the opportunity to state egalitarian and nonprejudicial views toward minorities and women were *more likely* to subsequently discriminate against these groups than those who did not have an opportunity to declare these views. A crucial area for future research is to explore how the content, framing, and communication of strategies and policies are most effectively combined with action in the management of diversity and discrimination.

The top leadership of the organization is perhaps among the most important of the structural factors. Obviously, discriminatory acts by CEOs, such as sexual harassment, would weaken diversity initiatives, whereas a charismatic leader who sets the example by strongly promoting diversity can have a powerful impact on the elimination of discrimination and the promotion of diversity. Less obvious is how a lack of strong commitment on the part of top management can undercut policies and strategies that promote diversity and tolerance. Indeed, the acts of the top management can send a signal that discrimination is acceptable even if the words would indicate otherwise. There is a growing literature on top-level leadership (Zaccaro & Klimoski, 2001), but relatively little attention has been given to how the leadership of CEOs and other top executives influence discrimination in the organization.

Finally, the nature of the human resource management function in an organization is a major influence on the extent to which discrimination occurs in an organization. Ostroff and Bowen (2000) described a strong HR system as one that "unambiguously creates the foundation for a particular type of climate to develop" (p. 236). Strong HR systems are those in which the HR practices are public, understandable, acceptable to employees, uniformly applied across employees and time, internally consistent, and widely applied. To the extent that the practices related to equal employment and affirmative action are implemented within the context of a strong HR system, the system will have more influence on the attitudes and behaviors of individuals. On the other hand, if the HR policies and practices related to diversity are implemented in the context of weak HRM systems, the attitudes and behaviors of individual employees shape the degree to which the organizational climate supports, tolerates, or discourages discrimination.

Group and Dyadic Factors Influencing Discrimination

At the group and dyad level, discrimination is often motivated by an actor's attempts in the social situation to restore equity in the distribution of outcomes (Adams, 1965) or to address unfair procedures used in distributing the outcomes (Folger & Martin, 1986). Yet, surprisingly little research exists on how perceptions of distributive, procedural, or interpersonal justice mediate discriminatory acts. Similar to distributive justice models is relative deprivation theory, which suggests that fairness of outcomes are judged against what persons want, what they believe they deserve, and what they believe others are receiving. Relative deprivation theory is particularly valuable in understanding when an oppressed group takes action to improve the situation and when they accept with contentment a state of disadvantage (Bernstein & Crosby, 1980; Major, 1994). A broader approach to discrimination in the I/O literature would give attention to the acceptance of discrimination by the victim as a potential problem.

In a group or dyadic situation, discrimination also can occur as response to a threat to identity. In its simplest form, social identity theory posits a basic need to think of one's self as belonging to groups with high positive worth. According to Tajfel and Turner (1979), when the social encounter is intergroup in nature, group loyalties override individual characteristics of the parties to the interaction. The person's perceptions are distorted such that more differences than really exist are seen within the group and fewer differences than really exist are seen within the outgroup (Ashforth & Mael, 1989). From this perspective, an act of discrimination and the response of the target to this act are both responses to the perceived threat to social identity. In self-categorization theory, acts of discrimination of member of the ingroup against an outgroup are more likely when persons in the group view themselves as members of a category rather than in terms of their individual attributes (Turner, 1982). Intergroup conflict can be functional when focused on substantive issues, but when motivated by what is seen as a potential destruction of one's self, it is likely to harm the organization and those involved (Northrup, 1989).

The social determinants of discrimination can emerge at the level of the group and take on a reality of their own. Norms are the collective standards of evaluation used by group members to evaluate the appropriateness of the behavior and attitudes of group members. Roles are expectations used in a group to define the behavior and attitudes expected of group members in individual positions. The cohesion of the group is the extent to which members of the group are bound through mutual liking and attraction. The status structure of the group reflects beliefs about the relative worth of group members. Acts of discrimination, expressions of prejudice, and stereotyping can reflect the response of individuals in the group to these group-level entities.

A crucial group and dyadic level of phenomenon is the self-fulfilling prophecy in which one person's expectations for another lead to treatment of another person that fulfills the original expectation. Perhaps no other social dynamic is as important as the self-fulfilling prophecy at the dyadic level, but there are aspects of this dynamic that are neglected in applications to organizational discrimination. For one, the expectations of the target can be self-fulfilling as might happen if the target of discrimination expected mistreatment and acted in a way that draws out the discriminatory treatment. Also, negative prejudices and stereotypes for a member of an outgroup can have the effect of evoking just the opposite of the behavior expected when the target person reacts against, rather than passively complies to, negative expectations. We need to know more about the boundary conditions determining when expectations lead to what was expected and when expectations can have the opposite effect. The target of discrimination may expect mistreatment and can act in a way that draws out the discriminatory treatment.

When we discuss discrimination at these levels, the *relationships* among individuals become crucial to understanding discrimination. It seems unlikely that discrimination would occur in the context of a close relationship characterized by friendship, but the nature of the relationship has been largely ignored. Pettigrew (1997) presented evidence from four nations that friendship causes lower prejudice rather than the opposite.

Individual Factors That Determine Acts of Discrimination

At the individual level, we can distinguish among cognitive, affective, and behavioral aspects of discrimination.

Cognitive Factors   People categorize people on the basis of their membership in a group and infer from this group membership the stereotypical attributes associated with the group. Perceivers attribute to the African American individual the characteristics of the typical Black, to an older individual the characteristics of the typical older person, to a gay man or a lesbian the characteristics of the typical gay or lesbian, to a woman the characteristics of the typical woman, and to a disabled individual the characteristics of other persons with that disability. The attribution of the characteristics of the group to the individual is guided by knowledge structures that have been acquired as a consequence of their socialization and their experiences with members of the group. These knowledge structures guide the encoding, inference, and retrieval of information on persons who are the target of discrimination.

The most common of the knowledge structures used in explaining discrimination are stereotypes. Fiske (1998) characterized the content of stereotypes along the dimensions of competence and likability. "According to bigots, there are two kinds of stereotyped groups: those one likes but disrespects (women, Blacks, Latinos, native peoples, the Irish, the

Mediterraneans, the elderly, the poor, the blind), and those one respects but dislikes (Asians, Jews, Germans, the wealthy, Whites, men)" (p. 380). Crucial to understanding stereotyping in organizations is understanding how stereotypes of groups work in conjunction with stereotypes of particular jobs to determine assessments of individuals. The stereotypes that people have regarding groups reflect the distribution of the various groups that they observe. So if older persons are seen as less competent, it is because they are less likely to be seen among the employed and more likely to be seen among the retired and disabled. If women are seen as lacking leadership potential, it is because they are disproportionately represented in subordinate positions rather than in leadership positions. If African Americans are stereotyped as less competent, it is because they are disproportionately represented in unskilled positions and underrepresented in skilled or higher level positions.

Discrimination in the assessments of applicants and employees can be described according to a prototype matching process (Heilman, 1983; Perry, 1994). The prototype matching approach involves comparing an individual to the prototypical incumbent for a given job. Persons are judged as more qualified to the extent that they are perceived as possessing the primary attributes associated with the prototype for the job. According to dual process theories, people automatically perceive the target in terms of the assigned category unless they are motivated to individuate the person and unless there are sufficient cognitive resources to devote to processing information on the target. When perceivers are "cognitively busy" as the result of competing mental tasks, they are more likely to discriminate (Martell, 1996). It is interesting to speculate as to how the immediate work environment of the individual potentially encourages or discourages discrimination as the result of "cognitive business." For instance, work involving extreme time pressure could potentially make the individual more vulnerable to outgroup derogation, prejudice, and stereotyping as the result of depleting mental resources needed to suppress these biases (Kruglanski & Freund, 1983).

The extent that information processing is controlled or automatic is another factor. If decision makers have little control over their categorization of others and are subject to unconscious processes, they are more likely to discriminate (Macrae, Milne, & Bodenhausen, 1994). Finally, stereotyping, prejudicial attitudes, and discrimination are more likely when there is little available information to make a judgment and when the available information is ambiguous (Heilman, Martell, & Simon, 1988). All of these findings would argue for structuring personnel assessments to encourage a thoughtful, piecemeal processing of information and of the individuation of the person assessed.

Affective Factors Many cognitive models of discrimination describe discrimination as guided by a process that appears rational, at least in intent, even if it falls far short of being optimal. An example would be discrimination against women in hiring for a traditionally male job because they are seen as lacking the requisite characteristics. Affective factors reflect a different process. In judging others, raters simply dislike the other person on the basis of idiosyncratic and particularistic biases without any semblance of rationality in their assessments. An important distinction that has emerged in the social psychological research is between implicit and explicit attitudinal responses (Dovidio & Hebl, this volume). Explicit attitudes are measured with self-reports and involve deliberative controlled responses in which people weigh the options. Implicit attitudes are measured using response time and involve processes that are automatic and uncontrolled. A somewhat similar distinction is made between automatic and innate emotional reactions (Zajonc, 1980) and emotions that result from cognitive appraisals (Lazarus, Kanner, & Folkman, 1980). It is interesting to speculate on how the physical work environment of an individual might arouse emotions and moods that, in turn, evoke prejudicial attitudes and discriminatory behaviors.

Behavioral Manifestations of Discrimination Discrimination is by definition behavior that can come in a variety of forms, both overt and covert. Dovidio and Hebl (in this volume) distinguish between formal discrimination, described as "explicit behaviors that are legally sanctioned (e.g., decisions regarding hiring, promoting, and firing employees" and interpersonal discrimination, described as a "less explicit form of discrimination, which may not be exhibited intentionally and involves more subtle interpersonal cues (e.g., eye contact, lack of warmth, shortened interaction length)." Explicit expression of prejudicial attitudes has been used to refer to self-reports of prejudice and has been contrasted with implicit prejudice in the form of reaction times.

Another form of discrimination is covert discrimination. Cleveland et al. (in the present volume) use as an example of covert sexism the humor and language that disguise attempts to put women in their place and express the dominance over women. Similarly, Colella and Stone (in the present volume) discuss how paternalistic behavior can be used as a seemingly benign form of discrimination against people with disabilities. Ambivalent racism, sexism, and attitudes toward those with disabilities were described as biases that consist of both positive and negative feelings regarding the target.

One view of discrimination at the individual level is that it is a serial process in which cognitions and affect are antecedent to and cause discriminatory behavior (see Dovidio & Hebl in this volume). Expectations for the

outcomes of a discriminatory act and the attitudes toward the discriminatory act itself lead to intentions to discriminate, and these intentions lead to
the discriminatory act. The process as depicted in such a model is a tightly
linked one but we suspect that the process is more frequently characterized by a loose coupling among the affective, cognitive, and behavioral
components. Thus, behavioral manifestations of discrimination occur that
are inconsistent with the cognitive and affective components, and individuals are unaware of the inconsistencies. Some of the existing models have
alluded to these conflicts and inconsistencies but little attention has been
given to them in the research.

Individual Differences   The question of whether there are traits that can
account for a stable predisposition to discriminate has been the subject of
considerable research but deserves more attention. There is some evidence
that expressions of prejudice are negatively related to cognitive ability
(Crandall & Eshleman, 2003; Meertens & Pettigrew, 1997). There are other
explanations, but one interesting possibility is that more intelligent persons
have more cognitive resources to devote to the suppression of prejudice
and stereotyping (Crandall & Eschleman, 2003).

The tendency for persons with one type of prejudicial attitude (e.g.,
heterosexism) to also hold other prejudicial attitudes (e.g., racism) is evidence in favor of a general prejudiced personality trait. Several personality constructs have been proposed to account for a general predisposition to discriminate. In the late 1940s, the construct of authoritarianism
was introduced to understand the anti-Semitism of the 1930s and 1940s
(Adorno, Frenkel-Brunswik, Levinson, & Sanford, 1950). Later, Altemeyer
(1996) proposed a variation of this construct that he called right-wing authoritarianism. Some of the characteristics of authoritarians are rigidity
in thinking, submission to authority, conformity to conventional values,
and aggression toward social deviants. Social dominance orientation was
recently proposed by Pratto, Sidanius, Stallworth, & Malle (1994) who described it as an acceptance of inequality based on the belief that group
hierarchies and competition for resources are inevitable. Those high on social dominance orientation are prejudiced toward a range of other groups,
whereas those low in social dominance orientation are characterized by a
concern for others' welfare, empathy, and tolerance. How prejudice and
discrimination map onto the big five personality dimensions still needs research, but it seems reasonable to hypothesize that those low on openness
and high on neuroticism are more prone to discriminate against members
of outgroups.

In addition to personality differences, prejudice is rooted in individual differences in belief systems and ideologies. The research is consistent in showing that individuals who are prone to prejudice tend to be

conservative in their values and political beliefs. This has been dealt with in several previous chapters. For instance, Ragans et al. (in this volume) presented evidence that heterosexism is more likely to be found among those who hold conservative religious beliefs (Kirkpatrick, 1993), conservative social philosophies (Heaven & Oxman, 1999), sexist attitudes (Stevenson & Medler, 1995), and beliefs that being gay or lesbian is a choice rather than a biological orientation (King, 2001). Similarly, the research on symbolic racism has clearly shown that individuals who hold negative racial attitudes are more likely to endorse conservative political beliefs (Sears, Van Laar, Carrillo, & Kosterman, 1997). In a recent meta-analysis, Jost, Glaser, Kruglanski, & Sulloway (2003) report that political conservatism is related to personality variables such as dogmatism, uncertainty avoidance, low openness to experience, fear of threat and loss, death anxiety, low integrative complexity, and low self-esteem. The relation of conservatism to prejudice reflects a resistance to change and a justification of inequality motivated by a general need to manage uncertainty and threat.

Perhaps no other set of findings in this volume is as likely to offend and evoke controversy as the research on belief systems and ideologies. We appreciate that those who hold sincerely felt and intelligently reasoned conservative beliefs might question evidence that conservatism is related to prejudice. However, these findings are misinterpreted if they are used to stereotype all conservatives as practicing or potential bigots. We would suggest that people seek ideological justifications when they are engaged in behavior that is inappropriate, and that ideologies of all varieties can be used in these justifications. Criminals, for instance, might find it convenient to use politically liberal views, such as the belief that crime is the result of poverty, and social injustice to justify their actions. We would not conclude that all liberals are criminals any more than we would be justified in concluding that all conservatives are racists. It just so happens that some conservative beliefs provide a convenient justification for racism and other prejudices. In these instances, the ideology appears to follow as a justification for the inappropriate behavior rather than as the cause of this behavior. In both cases, one could argue that the ideology is misused. Moreover, it has not been shown that those with left-wing political views are generally unbiased whereas those with right-wing views are generally biased in their assessments of others. Rather some evidence would suggest that they are both biased but perhaps in different directions (Lavasseur, 1998). There is some evidence that whereas politically conservative or right-wing authoritarians are biased against the underdog, politically liberal or left-wing authoritarians are biased in favor of the underdog and against persons from high status groups.

Functional Bases of Discrimination   A potentially useful approach at the individual level is to explore the underlying functions that discriminatory acts may serve. In the original functional theory of attitudes, Katz (1960) distinguished among attitudes based on knowledge, ego-defensive, social adjustment/utilitarian, and value expression. Although seldom cited in the current literature on discrimination, the model seems quite appropriate for understanding discrimination in the workplace.

Discrimination can be rooted in informational needs such as the reduction of uncertainty, in which case the discriminatory behavior is based on incorrect beliefs and faulty information. In this case, prejudice and the discrimination reflect ignorance, and education may be the most effective intervention. In the case of utilitarian-based discrimination, the discriminatory acts originate from efforts to obtain rewards and avoid punishments. In an organization that has a hostile climate toward women, men who are egalitarian may engage in harassing behavior to "get along" in that climate. Perhaps the hardest to change are attitudes that are rooted in ego-defensive and value-expressive functions. Discrimination that is ego-defensive in nature is based on the individual's attempts to protect self-esteem and defend against threats to self-esteem. From this perspective, discrimination can be rooted in the individual's self-concept and may require what amounts to therapy. Thus, the sexism of some individuals may reflect the threat that highly competent women pose to the masculinity of the perpetrator. Functional attitude theory appears to offer some distinct predictions for individual-level differences in discrimination and some interventions to deal with discrimination that deserves the attention of researchers on workplace discrimination.

Internal Conflict Among the Cognitive, Affective, and Behavioral Components

Although these internal conflicts have been a primary focus of recent theories of discrimination, Gunnar Myrdal (1944) brought attention to these inconsistencies over 50 years ago. He noted that the problem of discrimination by Whites against African Americans in America would be simple to solve if it were simply a conflict between moral and immoral people:

> The essence of the moral situation, is however, that the conflicting valuations are also held by the same person. The moral struggle goes on within people and not only between them. As people's valuations are conflicting, behavior normally becomes a moral compromise. There are no homogeneous 'attitudes' behind human behavior but a mesh of struggling inclinations, interests, and ideals, some held conscious and some suppressed for long intervals but all active in bending behavior in their direction. (p. lxxx)

It seems useful to differentiate among different types of discrimination and prejudice on the basis of internal conflicts along the dimensions of public or private, intended or unintended, conscious or unconscious, and stable or unstable. Blatant discrimination is characterized by public, intended, conscious manifestations that are under the control of the person and stable across time and situations. By contrast, the most subtle forms of discrimination involve private, often unconscious and unintended manifestations that are not under the control of the person and unstable across time and situations. Several varieties of subtle discrimination have been proposed. All of these were initially directed toward an understanding of White racism toward Black persons, but the underlying concepts are easily extended to other forms of discrimination.

1. *Symbolic racism.* Sears and his associates (Sears, Henry, & Kosterman, 2000) propose in their theory of symbolic racism that Whites are still prejudiced toward Blacks but open expression of these beliefs is seen as unacceptable. Instead, prejudice is communicated symbolically via ideological beliefs that are opposed to the interests of Black persons. For instance, opposition to busing, affirmative action, and welfare become ways of expressing in a socially acceptable way anti-Black attitudes. This could be a conscious, intended "cover-up" of deeply held prejudices. More likely the opinions are ways of justifying prejudices that the individual denies and that evoke guilt and discomfort.

2. *Modern racism.* McConahay (1983) built on symbolic racism to propose that people are conditioned to have prejudices, but it is unacceptable to hold these views. In the face of the social prohibitions against prejudicial beliefs and discriminatory actions, racism is expressed in the form of beliefs that have the appearance of reasoned positions but that place African Americans at a disadvantage. Those who express these beliefs are often unaware of the racism that motivates them. These notions were extended to sexism by Swim, Aikin, Hall, and Hunter (1995).

3. *Ambivalent racism.* On the basis of the theories of ambivalent racism (Katz & Hass, 1988) and ambivalent sexism (Glick & Fiske, 1996), people have mixed feelings about the target group and experience conflict as the result of these opposing emotions. They have positive feelings toward Black individuals, for instance, in that they recognize their disadvantages and feel sympathetic toward them, but at the same time they hold negative feelings in the form of beliefs that they possess a number of negative attributes such as laziness or deviancy. Katz and Hass (1988) attempted to directly measure this ambivalence by separately measuring pro- and anti-Black attitudes. These mixed and conflicted feelings are rooted in conflicting underlying ideological stances. Thus, people have a belief in the Protestant

work ethic in which they value independence and hard work at the same time they hold humanitarian and egalitarian views. To the extent that people simultaneously hold intensely felt opposing feelings, their behavior toward the target group becomes more variable and unstable. When the target person does well, they may be rewarded even more than a White person but when they perform poorly they are punished more severely. The concept of ambivalent racism has been extended to the understanding of sexism (Glick & Fiske, 1996) and ambivalence amplification in response to persons with disabilities (Katz, 1981; Katz & Hass, 1988; Katz & Glass, 1988).

4. *Aversive racism.*   Another version of subtle racism is aversive racism. According to Gaertner and Dovidio (1986), Whites endorse egalitarian values but have been socialized to hold negative views of Blacks and other minorities. These prejudices are aversive to Whites and as a consequence they are often unconscious. When the situation allows them to discriminate in a way that can be justified on the basis of nonracist reasons, they discriminate, but they do so in a way that allows them to maintain an unprejudiced self-image. Prejudice nevertheless leaks into nonverbal behavior.

5. *Dissociation model of racism.*   Devine (1989) proposed that cultural stereotypes that depict Blacks in a negative light are learned as the result of early socialization and are automatically activated. Personal beliefs about Blacks and other minorities develop later and are under the person's conscious control. This is called the dissociation model because there is a discrepancy between the culturally rooted stereotypes of Blacks and other minorities and the personal, conscious beliefs of the person. The former are generally negative but the latter reflect conformity to social norms against prejudicial beliefs and are more positive. The level of prejudice held by an individual dictates the amount of control the person has over his or her stereotypes. Negative stereotypes are activated in persons who are low on prejudice, but they can exert control over these feelings and as a consequence are guided by their more egalitarian personal beliefs. Persons who are high on prejudice, however, will be less successful in controlling their feelings.

TYING TOGETHER THE MULTILEVEL FACTORS IN A DYNAMIC, RECURSIVE MODEL

Now that we have presented various antecedents of discrimination in the workplace at the level of the individual, the group, the organization, and the environment, the question is how to pull these seemingly disparate elements together into a common framework that can allow for a general understanding of discrimination. We would suggest several directions for these future efforts.

Multilevels

Discrimination can occur at the level of individual acts of discrimination or at higher levels such as institutional discrimination or intergroup discrimination. It is at the individual level that discrimination exists in its most concrete, tangible form. Discrimination at the organizational level is an abstraction and based to a large extent on aggregates of what occurs at the individual and group levels. This is not to imply, however, that higher level discrimination is unimportant.

Reciprocal Causation

The typical models presented to describe discrimination presents a serial process that stops with the act of discrimination and is nonreciprocal. This type of model is not always inappropriate, but it is usually incomplete. The research we do is important in demonstrating individual causal links, but it is almost always the case in social behavior that variables at each level influence each other. Causality is also reciprocal across levels. Lower level factors can shape higher level factors and, in turn, higher level factors influence lower level factors. Rather than propose a purely serial chain of events, a model is needed that takes into account reciprocal causal links and the potential for causal leaps across levels. In systems characterized by reciprocal causation, cause and effect are intertwined, and it is meaningless to ask for original causes.

There are numerous examples of this reciprocal causation in discrimination. We again return to Myrdal (1944) who observed reciprocal causation at the societal level. White prejudice and discrimination kept African Americans at a low standard of living and their low standard of living, in turn, confirmed the prejudices of Whites. This mutual causation has important implications.

> If either of the factors changes, this will cause a change in the other, too, and cause of a process of interaction where the change in one will continually be supported by the reaction of the other factor. The whole system will be moving in the direction of the primary change, but much further. This is what we mean by cumulative causation. (Myrdal, 1944, pp. 75–76)

Another example is the reciprocal relationship between discrimination and reputation. For instance, accumulated individual acts of discrimination or a few highly visible acts may have consequences at the level of the organization in the form of a spoiled reputation. Once a firm develops a reputation as a place that is unfriendly to minorities, women, people who are disabled, or gays and lesbians, it becomes harder to recruit and attract employees from these groups to work in the organization. With increasing homogeneity of the organization's workforce, stereotypes of the ideal employee become increasingly similar to the prototypic majority group member and less similar to those in minority and disadvantaged groups. The stereotypes lead to discriminatory practices that further soil the firm's reputation and perpetuate the problem.

Dynamic Process

Events such as these describe a closed cycle that becomes self-perpetuating once it emerges. The dynamic model proposed by Sidanius and Pratto (Pratto, 1999) serves as a potential beginning point for an integrative model of discrimination in the organization. They proposed that inequality among groups exists because of the assembling of cognitive biases, prejudicial personalities in the form of social dominance orientation (SDO), discrimination, and culture. Because everything influences directly or indirectly everything else in this model, there is overdetermination. This redundancy means that the system can continue even if some of the processes are disrupted.

> The model implies that group inequality does not exist merely because of cognitive biases, or because it is part of culture, or because of certain prejudiced personalities, or because of discrimination but because all of these work together. . . . . . if people observe group differences, they will form and use stereotypes which can cause them to discriminate, which would result in group differences. Starting at any of these three stages (group differences, stereotypes, or discrimination) will start the whole feedback cycle, so a given component can assemble the system. (pp. 248–249)

The Dilemma of the Individual in the Crossfire

The social psychological models of subtle discrimination posit conflicts that are internal to the individual; only recently has there been some recognition that conflicts also originate in the context of the individual (cf. Crandall & Eschelman, 2003). If we acknowledge that discrimination occurs in complex multilevel settings, the research and theory will need to go even further in the direction of acknowledging that individuals are often caught in the crossfire among competing and inconsistent internal and external pressures to discriminate or to not discriminate.

One conflict is between environmental and individual level factors. Thus, an individual may be personally inclined to discriminate against a minority, but environmental forces (e.g., labor shortage) may constitute a strong pressure against discrimination. Conflict can also occur between organizational-level and individual-level factors. An example is an individual with egalitarian views and behavior in an organizational climate that is nonsupportive of diversity and perhaps hostile to minorities and other groups. Conflict also occurs at the level of the group to which the individual belongs. Peer pressure to go against one's personal inclinations to discriminate or not discriminate is another source of conflict. We can also conceive of conflict among factors at the levels of the environment and the organization, the group and organization, and the group and the environment.

SOLUTIONS TO UNFAIR DISCRIMINATION IN ORGANIZATIONS

We have discussed some of the potential causes of discrimination in organizations and the possibility that individual acts of discrimination reflect one or more levels of causes. We now turn to the question of how to deal with discrimination. In recent years, much has been written about the economic benefits of having a diverse workforce. A diverse workforce is said to allow greater customer service (Robinson & Dechant, 1997); the ability to recruit the most talented applicants (Cox, 1993; Kim & Gelfand, 2003); greater use of the talents of people in the organization (Wentling & Palmas-Rivas, 1997); reduced turnover, absenteeism, and discrimination suits (Jackson & Alvarez, 1992); and increased workforce productivity and creativity (Cox, Lobel, & McLeod, 1991; Jackson & Alvarez, 1992). These and other benefits are believed to create a competitive advantage for the firm (Cox & Blake, 1991). Efforts to reduce and eliminate discrimination help to achieve a diverse workforce and the benefits associated with diversity.

Not only does diversity have benefits but also discrimination appears to have a variety of negative effects. The work on relational demography demonstrates that differences among people are associated with a variety of negative social processes and a common explanation is that stereotyping, prejudice, and discrimination mediate these effects (Riordan et al., in this volume). The experience of discrimination is negatively related to a variety of work-related attitudes. For instance, the experience of discrimination is negatively related to job satisfaction, organizational commitment, organizational citizenship, job involvement, career commitment, organization-based self-esteem, and satisfaction with opportunities for promotion. The experience of discrimination is positively related to feelings of powerlessness, turnover intentions, stress, and health problems.

The Dilemma of the Business Case Against Discrimination

The evidence seems clear that unfair discrimination can have negative consequences, whereas organizations can reap financial rewards from a diverse workforce. However, there are limits to the business case and dangers in overemphasizing it. Racial and ethnic diversity do not automatically bring benefits and can have a negative impact on business performance if managed poorly (Hansen, 2003; Sacco & Schmitt, 2003). In the most comprehensive examination of the business case for diversity, Kochan and his colleagues (2003) concluded that there is no justification for the assertion that diversity in the workforce necessarily leads to better performance on financial measures such as their profits, revenue costs, and return on investments. One could even argue that focusing too much attention on the return on investment in efforts to increase diversity and eliminate discrimination may have the unintended consequence of harming these efforts. Imagine going back in time and in the midst of the debate over slavery and child labor. Rather than resting the arguments against these practices solely on the issue of their economic viability, one would no doubt muster moral and ethical arguments against these practices. Similarly, opposition to discrimination and the support for diversity are ultimately ethical positions in which decisions regarding how to treat people are dictated by basic values and the desire to do the right things rather than solely by economic utility. Moreover, resting the case for diversity and against discrimination solely on economic returns runs the risk of a backlash against these efforts if the economic case cannot be made.

The Dilemma of the Necessity for Discrimination

Another complication is that some degree of discrimination is functional and even essential. To accurately perceive the social environment and the people who constitute this environment requires that we categorize and stereotype. Seeing what people share in common is fundamental to identifying the meaningful differences among them. We would go further. Maintaining social control requires that we are able to distinguish among employees and perhaps stigmatize them on the basis of their behavior. For instance, stigmatizing to some extent employees who are dishonest and irresponsible would seem appropriate in maintaining a productive climate. Finally, discriminatory behavior is essential to differentiating among people to make fair and reasonable decisions that further the goals of the organization while meeting the needs of employees. When there are scarce resources, hard decisions have to be made such as determining which employees are given higher salaries and in these situations differentiation is needed to allow a fair distribution of outcomes.

To act as though there are no differences among employees would not only threaten the ability of the organization to achieve its goals in an efficient and productive fashion, but would make it difficult to treat people fairly. The work of industrial and organizational psychologists should enable decision makers in organizations to make accurate distinctions among people so as to provide rational and fair bases for differentiating among persons in the workplace. Indeed, the pursuit of construct valid measures of work-related attributes should provide methods of differentiating among people that are alternatives to surface features such as gender, physical status, age, and appearance that can have the effect of denying opportunity to entire groups. At the same time, I/O psychologists must be constantly aware that their procedures, findings, and theories can be intentionally or unintentionally used to deny opportunity and to rationalize inequalities.

The Dilemmas of a Colorblind Organization

We have seen in the reviews of the discrimination literature ample evidence that bringing attention to racial, gender, and other differences can activate stereotypes and prejudices. Making explicit procedures that are aimed at improving the condition of minorities and other disadvantaged groups can stigmatize the groups that the efforts are intended to help (Heilman and Haynes, in this volume). These risks would argue for treating each employee as an individual with no mention of demographic and other group membership. However, there are dangers in this approach as well.

The message of the research on subtle discrimination is that slight changes in procedures can potentially provide a justification for and actually encourage discrimination. For example, avoiding all mention of racial differences in employee hiring may convince people in the organization that their decisions are free of prejudice. This feeling might actually create a climate in which discrimination occurs without compunction because people are convinced of the rationality of their actions. According to Darley (2001) the mere "existence of corporate codes can cause superiors to assume that the codes are much on the minds of the subordinates, and of course this assumption may not be true.... The superior assumes that he or she has communicated such ethical precautions far earlier; therefore, they do not need to be a part of the present communication" (pp. 40–41). Another potential problem is that it is impossible for employees to avoid attending to each others' racial, gender, and other differences especially if these individuals who possess these characteristics are in the minority. The research on ironic processes suggests that efforts to get people to avoid attending to factors such as race can actually result in people being influenced even more than would be the case if nothing were said (Macrae, Bodenhausen, Milne, & Jetten, 1994). Finally, trying to create a colorblind organizational culture may discourage open dialogue about differences when such dialogue could provide a constructive basis for encouraging diversity. In a multicultural society that values diversity, it would appear important to allow people to retain their group identities at the same time that we take steps to provide equal opportunity and eliminate unfair discrimination. The specific interventions that will allow this to occur have yet to be researched.

Strategies for Combating Discrimination

To avoid unrealistically optimistic expectations, we should acknowledge that discrimination can yield economic rewards, that it is necessary to differentiate among employees, and that workplaces can never be truly colorblind. With these dilemmas in mind, we can identify several potential strategies for dealing with the problem of discrimination.

The traditional HR functions provide the most direct means of solving the problem of discrimination at the level of the individual antecedents. Arthur and Doverspike (in this volume) suggest two major approaches by which organizations can change their practices in order to reduce discrimination and increase diversity in staffing, human resource development, and performance management.

The first strategy is to use HR procedures that minimize adverse impact against minorities, women, and other groups. HR practices can lead to inequalities among groups in valued outcomes such as selection/hiring, pay, promotions, appraisals, and access to training. The crucial question is how HR practices can be altered or improved in ways that reduce adverse impact and increase the representation of members of affected groups in organizations, while maintaining the validity of the practices. There is substantial research to allow the evaluation of the potential adverse impact of cognitive ability tests on racial, gender, and age groups. There is less research on the potential adverse impact of noncognitive tests, and this is a deficiency that clearly needs to be addressed.

The second strategy according to Arthur and Doverspike is to reduce discrimination by changing the behavior of majority group employees in the workforce. In staffing, one might consider the possibility of selecting employees who are less likely to show discrimination in the workplace and are perhaps appreciative of diversity (Douthitt, Eby, & Simon, 1999). Although this approach warrants consideration, there are numerous pitfalls of selecting on the basis of propensity to discriminate. For one, the use of measures of the propensity to discriminate seem likely to adversely influence groups of employees. Symbolic racism, for instance, would suggest screening out employees with conservative beliefs, an approach that not only is unfair but potentially illegal. Perhaps a better approach is to incorporate into appraisal procedures dimensions that ensure nondiscriminatory behavior is encouraged and discriminatory behavior is discouraged. Perhaps the most common and realistic intervention aimed at the majority members of the workforce is training to increase the appreciation for diversity and sensitivity to discriminatory behaviors. Here again, we find little research on the relative effectiveness of these alternative approaches to reducing discrimination of the majority group members.

We would add to these two primary HRM interventions a third in the form of efforts to change the behavior, knowledge, attitudes, skills, and other characteristics of the persons who are targets of discrimination. For instance, one could recruit, select, and train potential targets so as to reduce the possibility that others will discriminate against them. Although there are situations in which such interventions are appropriate, caution must be observed lest this type of intervention places blame on the victim of discrimination and is used to justify the behavior of those who perpetuate the discrimination.

We would hope that in future scientific research the same amount of effort and enthusiasm is invested in constructing measures that are free of adverse impact as has been invested in improving the validity and reliability of these measures. I/O psychology and HRM research can provide the techniques, theories, and knowledge that allow assessments that go below the surface to enhance the understanding, prediction, and management of organizational behavior. At best, discrimination on the basis of factors such as demographics, sexual orientation, appearance, and physical condition are very crude indicators of how people will perform in organizations. A message of scientific research and practice in I/O psychology is that organizations can and must do better than this.

The changes in HRM procedures discussed by Arthur and Doverspike (in this volume) are probably most suitable in addressing the individual-level antecedents of discrimination. When the antecedent factors are at the group, organizational, and environmental levels, other interventions are needed in addition to HRM approaches. In these cases, insight is more likely to come from the organizational development and change literatures. With time and contact, diversity should lead to higher performance as employees develop deeper level interpersonal understanding and go beyond surface characteristics such as demographics (Harrison, Price, & Bell, 1998; Pelled, Eisenhardt, & Xin, 1999). However, as Allport (1954) observed, mere contact is seldom sufficient. Intergroup contact is more likely to eliminate prejudice if it involves interaction among members of the groups that is intimate, equal in status, supportive, and cooperative. One could hypothesize that close, high-quality relationships in the form of friendships among employees mediate the impact of these conditions. Wright, Aron, McLaughlin-Volpe, and Ropp (1997) demonstrated under laboratory conditions the effectiveness of a relationship building exercise in reducing intergroup bias. A potentially fruitful direction for future research is to explore whether similar relationship building interventions could be used in the workplace to deal with discrimination and prejudice.

At an even deeper level than dyadic and group relationships, interventions to reduce discrimination involve changes in social identity. Brewer and Miller (1996) proposed a three-step process to reduce prejudice consisting of decategorization, recategorization, and subcategorization. In the first step, persons are encouraged to think of each other as individuals rather than as members of groups (decategorization). The next step is recategorization in which group members are encouraged to tolerate multiple social identities and to develop a superordinate identity perhaps as the result of a superordinate goal. The third step involves subcategorization in which "multiple social identities coexist constructively" through "ground rules for social interaction" that "preserve social identities while encouraging cooperation." To accomplish these objectives requires increasing the value placed on diversity by employees and changing their perceptions so that they see diversity as an opportunity rather than as a threat.

The practical implications of a recursive dynamic model are clear if there is a chance to design a workgroup, a task, or an organization in a greenfield situation. To minimize unfair discrimination, we would want to create conditions in which intergroup cooperation is rewarded and the focus is on superordinate goals. What is done once intergroup conflict has emerged is less clear. It may require doing more than simply training people to appreciate diversity, but also organizational development interventions to change the system. At the organizational level of intervention, we confront perhaps the most controversial approach to dealing with discrimination— changing the fundamental ways in which we define career success and the criteria by which we evaluate employees on the basis of these criteria. For instance, Cleveland et al. (in this volume) suggest that the neglect of work–family balance, in the criteria traditionally used to evaluate success in organizations, is at the heart of gender bias. An issue that has received attention in the popular literature is whether organizations need to change structurally to ensure that more women rise to the top managerial ranks (Tischler, 2004). This is a question that deserves much more attention in the I/O research.

SOME FUTURE DIRECTIONS

In looking back at the research on discrimination, it is apparent that much has been learned but several new directions are warranted. A major factor inhibiting progress is that the research on discrimination is segregated into different types of discrimination. This segregation is warranted to the extent that each type involves separate issues and a historical context that set it apart. Nevertheless, there are too few attempts to explore the common dynamics and generate an integrative framework. What follows are several suggestions to facilitate this integration.

The Underlying Dimensions of Stigmatizing Attributes

An important step in the direction of developing an integrative framework would be the development of a taxonomy of stigmatizing attributes. Social psychologists have suggested several dimensions of stigma that would seem to have relevance to the workplace (Dovidio, Major, & Crocker, 2000; Fiske, 1998; Deaux, Reid, Mizrahi, & Ethier, 1995; Jones, Farina, Hastorf, Markus, Miller, & Scott, 1984). These include attributes of a stigma such as the (a) agentic and communal components, (b) aesthetic qualities, (c) visibility, (d) changeability, (e) existential threat, and (f) personal responsibility. Discrimination in the workplace, however, occurs in a context that includes the job, the supervisor, coworkers, customers, and the organizational culture or climate. Research is needed on underlying dimensions that influence perceived fit to these various workplace contexts.

The Combined Effects of Stigmatizing Attributes

People do not belong to just one group but are members of multiple groups. What is the consequence of being both Black and female, or disabled and older on reactions of perceivers? Gender, race, sexual orientation, age, and disability may have cumulative effects or may interact in influencing workplace discrimination. Sidanius and Pratto (1999) present what they refer to as the subordinate male target hypothesis (SMTH) in which men from a subordinate group are subject to greater discrimination than women from a subordinate group. The other side of the coin is how various group memberships influence self-identity. Any one person can potentially identify themselves in multiple ways and an important question is what determines the particular attributes that become the source of self-identification. Research is needed to determine what influences the salience of a particular identity and the impact on the strategies that are used in dealing with workplace discrimination.

The Influence of Ideologies in the Workplace

Another issue is how values of the majority *vis à vis* the minority influence discrimination toward the outgroup. One thesis that has run through several theories of racism is that racial minorities are discriminated against to the extent that they are seen as violating central values of the culture. In the United States, these values include individualism and self-reliance, the work ethic, obedience, and discipline (Katz & Hass, 1988; Kinder & Sears, 1981). Belief systems have been given little attention by HR and I/O researchers but appear to be powerful antecedents of not only race discrimination but also a variety of other forms of discrimination. For instance, negative reactions to the obese is associated with a belief in the work ethic suggesting that persons who ascribe to the work ethic are more likely to attribute obesity to the lack of character or effort of the person (Crandall, 1994).

Discrimination from the Perspective of the Target

A small but growing literature has addressed the experience of those who are targets and the impact on their occupational success, physical health, and psychological well-being (Swim & Stangor, 1999). One could argue that the perception that one is the target of discrimination is as important as the objective occurrence of discrimination. Moreover, seeing one's self as a victim of discrimination can be a major source of stress that seems likely to harm the individual's mental and physical well-being. Research is needed to explore the effectiveness of alternative means of coping with the stress of discrimination in the workplace.

The Management of Stigmatized Identities in the Workplace

How potential or actual victims of discrimination manage impressions in the workplace is another important question for future research. This is an issue that has been examined mostly with regard to gay and lesbian and disabled persons who must decide whether to disclose or not and how to manage the impressions of their stigma once there is disclosure. Employees who are racial minorities, women, and older also engage in impression management in dealing with discrimination. Consequently, we need to go beyond impression management of gays and lesbians and disabled persons to explore the factors related to the success with which employees with other stigmatizing attributes use tactics and strategies in managing what others think of them.

Discrimination from the Perspective of the Discriminator

Relatively little attention has been given to how the targets of discrimination cope with discrimination. Even less attention has been given to how those who are potential discriminators deal with pressures on them with regard to discrimination. As previously observed, these pressures are not only internal as depicted in the models of subtle discrimination (e.g., aversive racism) but can also originate external to the person in the environment, the organization, and the group. For example, what does a relatively unprejudiced employee do in the presence of fellow employees trading racist jokes? Or how does an egalitarian male employee respond to the sexist behavior of his male colleagues in an organizational climate that is hostile to women? In addition to informing employers on how to minimize the occurrence of discrimination, the research of I/O psychologists could provide the basis for advising employees on how to effectively work within such a work context.

Discrimination as an Implicit Process

The emphasis in the research on workplace discrimination has been on explicit measures such as observations of discriminatory actions or public statements of opinions and judgments. The social psychological research on discrimination, prejudice, and stereotyping has embraced implicit measures, and we would suggest that research in I/O psychology should give more attention to these procedures. An example of implicit measurement of prejudice can be found in Dovidio, Kawakami, Johnson, Johnson, & Howard (1997). They used a semantic priming task in which they subliminally primed the participants with a black face, a white face, or a neutral face and then presented the participants with positive or negative word. The task was to press a yes or no key to indicate whether the word was descriptive of a person or a house. The measure of implicit prejudice was the latency of response in pressing the key. Specifically, high prejudice was indicated by faster responding to negative words following black face primes relative to the white face primes and faster responding to positive words following white face primes relative to back face primes. The underlying assumption of these types of implicit measures is that negative associations with Black persons on the part of White persons are deeply ingrained, and as a consequence the processing of inconsistent pairings of information (positive words with Blacks, negative words with Whites) is slower.

The use of implicit measures would add considerable to the understanding of workplace discrimination. How far the interpretation of findings with these measures should be taken is still subject to considerable controversy. Even more controversial is whether such measures can be used for applied purposes. Paetzold (in this volume) suggests a deemphasis of intention in the legal theory of disparate treatment discrimination based on the research findings with the implicit measures. Can we go even further and argue that implicit measures should be used on a routine basis to assess prejudicial attitudes or the propensity to discrimination instead of or in addition to explicit, self-report measures? We doubt the ethics of using implicit measures to identify persons who are likely to discriminate for purposes of selection, appraisal, or remediation. In the end, we need to rely on what people intend to do or actually do in assessing people on how much they actually discriminate even if there are unconscious and even uncontrollable inclinations to discrimination. As suggested by Devine (1989) in her dissociation model, we all have prejudicial inclinations but differ in our proclivities and our ability and motivation to suppress these proclivities. It is the outcome of the internal conflict between the initial urge to discriminate and the prohibitions against such discrimination rather than the initial urge alone that provides a valid basis for personnel action.

Discrimination as a Complex Process

Industrial and organizational psychologists have often seen discrimination in terms of adverse impact. In other words, discrimination is defined by one group receiving more or less of an important outcome. Although adverse impact is important, an overemphasis on the numbers leaves out important components. As open systems, organizations are characterized by multifinality, and discrimination can occur the form of behaviors, attitudes, and feelings that on the surface may appear to be altruistic and caring. For example, discrimination can occur not only in the form of hostility and other negative behaviors but also in the form of positively inflated evaluations, unrealistically positive feedback, overzealous helping, assignment of easy tasks, pity, and babying. The outcome of both well-intentioned and not so well-intentioned discrimination can harm by stigmatizing the target; inducing feelings of incompetence, helplessness, and passivity; and preventing the acquisition of basic knowledge, skills, and abilities. Clearly, research is needed to explore these and other complexities associated with discrimination in the work place.

IN CONCLUSION: INEVITABILITY AND HOPE

In conclusion we wish to state perhaps the most fundamental dilemma in the issue of discrimination and prejudice. On one hand, discrimination is inevitable. The targets may change, but discrimination itself will continue in other forms. Thus, even as bias against Blacks, gays and lesbians, older persons, persons who are disabled, and women may decline, biases against other groups will emerge. The reason for this is that dynamics associated with discrimination are deeply ingrained in how people construe their social world, how they view themselves as individuals, and how they deal with one another. Like it or not, to be human is to discriminate in one form or another. The chapters in this book cover several of these fundamental dynamics such as the denigration of outgroups, enhancement of one's ingroup, stereotyping, and stigmatization. These and other dynamics seem likely to outlive the specific types of discrimination that are salient at a particular point in history.

On the other hand, we firmly believe that there is reason for optimism. Each of the bases of discrimination examined in this book is historically bound. The good news is that with the passing of time and laws, we fully expect that discrimination against some or all of the groups will decline. Our hope is that this book will help speed the demise of the discrimination that has served as a barrier to achieving the benefits of diversity in the workplace. In doing so we also hope that this book will become dated quickly and that in the near future readers will look upon discrimination on the basis of race, gender, age, sexual orientation, appearance, personality, and disability as odd relics of the past.

REFERENCES

Acemoglu, D., & Angrist, J. D. (2001, October). Consequences of employment protection? The case of the Americans with Disabilities Act. *The Journal of Political Economy, 109*, 915–957.

Adams, J. S. (1965). Inequity in social exchange. In L. Berkowitz (Ed.), *Advances in experimental social psychology* (Vol. 2, pp. 267–299). New York: Academic Press.

Adorno, T. W., Frenkel-Brunswik, E., Levinson, D. J., & Sanford, R. N. (1950). *The authoritarian personality*. New York: Norton.

Albelda, R., Drago, R. W., & Shulman, S. (1997). *Unlevel playing fields: Understanding wage inequality and discrimination*. New York: McGraw-Hill.

Allport, G. W. (1954). *The nature of prejudice*. Reading, MA: Addision-Wesley.

Altemeyer, B. (1996). *The authoritarian specter*. Cambridge, MA: Harvard University Press.

Ashforth, B. E., & Mael, F. (1989). *Social identity theory and the organization. Academy of Management Review, 14*, 20–39.

Badgett, L. (1996). The wage effects of sexual orientation discrimination. *Industrial and Labor Relations Review, 48*, 726–739.

Baron, J. N., Mittman, B. S., & Newman, A. E. (1991). Targets of opportunity: Organizational and environmental determinants of gender intergration within the California civil services. 1979–1985. *American Journal of Sociology, 96*, 1362–1401.

Becker, G. S. (1971). *The economics of discrimination.* Chicago: The University of Chicago Press.

Bendick, M., Jr., Jackson, C., Reinoso, V., & Hodges, L. (1991). Discrimination against Latino job applications: A controlled experiment. *Human Resource Management, 30*, 469–484.

Bendick, M., Jr., Jackson, C., & Romero, J. H. (1996). Employment discrimination against older workers: An experimental study of hiring practices. *Journal of Aging and Social Policy, 8*, 25–46.

Bernstein, M., & Crosby, F. (1980). An empirical examination of relative deprivation theory. *Journal of Experimental Social Psychology, 16*, 442–456.

Bobo, L., & Kluegel, J. R. (1993). Opposition to race-targeting: Self-interest, stratification, or racial attitudes? *American Sociological Review, 58*, 443–464.

Brewer, M. B., & Miller, N. (1996). *Intergroup relations.* Pacific Grove, CA: Brooks-Cole.

Catalyst. (1993). *Successful initiatives for breaking the glass ceiling to upward mobility for minorities and women.* New York: Catalyst.

Catalyst. (2000). *Census of women corporate officers and top earners.* New York: Catalyst.

Cohn, S. (2000). *Race and gender discrimination at work.* Boulder, Colo: Westview Press.

Cohn, T. H., Jr., & Blake, S. (1991). Managing cultural diversity: Implications for organizational competitiveness. *The Executive, 5*, 45–56.

Colella, A., & Varma, A. (2001). The impact of subordinate disability on leader-member exchange dynamics. *Academy of Management Journal, 44*, 304–315.

Cox, T. H., Jr., (1993). *Cultural diversity in organizations: Theory, research and practice.* San Francisco: Berrett-Koehler.

Cox, T. H., Lobel, S., & McLeod, P. (1991). Effects of ethnic group cultural difference on cooperative versus competitive behavior in a group task. *Academy of Management Journal, 34*, 827–847.

Cox, T. H., & Blake, S. (1991). Managing cultural diversity implication for organizational competitiveness. *Academy of Management Executive, 5*, 45–57.

Crandall, C. S. (1994). Prejudice against fat people: Ideology and self-interest. *Journal of Personality and Social Psychology, 66*, 882–894.

Crandall, C. S., & Eshleman, A. (2003). A justification-suppression of the expression and experience of prejudice. *Psychological Bulletin, 129*, 414–446.

Darley, J. M. (2001). The dynamics of authority influence in organizations and the unintended action consequences. In J. M. Darley, D. M. Messick, & T. R. Tyler (Eds.), *Social influences in ethical behavior in organizations* (pp. 37–52). Mahweh, NJ: Lawrence Erlbaum Associates.

Deaux, K., Reid, A., Mizrahi, K., & Ethier, K. A. (1995). Parameters of social identity. *Journal of Personality and Social Psychology, 68*, 280–291.

Devine, P. G. (1989) Stereotypes and prejudice: Their automatic and controlled components. *Journal of Personality and Social Psychology, 56*, 5–18.

DiMaggio, P. J., & Powell, M. S. (1983). The iron cage revisited: Institutional isomorphism and collective rationality in organizational fields. *American Sociological Review, 48*, 147–160.

Dipboye, R. L. (1985). Some neglected variables in research on unfair discrimination in appraisals. *Academy of Management Review, 10*, 116–127.

Dipboye, R. L., & Flanagan, M. (1979). Research settings in industrial and organizational psychology: Are findings in the field more generalizable than in the laboratory? *American Psychologist, 34*, 141–150.

Dobbin, F. R., Sutton, J. R., Meyer, J. W., & Scott, W. R. (1993). Equal opportunity law and the construction of internal labor markets. *American Journal of Sociology, 99*, 396–427.

Douthitt, S. S., Eby, L. T., & Simon, S. (1999). Diversity of life experiences: The development and validation of a biographical measure of receptiveness to dissimilar others. *International Journal of Selection and Assessment, 7,* 112–123.

Dovidio, J. F., Kawakami, K., Johnson, C., Johnson, D., & Howard, A. (1997). On the nature of prejudice: Automatic and controlled processes. *Journal of Experimental Social Psychology, 33,* 510–540.

Dovidio, J. F., Major, B., & Crocker, J. (2000). Stigma: Introduction and overview. In T. F. Heatherton, R. E. Kleck, M. R. Hebl, & J. G. Hull (Eds.), *The social psychology of stigma* (pp. 1–28). New York: Guilford.

Edelman, L. B. (1990). Legal environments and organizational governance: The expansion of due process in the American workplace. *American Journal of Sociology, 95,* 1401–1440.

Edelman, L. B. (1992). Legal ambiguity and symbolic structures: Organizational mediation of civil rights law. *American Journal of Sociology, 97,* 1531–1576.

Fiske, S. (1998). Stereotyping, prejudice, and discrimination. In D. Gilbert, S. Fiske, & G. Lindzey (Eds.), *The handbook of social psychology* (Vol. 2, 4th ed., pp. 357–411). New York: McGraw-Hill.

Folger, R., & Martin, C. (1986). Relative deprivation and referent cognitions: Distributive and procedural justice effects. *Journal of Experimental Social Psychology, 22,* 531–546.

Gaertner, S. L., & Dovidio, J. F. (1986). The aversive form of racism. In J. F. Dovidio and S. L. Gaertner (Eds.), *Prejudice, discrimination, and racism* (pp. 61–89). San Diego, CA: Academic Press.

Glick, P., & Fiske, S. T. (1996). The Ambivalent Sexism Inventory: Differentiating hostile and benevolent sexism. *Journal of Personality and Social Psychology, 70,* 491–512.

Goodstein, J. D. (1994). Institutional pressures and strategic responsiveness: Employer involvement in work-family issues. *Academy of Management Jouirnal, 37,* 350–383.

Hansen, F. (2003, April). Diversity's business case doesn't add up. *Workforce, 82*(4), 28–33.

Harrison, D. A., Price, K. H., & Bell, M. P. (1998). Beyond relational demography: Time and the effects of surface- and deep-level diversity on work group cohesion. *Academy of Management Journal, 41,* 96–108.

Heaven, P., & Oxman, L. N. (1999). Human values, conservatism and stereotypes of homosexuals. *Personality and Individual Differences, 27,* 109–118.

Heilman, M. E. (1983). Sex bias in work settings: The lack of model fit. In B. M. Staw & L. L. Cummings (Eds.), *Research in organizational behavior* (Vol. 5, pp. 269–298). Greenwich, CT: JAI.

Heilman, M. E., Martell, R. F., & Simon, M. C. (1988). The vagaries of sex bias: Conditions regulating the undervaluation, equivaluation, and overvaluation of female job applicants. *Organizational Behavior and Human Performance, 23,* 360–372.

Henry, P. J., & Sears, D. O. (2002). The symbolic racism 2000 scale. *Political Psychology, 23,* 253–283.

Hofstede, G. (2001). *Culture's consequence: Comparing values, behaviors, institutions, and organizations across nations* (2nd ed.). Thousand Oaks, CA: Sage.

Ibarra, H. (1993). Personal networks of women and minorities in management: A conceptual framework. *Academy of Management Review, 18,* 56–88.

Jackson, S. E., & Alvarez, E. B. (1992). Working through diversity as a strategic imperative. In S. E. Jackson & Associates (Eds.), *Diversity in the workplace* (pp. 13–29). New York: Guilford.

James, K., Lovato, C., & Khoo, G. (1994). Social identity correlates of minority workers' health. *Academy of Management Journal, 37,* 383–396.

Jones, E. E., Farina, A., Hastorf, A. H., Markus, H., Miller, D. T., & Scott, R. A. (1984). *Social stigma: The psychology of marked relationships.* New York: Freeman.

Jost, J. T., Glaser, J., Kruglanski, A. W., & Sulloway, F. J. (2003). Political conservatism as motivated social cognition. *Psychological Bulletin, 129,* 339–375.

Kanter, R. M. (1977). *Men and women of the corporation.* New York: Basic Books.

Kato, P., & Mann, T. (eds). *Handbook of diversity issues in health psychology.* New York: Plenum.

Katz, D. (1960). The functional approach to the study of attitudes. *Public Opinion Quarterly, 24,* 163–204.

Katz, I. (1981). *Stigma: A social psychological analysis.* Hillsdale, NJ: Lawrence Erlbaum Associates.

Katz, I., & Glass, D. C. (1979). An ambivalence amplification theory of behavior toward the stigmatized. In W. Austin & S. Worchel (Eds.), *The social psychology of intergroup relations.* Monterey: Brooks/Cole, pp. 55–70.

Katz, I., & Hass, R. G. (1988). Racial ambivalence and value conflict: Correlational and priming studies of dual cognitive structures. *Journal of Personality and Social Psychology, 55,* 893–905.

Kim, S. S., & Gelfand, M. J. (2003). The influence of ethnic identity on perceptions of organizational recruitment. *Journal of Vocational Behavior, 63,* 396–116.

Kinder, D. R., & Sears, D. O. (1981). Prejudice and politics: Symbolic racism versus racial threats to the good life. *Journal of Personality and Social Psychology, 40,* 414–431.

King, B. R. (2001). Ranking of stigmatization toward lesbians and their children and the influence of perceptions of controllability of homosexuality. *Journal of Homosexuality, 41,* 77–97.

Kirkpatrick, L. A. (1993). Fundamentalism, Christian orthodoxy, and intrinsic religious orientation as predictors of discriminatory attitudes. *Journal for the Scientific Study of Religion, 32,* 256–268.

Kochan, T., Bezrukova, K., Ely, R., Jackson, S., Aparna, J., Jehn, K., Leonard, J., Levine, D., & Thomas, D. (2003). The effects of diversity on business performance: Report of the diversity research network. *Human Resource Management, 42,* 3–21.

Korman, A. K. (1976). Hypothesis of work behavior revisited and an extension. *Academy of Management Review, 1,* 50–63.

Kruglanski, A. W., & Freund, T. (1983). The freezing and unfreezing of lay-inferences: Effects of impressional primacy, ethnic stereotyping, and numerican anchoring. *Journal of Experimental Social Psychology, 19,* 448–468.

Lavasseur, J. B. (1998, February). Authoritarianism and political orientation: Validation of a left-wing authoritarianism scale. (Unpublished dissertation, University of Maine). *Dissertation Abstracts International: Section B: The Sciences & Engineering, 58*(8-B), 4524.

Lazarus, R. S., Kanner, A. D., & Folkman, S. (1980). Emotions: A cognitive phenomenological analysis. In R. Plutchik & H. Kellerman (Eds.). *Emotion: Theory, research and experience* (Vol. 1, pp. 199–214). New York: Academic Press.

Leonard, J. S. (1984). The impact of affirmative action on employment. *Journal of Labor Economics, 2,* 439–463.

LeVine, R. A., & Campbell, D. T. (1972). *Ethnocentrism: Theories of conflict, ethnic attitudes, and group behavior.* New York: Wiley.

Lloyd, W. S. (2003). Tough economy may test newspapers' commitment to diversity. *Newsroom Diversity* [Online]. Available: http://www.freedom.forum.org/templates/document. asp?documentID=15622.

Macrae, C. N., Bodenhausen, G. V., Milne, A. B., & Jetten, J. (1994). Out of mind but back in sight: Stereotypes on the rebound. *Journal of Personality and Social Psychology, 67,* 808–817.

Macrae, C. N., Milne, A. B., & Bodenhausen, G. V. (1994). Stereotypes as energy-saving devices: A peek inside the cognitive toolbox. *Journal of Personality and Social Psychology, 66,* 37–47.

Major, B. (1994). From social inequality to personal entitlement: The role of social comparisons, legitimacy appraisals, and group membership. In M. Zanna (Ed.). *Advances in Experimental Psychology* (Vol. 26, pp. 293–355). New York: Academic Press.

Martell, R. F. (1996). What mediates gender bias in work behavior ratings? *Sex Roles, 35*, 153–169.

McConahay, J. B. (1983). Modern racism and modern discrimination: The effects of race, racial attitudes, and context on simulated hiring decisions. *Personality and Social Psychology Bulletin, 9*, 551–558

Meertens, R. W., & Pettigrew, T. F. (1997). Is subtle prejudice really prejudice? *Public Opinion Quarterly, 61*, 54–71.

Monin, B., & Miller, D. T. (2001). Moral credentials and the expression of prejudice. *Journal of Personality and Social Psychology, 81*, 33–43.

Myrdal, G. (1944). *An American Dilemma*. New York: Harper & Row.

Northrup, T. A. (1989). The dynamic of identity in personal and social conflict. In L. Kriesberg, T. A. Northrup, and S. J. Thorson (Eds.), *Intractable conflicts and their transformation* (pp. 55–82). Syracuse, NY: Syracuse University Press.

Oliver, C. (1991). Strategic responses to institutional pressures. *Academy of Management Review, 16*, 145–179.

Ostroff, C., & Bowen, D. E. (2000). Moving HR to a higher level: HR practices and organizational effectiveness. In K. J. Klein & S. W. J. Kozlowski (Eds.), *Multilevel theory, research, and methods in organizations: Foundations, extensions, and new directions* (pp. 211–266). San Francisco: Jossey-Bass.

Pelled, L. H., Eisenhardt, K. M., & Xin, K. R. (1999). Exploring the black box: An analysis of work group diversity, conflict, and performance. *Administrative Science Quarterly, 44*, 1–28.

Perry, E. L. (1994). A prototype matching approach to understanding the role of applicant gender and age in the evaluation of job applicants. *Journal of Applied Social Psychology, 24*, 1433–1473.

Perry, E. L., & Davis-Blake, A. (1994). Explaining gender-based selection decisions: A synthesis of contextual and cognitive approaches. *Academy of Management Review, 19*, 786–820.

Pettigrew, T. F. (1997). Generalized intergroup contact effects on prejudice. *Personality and Social Psychology Bulletin, 23*, 173–185.

Pratto, F. (1999). The puzzle of continuing group inequality: piecing together psychological, social, and cultural forces in social dominance theory. In Mark P. Zanna (Ed.), *Advances in experimental social psychology* (pp. 191–263). San Diego: Academic Press.

Pratto, F., Sidanius, J. Stallworth, L. M., & Malle, B. F. (1994). Social dominance orientation: A personality variable predicting social and political attitudes. *Journal of Personality and Social Psychology, 67*, 741–763.

Ragins, B. R., & Sundstrom, E. (1989). Gender and power in organizations: A longitudinal perspective. *Psychological Bulletin, 105*, 51–88.

Robinson, G., & Dechant, K. (1997). Building a business case for diversity. *Academy of Management Executive, 11*, 21–31.

Runkel, P. J., & McGrath, J. E. (1972). *Research on human behavior: A systematic guide to method*. New York: Holt, Rinehart & Winston.

Sacco, J. M., & Schmidt, N. W. (2003). *The relationship between demographic diversity and profitability: A longitudinal study*. Paper presented at the 18th Annual Conference of the Society for Industrial and Organizational Psychology, Orlando, FL.

Scott, F. A., Berger, M. C., & Garen, J. E. (1995). Do health insurance and pension costs reduce the job opportunities of older workers? *Industrial and Labor Relations Review, 48*, 775–791.

Scott, R. (1995). *Institutions and organizations*. Thousand Oaks, CA: Sage.

Sears, D. O., Henry, P. J., & Kosterman, R. (2000). Egalitarian values and contemporary racial politics. In D. O. Sears, J. Sidanius, & L. Bobo (Eds.), *Racialized politics: The debate about racism in America* (pp. 75–117). Chicago: University of Chicago Press.

Sears, D. O., Van Laar, C., Carrillo, M., & Kosterman, R. (1997). Is it really racism? The origins of white americans' opposition to race-targeted policies. *Public Opinion Quarterly, 61,* 16–53.

Seglin, J. L. (2002, May 17). *How to get a company's attention on women's pay.* New York Times, p. 4, section 3.

Seidel, M., Polzer, J. T., & Stewart, K. J. (2000). Friends in high plces: The effects of social networks on discrimination in salary negotiations. *Administrative Science Quarterly, 45,* 1–24.

Shea, T. F. (2003). Work-life professionals face rising tensions in a nervous economy. SHRM Online: Society for Human Resource Management [Online]. Available http://www.shrm.org/hrnews_published/archives/CMS_003785.asp.

Sidanius, J., & Pratto, F. (1999). *Social dominance.* New York: Cambridge University Press.

Siegelman, P. (1999, March). Racial discrimination in "everyday" commercial transactions: What do we know, what do we need to know, and how can we find out? In M. Fix & M. A. Turner (Eds.), *A national report card on discrimination: The role of testing.* Washington, DC: Urban Institute.

Stevenson, M. R., & Medler, B. R. (1995). Is homophobia a weapon of sexism? *Journal of Men's Studies, 4,* 1–8.

Stone, E. F., Stone, D. L., & Dipboye, R. L. (1992). Stigmas in organizations: Race, handicaps, and physical unattractiveness. In K. Kelley (Ed.), *Issues, theory, and research in industrial and organizational psychology* (pp. 385–457). Amsterdam, Netherlands: North-Holland, Elsevier Science Publishers.

Swim, J. K., Aikin, K. J., Hall, W. S., & Hunter, B. A. (1995). Sexism and racism: Old-fashioned and modern prejudices. *Journal of Personality and Social Psychology, 68,* 199–214.

Swim, J., & Stangor, C. (Eds.). (1999). *Prejudice: The target's perspective.* San Diego, CA: Academic Press.

Tajfel, H., & Turner, J. C. (1979). An integrative theory of intergroup conflict. In W. G. Austin and S. Worchel (eds). *The Social Psychology of Intergroup Relations* (pp. 33–47). Monterey, CA: Brooks/Cole.

Tamen, J. F. S. (2002). Florida companies recommit to diversity as economy recovers. *RaceMatters.org.* [Online]. Available: http://www.racematters.org/southfloridaavenuecoalition.htm.

Tischler, L. (2004, February). Where are the women? *Fast Company, 79,* p. 52.

Tolbert, P., & Zucker, L. (1983). Institutional sources of change in the formal structure of organizations: The diffusion of civil service reform, 1880–1935. *Administrative Science Quarterly, 28,* 22–39.

Turner, J. C. (1982). Towards a cognitive redefinition of the social group. In H. Tajfel (Ed.), *Social identity and group relations* (pp. 15–40). Cambridge, MA: Cambridge University Press.

U.S. Census Bureau (August 22, 2002). Table 3: Work experience and mean earnings in 2000—work disability status of civilians 16 to 74 years old, by educational attainment and sex: 2001. Washington, DC: Author.

U.S. Department of Labor Bureau of Labor Statistics (2003a). Annual averages—Household data, employed persons by detailed occupation, sex, race, and Hispanic origin. [On-line]. Retrieved October 8, 2003, from http://www.bls.gov/cps/cpsa2002.pdf.

U.S. Department of Labor Bureau of Labor Statistics (2003b). Annual averages—Household data, employment status of the civilian noninstitutional population 25 years and over by educational attainment, sex, race, and Hispanic origin. [On-line]. Retrieved October 8, 2003, from http://www.bls.gov/cps/cpsa2002.pdf.

U.S. Equal Employment Opportunity Commission (2003, February 6). Charge statistics FY 1992 through FY 2002. [On-line]. Retrieved October 8, 2003, from http://www.eeoc.gov/state/charges.html.

Warner, R. L., & Steel, B. S. (1989). Affirmative action in times of fiscal stress and changing value priorities: The case of women in policing. *Public Personnel Management, 18,* 291–309.

Wentling, R. M., & Palma-Rivas, N. (1997). Barriers to diversity initiatives. Current status of diversity initiatives in selected multinational corporations (Diversity in the Workforce Series Repport #3). [On-line]. Available http://ncrve.berkeley.edu/Abstracts/MDS-936/MDS-936-Barriers.html.

Wright, S. C., Aron, A., McLaughlin-Volpe, T., & Ropp, S. A. (1997). The extended contact effect. Knowledge of cross-group friendships and prejudice. *Journal of Personality and Social Psychology, 73,* 73–90.

Zaccaro, S. J., & Klimoski, R. J. (Eds.). *The nature of organizational leadership: Understanding the performance imperatives confronting today's leaders.* San Francisco: Jossey-Bass.

Zajonc, R. B. (1980). Feeling and thinking: Preferences need no inferences. *American Psychologist, 38,* 151–175.

Author Index

Subject Index